Competition Law Today

'[T]he volume will become necessary reading for all those ... who intuitively understand the importance of the subject but would like to get deeper into [it]. [Vinod Dhall] should be congratulated for ... bringing together these expert writings in one place.'

—Rajiv Kumar
Vice Chairman, National Institution for Transforming India (NITI) Aayog

'*Competition Law Today* gathers together an extraordinary series of essays on the major competition law issues today. It is essential reading now and will be an important reference work for many years to come.'

—Bernard J. Phillips
Former Head, Competition Division, Organization for Economic Cooperation and Development

'[A] highly useful compendium... . The essays in this publication ... will be an invaluable aid to the development of the law in India and also of interest abroad.'

—Dipankar P. Gupta
Senior Advocate and Former Solicitor General of India

Competition Law Today

Concepts, Issues, and the Law in Practice

Second Edition

edited by

VINOD DHALL

OXFORD
UNIVERSITY PRESS

OXFORD
UNIVERSITY PRESS

Oxford University Press is a department of the University of Oxford. It furthers the University's objective of excellence in research, scholarship, and education by publishing worldwide. Oxford is a registered trademark of Oxford University Press in the UK and in certain other countries.

Published in India by
Oxford University Press
2/11 Ground Floor, Ansari Road, Daryaganj, New Delhi 110 002, India

First Edition published in 2007
Second Edition published in 2019

ISBN-13: 978-0-19-948666-3
ISBN-10: 0-19-948666-2

Typeset in Adobe Garamond Pro 11/13
by Tranistics Data Technologies, New Delhi 110 044
Printed in India by Replika Press Pvt. Ltd.

To

Manju, Radhika, and Sonali,

who helped me stay the course.

Contents

PART III: COMPETITION LAW, ECONOMICS, AND POLICY

PART IV: COMPETITION LAW IN SOUTH ASIA

Foreword to the Second Edition

It is indeed a great pleasure for me to welcome the second edition of Vinod Dhall's book, *Competition Law Today*. The first edition was published shortly after the Competition Act of India was enacted. It was then the first book on the subject in India and it made a significant contribution to creating greater awareness of the law, its purpose, and principles. This second edition will further enrich the pool of knowledge and experiences on the subject. The contributing authors are globally recognized competition law experts hailing from various countries; their chapters cover a comprehensive range of topics and also cover the competition laws of several leading jurisdictions. Put together in a single volume, this book constitutes the most valuable resource of knowledge on competition law.

In India, the objectives of competition law may be traced to Article 39 of the Directive Principles of our Constitution, which enjoins the state to ensure that the ownership and control of the material resources of the community are so distributed as best to subserve the common good, and further that the operation of the economic system does not result in the concentration of wealth and means of production to the common detriment. In many countries, the competition law is seen as the bedrock of economic democracy. In the United States, Justice Thurgood Marshall observed (in *United States* v. *Topco Inc*) that 'Antitrust laws ... are the Magna Carta of free enterprise. They are as important to the preservation of economic freedom and our free enterprise system as the Bill of Rights is to the protection of our fundamental personal freedom.' In Germany, the competition law has been likened to the constitution of the German economy. The ordo-liberal viewpoint that witnessed its emergence in a war-struck Germany recognized that there was a deep relation between the success of an economy and the legal and political conditions of a country.

The erstwhile Monopolies and Restrictive Trade Practices Act (MRTP Act), 1969 rarely functioned as a truly economics-based competition law, and was often reduced to an instrument of the state to exercise control over businesses. It was eventually realized that the MRTP Act, 1969 had been rendered archaic and redundant and could not cope with the new market realities.[1] It was repealed and replaced by the Competition Act, 2002. But the new Act's enforcement was held up for long by constitutional challenges and the process of amendments.

The Act's objectives are expressed in its Preamble:

> To provide, keeping in view of the economic development of the country, for the establishment of a Commission to prevent practices having adverse effect on competition, to promote and sustain competition in markets, to protect the interests of consumers and to ensure freedom of trade carried on by other participants in markets, in India and for matters connected therewith or incidental thereto.

The overriding concern is to preserve competition in the markets, but notably doing so in the Indian economic context. It is different from the MRTP Act, 1969 not only in its overarching philosophy but also in specific provisions.

India's Competition Act is on par with similar laws in other jurisdictions. It protects the process of competition in the markets by prohibiting anticompetitive agreements, especially cartels and abuse of dominance, and by regulating large mergers. The widely accepted economic principles underlying competition law are embedded in its provisions. Other than naked cartels amongst competitors, other prohibitions are founded on economic analysis and the rule of reason such as vertical agreements, abuse of dominance, and mergers. In the case of mergers, the thresholds for being caught in the jurisdiction of the Competition Commission are amongst the highest in the world; thus, most mergers need not be cleared with the Competition Commission. As noted by experts, 'Competition Law exists to protect competition not competitors.'[2]

The command and control regime that was the overriding structure of India's economic policies since Independence ultimately proved counterproductive and stunted our economic growth for decades. Economic reforms were late in coming, but their benefits were soon reflected in the GDP growth

[1] 'Ninety Third Report', *The Competition Bill*, 2001.

[2] Charles James, assistant attorney general, USA, in *Program on Antitrust Policy in the 21st Century*, 2002, at the European Commission and the US Mission to the European Union.

breaking out of the unkindly called 'Hindu rate of growth'. Our competition law too was a component of the economic reforms process. In fact, continuation of the economic reforms is the need of the hour.

Competition is fundamental to a market-based economy; it leads to higher efficiencies, both productive efficiency and allocative efficiency. It also enhances dynamic efficiency by incentivizing innovation and thereby promoting the development of new products and technological growth. It compels companies to be more efficient in order to survive and grow in a competitive environment. It is against unjustified entry barriers, and thereby seeks to provide equal opportunity for all to compete and grow. Ultimately, competition benefits the consumers by increasing choice of products and services at affordable prices.

There are empirical studies that show the effect of competition-based policy on economic growth. In several countries, such as USA, Australia, New Zealand, and United Kingdom, studies have observed that consequent to pro-competition policies or reforms, the economy benefitted in different ways such as higher growth, increased level of employment, and lower prices. In the long run, competition-oriented policies can help reduce poverty too.

Maintaining a competitive market is not easy since there can be market failures when firms may try to enter into arrangements that obstruct competition. Competition law lays down an effective and sound legal framework for the state to foster competition. Professor W. Lachmann has observed, 'Competition is not a weed that grows even if left alone; rather it is a cultural plant and needs continuous government attention.'[3] The law compels enterprises to gear up to face the challenges that are thrown up by globalization. Michael Porter has remarked: 'It is difficult to visualize a business emerging as a global champion if it has not had to face competition at home.'[4]

The Competition Act also gives to the Competition Commission the responsibility for competition advocacy. This includes looking at government policies and processes and how far these inhibit or enhance competition. It is expected that the Commission will take up such matters with the government and advocate a more pro-competitive approach, unless there are exceptional circumstances or larger considerations of public interest when this may not be feasible or desirable. This will facilitate more competitive structures in the market. Besides yielding better outcomes, competition-based

[3] W. Lachmann, 1999. *UNCTAD Series on Issues in Competition Law and Policy*, Nuremberg University.

[4] Michael Porter, 1990. 'The Competitive Advantage of Nations and Regions.', *Harvard Business Review*, Harvard University, March–April 1990 Issue.

policies and processes also ensure greater transparency and even-handedness in governance. This has been evident in the difference between the way in which natural resources such as spectrum and coal have been allocated by the government under the discretionary system in the past and the auction mode now promoted by the government. Similarly, in public procurement of goods, services, or works, competition should be one of the overarching principles.

Any law is as good as its enforcement. Since the start of enforcement in May 2009, the Competition Commission has had to deal with a variety of cases—cartels and other types of agreements, abuse of dominance as well as mergers; it has passed a large number of orders in these cases. But when seen in perspective, the Commission is in its infancy and necessarily is on a learning curve. There is, however, a wealth of international experience, as reflected in this book, from which it can benefit, and in fact is doing so. It is expected that as the Commission's work progresses, it will gain in professionalism, economic analysis, and technical skills. Its enforcement must keep in mind the state and features of the Indian economy as the preamble of the Act specifically refers to. Most importantly, its approach to mergers can impact the Indian economy if there are avoidable delays or road blocks.

Vinod Dhall has been deeply associated with the Indian competition law since its inception—first at the policy stage in government when the bill was framed and enacted, then during his tenure at the Competition Commission, and finally as an independent expert in the field in India. He had kept alive the competition law flame when it was confronted with daunting challenges in its initial stages. As a result, he has a 360 degree view of the law. Fittingly, therefore, he has taken the initiative to compile this book and produce a timely revised edition. I trust his efforts will continue in the future as well, much to the service of the various stakeholders in competition law.

Arun Jaitley
Minister of Finance and Corporate Affairs
Government of India

Foreword to the First Edition

I am indeed very pleased to write the foreword to this very timely publication. Vinod Dhall has taken extraordinary pains to edit this collection of essays, which provides a comprehensive view of the various facets and dimensions of competition law.

It is being increasingly recognized that markets have an important role to play in any economy. Economic theory clearly brings out the benefits that flow from a competitive market system. As the role of the market expands, the role of the state also undergoes a change. In any economic system, the state can play three roles: (a) as a producer of marketable goods and services, (b) as a producer of 'public goods' and 'merit goods', and (c) as a regulator of the system. As the state reduces its role in the production of marketable goods and services and yields to the market, its role as a 'regulator' and 'facilitator' gets enhanced. Among other things, the regulatory role of the state demands action to maintain competitive conditions in the market. Efficiency is associated with competition and the markets can fulfil their functions efficiently only if they remain competitive. Legislation is, therefore, required to prevent the degeneration of the markets to a monopolistic or a near-monopolistic situation. Competition law is a framework of legal provisions designed to maintain competitive market structures. Competition laws in general seek to (a) prohibit anti-competition agreements, (b) prevent abuse of dominant position, and (c) regulate mergers and acquisitions. By now, there is a wealth of knowledge available on how to deal with these issues in terms of design and output. Several countries in the developing world have a long history of the operation of competition laws.

In India too, in the wake of economic liberalization begun in 1991, there is a growing emphasis on the measures required to keep the markets competitive. India enacted an appropriate competition law in 2002, even though some of its provisions are yet to come into force. We, in India, need to learn from the experience of other countries in this regard. It is in this context that this book, which draws from global experience, is timely, relevant, and welcome.

The editor should be commended for undertaking this effort. He has for long studied the problems associated with competition law. This book contains contributions from some of the leading experts in the field. They are professionals who have witnessed or influenced the growth of competition law over the last few decades. Their contributions make this book a formidable collection of expert opinion. These contributions examine not only the critical issues relating to competition law but also the experience of different countries in dealing with these issues.

I welcome this book heartily and am sure it will be read with profit by anyone interested in competition law and policy not only in India, but also abroad.

C. Rangarajan
Former Chairman
Economic Advisory Council to the Prime Minister
Government of India

Law and Economics

Fali S. Nariman

The publishers have a purpose in interposing this diversionary piece between the 'Foreword' and the 'Preface'—and as a prelude to the entirety of the book's contents. Wine tasters know that before savouring good wine one must have a few sips of water. The wine tastes the better for it. My role is to provide those sips of water. What I have to say might have little to do with competition law, but it has much to do with the need for lawyers to be better equipped with the knowledge and experience of disciplines other than law.

Lawyers, more than their brethren in other professions, must be equipped in what (for want of a better expression) is called 'significant learning'—learning which is more than a mere accumulation of facts, learning which makes a difference in the individual's behaviour in society, in the course of action pursued, in attitudes, and in approaches.

Knowledge of the law is not an end in itself. It is a means for equipping the inquiring mind with a liberal education. There is some stress between what society demands of lawyers and what legal education can provide: the gap is significant, if only because pearly words of wisdom of legal sages of the past have been ignored.

Back in the seventeenth century, Serjeant Finch (in those days senior lawyers were known as 'serjeants') picturesquely expressed the affinity of law and other disciplines. He said that 'the sparks of all sciences are rolled up in the ashes of the law'. Also, the oft-quoted (but much-neglected) jurist of the eighteenth century William Blackstone said that 'general academic education must be a first step to the profession of the common law—for sciences are of a sociable disposition and flourish best in the neighbourhood of each other;

nor is there any branch of learning but it may be helped and improved by assistance drawn from other arts'.[1] Of course, Blackstone thought in terms of history and philosophy, but what he said was applicable to other branches of knowledge as well.

In the nineteenth century the great American Judge Oliver Wendell Holmes reminded men of the law (there were no women in the legal profession then): 'To be master of any branch of knowledge, you must master those which lie next to it.'[2] And in the 1940s E.C.S. Wade, in an inaugural lecture in Cambridge, urged that 'we should teach (and practise) law as a great human institution serving social and economic ends and in relation to the world in which we live.'[3]

Sir Walter Scott had been trained to become a lawyer, but his interests were in literature. He wrote novels. In *Guy Mannering*, he showed that he had not forgotten his early impressions of what a lawyer should aspire to become: the hero in the novel visits the house of a Scottish lawyer (Counsellor Pleydell), and is shown into the lawyer's study, the walls of which are lined with a collection of the classics and other tomes on varied subjects. 'These', says Pleydell, 'these are the tools of my trade. A lawyer without history or literature is a mechanic, a mere working mason. If he possesses some knowledge of these he may venture to call himself an architect.' If a lawyer is to be at all worthy of the society which he (or she) serves—then the yearning must be to become an 'architect' in the law, not to remain a mere mason!

It is more or less common ground amongst juristic thinkers of today that law is an instrument, or a range of instruments through which men and women seek to achieve certain purposes in society. Judges do this all the time—when interpreting statutory instruments: the modern trend is to give a purposive interpretation to words used in legislation. 'Globalization' is the new buzzword of our age and judges are already building a global community of law—national and international. Judges are networking, and becoming increasingly aware of one another's decisions. The most informal level of transnational judicial contact is knowledge of foreign and international judicial decisions and willingness to reach out and cite them. Justice Sandra Day O'Connor (the first woman judge to be appointed on

[1] William Blackstone. 1765. 'Introduction, "On the Study of Law"', *Commentaries on the Laws of England*, I.

[2] Oliver Wendell. 1886. 'Law as a Profession', *American Law Review* 20, pp. 741–2.

[3] E.C.S. Wade. 1945–7. 'The Aims of Legal Education', *Cambridge Law Journal* 9, p. 286 at 288.

the US Supreme Court) once chided American lawyers and judges about their insularity in ignoring foreign law and predicted that she and her fellow justices would find themselves 'looking more frequently to decisions of other Constitutional Courts'.

The legal world has become a global village and the vast proliferation of laws—national and international—as well as treaties and conventions on a wide range of subjects must receive at least a nodding acquaintance from a true votary of the law. The lawyer of today has to meet and contend with challenges beyond the law: challenges to the lawyer's traditional role as an intermediary between litigants and courts of justice. Many decades ago, when the then Chief Justice of Australia, Owen Dixon, was asked whether it was any part of the duty of a lawyer to contribute towards the progress of society, he said that it was not: the duty of a lawyer (he said) was to keep a hand on and hold steady the framework and foundations of the law. However, that was long, long ago. The quickening pace of technological advance and a new sense of service and duty to society have replaced the old model. In a message to a conference of lawyers in New Delhi in 1985, then Secretary General of the Commonwealth, Sir Shridath Ramphal, reminded us that we are 'heirs to a noble tradition of intellectual inventiveness': a nice, well-rounded phrase of great use to the lawyer practising in this new millennium; it matters not in which part of the globe.

We live in an age in which there is much economic legislation—after all the welfare of the people is the professed objective of every civilized state. Yet, there are vast expanses of uncharted ignorance amongst lawyers and judges—particularly about economics. Competition law is about economics—it has grown at a phenomenal pace in recent years—mainly in response to changes in economic behaviour witnessed in many places around the globe. There are now more than a hundred different systems of competition law in the five continents of the world—in countries with different types of economies: activities that were once regarded as state monopolies—telecommunications, energy, transport, broadcasting, postal services, and the like—have now become the subject of scrutiny and regulation under competition law. Even activities such as sports, entertainment, and the media are within its sweep. Competition law is the hand-maiden of modern economics: and economics motivates laws which in turn drive the economy; the bundle of laws that reflect societal values is now known as 'sociological jurisprudence'.

Since competition law is about economic behaviour, it is essential that the regulator, the civil servant, the judge, and lawyer be acquainted with, and become proficient in the application of economic concepts to the needs of society: *Competition Law Today* is about economic concepts. One of the contributors[4] to this book has mentioned US Supreme Court Justice Brandeis. He had, as lawyer and social activist, given his name to 'the Brandeis Brief'—a well-researched document submitted to courts when the constitutional validity of social and economic legislation, or its interpretation, is involved.[5] It is reported that Justice Brandeis had said: '[A] lawyer who has not studied economics ... is very apt to become a public enemy', a little exaggerated, I think, a trifle harsh perhaps, but not inappropriate! As Lord Keynes used to say: 'Words have sometimes to be harsh since they represent an assault on the thoughts of the unthinking.'

Fali S. Nariman
Senior Advocate
Supreme Court of India and
President of the Bar Association of India

[4] Richard Whish. 2005. *Competition Law* (5th ed.), Oxford University Press, Oxford.

[5] As Counsel before the US Supreme Court in *Muller* v. *Oregon* (1908), Louis Brandeis, then a well-known attorney, submitted a lengthy brief supporting the constitutionality of a statute enacted by the legislature of Oregon that limited the hours per day that women could work in laundries and other industries. Brandeis used it to demonstrate that there was a reasonable basis for the Oregon statute. It compelled the Supreme Court of the US to consider data that state legislators had employed in drafting reform-laws. The 'Brandeis brief 'soon became a staple of litigation in the US—it is still used by lawyers to attack or support wide-ranging economic legislation.

Preface

As countries across the world have been shifting to market economies, they have, as a corollary, been adopting, or modernizing, competition laws. Interest in this area of economic law has therefore been expanding.

India took up economic reforms in earnest in the early 1990s, and in the second phase of the reforms, it enacted a new competition law to replace the Monopolies and Restrictive Trade Practices (MRTP) Act, 1969, which had become obsolete in certain respects. The Competition Act, 2002, came on the statute book in January 2003. It is in economic terms a more sophisticated law and covers the three standard limbs of competition law—anticompetitive agreements, abuse of dominance, and merger regulation; it also mandates the Competition Commission of India to undertake competition advocacy.

Years of government controls and protective regimes have left India with a weak competition culture. As a governing principle for the markets, competition may be said to be only now gaining acceptance. However, there are still sceptics about the need for a competition law seeing it as an unnecessary intervention in the markets; trust in antitrust is faint. Outside select corridors of academia, law firms, and policymaking circles, it may be difficult to find adequate understanding of competition law, of its economic context, its substantive provisions, the role of economic analysis in determining competition cases, interface of competition law with intellectual property rights, the relationship of the competition authority with sector regulators, and many other issues.

Such an environment is hardly conducive to the effective implementation of the Competition Act. This book has been undertaken to contribute to an extent, however small, towards enhancing the knowledge base on the subject of competition law in India. It has been designed to help practitioners including lawyers, chartered accountants, company secretaries, and cost and works accountants, all of whom are eligible to appear before the Competition

Commission of India, courts, company compliance officers, academicians and students of competition law, staff of the Competition Commission and other statutory regulators, and policymakers in India, to better understand the basics of competition law. However, the broad coverage of its contents could well be of interest to readers in other countries.

The objective of bringing out this book has dictated its structure. At the outset, there is an overview of competition law, which broadly covers the history, objectives, and substantive provisions of the law, its relationship with regulated sectors of the market, the economics of the law, its international dimension, and competition law in developing countries. The overview does not delve into the nuances of the law, which are more thoroughly examined in the other chapters that deal with specific aspects of competition law; it provides only a framework for the rest of the book.

Part I provides a generic treatment of the substantive provisions of competition law. The first three chapters explain the three core activities covered by competition law, that is, cartels and other anticompetitive agreements, abuse of dominance, and merger control. The other chapters deal with leniency programmes, increasingly being used in pursuing cartels; the complex interface between competition law and intellectual property rights; exemptions and exceptions; competition advocacy, increasingly a part of competition dialogue; the vexatious issue of the interrelationship between competition law and sector regulation; attributes of a successful competition authority; and the much-debated international dimension of competition law.

Part II describes the competition laws and practices of important jurisdictions in the world, covering both industrialized and developing countries. Amongst the industrialized nations, the two most important jurisdictions are covered: the USA, to which the origin of modern competition law is usually traced, and the European Union, which has one of the most active supranational competition regimes. This part also includes some other important competition regimes including Australia, Germany, and the UK, where competition law has witnessed substantial growth. Among the newer competition jurisdictions, some that have gained significant recognition have been covered such as Mexico, South Africa, and South Korea.

Competition law is about economics, which underlies its key concepts. This point is clearly evident from the treatment of the various subjects by the contributors of this book. Specifically, the integral relationship between the two disciplines is explored in Part III, along with the interface between competition law and industrial policy.

The first three parts together traverse the canvas of competition law and provide the setting for Part IV, which deals with competition law in India. Here, one chapter is about the evolution of the law, and the last three chapters explain the Competition Act, 2002, at length.

It would be preposterous to claim that this book covers every issue in competition law, which is a vast and growing subject. However, it is hoped that the above treatment is deep enough to give readers a better appreciation of the Indian law, and enable them to view the Indian law in a broader, global context.

The contributors are reputed professionals in the field. They include professors and other scholars, judges, chairpersons, members, or senior officers of competition authorities, senior staff members of multilateral bodies, and partners of law firms that have an established practice in this area. They belong to different continents and countries, both industrialized and developing, and cover most of the important competition regimes in the world. Together they represent an impressive array of scholarship and experience in competition law.

Bringing out this book has been a pleasurable enterprise, though by no means an easy one. I cannot adequately express my appreciation of the cooperation I received from the contributing authors, who readily agreed to write their respective chapters. Before starting this work, I discussed the proposal with several of them. They provided critical advice and unstinted support, and helped to refine and improve the structure of this volume. I believe the backdrop to this cooperation is provided by the evolution of an international competition law community, whose members have an unselfish interest in enriching the body of competition law experiences. This volume is a testimony to this community at work.

I have accumulated deep debts in bringing out this book, and I can scarcely hope to acknowledge all of them. I profited greatly from the comments given by Eleanor M. Fox on both my chapters, and by Richard Whish and Valentine Korah on my chapter on Indian competition law. Mallika Ramachandran helped with painstaking research and other assistance. Vikram Sawhney and Manju Dhall helped tone up the text with thoughtful suggestions. Colleagues at the Ministry of Company Affairs, Government of India, and the Competition Commission of India have been supportive in a variety of ways. I would also like to thank the editors at Oxford University Press. Finally, the support by Arun Jaitley, C. Rangarajan, and Fali S. Nariman, by writing the 'Foreword to the Second Edition', the 'Foreword to the First Edition', and the special piece on 'Law and Economics', respectively, has been most valuable.

For the sake of good order, I should add that the views expressed in this book by the contributing authors are not attributable to me, nor to the Competition Commission of India, of which I am currently a member. Similarly, the views expressed by me here and in my chapters are my personal views and not necessarily those of the Competition Commission of India.

Vinod Dhall
January 2007

Cases

Abbreviations

'the 1998 Act'	The Competition Act, 1998 (United Kingdom)
'the 2002 Act'	The Enterprise Act, 2002 (United Kingdom)
'Division'	United States Department of Justice Antitrust Division
'the Tribunal'	Competition Appeal Tribunal (United Kingdom)
AAG	Assistant Attorney General (US Department of Justice Antitrust Division)
ACCC	Australian Competition and Consumer Commission
AGCM	Autorità Garante della Concurrenza e del Mer Cato (Italian Competition Authority)
AIR	All India Reporter
ANC	African National Congress
ANZCERTA	Australia New Zealand Closer Economic Relations Trade Agreement
AOD	Abuse of Dominance
APEC	Asia Pacific Economic Cooperation
BA	British Airways
CAA	Civil Aviation Authority (United Kingdom)
CARICOM	Caribbean Common Market
CB	Competition Bureau (Canada)
CC	Competition Commission (United Kingdom)
CBCPI	Capacity Building and Competition Policy Implementation subgroup (International Competition Network)
CCI	Competition Commission of India
CFC	Federal Competition Commission (Mexico)
CFTC	Commodities Futures Trading Commission

CLWP	Commission's Legislative and Work Program (EC Directorate General Competition)
CMLR	Common Market Law Reports
CMO	Common Market Organization
COFEMER	Federal Regulatory Improvement Commission (Mexico)
COMESA	Common Market for Eastern and South Africa
DCA	Danish Competition Authority DG Competition Directorate General Competition
(European Union)	
DOJ	Department of Justice (United States)
EC	European Community
ECJ	European Court of Justice
ECMR	European Commission's Merger Regulation
ECN	European Competition Network
ECR	European Court Reports
EEA	European Economic Area
EEC	European Economic Community
EFTA	European Free Trade Agreement
EU	European Union
FCA	Finnish Competition Authority
FRAND	Fair, Reasonable, and Non-discriminatory
FTA	Free Trade Agreement
FTAIA	Foreign Trade Antitrust Improvements Act (United States)
FTC	Federal Trade Commission (United States)
GATS	General Agreement on Trade in Services
GATT	General Agreement on Trade and Tariffs
HCC	Hard Core Cartels
HCI	Heavy and Chemical Industries
HHI	Herfindahl-Hirschmann Index
HMT	Hypothetical Monopolist Test
HSR	Hart-Scott-Rodino Act (United States)
IA	Impact Assessment
ICN	International Competition Network
INTERPOL	International Criminal Police Organization
IPRs	Intellectual Property Rights
ITO	International Trade Organization

JFTC	Japanese Fair Trade Commission
KFTC	Korean Fair Trade Commission
LCFE	Federal Law of Economic Competition (Mexico)
M&A	Mergers and Acquisitions
MDW	Minimum Daily Wages
MERCOSUR	South American Common Market
MIC	Monopolies Inquiries Committee (India)
MLAT	Mutual Legal Assistance Treaty
MMC	Monopolies and Mergers Commission (United Kingdom)
MOU	Memorandum of Understanding
MRFTA	Monopolies Regulation and Fair Trade Act (Korea)
MRTP	Monopolies and Restrictive Trade Practices (India)
MRTPC	Monopolies and Restrictive Trade Practices Commission (India)
MTPs	Monopolistic Trade Practices
NAFTA	North American Free Trade Agreement
NCA	National Competition Authority
NCP	National Competition Policy (Australia)
NEDLAC	National Economic Development and Labour Council (South Africa)
OECD	Organization for Economic Cooperation and Development
OFCOM	Office of Communications (United Kingdom)
OFGEM	Gas and Electricity Markets Authority (United Kingdom)
OFT	Office of Fair Trading (United Kingdom)
OFWAT	Office of Water Services (United Kingdom)
OMB	Office of Management and Budget (United States)
OPEC	Oil Producing and Exporting Countries
ORR	Office of Rail Regulation (United Kingdom)
R&D	Research and Development
Raghavan	High-Level Committee on Competition Policy and Committee Law (India)
RIS	Regulatory Impact Statement
RLFCE	Regulations for Implementing the Federal Law of Economic Competition (Mexico)

RPM	Resale Price Maintenance
RTPs	Restrictive Trade Practices
SCC	Supreme Court Cases
SCP	Structure-Conduct-Performance
SMEs	Small and Medium Sized Enterprises
SSNIP	Small but Significant Non-transitory Increase in Price
TCA	Turkish Competition Authority
TOR	Terms of Reference
TRIPs	Trade Related Intellectual Property Rights
UNCTAD	United Nations Conference on Trade and Development
UNCTAD RBP	Set of Multilaterally Agreed Equitable Principles and Rules for the Control of Restrictive Business Practices
UTPs	Unfair Trade Practices
WTO	World Trade Organization

Overview*

Key Concepts in Competition Law

Vinod Dhall

Competition law has grown enormously in recent years, especially since the early 1990s. The growth has been both in terms of geographical regions that have adopted competition law, as well as in the range of economic activities now subject to competition law. As an increasing number of countries have undertaken economic reforms and embraced the market economy, many of them have also introduced competition law to maintain competition in their markets. Also, many economic activities that were earlier state monopolies or natural monopolies and were shielded from competition are now subject to competition law. Similarly, professions such as medicine or law that have been more or less self-regulated are also now feeling the reach of competition law.

With the growing integration of the global economy, any anticompetitive activity can have effects across national borders. Competition law has, therefore, become an important part of international trade dialogue. Cooperation on competition issues figures in an increasing number of bilateral or regional trade agreements. It was one of the contentious issues in the Doha round of WTO negotiations, till it was dropped from the agenda. Apart from UNCTAD, which has been studying competition issues for a long time, newer international forums have grown in recent years for debate on competition

* The views expressed here are the author's own and do not reflect those of the Competition Commission of India.

matters, most notably OECD's Global Forum on Competition and the International Competition Network (ICN).

History of Competition Law

The history of modern competition law is generally traced to the United States, where the Sherman Act was enacted in 1890[1] out of the growing concern about the formation of trusts by American companies wherein owners of stocks held in competing companies transferred those stocks to trusts which then controlled the activities of those competitors[2] with the view to coordinate their activities in regard to pricing, output, or other areas and, thereby, to dominate the market. Such trusts were formed, for example, in oil, sugar, whiskey, and metals. The Sherman Act, 1890, prohibited contracts, combinations, or conspiracies in restraint of trade,[3] and also prohibited monopolization or attempts or conspiracies to monopolize.[4] The Sherman Act was a simple, short statute. As intended, it was interpreted by case law. Some of the deficiencies of the law were sought to be made up through the Clayton Act, 1914, which contains provisions for merger control and also against tying, price discrimination, and exclusive dealing. The Federal Trade Commission Act was enacted in 1914 to set up an autonomous enforcement agency. In the wake of the tide of anti-competitive mergers in the 1940s, the Clayton Act was amended through the Celler–Kefauver Act, 1950, to further strengthen control over mergers.

The years of World War II witnessed the operation of huge cartels, both at the national and international levels. After the war, therefore, antitrust was looked upon also as a check against private corporate power. Antitrust legislation was introduced in Germany in 1957, attributed to the influence of both the ordoliberal philosophy of the Freiburg school and the Marshall Plan. Similarly, antitrust law was introduced in Japan in 1947;[5] however, it

[1] Canada enacted its first law in 1889 and some states of the United States too had earlier laws but, on account of their limited effectiveness, they have not acquired comparable significance in antitrust history. See also para 4.1.4 (2000). 'Report of the High Level Committee on Competition Policy and Law in India' (Raghavan Committee).

[2] See Jones, Allison and Brenda Sufrin. 2002. *EC Competition Law: Text, Cases and Materials*, Oxford University Press, Oxford.

[3] Section 1, Sherman Act, 1890.

[4] Section 2, ibid.

[5] The Japanese Antimonopoly Act, 1947, see Fox, Eleanor M. 2002. *Competition Law*, in Lowenfeld, Andreas N.: *International Economic Law*, Oxford University Press, Oxford, pp. 340–83.

is generally felt that in Japan, the law did not take root for many years due to the tacit acceptance of cooperative business practices and government–business collaboration prevailing in the country. In the United Kingdom, the Monopolies and Restrictive Practices (Inquiry and Control) Act was enacted in 1948.

In 1957, the treaty of Rome was signed by six European nations[6] bringing into existence the European Economic Community (EEC). Competition law was incorporated into this treaty in the form of Articles 85 and 86 (later renumbered Articles 81 and 82). These articles prohibit anticompetitive agreements and abuse of dominant position respectively. Other related articles prohibit the particular states from restraining the European internal market or giving state aid that distorts competition,[7] and extend the competition law to state-owned enterprises.[8] Later, in 1989, the European Commission adopted the Merger Regulation[9] to control anticompetitive mergers. The enforcement of the EU competition law was to be done through the European Commission; subsequently the administration has been decentralized through 'modernization'[10] of the EU law, and a greater role has been given to the national competition agencies in the enforcement of Articles 81 and 82.

In the 1990s, as the economies of the East European countries were overhauled to give way to market-based economies, these countries progressively introduced their own competition laws. Many developing countries also adopted competition legislation, including countries in Latin America, Africa, and Asia. Amongst the countries that have most recently adopted a competition law are Singapore, Vietnam, and India (though the Indian law at the time of writing has not been fully brought into force). China is also in the process of adopting a competition law. The number of countries having a competition law has risen to over 100 from only about 40 in the early 1990s.

Objectives of Competition Law

There is some controversy about what are or should be the objectives of competition law. However, there is broad agreement that the principal objective is to make the market economy work better by stopping private power from obstructing markets. In this way, the principal objective is to maintain

[6] Namely, Belgium, Netherlands, Luxembourg, France, Italy, and West Germany.

[7] Articles 28–31, Article 87 of the EC Treaty.

[8] Article 86 of the EC Treaty.

[9] Regulation 4064/89.

[10] Regulation 1/2003.

and protect the competitive process since competition promotes efficiency including dynamic efficiency, increases consumer welfare, and contributes to the progress of the economy as a whole. On the other hand, firms tend to restrict competition through means such as collusive agreements to fix prices and outputs, exploitative and exclusionary measures, and seek mergers and other forms of combinations to gain or augment market power. Such market failures undermine the benefits of free and fair competition in the economy and, therefore, need to be prohibited through legal devices provided by the competition law.

Competition law may subserve some supplementary objectives. One of these is freedom of trade, which has been viewed as the economic counterpart of political democracy. This is the theme of preserving pluralism and distribution of market power; both these objectives reflect the once prevailing fear of allowing concentration of economic power in the hands of a few market agents. While competition law has been mainly aimed at countering private restraints to competition, in recent years the objective has expanded also to lessening the adverse effects of government intervention in the market place.[11]

Competition law may also recognize other objectives and may, therefore, allow exemptions to serve such objectives. For example, the law may allow for the protection of small and medium enterprises or for the development of less developed regions. In South Africa, the law specifically seeks the objective of increasing the participation of black-owned businesses in the economy.[12]

Substantive Provisions of Competition Law

Competition law, almost everywhere, prohibits three kinds of activities, namely anticompetitive agreements, abuse of dominance (or monopolization), and anticompetitive mergers.

Anticompetitive Agreements

Anticompetitive agreements between enterprises that restrict competition fall into two categories: 'horizontal agreements', which are those between enterprises at the same stage of the supply chain, for example, agreements

[11] Khemani, R. Shyam, et al. 1999. 'Objectives of Competition Policy', in World Bank/OECD: *A Framework for the Design and Implementation of Competition Law and Policy*, World Bank/OECD, p. 2.

[12] See Preamble to the Competition Act of South Africa, available at http://www.compcom.co.za/thelaw/thelaw_act_competition_acts.asp?level=1&child=1.

between manufacturers of the same product like tyres or cement; and 'vertical agreements', which are between enterprises at different stages of the supply chain, for example, between a manufacturer and a distributor or a retailer. Usually, it is the horizontal agreements that cause the greatest concern to competition authorities.

Cartel

A cartel is a horizontal agreement to fix prices, allocate customers or territories and restrict output or rig bids. A cartel is regarded as the most pernicious form of violation of competition law since it unequivocally damages competition and causes loss to the economy and to consumers. Owing to the seriousness of cartels, they are subject to the *per se* rule[13] in many jurisdictions, for example, in the laws in the US[14] and in the European Union.[15] Accordingly, a cartel is considered to be inherently anticompetitive and injurious to the public without any need to determine whether it has actually injured competition. In many jurisdictions it is treated as a criminal offence subject to prison terms for the individuals involved in the crime. This is the case, for example, in the United States, Canada, Japan, Ireland, Korea, Norway, the Slovak Republic, Germany (only for collusive tendering) and, since recently, in the United Kingdom. It is believed that in Australia too a proposal for amendment is likely to treat cartels as a criminal offence. Even in countries where it is not treated as a criminal offence, the penalties reserved for cartels could be particularly high.

Cartels are not easy to detect since the colluding parties go to great lengths to cover their tracks. Therefore, competition agencies have been resorting to and seeking greater investigative powers for unearthing evidence, such

[13] The 'per se' rule is the judicial principle that a trade practice violates the Sherman Act simply if the practice is a restraint of trade, regardless of whether it actually harms anyone, Black's Law Dictionary (7th ed.), p. 1162.

[14] Price-fixing, market allocation, output limitation, etc. are subject to the per se rule in the United States. See *White Motor Co.* v. *United States* 372 US 253 (1963); *N.C.A.A.* v. *Board of Regents of the University of Oklahoma* 468 US 85 (1985); *Federal Trade Commission* v. *Superior Court Trial Lawyers Association* 493 US 411 (1990); *United States* v. *Topco Associates Inc* 405 US (1972); *Copperweld Corporation* v. *Independence Tube Corp.* 467 US 752 (1984), etc.

[15] In EU law, the prohibition in Article 81 applies in particular to, inter alia, agreements to directly or indirectly fix purchase or selling prices or any other trading conditions; agreements to limit or control production, markets, technical development or investment; and agreements to share markets or sources of supply.

as 'dawn raids' and the power to order production of documents or summon witnesses. In the case of the famous global lysine cartel, agents of the Department of Justice along with FBI agents simultaneously raided the offices of ADM (the cartel leader) across the country. To help them nail the cartel they had taped telephone conversations and video-taped meetings held in secret locations. The directorate general of Competition of the European Commission, recently acquired the power of 'dawn raids'.

A relatively recent development in competition law has been the use of leniency provisions (called the amnesty programme in the US) to detect or investigate cartels. This allows the court or the competition authority to offer lenient treatment to any party to the cartel that blows the whistle on the cartel and provides substantial information and fully cooperates with the authority. The leniency provision has led to a quantum jump in the detection and successful investigation of cartels. It has proved a powerful tool in the hands of authorities, offering a huge incentive to the cartel members to abandon the cartel and be the first to reach the door of the competition authority. The fear of the 'empty seat at the table' has aggravated the inherent instability of cartels.

Economic theory points to certain conditions that are conducive to the formation of cartels. These include homogeneity of the product, high concentration in the market (which implies large shares for the big players), and high entry barriers. Other facilitating conditions include a large number of buyers, relative equality of production costs amongst firms and relatively stable or predictable demand conditions. Cartels tend to emulate the position of a monopolist by attempting to raise their prices and lower output, or do both. Cartels have all along been a familiar phenomenon in the market place. Recent years, however, have witnessed a hardening of the attitude of authorities against cartels. Countries or their competition authorities have also been collaborating with each other in acting against hard-core cartels, especially global cartels. Prominent examples of recently detected global cartels are the lysine cartel, vitamins cartel, and the graphite electrode cartel.

Developing countries are particularly vulnerable to the damage from global cartels. A World Bank Background Paper shows that in 1997 developing countries imported US$ 81.1 billion worth of goods from industries which had seen a price fixing conspiracy during the 1990s.[16] Those

[16] Levenstein, Margaret and Valerie Suslow. 2001. 'Private International Cartels and their Effect on Developing Countries', Background Paper for World Bank's World Development Report, available at http://www.worldbank.org/wdr/2001/bkgroundpapers/levenstein.pdf.

imports represented 6.7 per cent of the imports and 1.2 per cent of the GDP in the developing countries and an even larger proportion of trade in the poorest developing countries for whom the 16 products in question represented 8.8 per cent of the imports.[17] Organization for Economic Cooperation and Development's Global Forum on Competition, 2001, contains a list of 26 cartel and bid rigging cases reported by 12 developing countries.[18] However, there are only a few examples of global cartels being successfully penalized in developing countries; the reasons for this are well known, such as limited capacity of the domestic competition agencies to investigate and unearth evidence, difficulty in securing cooperation of the corresponding agencies in industrialized countries, and limitations in the law.

Anticompetitive Non-cartel Horizontal Agreements

Every horizontal agreement imposes some restraint on the commercial conduct of the parties. But all agreements need not be naked restraints of trade. There may be agreements between firms that are entered into with some efficiency objective, for example, for research and development. Competition laws do not prohibit these outright and generally adopt a liberal attitude towards them. Such cases may be examined under the 'rule of reason' to determine whether they have any anticompetitive effects, and if so whether there are outbalancing pro-competitive benefits, including efficiencies. Horizontal agreements, not amounting to cartels, may be of various kinds, as explained below.

Trade associations undertake activities to further the broader interests of the particular industry, for example, training; raising members' awareness about tax or other laws; lawfully lobbying the government on tax, tariffs, or other issues; educating members about new developments in technology or potential problems about the products; undertaking research and development; and addressing common problems like anti-dumping. However, often a trade association can function as a vehicle for cartel-type agreements whose main objective may be to manipulate the market through fixing prices, allocating territories, or rigging bids. Frequent meetings or exchange of information in trade associations can facilitate such cartel agreements. It is thus important

[17] Ibid.

[18] OECD. 2001. 'Global Forum on Competition: Summary of Cartel Cases Described by Invitees', available at http://www.oecd.org/dataoecd/41/30/2491386.pdf.

for associations to be wary of the boundaries of their legitimate activities vis-à-vis the competition law.

Some associations are set up for the purpose of coordinating the activities of members in the export markets with a view to economizing on the high costs involved in export marketing, such as in advertising. But the dividing line between coordinating for economic efficiency and for cartel activity may be blurred. The jurisdiction of the competition laws of most countries does not extend to activities that impact only overseas markets. In fact, some countries have special legislation authorizing export associations, so long as these do not have negative spill over effects in the domestic markets; this is the case, for example, in the United States.[19]

Firms often enter into a joint venture for a specific purpose, for example, to promote research or to undertake the joint manufacture of a new component needed by all the participating firms. Individually, such a venture may be beyond the resources of any single firm and it may enable the sharing of costs or resources and thus be efficiency enhancing. A joint venture may take different forms, for example, setting up a jointly owned new legal entity like a company or setting up a joint team or simply a joint activity. The legal form is not important. However, joint ventures may often contain provisions that restrict competition in order to make a cooperative activity work. Therefore, the competition authority must determine whether the visualized restrictions are reasonable and necessary to achieve the pro-competition purpose of the joint venture, or whether the same arrangement can be accomplished with less restrictions on the parties' freedom to compete.

Firms may enter into specialization agreements in which each participating firm agrees to concentrate on the activity in which it enjoys greater efficiency, and withdraws from the other activities in favour of other participating firms. For example, a firm may agree to manufacture only heavy-duty trucks while the other firm may produce only light commercial vehicles. Under some nations' laws these agreements are subject to analysis in the same way as joint ventures. Other nations may condemn them per se, if the firms have no integrative functions.

There may be horizontal agreements to restrict advertising, provide for information exchange, or adopt common standards. Such facilitating practice

[19] The Webb-Pomerene Export Trade Act provides antitrust immunity for the formation and operation of associations of otherwise competing businesses to engage in collective export sales. The immunity conferred by the statute does not extend to actions that have an anticompetitive effect within the United States or that injure competitors of members of export associations. See Antitrust Division Manual, Chapter 2, available at http://www.usdoj.gov/atr/foia/divisionmanual/ ch2.htm.

agreements are usually evaluated on the basis of how likely they are to lead to oligopolistic coordination and raise prices.[20]

Restrictions on false or misleading advertising are understandable, but restrictions on advertising as such could adversely impact competition. Advertising serves a purpose of enabling the business to make known the quality, price, and other features of its product to customers. Such restrictions could thus raise entry barriers.

Setting standards is beneficial for the consumer, especially those standards that relate to health and safety. They maintain quality and performance levels and promote compatibility of products. But they could also be misused to shut out competition by raising entry barriers (for example, by setting unjustifiably high standards, or obstructing certification processes). These could also artificially raise prices.

Information exchange by itself can generate efficiencies, for example, information about market trends, development of new technologies, or products or processes.

However, information exchange could equally reflect an implicit collusion that is being used by the colluding parties to set prices or divide markets or customers, especially if the information is about forward-looking data.

Anticompetitive Vertical Agreements

Vertical agreements lead to an integration of distinct businesses, a kind of loose vertical merger of the businesses without creating a single legal entity. In practice, the main concern of competition agencies has been the restraints placed on retail distribution. Common types of vertical agreements are: tie-in agreements, exclusive dealing agreements (also known as exclusive supply agreements), exclusive distribution agreements, and resale price maintenance. These and other vertical agreements are of particular concern where these are imposed by a dominant enterprise on distributors. Thus, while in some jurisdictions, some vertical agreements are dealt with under the provisions related to anticompetitive agreements, in other jurisdictions these are covered by provisions related to abuse of dominance.

Tie-in agreements are those where the distributor is obliged to accept along with a product (tying product), another product (tied product), for example, a software along with the hardware or, an experience older Indian consumers would be familiar with, a cooking gas burner along with a cooking

[20] See Meyerman, Gerald, Mary Jean Moltenbrey, Judy Whalley, et al. 1999. 'Agreements', in World Bank/OECD supra, n. 11, p. 31.

gas cylinder. An exclusive dealing agreement is one where the distributor is prohibited from dealing in competing products. Under exclusive distribution agreements, the distributor is confined to dealing only in a certain area or with certain customers, for example, the distributor may be prohibited from dealing with customers from outside the country. Resale price maintenance occurs when the distributor is obliged to not sell below a given price.

Enterprises in developing countries have often faced the adverse impact of such vertical restraints imposed by powerful multinational companies including exclusive dealing agreements or exclusive distribution agreements, for example, when enterprises were restrained from dealing with countries where the multinational companies had arrangements with other distributors.

According to Fox,[21] in the 1960s and 1970s, the law in the USA 'broadly condemned vertical restraints on grounds that they lessened the autonomy of dealers and foreclosed firms from the economic opportunity to supply significant customers and market segments.' But, by the middle to the end of the 1970s, the US law moved away from this view. In a watershed decision in *Continental TV Inc.* v. *GTE Sylvania*,[22] the Supreme Court ruled that the law must rely on economic concerns, not social or political concerns. It observed that vertical restraints may be efficient and thereby enhance inter-brand competition. Thus, both the beneficial and the harmful aspects have to be carefully balanced. For this reason, such violations are treated according to the 'rule of reason' in most countries. A not uncommon exception is resale price maintenance (minimum vertical price fixing), which is sometimes illegal on its face, and sometimes illegal on its face if engaged in by a dominant firm. This is because resale price maintenance may be used to facilitate a cartel or for single firm exploitation. Tie-ins are similarly treated. Where a firm with market power forces buyers of one product to accept another product, this conduct may be illegal; or illegality may turn on rule of reason analysis. The United States currently has a per se rule against minimum resale price maintenance; it has a modified per se rule against forced tie-ins by a firm with market power, but the recent trend is towards dilution of this approach and courts seem willing to consider the defendant's arguments that the tie was efficient and did not harm competition.

Anticompetitive Agreements–Block Exemptions

Some competition authorities have issued block exemptions, exempting thereby a class of agreements automatically from formal intervention by or

[21] See, Fox supra, n. 5, p. 226.

[22] 433 US 36 (1977), See also chapter 'Competition Law in the United States of America' by Stephen Calkins.

approval from the authority. Such block exemptions create a safe harbour for common types of agreements and remove uncertainty in the sense that the parties know that if their agreement falls within the block exemption, it would be saved from challenge. The European Commission has adopted block exemptions for agreements relating to specializations,[23] research and development,[24] technology transfer,[25] motor vehicle distribution,[26] and some others.[27] Apart from bringing greater certainty for the market players, such block exemptions also conserve the limited resources of the competition authority which would otherwise be spent on dealing with individual cases of such agreements.

Abuse of Dominance

The traditional definition of 'dominance' is that it relates to a position of economic strength enjoyed by an enterprise in the relevant market which enables it to prevent effective competition by affording it the power to behave independently of competitors and of customers.[28] Thus, dominance incorporates two characteristics: first, the ability of the enterprise to behave independently of customers or competitors, thereby allowing it to exploit customers (exploitative abuse), and second, to exclude competitors (exclusionary abuse). In a particular case, before abuse can be established, it will be necessary to determine that the enterprise is dominant. This involves two important exercises: one, to define the relevant market, and two, to assess whether the enterprise is dominant in the relevant market.

Relevant Market

The relevant market identifies the products or services which are such close substitutes for each other that they operate as a competitive constraint on the conduct of the suppliers thereof; it sets the framework within which dominance is to be determined.

[23] Regulation 2658/2000.

[24] Regulation 2659/2000.

[25] Regulation 772/2004.

[26] Regulation 1400/2002.

[27] See Rodger, Barry and Angus MacCulloch. 2004. *Competition Law and Policy in the EC and UK* (3rd ed.). Cavendish Publishing Ltd, p. 154.

[28] See *United Brands and United Brands Continental BV* v. *Commission of the European Communities* [1978] 1 CMLR 429 and *Hoffman-La Roche* v. *Commission* [1979] 3 CMLR 211.

The determination of the relevant market is of crucial importance. Several competition authorities have laid down the process they will follow in defining the relevant market. The relevant market comprises of two elements: the relevant product market and the relevant geographic market.

The relevant product market comprises all products that are in competition with the product in question. If the product market is drawn too narrowly it may exclude from consideration products that could compete, and this will increase the likelihood of the enterprise being found dominant; the reverse would be the case if the product market is defined too broadly. In determining the relevant product market, it is common to use certain economic tools. One such tool is the SSNIP test (acronym for Small, but Significant, Non-transitory Increase in Price), also called the 'hypothetical monopolist test'. Under this test, the question asked is that if the price of the product were increased by a factor of around 5 to 10 per cent, which other products would the customer switch to; all such products would be covered by the relevant product market. The SSNIP test has a major drawback known as the 'cellophane fallacy'[29] in determining the relevant product market in abuse of dominance cases. This refers to the situation where a dominant enterprise has already raised price to a non-competitive level; a further rise of say 5 to 10 per cent may result in demand substitution by a product which might not have been regarded as a substitute at a lower, competitive price. Thus, this could lead to an unjustifiably broad determination of the market, which would be favourable to the defence of the dominant firm.

Another test is the interchangeability of products. This examines a number of factors such as the physical characteristics of the product, the cross elasticity of demand, its intended use and its price, and the supply side interchangeability. In the landmark *United Brands* case,[30] the European Court of Justice laid down certain tests for defining the relevant product market. For example, it accepted that compared to other fruits, the banana constituted a separate market due to its softness and year-round availability making it particularly suitable for old people and small children, and the relevant product market did not include other fruits. In the *Staples/Office Depot* merger case,[31] the US court found that a relevant product submarket is only the consumable

[29] 'Cellophane fallacy' refers not to the product cellophane but the US case in which the fallacy was discussed, that is, *United States* v. *E.I. Du Pont de Nemours and Co.* 118 F Supp 41 (D Del 1953); aff'd 351 US 377 (US Sup Ct 1956).

[30] *United Brands Continental BV* v. *Commission of the European Communities* [1978] 1 CMLR 429 Rodger and MacCulloch (2004), ibid. at n. 28, p. 87.

[31] See http://www.ftc.gov/opa/1997/06/unofficial.htm.

items sold by office supply super stores, and did not include other products or products sold by department stores such as Walmart. In this reduced product market, Staples and Office Depot together enjoyed around 80 per cent in most local markets. This meant that the merged entity would have been a dominant firm in the relevant market, and prices would probably have gone up. The proposed merger did not go through.

The relevant geographic market is regarded as that part of the relevant market that identifies physical regions in which the firms might compete.[32] If a firm can raise prices and cut production without causing a quick influx of supply to the area from outside sources, that firm is operating in a distinct geographic market.[33]

Dominant Position in Relevant Market

After the relevant product and geographic markets are determined as above, the next issue is to determine if the enterprise enjoys a dominant position in the relevant market. A number of factors are usually examined in this exercise. Market share is an important factor, though not the only one. Along with the market share of the enterprise, it is necessary to see the market shares of its competitors, especially the near rivals. For instance, if the market share of the enterprise is 40 to 45 per cent, and that of its close rivals is about 30 per cent each, the rivals might constrain its action and the enterprise might not be dominant. But if the share of the nearest rival is only around 16 per cent, the likelihood of a constraining effect is more remote and the enterprise is more likely to be dominant. In *United Brands*,[34] the court examined the market share of United Brands, the market share of its next competitor, the extent of vertical integration of the enterprise, its technological advantages and its resources. After considering the combination of these factors, the court concluded that the hold of United Brands over the market was such that it enjoyed a dominant position.

It is also necessary to examine the entry barriers, such as legal restrictions, entry costs, and sunk costs (costs incurred that the enterprise would lose in the event it has to exit the market). A common view is that any cost that a prospective entrant has to bear is an entry barrier. But, some regard only those costs as entry barriers which are in excess of the entry costs borne by the incumbent enterprise. The concept of sunk costs is important for a

[32] *Black's Law Dictionary* (7th ed.), p. 983.

[33] Ibid.

[34] Ibid. at n. 28.

prospective entrant. For example, it may be possible for some entrants to carry their equipment elsewhere and utilize it for manufacture in some other area or for some other product, thereby reducing their sunk costs. But the entrants may not similarly be able to recover the advertisement expenditure already incurred for that product, which would therefore be included in sunk costs.

Abuse

An enterprise abuses its dominant position when it resorts to an anticompetitive practice to maintain or increase its position in the market, especially when such practice is not a response to the market, and when it has a significant effect on competition. In the EU, such abuse is prohibited under Article 82 of the EC Treaty, which also lists some examples of abuse, namely unfair pricing, restriction of production or output, and imposing discriminatory or unnecessary terms in dealings with trading partners.[35] The European court has held that the concept of abuse is an objective concept regarding behaviour of an undertaking in a dominant position, which is such as to influence the structure of a market where, as a result of the very presence of the undertaking in question, the degree of competition is weakened and which through recourse to methods different from those which condition normal competition in products or services on the basis of transactions of commercial operators has the effect of hindering the maintenance of the degree of competition still existing in the market or the growth of that competition.[36]

Abuse of dominant position may be of two types: exploitative and exclusionary. Exploitative abuse refers to excessive or monopoly pricing where the enterprise, not being restrained by competitive pressures, is able to charge a high price and reap 'monopoly profits', though it is not always easy to decide what price is excessive. Similarly, the enterprise may abuse its dominance by imposing unfair conditions other than price.

Most abuses of dominant position are of an exclusionary nature. A dominant enterprise may resort to tying-in, which may have the effect of excluding competitors in the tied product market since customers are forced to buy the tied product from the dominant enterprise. Or the dominant enterprise may refuse to supply the product or service to a customer; since the enterprise is dominant, this could leave very little choice to the customer.

[35] Glossary of Terms used in the EU Competition Policy, Directorate General for Competition, Brussels, July 2002.

[36] *Hoffman-La Roche* v. *Commission* [1979] 3 CMLR 211.

In some cases, where the dominant enterprise holds an 'essential facility', this could amount to foreclosing the market for the competitor. Access to an 'essential facility' has been a particularly controversial area of competition law. Courts have often granted access to an 'essential facility' where competition would not be possible without such access. For example, an electricity transmission line or a gas pipeline could be regarded as an essential facility. In the case of *London-European/Sabena*,[37] the court held that Sabena was abusing its dominance by not allowing London–European (a new airline) access to its computerized reservation system. In *Oscar Bronner*,[38] however, the court observed that it was not difficult for Bronner (a daily newspaper in Austria) to set up an alternative distribution system and declined to order access to the rival's distribution system. The Court set out the following conditions for the applicability of the 'essential facility' doctrine:[39]

- The facility must be indispensable to carrying on the entrant's business, in that there are no potential substitutes; and
- There must be technical, legal, or economic obstacles which make it impossible or unreasonably difficult to replicate the facility.

There is some tension between free trade and markets on the one hand and intellectual property rights (IPRs) such as patents and copyrights. An IPR is given to reward and encourage innovation and give to the holder thereof the exclusive right to its use, a kind of legal monopoly. But it is important that this right is not used to stifle competition. According to Fox, in the US in the 1960s and 1970s, and in the European Community in the 1970s and 1980s, the owner of an IPR was characterized as a monopolist and faced significant constraints. However, over time, in the USA, an IPR came to be regarded with deference rather than with suspicion. Earlier guidelines which enjoined the IPR holder not to tie-in, not to require grant backs, or not to charge royalties after the expiry of the patent were replaced by significantly relaxed guidelines. Similarly, the regulations of the European Commission were relaxed in favour of IPR holders; overall Fox believes, the EC shows less reluctance than US authorities to privilege IPR holders.[40]

[37] Commission decision 88/589/EEC, OJ1988, L317/47; [1989] 4 CMLR 662 cited at p. 107. Rodgers and MacCulloch (2004), ibid.

[38] *Oscar Bronner* v. *Media Print* [1998] ECR I-7791; [1999] 4 CMLR 112 cited in Rodgers and MacCulloch (2004), ibid.

[39] Ibid.

[40] See Fox supra, n. 5, p. 226.

While in most jurisdictions, including the European Union, the term used is abuse of dominance, in the US, the counterpart term is monopolization or attempted monopolization, which is prohibited under section 2 of the Sherman Act. In this area the contrast between the US and the EC approaches is most marked. Dominance under the EC law seems to require less market power than monopoly under US law.[41] The US law is more tolerant of monopolist behaviour, recognizing that monopoly firms also have the liberty to compete and engage in hard competition, even if it may lead to the extinction of rival firms. The US law focuses on harm caused to consumers and not the harm caused to competitors, while the EC approach so far seems to be that if competitors are unreasonably harmed, it would amount to harming competition. The US also has certain prophylactic rules, for example, on the right to refuse to deal, to change product design, or lower price.

Mergers

In competition law, the term 'merger' is used in a broad sense covering combinations of enterprises in various forms, for example, a merger proper, amalgamation, acquisition of shares, voting rights, or assets, or acquisition of control over an enterprise. Mergers are a normal activity within the economy and are a means for enterprises to expand business activity. However, some mergers could adversely affect competition. The principle for exercising merger control is that if a merger is likely to give rise to market power, it is better to prevent this from happening than to control the exercise of market power after the merger has taken place, that is to say, prevention is better than cure. Also, the social and economic cost of de-merging the firms after the merger is usually very heavy and thus not an easy option for competition authorities. Further, enterprises should not be allowed to evade the competition law by using the merger route to achieve an agreement between themselves which would have been found to be anticompetitive by a competition authority.

Mergers fall into one of three categories: horizontal mergers, vertical mergers, and conglomerate mergers. Horizontal mergers are between enterprises that are existing or potential competitors, being at the same level in the supply chain, for example, two manufacturers, two distributors, or two retailers of the same product. Vertical mergers are between enterprises at different levels in the supply chain, for example, a merger between a manufacturer and a distributor or retailer of the same or substitutable product. Conglomerate mergers are between enterprises which have neither horizontal nor vertical

[41] See Fox, ibid.

relationship, for example, between enterprises manufacturing or distributing different products.

Usually, competition authorities are most concerned with horizontal mergers. These can have two kinds of anticompetitive effects, unilateral effects or coordinated effects. A merger may lead to a monopoly (in an extreme case) or otherwise create an enterprise with substantial or substantially increased market power. The enterprise can then overcharge, or otherwise unilaterally abuse its dominant position. Or a merger may decrease the number of competing enterprises and make it easier for the remaining enterprises to coordinate their behaviour in terms of price, quantity, or quality, that is, a cartel-type arrangement. This is likely to be easier in markets for homogeneous products.

The adverse impact of vertical mergers on competition is comparatively less. Also they may bring benefits for the merging enterprises and for consumers, which is less likely and less convincing in the case of horizontal mergers. However, in certain circumstances, vertical mergers can attract action by competition authorities. For example, if a dominant enterprise acquires sources of raw materials, this enterprise could deny access to raw materials to competitors or potential competitors; such a merger could also facilitate collusion.

Generally, conglomerate mergers are not considered potentially anticompetitive. However, some competition authorities are wary of mergers that may produce a conglomerate with great financial and market power and with deep pockets. Sometimes conglomerate mergers could give rise to a situation of 'mutual forbearance', where each enterprise may independently decide to compete less vigorously with the other in that section of the market where its position is relatively weak, thereby leading to a situation of peaceful co-existence rather than vigorous competition.

Experience worldwide shows that only in a small proportion of cases do competition authorities find it necessary to intervene in order to block or modify a merger; in the majority of cases such intervention is not found to be necessary.

Merger analysis differs from the analysis of anticompetitive agreements or of abuse of dominance in an important way: in the case of mergers, the authority is trying to look into future performance or behaviour rather than into existing or past behaviour. Also, in the case of mergers, timely completion of the inquiry becomes important so as not to unnecessarily hold up a proposed merger. Many competition laws, therefore, provide for a time limit for the completion of a merger inquiry; if not completed in that time, the law may provide that the merger is deemed approved.

Some competition authorities have issued merger guidelines describing the process they will use in analysing the merger. Well known are the 1997 guidelines for horizontal mergers of the US Department of Justice and the Federal Trade Commission.[42] These provide for a five-step process consisting of market definition, identification of enterprises and their market shares, identification of potential adverse effects, entry barriers, and generation of efficiencies. Guidelines of other competition authorities may differ in detail, but they are broadly consistent in their approach.[43]

Determining the relevant market (relevant product market and relevant geographic market) in a merger case is important as in an abuse of dominance case. A flawed determination of the market can give a completely distorted picture of the likely power that would be enjoyed by the merged entity.

Next, it is necessary to identify the enterprises active in the relevant market or that are potential competitors in the market and to assess the market shares of these enterprises. A very high market share of the merged enterprise, particularly in a concentrated market, may restrict competition. Competition authorities usually carry out a concentration analysis using economic tools such as the concentration ratio (of the top few firms, usually the top four) or the Herfindahl–Hirschman Index (HHI). The US guidelines use the HHI to determine whether the market has low, medium, or high level of concentration and also contain a benchmark of how much increase in the HHI in each of the above instances would give rise prima facie to competition concerns, and therefore would warrant further analysis.

The next step is to identify the potential adverse effects, including unilateral effects and coordinated effects. In the case of horizontal mergers, the apprehension of the competition authorities is often that a monopoly or a dominant firm would emerge which could easily raise prices and/or reduce output or resort to other unilateral or coordinated effects. For example, in the case of the proposed merger between Staples and Office Depot, the US FTC noted that in geographic areas where only one of the three office supply superstores was present, the price was significantly higher than the price in areas where two of the firms were present, and in many localities the merged firm would be the only office supply superstore left. Thus, there was a concern that the merged firm could raise prices significantly above the competitive level.

[42] Horizontal Merger Guidelines, available at http://www.usdoj.gov/atr/public/guidelines/horiz_book/toc.html.

[43] Bamford, Peter, David Elliott, Russel Pittman, and Margaret Sanderson (1999): in World Bank/OECD (1999) supra, n. 11, p. 46.

It is important to determine how easy or difficult it is for new firms to enter the market in response to monopolistic pricing or other monopolistic conduct, that is, to determine the entry barriers. This analysis is similar to that in the case of abuse of dominance.

It is usual for merging parties to claim gain in efficiencies through a merger and in addition, to claim that such gain in efficiencies would be shared with the consumers. A relevant consideration is also the 'failing firm' defence, that is to say, if a firm is likely to go out of business anyway, the consumer would not be harmed if that firm would be acquired by an existing competitor.

Most competition laws require prior notification of the merger to the competition authority. In a few countries like India, the UK, and Finland, prior notification is not mandatory but optional.

Remedies

In the case of anticompetitive agreements, including cartels, and abuse of dominant position, the range of remedies provided in the law usually includes the following:

1. The authority or court passes an order to cease the offending practice and to desist from re-entering the practice, usually referred to as a 'cease and desist' order.
2. Many laws provide that an anticompetitive agreement shall be deemed void, that is to say it had never existed. This means that a party to the agreement can no longer enforce it before a court or other authority and cannot sue to recover from the other party or parties the benefits that it may claim to have been entitled to under the agreement.
3. The law usually allows the authority or court to impose monetary penalties. The maximum penalty may be prescribed in absolute terms or, as is common in the modern laws, as a percentage of annual revenues (that is, turnover). For example, in the laws of the EU, UK, and India the maximum penalty is 10 per cent of the turnover. Most laws allow penalties on worldwide turnover; however, in actual practice, so far penalties have been related generally to turnover within the country or region.

   The quantum of the fine in an individual case may depend upon criteria such as the gravity of the violation, the length of time over which the violation has continued, whether it was a repeat offence, the extent of damage caused to the economy, the amount of unlawful profit made, the involvement of senior management, and so on. In the UK, if an enterprise has a competition law compliance programme, this is regarded as a mitigating factor; on the other hand, if directors or senior management were involved in the offence, this is regarded as an aggravating factor.[44]

4. The authority or court may even require compulsory licensing of technology or the compulsory provision of access to an 'essential facility' with a view to establish competition in the market in which it was being suppressed or the enterprise may be ordered to take any other action necessary to ensure fair competition in the market, for example, the Indian Competition Act, 2002, empowers the Competition Commission of India to 'pass such other order as it may deem fit'.
5. The law may also provide for the award of compensation or damages. The US law has the well-known 'treble damages' provision whereby the compensation claim could be up to three times the loss caused to the injured party.[45]
6. Sometimes the complainant and the defendant may arrive at an informal settlement with the involvement of the competition authority or court. If it is a private dispute, such settlement may be preferable as it could avoid lengthy legal proceedings that impose huge costs on the parties.
7. In the case of cartels, stiffer penalties designed to have a deterrent effect are usually provided. In the UK, in the case of cartels, the amount of fine has no upper ceiling.[46] Under the Indian law, the normal ceiling on the fine is 10 per cent of the turnover (annual revenues); but for a cartel the fine may be 10 per cent of the turnover or three times the profit made by the cartel, whichever is higher.[47]
8. In an increasing number of countries, cartelization is treated as a criminal offence punishable with imprisonment, in addition to other penalties.

   As many as nine OECD countries have such a provision; Australia is also said to be considering an amendment in this regard. In the UK, in addition to the unlimited fine and the prison term, offending individuals can be disbarred from holding the position of director or like positions for 15 years.[48]

[44] OFT. 2005. 'How your Business can Achieve Compliance', available at http://www.oft.gov.uk/nr/rdonlyres/78ad1280–4eb8–46d4-a52b-207f9afeaae1/0/oft424.pdf.

[45] Section 4 of the Clayton Act, 1914.

[46] Section 190 Enterprise Act, 2002. According to Section 190 (1) (a), a person guilty of an offence under section 188 of the Enterprise Act (cartel offence), on conviction on indictment will be liable to imprisonment for a term not exceeding five years or to a fine, or to both.

[47] Section 27(b) of the Indian Competition Act, 2002.

[48] Section 204, Enterprise Act, 2002 (United Kingdom).

9. In many laws, a fine may be imposed not only on the enterprise but also on an employee. However, the ceiling for a fine in the case of an individual may be substantially lower than in the case of a company. In the US, the maximum fine for a company is US$ 100 million whereas in the case of an individual it is US$ 1 million. In India, the law provides that in the case of a contravention, 'every person who at the time the contravention was committed, was responsible to the company for the conduct of the business of the company, as well as the company, shall be deemed to be guilty of the contravention and shall be liable to be proceeded against and punished accordingly'.[49] Thus in the Indian law, on the face of it, no distinction has been made between the maximum penalty that can be imposed on an individual and on a company.

In the case of mergers, three kinds of remedies are normally open to authorities if the merger is found to be potentially anticompetitive. The merger may be prohibited in its entirety or if it has already taken place, the unusual step of de-merging the merged entity may be ordered. Alternatively, the merger may be allowed with certain remedies like the divestiture of an operation. The authority may also pass an order regulating the conduct of the merged entity to prevent anticompetitive effects. The first two remedies are regarded as structural while the third is behavioural. Behavioural remedies are less popular with authorities because of the difficulty in monitoring them.

Competition Advocacy

Competition law is generally aimed against private restraints on trade, that is, against anticompetitive acts of private parties. However, there are restraints that may arise from acts of governments acting in their sovereign capacity or of regulators acting in their statutory capacity. Government departments acting in a commercial capacity are usually covered by the competition law as much as private players, unless the competition law exempts such activities from its purview. Where government departments act in their sovereign capacity, these acts usually fall outside the jurisdiction of the competition law. But here competition authorities could have an advocacy role whereby they could bring to the notice of government the anticompetitive fallout of their policies, and suggest suitable changes to such policies. In some countries, the law specifically mandates or allows the competition authority to take such advocacy measures, for example, in India,[50] the United Kingdom,[51] and

[49] Section 48 (1), the Indian Competition Act, 2002.

[50] Section 49, Indian Competition Act, 2002.

[51] Sections 6 and 7, Enterprise Act, 2002.

Australia.[52] The extent to which the competition authority can intervene as part of its advocacy role may vary according to the provision of the law. In some cases the law may provide that the competition authority may give its opinion upon being asked to do so by the government, and the government may give due consideration to the opinion. But the law could also allow the competition authority to give its opinion on its own motion.

Even where there is no specific provision in the law, there may be nothing to prevent the competition authority from sending its opinion to the government on a matter that involves a policy or legislation that has anti-competitive effects. However, in this case, the opinion may not have the same statutory standing as when there is a specific provision in the law allowing such intervention.

Government policies and practices that may directly impinge on the state of competition in the markets include, for example, policies in the areas of: international trade and import tariffs, industrial and foreign investment, protection to small and medium enterprises, government procurement, deregulation of infrastructure industries, privatization of state enterprises, and state subsidies. Competition authorities could influence these policies with the view to expanding the space for competition in the economy. Competition law by itself may not be sufficient to bring about contested markets; the role of government policy is crucial.

Many countries have only recently migrated to the market economy from a government-controlled economy. This is particularly true of several developing countries. In many of these countries, therefore, the culture of competition is weak, not merely within government but also within the private sector itself. For this reason, compliance with the competition law may also be poor. In such countries, the competition authorities have the additional task of spreading awareness about the competition law and its benefits for the economy as a whole and for the consumers. Such efforts can advance the levels of compliance, and also reduce the need for direct intervention by competition authorities in individual cases.

This could help in ensuring the optimal use of the limited resources of competition authorities.

Competition authorities also seek to educate the parties about their understanding of the law and their approach to its enforcement. Thus, many authorities put out guidelines on specific areas of the law, for example, control of mergers, or application of the leniency provision to cartel cases, or the treatment of joint ventures. This helps to enhance transparency and reduce uncertainty in the minds of the affected parties and also promotes compliance.

52 Section 28, Trade Practices Act, 1974.

Role in Regulated Sectors

Recent years have witnessed major liberalization of national economies. In both industrialized countries and developing nations, state-owned monopolies are being wholly or partly privatized. This has led to private monopolies substituting public monopolies, which is not in the best interest of the consumers. Further, there are sectors depending on networks such as telecommunications, water supply, electricity, and gas distribution; these networks cannot be easily duplicated. These are also natural monopolies as the market may not support the existence of more than one economic supplier. In many sectors, there is the issue of providing 'universal service' such as in the postal service, telecommunications, and water; this means that these services have to be provided to every customer who desires them. The usual solution to these problems is to subject these sectors to regulation. This typically involves setting up of an authority in the shape of a sector regulator which will control or regulate prices, quality, and other service conditions and also oversee the social obligations of the enterprises, such as providing universal service.

The role of competition authorities in regulated sectors of the economy and their relationship with sector regulators has been a subject of much debate, within countries and in international forums. Different models exist across countries, which give varying degrees of intervention powers to the competition authorities. In some countries, such as Australia and New Zealand, the reach of the competition authority is wide. In Australia, certain sector regulators such as the telecom and electricity regulators have been merged into the Australian Consumer and Competition Commission (ACCC). In New Zealand, competition issues are dealt with by the economy-wide competition authority under the Commerce Act, rather than by a sector regulator. In Mexico, before the sector regulator can undertake economic regulation of the sector (as opposed to regulation purely in technical matters), it needs an opinion from the competition authority stating that there is no effective competition in the sector. If the competition authority further is of the opinion that a certain player is dominant in the sector, the sector regulator could impose obligations on such dominant player. In South Africa, at first, the 1998 Competition Act excluded 'acts subject to or authorized by other legislation'. Consequently, the application of the Competition Act to regulated sectors was in doubt till the Act was amended in 2000. The amended Act calls for establishing agreements regarding working relationships between competition authorities and sector regulators.[53] In the UK, the law gives concurrent

[53] See OECD. 2003. 'OECD Peer Review: Competition Law and Policy in South Africa', available at http://www.oecd.org/dataoecd/43/58/34823812.pdf.

powers for the enforcement of the competition law to the competition authority and the sector regulators, and there are administrative arrangements to decide which authority is best suited to take up a particular case. There would be very few countries where the jurisdiction of the competition law and the competition authority is expressly excluded from the regulated sectors. Many laws even provide for consultations to be undertaken between the competition authority and the sector regulators. Whether or not the law has such a provision, it is a healthy practice for the competition authority and the sector regulators to undertake mutual consultations. Both authorities have their respective strengths, and consultations can enable the strengths of both to be applied to an individual case. Consultations also can discourage forum-shopping by parties.

Competition Law and Economics

Competition law is an economic law; it is about the economic behaviour of agents. Economics provides a theoretical basis for the law; it also provides the tools with which to analyse markets and competition within them.[54]

For a proper appreciation of the competition law, it is important to have an understanding of the economic concepts inherent in the law. As Brandeis J. once said, 'A lawyer who has not studied economics...is very apt to become a public enemy.'[55]

Competition in the economic sphere denotes the process of rivalry between firms for the patronage of customers. Khemani et al. define competition as a situation in which firms or sellers 'independently strive for buyers' patronage in order to achieve a particular business objective, for example, profits, sales, or market share'.[56] The European Commission also defines it in identical terms.[57] Richard Whish refers to competition in the commercial world as 'a striving for the custom and business of people in the market place'.[58] In this

[54] See Doern, G. Bruce and Stephen Wilks. 2001. *Comparative Competition Policy—National Institutions in a Global Market,* Oxford University Press.

[55] Quoted in Whish, Richard. 2005. *Competition Law* (5th ed.) Oxford University Press, p. 1.

[56] Khemani et al. (1999) supra, n. 11, p. 4.

[57] Glossary of terms used in EU Competition Policy, Director General for Competition, Italy, 2002, available at http://europa.eu.int/comm/competion/general_info/glossary_en.html.

[58] See Whish (2005) supra, n. 55, p. 23. For another definition, see, Consumer International: The Consumer Guide to Competition: A Practical Notebook, March 2003.

sense, competition is the equivalent of rivalry between firms; this rivalry may be in different forms such as for price, service, or a combination thereof, or other factors.

Competition is at the heart of the market-based economy. The debate about the relative merits of a market-based economy versus a state controlled, planned economy that raged for decades seems to have been broadly settled in favour of the former. Countries across the globe are reforming their economies, and undertaking privatization and deregulation. As they do so, the forces of competition come increasingly onto the centre stage of the economy.

A perfectly competitive market requires that there should be a large number of sellers and buyers, each seller, therefore, having only a small share of the market. Further, the product should be homogeneous, there should be no entry or exit barriers or information asymmetries, and both the seller and buyer should have access to the market. In such a market, sellers are price-takers, not price-makers, and the price of a product equals its marginal cost; each supplier makes only a normal profit.

A perfectly competitive market is said to achieve allocative efficiency and productive efficiency. The combined effect of allocative and productive efficiencies is that society's welfare overall is maximized. Consumer welfare is also maximized in such a situation. Allocative efficiency is achieved when the goods are produced in the quantities desired by society; and it is not possible to make any one better off without making someone else worse off. Productive efficiency is achieved when goods are produced at the lowest possible cost, that is, as little of society's wealth is expended in the production process as is necessary. Competition also enhances dynamic efficiency in that it spurs innovation, development of new products, and technological growth.

If perfect competition is at one end of the spectrum, at the other end is monopoly. Here, there are many buyers but only one seller, who is a monopolist and who is in a position therefore, to increase prices and reduce the volume of supply. In this situation there is allocative inefficiency which is also referred to as dead-weight loss. In economic theory, however, the objection to monopoly is not only that the monopolist is able to charge excessively and reduce production, but also that monopoly is inefficient. The inefficiency arises out of higher costs, for example, through higher remuneration and excessive staff. A monopolist may also waste resources by maintaining excess capacity or indulging in excessive product differentiation. This situation is also referred to as X-inefficiency; the term first used by Liebenstein.[59]

[59] Liebenstein. 1966. 'Allocative Efficiency vs X-Efficiency'. 56 *American Economic Review,* 392–415 quoted at p. 5, Whish, Richard supra, n. 56.

A weakness of the competition theory, however, is that in the real world neither perfect competition nor a perfect monopoly exists. Perfect competition is based on assumptions (mentioned above) that are unlikely, if not impossible, to be found in real life, where the situation is likely to be somewhere between these two poles of perfect competition and a monopoly. Nevertheless, perfect competition is a model which is still useful to demonstrate the concept of productive and allocative efficiencies and as a benchmark against which to measure the actual situation in the market. Short of perfect competition, therefore, other more realistic concepts have evolved over the years. For example, some economists have settled for the concept of 'workable competition', evolved by Clark in 1940.[60] This concept considers it worthwhile to aim to produce the best competitive arrangements that are practically attainable. Some economists have advanced the theory of 'contestable market' according to which firms are constrained by competitive forces, provided entering into the market is free and exit is costless; that is, the incumbent enterprise must be wary of a 'hit-and-run' entry by competitors. The EC competition law uses the expression 'effective competition' though what is meant by the term has not been spelt out.

Another weakness in the competition theory is that in certain situations, competition may in fact not yield the best result in terms of efficiencies, as for example, where the economies of scale support the existence of only one enterprise. Further, in the case of certain industries, there exists what is called the 'network effect', that is, the utility of a product or service increases with the increase in the number of consumers, for example, in telecommunications or personal computer operating systems. Thus, the network effect could in certain situations, indicate that it is more beneficial to have only one or a few producers of products or providers of services.

In the US, two important economic schools of thought have greatly influenced competition law and policy. In the 1950s, the structure–conduct–performance concept was developed by what has come to be known as the 'Harvard school' of thought, attributed to E.S. Mason and J.S. Bain. According to this school, the market structure influences conduct which, in turn, influences performance. Concentrated markets are regarded as quite susceptible to economic power and its exercise. Antitrust law is regarded as an important tool to protect the market. This school gives to competition law a more interventionist role and places less confidence in the markets. According to this view, competition policy should be concerned with structural remedies rather than behavioural remedies.

[60] Clark. 1940. 'Towards a Concept of Workable Competition'. 30 *American Economic Review*, 241–56 quoted at p. 14, Whish, Richard supra, n. 56.

In the 1970s and 1980s, the ascendancy of the 'Chicago school' of thought produced a revolution in antitrust thinking. The 'Chicago school' focuses on the pursuit of efficiency as the sole goal of antitrust; efficiency consisting of allocative efficiency and productive efficiency. According to this view, most markets are competitive, and entry barriers are more imagined than real; a monopolist's position is quickly eroded and firms are rational in their pursuit of profit maximization. The Chicago school believes that antitrust policy should be less interventionist than demanded by the structure-conduct-performance paradigm. The Harvard school saw concentration as the evil. The Chicago school does not worry about concentration so much, and thinks government intervention is usually clumsy and inefficient. Therefore the foundation is not concentration but non-intervention unless the plaintiff can show price raising outcomes from specific conduct or transactions. But the Chicago school itself spans a spectrum, with some applying more robust market premises than others.

Both the 'Harvard' and 'Chicago' schools have left their stamp on antitrust thinking. However, recent years seem to have witnessed a rapprochement between the two. It is being increasingly recognized that while economics may provide the tools for analysis and it may also indicate what questions to ask, it does not always yield definitive answers, and it does not provide space for society's values to be taken into consideration.

The European tradition of competition law owes much to the German ordoliberal school of thought, also referred to as the Freiburg school. This sees competition law almost as part of an 'economic constitution'. It believes that competition is necessary for economic welfare and that economic freedom is necessary for political freedom. It stresses the necessity to disperse private economic power so as not to influence political power. The ordo-liberal school had a profound influence on the early decisions in European competition law and could account for its greater concern in protecting the freedom of competitors to compete on merits.

Competition law employs a number of economic tools in analysing individual cases; for example, an important starting point in analysing a case is to determine the relevant market, the purpose of which is to identify the products and services which are such close substitutes for one another that they operate as a competitive constraint on the conduct of the supplier of those products and services. The relevant market comprises of the relevant product market and the relevant geographic market. As discussed earlier, an economic tool usually employed in determining the relevant product market is the SSNIP test (also called the hypothetical monopolistic test) to determine the demand side or supply side substitutability of the product. Also, economic tools are used for determining the entry barriers which may include determining the economies of scale, extent of product differentiation, extent of capital requirement, and predatory behaviour.

Some empirical studies have tried to measure the gains from competition in the markets. In a contemporaneous review in the United States of deregulation of natural gas, long-distance telecommunications, airlines, trucking, and rail, it was reported that real prices dropped at least 25 per cent and sometimes close to 50 per cent within 10 years of deregulation in those industries. The annual value of consumer benefit from such deregulation was estimated to be approximately US$ 5 billion in the long-distance telecommunication industry, US$ 19.40 billion in the airline industry, US$ 19.60 billion in the trucking industry, and US$ 9.10 billion in the rail industry. At the same time, there were improvements in the quality of service.[61] A study by the Australian Productivity Commission, quoted by OECD, estimates that Australian household 'annual incomes are, on average, around A$ 7,000 higher as a result of competition policy'.[62] The same OECD document also quotes a study that estimates that pro-competition policy developments in New Zealand and the UK have added around 2.5 percentage points to their employment rate over the period 1978–98; countries with more modest reforms, such as Greece, Italy, and Spain added only 0.5–1 per cent to the employment rate.[63] Another study finds that 'reforms promoting private governance (that is, privatization) and competition tend to boost productivity. In manufacturing, gains to be expected from lower entry barriers are greater the farther a given country is from the technology leader.[64]

Two elements are required to maintain competition in the economy: a competition policy and a competition law. Competition policy refers generally

[61] Robert Luke, J. 1997. 'Economic Deregulation and Customers Choice: Lessons for the Electricity Industry, George Messing University Centre for Market Process', quoted in Crampton, Paul. 2003. *Competition and Efficiency as Organizing Principles for all Economic and Regulatory Policy Making*, OECD-IADB, April 2003.

[62] OECD. 2005. 'The Relationship between Competition Authorities and Sectoral Regulators', Document No. DAF/COMP/GF (2005)2 for Global Forum on Competition, OECD February, 2005, p. 3, available at http://www.oecd.org/dataoecd/8/61/237607.pdf.

[63] Nicoletti, Guiseppe and Stefano Scarpetta. 2001. 'Interaction between Product and Labour Market Regulations: Do They Affect Employment? Evidence from OECD Countries', OECD Economics Working Papers, quoted in OECD (2005), ibid.

[64] Nicoletti, Guiseppe and Stefano Scarpetta. 2003. 'Regulations, Productivity and Growth: OECD Evidence', World Bank Policy Research Working Paper No. 2944, January 2003 quoted in OECD (2005), ibid.

to a set of government measures that enhance competition, give primacy to market forces, facilitate entry and exit, reduce administrative controls, and minimize regulations. Competition law refers to a statute to prohibit and penalize anticompetitive practices and regulate potentially anticompetitive mergers. The two elements are mutually complementary, one trying to promote a market-based economy as opposed to controlled or regulated economy, the other trying to remove impediments that may be placed by market players in the functioning of the economy.

The International Dimension

One of the controversial areas of competition law has been its extra-territorial reach. As the world economy becomes more globalized, an anticompetitive act of a firm may have effect not only in the country where it is located, but even in other countries, where it has business activities. In most countries, the legal view taken is that the domestic competition law captures such acts even if the guilty enterprise is not located in the country, provided that the anticompetitive act has an effect in the country. This doctrine is also referred to as the 'effects doctrine' or the principle of 'extra-territoriality'. This doctrine was first used in any significant manner by the US courts. An early case[65] related to the aluminium cartel, in which the US authorities sued not only the US firm Alcoa, but also the Canadian firm Aluminum Limited. This assertion of jurisdiction was resented by many other countries that saw this as an invasion of their sovereignty. Some of these other countries even enacted laws[66] to block discovery of evidence needed by overseas authorities for prosecuting such cases. The UK, for example, enacted the British Protection of Trading Interests Act, 1980. Adverse reaction led to a modification in the US position, and though the reach of the US law was never really restricted, the courts' approach was that all factors should be weighed, including conflict with foreign law and policy, and that to invite intervention the foreign firm's alleged anticompetitive conduct must have a direct, substantial, and reasonably foreseeable effect in the US market.[67]

In time, the US enacted the Foreign Trade Antitrust Improvements Act, 1982, which clarified as above the extra-territorial reach of the US law regarding foreign commerce other than import commerce, that is to say,

[65] *United States* v. *Aluminum Company of America* 148 F 2d. 416, of Fox supra, n. 1, p. 225.

[66] See Fox supra.

[67] See Fox supra, pp. 225–6.

for intervention, there must be direct, substantial, and foreseeable effect on US domestic or certain export commerce. For matters harming only foreign nations, there is no jurisdiction under US law.

The European courts too have asserted the effects doctrine in several cases involving overseas firms. For example, the European authorities intervened in the merger between Boeing and McDonnell Douglas[68] and in the merger between General Electric and Honeywell[69] on grounds of their potential anti-competitive effect in European markets. Similarly, the European Commission took action against Microsoft for abuse of its dominant position in the personal computer operating systems market, and imposed a heavy penalty on the firm.

The effects doctrine is now not questioned in international competition law to the extent that nations may, if they wish, take jurisdiction over offshore conduct that harms their markets. The competition laws of many nations have specific provision to this effect, for example, India, Germany, and EU.[70]

The OECD Guidelines for Multinational Enterprises expressly caution these enterprises to take into account the competition laws of not only the countries in which they operate, but also those countries where their acts may have effect.[71]

A connected matter here is of international cooperation in the enforcement of competition law, an issue brought into greater focus by the growing globalization of trade. Increasingly, competition cases involve more than one competition law jurisdiction such as global cartels, cross-border mergers, and abuse of dominance by multinational corporations. A competition authority may find itself unable to tackle a competition problem where it arises from actions of firms located overseas, or it may risk taking action which affects the interests of other countries. This has underlined the necessity for competition authorities to cooperate with each other. In recent years, a number of bilateral cooperation agreements have come into existence. Most of these involve the more industrialized nations. Also, several regional trade agreements incorporate cooperation on competition issues, for example, the European Community, and the North American Free Trade Agreement (NAFTA). The level of cooperation visualized in these agreements varies

[68] (1997) OJ L 336/16.

[69] Case COMP/M. 2220, Commission decision 2004/134/EC: Case T-210/01 (Ct. of First Instance 14 December 2005), available at http://www.curia.eu.int/en/content/ juris/index.htm. [GE/Honeywell Judgment].

[70] See Fox supra.

[71] Ibid.

greatly. Some of the agreements contain only general provisions encouraging cooperation. But some others contain more detailed and specific provisions, such as the mutual notification of cases, exchange of information, collection of evidence, confidentiality of information exchanged, and so on. The agreements may contain provisions of negative comity (respect for the other party's enforcement) and positive comity (either party can request the other to take action in a particular case). One of the more well-known agreements is that between the USA and the EC. The two authorities have cooperated, or at least consulted, in a number of high-profile cases such as the merger cases of AOL–Time Warner, GE–Honeywell, and Boeing–McDonnell Douglas, though the two authorities may have differed in their conclusions in some of these cases, which also brought out the limitations of these cooperation agreements.

The only multilateral agreement on competition law is the United Nations Set of Multilaterally Agreed Equitable Principles and Rules for the Control of Restrictive Business Practices (the UN set) brought about under the aegis of UNCTAD. This is however, not a binding agreement; it only recommends certain general principles to member countries. The objectives of the UN set include: to ensure that restrictive business practices do not impede or negate the realization of benefits that should arise from the liberalization of tariff and non-tariff barriers affecting world trade, particularly those affecting the trade and development of developing countries; to attain greater efficiency in international trade; to protect and promote social welfare; and to provide a set of multilateral principles and rules for the control of restrictive business practices which will facilitate the adoption and strengthening of laws and policies in this area at the national and regional levels.[72] The UN Set includes principles with regard to preferential or differential treatment for developing countries; principles and rules for enterprises including transnational corporations; principles and rules for states at national, regional, and sub-regional levels; and international measures and international institutional machinery. Efforts by the EC and some others to include competition law and policy in the WTO negotiations with the view to have a multilateral framework did not succeed as many countries had serious reservations about this proposal; many developing countries did not feel sufficiently prepared to enter into negotiations with highly expert counterparts and wished to maintain sufficient 'policy space'

[72] See Objectives, United Nations Set of Multilaterally Agreed Equitable Principles and Rules for the Control of Restrictive Business Practices, available at http:// r0.unctad.org/en/subsites/cpolicy/docs/CPSet/cpsetp4.htm.

for themselves.[73] In the near future, it appears that only limited cooperation on the lines of existing bilateral and regional agreements may be possible, and the development of a multilateral framework seems unlikely at this stage.

Competition Law in Developing Countries

The two dominant influences today on competition law are of the US and the EC. The US tradition of antitrust is the older of the two and has had some influence on the evolution of the law in Europe as well. The US has a more non-interventionist version of competition law based on greater trust in the markets. The EC law diverges from the US law mainly in its treatment of abuse of dominant position, and shows greater concern in protecting competitors from unfair treatment that blocks competition on the merits. It also takes into account objectives other than economic efficiency, such as integration of the European common market and state aids.

Developing countries face a host of problems, such as the removal of poverty and reduction in the extreme disparities in incomes and standards of living. They also have relatively poorly developed social services and business infrastructure. Developing markets exhibit some distinct characteristics such as higher entry barriers, higher concentration ratios, greater instances of dominance particularly by erstwhile public-sector monopolies, fragmentation of the national market, marked asymmetries of information, presence of small scale and cottage enterprises providing livelihood to large numbers of people and sub-optimal size of firms. Further, the resources at the command of enforcement agencies in developing countries are meagre compared to the resources available to competition authorities in industrialized countries, and the former's experience in enforcement of the law is limited.

The question often arises whether these characteristics of developing countries warrant a different or modified approach to the enforcement of competition law. For example, should the law seek to protect domestic competitors from being overwhelmed by the more powerful multi-national corporations? To what extent must the law accommodate arrangements by the state or by small scale enterprises to coordinate their activities with the view to providing meaningful competition to larger enterprises? For example, in countries such as India, there are small scale industries development corporations, owned by the State, that pool marketing activities of small scale industries:

[73] See UNCTAD document TD/B/COM.2/CLP/45/Rev.1 dated 9 September 2005.

should such pooling give rise to competition concerns? Governments in developing countries (and even in Europe) provide incentives for the growth of disadvantaged regions. Should competition law allow an anticompetitive agreement or an abuse of dominance to be justified on such considerations? Competition law provides exemptions—should there be more exemptions in developing countries?

Singh and Dhumale have suggested that development friendly competition policies need to have different objectives from those normally posited for advanced economies; such policies also need to be specific to the stage of a country's economic and industrial development as well as its institutional and governance capacities.[74] Fox is of the view that raising questions such as the above is relevant in view of the special characteristics of developing markets. In her opinion, in the case of many egregious anticompetitive practices such as cartels and boycotts in aid of cartels, there is no reason to seek differential rules. Practices that are clear violations in developed countries are often targeted at developing countries and are harming their people and their development. However, in certain other cases, the market characteristics of developing countries tend to be different, and therefore the efficient rule for certain industrialized countries might not be efficient rule for developing countries. For example, the US predatory pricing rule was adopted against a background of robust goods markets, well-functioning capital markets, and relative ease of entry. Monopolization by predatory pricing is likely to be easier and more sustainable in developing countries. At the same time, however, the freedom of low pricing might be all the more valuable in developing countries. Fox's claim is not that the best rule for developing countries is obvious but that general economic context is always relevant and that trade-offs should be considered by developing countries in terms of what they think is best for them. Fox suggests active engagement by the developing countries in the current debate about convergence of antitrust standards in the world or else their views could go by default.[75]

Experiences across the globe demonstrate that markets, whether in developed or developing countries, are subject to failures in broadly similar ways. The practices of cartelization, abuse of dominance, and anticompetitive mergers are as much prevalent in developing countries as in the developed economies. OECD's Global Forum on Competition, 2001, contains a list

[74] UNCTAD (2002). G-24 Discussion Paper No. 18, September 2002, UNCTAD/GDS/MDPB/G24/18.

[75] See chapter 'Conflicts, Convergence, Cooperation, and World Competition Law' by Eleanor M. Fox in the 2007 edition of *Competition Law Today*.

of 26 cartel and bid rigging cases reported by 12 developing countries; these cases were suspected in diverse sectors of the economy such as transportation, phone cards, gasification, engineering construction, milk products, aviation, courier services, drugs, and electrical energy.[76] At the OECD Global Forum on Competition, 2005, participating developing countries provided information on nine specific cases of actual or alleged abuse of dominant position in nine developing countries; these cases related to the regulated or partially regulated sectors of the economy such as insurance, telecommunications, electricity, pharmaceuticals, and marine ports.[77] Jenny has observed on the basis of empirical evidence that 'the scope of anti-competitive activity in developing countries is staggering in terms of the type of practices (cartels, abuses of dominance, vertical restrictions to competition or anticompetitive mergers), the sectors affected (bread, chicken, beer, retail distribution, cement, aluminium, steel, telecommunications, railways, bus services, freight, professional services) and potential harm to economies'.[78] In India, the Monopolies Inquiry Commission, set up by the Government of India in 1964, highlighted many years back the prevalence of anticompetitive practices in various areas of the economy.[79]

Developing economies are, if anything, more vulnerable to the impact of anticompetitive activities than industrialized nations, whether these activities arise from domestic or overseas enterprises. The enforcement of competition law is, therefore, as much a necessity in emerging economies as in the industrialized nations. The law needs to have the standard provisions against harmful anticompetitive activities of the kind that prevail there, which are similar to anticompetitive activities in developed economies. In the enforcement of the law, the economic context is always relevant, and questions such as those above would arise for consideration. For instance, there could be greater

[76] OECD. 2001. Global Forum on Competition: Summary of Cartel Cases Described by Invitees, available at http://www.oecd.irg/dataoecd/41/30/2491386.pdf.

[77] OECD. 2005. Global Forum on Competition: Key Issues for Discussion in Technical Sessions, DAF/COMP/GF/(2005) 3/ANN1.

[78] Jenny, Frederic. 2005. 'Anticompetitive Practices in Developing Countries: Lessons from Empirical Evidence'.

[79] Report of the Monopolies Inquiry Commission, 1965. The Commission had been set up by the Government of India by notification dated 16 April 1964, to inquire into the extent and effect of concentration of economic power in private hands, and to suggest legislative and other measures that might be considered necessary in the light of such inquiry. Following the report of the Committee, the Monopolies and Restrictive Trade Practices Act, 1969, was enacted.

tension, than in developed nations, between competition law and other policies such as industrial policy and social policies, more particularly in cases of abuse of dominant position or merger control. The Indian Competition Act, 2002, in its preamble, specifically provides for the Act to keep in view the economic development of the country.[80] However, no standard formula can be set forth on how to balance the conflicting considerations. On the other hand, caution has to be exercised that such debates should not lead to the dilution of the competition law to such an extent as to compromise its effectiveness, or to insert in it so many different objectives as to affect the clarity of the law and render it confusing.

The history of competition law is over a century old, but the law has witnessed phenomenal growth in recent years. As countries have embraced the market economy they have also brought in competition law, which is integral to a market economy. Economics provides a theoretical basis for the law; it also provides the tools with which to analyse markets and competition within them.[81] Competition tends to maximize consumer welfare and efficiency. Even if perfect competition is unlikely in the market, it is a useful model to serve as a benchmark against which to measure the actual situation in the market.

The principal objective of competition law is to maintain and protect the competition process, though there could be other objectives as well. Competition law prohibits market players from entering into cartels or other anticompetitive agreements and from an abuse of dominant position. It also includes merger control. The law provides a range of remedies.

Increasingly, competition law includes the mandate to undertake competition advocacy.

There has been controversy about whether the prevailing models of competition law, amongst which the US and the EC models are predominant, are suited to the special characteristics of developing economies. Developing economies are even more vulnerable to the harm caused by anticompetitive activities than industrialized countries. The fundamental principles of competition law have broad applicability, that is, against collusive practices,

[80] The preamble to the Competition Act, 2002 No. 12 of 2003 states 'An Act to provide, keeping in view the economic development of the country, for the establishment of a Commission to prevent practices having adverse effect on competition, to promote and sustain competition in markets, to protect the interests of consumers and to ensure freedom of trade carried on by other participants in markets, in India, and for matters connected therewith or incidental thereto'.

[81] See Doern, G. Bruce and Stephen Wilks. 2001. *Comparative Competition Policy—National Institutions in a Global Market*, Oxford University Press, Oxford.

against abuse of dominance, and merger control. The economic context is always relevant, but care has to be taken not to allow the debate to dilute the competition law to such an extent as to compromise its effectiveness.

This chapter has attempted to give only a broad picture of competition law. It has not delved into the nuances of the law, which are many, but has aimed to provide a framework and perspective for the other chapters of this book which deal with a broad range of specific subjects relating to competition law.

PART I

COMPETITION LAW

Substantive Provisions and Major Issues

1

Control of Cartels and Other Anticompetitive Agreements*

Richard Whish

A system of competition law which is intended to protect the process of competition is typically concerned with three issues: first, anticompetitive agreements that have the object or effect of preventing, restricting, or distorting competition; second, abusive behaviour by a monopolist or dominant firm with significant market power that could be harmful to consumer welfare; and third, mergers that would reduce (or which have reduced) rivalry between firms in the market, again with detrimental consequences for consumer welfare. A further feature of some, but by no means all, systems of competition law is the establishment of a 'competition advocacy' role for competition authorities, whereby they keep under review and, where appropriate, comment upon restrictions of competition for which the state is responsible, for example, through legislation, regulation, or the provision of state aid; these are often referred to as 'public restrictions'. This chapter is concerned with the first of these issues, the control of anticompetitive agreements. In particular, it discusses the prohibition of 'hard-core' horizontal agreements, often referred

* The author would like to acknowledge the helpful research assistance of Avinash Amarnath of Vinod Dhall-TT&A, New Delhi, in the preparation of this chapter.

to as cartels, although it also considers the extent to which vertical agreements may present a threat to consumer welfare. The widespread condemnation of cartel agreements, the important lead that the Organization for Economic Cooperation and Development (OECD) has taken in the fight against cartels, and some legal points about anti-cartel legislation and judicial practice are noted and discussed, while providing details of recent cartel cases from a number of jurisdictions around the world with a special focus on India. Some of the contemporary issues facing competition authorities in their fight against cartels are considered; it will be noted in passing that not all horizontal agreements between competitors are necessarily to be condemned; the chapter will conclude by briefly discussing the extent to which vertical agreements are a source of competition law concern.

Widespread Consensus against Cartels

There are approximately 130 systems of competition law in the world today. Some of these laws date back more than a century; for example, the US enacted the Sherman Act in 1890. The competition rules of the European Union were adopted by the Treaty of Rome in 1957, the same year as the German Act against Unfair Restraints of Competition. Competition law in the United Kingdom began with the Monopolies and Restrictive Practices (Inquiry and Control) Act of 1948. The first competition law in Japan was the Act Concerning Prohibition of Private Monopoly and Maintenance of Fair Trade of 1947. Since the beginning of the 1990s the number of systems of competition law has proliferated. Competition law can now be found in all six continents, and in all kinds of economies—large, small, continental, island, advanced, developing, industrial, trading, agricultural, liberal, and post-communist. Important recent statutes include the Malaysian and Pakistani Competition Acts of 2010, the Ecuadorian Organic Law for Regulation and Control of Market Power of 2011, the Hong Kong Competition Ordinance of 2012, and the Philippine Competition Act of 2015. Not surprisingly, these laws differ in various respects: however, if there is one feature that unites them, it is that they all condemn 'hard-core' cartel agreements, even if they may differ in the ways in which such agreements may be prosecuted and punished.

There are many complex issues that arise in systems of competition law, for example, the extent to which the unilateral conduct of firms with market power should be controlled; the price which a competitor or customer should pay for access to an 'essential facility', such as a gas pipeline or seaport; the relationship between intellectual property law and competition law; the extent to which mergers should be prohibited, or transactions modified, because of potential harm to competition. These are issues that have kept policy makers, competition authorities, and scholars occupied for many years and have led to the publication of literally thousands of books, articles, consultations, green papers, white papers, decisions, and judgments. These are often matters of the greatest complexity, and have great intellectual fascination. However, it is important not to lose sight of a very simple fact about competition policy, which is that the most obvious target of any system of law should be agreements between independent firms that are restrictive of competition. The humdrum cartel that fixes the price of cement, or air fares, or insurance premiums does not provoke the same kind of intellectual debate as predatory pricing, tying and bundling, loyalty rebates, or the fair, reasonable and non-discriminatory (FRAND) licensing of standard-essential patents; and yet cartels are surely the most obviously harmful anticompetitive practice known to competition law, and they are one of the prime targets of competition authorities.

Writing in 1776, Adam Smith famously remarked in *The Wealth of Nations* that: 'People of the same trade seldom meet together, even for merriment and diversion, but the conversation ends in a conspiracy against the public, or in some contrivance to raise prices.'

Evidence suggests that the tendency of competitors to meet in smoke-filled rooms—or perhaps now in smoke-free Internet chat-rooms—is just as strong today as it was in the eighteenth century; cartels appear to be alive and kicking throughout the world. The phenomenon described by Smith was not a new discovery in 1776. Cartels were recognized—and prohibited—in ancient India: Kautilya's *Arthashasthra*, an ancient Indian treatise on statecraft and economic policy, recognized cartel activity as a public offence as far back as 400 BC. In the days of the Eastern Roman Empire (Byzantium), the Constitution of Zeno of AD 483 punished price fixing in relation to clothes, fishes, sea urchins, and other goods with perpetual exile, usually to Britain. There is no reciprocal provision in Britain today, since exile to Rome for infringing competition law would be unlikely to have a sufficient deterrent effect on the average British sales director: indeed a trip to the eternal city would be more likely to act as an incentive. Adam Smith's comment in 1776 was clearly correct: cartels have thrived through the centuries, often with implicit or even explicit support from governments. Even the adoption of competition laws with tough sanctions, including imprisonment, has not been sufficient to suppress cartel activity, as is demonstrated by the number of prosecutions that have been brought in recent times. Some important examples of cartel cases from around the world in the last few years, with a special focus on India, are provided in the section on recent action against cartels, given later in the chapter. There is a very real sense today among the world's competition authorities that, if competition law is about one thing above all, it is the detection and punishment of hard-core cartels.

In the European Union Mario Monti, the former commissioner for competition, once described cartels as 'cancers on the open market economy', and the Supreme Court in the US has referred to cartels as 'the supreme evil of antitrust'.[1] In the USA, in particular, it is customary to hear cartels described as 'nothing other than theft'. Hew Pate, formerly the assistant attorney general with responsibility for competition law and policy at the Department of Justice, has said:

> Especially for countries that have taken up antitrust enforcement relatively recently, there can be no sounder way to develop a strong competition culture than to place primary emphasis on cartel enforcement. Consumers will benefit. Businesses that rely upon commodity inputs will benefit. Taxpayers and governments will benefit when bid-rigging is curtailed. And unlike other more subtle or controversial areas of competition law, there is no danger here that government intervention might have anti-competitive effects.[2]

These are simple, but striking, statements. The mysteries of some aspects of competition policy should never be allowed to obscure the simplest fact of all: that competitors are meant to compete with one another for the business of their customers, and not to cooperate to distort the process of competition. The electorate in a properly functioning democracy votes for the party that it prefers; the customer in an efficient market votes by choosing from a range of competitors on the basis of price, quality, and standard of service. Suppliers must not commit a fraud on their electorate by artificially restricting choice to their own collective advantage.

Unfortunately, however, it appears that in many sectors in numerous countries around the world, collective action which would squarely be caught as a cartel under most modern competition laws is still regarded as a normal way of doing business, a continuation of the way in which business has traditionally been conducted. A striking example of this is the way in which pharmaceutical stockist trade associations function in India. It is a well-accepted practice that, if a pharmaceutical company wishes to appoint a stockist in India, it must obtain a no-objection certificate from the regional

[1] See *Verizon Communications Inc.* v. *Law Offices of Cur tis Trinko*, available at www.supremecourtus.gov/opinions.

[2] See www.usdoj.gov/atr/public/speeches.

stockist trade association. Failure to do so results in calls for collective boycott of the stockist. The trade associations have also traditionally fixed the trade margins that can be earned by an individual stockist. Of course, such conduct is simply not acceptable in a competitive market. There have been at least 10 infringement decisions of the Competition Commission of India (CCI) dealing with these practices, and there are a few more pending investigations against various pharmaceutical stockist trade associations in India.[3]

The Position of the OECD in Relation to Cartels

The OECD has been at the forefront of policy in relation to cartels. This in itself reflects an obvious but important point, that cartels are often international in nature whereas, for the most part, systems of competition law are purely national in scope. The rules of the European Union are an important exception, since they apply throughout the 28 Member States as well as 3 Contracting States of the European Economic Area. International business phenomena, such as cartels necessitate an international response, and the OECD is in an important position to give a lead in this respect.

In 1998, the OECD adopted a *Recommendation of the Council Concerning Effective Action against Hard Core Cartels* in which it called upon its member countries to ensure that their laws 'effectively halt and deter hard-core cartels', and invited non-member countries to associate themselves with the *Recommendation* and to implement it. In particular, the *Recommendation* said that countries should provide for effective sanctions of a kind and at a level to deter firms and individuals from participating in such cartels, as well as effective enforcement procedures to detect and remedy hard-core cartels. The *Recommendation* defined a hard-core cartel as: 'An anti-competitive agreement, anti-competitive concerted practice, or anti-competitive arrangement by competitors to fix prices, make rigged bids (collusive tenders), establish output restrictions or quotas, or share or divide markets by allocating customers, suppliers, territories, or lines of commerce.'[4]

Subsequently, the OECD has published a number of documents which are of particular interest to the issue of anti-cartel enforcement. In its 2001 *Report on Leniency Programmes to Fight Hard Core Cartels*, the OECD discussed the need to penetrate the cloak of secrecy that surrounds hard-core cartels, and the contribution that the encouragement of whistleblowers can make to this need. It noted that the seriousness of the penalties, including the

[3] As on 23 January 2016, see www.cci.gov.in.

[4] The OECD materials cited are available at www.oecd.org.

risk of personal liability, can be a powerful motivating factor in encouraging whistleblowing or leniency applications. It considered the procedures that are required for an effective and fair leniency programme, and noted the need for strong protection against unauthorized disclosure of information provided by leniency applicants. Whistleblowing and leniency applications are discussed later in this chapter.

In its 2002 *Report on the Nature and Impact of Hard Core Cartels and Sanctions against Cartels under National Competition Laws*, the OECD noted that the worldwide economic harm from cartels is very substantial, though hard to quantify: it was estimated that 16 large cartel cases investigated in the US may have caused economic harm in excess of US$ 55 billion. Firms go to great lengths to keep cartel agreements secret, and are in some cases explicit in their contempt for the competitive process. The principal purpose of sanctions in cartel cases is deterrence. Strong sanctions against enterprises and individuals increase the effectiveness of leniency programmes. The report also noted that, although there is a move towards the imposition of larger penalties for infringement of anti-cartel legislation, sanctions had yet to reach the required level for deterrence.

In *Hard Core Cartels: Recent Progress and Challenges Ahead*, published in 2003, the OECD examined the harm that arises from cartels: whilst acknowledging how difficult it is to quantify such harm, it found that it amounted to billions of dollars worldwide each year. It also reviewed recent progress in the fight against cartels, which it found to be significant: new laws had been passed, sanctions had been increased, and most countries were now aggressively prosecuting cartels. However, the OECD was of the view that more still needed to be done in relation to sanctions which, in its view, were still not severe enough; and stressed the need for greater international cooperation in combating cartels which, as noted earlier, often transcend national boundaries.

In its 2005 *Third Report on the Implementation of the 1998 Recommendation*, the OECD focused on four topics: progress in fighting cartels; public awareness of the harm caused by cartels; effective sanctions, in particular against individuals; and international cooperation in cartel cases. The report again noted that there had been considerable progress, but nevertheless concluded that much remains to be done. In particular, more countries should expand their awareness programmes, and work more extensively with procurement officials in an effort to fight bid rigging. The report also noted that countries should seek opportunities to further increase corporate fines, and consider introducing sanctions against individuals, including criminal sanctions. The report identified opportunities to enhance international cooperation in cartel investigations, and highlighted in particular the OECD Competition Committee's *Best Practices for the Formal Exchange of Information between Competition Authorities in Hard Core Cartel Investigations*. The Committee believes that member countries of the OECD should generally support information exchanges and should, in accordance with their laws, seek to simplify and expedite the process for exchanging information in order to avoid imposing unnecessary burdens on competition authorities and to allow an effective and timely information exchange. The *Best Practices* address the issues of the authority of a requested competition authority to exchange information; provisions concerning confidentiality; use and disclosure of information in the requesting jurisdiction; protection of legal professional privilege; and the giving of notice to the source of any exchanged information.

In its 2012 *Recommendation on Fighting Bid Rigging in Public Procurement*, the OECD called for member countries to assess their public procurement laws and practices at all levels of government in order to promote more effective procurement and reduce the risk of bid rigging in public tenders. The *Recommendation* included *Guidelines for Fighting Bid Rigging in Public Procurement*. These *Guidelines* are aimed at helping governments to improve public procurement by fighting bid rigging. They are designed to reduce the risks of bid rigging through careful design of the procurement process and to detect bid rigging conspiracies during the procurement process. The Guidelines include two checklists: a *Checklist for Detecting Bid Rigging in Public Procurement* and a *Checklist for Designing the Public Procurement Process to Reduce the Risks of Bid Rigging*.

In 2014, the OECD issued a *Recommendation Concerning International Co-operation on Competition Investigations and Proceedings* replacing the earlier recommendation of 1995 on the same issue. In the most recent *Recommendation*, the OECD calls for governments to develop their competition laws and practices so as to promote further international cooperation among competition authorities and reduce the harm arising from anti-competitive practices and mergers with anticompetitive effects. Although international cooperation has been at the core of the OECD agenda for several years, the OECD noted that a survey conducted by it in conjunction with the International Competition Network showed that very few jurisdictions, in fact, co-operated with other jurisdictions in competition law enforcement, in particular due to legal and/or practical limitations to such co-operation. The *Recommendation* contains two primary sections offering enforcers new and innovative solutions: first, a section calling for the adoption of national provisions that allow competition agencies to exchange confidential information without the need of seeking prior consent from the source of the information (so called 'information gateways'); and second, a section calling for enhanced co-operation in the form of investigative assistance, including the possibility, for example, to execute dawn raids (inspections of premises), requests for information, and witness testimonies on behalf of another agency. Other sections cover issues, such as a commitment to effective cooperation by restricting legislation that might impede cooperation between competition authorities, notifications of investigations by competition authorities to each other and coordination of investigations.

Anti-cartel Legislation and Judicial Practice

There is a high degree of consensus as to the types of horizontal agreements that should be treated as hard-core cartels. The OECD definition has been given earlier in the chapter. Chapter III of United Nations Conference on Trade and Development's (UNCTAD) Model Law on Competition of 2004[5] suggests that the following practices should be prohibited:

1. Agreements fixing prices or other terms of sale, including in international trade;
2. Collusive tendering;
3. Market or customer allocation;
4. Restraints on production or sale, including by quota;
5. Concerted refusals to purchase;
6. Concerted refusals to supply; and
7. Collective denial of access to an arrangement, or association, which is crucial to competition.

If one turns to actual laws forbidding cartels, a typical list of prohibited practices can be found in Article 101(1)(a)–(c) of the Treaty on the Functioning of the European Union (TFEU),[6] which refers to agreements which:

1. directly or indirectly fix purchase or selling prices or any other trading conditions;
2. limit or control production, markets, technical development, or investment;
3. share markets or sources of supply.

[5] See www.unctad.org.

[6] Equivalent to Article 81(1)(a)–(c) of the EC Treaty, which the TFEU replaced.

This list is closely reflected in Section 34(2) of the Singaporean Competition Act of 2004 and Section 3(3) of the Indian Competition Act of 2002, which usefully refers to a further obvious cartel practice, that of bid rigging and collusive bidding. As one reviews other systems of competition law, it is striking how similar most pieces of legislation are in the examples that are given of prohibited horizontal agreements.

Of course the crucial issue is how effectively these provisions are applied in practice, and it is also striking to see the extent to which competition authorities and courts around the world have had to grapple with very much the same problems of interpretation of anti-cartel legislation. Obvious points that emerge from the decision-making process are: first, that a horizontal agreement may restrict competition between the parties to the agreement itself, but may also restrict competition between the parties to the agreement and other operators in the market. It follows that competition law prohibits not only a price-fixing agreement between producers, but also action taken to eliminate third parties from the market; the concerted refusals to deal and the collective denial of access in the UNCTAD Model Law are examples of such behaviour. A second point is that systems of competition law recognize that the expression 'agreement' in this context does not refer only to written and legally enforceable agreements. It also applies to informal agreements, 'gentlemen's agreements', oral agreements, and to simple understandings, irrespective of whether they are intended to be legally enforceable and whether there is any enforcement mechanism for infringement. Competition law, typically, also applies to so-called 'concerted practices' whereby the parties substitute practical cooperation between themselves for the risks inherent in competition. The activities of trade associations—for example, when adopting rules for their members or making recommendations to them—are also covered by the rules against anticompetitive agreements.

A third point is that systems of competition law usually make a distinction between agreements which have as their *object* the restriction of competition and those that have an anticompetitive *effect*. This is an important distinction, in particular for competition authorities: their resources may be limited and they often face considerable difficulties in proving the existence of a cartel. Competition laws often identify certain types of agreements as having an anticompetitive object, with the consequence that the competition authority is absolved from the need to demonstrate, for example, that horizontal price fixing produces anticompetitive effects. To that extent the authority's resources can be focused on proving the existence of the cartel agreement; it is spared the need to prove effects as well. The agreements in the 'object box' typically will be similar to those set out in the UNCTAD

Model Law set out above. In US law, much the same dichotomy exists between agreements that are 'per se' illegal under Section 1 of the Sherman Act and those that are subjected to a more elaborate analysis under the so-called 'rule of reason'. The Indian Competition Act also makes a distinction between agreements that are 'presumed' to cause an appreciable adverse effect on competition and those where the CCI has to prove such an effect under the rule of reason. The Indian legislation usefully sets out the factors that the CCI must take into account while conducting rule of reason analysis.[7]

A final point that should be made about judicial practice in relation to cartels is that courts have developed the idea that a number of firms can have been party to a single overall cartel agreement that has lasted for many years, and for which they all bear responsibility. This can be important in practice. It may be that there has been cartelization of a particular product market for many years, but that the participants in the cartel have fluctuated over time, the geographical extent of the cartel may have changed, and the types of cartel behaviour may have altered. If one were to analyse such a situation as consisting of several discrete cartels, involving different firms, areas, and practices, a competition authority may have to launch several investigations; and it might be that some of the illegal practices are so far in the past that rules of limitation prevent an investigation altogether. On the other hand, if such a situation can be regarded as a single overall agreement that has been continuously in existence, only one investigation will be needed and it is much less likely that a limitation problem will arise. The law in the EU is explicit that the European Commission may proceed against a single overall agreement in this way.[8]

Recent Action against Cartels

The commitment of competition authorities around the world to the detection and prohibition of cartels is demonstrated by the number of cases that have been decided in recent years, in many of which the sanctions imposed have been very significant. Some of the significant cartel developments in India are described ahead. Further, some of the most important and interesting ones from jurisdictions around the world are described in Box A.

[7] See Section 19(3) of the Indian Competition Act, 2002.

[8] See Whish and Bailey. 2015. *Competition Law* (8th ed.), Oxford University Press, pp. 107–10.

Box A

India

Section 3(3) of the Indian Competition Act containing the cartel prohibition came into effect in May 2009. Between May 2009 and January 2016, the CCI found 46 cases of infringement of Section 3(3). The most notable amongst these was the *Cement* decision,[9] where the fines on 11 cement companies and a trade association for price fixing and limiting output amounted to about INR 63 billion (about US$ 1 billion). In this case the CCI found no direct evidence of price fixing. However, it held that circumstantial evidence can be indicative of an agreement under Section 3. The CCI found that the parallelism in prices and dispatch along with communications among the parties through an association, the Cement Manufacturer's Association, which also collected information on retail prices, in conjunction with the oligopolistic structure of the market was sufficient circumstantial evidence from which to infer an agreement to fix prices. On appeal the decision was set aside by the Competition Appellate Tribunal (COMPAT) on due process grounds: as the Chairman of the CCI, who did not attend the oral hearings of the parties, had added his signature to the final decision thereby violating the rule that 'he who hears must decide'. As a consequence the matter was remitted back to the CCI for fresh oral hearings and decision. An interesting contrast to the *Cement* cartel decision is the *Tyres*[10] case. As in the *Cement cartel* decision, there was no direct evidence of price fixing in *Tyres*. The CCI found that while the tyre market, being oligopolistic in structure, superficially displayed certain characteristics of a cartel, the circumstantial evidence available was not sufficient to establish a cartel agreement amongst the tyre manufacturers.

More recently the CCI imposed penalties of approximately US$ 38.6 million in total on three airlines, Jet Airways, InterGlobe Aviation (which operates under the brand 'Indigo'), and Spice Jet, finding that they were guilty of fixing the rates of fuel surcharges in relation to the carriage of air cargo.[11] This was another decision of the CCI based on purely

[9] *Builders' Association of India* v. *Cement Manufacturers' Association and Ors* Case No. 29/2010; the decisions of the CCI are available at www.cci.gov.in.

[10] *All India Tyre Dealers Federation* v. *Tyre manufacturers*, MRTP Case RTPE No. 20/2008

[11] *Express Industry Council of India* v. *Jet Airways (India) Ltd and Ors*, Case No. 30/2013.

circumstantial evidence. The CCI found that a pattern of parallelism existed in the increases of the surcharges by the three airlines and that the only possible explanation for such parallel movement was that a cartel existed between the airlines. The significance of this decision lies in the change in the evidentiary standard in cartel cases involving price parallelism and circumstantial evidence. In previous cases, the CCI had observed that mere price parallelism would constitute insufficient evidence to establish a cartel and that certain 'plus factors' would be needed to corroborate the price parallelism. However, in the fuel surcharges case, the CCI seems to suggest that price parallelism alone can constitute sufficient evidence of a cartel if there is no other possible explanation for such parallelism other than a cartel.

In another recent decision the CCI imposed a penalty of approximately US$ 105.7 million on four public sector insurance companies, owned by the Government of India, for indulging in bid rigging. The CCI found direct evidence in this case, such as minutes of meetings between the companies.

A notable area where the CCI has adopted several infringement decisions is bid rigging in public procurement. In the *Aluminium Phosphides* case[12] the CCI imposed penalties totalling to INR 3.1 billion (approximately US$ 50 million) on three suppliers of aluminium phosphide tablets for bid rigging in relation to supplies to the Food Corporation of India, a public body responsible for storing food grains intended for public distribution. On appeal the COMPAT substantially reduced the penalties to about INR 100 million (approximately US$ 1.5 million). This is because the COMPAT held that in the case of multi-product companies, such as the appellants in the present case, only the turnover arising from the product to which the infringement relates, that is to say the 'relevant turnover', should be taken into consideration while imposing a penalty. A more detailed discussion on the principle of 'relevant turnover' and the COMPAT's decision follows in the section on 'Sanctions'. In the *LPG Cylinders* case,[13] the CCI imposed penalties of INR 1.6 billion (approximately US$ 26 million) on 48 manufacturers of cylinders for storing and transporting liquefied petroleum gas for bid rigging in relation to supply to a public sector oil company in India. On appeal the COMPAT upheld the decision of the CCI on the substantive finding of infringement but

[12] *In re: Aluminium Phosphide Tablets Manufacturers*, Suo Moto Case No. 02/2011.

[13] *In re: Suo Motu Case against LPG Cylinder Manufacturers.*

remanded the case back to the CCI to re-hear the parties on the question of penalties as the COMPAT found that the CCI had not given adequate reasoning in its order for the quantum of penalty and had adopted an arbitrary approach in calculating it. The COMPAT directed the CCI to re-hear the parties keeping in mind the principle of 'relevant turnover' and the need to consider mitigating factors.[14] The CCI on re-hearing the parties substantially upheld its original penalties on the ground that none of the companies had put forward evidence to show that they were multi-product companies, thereby eliminating the need to consider 'relevant turnover', or that there were valid mitigating factors justifying a lower penalty.

Apart from the previously mentioned cases, the CCI has penalized several trade associations for collective actions, such as boycotts and the fixing of trade margins. As discussed earlier, there have been as many as 10 infringement decisions of the CCI against various pharmaceutical stockist trade associations as of January 2016. Similarly, there have been as many as 10 infringement decisions against film distributor trade associations.

It is noteworthy that, although the CCI has had a leniency program since 2009, none of its infringement decisions to date resulted from a leniency application. This can be attributed to lack of awareness of the leniency program amongst some businesses; others may consider that the risk of detection is insufficiently great to warrant such an application.

Argentina

In July 2005, five cement companies were prosecuted in Argentina for a cartel that lasted for 18 years, from 1981 to 1999. The companies agreed on a market division that was closely monitored by their trade association. The respondents were fined US$ 107 million, the largest antitrust fine in the nation's history.[15]

Australia

On 25 February 2011, the Federal Court ordered fines of A$ 4.2 million against Asia Pulp & Paper Company Ltd (Singapore) and PT Indah Kiat Pulp and Paper Tbk (Indonesia) for fixing the prices of uncoated woodfree folio and cut-size paper (UWF paper). The Court fined the companies

[14] Order of COMPAT, 20 December 2013, available at www.compat.nic.in.

[15] See www.unctad.org/en/docs.

despite the cartel being operated overseas because it covered supply to customers in Australia.[16]

Brazil

On 28 May 2014, Administrative Council for Economic Defence (CADE), the Brazilian competition authority, found a cartel in relation to cement and fined six companies, six individuals, and three associations a total of BLR 3.1 billion (approximately US$ 1.1 billion). Interestingly, CADE also imposed a structural remedy, directing that the companies divest certain assets and not operate in the cement sector for a period of five years.[17]

European Commission

On 19 March 2014, the European Commission imposed fines totalling EUR 953 million on two European companies and four Japanese companies for price fixing, colluding on requests for quotations and for annual price reductions from customers and exchanging commercially sensitive information in relation to automotive bearings. The cartel came to light when Japanese company, JTEKT, blew the whistle to the European Commission.[18] This decision was part of the Commission's wide-ranging investigation into the automotive parts sector, which resulted in two other cartel findings, one in wire harnesses for cars (the fines totalled EUR 141 million) and one in the flexible foam used in car seats (fines totalled EUR 114 million). The European Commission is investigating more products, such as airbags, safety belts and steering wheels, air conditioning and engine cooling products, and lighting systems and exhaust systems.[19] Cartels in the auto parts sector are being investigated in several major jurisdictions including the US, EU, and Japan.

In the year 2015[20] the European Commission adopted five decisions on cartels, in which the fines totalled EUR 364.5 million.[21] This was an unusually low level of fines for the Commission: the lowest level since 2000. However, it would be wrong to infer from this that

[16] See www.accc.gov.au.

[17] See www.cade.gov.br.

[18] Details of the Commission's decisions can be found at www.europa.eu/rapid

[19] See www.europa.eu/rapid/press-release.

[20] As of 21 October 2015.

[21] See www.ec.europa.eu/competition/cartels/statistics.

the Commission has decided to take a softer line: there are many cartel investigations 'in the pipeline' that are likely to result in very high fines; and 2015 saw the handover from Vice President Joaquin Almunia to the new Commissioner, Margrethe Vestager, which probably resulted in an interruption in the normal flow of decisions as the new Commissioner settled into her post.

France

On 15 December 2015, the French Competition Authority fined 20 delivery service companies a total of EUR 672.3 million for coordinating on annual price increases that they charged to their respective clients. This information-sharing process, which occurred between September 2004 and September 2010, mainly took place during meetings held within the framework of a professional trade union body, TLF, which was also fined.[22]

Germany

On 31 March 2014 the Bundeskartellamt in Germany imposed fines amounting to approximately EUR 338 million on 11 beer manufacturers, a trade association, and 14 individuals for operating a cartel to increase the prices of draught beer and bottled beer.[23]

Japan

On 18 March 2014 the Japanese Fair Trade Commission ordered five shipping companies to pay fines amounting to Japanese Yen 22.7 billion (approximately US$ 191.3 million) for fixing freight rates and refraining from bidding against each other with respect to particular international ocean shipping services for the transportation of automobiles.[24]

South Korea

On 2 October 2015 the Korean Fair Trade Commission imposed fines of Korean Won 28.66 billion (approximately US$ 23.9 million) on

[22] See www.autoritedelaconcurrence.fr.

[23] See www.bundeskartellamt.de.

[24] See www.jftc.go.jp/en/pressreleases.

four companies for agreeing in advance on the winning bidder and bidding prices for the construction of a railway line placed by the Korean Rail Network Authority.[25]

UK

In 2014 the Office of Fair Trading (OFT), UK imposed a fine of £ 370,226 on pharmaceutical group Hamsard for entering into a market-sharing agreement with pharmaceutical company Celesio AG and its subsidiary Lloyds. The case came to light as a result of Lloyds blowing the whistle. Accordingly, Lloyds was not fined under the OFT's leniency policy.[26]

USA

From 2011 the US Department of Justice commenced a major investigation into alleged price fixing and bid rigging by several manufacturers of automotive parts. As of February 2014, 26 companies had pleaded guilty or agreed to plead guilty and agreed to pay a total of more than US$ 2 billion in criminal fines. Additionally, 28 individuals had been sentenced to terms of imprisonment.[27] The US$ 425 million fine against Bridgestone Corporation is the fourth-largest criminal antitrust fine ever imposed in the US against a single company.[28]

Current Issues

As suggested earlier in this chapter, there is very little debate today as to whether hard-core cartels should be illegal—there is widespread agreement that they should be. Rather the important policy questions are:

- What sanctions are necessary in order to deter firms from entering into cartel agreements in the first place, and should sanctions be available against individuals as well as companies?
- What additional tools are needed to assist competition authorities in detecting and prohibiting cartels?

[25] Press Release No. 248, available at www.eng.ftc.go.kr/bbs.do.

[26] See www.webarchive.nationalarchives.gov.uk; www.oft.gov.uk/news-and-updates/press.

[27] See www.justice.gov/atr/public/press_releases.

[28] See www.justice.gov/atr/public/division-update/2014/criminal-program.html.

- To what extent can 'whistleblowing' or 'leniency' programmes assist in the detection of cartels?
- Should competition authorities go so far as to give rewards to informants providing information about anticompetitive behaviour?
- What should be done to stamp out international cartels that have effects in many different countries, given that national laws apply only to harms that occur within the national jurisdiction, and that some countries do not have anti-cartel laws at all?

Sanctions

As noted earlier, the OECD has repeatedly pointed out the need for effective sanctions to deter cartel behaviour, and has broached the subject of whether countries should introduce provisions directed at individuals as well as firms. The cases cited in the previous section demonstrate that the level of penalties being imposed on firms is now substantial, and it can be anticipated that this trend will continue. The interesting development to watch for in the years ahead will be to see whether more countries pursue the idea of introducing criminal sanctions against individuals and, more specifically, whether those sanctions include imprisonment as well as the imposition of fines. Several countries—for example, Canada, France, Germany (for collusive tendering), Ireland, Japan, Korea, Mexico, Norway, the Slovak Republic, and the US—already provide for criminal sanctions, including in some cases terms of imprisonment, to be imposed on individuals where they bear responsibility for the operation of hard-core cartels. As a deterrent, there is no question that in the US, for example, being in prison rather than with the family on Thanksgiving Day is going to have a greater deterrent effect than the imposition of a corporate fine, no matter how large that fine might be. There are no criminal sanctions under EU law. However, the UK Enterprise Act, 2002 introduced two provisions designed to encourage individuals to ensure compliance with competition law. First, Section 188 of the Act established the 'cartel offence', the commission of which can lead, on indictment, to a term of imprisonment of up to five years and/or an unlimited fine; changes were made to Section 188 by the Enterprise and Regulatory Reform Act, 2013, removing the requirement for the prosecution to prove that the person responsible for the cartel behaviour was acting 'dishonestly'.[29] Second, Section 194 of the Act introduced the possibility of company directors being

[29] It is also possible that some cartel activity might be criminal at common law in the UK, for example, as a conspiracy to defraud.

disbarred from office for a period of up to 15 years where they know, or ought to have known, that their company was guilty of an infringement of EU or UK competition law. These important provisions attempt to address the problem that the imposition of fines—even very substantial ones—on companies may not have a sufficiently deterrent effect, especially where the cost of the fines is simply transferred to customers through higher prices; and that if a fine is so large that it results in the insolvency and liquidation of a company, it would result in the loss of a competitor from the market, a somewhat perverse achievement for a system of competition law. The criminal sanction is a very important feature of the US law on cartels; there have been many high-profile cases in recent years in which senior executives of major companies have had to serve terms of imprisonment. Since May 1999, more than 107 individuals have served, or are serving, prison sentences in cases prosecuted by the Antitrust Division of the Department of Justice, and several of these individuals were foreign.[30]

The deterrent effect of competition law may be increased further if the victims of cartel behaviour can seek redress through the courts for the economic harm that they have suffered. Private enforcement is a very important part of the system in the US, and the European Commission in December 2005 published a Green Paper that explores the question of whether action should be taken to facilitate more litigation in the civil courts in Europe.[31] This was followed by a White Paper in 2008 which made certain specific recommendations with the objective of ensuring that all victims of infringements of EU competition law have access to truly effective mechanisms for obtaining full compensation for the harm they have suffered.[32] These recommendations were ultimately adopted as a directive on 26 November 2014, which must be implemented by 16 December 2016.[33]

In India, for cartels, the CCI is empowered to impose penalties of up to 10 per cent of the average turnover of an enterprise for the last three financial years or up to three times the profit of an enterprise for each year of continuance of

[30] See speech by Scott Hammond, Deputy Assistant Attorney General for Criminal Enforcement at the DoJ, 16 November 2005, available at www.usdoj.gov/atr/public/speeches.

[31] See Green Paper on 'Damages Actions for Breach of the EC Antitrust Rules', available at www.europa.eu.int/comm/competition.

[32] See White Paper on 'Damages Actions for Breach of the EC Antitrust Rules', available at www.eur-lex.europa.eu.

[33] See www.ec.europa.eu/competition/antitrust.

the cartel agreement, whichever is higher.[34] The legislation allows for similar penalties to be imposed on individuals responsible for the operation of the enterprise at the time of infringement.[35] The legislation also allows follow-on damages actions to be brought by affected parties before the COMPAT, following a finding of infringement by the CCI or the COMPAT.[36] Given that India is still a relatively nascent competition jurisdiction, it is still grappling with some fairly basic questions of fining policy.

While the CCI has imposed some significant penalties on enterprises using these powers, the CCI has been kept in check by the COMPAT, which has directed that the CCI must adopt reasoned orders after considering any relevant aggravating and mitigating factors.

In a landmark decision in the *Aluminium Phosphides* case the COMPAT, relying on international practice, such as the EU fining guidelines, held that in the case of multi-product companies, the penalty can only be imposed by reference to the 'relevant turnover', that is to say the turnover arising from the product to which the infringement relates. It follows that the maximum penalty that can be imposed on an enterprise is 10 per cent of its relevant turnover and not its total turnover. This principle was reiterated by the COMPAT in a recent decision in *Hiranandani Hospital* v. *CCI and Anr.*[37] By applying the 10 per cent cap to the relevant turnover itself, the COMPAT has greatly limited the ability of the CCI to impose fines that would deter enterprises from infringing the competition rules. The approach of the COMPAT seems to go against the wording of Section 27 of the Competition Act, which does not restrict the meaning of the expression 'turnover'; the Act appears to confer a wide discretion on the CCI to impose fines. The CCI has appealed to the Supreme Court against the order of the COMPAT in the *Aluminium Phosphides* case and has continued with its earlier practice of imposing penalties calculated by reference to total turnover, until the disposal of the appeal.

The CCI has exercised its power to fine individuals in a few recent cases against trade associations where penalties were imposed on the individual office bearers of the trade association.[38]

[34] Section 27(b) of the Indian Competition Act.

[35] Section 48 of the Indian Competition Act.

[36] Section 53N of the Indian Competition Act.

[37] Appeal No. 19/2014, available at www.compat.nic.in.

[38] See, for instance, the CCI's decisions against *Chemists and Druggists Association, Ferozepur*; *Bengal and Chemist Druggist Association*; and *Indian Jute Mills Association*, all available at www.cci.gov.in.

Although no follow-on damages actions have been brought in relation to cartel decisions of the CCI or COMPAT so far, the first damages action under the legislation was brought recently against the National Stock Exchange by MCX-SX, a competitor, after the CCI found that the National Stock Exchange had abused its dominant position by indulging in predatory pricing.[39]

Tools

Firms that participate in cartels are usually fully aware of the unlawfulness of their conduct. They know, therefore, that they should avoid the creation of incriminating documents that would be discovered by a competition authority when conducting surprise inspections (dawn raids). They will often arrange to meet in jurisdictions where they are unlikely to be scrutinized by competition authorities and they may use code names and resort to other practices to avoid detection. It follows that competition authorities may find it very difficult to compile evidence that will satisfy a court to the required standard of proof that there has been illegal behaviour. For this reason, a lot of thought has been given to the question of what additional tools are needed to enable competition authorities to operate effectively. Without doubt the adoption of whistleblowing and leniency programmes has been immensely important in this respect—most cases in the US and the EU in recent years have originated in a whistleblower approaching the Department of Justice or the European Commission. This is discussed briefly in the following section and more extensively later in this book.

In the Netherlands, the Dutch Competition Authority launched a major initiative to bring an end to cartels in the construction sector by encouraging firms to admit their involvement and seek leniency, and the Dutch Government lent its support to the campaign. In its report for 2004, the Authority reported that 481 companies had decided to 'come clean' and notify their illegal behaviour to it.[40] In the UK, the OFT launched, in November 2005, the 'Come Clean on Cartels Month', in which it urged businesses, and in particular small- and medium-sized enterprises, to make a clean break with any anticompetitive agreements they may be involved in.[41] The advantage of initiatives such as these is that media attention, peer pressure, and the threat of sanctions may lead firms to acknowledge the unlawfulness of their behaviour

[39] See www.compat.nic.in.

[40] See www.nmanet.nl/Images?Annual%20Report.

[41] OFT Press Release 206/05, 2 November 2005.

and come to terms with the risks that they run by participating in cartel activity. The Dutch example is a striking illustration of what a campaign of this kind can achieve.

A serious problem that faces competition authorities is the difficulty of obtaining evidence which, of course, is why the whistleblower has such an important role to play, as it may be able to provide an authority with richly informative data about meetings, contacts, the participants in the cartel, and the range of practices covered. It is vital that competition authorities be given the powers of investigation needed to track down evidence of sufficient quality to satisfy the standard of proof set by the law. At the very least, authorities need the power to request information and conduct unannounced 'dawn raids', including, where appropriate, of people's homes. It is also important that information stored electronically can be retrieved, which means that competition authorities must have staff, or access to individuals, with the necessary skills to achieve this. Further tools may also be needed, however, if the system of law is to be fully effective. This is why, in some jurisdictions, powers exist to listen to telephone conversations; to maintain surveillance, for example, of office premises in order to monitor who is attending meetings there; and even to require people to attend meetings of a cartel and report back to the competition authority of what took place.[42]

Whistleblowing and Leniency

A crucial tool in the detection of cartels includes the policy of encouraging whistleblowers to approach the competition authorities with information about a cartel. Subject to a series of conditions, such as that the whistleblower will cooperate with the investigation of the authority in question and that it was not a ringleader of the cartel, complete immunity will be available from any penalty that might otherwise have been imposed. Amnesty programmes have been implemented in many jurisdictions, and have proved to be highly successful. For example, the European Commission received 49 applications for immunity and leniency in 25 different cases in 2004.[43] Whistleblowing and leniency applications are discussed in Chapter 4.[44]

[42] On the powers to this effect in UK law, see Whish and Bailey, *Competition Law*, pp. 458–9.

[43] Saarela and Malric-Smith. 2005. *Competition Policy Newsletter*, Summer, p. 43.

[44] See the chapter 'Leniency Programmes in Competition Law' by Paul Crampton and Graham Reynolds.

Incentives and Rewards

Under US law, the Civil False Claims Act enables a private citizen to bring an action in the name of the US government, claiming fraud by government contractors and other entities that use government funds, and the litigant is then able to share in any money received. This legislation was used in the case of a bid-rigging cartel for wastewater treatment projects in Egypt funded by United States Agency for International Development (USAID), representing the first time that the legislation had been used to expose a large multinational cartel.[45] In South Korea, the Korean Fair Trade Commission has established a reward system for those who report or give information about competition law violations. A 'Reward Review Committee' has been established to ensure a fair and transparent process for determining reward eligibility. The identification of informants is kept confidential.[46] A reward of 66.87 million won (about US$ 63,700) was paid in June 2005 to a person who provided decisive evidence in a welding rod cartel case, the largest reward so far to have been given.[47]

Cartels and Globalization

The OECD has pointed out that cartels are an increasingly international phenomenon and that they thwart the gains that should follow from global market liberalization. In recent years, several cartels have come to light which had a genuinely global reach: auto parts, the vitamins, graphite electrodes, lysine, and citric acid cartels are obvious examples of this. In the OECD's view, increased cooperation is needed between antitrust authorities to combat such cartels. Formal and informal cooperation between competition authorities has become much more common in recent years, as the recent simultaneous investigations of firms in several jurisdictions found to have taken part in a cartel in auto parts has demonstrated.

There are many formal cooperation agreements in place between major competition law jurisdictions, such as the US, Canada, the EU, Australia, and Japan. India has also recently concluded cooperation agreements with the competition agencies of the US, the EU, Canada, Australia, and Russia. Such agreements may deal with a range of matters, including the provision of assistance in obtaining evidence located in a foreign jurisdiction, obtaining testimony from witnesses, and collecting fines. A particular

[45] See speech by Bill Kovacic, available at www.ftc.gov/speeches.

[46] See www.ftc.go.kr/data/hwp/rewardsystem.doc.

[47] See www.ftc.go.kr/data/hwp/informant_reward.doc.

issue is that national law may contain restrictions on the extent to which sensitive and confidential information may be shared with agencies in other countries, and yet that information may be precisely the kind that competition authorities would wish to exchange. It is likely that there will be amendments to national systems of law that impede the exchange of information of this kind. In the meantime, the OECD has published *Best Practices for the Formal Exchange of Information between Competition Authorities in Hard Core Cartel Investigations*[48] and the *Recommendation concerning International Co-operation on Competition Investigations and Proceedings*.[49]

An additional important feature of the global campaign against cartels is the annual 'anti-cartel enforcement workshop' that brings together cartel investigators and prosecutors from around the world. The first such workshop was held in the autumn of 1999 in the US, attended by representatives of competition authorities from 25 countries, to share learning and experience on how to address the problem of international cartels. Subsequent workshops were held in the UK, Canada, Brazil, and Belgium. The International Competition Network (ICN) established a Cartel Working Group at its meeting in Seoul in 2004 in recognition of the need for competition authorities to work more closely together in the fight against international cartels. Two sub-groups were created, one to work on the basic concepts involved in the fight against cartels and the other on the development and refinement of practical enforcement techniques. The fifteenth ICN cartel workshop took place in Cartagena, Colombia in 2015.

As already noted, some systems of competition law include the possibility of custodial sentences being imposed on individuals, and this can be significant in the punishment of international cartels. The US has not hesitated to seek the extradition of individuals in foreign companies whom it considers to have infringed its anti-cartel legislation. Furthermore, the Department of Justice in the US has adopted a policy of placing indicted individuals, accused of violating the Sherman Act, on a 'Red Notice' list maintained by the International Criminal Police Organization (INTERPOL), with the result that they might be arrested when attempting to cross a national boundary and extradited to the US for prosecution.[50]

48 See www.oecd.org/dataoecd/1/33/35590548.pdf.

49 See www.oecd.org/daf/competition/2014-rec-internat-coop-competition.pdf.

50 See speech by Scott Hammond, Deputy Assistant Attorney General for Criminal Enforcement at the DoJ, 16 November 2005, available at www.usdoj.gov/atr/public/ speeches/213247.htm.

Not All Horizontal Agreements Are 'Hard-Core'

An important comment that needs to be made about horizontal agreements is that there may be circumstances in which competitors cooperate with one another in a way that delivers economic benefits, not just for themselves, but for consumer welfare as well. Not all horizontal agreements are necessarily bad. Hard-core cartels of the kind described earlier are always bad for consumer welfare, but other horizontal agreements—for example, between pharmaceutical companies to combine their research and development efforts in order to develop new and better drugs, or between two small- or medium-sized businesses to produce products on a joint basis, thereby achieving economies of scale—may be beneficial. The OECD's 1998 *Recommendation*[51] stated that the definition of a hard-core cartel: does not include agreements, concerted practices, or arrangements that...are reasonably related to the lawful realization of cost-reducing or output-enhancing efficiencies.

Chapter 3 of the UNCTAD Model Law[52] states that: 'Practices falling within paragraph 1 (restrictive agreements or arrangements), when properly notified in advance, and when engaged in by firms subject to effective competition, may be authorized or exempted when competition officials conclude that the agreement as a whole will produce net public benefit.'

The fact that not all horizontal agreements are pernicious explains why, for example, Article 101(3) of the TFEU provides that agreements that restrict competition under Article 101(1) may nevertheless be legal. This would be the case where an agreement contributes to an improvement in the production or distribution of goods or in technical or economic progress, provided that various conditions—that consumers get a fair share of the resulting benefit, that the agreement does not contain any restrictions that are dispensable, and that the agreement does not substantially eliminate competition—are satisfied. Similarly, under US law it is only 'hard-core' cartels that are per se illegal; other horizontal agreements are subject to a so-called 'rule of reason', according to which the pro and anticompetitive effects of an agreement are balanced against one another in order to deter mine whether it is illegal. The Indian legislation seems to envisage a similar position as it contains a general prohibition against agreements which cause or are likely to cause an appreciable adverse effect on competition in India and a specific provision which lays down a presumption of appreciable adverse

[51] See www.oecd.org.

[52] See www.unctad.org.

effect on competition for certain specified hard-core horizontal agreements, such as price fixing, limitation of output, market sharing, and bid rigging. Arguably, all horizontal agreements falling outside this list will be subject to a rule of reason analysis under the general prohibition. A helpful discussion of issues relevant to the analysis of horizontal cooperation agreements has been published by the European Commission in its *Notice on horizontal cooperation agreements*.[53]

Vertical Agreements

Vertical agreements, that is to say agreements between firms that operate at different levels of the market, may also be harmful to competition, although this is only likely to be the case where one or both of the parties to the agreement have significant market power. Indeed, most vertical agreements increase consumer welfare.

Set out below is a brief description of the spare parts decision of the CCI which is India's first major infringement decision in relation to vertical agreements.

India

In August 2014, the CCI imposed penalties totalling INR 25.44 billion (approximately US$ 400 million) on 14 car manufacturers in India for entering into anticompetitive vertical agreements in relation to the supply of spare parts for their cars. The CCI found that the car manufacturers had entered into a series of agreements with local original equipment suppliers of spare parts and authorized dealers, which resulted in each car manufacturer being the sole channel for sale of spare parts of its own brand. The CCI concluded that these agreements result in exclusive distribution and a refusal to deal.[54]

Many systems of competition law prohibit the practice of resale price maintenance, whereby a supplier of products dictates a fixed or minimum price at which they may be resold. Some examples of resale price maintenance cases in recent years from jurisdictions around the world are set out in Box B.

[53] See www.europa.eu.int/comm/competition/index_en.html.

[54] See www.cci.ord.in.

Box B

Australia

On 10 December 2010 IGC Dorel, a child care product maker and its sales representative admitted to resale price maintenance and agreed to pay penalties of A$ 80,000 and US$ 20,000, respectively.[55]

Japan

On 22 June 2009 the Japanese Fair Trade Commission issued a cease and desist order against Seven-Eleven Japan Co. Ltd, a company engaged in franchising of convenience stores as it had forced certain franchisees who practiced or intended to practice discount sales to stop such discount sales.[56]

New Zealand

In March 2006 the New Zealand Commerce Commission successfully prosecuted computer parts and systems wholesaler, Morning Star Computer Limited for preventing computer parts resellers from advertising its products below certain fixed prices. The company was fined New Zealand $ 50,000.[57]

South Africa

On September 2005, Italtile, a ceramic and tile retailer, agreed to pay a penalty of ZAR 2 million following a Competition Commission finding that it had engaged in resale price maintenance by setting selling prices to franchisees.[58]

[55] See www.australiancompetitionlaw.org/cases/2010doral.html.

[56] See www.jftc.go.jp.

[57] See www.comcom.govt.nz.

[58] See www.business.iafrica.com.

Exclusive dealing agreements may also infringe competition law, for example, where a supplier agrees to deal with only one distributor in a particular territory, or where a distributor is required to purchase products exclusively from one supplier, thereby foreclosing access to the market for other suppliers. However, agreements of this kind may have pro as well as anticompetitive effects, and a detailed market analysis is usually needed to determine whether the agreement is unlawful. A further example of a vertical agreement that might be restrictive of competition is one whereby a supplier requires a customer to purchase one product as a condition of acquiring another, often referred to as a 'tie-in' transaction. Again, however, careful analysis is needed to determine whether such agreements actually have anticompetitive effects. Where vertical agreements of this kind are entered into between a dominant firm and a supplier or purchaser, it is possible that this may amount to an abuse of a dominant position on the part of the dominant firm, even if the agreement does not infringe the provisions on anticompetition agreements.

Competition authorities around the world are more determined today than they have ever been to eradicate hard-core cartels. Evidence of recent action in this area demonstrates that cartel behaviour is far from uncommon, and it seems that even the possibility of substantial fines is insufficient to deter firms from infringing the law. In the years ahead, the debate will be about the additional tools that are needed to make the battle against cartels more effective, and it is likely that more countries will decide that custodial sentences against individuals are, ultimately, the most effective deterrent.

2

Abuse of Dominant Position*

Emerging Enforcement Issues and Approaches

Robert D. Anderson and Alberto Heimler

The application of competition law provisions relating to abuse of dominant position is a challenging area of competition policy implementation for enforcement authorities, whether old or new. Both economic theory and enforcement experience underline the challenges that are posed for such authorities in reaching sound conclusions in abuse cases. Moreover, the stakes can be high: inappropriate decisions or enforcement approaches that depart from established practices can potentially interfere with efficient business conduct or create uncertainty and thereby deter beneficial investments and innovation.

At the same time, well-conceived abuse of dominance (AOD) cases can be among the most economically significant cases that are brought by competition

* This chapter is an updated and substantially revised version of an earlier chapter by the authors entitled 'Abuse of Dominant Position: Enforcement Issues and Approaches for Developing Countries', published in Vinod Dhall. 2007. *Competition Law Today: Concepts, Issues and the Law in Practice*, Oxford University Press India, Delhi. Anderson thanks Pierre Arhel and Hélène Chaudriller for their help in finalizing the chapter. It has been prepared strictly in the authors' personal capacities. The views expressed should *not* be attributed to the organizations with which they are affiliated.

agencies in any country. They may, at least in some cases, be directly linked to the addressing of structural problems that are critical to establishing healthy market economies in such countries (Anderson and Heimler 2007; Anderson and Jenny 2005; Osakwe 2001). In addition to many other impacts, they can assist in addressing infrastructure monopolies that impede the competitiveness of developing countries' exporters (International Trade Centre 2012; Pittman 2009). As such, they are significant not only for competition but also for development and trade (Anderson and Heimler 2007; Anderson and Müller 2013).

For these reasons, and as will be elaborated herein, it is important that competition authorities take a nuanced and informed approach to enforcement in this area, drawing on both economic theory and relevant international experience. The purpose of this chapter is to facilitate such an approach, by drawing together relevant aspects of economic learning and case developments.

The remainder of the chapter is organized as follows. The section 'Analytical Steps in the Development of AOD Cases' sets out the main analytical steps and considerations that arise in the development of most AOD cases. The focus here is on economic principles, insights, and evaluation approaches that, in our experience, are relevant to abuse or monopolization cases in all countries, rather than on any particular legal approach.

The section 'The Crux of the Matter: Distinguishing Actual Anticompetitive Abuses from (potentially) Efficient Business Practices' carries forward the analysis with reference to what we see at the crux of the matter, namely distinguishing actual anticompetitive abuses from potentially efficient business practices. The last section provides concluding remarks.

Analytical Steps in the Development of AOD Cases

AOD provisions typically embody four common elements. First, it is necessary to establish the existence of a dominant position held by a firm or (where relevant) a group of firms in a market. This, in turn, normally requires the delineation of the 'relevant market(s)' in which such a position is held. Second, it is necessary to identify specific practices that are harmful to competition. Third, the overall effects of such practices in the relevant market(s) are assessed. Fourth, and very importantly, consideration must be given to the matter of appropriate remedies and practices that have been found to be harmful to competition. This section of the chapter will address and reflect upon the application of each of these elements, with reference to relevant aspects of economic theory, law, and enforcement experience.

To be sure, the content and application of the previously referenced elements varies across jurisdictions. For example, under some countries' laws, the existence of a dominant position can be inferred largely or entirely on the basis of market shares. Other countries' statutes or enforcement guidelines require consideration of various factors that influence the ability of firms to exercise market power, for example, entry conditions. A further important distinction is that in some jurisdictions the mere charging of high prices or other 'exploitative' acts may be treated as abuses, while in others the law focuses on conduct that prevents other firms from competing effectively in markets (that is, exclusionary abuses). Another way in which national laws differ is in the treatment of efficiency claims or defences based on business justification. In the laws of some jurisdictions, there is an explicit statutory exception for such claims; in others, the question of business justification is intertwined with the evaluation of whether the practices under challenge are, indeed, likely to lessen competition (Anderson and Heimler 1999). Finally, in some jurisdictions only a single firm can become dominant, while in others a group of firms can also be treated as jointly dominant. We, nonetheless, consider that the analytical steps outlined in this section are of central importance in most if not all abuse cases, even taking due account of relevant statutory requirements.

Both economic theory and case experience underline the challenges that are posed for competition authorities in reaching sound conclusions in abuse (or monopolization) cases. It is important, in this regard, to recall that firms can achieve a dominant position in a market legitimately, for example, through innovation, superior production or distribution methods, or simply through greater entrepreneurial efforts. Moreover, many practices that appear on the surface to be anticompetitive (for example, tying, predation, or exclusive dealing requirements) can serve legitimate pro-competitive purposes at least in some circumstances. Reflecting this ambiguity in addition to differing legal standards, even established competition authorities with experience in this area sometimes reach different conclusions regarding the effects of particular practices and the remedies that are appropriate in particular cases (see, for example, the references to international divergences regarding the various *Microsoft* cases, given later in the chapter). Experience also warns us of the 'chilling effects' (that is, deterrence of healthy competition and innovative business strategies) that may result from the mistaken application of AOD provisions to either: (a) aggressive but healthy competition on the merits, for example, through price-cutting that is vigorous but unlikely to prevent future entry or re-entry to markets by competing firms; and (b) benign but complex marketing strategies.

Beyond the previously noted conceptual problems which are relevant to developed and developing economies alike, the application of legal provisions relating to AOD in developing or transition economies entails particular challenges. Some of these relate to (a) inadequate information bases and statistics which are important for the analysis of AOD and other 'rule of reason' cases; (b) a lack of experience with the operation of markets, which may tempt the authority to over-enforce; and (c) relatively new and sometimes overwhelmed judicial institutions which may compromise the enforceability of remedial orders (Beato and Laffont 2003).

For these and other reasons, in the 1990s some authors recommended that new competition agencies forgo the implementation of AOD provisions in their early years, at least until they gained experience in respect to other aspects of competition law (for example, Godek 1992; Willig 1992). We do not agree that it is appropriate to ask developing or transition countries to deny themselves a tool which is used by most developed countries and which, indeed, may be essential to deal with infrastructure and other monopolies or abusive conduct that, potentially, can undermine economic growth and the intended benefits from privatization, trade liberalization, and related economic reforms. Recent scholarly analyses underline the importance of pro-competitive reforms in developing countries, particularly in infrastructure sectors, as a tool of growth and development (Beato and Laffont 2003; Laffont 2005; see also Anderson and Müller 2014; International Trade Centre 2012). Competition law provisions regarding abuse of dominant position have an important role to play in this area. Moreover, at least in the case of Central and East European countries, the available evidence does *not* support a finding that AOD provisions have been systematically over-used, even in the early years of transition (Pittman 2004). Rather, there are indications that relevant authorities have themselves increasingly tended to curtail the bringing of questionable cases involving alleged exploitative abuses, and have also exercised restraint in regard to exclusionary abuse cases (Kovács and Reindl 2013).

We, nonetheless, share the view that care is warranted to prevent the misuse of enforcement powers in this area. To avoid deterring efficient business practices, the conduct under evaluation in abuse cases (for example, allegations of predatory price-cutting, the use of loyalty rebates and tying arrangements and others) should normally be evaluated on a case-by-case basis, taking account of both pro and anticompetitive explanations for the behaviour under examination. In addition, in analysing cases in developing economies, account should be taken of the special characteristics of such economies, such as, at least in some cases (a) thinly developed capital markets; (b) high entry barriers due to inadequate distribution channels and other business infrastructure; (c) in some countries, intrusive regulatory and licensing regimes; (d) more extreme asymmetries of information than normally occur in developed economies, in both product and credit markets; and (e) a greater proportion of local (non-tradable) markets (Anderson and Jenny 2005; Beato and Laffont 2003). Abuse of dominance cases can also have an important interface with regulatory regimes or other government measures (for example, licensing restrictions) that inhibit entry to markets or enhance the power of incumbent firms. In such cases, authorities may wish to consider appropriate competition advocacy activities as an adjunct or alternative to the enforcement of AOD provisions.

Determining the Existence of a Dominant Position

In recent years, the practice of defining a dominant position independently from the specific abusive practice under consideration has been repeatedly criticized. For example, economists serving on the Economic Advisory Group on Competition Policy of the European Commission's DG Competition have argued in a paper for the Commission (EAGCP 2005) that 'in terms of procedure, the economic approach implies that there is no need to establish a preliminary and separate assessment of dominance. Rather, the emphasis is on the establishment of a verifiable and consistent account of significant competitive harm, since such an anticompetitive effect is what really matters and is already proof of dominance'. On this basis, the economists proposed that the Commission abandon its practice of first establishing dominance and then evaluating its possible abuse. In its subsequently issued guidelines on exclusionary abuse issues (European Commission 2009), the Commission declined to follow this advice. The main reason cited was that the position urged by the advisory group would increase uncertainty and, as a result, would distort the incentives of possibly dominant firms to respect the rules.

In our view, the decision of the European Commission was a sound one. It enhances predictability for businesses while, nonetheless, respecting the Advisory Group's underlying concern. All rules prohibiting the abuse of a dominant position have indeed two parts. The first is that a firm needs to be dominant for the legal provision to apply and the second that its abusive conduct is prohibited. To be sure, what really matters is the second part. Whichever definition of dominance is adopted, what really should be prohibited is what the EAGCP rightly references, namely 'the establishment of a verifiable and consistent account of significant competitive harm'. Providing firms with a definition of dominance signals to them that they are potentially subject to the prohibition of abuse and, therefore, they should comply with it.

If dominance is not defined, or it is impossible to identify ex-ante, a firm, not knowing that a given practice may lead to significant competitive harm, may violate the rules against abuse, but the uncertainty surrounding the fact that it is subject to the rules reduces the ex-ante incentives to respect them. The public interest requires, therefore, dominance to be defined so that compliance is increased. If the definition of dominance is large and the firm is indeed not dominant, even though we mistakenly presumed so, then the conduct under consideration would not be considered abusive because it would not produce a 'significant competitive harm'.

Delineating the Relevant Markets

Careful delineation of the relevant product and geographic markets is critical to the sound development of most competition law cases, including abuse cases. In abuse cases, typically, it is necessary to delineate both: (a) the market(s) in which the firm under investigation has a dominant position; and (b) the market(s) in which the conduct under investigation has its anticompetitive effects (note that these are not always the same). The delineation of relevant markets facilitates the assessment of competitive effects and, as a result, often has an important bearing on the overall disposition of a case. A narrow definition of a market will tend to result in higher market shares for incumbent firms, often important in establishing a presumption of market power and, therefore, in facilitating a finding that the practices under consideration are indeed anticompetitive. By contrast, a wide definition of the relevant market will tend to result in lower market shares and, consequently, militate against a finding that the practices under examination are anticompetitive.[1]

As White (2006) points out, market definition in abuse of dominant position or monopolization cases lacks a guiding theory or paradigm such as that which is routinely and satisfactorily employed in merger cases, namely the 'hypothetical monopolist' or Small but Significant Non-transitory Increase in Price (SSNIP) test (see also Anderson, Daniel, and Heimler 1999). The latter asks whether consumers, faced with a 'SSNIP', could easily switch to an alternative product or another supplier. If the answer is yes, then the alternative product or source of supply is included in the relevant market for the case.

[1] Note, however, the important conceptual difficulties that can arise in defining markets in abuse or monopolization cases, as discussed later in the chapter. In some cases, the direct evaluation of anticompetitive effects using modern econometric tools may be a viable alternative to traditional market delineation. See related discussion in section 'Delineating the Relevant Markets'.

The hypothetical monopolist test is well-suited for most merger cases and for other competition law cases in which the focus is on a *prospective* exercise of market power (that is, one which will occur in the future, as a result of the merger). In abuse cases, it often generates misleading results. In fact, in any case which is principally concerned with past or current, and not future, behaviour (which is normally the case in regard to abuse or monopolization cases), use of the hypothetical monopolist approach is likely to generate misleading results, as a result of a conceptual error known as the 'cellophane fallacy' (Landes and Posner 1981; Stocking and Mueller 1955). The latter term recognizes that in any situation where price is already above the competitive level, evidence of consumer substitution in favour of other products (or suppliers from adjoining geographic regions) may simply reflect the fact that the firm under investigation is already pricing in the elastic range of the demand curve—a normal practice for a firm with significant market power (Anderson, Khosla, and Monteiro 1996; Baker 2006; White 2006). Hence, in abuse or monopolization cases focused on the past or present conduct of a firm, the hypothetical monopoly test cannot distinguish between a market which is already effectively monopolized and a genuinely competitive market. Abuse cases are particularly susceptible to the Cellophane Fallacy, since in order for a violation to exist a firm needs to be dominant and therefore it is to be expected that its prices will normally be above competitive levels.

Where does this conundrum leave the officials responsible for developing cases and administering legal provisions on AOD? In some cases, it may be possible or even preferable to focus on direct evidence of market power and/or anticompetitive effects. However, this approach has its own intrinsic difficulties (see discussion in section 'Direct Evaluation of the Existence of Market Power (Dominance)'). In many cases, it will be necessary to delineate the relevant markets largely or entirely on the basis of the functional characteristics of the product(s) and on consumer behaviour patterns. These may include physical characteristics of the product, uses to which the product is suited, and evidence about buyers' willingness to switch from one product to another as relative prices change. Similarly, defining the relevant geographic market will often be based on factors such as transportation costs and perishability that limit the ease with which products can be moved over long distances.

The foregoing approach, to be sure, will not always be satisfactory to econometricians who (correctly) emphasize that substitution possibilities cannot be definitively assessed without regard to pricing considerations. It is, nonetheless, an approach that has been relied upon extensively in most jurisdictions, and may be the only approach that is realistically available in some cases (Anderson, Khosla, and Monteiro 1996).

Assessing Whether the Incumbent Firm(s) Enjoy a Dominant Position in (At Least Some of the) Relevant Market(s)

Once the relevant markets have been defined, establishing whether the firm(s) under investigation occupies a dominant position is relatively straightforward. This depends on two main factors: the market share of the dominant firm and entry conditions. In general, the greater the market share of an alleged dominant firm, the more likely it is to exercise market power. In our view, it is impossible to set out market share thresholds at which a firm can, with absolute confidence, be deemed to have or not have significant market power. It is unlikely, however, that a firm with a market share of less than 35 per cent would have the ability to reduce output or impose a significant price increase above the competitive level. Conversely, where a firm has a market share of 65 per cent or more, it may well be in a position to exercise market power depending on the existence of significant entry barriers and other considerations.[2]

As to the assessment of entry conditions, the question of interest for enforcement officials is whether entry by new competitors is likely to prevent the exercise of substantial market power by the dominant firm. Contrary to merger analysis where enforcement aims at impeding price increases, in abuse cases enforcement aims at impeding that prices are kept artificially high. Therefore, the question will be why entry does not occur.

Indeed, in the absence of regulatory/legal impediments to entry, the focus will be on 'sunk costs' (for example, specialized physical assets) that delay or impede entry by new competitors. There are, however, two special considerations that apply in abuse cases. First, as in defining relevant markets, assessment of entry conditions should take into account the theory of the case. Barriers that would be ineffective if prices were raised higher than prevailing levels may still be relevant in assessing the impact of exclusionary practices that prevent prices from falling below current levels.

Second, in abuses cases, the conduct under investigation itself may constitute the principal deterrent to new entry. The ability of firms to deter entry through behavioural as opposed to structural barriers is increasingly recognized (Ordover and Saloner 1989)—indeed, it is the essence of many abuse or monopolization cases. Entry-deterring conduct may include many or most of the practices that are typically dealt with as abuses—for example, predatory pricing, exclusionary contractual provisions, tying requirements, and use of

[2] For example, in addition to its own market share, a firm's ability to exercise market power may also depend on the size of other firms in the market. Factors such as the degree of vertical integration in the market may also be relevant.

fighting brands. The significance of this point is that valid cases of abuse may sometimes involve markets in which there are few or (in principle) no barriers in the more traditional, structural sense of specialized physical assets.

Third, especially with respect to exclusionary abuses, a market analysis is necessary in order to check whether entry occurred in the past and whether competitors were able to grow. If the answer is yes, dominance could be reasonably excluded, unless entry occurred when the abusive practice was not in place.

Fourth, the lack of capacity may make it very difficult for a company to increase its market shares. However, this is not necessarily a sign that the company is not dominant because the exclusionary abusive practice may make it possible to artificially keep existing market shares, even though the lack of capacity may not allow the company to grow.

Direct Evaluation of the Existence of Market Power (Dominance)

As an alternative to delineating markets and then assessing the existence of dominance via the indirect route of constructing market shares, in some cases it may be preferable to look for direct evidence of the existence of market power in the form of abnormally high profits or prices. Certainly, where these are present, the authority should take note of this. It should be emphasized, however, that accounting profits by themselves do not provide reliable evidence of market power, nor does the absence of such profits necessarily signal a lack of market power. There are at least two reasons for this. First, accounting profit rates are often affected by tax measures, transfer pricing, etc. Second (and perhaps surprisingly), monopolists do not always earn high profits even in the economic sense. One of the most important consequences of a lack of competition in a market can be resulting productive inefficiencies and a lack of technological progress. In addition, dominant firms, especially firms that enjoy a legal monopoly, often engage in rent-sharing activities with workers and suppliers, resulting in higher costs, not necessarily higher profits (see, for related discussion, Bain 1941; Fisher and McGowan 1983).

Identifying and Evaluating Alleged Abuses

In any AOD case, a central analytical challenge will concern the identification and evaluation of specific (alleged) anticompetitive practices. These may include, inter alia, a wide range of possible exclusionary practices and, in some jurisdictions, also 'exploitative' abuses such as the charging of high prices. The range of possible exclusionary practices—which are increasingly viewed as the 'main' anticompetitive acts with which laws on AOD should be concerned—include practices such as refusals to deal; predatory pricing; the use of loyalty discounts; tying arrangements or 'bundling'; raising rivals' costs; and many other practices. However, whether the use of such practices is indeed exclusionary in particular cases is a question that often is not straightforward and, at the least, requires consideration of a range of contextual factors and possible explanations. It is also a matter regarding which recent case decisions offer significant insights. An in-depth discussion of these questions, building on recent jurisprudence and enforcement experience, is provided in the section 'The Overall Assessment of Market Effects: Restrictions of Competition vs. Superior Efficiency'.

Overall Assessment of Market Effects: Restrictions of Competition vs Superior Efficiency

As pointed out earlier, a central challenge in AOD or monopolization cases is to ensure that the law does not inadvertently curb efforts to achieve superior efficiency or the adoption of efficient business practices. Firms may achieve a dominant position through methods that are perfectly legitimate (through innovation, adoption of superior production or distribution methods, or greater entrepreneurial efforts). Moreover, many practices that appear to be anticompetitive (vertical market restraints, discounting, or tying) can serve legitimate pro-competitive purposes.

Alleged exclusionary abuses of a dominant position can usefully be considered with reference to a two-prong test. First of all, it should be established that, as a result of the practices under examination, an equally efficient competitor cannot profitably remain in the market. Second, there should not be offsetting advantages for consumers. This second pillar of the evaluation of an abuse should not be required in all circumstances. For example, in the case of price abuses (predation, discounts, mixed bundling), proof that an equally efficient competitor has been excluded may be sufficient. On the other hand, for non-price abuses (bundling, tying, refusal to deal, etc.), efficiency considerations (reduction of transaction costs for consumers, innovations, etc.) may well offset any negative effect on competition originating from the exclusion of equally efficient competitors and need to be considered carefully.

Another useful analytical approach is to consider the effects of practices with reference to the dynamics of an industry. If a practice is efficiency enhancing, then small as well as large firms will have an incentive to adopt it. In this regard, it is relevant to ask: did the firm engage in the practice when it was smaller? Or, if the firm never was small, do its smaller rivals engage in the practice? If such firms do not exist, do firms of all sizes in the same industry in other countries (or similar industries in the same country) engage in the practice? Have the firms that have recently grown used the alleged abusive practice? If so, then the alleged practice may be important to those changes, and it may be counterproductive for competition authorities to intervene.

Developing Appropriate Remedies in AOD Cases

A point worth stressing is the usefulness of giving preliminary consideration to the question of remedies even in the earliest stages of developing a case, well before the agency may be ready to initiate formal proceedings. Although views concerning the remedies appropriate to a particular matter can certainly evolve as other aspects of the case are developed, if in fact, there is no practical remedy for an apparent abuse (that is, one that clearly improves the situation and does not entail excessive monitoring costs), then there is no point in devoting scarce public resources to pursuit of the case (see, for useful elaboration, Kovacic 1999). Thinking about appropriate remedies can also be useful in evaluating the effects of the conduct under examination in that it provides a point of comparison between the current functioning of the market and an alternative 'ideal' scenario.

Remedies in AOD cases typically comprise one or more of the following types of measures: (a) behavioural orders prohibiting the continuation of specific actions or behaviour; (b) the levying of fines or financial damages on firms that have engaged in such conduct; (c) divestiture of specific assets of the firm(s), including vertical disintegration, for the purpose of re-establishing competition in the market; (d) other 'proactive' measures such as mandating access to essential facilities and compulsory licensing (at prices that would not exclude an equally efficient competitor). Probably, the most common are the first category of measures—that is, orders prohibiting the continuation of specific actions or behaviour. One reason for the popularity of such orders is that they generally are less intrusive and more easily accommodated by the firms on whom they are imposed. However, by themselves, they also may not be sufficient either to deter similar abuses by other firms or to restore competition in the markets affected by the anticompetitive conduct. For this reason, other measures such as structural divestiture may need to be considered. Where simple orders prohibiting abusive conduct are imposed, it is important that they be sufficiently clear and specific at least to prevent recurrences. For example, if the core abuse relates to the use of loyalty rebates to exclude potential competitors, guidance must be provided as to the circumstances in which such rebates will and will not be considered acceptable. A mere prohibition of 'continued anti-competitive conduct' will not suffice.

The second type of remedial measure listed earlier, namely fines, has clear advantages vis-à-vis simple prohibitory orders in deterring similar conduct by other firms. However, while fines are an appropriate remedy in many cases (imprisonment for abuse-type violations exist only in a very few jurisdictions), they are not appropriate in circumstances where there is no culpable intent. For example, the firm responsible for the abuse(s) may have believed its behaviour to be completely legitimate, not having been aware that it had reached a dominant position. In such cases, fines are generally inappropriate. Furthermore, even if the firm knew it was dominant, the practice considered abusive may have been of a novel nature and not yet covered by the existing case law. In such circumstances, a fine would be inappropriate because it would not have been anticipated by the firm and therefore could not serve any deterrent function.

On the other hand, where a case involves flagrant, premeditated anticompetitive conduct (for example, harassment or threats of violence to potential entrants) or violates known standards that have been clearly enunciated in relevant guidelines or case decisions, it may be appropriate to seek/impose fines or other punitive sanctions. In extreme cases, efforts by incumbent firms to deter entry by potential rivals may extend to outright criminal conduct (for example, threats to the safety of individuals or corporate facilities). In such circumstances, competition agencies should report the case to the police or other relevant authorities to bring criminal charges. In addition, criminal proceedings for contempt of court may be appropriate in circumstances where a previous remedial order has been flagrantly ignored by the relevant firm(s).

Fines are meant to achieve deterrence, at least in those jurisdictions where damages are prohibited by law from being punitive. Deterrence means that the expected value of the fine, taking into consideration the probability of being caught, which in the case of AOD is in general quite high because the affected firm is well aware of its existence and could easily report the practice to the competition authority, should exceed the expected gains originating from the violation. Heimler and Mehta (2012) provide orders of magnitude estimates of the levels of fine able to achieve deterrence in the case of an AOD. First of all, in the case of an abuse the expected increase of profits originating from the violation is generally modest because the abuse is only meant to increase the already high market power that dominance ensures. Furthermore, the level of the fine should in general achieve deterrence at percentages of affected sales that are around half those necessary for cartels. Heimler and Mehta (2012) suggest in the case of AOD fines between 3 and 7 per cent of affected sales.

A related but different set of issues is raised by the assessment of monetary damages—that is, amounts that must be paid by a firm which has been found to have engaged in abusive conduct to firms or individuals that have suffered financial losses as a result of the impugned conduct. The clear benefit of requiring damages to be paid is deterrence, reinforcing the effect of fines—that is, firms in similar circumstances in other markets will be deterred from engaging in the same conduct, lest they also be forced to pay damages. However, there is also a risk that the availability of damages will encourage the use of competition law enforcement for purposes of rent-seeking—that is, the making of complaints by one firm against the other purely for purposes of pecuniary gain.

Another kind of remedy that may merit consideration in particular cases is structural divestiture—that is, the actual separation of individual components of the business of the firm(s) whose conduct has been found to be abusive. In most cases, divestiture will probably take the form of vertical disintegration (that is, separation of a firm's assets according to vertical stages of production).[3] Such a remedy may be particularly relevant where competitors in one market (for example, alternative electricity generators or telephone service provider) require access to a monopoly component (the transmission line in electricity or the local loop in telephone services) that is owned and controlled by a vertically integrated dominant firm. The usefulness of vertical disintegration as a remedy arises from the fact that continuing exclusionary practices by vertically integrated firms are difficult to detect and deter because they may take many forms (including, for example, subtle reductions in the quality of access provided to competitors, for strategic purposes). For this reason, a mere prohibition of exclusionary conduct or requirement to provide inter-connection on equal terms can be difficult to enforce.

In contrast, vertical ownership separation (that is, divestiture) eliminates the incentive to discriminate against competitors (see, useful discussion, OECD [2001a]). In this way, it can:

- limit the need for access regulation that is difficult, costly, and only partially effective;
- stimulate innovation and efficiency in the competitive services;
- eliminate the incentive on the incumbent operator to abuse its dominant position by impeding entry of competitors; and
- eliminate the risk of cross subsidization (see further details, OECD [2001b]).

[3] Note, however, that divestitures imposed by the US courts in the early years of enforcement of Section 2 of the *Sherman Act* (for example, in the *Standard Oil* case) often had a horizontal as well as a vertical aspect.

Divestiture is sometimes depicted as a 'radical' or 'extreme' remedy. Indeed, it should not be imposed without careful analysis of the likely results and implications for production and other efficiencies. It is worth pointing out, however, that established competition agencies have imposed remedies of this nature in some notable cases. For example, probably the most far-reaching structural remedies that have ever been adopted in an AOD or monopolization case were those imposed in *US* v. *AT&T*, the case brought by the US Department of Justice against the then-dominant US telecommunications carrier in the 1970s and concluded in 1982. The case was settled through a consent decree that broke the existing AT&T Corporation into a large number of constituent parts, including Regional Bell Operating Companies (RBOCs) and a long-distance carrier that retained the original company's name. The break-up was considered necessary, inter alia, to eliminate the scope for predation and incentive for inefficient cross-subsidization resulting from the original company's operating simultaneously in regulated and unregulated markets (see, for useful discussion, Brennan 1987). On the whole, the AT&T break-up has been assessed by commentators in very positive terms, as ushering in an era of far-reaching innovation, efficiency gains, and price decreases, overall very beneficial for consumers (Kahn [2004] provides a useful discussion).

Full structural separation is not, however, without its own potential downsides. For example, it may not allow the exploitation of economies of scope from integrated operation, it may increase transaction costs for consumers, may reduce system reliability, and may reduce the incentive to innovate for the separated monopoly component. There is some evidence that structural separation may be beneficial in industries such as gas and electricity, where competition may be forthcoming. On the other hand, more care should be exercised in the case of industries like rail where competition, especially competition in passenger services, is difficult to develop. As for telecommunications, technical progress is continuously reducing the boundaries of natural monopoly, so that it is difficult to precisely identify the monopoly components of the industry once and for all, in order to separate them. Recently, functional separation, a less intrusive and less costly way to achieve the objectives of full (ownership) vertical separation, has been put forward in the United Kingdom first and then in other countries as well (OFCOM 2004). By imposing separation between different divisions within the same firm, but under different management incentive schemes, functional separation ensures that decisions on the terms of access are neutral with respect to whether the entity requiring access is a competitor or an internal division of the integrated company.

Still another remedy that is often considered in cases involving network industries, sometimes as an alternative to divestiture, is the mandating of access to facilities that are deemed to be essential. In the US, the 'essential facilities doctrine' permits the mandating of access in cases where the following four criteria are met: (a) control of the essential facility by a monopolist; (b) a competitor's inability practically or reasonably to duplicate the facility; (c) the denial of the use of the facility to a competitor; and (d) the absence of a valid business justification for denial of access.[4]

As has been discussed extensively in relevant literature, the application of the essential facilities doctrine raises complex questions relating, for example, to the pricing and other characteristics of the services to be provided. An overly expansive approach to questions of essential facilities can discourage firms from investing in new goods and services for fear that they could not earn an adequate return. Reflecting this, in its recent opinion in the *Trinko* case, the US Supreme Court emphasized that there is no general duty of firms to cooperate with competitors under US antitrust law. It came close to rejecting the availability of the essential facilities doctrine in cases where a court order to share facilities would require complex judicial oversight and observed that the decision in *Aspen Skiing* is 'at or near the outer boundary of [liability under US monopolization law]' (see, for related discussion, McDonald 2004).

Despite these reservations, authorities likely will continue to seek access to essential facilities as a remedy for abuse of dominant position in at least some cases. Such a remedy may still be the most attractive option particularly in circumstances where vertical divestiture is precluded by overwhelming technical efficiencies from vertical integration. A key challenge in such cases is to set an appropriate price for the services to be provided. Without minimizing the problems inherent in setting such a price, one possible approach to this issue is given by the so-called Efficient Component Pricing Rule (ECPR) (Baumol and Sydak 1994). Under this approach, the incumbent operator's price to final consumers is accompanied by an access charge low enough to allow equally efficient competitors to compete (and equal to the final price minus avoided cost). This is important because simply eliminating the price squeeze would lead to higher final prices for consumers. It would be ironic (and self-defeating) if antitrust enforcement would lead to such a result.

[4] *MCI Communications Corp.* v. *AT&T*, 708 F.2d 1081, 1132–33 (7th Cir. 1983). It should be noted that the essential facilities doctrine concerns the availability of a remedy and not a finding of liability; before access can be granted under this doctrine an underlying antitrust violation must be shown.

The reference to ECPR as the proposed antitrust standard for access charges is a direct consequence of the core objective of antitrust enforcement in abuse cases, that is, to avoid unjustifiable exclusion of competitors. Fairness is a different standard and should be pursued by regulation. This point is not always clear to enforcers. For example, in the 2004 Microsoft case, the European Commission had ordered that Microsoft license the use of the relevant information for interoperability on 'reasonable and non-discriminatory terms'. As Heimler (2014) argues, reasonableness should not be an antitrust standard because it can erode the incentive to 'innovate around the monopoly' to which access is mandated, thereby reducing competition in the future.

The Crux of the Matter: Distinguishing Actual Anticompetitive Abuses from (Potentially) Efficient Business Practices

As already noted in section 'Identifying and Evaluating Alleged Abuses', a central analytical challenge in all abuse cases concerns the identification and evaluation of specific (alleged) anticompetitive practices. Whether such practices are indeed exclusionary in particular cases is a question that often is not straightforward and, at the least, requires consideration of a range of contextual factors and possible explanations. This section of the chapter is concerned with this crucial aspect of competition analysis in AOD cases.

Two broad categories of business conduct have traditionally been recognized as (potentially) abusive by competition laws and enforcement agencies: (a) exclusionary abuses, in which a firm attempts to prevent the entry or expansion of new competitors in the relevant markets or (in more extreme cases) to drive existing competitors out of the market; and (b) exploitative abuses, in which a firm takes advantage of its market power by charging excessively high prices to its customers, discriminating among customers, paying low prices to suppliers, etc. Of course, if the objective of excessively high prices (for example, high access prices to a network) is to exclude competitors from the market, then these high prices are considered to be exclusionary, not exploitative. Exploitative abuses are defined to be abuses to customers, not competitors.

The trend, in recent years, has been for enforcement agencies to give higher priority to the prevention of exclusionary as opposed to exploitative abuses.[5] There are a number of reasons for this. To begin with, in the case of exploitative abuses it is often difficult to say clearly what is an acceptable exercise of

[5] In some jurisdictions, notably the US, only exclusionary abuses are addressed under the relevant legal provisions (in this case, Section 2 of the Sherman Act).

market power. For an enforcement agency, it is almost impossible to define the 'right' price that a dominant firm should charge for the sale of products or services, since accurate and timely information on costs and demand is generally unavailable or expensive to acquire. In addition, antitrust intervention against 'excessive' prices can have the perverse effect of inhibiting competition since it may deter entry to the relevant markets by new competitors. Moreover, if firms expect that antitrust authorities may establish an upper ceiling on the prices they would be allowed to charge, if they grow and capture a sizable share of a market, their incentives for innovation and entry into new markets will be diminished, damaging consumer welfare in the long run. As for using exploitative abuses in order to impose a fair behaviour on a dominant company, antitrust enforcement is no longer considered the most appropriate tool for achieving it, since taxation and regulation are much more effective. However, an argument has been made that the use of competition law provisions as a residual tool of price regulation may have merit in a transition economy setting, even if it is not viewed as an optimal policy in a mature economy (Ordover and Pittman 1993). For this reason and because exploitative abuses still figure in the laws of many jurisdictions, both types of abuses are considered ahead.

Identifying and Evaluating Alleged Exclusionary Abuses

In a recently published handbook on antitrust economics, Bernheim and Heeb (2015) start their chapter, which is meant to establish a framework for the analysis of exclusionary conduct, by denouncing what they call 'a lack of any consensus on principles' over what an abuse should be and concluding that it may lead Courts to 'inadvertently establish economically counterproductive precedents'. They, nonetheless, believe that it is possible to identify a common thread that characterizes all exclusionary conduct. In particular, they suggest that what identifies an abuse is the fact that an exclusionary arrangement between the market leader and one of its customers 'reduces the benefits that other customers can expect to derive from vendor competition' (Bernheim and Heeb 2015: 8). In other words, the exclusion is not an abuse because a competitor is excluded via a contract but because such exclusion affects the competition that will take place in the market. This formulation draws upon and gives operational content to the widely-held precept that 'competition law is intended to protect the competitive process and not competitors as such'.

Vickers (2005) identifies three economic standards that can be used to categorize the legal provisions and the case law developments on abuse of market power of most jurisdictions: the 'sacrifice test', the 'as efficient competitor test', and the 'consumer harm test'. The sacrifice test is the broadest and the most discretionary of the three. It identifies as abuse any behaviour by a dominant firm that would be 'profitable, or make business sense, but for its tendency to eliminate or lessen competition'. Under this definition, all that seems to matter is that the dominant firm had the intention to eliminate or to lessen competition, a standard that is hardly useful for distinguishing between procompetitive or anticompetitive behaviour because the wish to eliminate its rivals is commonplace among firms. Moreover, intent is one thing; realization is another. Hence, in order for sacrifice to become a standard of proof, a benchmark needs to be found with respect of which such a sacrifice is assessed, a difficult, if not impossible, task.

The efficient competitor and the consumer harm tests identify the benchmark under which an abuse can be identified. In particular, as Vickers (2005) points out, the as efficient competitor test defines as exclusionary only those practices that exclude as efficient rivals and therefore it is a standard under which competition, as opposed to competitors, is protected. Finally, according to the consumer harm test, the 'law against exclusionary practices by dominant firms should prevent the exclusion of rivals whose presence enhances consumer welfare' (Vickers 2005: 258). In practice, the consumer harm test would imply that conduct is not exclusionary unless it can be shown to have the effect of raising prices and reducing output, again a very broad standard.

Our view is that the as efficient competitor and the consumer harm tests can usefully be combined in a sequence. First, in order to identify an abuse the possibility that the practice under investigation would exclude an equally efficient competitor should be proved. As a second step, the authority should then ask whether consumers are harmed; only if the answer is yes should it conclude that an abuse has occurred.

The following provides a discussion of competition and efficiency considerations that arise in regard to particular examples of abusive practices, specifically: (a) refusals to deal; (b) predatory pricing; (c) the use of loyalty discounts and rebates; (d) tie-ins and bundling; and (e) raising rivals' costs.

Refusal to Deal

We address the issue of refusal to deal first because of its central role in the cases reviewed in section 'Analytical Steps in the Development of AOD Cases' and its perceived importance to developing countries. We note, nonetheless, that this issue is economically complex and is probably the single most controversial aspect of the law of AOD (for example, McDonald 2004); agencies are well-advised to proceed cautiously in this area.

Indeed, in most jurisdictions, competition law does not impose on firms a general duty to deal, and economic theory would not support such an approach. When a firm (even a dominant one) refuses to deal with a customer (as opposed to a competitor), in most circumstances, an intervention by a competition authority may not be justified. The underlying hypothesis is that refusing an opportunity for profit is not rational for any firm, including dominant ones, and that if it is done there are usually other justifications for it.

On the other hand, refusal to deal with a competitor may be an abuse, for example, when a vertically integrated dominant firm refuses to supply to a competitor downstream an essential input that it controls. In these circumstances, the refusal can impede the development of competition in the downstream market. In general, to assess abuse in cases involving refusal to deal it is necessary to look at: the market power of the firm, the rationale for the refusal, and the resulting competitive harm. As always, it is critical to properly verify that access be really indispensable for effectively competing. First of all, there might be alternatives in the market so that the shut-out firm can sidestep the refusal and still be an effective competitor, then the refusal to deal should not be considered anticompetitive. Furthermore, when this is not possible, it may be that the facility could be duplicated at reasonable cost in a reasonable time. Finally, there may be objective justifications for the refusal, such as lack of capacity or that the customer is not trustworthy.

In order to develop a useful body of case, law competition agencies should be careful not to mistake injury to competition with injury to individual competitors. Orders requiring firms to provide mandatory access to 'essential' facilities should be sought only when the benefits of providing such access clearly outweigh the costs. Authorities should avoid embracing an excessively broad 'essential facilities doctrine,' that is, routinely compel firms to deal with rivals, which often benefits competitors but not competition. Such a rule can discourage firms from investing in new goods and services for fear that they could not earn an adequate return (for a useful discussion of these and other problems associated with the doctrine of essential facilities, Werden 1987).

In the US, two opinions by the Supreme Court from previous decades (the *Aspen*[6] and *Kodak*[7] cases) shed light on this issue, suggesting that refusal

[6] *Aspen Skiing Co.* v. *Aspen Highlands Skiing Corp.*, 472 U.S. 585, 602 (1985).

[7] *Eastman Kodak Co.* v. *Image Technical Service Inc.* 504 U.S. 451 (1992).

to deal can be an abuse when access is denied after having been granted in the past.[8] As Baker (1999) notes, in both cases the refusal was deemed abusive only insofar as: (a) a rival was substantially excluded; (b) the mechanism for doing so was disruption of a collaborative and complementary relationship; and (c) the firm engaging in the conduct lacked a satisfactory business justification. In its subsequent decision in *Trinko* v. *Verizon*,[9] the Supreme Court held that when a binding regulatory obligation to deal is in place, refusal to deal should not be considered an antitrust law violation. More generally, the Court's opinion in *Trinko* emphasizes the intrinsic difficulties involved in the use of mandatory access as an antitrust remedy and makes clear that there is no general duty of firms to cooperate under US antitrust law (McDonald 2004).

Although US and EC case law and policy on refusals are sometimes characterized as being widely divergent (for example, McDonald 2005), the differences can also be over-stated (Anderson 2011). The 1998 European Court of Justice (ECJ) decision in *Bronner*[10] suggests that the EC and US approaches are more convergent than is sometimes suggested. *Bronner* originated from the refusal by *Mediaprint*, a major Austrian newspaper publisher, to provide access to its local distribution network to a much smaller rival, Oscar Bronner. The Court held that a refusal to deal is an abuse of a dominant position when it is 'likely to eliminate all competition in the [...] market [...] [is ...] incapable of being objectively justified, but also that the [refused] service [...] be indispensable to carrying on that person's business, inasmuch as there is no actual or potential substitute'. In the circumstances of the case, the Court held that Oscar Bronner had not been able to demonstrate that the distribution network for which it requested access was indeed indispensable for entry. Consequently, the Court concluded, the refusal to deal was not an abuse.

Where the United States and Europe appear to differ the most is in their treatment of refusal to deal by intellectual property owners (that is, refusal

[8] *Aspen* dealt with a situation in which three of four downhill skiing areas in a prestige location (Aspen, Colorado) were owned by a dominant firm which terminated a pre-existing joint ticket arrangement with a firm owning the fourth area; *Kodak* dealt with the taking of steps by the Kodak corporation to make it more difficult for independent service organizations to service Kodak photocopiers, in part by denying access to copier replacement parts.

[9] *Verizon Communications Inc.* v. *Law Offices of Curtis V. Trinko, LLP*, 540 U.S. 682 (2004).

[10] *Oscar Bronner GmbH & Co. K.G.* v. *Mediapring Zeitungs und Zeitcshriftenverlag GmbH & Co. K.G.*, Case C-7/97, 1998 E.C. R. I-7791, [1999] 4 C.M.L.R. 112.

to license). In the US, established case law indicates that there is very strong or possibly absolute prerogative of patent holders to refuse to license their technology. The 1995 Antitrust Guidelines for the Licensing of Intellectual Property of the United States Department of Justice and Federal Trade Commission, while emphasizing that intellectual property is not different from physical property in terms of its being subject to antitrust liability, are reluctant to admit that refusal to deal by IP owners could be anticompetitive. In contrast, the ECJ in the *Magill* case[11] has defined criteria for requiring access to IP and has confirmed them in the *IMS Health* case.[12] These criteria stipulate that, in order for a refusal to license to be treated as an abuse, the following requirements must be met: (a) there must be no actual or potential substitute for the IP-protected product in the relevant market; (b) there can be no business justification for the exclusion; and, perhaps most importantly, (c) a new product must be denied to consumers because of the refusal.[13]

The Court's third requirement is the only one specific to intellectual property. The case law developed so far in Europe does not identify precise criteria for defining what is actually 'new', arguably leaving intellectual property owners, including prospective ones, in a state of uncertainty as to the extent of exclusionary power they are entitled to when granted a patent.

However, the European Courts clearly rejected the notion that the mere presence of intellectual property rights by themselves satisfy, as Microsoft had argued in defence, the burden a dominant firm has to supply objective justifications when it refuses to license.

[11] The 1995 *Magill* case originated from the refusal by Irish television stations to license their copyrighted program listings to Magill that wanted to publish a weekly guide, while the TV stations were only making available daily guides. See ECJ Joined cases C-241/91 P and C-242/91 P *Radio Telefis Eireann (RTE) and Independent Television Publications Ltd (ITP)* v. *Commission (Magill)* [1995] ECR 743.

[12] The 2004 case originates from the refusal by IMS Health to make available to competitors a very detailed system of classification of German pharmacies that was the standard producers of pharmaceuticals used for their marketing strategies. See ECJ Case C-418/01, *IMS Health GmbH & Co. OHG* v. *NDC Health GmbH & Co. KG*, [2004] ECR I-5039.

[13] These criteria were confirmed by the Court of First Instance dismissal of Microsoft's application to annull the Commission decision, *Microsoft* v. *Commission*, Judgement of the Court of First Instance 17 September 2007 in Case T-201/04, available at: http://curia.europa.eu/juris/showPdf.jsf;jsessionid=9ea7d0f130de80129481efcf45c4bf29fb00d285c5bd.e34KaxiLc3eQc40LaxqMbN4ObhqMe0?text=&docid=62940&pageIndex=0&doclang=EN&mode=lst&dir=&occ=first&part=1&cid=42310.

Proceedings in the 2004 European Commission case against the Microsoft Corporation provide further scope for reflection.[14] A key aspect of this case concerned the refusal by Microsoft to provide competitors with information relating to its operating system source code which, it was alleged, was necessary for the development of competing software products.[15] Although the relevant information may have been protected by intellectual property rights, the Commission considered it essential for allowing the development of competing applications so that they could run smoothly on Windows. The Commission's treatment of the first two requirements that the Court had developed in *IMS* was straightforward: it found, on the facts, that there was no substitute for the IP-protected product in the relevant market and that no satisfactory business justification for the exclusion had been shown. As to the third requirement enunciated in *Magill* and *IMS* (that a new product must be denied to consumer), this does not appear to have been considered explicitly in the Commission's decision. Perhaps, this signals that this requirement can be met on the basis of a denial of a potential as opposed to an actual new product.

Before concluding our discussion on refusal to deal, a final observation on access prices is appropriate. Indeed, an obligation to provide access to a competitor has to be associated with an indication of the maximum price above which access would become unprofitable, so as to make sure that access at excessively low prices would not reduce the incentives to invest or to innovate on the part of essential facility owners. The 'price minus avoidable cost' rule, or Efficient Component Pricing Rule (ECPR), originally introduced by Willig (1979) and further developed by Baumol and Sydak (1994) and Baumol and Willig (1995), addresses exactly this question and, by preserving the profits of the facility owner, maintains the right incentives to invest/innovate. By pricing above the ECPR an equally efficient competitor of the dominant firm would be kept out of the market. This 'squeezing' strategy represents a different abuse than refusal to deal (even though the effects of the practice are the same) and will be discussed in the section 'Predatory Pricing'. A related discussion is provided in the section on 'Tie-ins and Bundling', later.

[14] European Commission Case No. COMP/37.792 Microsoft of 24.3.2004; confirmed in CFI, 17 September 2007, Microsoft, Case T.201/04.

[15] Another aspect of the case, concerning the bundling of Microsoft's Media Player software with its operating system, is discussed later in the sub-section on tie-ins and bundling.

Predatory Pricing

Predatory pricing refers to a dominant firm's practice of selling its products at prices below cost so as to drive competitors out of a market and successfully monopolize it, in the expectation of eventually achieving higher-than-competitive profits. Economists today (and many competition officials) approach allegations of predatory pricing with a healthy degree of scepticism. This reflects a widespread view, supported by relevant scholarly literature, that predatory strategies are costly to implement and uncertain in the pay-offs that they yield (see, for development of this basic perspective, Easterbrook (1981) and references cited therein). In particular, predatory price-cutting and/or capacity expansions are unlikely to be profit-maximizing strategies for the firms involved in the absence of barriers that prevent subsequent entry (or re-entry) of competitors. This is because the possibility of such (re-)entry will prevent the alleged predator from eventually raising its prices above competitive levels, as it must do if its losses from the period of predation are to be worth the cost.

In many jurisdictions, the assessment of alleged predatory conduct increasingly emphasizes the identification of barriers to re-entry and the consequent feasibility of 'recoupment'. This is the case, for example, in the US (see, for example, the leading US decision on this matter, *Brooke Group Ltd.* v. *Brown and Williamson Tobacco Corp.*, 509 U.S. 209, 113 S. Ct. 2578 [1993]). Under this approach, predation is condemned not because it results in lower prices now, but because it is likely to lead to reduced output and higher prices in the future and, therefore, ultimately harm consumers. This approach is also being given increasing weight in the European Community (EC). Although explicit proof of recoupment is not yet required in the EC, in its judgment in *Tetra Pak II* v. *Commission* (Case C-333/94 P, *Tetra Pak International SA* v. *Commission*, 1996 E.C.R. I-5951) the ECJ noted that 'according to the specific circumstances of the case,' it was not necessary to prove recoupment. By explicitly stating that recoupment did not need to be proven in the specific circumstances of the case, the *Tetra Pak II* judgment implies that recoupment does need to be proven in most other cases *(id.* at para. 44).

Indeed, the European Commission guidelines of 2009 acknowledge the necessity of establishing recoupment, suggesting that

> generally speaking, consumers are likely to be harmed if the dominant undertaking can reasonably expect its market power after the predatory conduct comes to an end to be greater than it would have been had the undertaking not engaged in that conduct in the first place, that is to say, if the undertaking is likely to be in a position to benefit from the sacrifice. This does not mean

> that the Commission will only intervene if the dominant undertaking would be likely to be able to increase its prices above the level persisting in the market before the conduct. It is sufficient, for instance, that the conduct would be likely to prevent or delay a decline in prices that would otherwise have occurred.

More importantly, according to the European Commission, '[I]dentifying consumer harm is not a mechanical calculation of profits and losses, and proof of overall profits is not required. Likely, consumer harm may be demonstrated by assessing the likely foreclosure effect of the conduct, combined with consideration of other factors, such as entry barriers. In this context, the Commission will also consider possibilities of re-entry' (European Commission 2009: 22).

In any case, while predation is a theoretically challenging subject, it is not very common to see genuine instances of predation. First of all, firms that consider engaging in predatory behaviour are certain to incur some costs in the initial period, while future benefits are uncertain. Furthermore, the strategy can be risky because these costs can persist for a long time if the prey does not exit the market as quickly as expected (and costs are much higher for the dominant firm than for its much smaller prey). The risk of false positives (an authority finds predation when in fact there is no predation) is therefore much higher than that of false negatives (an authority finds no predation when in fact there is predation).

In order to reduce the risk of false positives, one should rely not only on identifying an appropriate measure of costs under which prices would indeed be predatory (prices being below average incremental costs), but, most importantly, on proving the possibility of recoupment, which would include recoupment obtained by establishing a reputation as a predator. As the US case law makes clear, recoupment implies proving that profits to be gained in the post-predation period must outweigh all losses.

Ordinarily, the necessity of actually proving recoupment is unlikely to be excessively burdensome for antitrust agencies. Most cases of predation are, in fact, related to practices of selective predation, that is, not across the board predation, but directed at customers more likely to switch to other suppliers. In these cases, recoupment does not necessarily occur over time, but it occurs continuously via infra-marginal units sold at above cost prices. In such cases, it is only necessary to prove that the practice is indeed exclusionary, that is the share of the market affected is sufficient to exclude competitors.

A similar analytical approach is appropriate in regard to price squeezing strategies. This type of abusive practice is particularly common when the dominant firm that controls a scarce input is fully integrated downstream where its competitors are also the buyers of that input (that is indispensable for them in order to enter). The abuse originates from the difference between the price downstream and the price of the scarce input being so low as not to allow profitable entry. More technically, when this difference is lower than the average total cost of an equally efficient competitor operating only downstream, then it is exclusionary. There are a number of problems associated with characterizing 'predatory' a price squeezing strategy, the most important being that the 'predator' is generally not pricing below costs. For example, price squeezing cases are most common in telecommunications where competitors downstream require access to the local loop. The exclusionary strategy originates from the way access charges are regulated. When these regulated access charges cover costs and a normal return to capital, then the incumbent vertically integrated operator has the incentive to consider only the marginal cost of access when deciding its final price downstream. The result is a price squeeze for competitors that have to pay the regulated access cost, but not necessarily losses for the incumbent.[16] As already noted, appropriate remedies can be difficult to identify in such cases.

Since the exclusionary strategy often originates from the way access prices are regulated, it is not always clear whether price squeezing is an antitrust or a regulatory offence. The recent opinion of the US Supreme Court in *Verizon* v. *Trinko*[17] clarifies the extent of antitrust jurisdiction in that country in cases where also the regulator is in charge. The case involved Verizon, a telecommunications incumbent operator that had refused access to the local loop to competitors at regulated access prices. Because these access prices were imposed by the US Telecom regulator (the Federal Communications Commission) to be equal to long run incremental costs, one of the arguments of the Supreme Court was that there was no antitrust infringement because these regulated access prices were much lower than those that would have prevailed in a regulation-free market (that is, right below the level where they would be exclusionary). The US Supreme Court opinion suggests that while the safe harbour for antitrust action is that access prices not be exclusionary, the regulator can establish even lower access prices.

One final issue in predation is whether a meeting competition defence should be allowed. The answer, in our view, is a qualified 'yes', in the sense

[16] See, for example, the European Commission case Comp/37.451, *Deutsche Telekom*, 'Price squeeze local loop Germany' (2003).

[17] *Verizon Communications Inc.* v. *Law Offices of Curtis V. Trinko* 124 S. Ct. 872 (2004), rev'g 305, F, 3d 89 (2nd Cir. 2002).

that it may be a defence only for prices between average variable costs and average total costs, but never for prices below average variable costs. Indeed, if meeting competition was allowed for prices below average variable costs, the below cost pricing prerequisite would be superfluous when it is most needed, that is, when a high-cost monopolist faces new, more efficient competitors.

Loyalty Discounts and Rebates

Firms can structure their discounting policies in different ways: standard quantity discounts, loyalty discounts granted in exchange for exclusivity, or target discounts where a discount is granted on all purchases after a pre-specified level of sales (which may differ for different retailers) has been reached. There is no consensus across jurisdictions on how to assess the abusiveness of discounts granted by dominant firms. In the European Community, the only proper justification for discounts is some objective measure of the cost savings associated with the corresponding level of sales. Otherwise, exclusionary effects are presumed. In the US, exclusionary effects of discounts have to be proven explicitly, not as a simple hypothesis or as a logical possibility.

For example, in 1999, in *Virgin/BA* (COMP/34.780), the Commission found British Airways' (BA) travel-agent discounting schemes abusive. In that case, which was confirmed by the Court of First Instance (CFI),[18] discounts were granted to travel agents according to predetermined, customized turnover targets. In order to prove the abuse, the Commission tried to show that BA discounts led to large increases in the margins an aggressive airline would have to leave to travel agents so as to make them indifferent to the BA offer. In particular, the Commission calculated the effect of the discounting scheme on a new entrant wishing to compete away 2 per cent of the BA market. However, in its calculation, the Commission did not consider that BA's market share was slightly below 50 per cent and declining and that a competitor also competed with other airlines—not just with British Airways. Furthermore, after showing that matching the discount was more costly to a new entrant, the Commission simply presumed that competing airlines (that were already in the market) did not have the ability to profitably match BA discounts. This is an unrealistic presumption at least because, irrespective of the discounting policy, Virgin, the company that initiated the case, was able to enter the market profitably and to gain quite substantial market shares in quite a short time.

[18] Case T-219/99, *British Airways plc* v. *Commission* (17 December 2003, not yet reported), upholding *Virgin/BA* supra, n. 16, appeal to the ECJ is pending as Case C-95/04, *British Airways* v. *Commission.*

In the US, a different result was reached in a similar case. In July 2001, the US Court of Appeals for the Second Circuit affirmed the summary judgment of the District Court, stating that a loyalty discount scheme by BA, allegedly used to exclude Virgin Atlantic Airways from the market, was not anticompetitive.[19] An analysis of the US Court of Appeals' judgment provides a good opportunity to identify the main differences underlying the approaches of the two jurisdictions. In particular, according to the US Court of Appeals, Virgin failed to demonstrate that BA's discounts to travel agents harmed competition, since they did not lead to lower output, higher prices, or decreased quality. Furthermore, no evidence was provided to support the argument that BA's discounting policy might lead to monopoly. A major point in the Court's judgment was that, during the period under consideration, there was no actual exclusion. On the contrary, Virgin was able to gain considerable market share (and profitably so), becoming a major player along the US-London routes.

Heimler (2005) argues that in the evaluation of discounting policies, greater reliance on economic analysis would strengthen decision-making in both jurisdictions. In particular, he suggests that discounts by a dominant firm should be considered abusive only if they would force an equally efficient competitor to price below costs. In particular, he suggests that 'the calculation of the below-cost character of discounts is made with respect to a small but significant increase in sales and refers to the price-cost margin of the dominant firm to ensure that exclusion is assessed with respect to an equally efficient competitor'. This approach, which is very similar to the one suggested in the 2009 European Commission 'Guidance on the Commission's enforcement priorities in applying Article 82 of the EC Treaty to abusive exclusionary conduct by dominant undertakings', provides a unified treatment of discounts, rebates, and predation. One important difference between discounts and across the board predation is that in the case of discounts recoupment is not a contentious issue since it can occur simultaneously, through the higher prices of infra-marginal units (Heimler 2005).

The Intel case provides a better understanding of how discounts may become exclusionary. Both the US Federal Trade Commission and the European Commission addressed, in relevant cases, the exclusionary nature of Intel's discounting practices. In 2009, the European Commission found that Intel Corporation abused its dominant position in the market for x86 CPUs, an essential component of computer memory. According to the Commission, Intel engaged in two types of abusive practices. 'First, Intel gave rebates to computer manufacturers—Dell, HP, NEC, Lenovo on condition that they

[19] United States Courts of Appeal for the Second Circuit, August Term 2000, decided 24 July 2001, Docket n. 99-9402. *Virgin Atlantic Airways Limited.*

bought all, or almost all, their x86 CPUs from Intel. Intel also made direct payments to Europe's largest PC retailer—Media Saturn Holding (MSH) on condition that it stocked only computers with Intel x86 CPUs. Second, Intel made direct payments to computer manufacturers—HP, Acer, Lenovo—to stop or delay the launch of specific products containing a competitor's computer chips and to limit the sales channels available to these products'.[20]

A similar decision against Intel, this time in the form of a consent decree, was adopted by the US Federal Trade Commission in 2010. The case was similar to the European one in key respects. The FTC alleged that Intel 'used anticompetitive tactics to cut off rivals' access to the marketplace and deprive consumers of choice and innovation in the microchips that comprise computers' central processing unit, or CPU'. Under the settlement, Intel, among other things was prohibited from: 'conditioning benefits to computer makers in exchange for their promise to buy chips from Intel exclusively or to refuse to buy chips from others; and retaliating against computer makers if they do business with non-Intel suppliers by withholding benefits from them'.[21]

The reasons why Intel's loyalty rebates were considered an abuse are captured effectively in the decision of the European Commission. There, the Commission posits that matching the gains Intel's customers would have made by benefitting from the conditional rebates, would have led Intel's main competitor, AMD, to price below cost for a small but significant increase in its sales. In other words, the abuse originates in a very specific hypothesis that the Commission makes on the functioning of the microchips market. The Commission believes that consumers are sensitive to the chip brand that is used in the computer they purchase. As a result, since Intel is dominant, the large part of the chips a computer manufacturer purchases would come from Intel. AMD could only have a small share which Intel abusively competes away with the discounting policy. This conclusion is only true if competition in the microchips market operates as the Commission suggests: each computer manufacturer would purchase most of the microchips from Intel and AMD could only aim at achieving a small share. On the other hand, whether AMD could compete away the whole demand of microchips of single manufacturers (which if it were possible would make the rebates not

[20] See the European Commission Press Release of 13 May 2009, 'The Intel antitrust case', available at http://ec.europa.eu/competition/sectors/ICT/intel.html.

[21] See the US Federal Trade Commission press release of 4 August 2010, 'FTC Settles Charges of Anticompetitive Conduct Against Intel', available at: http://www.ftc.gov/news-events/press-releases/2010/08/ftc-settles-charges-anticompetitive-conduct-against-intel.

abusive), that is, maintaining its share in the overall market for microchips by concentrating its sales to a few manufacturers, not by selling that share to each manufacturer, is not discussed in the Commission decision.

Tie-ins and Bundling

A tie-in is the sale of one product (the tying good) on the condition that the buyer purchase another product (the tied good). Bundling refers to situations where a package of two or more of products is offered. If only the bundle is offered and not its individual components then bundling is called 'pure', otherwise it is 'mixed'. With tying the quantity of the tied good is not predefined, while with bundling the 'package' cannot generally be customized and the number of units of the bundled goods is fixed. Furthermore, while tying is based on a contract, bundling may also originate from technological integration so that unbundling may not be that simple.

Mixed bundling, a situation where a bundle is discounted with respect to the price of its individual components, is abusive only in so far as an equally efficient competitor, offering only some of the components, could compete only at a loss against the discounted bundle. The analysis to be performed in order to identify an abuse is the same as that suggested for discounts and rebates.

Tying and bundling should not be considered abusive if the firm lacks market power in the tying good. Even when the firm has market power, establishing that a tie-in or a bundle is in fact abusive requires detailed analysis of its purpose and the market context. Sometimes two products are vertically related, with one being an input to the production of the other. In such circumstances, tying/bundling can reduce the overall net price paid by consumers (that is, eliminating inefficiencies originating from double marginalization). Tying may be motivated by the firm's desire to maintain or increase its reputation for quality or reliability. This should not be considered abusive since it increases efficiency and market demand.

Tying and bundling raise concerns for competition policy when they foreclose the tied market to equally or more efficient competitors. This might be the case, for example, when a tie-in raises entry barriers to competitors thereby permitting the exercise of market power in the tied market. Tying can also be used to evade price regulation on the tying good. Suppose a dominant firm has market power in its primary product. Suppose further that the dominant firm's price is regulated, which effectively prevents it from earning all of the monopoly profits that it could if there were no regulation. The dominant firm would have an incentive to sell its regulated product only on condition that another product is purchased (whose price is not regulated) and then set the price of the bundle to capture all monopoly profits in the regulated good.

The competition authority must determine whether the tie-in or the bundle determines the anticompetitive lock-in of—sometimes imperfectly informed consumers or whether the exclusion of competitors is nonetheless efficient, improving consumer welfare. If, for example, the cost of replacement parts is substantial in relation to the price of the durable good, as, say, with a motor car, the replacement parts market might not constitute a properly defined relevant market. What this means is that consumers, worried about the future cost of replacement parts, would consider this cost at the time of purchase and switch to a different brand should they be charged excessive prices in the replacement parts market. In such circumstances, a possible tie (imposing to consumers that repairs could only be made at an authorized dealership) could not be technically defined a 'tie in', since there is only one relevant market involved, not two. In other words, if consumers would consider at the time of purchase of a durable good all the costs they would incur in its life, then the tie should not be worrisome for antitrust authorities since competition in the primary market (if it exists) would already discipline the firm. On the other hand, if replacement parts constitute a separate relevant market, then restricting the categories of customers authorized to purchase replacement parts could be a tie-in. The analysis should then consider whether there is a consumer welfare justification for the tie-in (for example, maintaining the high-quality reputation of a brand by impeding sub-standard repairs that the owner of the durable cannot identify as such). Otherwise the tie-in is abusive.

Tie-ins and bundling have been an important consideration in various cases relating to practices of the Microsoft Corporation. In a case initiated in the early 1990s (the so-called Licensing case), the US Department of Justice and Microsoft entered into a consent agreement to settle the Department's allegations that Microsoft had violated antitrust laws by engaging in certain contractual practices with computer manufacturers. A central allegation made by the department was that Microsoft

> used monopoly power to induce personal computer (PC) manufactures into anticompetitive, long-term licenses under which they must pay Microsoft not only when they sell PCs containing Microsoft's operating systems but also when they sell PCs containing non-Microsoft operating systems. These anti-competitive long-term licenses have helped Microsoft maintain its monopoly. By inhibiting competing operating systems' access to PC manufacturers,

> Microsoft's exclusionary licenses slow innovation, raise prices, and deprive consumers of an effective choice among competing PC operating systems'[22]

In a subsequent case initiated in 1998, the Department of Justice alleged that Microsoft, by bundling Windows with Internet Explorer, was excluding Netscape and other potential entrants from the browser market and was extending its monopoly in personal computer operating systems into Internet browsing software.[23] The case ended in 2002 with a settlement between the Department and Microsoft which, among other obligations, imposed on Microsoft a requirement to provide software developers with the interfaces needed to inter-operate with the operating system, allowing them to effectively compete with Microsoft. A number of aspects of the case are of interest. First, as Professor and former Judge Robert Bork (1998) argued at the time, Microsoft's bundling of its browser to the Windows operating system appeared to be aimed directly at excluding Netscape—which otherwise could have developed a competing operating system—from the market. For this reason, Bork, who is not normally considered as an advocate of activist antitrust policy except perhaps with respect to horizontal cartels, concluded that the case was much different from a pure bundling one and that Microsoft's bundling strategy was indeed dangerous to competition. Although Bork's arguments were not fully reflected in the 2002 Final Judgment, they were instrumental in suggesting that Microsoft's practices in this case were anticompetitive. Yet, the case also shows that pure bundling, even by a quasi-monopolist, may nonetheless also provide consumer benefits (that is, the convenience of purchasing complementary products as a package). In practice, it can be difficult to calculate these benefits and, more importantly, to assess how large they are in relation to the exclusionary effects.

In the course of the *Microsoft* proceedings, Professor Elhauge (2002) made the interesting suggestion that consumer benefits be calculated in an objective way and that pure bundling should be prohibited when it excludes an equally efficient competitor and its technological benefits are not demonstrated. With specific reference to the *Microsoft* case, he suggested that the bundling of the Windows operating system and Internet Explorer did not produce any technological benefit on the basis that bundling actually reduced the efficiency (speed) of the computer on which the new system was installed (even though

[22] See *U.S.* v. *Microsoft*, 'Competitive Impact Statement', Civil Action No. 94-1564, 27 July 1994.

[23] See Department of Justice Press Release (1998). Available on the Department of Justice website at http://www.usdoj.gov/atr/public/press_releases/1998/1764.htm.

it reduced it by a degree unnoticeable to most users). While intrigued by the possibility of an objective measure of consumer harm, we are doubtful that a mechanical approach like the one proposed by Elhauge (2002) in this case is a sound measure of consumer harm, given the wide discretion involved in choosing a single characteristic of performance (speed).

The US proceedings relating to bundling of the Windows operating system and the Internet Explorer browser triggered wide discussion on the exclusionary effects of bundling. In the following years, possibly as a consequence of that discussion, antitrust authorities in a number of other jurisdictions initiated cases against Microsoft on broadly similar grounds. For example, pure bundling between the Windows operating systems and the Media Player function was deemed abusive in a 2004 European case.[24] In that case, the European Commission determined that Microsoft was dominant in the tying market of operating systems and that there were no economies flowing from integration with the tied media player market because 'distribution costs in software licensing are insignificant [and] a copy of a software programme can be duplicated and distributed at no substantial effort'. On the other hand, the Commission argued, 'the importance of consumer choice and innovation regarding applications such as media players is high'; on this basis, the elimination of competition in media players was considered to produce negative effects on consumers.

A significant perceived problem with the remedies adopted by the EU in this case was that the Commission's decision obliged Microsoft to offer to consumers also an unbundled version of the Windows XP operating system that would not have Media Player bundled with it, but did not require that the prices of the two versions be substantially different. The decision simply forbade Microsoft to offer the bundled version at a discount. As a result, Microsoft offered the two versions of the Windows XP operating system at effectively the same price. The unbundled version was only purchased by consumers that expressly did not want Media Player. As could have been expected, by April 2006 Microsoft had only sold 1787 copies of the unbundled version of Windows XP[25] all over Europe, around 0.005 per cent of all sales of Windows XP.[26]

More generally, the problem with prohibiting pure bundling is that the evaluation of the trade-off between technological integration, the elimination

[24] European Commission Case No. COMP/37.792 Microsoft, 24 March 2004.

[25] As reported by Gavil and First (2014), p. 251.

[26] Sherer (2008) suggests that the European Commission should have set the prices of the bundled and unbundled versions of Microsft XP in proportion to the R&D expenses incurred in the preparation of the Windows media player, which meant a price difference between the two of around 15 per cent.

of competition, and consumer harm is intrinsically difficult. It requires an understanding of the possible directions of technical progress and an assessment of uncertain long-term consumer benefits. Furthermore, effective remedies that do not cause inconvenience to consumers are not easy to identify.

Raising Rivals' Costs

Raising rivals' costs may be less costly than predatory pricing as a means of excluding competitors from the market, because it may not require a direct reduction in profits for the dominant firm. The 1961 *Pennington* case in the US is a classic example. This case involved the strategic use of collective bargaining arrangements by a dominant firm. It was alleged that higher wages industry wide were actively encouraged by large producers to increase the costs of smaller, marginal firms in the US coal-mining industry. A high wage level for the industry benefited capital-intensive firms, since it had a proportionally smaller impact on their costs than on smaller, labour-intensive competitors (Williamson 1968). But it is difficult to actually prove that a dominant firm accepted high wages for its employees just for the sake of raising the costs of its competitors.

Other possible examples of raising the costs of a small rival include engaging it in litigation (fixed costs weigh more on a small budget), or strategically advertising to such a degree that it raises sunk-cost investments for small rivals and potential entrants. With advertising, however, such expenses should be more properly considered as an investment in the reputation of the firm. Moreover, a firm's reputation may not be limited to the market to which the advertisement is directed. Thus, many firms that have gained a reputation in one market use it to enter a different market. For instance, firms with high standing in the fashion industry have used their reputation to move into other markets, such as perfumes or shoes.

Other Possible Exclusionary Abuses

The foregoing discussion of examples of exclusionary abuses is by no means exhaustive. Other possible examples might include: (a) exclusive dealing or other vertical restraints when employed by a dominant firm; (b) the pre-emption of scarce facilities in a market; (c) predatory investments; (d) boycott of competitors; and (e) exclusionary branding or patent extension strategies. As with the practices that have been discussed so far, evaluation of these practices would involve steps such as the degree to which the firm engaging in the practice wields market power, the effectiveness of the practice as a tool for excluding competitors, and alternative (pro-competitive) business justifications.

Identifying and Evaluating Alleged Exploitative Abuses

The purpose of any law, including antitrust, is to give clear guidance to firms on what they are allowed to do and on what is prohibited. In this sense, all laws are expected to provide an ex-ante guidance. The reason is that if we would know only afterwards what is prohibited, the law would have no deterrence effect. Of course, laws can be quite general, which indeed is the case in regard to some antitrust provisions. In these circumstances, legal certainty must be provided through the development of case law and by legal and economic analysis. Abuse of dominance represents a particularly difficult area in which to provide certainty, for the reason that laws do not define precisely neither dominance nor what is abusive. In our view, this is unavoidable, since with a mechanical rule many pro-competitive behaviours might be penalized and, at the same time, many abusive practices would not be identified.

The difficulties related to the identification of an abuse are enhanced in the case of possible exploitative abuses. Here, the issue is not only providing guidance on when the exercise of market power with respect to the customers of a dominant firm is 'abusive', but also identifying a threshold below which the behaviour is no longer abusive. The equally efficient competitor standard that was developed for exclusionary abuses is not extendable to exploitation and another one cannot be identified. We will briefly discuss two practices, excessive prices and discrimination that are the most frequent ones to be taken up by competition authorities as exploitative.

Charging of Excessive Prices

The problem is that prices may be high for many reasons, including surges in demand, high unit costs, and exercise of market power. To prevent a dominant firm from abusing its position, antitrust enforcers should be more concerned with the reasons that lead to high prices and profits than with the prices themselves. This is only partly because it can be difficult and time consuming for a government agency to determine a firm's costs, which must be known to judge whether prices charged are excessive and to set the 'right' price. It can be particularly difficult to determine costs when a firm produces many different products and common costs have to be allocated to each one. As also noted earlier, in a market economy profits serve a critical function: when firms earn high profits, they create an incentive for others to enter the industry. When firms earn relatively low profits, they have an incentive to exit. By responding in this way, firms are more likely to produce goods and services that are highly valued by consumers and good for consumers and firms. When government agencies regulate prices, the crucial role played by profits in providing incentives to enter and exit may be short-circuited.

There are, of course, some industries in which the market can support only one firm even when there are no legal barriers to entry (that is, natural monopolies). Such a situation can arise when economies of scale or economies of scope (or both) are so pervasive that the costs of production are lowest when a single firm supplies the market. Possible examples are electricity transmission and local water supply. In Western economies, the prices and practices of natural monopolies are often not under the jurisdiction of the competition agency but are supervised by industry-specific regulators. Where a regulatory agency does not exist, the competition authority may be considered responsible for ensuring that the industry does not charge excessively high prices. However, contrary to a regulator, an antitrust authority would usually not be able to intervene ex-ante and directly impose competitive prices. The antitrust authority would only block prices that are excessive (whatever that may mean) without being able to impose a specific price schedule on the dominant firm. Indeed while regulation prescribes, antitrust laws only identify what is prohibited and as a consequence, when competition is completely missing, the enforcement of antitrust law is not the most effective solution. Of course, when excessive prices are exclusionary of competitors, it is much easier to identify the level of prices that triggers such exclusions and both antitrust authorities and regulators can exercise appropriate supervision.

In Sweden, tele-heating prices were not regulated. The prices of such services charged by Fortum Värme in Stockholm were considered excessive and the antitrust authority initiated proceedings against AOD in around 2005.[27] The most difficult aspect of the case was to find a generally accepted method by which to assess the excessive price claims. Since tele-heating is a byproduct of the production of electricity, the most difficult part of the case was to identify the 'proper' way to allocate common costs. In particular, the Swedish Authority tried to apply to district heating the two-part excessive price test developed by the ECJ in the 1978 United Brands case.[28] That case centred around the price of bananas in the different member states of the

[27] See Swedesh Competition Authority Ref. No. 521/2007 and 945/2005.

[28] Judgment of the Court of 14 February 1978. *United Brands Company and United Brands Continentaal BV* v. *Commission of the European Communities*. Chiquita Bananas. Case 27/76, available at: http://curia.europa.eu/juris/showPdf.jsf?text=&docid=89300&pageIndex=0&doclang=EN&mode=lst&dir=&occ=first&part=1&cid=18192.

European Union and the Court introduced a test based on two stages. First of all, for a price to be considered abusively high, it needs to be associated with 'high profits' (unfair prices in itself). Furthermore, the price charged by the dominant firm needs to be abnormally high in comparison to that charged by competitors (unfairness in comparison).

The ECJ's approach in the United Brands case was not appropriate to the Swedish heating services case, for several reasons. First of all, since district heating is a natural monopoly, there are no competing products; therefore, it was impossible to apply the unfairness in comparison test. Furthermore, given that district heating facilities are used to produce both electricity and heat, the question is how the costs should be allocated between these two outputs. Additionally, it is necessary to allocate the investment over time, since profitability is not constant in time and was even negative in early years. The calculation was impossible to perform because contrary to regulation, which adopts an ex-ante approach, excessive prices in AOD cases have to be compared to 'optimally' determined fair prices and, unfortunately, there was no strong theory over which to rely. This is why the very simple commitment adopted (transparency of pricing conditions) was actually the only possibility.

Price Discrimination

Price discrimination is the practice of a seller charging different prices according to the profile of the customer and in the absence of appreciable cost differences that might justify different prices. A discriminatory strategy can also involve charging the same price to customers even though there are different costs of supplying them. With price discrimination, a firm may earn higher profits than when it charges a single price (net of costs) to all consumers. Some extra profits may come from increased sales; thus, price discrimination can increase a firm's total production. Price discrimination requires that a firm identifies different consumers who are willing to pay different prices. The firm must also be able to prevent arbitrage, that is, prevent the disadvantaged consumers from purchasing the product from the consumers who buy it at a favourable price.

It should be emphasized that the practice of price discrimination is not necessarily harmful to consumer welfare. In theory, discrimination can be exclusionary when a dominant firm charges lower prices to buyers more likely to switch to other suppliers. It is difficult, however, to distinguish this practice from that of a firm selling to customers willing to pay only a lower price and not the non-discriminating price. This practice (referred to in the economic literature as third-degree price discrimination) can result in more customers being supplied than would be the case with a single price for everyone.

The European Commission has frequently dealt with price discrimination strategies by dominant firms as an abuse. In many of its cases against abusive exclusionary discounts, it has also considered as abusive or potentially abusive the fact that the use of such discounts led the dominant firm to charge different prices to otherwise similarly-situated customers. Such 'discrimination' has been treated as a separate violation of competition rules because it allegedly restricts competition downstream.[29] However, as Heimler (2005) argues,

> the Commission never asks why it would be in the interest of a supplier to reduce competition among its customers, provided that a reduction of competition downstream reduces sales upstream. Furthermore, applying discount rates, independent of the size of the retailer and in some sense in proportion to its sales efforts, tends to increase, not decrease, competition among retailers, eliminating possible disadvantages that a small retailer would possibly have with respect to a larger one. Such discrimination at least at first sight, looks pro-competitive.

Furthermore, in many cases, what appears to be price discrimination may be explained by differences in the cost of serving different consumers. For example, consumers who pay higher insurance premiums or higher interest rates may be more risky and thus more costly to supply than consumers who pay lower rates. In other cases, price differences for what appears to be the same product can be explained by quality differences. To rule out such cost-based or demand-based explanations, competition agencies would have to estimate a firm's costs. But it is well known that such analysis can be time-consuming and uncertain. For these reasons, we counsel against giving high priority to price discrimination investigations as an aspect of AOD.

***

The application of competition law provisions relating to abuse of dominant position is a particularly challenging area of competition policy implementation for enforcement authorities, old and new alike. Economic theory and enforcement experience underline the challenges that are posed for such authorities in reaching sound conclusions in abuse cases. At the same time, well-conceived AOD cases can be among the most economically and

[29] See, for example, Commission Decision 2000/74/EC, Virgin/British Airways, 2000 O.J. (L 30) 1.

developmentally significant ones that are brought by competition agencies in emerging and developing countries, to the extent that they address structural problems that are critical to establishing healthy market economies in such countries.

Recent experience with respect to the enforcement of AOD provisions indicates that the bulk of cases in both developed and developing economies are in the category of exclusionary abuses. Exploitative abuses are difficult to prove because the benchmark above which exploitation is found is almost impossible to identify. On the other hand, for exclusionary abuses economic analysis provides the necessary tools for evaluating whether the practice should be prohibited or not. The use of economic analysis as a tool for identifying an exclusionary abuse is coherent with the objective of ensuring that firms are informed on what is or is not prohibited. For any legal prohibition, including of course antitrust prohibitions, it is vital that its content be known ex-ante, enabling firms' behaviour to be in full conformity with the law.

A key challenge in applying AOD provisions arises from the fact that they address behaviours that are prohibited only insofar as they are adopted by a dominant firm. Without dominance, there is no abuse; moreover, defining a dominant position requires, by itself, a careful analysis. Exclusionary abuses are common especially in industries that are opening up to competition and where incumbent dominant firms have strong incentives to keep competitors out. This is why the antitrust laws of all countries, especially countries at the start of a competition-oriented process of reform, should prohibit exclusionary abuses and provide for sanctions that are sufficient to guarantee deterrence.

This chapter adopts the view that the threshold of exclusion is reached at the point where an equally efficient competitor is unable to profitably replicate the offer of a dominant firm. In the case of price abuses (predation, discounts, mixed bundling), once it is proved that an equally efficient competitor is excluded, further analysis should not normally be required. In contrast, for non-price abuses (bundling, tying, refusal to deal, etc.), efficiency considerations (reduction of transaction costs for consumers, innovations, etc.) may very well offset any negative effect on competition originating from the exclusion of equally efficient competitors. For these practices, the analysis should also include an evaluation of whether consumers are harmed and should only conclude that there is an abuse if the answer is positive.

Our analysis also highlights the importance of careful choices in regard to the remedies adopted in abuse cases. Care should always be taken to avoid imposing greater costs than those incurred by the anticompetitive conduct. For example, the most effective way to establish competition in a market might be to break up a dominant firm. However, if this remedy would prevent the realization of overwhelming economies of scale or scope, then it would not be a responsible remedy for any agency to seek. Similarly, an investigation may determine that vertical market restraints (for instance, tied selling or exclusive dealing) have prevented the beneficial entry into a market by new competitors. Vertical market restraints, however, may also serve legitimate pro-competitive purposes, such as preventing free riding. Remedies in such cases should seek to deter anticompetitive conduct while permitting contractual restrictions that achieve genuine efficiencies.

Lastly, it is true that competition law provisions relating to AOD are often general and may not precisely identify what is prohibited. This highlights the need for appropriate case law, economic and legal analysis, guidelines by competition authorities, and scholarly papers. At an appropriate time, international agreements may be needed to adapt these general rules to the intricacies of relevant cases, especially where (as is increasingly the case) the conduct involved transcends national borders. This chapter has sought to contribute to potential developments in this area by highlighting emerging trends and enforcement approaches that are well-grounded in economics and/or international experience.

Bibliography

Anderson, Robert D. 2011. 'Systemic Implications of Deeper TransAtlantic Convergence in Competition/Antitrust Policy', in Simon J. Evenett and Robert M. Stern (eds), *Systemic Implications of Transatlantic Regulatory Cooperation and Competition*, Chapter 7. Singapore: World Scientific Publishing.

Anderson, Robert D. and Alberto Heimler. 2007. 'What Has Competition Done for Europe? An Inter-Disciplinary Answer', *Aussenwirtschaft (the Swiss Review of International Economic Relations)*, 62(4), pp. 419–54.

Anderson, Robert D., Timothy Daniel, and Alberto Heimler with Thinam Jakob. 1999. 'Abuse of Dominance', *A Framework for the Design and Implementation of Competition Policy*. Washington, DC: World Bank Publications.

Anderson, Robert D. and Frédéric Jenny. 2005. 'Competition Policy, Economic Development and the Possible Role of a Multilateral Framework on Competition Policy: Insights from the WTO Working Group on Trade and Competition Policy', in Erlinda Medalla (ed.), *Competition Policy in East Asia*. Oxon: Routledge/Curzon.

Anderson, Robert D., S. Dev Khosla, and Joseph Monteiro. 1996. 'Market Definition in Abuse of Dominant Position Cases under the Canadian *Competition Act*'. Reprinted in 'Canada', OECD Committee on Competition Law and Policy, *Proceedings of a Roundtable on Abuse of Dominant Position*, pp. 89–112. Paris: OECD.

Anderson, Robert D. and Anna Caroline Müller. 2014. 'Competition Policy and the Multilateral System: Three Propositions, an Observation and Some Questions for Reflection', in Philip Lowe and Mel Marquis (eds), *European Competition Law Annual 2012*. West Sussex: Hart Publishing.

———. 2013. *Competition Policy and Poverty Reduction: A Holistic Approach*, WTO Staff Working Paper No. ERSD-2013-02, 20 February.

Bain, Joe S. 1941. 'The Profit Rate as a Measure of Monopoly Power', *Quarterly Journal of Economics*, 55(2), pp. 271–93.

Baker, Jonathan. 1999. 'Promoting Innovation and Competition through the *Aspen/Kodak* Rule', *George Mason Law Review*, 7, pp. 500–3.

———. 2006. 'Market Definition', mimeo.

Baumol, William J. and Gregory J. Sydak. 1994. 'The Pricing of Inputs Sold to Competitors', *The Yale Journal of Regulation*, 11(1), pp. 172–202.

Baumol, William J. and Robert Willig. 1995. 'Notes on the Efficient Component Pricing Rule', Paper presented at the *Montreal Conference on Regulated Industries*.

Beato, Paulina and Jean-Jacques Laffont. 2003. *Competition Policy in Regulated Industries: Approaches for Emerging Economies*. Washington, DC: Inter-American Development Bank.

Bernheim, Douglas R. and Randal Heeb. 2015. 'A Framework for the Economic Analysis of Exclusionary Conduct', in Blair, Roger D. and Sokol, Daniel D., eds., *The Oxford Handbook of International Antitrust Economics*, 2, pp. 4–39. Boston: MIT Press.

Bork, Robert H. 1998. 'The Most Misunderstood Antitrust Case', in *The Wall Street Journal*, 22 May. Available at https://www.wsj.com/articles/SB895785768291704000.

Brennan, Timothy. 1987. 'Why Regulated Firms Should Be Kept Out of Unregulated Markets: Understanding the Divestiture', in *U.S.* v. *AT&T.' Antitrust Bulletin*, 32(3), pp. 741–93.

EAGCP. 2005. An economic approach to Article 82, available at: http://ec.europa.eu/dgs/competition/economist/eagcp_july_21_05.pdf.

Easterbrook, Frank H. 1981. 'Predatory Strategies and Counter-Strategies', *University of Chicago Law Review*, 48(2), pp. 263–337.

Elhauge, Einer. 2002. 'Tunney Act Comment on the Proposed Settlements between the United States and Microsoft', available at http://www.justice.gov/atr/cases/ms_tuncom/major/mtc-00027209.htm.

European Commission. 2009. 'Guidance on the Commission's Enforcement Priorities in Applying Article 82 of the EC Treaty to Abusive Exclusionary Conduct by Dominant Undertakings', Communication from the Commission.

Fisher, Franklin M. and John McGowan. 1983. 'On the Misuse of Accounting Rates of Return to Infer Monopoly Profits', *American Economic Review*, 73(I), pp. 81–97.

Gavil, Andrew L. and Harry First. 2014. *The Microsoft Antitrust Cases*. Boston: The MIT Press.

Godek, Paul. 1992. 'Protecting Eastern Europe from Antitrust', *Regulation*, 15(4), p. 4.

Heimler, Alberto. 2005. 'Below-Cost Pricing and Loyalty Discounts: Are They Restrictive and, if so, When?', *Competition Policy International*, 1(2), Autumn, pp. 149–72.

———. 2014. 'Antitrust Enforcement and Regulation: Different Standards but Incentive Coherent?', in I. Lianos, T. Cheng, and D. Sokol (eds), *Competition and the State*. Redwood City: Stanford University Press.

Heimler, Alberto and Kirtikumar Mehta. 2012. 'Violations of Antitrust Provisions: The Optimal Level of Fines for Achieving Deterrence', *World Competition*, 35(1), pp. 103–19.

International Trade Centre (R. Anderson, F. Jenny and A. Müller, principal authors). 2012. *Combatting Anti-Competitive Practices*, available at: http://www.intracen.org/layouts/three-column.aspx?Pageid=45836&id=62357.

Kahn, Alfred E. 2004. *Lessons from Deregulation*. Washington: AEI-Brookings Joint Center for Regulatory Studies.

Kovacic, William E. 1999. 'Designing Antitrust Remedies for Dominant Firm Misconduct', *Connecticut Law Review*, 31(4), pp. 1285–1319.

Kovács, Csaba and Andreas P. Reindl. 2013. 'The Evolution of the Hungarian Competition Regime: 2 Decades of Dynamic Change and Continuity', in David Lewis, *Building New Competition Law Regimes: Selected Essays*. Cheltenham, UK – Northampton, MA, USA: Edward Elgar.

Laffont, Jean-Jacques. 2005. *Regulation and Development*. Cambridge: Cambridge University Press.

Landes, William M. and Richard A. Posner. 1981. 'Market Power in Antitrust Cases', *Harvard Law Review*, 5, March, pp. 937–96.

McDonald, J. Bruce [then US Deputy Assistant Attorney-General for Antitrust]. 2004. 'Antitrust Division Update: Trinko and Microsoft' (Before the Houston Bar Association Antitrust and Trade Regulation Section, April).

———. 2005. 'Section 2 and Article 82: Cowboys and Gentlemen' (College of Europe Global Competition Law Centre, Second Annual Conference, The Modernization of Article 82, Brussels, 16–17 June).

OECD. 2001a. *Recommendation of the Council Concerning Structural Separation in Regulated Industries*. Paris: OECD.

———. 2001b. 'Restructuring Public Utilities for Competition'. Paris: OECD.

OFCOM. 2004. 'Strategic Review, Phase 2 Consultation Document', 18 November.

Ordover, Janusz and Russell Pittman. 1993. 'Comments on Competition Policy during Transformation of a Centrally Planned Economy', in Barry Hawk (ed.), *International Antitrust Law and Policy*, pp. 533–8. New York: Annual Proceedings of the Fordham Corporate Law Institute.

Ordover, Janusz A. and Garth Saloner. 1989. 'Predation, Monopolization and Antitrust', in Richard Schmalensee and Robert Willig (eds), *The Handbook of Industrial Organization*. Amsterdam: Elsevier.

Osakwe, Chiedu. 2001. *Poverty Reduction and Development: The Interaction of Trade, Macroeconomic and Regulatory Policies*, 10th Joseph Mubiru Memorial Lecture Organized by the Bank of Uganda.

Pittman, Russell. 2004. 'Abuse-of-Dominance Provisions of Central and Eastern European Competition Laws: Have Fears of Over-Enforcement Been Borne Out?', *World Competition*, 27(2), pp. 245–57.

———. 2009. 'Competition Issues in Restructuring Ports and Railways' EAG 09-6 (November 2009), available at: www.justice.gov/atr/public/eag/251856.pdf.

Scherer, Frederic M. 2008. 'Prices and profits in dominant firm adjudication', Faculty Research Working Paper Series, Harvard Kennedy School, RWP08-051.

Stocking, George W. and Willard F. Mueller. 1955. 'The Cellophane Case and the New Competition', *American Economic Review*, 45(1), pp. 29–63.

Vickers, J. 2005. 'Abuse of Market Power', *Economic Journal*, 115(504), pp. 244–61.

Werden, Gregory. 1987. 'The Law and Economics of the Essential Facilities Doctrine', *Saint Louis University Law Journal*, 32(Winter), pp. 432–80.

White, Lawrence J. 2006. 'Market Definition in Monopolization Cases: A Paradigm is Missing', in Wayne D. Collins (ed.), *Issues in Competition Law and Policy*. Chicago: American Bar Association.

Williamson, Oliver E. 1968. 'Wage Rates as a Barrier to Entry: The Pennington Case in Perspective', *Quarterly Journal of Economics*, 82(1), pp. 85–116.

Willig, Robert. 1979. 'The Theory of Network Access Pricing', *Issues in Public Utility Regulation*, 109, pp. 109–52.

———. 1992. 'Anti-monopoly Practices and Institutions', in Christopher Clague and Gordon C. Rausser (eds), *The Emergence of Market Economies in Eastern Europe*. Cambridge: Blackwell.

3

Merger Control*

Alan H. Goldberg

International comparisons of merger control are of increasing importance because, as the opportunities for business and trade extend beyond national borders, so too must merger control look beyond the confines of the nation state. This chapter looks at some nations with a relatively long history of merger control—Australia, New Zealand, the United Kingdom, the United States of America, Canada, South Africa, and the European Union—to illustrate current approaches to merger control.

A merger is, broadly speaking, a transaction that brings about a change in control of different business entities enabling one business entity effectively to control a significant part of the assets or decision-making processes of another. Mergers occur between business entities engaged in activities at the same level of the manufacturing or distribution chain, known as horizontal mergers, as well as between business entities engaged in activities at different stages of the manufacturing or distribution chain, known as vertical mergers.

* Reproduced from 'Merger Control', published in Dhall, V. (ed.). 2007. *Competition Law Today: Concepts, Issues, and the Law in Practice* (first ed.), Oxford University Press, New Delhi.

The author acknowledges the assistance provided by Verity Quinn, Associate to the President of the Australian Competition Tribunal, in the preparation of this chapter.

Mergers attract the attention of competition policy-makers because they generally have implications for the concentration of, and ability to use, market power, which, in turn, can impact negatively upon competition. Market power describes the ability of a business entity to act unconstrained by rivals and potential rivals in both price and non-price conduct. Mergers impact upon the concentration and use of market power because they lead to:

- a reduction in the number of business entities operating in a market; and
- an increase in the market share controlled by the merged entity,

and, in the case of vertical mergers, they can lead to increased control by the merged entity over a vertical activity in the production and distribution chain.

As a result, a merged entity may be able to exercise increased market power, or the smaller number of business entities remaining post-merger may be able to coordinate their activities. In turn, this may lead to prices being raised above the level that would otherwise exist in a competitive market, restricted output, diminished innovation, increased barriers to entry and expansion, rival business entities being eliminated, rivals' costs being raised, and other behaviour damaging to the competitive process. Accordingly, competition law seeks to prohibit mergers which are likely to bring about a concentration of market power or an enhanced ability to use market power.

However, mergers can also be an effective means of generating efficiencies and achieving public-interest type benefits. For example, mergers can be an effective means of generating economies of scale and of scope, resulting in the production of products at a lower cost or of higher quality. Mergers can also help businesses to combine research and development in a more effective manner to create new or improved products. Mergers can also facilitate the achievement of national policy objectives. For example, mergers may enhance growth in national markets and exports. Accordingly, merger control regimes need to ensure that beneficial mergers are permitted to proceed and are not unduly hampered by regulation.

Merger control needs to be designed to prohibit mergers which are likely to be anticompetitive and to permit mergers which are likely to be beneficial. This requires a delicate balancing act. Getting the balance between prohibition and permission right is important as an overly restrictive approach to merger control can prevent beneficial mergers proceeding, entrench existing inefficient market structures, and limit incentives for new investment; whilst an overly permissive approach to merger control can entrench monopoly elements.[1]

[1] For a detailed discussion, see Michal S. Gal. 2003. *Competition Policy for Small Market Economies*, pp. 195–6.

A number of approaches have been adopted by national competition regimes in their quest to achieve the right balance between prohibition and permission in merger control. As nations learn from their own and one another's experiences, common trends are emerging, particularly in the substantive concepts used to assess what types of mergers ought to be prohibited and what types of mergers ought to be permitted. Increasingly, competition policy-makers are focusing upon harmonization of merger control across nations, but significant differences do remain. This is primarily due to the fact that competition policy is influenced by a number of goals, only some of which are common across nations. Further, different resources and levels of expertise dictate the extent to which national competition regimes can employ complex and resource-intensive processes.

Regulatory Frameworks

The administration of merger control is generally carried out by specialist statutory bodies, with responsibility for enforcement often being entrusted to quasi-judicial specialist tribunals in conjunction with courts of general jurisdiction. This structure reflects the fact that merger control requires more than just an understanding of the laws used to regulate mergers—it also requires an understanding of the economic concepts and business realities underlying the operation of such laws.

By way of example, in Australia the Australian Competition and Consumer Commission (ACCC), an independent statutory body, investigates mergers and has the power to grant informal and formal clearances of mergers. Parties can seek authorization determinations from the Australian Competition Tribunal, a quasi-judicial body made up of judges of the Federal Court of Australia and lay members with experience in industry, commerce, economics, law, or public administration. Determinations of the Australian Competition Tribunal can be reviewed by the Full Federal Court of Australia on matters of law and procedure. Similarly, in the United Kingdom, the Office of Fair Trading (OFT), an independent government department, investigates mergers and may clear a merger or refer a merger to the Competition Commission. Upon receiving a reference from the OFT, the Competition Commission, which is a statutory body made up of lawyers, economists, accountants, and administrators, determines whether or not the merger should be permitted. Appeals from decisions of the OFT and the Competition Commission can be made to the Competition Appeal Tribunal, a quasi-judicial tribunal consisting of High Court judges and members with experience in such areas as law, economics, accountancy, and business. Appeals on points of law can be made from decisions of the Competition Appeal Tribunal to the Court of Appeal, the Court of Session, or the Court of Appeal in Northern Ireland, depending upon where the case arises.

In addition to specific competition legislation, it is quite common for competition authorities to issue guidelines which explain the approach they will take to administering the legislation. While they do not have the force of law, these guidelines are important to an understanding of the practical operation of merger control.

Unlike many other activities regulated by competition law, mergers are generally not viewed as prima facie anticompetitive. Many merger control regimes prohibit only those mergers which are likely to have a particular impact on market power in particular, or on competition in general.[2] This approach has been adopted in Australia, New Zealand, the United States of America, Canada, the United Kingdom, South Africa, and the European Union.

Many merger control regimes impose mandatory pre-merger notification for mergers of a certain size.[3] In the United States of America, pre-merger notification is required for mergers valued above certain monetary thresholds.[4]

In Canada, notification is required for mergers which meet certain party-size and transaction-size thresholds.[5] In South Africa, notification is required for 'intermediate' and 'large' mergers which are defined by reference to turnover and asset thresholds.[6] In the European Union, notification is required for mergers with a 'Community dimension,' defined by reference to geographical turnover thresholds.[7] Applying such criteria for notification lessens the administrative burden for competition authorities, compared with mandatory notification of all mergers. It also enables competition authorities to identify and focus upon the mergers which are most likely to be of concern.

Other merger control regimes, such as those of Australia, New Zealand, and the United Kingdom, do not impose mandatory notification requirements

[2] Some merger control regimes do, however, apply a prohibition on all mergers, save for those which are specifically permitted. See, for example, s 27 of Kenya's Restrictive Trade Practices, Monopolies and Price Control Act, 1989.

[3] Some merger control regimes, for example, Kenya, require notification of all mergers, regardless of size or character.

[4] See s 7A of the Clayton Act 15 U.S.C. §18 (1988).

[5] See ss 109–10 of the Competition Act RS, 1985.

[6] See s 11 of the Competition Act, 1998 and the Notice by the Minister of Trade and Industry in Terms of the Competition Act, 1998 (Act 89 of 1998).

[7] See Arts 1(2), 1(3), and 4 of the Council Regulation (EC) No. 139/04 of 20 January 2004 on the control of concentrations between undertakings.

for any type of merger. Instead, merging parties may voluntarily opt to notify competition authorities. The availability of merger clearance, which gives merging parties certainty that the competition authority will not seek to prevent the merger if it proceeds, can make voluntary pre-merger notification an attractive option despite the various costs involved, and is available in Australia, New Zealand, and the United Kingdom.

In recognition of the potential for mergers to have both anticompetitive and beneficial effects, merger control requires a number of distinct tests or conceptual analyses—designed either as separate avenues or incorporated as one multi-part test—to assess whether a merger ought to be prohibited or permitted.

Australia and New Zealand are examples of regimes which employ a number of separate avenues for assessing the likely impact of a merger. In Australia, there is an informal and formal clearance process,[8] and in New Zealand there is a formal clearance process,[9] whereby the competition authorities make an initial assessment of whether the merger is of the type likely to be prohibited due to its anticompetitive effects. Both nations also provide the opportunity for merging parties to seek formal authorization on the grounds of the likely benefits the merger will bring about.[10] In Australia, the Australian Competition Tribunal assesses whether the benefits to the public likely to result from the merger are such that the merger ought to be permitted. This assessment involves weighing the anticompetitive effects of the merger against the potential benefits of the merger. In New Zealand, the authorization process requires the competition authority first to be satisfied that the likely anticompetitive effects of the merger are such that it is the type of merger specifically prohibited by legislation, and then to engage in a weighing of the anticompetitive effects of the merger as against its potential benefits.

Clearance is also available in the United Kingdom once pre-merger notification or an informal submission has been made.[11] Unlike the Australian and New Zealand regimes, there is no separate avenue for merging parties to

[8] See Australian Competition and Consumer Commission, Merger Guidelines, June 1999 and Australian Competition and Consumer Commission, Guideline for Informal Merger Reviews, October 2004.

[9] See s 66 of the Commerce Act, 1986.

[10] See s 95AT of the Trade Practices Act, 1974 (Cth) and s 67 of the Commerce Act, 1986, respectively.

[11] See ss 22 and 33 of the Enterprise Act, 2002 and the Office of Fair Trading, Mergers—Procedural Guidance, May 2003.

make an application for authorization. Instead, the likely benefits of a merger are taken into account in assessing whether the merger is of a type prohibited by legislation.[12]

Other merger control regimes, such as those employed in Canada, the United States of America, South Africa, and the European Union, do not provide for separate avenues by which merging parties can specifically seek clearance of a merger (on the basis that it is not of a type specifically prohibited by legislation because of its anticompetitive effects) or authorization (on the grounds of the benefits likely to result from the merger). Rather, the likely anticompetitive effects and the likely benefits of a merger are considered as part of the one multi-part assessment made by competition authorities in determining whether or not to permit the merger or impose conditions upon its implementation. Efficiencies and other benefits are generally considered as one factor in a weighing process, or in the form of a defence to anticompetitive effects.

In Canada, competition legislation provides that the relevant competition authority cannot make an order prohibiting or dissolving a merger if it finds that the merger is likely to bring about efficiency gains which would offset the anticompetitive effects of the merger.[13] In the United States of America, guidelines issued by the competition authorities indicate that efficiencies are a relevant consideration in assessing the impact of a merger on competition, noting that efficiencies can in fact serve to promote competition.[14] In South Africa, in determining whether a merger is of the type specifically prohibited due to its anticompetitive effects, the competition authority is required by legislation to determine whether there are efficiencies which offset the anticompetitive effect in any event, or whether the merger can otherwise be justified on substantial public interest grounds.[15] In the European Union, competition authority guidelines indicate that efficiencies are considered as part of the competition authority's substantive assessment of the effects of the merger.[16]

Reflecting the fact that competition law has no desire to restrict beneficial mergers from proceeding, practices and legislative provision for open dialogue

[12] See ss 22, 33, 35, and 36 of the Enterprise Act, 2002.

[13] See s 96 of the Competition Act RS, 1985.

[14] See Section 4 of the United States Department of Justice and the Federal Trade Commission, 1992 Horizontal Merger Guidelines (with 8 April 1997, Revisions to Section 4 on Efficiencies).

[15] See s 12A of the Competition Act, 1998.

[16] See European Commission, Guidelines on the Assessment of Horizontal Mergers under the Council Regulation on the Control of Concentrations between Undertakings, 5 February 2004 at [77].

and negotiated outcomes between competition authorities and merging parties facilitate the implementation of beneficial mergers. Many competition authorities have developed a practice of indicating any competition concerns they have with proposed mergers and allowing merging parties the opportunity to take steps to address any concerns prior to a decision being made as to whether the merger should be prohibited or permitted. It is common practice for competition authorities to provide informal, confidential guidance to merging parties prior to notification.

Many legislative regimes also provide for mergers to be permitted subject to conditions or the provision of undertakings which address any competition concerns of the authorities. For example, in the United Kingdom, the OFT may accept an undertaking from the merging parties addressing any competition concerns in lieu of referring the merger to the Competition Commission.[17] In the European Union, the competition authority may impose conditions and obligations on the merging parties as part of its declaration that the merger is compatible with the Common Market and therefore permissible.[18]

Substantive Tests for Prohibiting Mergers

Merger control is necessary because mergers can lead to the concentration of market power in a business entity and can enhance a business entity's (or a group of business entities') ability to use market power in a manner which impedes competition. Given the underlying rationale for merger control, it is not surprising that merger control regimes generally assess which mergers will be prohibited by reference to the level of impact the merger is likely to have on competition, or by reference to the degree of market power the merged entity will acquire.

A common test applied in merger control regimes is whether a merger is likely to result in a 'substantial lessening of competition' in a given market. In Australia and New Zealand, mergers which would have the effect, or likely effect, of 'substantially lessening competition' in a national market are prohibited.[19] In Canada, any merger which 'prevents or lessens, or is likely to prevent or lessen, competition substantially' in or among a (broadly defined)

[17] See s 73 of the Enterprise Act, 2002.

[18] See Art. 8 of the Council Regulation (EC) No. 139/04 of 20 January 2004 on the control of concentrations between undertakings.

[19] See s 50 of the Trade Practices Act, 1974 (Cth) and s 47 of the Commerce Act, 1986, respectively.

trade, industry, or profession, is prohibited.[20] South Africa applies a similar prohibition to mergers which 'substantially prevent or lessen competition' in a national market.[21] In the United Kingdom, mergers which meet certain turnover or share of supply thresholds are prohibited if they result, or may be expected to result, in a 'substantial lessening of competition' within a national market for goods or services.[22]

Whilst market power issues are able to be taken into account as part of the tests outlined above, some merger control regimes make explicit reference to market power issues of monopoly and dominance in addition to the level of impact the merger has or is likely to have on competition in their prohibition tests. In the United States of America, mergers are prohibited where 'the effect of such acquisition may be substantially to lessen competition, or to tend to create a monopoly.'[23] In the European Union, mergers are effectively prohibited if they 'significantly impede effective competition in the Common Market, or in a substantial part of it, in particular as a result of the creation or strengthening of a dominant position'.[24]

Many competition authorities place considerable emphasis upon market share and market concentration when applying the prohibition test, irrespective of whether the prohibition test is framed in terms of concentration of market power. Market share and market concentration are relatively simple to measure, and (subject to available data) easy to apply, making this an attractive measurement of a merger's likely impact on a market.

In Australia and South Africa, there is legislative provision for the level of concentration in a market to be taken into account by the competition authority in assessing whether the merger is likely to lead to a substantial lessening of competition.[25]

Further, competition authority guidelines in Australia refer to specific market share thresholds which, if exceeded, indicate that the merger is likely to result in a substantial lessening of competition. The guidelines specify that this occurs where, post-merger:

[20] See s 92 of the Competition Act RS, 1985.

[21] See s 12A of the Competition Act, 1998.

[22] See ss 22, 33, 35, and 36 of the Enterprise Act, 2002.

[23] See s 7 of the Clayton Act 15 U.S.C. § 18 (1988).

[24] Article 2(3) of the Council Regulation (EC) No. 139/04 of 20 January 2004 on the control of concentrations between undertakings.

[25] See s 50(c) of the Trade Practices Act, 1974 (Cth) and s 12A(2)(c) of the Competition Act, 1998, respectively.

- the combined market share of the four (or fewer) largest firms in the relevant market (or four-firm concentration ratio) will be 75 per cent or more and the merged firm will supply at least 15 per cent of the relevant market; or
- the merged firm will supply 40 per cent or more of the relevant market.[26]

Similarly, in New Zealand,[27] the United States of America,[28] Canada,[29] the United Kingdom,[30] and the European Union,[31] guidelines issued by the relevant competition authorities establish thresholds based on market share and/or market concentration to indicate whether the competition authority is likely to view the merger as having a substantial impact on competition.

There are obvious advantages in using market share and market concentration criteria as these offer a low-cost screening method which is easy to administer and offer predictability to merging parties. However, there is growing recognition that although market share and market concentration are useful in identifying potentially problematic mergers, analysis of factors indicative of market conduct and market dynamics enable a more accurate assessment of a merger's likely effect on competition and market power issues to be made.

Many competition authorities look to a combination of structural and strategic factors to assess a merger's likely impact on market power and, more generally, competition. Other factors which are often considered include:

- barriers to entry, expansion, and exit (structural, regulatory, and strategic);
- additional sources of potential competition;

[26] See Australian Competition and Consumer Commission, Merger Guidelines, June 1999, at [5.95].

[27] See New Zealand Commerce Commission, Mergers and Acquisitions Guidelines, 1 January 2004, at [5.3].

[28] See Section 1.5 of the United States Department of Justice and the Federal Trade Commission, 1992 Horizontal Merger Guidelines (with 8 April 1997 Revisions to Section 4 on Efficiencies).

[29] See Canadian Competition Bureau, Merger Enforcement Guidelines, September 2004, at [4.12].

[30] See United Kingdom Office of Fair Trading, Mergers: Substantive Assessment Guidance, May 2003, at [4.2]–[4.4] and United Kingdom Competition Commission, Merger References: Competition Commission Guidelines, June 2003, at [3.4], [3.10], [3.22], and [3.24].

[31] European Commission, Guidelines on the assessment of horizontal mergers under the Council Regulation on the control of concentrations between undertakings, 5 February 2004, at [14], [17]–[20], and [22]–[57].

- countervailing power in the market, including the sophistication of buyers, suppliers, or others in a position to discipline market players;
- excess capacity;
- ability of, and capacity for, firms to innovate;
- the objectives and culture of the firms in the market, including firms' commitment to the market;
- views of the future development of the market and appropriate strategies for meeting future development of the market;
- the history of pricing behaviour in the market and the extent to which transparent prices are available;
- the changing market demand or supply of inputs;
- the degree of homogeneity of firms and products;
- the existence of institutions and practices that may aid coordination;
- the stability of demand and costs;
- the stability of market shares over time;
- short-term financial pressures on firms; and
- the extent to which small firms on the fringe of the market might embark on large scale or more developed production.

These factors, whilst generally more difficult to measure, are aimed at predicting market behaviour and dynamics so that a more accurate assessment of the likely impact of the merger on competition can be made.

Importantly, any assessment of a merger's impact on competition or market power issues must be made in the context of a well-defined national market. Market definition is designed to help the competition authority assess the degree of market power which the merged firm will possess. In defining a market, the competition authority is identifying the competitive constraints which will operate upon the price and non-price conduct of the merged firm. For ease of analysis, market definition is often broken up into a number of market dimensions, including:

- the product dimension;
- the geographic dimension;
- the functional dimension;
- the temporal dimension; and
- the customer dimension.

Substantive Tests for Permitting Mergers

Recognizing that mergers can have beneficial, as well as anticompetitive, effects, merger control regimes need to incorporate a mechanism for considering what benefits are likely to arise from a merger and assessing whether these effectively outweigh any anticompetitive effects.

Concepts of efficiencies and benefits are commonly employed in competition legislation. Such concepts are sometimes incorporated as relevant factors to be taken into account in assessing whether the prohibition test is met. Sometimes they are treated as a form of defence. They can also arise as part of a separate avenue for permitting mergers such as in an authorization application.

With regard to efficiencies, it is common for competition authorities to take into account only those efficiencies that are merger-specific, not achievable by less anticompetitive means than that posed by the merger, and achievable in a relatively short time frame. A recent report by the International Competition Network reviewing merger control in twelve jurisdictions (including Australia, New Zealand, Canada, the United States of America, the United Kingdom, and the European Union) observed the following common trends in the types of efficiencies competition authorities will take into account:

- Productive efficiencies are regularly taken into account by competition authorities.
- Dynamic or innovative efficiencies are also relatively well-accepted by competition authorities, although they pose greater evidentiary difficulties than productive efficiencies.
- Distribution and promotional efficiencies, transactional efficiencies, and demand-side network effects have had limited acceptance by some competition authorities.
- Procurement, management, and capital cost savings are generally disregarded by competition authorities.[32]

Beyond this broad consensus, the treatment of efficiencies in merger control is highly controversial. Efficiencies raise practical difficulties of proof and quantification. They also raise issues as to whether the beneficiaries of any savings and improvements generated are relevant when considering which efficiencies should be taken into account. The issue of what welfare standard competition authorities should apply—explicitly raised in efficiencies analysis—delves into the political realm and its resolution depends to a large extent upon national policy objectives extending beyond merger control and indeed, beyond competition law itself.

[32] International Competition Network Merger Working Group: Analytical Framework Subgroup, Project on Merger Guidelines, April 2004, pp. 14–23 of Chapter 6. Available at http://www.internationalcompetitionnetwork.org/seoul/analysisofmerger.html.

Many competition authorities recognize that efficiencies may counter the lessening of competition which might otherwise be thought to arise from a merger based on indicators such as market share and market concentration. In Australia, competition authority guidelines state that it is unlikely that a merger will be found substantially to lessen competition for the purposes of the prohibition test where efficiencies exist which:

- enable the merged firm to compete better and enhance competition in a market;
- create a new or enhanced competitive constraint on the unilateral conduct of other firms in the market;
- undermine coordinated conduct in a market; and
- result in lower or unchanged prices, increased output, or higher quality goods or services.[33]

Similarly, competition authority guidelines in New Zealand indicate that efficiencies are a relevant factor in assessing whether a substantial lessening of competition is likely to result from a merger.[34]

In Canada, competition legislation explicitly provides that a merger will not be found to prevent or lessen competition substantially if it generates 'gains in efficiency' that will be greater than, and will offset, any negative impact on competition.[35]

Similarly, in South Africa, competition legislation provides that if it appears that a merger is likely substantially to lessen competition, then the competition authority must determine 'whether or not the merger is likely to result in any technological, efficiency, or other pro-competitive gain which will be greater than, and offset, the effects of any prevention or lessening of competition, that may result or are likely to result from the merger, and would not likely be obtained if the merger is prevented.'[36]

The United Kingdom uses distinct terminology, referring to 'relevant customer benefits', but this term seems to encompass matters taken into account by other competition authorities in considering the concept of efficiencies. By way of illustration, competition authority guidelines identify the following as 'relevant customer benefits':

[33] Australian Competition and Consumer Commission, Merger Guidelines, June 1999, at [5.172]–[5.173].

[34] New Zealand Commerce Commission, Mergers and Acquisitions Guidelines, 1 January 2004, at [7.4].

[35] See s 96 of the Competition Act RS, 1985.

[36] See s 12A(1) of the Competition Act, 1998.

- Economies of scale in production or distribution where the prospective cost reductions can be expected to result in prices lower than if the merger did not take place.
- Enhancement of innovation through economies of scale, specialization in research and development, or the pooling of risks.
- Benefits to a network by way of improved or extended services.
- Improved coordination, lower transaction and inventory costs, or the removal of double marginalization in vertical mergers.[37]

Such relevant customer benefits are considered as part of the assessment of whether a substantial lessening of competition has occurred for the purposes of the prohibition test. Interestingly, guidelines issued by United Kingdom competition authorities indicate that relevant customer benefits will be taken into account where, although they do not avert a substantial lessening of competition, will nonetheless be passed on to consumers in the form of customer benefits.[38]

Less explicit reference is made to efficiencies in the European Union, where competition legislation provides that where the competition authority is considering whether a merger significantly impedes effective competition in the Common Market, regard must be had to 'the development of technical and economic progress provided that it is to consumers' advantage'.[39]

In the United States of America, the relevance of efficiencies are cautiously acknowledged in guidelines issued by the competition authorities.[40] Whilst efficiencies have an accepted role in assessing whether a merger is likely to be found to be anticompetitive, the guidelines state that 'efficiencies are most likely to make a difference in merger analysis when the likely adverse competitive effects, absent the efficiencies, are not great. Efficiencies almost never justify a merger to monopoly or near-monopoly'.[41]

[37] United Kingdom Competition Commission, Merger References: Competition Commission Guidelines, June 2003, at [4.41]–[4.44].

[38] For a detailed discussion, see Christian Ahlborn and Dan Goyder, 'United Kingdom', in J. William Rowley and Donald I. Baker (eds), *International Mergers: The Antitrust Process* (3rd ed.), 2004, vol. III at [63.017].

[39] See Art. 2(1)(b) of the Council Regulation (EC) No. 139/04 of 20 January 2004 on the control of concentrations between undertakings.

[40] See Section 4 of the United States Department of Justice and the Federal Trade Commission, 1992 Horizontal Merger Guidelines (with 8 April 1997 Revisions to Section 4 on Efficiencies).

[41] See Section 4 of the United States Department of Justice and the Federal Trade Commission, 1992 Horizontal Merger Guidelines (with 8 April 1997 Revisions to Section 4 on Efficiencies).

The concept of 'public benefit' is also used in merger control to identify which mergers ought to be permitted. It appears to be a broader term than efficiencies as it takes efficiencies into account but can also encompass national policy objectives such as the enhancement of national markets.

In Australia and New Zealand, the concept of public benefit arises as part of a separate avenue for seeking permission for a merger. In Australia, 'public benefit' is considered as part of a weighing exercise undertaken when parties apply for authorization of a merger.[42] The Australian Competition Tribunal assesses whether the likely public benefit of the merger would outweigh the likely anticompetitive effects. The term 'public benefit' is broadly defined by legislation to include a significant increase in the real value of exports, a significant substitution of domestic products for imported goods, and 'all other relevant matters that relate to the international competitiveness of any Australian industry'.[43] Competition authority guidelines indicate that efficiencies are also relevant to the public benefit test for authorization.[44]

Similarly, in New Zealand, the concept of public benefit is considered as part of an authorization test.[45] In an application for authorization, if the competition authority is satisfied that the merger is likely substantially to lessen competition, then it must consider whether the merger is likely to generate a public benefit that would outweigh the merger's detrimental impact upon competition. New Zealand's competition legislation explicitly states that public benefit includes 'any efficiencies' likely to result from the merger.[46]

Although there is no separate authorization procedure available in South Africa, South African competition legislation provides that where it appears that a merger may result in a substantial lessening of competition, the competition authority must consider whether the merger is nevertheless justified on 'substantial public interest grounds'.[47] The legislation further provides that when determining whether a merger can be justified on substantial public interest grounds, the competition authority must consider the effect that the merger will have on:

- a particular industrial sector or region;
- employment

[42] See s 95AZH of the Trade Practices Act, 1974 (Cth).

[43] See s 95AZH (2) of the Trade Practices Act, 1974 (Cth).

[44] See Australian Competition and Consumer Commission, Merger Guidelines, June 1999.

[45] See s 67 of the Commerce Act, 1986.

[46] See s 3A of the Commerce Act, 1986.

[47] See s 12A(1) of the Competition Act, 1998.

- the ability of small businesses, or firms controlled or owned by historically disadvantaged persons, to become competitive; and
- the ability of national industries to compete in international markets.[48]

These examples highlight the way in which the broad concept of 'public benefit' is sometimes used to effect nation-specific policy goals through merger control.

The Future of Merger Control

Globalization of economic markets has led to an inability of instruments of national merger control to deal with international merger activity. Historically, merger control has been a product of the nation state, with attempted extra-territorial application of national laws, combined with piece-meal bilateral cooperation, being the traditional approach to multi-national mergers. There is now widespread acknowledgement that the traditional approach is insufficient to deal with the growing incidence of multi-national mergers. Multiple legal tests and regulatory hurdles can prove prohibitively costly and complex. To ensure that beneficial mergers are not unduly hampered, there must be some form of harmonization of merger control on an international scale.

There is already much common ground. Many competition policy-makers have opted for a form of prohibition test which focuses upon the impact a merger will have on the level of competition, which includes market power issues. Many competition authorities now employ similar analytical approaches to assessing a merger's impact on competition, incorporating both structural and strategic market factors, and to market definition.

Efficiencies and public benefit are key concepts in the analytical frameworks used to permit mergers in many national merger control regimes.

The development of a broadly consistent approach to merger control across nations is aided by multinational institutions such as the International Competition Network—which has undertaken useful comparative studies of various aspects of merger control and developed a set of guiding principles and best practices—and the Organization for Economic Cooperation and Development, the World Bank, and the United Nations Conference on Trade and Development—which have developed model competition laws. It is also enhanced by the increasing use of bilateral agreements and information and personnel exchanges between national competition authorities.

48 See s 12A(3) of the Competition Act, 1998.

However, there remain some major issues to be overcome before effective harmonization can be achieved. For example, the differential impact of multinational mergers in different national jurisdictions will need to be addressed. Assessment of the anticompetitive impact and potential benefits of multi-national mergers may have to be extended beyond national jurisdictions, and, if this is to be done, frameworks for benefit sharing across relevant nations may have to be developed. Another example is the treatment of efficiencies in merger analysis, where standards for identifying what types of efficiencies will be taken into account and what evidentiary requirements must be met in order for efficiencies to be given weight are in their infancy within national merger control regimes, let alone consistent standards being developed at the international level.

Furthermore, the use of merger control to achieve nation-specific policy objectives means that there will never be complete consensus across nations. There are also the perennial difficulties involved in attempting to apply a one-size-fits-all approach to nations with different market size, political orientation, and resources.

Given that considerable conceptual similarities already exist across national merger control regimes, whilst acknowledging that some elements of merger control are not amenable to international standardization, the future of merger control appears to be one in which broad harmonization of conceptual approaches, assisted by formal and informal cooperation between national competition authorities, will prevail. National concerns remain a primary focus of merger control, but international consensus and cooperation are now also firmly on the agenda.

4

Leniency Programmes in Competition Law*

Paul Crampton and Graham Reynolds

It is increasingly recognized that the remarkable increase in the number of successful hard-core cartel (HCC) cases as well as in the level of fines imposed in those cases in jurisdictions, such as the US, the European Union, and Canada is largely attributable to refinements that have been made to the leniency programmes in those jurisdictions.

A leniency programme is a policy that offers immunity (sometimes referred to as amnesty), in return for the leniency applicant being either (a) the first to disclose the existence of illegal conduct, or (b) the first to begin cooperating with the enforcement agency after it has received a complaint or commenced an investigation but before it has obtained sufficient evidence to establish that a contravention has occurred. In both situations, full, frank, and expeditious cooperation are required in return for leniency.[1]

* Reproduced from 'Leniency Programmes in Competition Law', published in Dhall, V. (ed.). 2007. *Competition Law Today: Concepts, Issues, and the Law in Practice* (first ed.), Oxford University Press, New Delhi.

[1] In some jurisdictions, such as the US, Australia, and Ireland, the leniency or amnesty programme technically applies only to full amnesty or immunity. Partial leniency is available pursuant to other policies. In other jurisdictions, the leniency programme explicitly covers both full and partial leniency. Partial leniency is

Leniency programmes exist in the increasing number of jurisdictions where HCC conduct is a criminal offence[2] as well as in jurisdictions, such as the European Union and many of its Member States, where HCC conduct is not subject to criminal sanctions.[3]

As a result of the success achieved with existing policies in the US, Europe, and Canada, as well as the international work on leniency programmes that has been taking place in forums such as the OECD,[4] the ICN,[5] and the European Competition Network,[6] many other jurisdictions have refined their prior leniency programmes or introduced new ones that incorporate many of the attributes of the best-in-class policies.[7]

This is not a fad of the developed world. Developing countries also are taking a greater interest in leniency policies. It is particularly important that they do so not only because of the greater relative harm that HCC behaviour can

---

discussed at the end of this chapter. The Canadian Competition Bureau's immunity policy focuses upon the Bureau's policy and procedures for recommending a grant of full immunity from prosecution. However, it also states that when a party does not qualify for immunity the Commissioner may recommend that the Attorney General grant another form of leniency. See Competition Bureau, Immunity Program Under the Competition Act, 2000, at paragraph 10, available at http://www.competitionbureau.gc.ca/internet/index.cfm?itemID=1752&lg=e.

[2] HCC conduct is a criminal offence in the US, Canada, Ireland, UK, Korea, Japan, and Mexico. The Australian Government also has announced that it will amend the Trade Practices Act, 1974 to introduce criminal penalties for HCC conduct. See http://www.treasurer.gov.au/tsr/content/pressreleases/ 2005/004.asp.

[3] See http://europa.eu.int/comm/competition/antitrust/legislation/authorities_with_leniency_programme.pdf.

[4] See, for example, OECD, *Fighting Hard-Core Cartels—Harm, Effective Sanctions and Leniency Programmes* (Paris: 2002). This is sometimes referred to as the OECD's Phase I Cartel Report.

[5] See, for example, ICN Cartel Working Group, Subgroup 2: Enforcement Techniques, Chapter 2, Drafting and Implementing an Effective Leniency Program (April 2005), available at http://www.internationalcompetitionnetwork.org/bonn/Cartels_WG/SG2_Enforcement_Techniques/Anti-Cartel_Enforcement_Manual.pdf.

[6] See, for example, the European Competition Authorities' Principles for Leniency Programmes (3–4 September 2001), available at http://www.tca.ie/eca.pdf.

[7] See generally, Kevin Arquit and Jacques Buhart (eds), Leniency Regimes—Jurisdictional Comparisons, (London: The European Lawyer Ltd, 2005); and OECD, Hard Core Cartels—Recent Progress and Challenges Ahead (2003), at 15–19, available at http://www.oecd.org/document/39/0,2340,en_2649_37463_2474407_1_1_1_37463,00.html. This is sometimes referred to as the OECD's Phase II Cartel Report.

cause in developing economies,[8] but also because of the greater vulnerability that such economies have to HCC conduct.[9]

One of the more fundamental objections to a leniency programme is that it allows lawbreakers to escape punishment. Jurisdictions that have enthusiastically adopted serious leniency programmes have overcome this objection by promoting a recognition of the contribution that an effective leniency programme can make to uncovering, punishing, and deterring HCC activity.[10] This contribution is briefly discussed below.

The elements of an effective leniency programme, as well as the other components of an anti-cartel enforcement framework that must exist before any leniency programme can be effective are then addressed. Broadly speaking, the other essential components include a serious commitment to punishing cartels and strong sanctions. The key attributes of the best-in-class leniency policies include certainty regarding the reward for being the 'first in', clearly defined conditions for obtaining leniency, transparency, and predictability regarding all other aspects of the programme, confidentiality, incentives to disclose the existence of other prohibited conduct, and the availability of leniency for individuals.

Then, processes for obtaining immunity are discussed, followed by a brief discussion on partial leniency.

The Contribution That Effective Leniency Programmes Can Make

The programmes uncover conspiracies that would otherwise go undetected. They elicit confessions, direct evidence about other participants, and leads that investigators can follow for other evidence too. The evidence is obtained

[8] See, for example, S. Evenett, M. Levenstein, and V. Suslow, 'International Cartel Enforcement: Lessons from the 1990s', Paper presented to the OECD's February 2002 Global Forum on Competition, at 6, available at http://www.oecd.org/dataoecd/55/3/1846165.pdf; and M. Levenstein and V. Suslow, 'Private International Cartels and Their Effect on Developing Countries', Background Paper for the World Bank's World Development Report 2001, at 12. See also S. Evenett, 'Private International Cartels and Developing Economies', presentation to the OECD's February 2002 Global Forum on Competition, available at http://www.oecd.org/dataoecd/48/2/2073938.pdf.

[9] See Mark Dutz, 'Competition Policy Issues in Developing and Transition Markets', Presentation to the OECD's February 2002 Global Forum on Competition, available at http://www.oecd.org/dataoecd/48/3/2073927.pdf.

[10] The Canadian experience with this issue is discussed in Paul Crampton, 'Canada's New Competition Law Immunity Policy—Warts and All', 28 *International Tax Journal*, 19 at 21 (2002).

more quickly, and at lower direct cost, compared to other methods of investigation, leading to prompt and efficient resolution of cases.[11]

HCC conduct is notoriously difficult to investigate. This is in part attributable to the fact that cartel participants are often aware that their conduct is unlawful and therefore they can go to great lengths to operate their arrangements in secret. Sometimes, the steps taken to conceal these arrangements can be quite elaborate. As a result, historically it was not uncommon for cartel cases to drag on for many years and even longer, particularly when subjected to constitutional or procedural wrangling in contested court proceedings.

This is all changing in jurisdictions with effective leniency programmes.[12] Enforcement authorities in those jurisdictions have found that such programmes can dramatically increase the success of efforts to uncover, punish, and deter HCC conduct without resorting to lengthy and costly court cases or other measures.

By substantially increasing the incentives for cartel participants to disclose the existence of the cartel and provide 'hot' documents and other important supporting evidence of meetings, telephone calls, and other communications, effective leniency programmes create a cartel destabilizing dynamic that can give rise to intense pressures to 'race to the door' of the enforcement authority.[13] For example, in the first 14 months after issuing its revised *Leniency Notice* in February 2002,[14] the European Commission received approximately 30 applications for full or partial leniency, a development that it has characterized as 'a tremendous success'.[15] Likewise, the (now former) Commissioner under the *Competition Act* (Canada) observed 'without

[11] OECD supra, n. 4, at 11.

[12] See generally OECD (2002) supra, n. 4; and OECD (2003) supra, n. 7.

[13] See, for example, Philip Lowe, Director General, DG Competition, European Commission, 'What's the Future for Cartel Enforcement', paper delivered at a conference on Understanding Global Cartel Enforcement, 11 February 2003, Brussels, at 3, available at http://europa.eu.int/comm/competition/speeches/text/ sp2003_044_en.pdf; and Scott Hammond, 'When Calculating the Costs and Benefits of Applying for Corporate Amnesty, How Do You Put a Price Tag on an Individual's Freedom?', presentation to the Criminal Justice Section of the American Bar Association, 8 March 2001, at 3, available at http://www/usdoj.gov/ar/public/speeches/7647.htm.

[14] Commission notice on immunity from fines and reduction of fines in cartel cases, OJ C 207 (2002/C 45/03) 19.2.2002, available at http://europa.eu.int/eur-lex/pri/en/oj/dat/2002/c_045/c_04520020219en00030005.pdf.

[15] Lowe supra, n. 13. See also Mario Monti, 'The Fight Against Cartels', Summary of talk to EMAC, Brussels, 11 September 2002, at 2 (Speech/02/384, available at http://europa.eu.int/rapid/pressReleasesAction.do?reference=SPEECH/02/384&for

hesitation' that the first full year of the Competition Bureau's revised leniency programme had been a success, with applications increasing to approximately one per month.[16] The following year, he reported that the Bureau had received 'more applicants than our current resources allow us to handle'.[17] In the US, where '[c]operation from leniency applicants has cracked more cartels than all other tools at [the Department of Justice's] disposal combined',[18] the results were even more dramatic. Within approximately five years of implementing, in August 1993, its current leniency programme, the Department of Justice (DOJ) reported that '[a]mnesty applications over the past year have been coming in at the rate of approximately two per month—a more than *twenty-fold* increase as compared to the rate of applications under the old Amnesty Program'.[19] More recently, the Korea Fair Trade Commission has reported 'a huge leap in the number of leniency applications' since revising its leniency policy in April 2005.[20]

Armed with evidence from the leniency applicant, enforcement authorities are finding it much easier to persuade other cartel participants to cooperate with investigations. This, in turn, substantially reduces the time and cost required to complete investigations. Increasingly often, the need for costly

---

mat=HTML&aged=0&language=EN&guiLanguage=en), where the early success of the current leniency programme was characterized as 'quite unprecedented'.

[16] Konrad von Finckenstein, 'Notes for an Address to the Annual Meeting of the National Competition Law Section of the Canadian Bar Association', 20 September 2001, available at http://www.competitionbureau.gc.ca/PDFs/ct02314e.pdf, at 5.

[17] Konrad von Finckenstein, 'Address to the Annual Meeting of the National Competition Law Section of the Canadian Bar Association', 3 October 2002, available at http://www.competitionbureau.gc.ca/internet/index.cfm?itemID=1145&lg=e.

[18] Scott Hammond, Deputy Assistant Attorney General for Criminal Enforcement, Slide Presentation to Working Party No. 3 of the OECD's Competition Committee, 18 October 2005, at slide 3, available at http://www.usdoj.gov/atr/public/ speeches/212269.htm.

[19] Gary Spratling, 'Making Companies an Offer They Shouldn't Refuse, The Antitrust Division's Corporate Leniency Policy—An Update', presented at The Bar Association of the District of Columbia's 35th Annual Symposium on Associations and Antitrust, 16 February 1999, at 2, available at http://www.usdoj.gov/atr/public/speeches/2247.htm.

[20] See Korea Fair Trade Commission, 'Recent Changes to Korea's Cartel Enforcement Regime', at paragraph 16, available at http://www.ftc.go.kr/eng/. See also a similar report by the Chairman of Japan's Fair Trade Commission, Kazuhiko Takeshima, 'Introductory Remarks', 4th Seoul International Competition Forum, at paragraph 3, available at http://www.jftc.go.jple-page.

contested proceedings also is entirely avoided, as cartel participants recognize that the prospects of prevailing in such proceedings are greatly reduced as a result of the evidence provided by the leniency applicant (as well as by other parties who subsequently decide to cooperate).

Other considerations that operate to induce expeditious cooperation by other cartel participants include a desire to: (a) obtain a reduced fine or other sanction (for example, imprisonment, in certain jurisdictions), especially in jurisdictions where enforcement authorities have adopted a practice of rewarding early cooperation more generously than late cooperation; (b) limit their exposure to proceedings initiated by private parties in the jurisdiction; (c) avoid complicating their position in other jurisdictions, such as the US, where the delicate balance of negotiations with class-action plaintiffs in treble damages proceedings can be adversely impacted by the disclosure of information about the cartel on the public record (that is, in court proceedings); (d) eliminate the uncertainty of judicial proceedings and reduce associated legal costs; and (e) avoid the adverse publicity that may be associated with the public disclosure of some of the more embarrassing types of information obtained by the enforcement authority.

By substantially reducing the incentives of all cartel participants to litigate, and increasing their incentives to fully and expeditiously cooperate, enforcement authorities are also finding themselves in a much stronger position to overcome jurisdictional obstacles associated with obtaining witnesses and evidence located abroad, as well as with investigating and ultimately sanctioning foreign cartel participants.[21]

Moreover, enforcement authorities increasingly are finding it easier to obtain information from their counterparts in other jurisdictions, pursuant to 'waivers' of confidentiality rights that have been provided by leniency applicants. This in turn has opened up increased scope for coordinated investigations (for example, dawn raids, witness interviews, and so on).

A further benefit of a leniency programme is that it can provide the opportunity to engage in covert operations, as perhaps best exemplified by the

[21] For example, in the US, 'roughly 50 per cent of corporate defendants in criminal cases brought by the Division were foreign-based'. Scott Hammond, 'An Update of the Antitrust Division's Criminal Enforcement Program', Presented at the ABA Section of Antitrust Law Cartel Enforcement Round table, 2005 Fall Forum, Washington, DC, 16 November 2005, at 3, available at http://www.usdoj.gov/atr/ public/speeches/ 213247.htm.

notorious 'lysine video tapes', which captured actual price-fixing and cartel discussions that took place at a series of different locations.[22]

In addition to all of the foregoing, enforcement authorities in jurisdictions with effective leniency programmes are finding themselves in a much stronger position to negotiate higher fines and (in the US) longer jail sentences. For example, at the time the existing leniency programme in the US was adopted in 1993, the highest antitrust fine that had ever been obtained was less than $ 3 million. By 2000, the Department of Justice was able to report that 'fines of $10 million or more have become almost commonplace with more than 30 imposed in the last five years. In fact, the Division has obtained fines of $100 million or more against five corporate defendants, including a $500 million fine against F. Hoffmann-La Roche ... for its participation in the worldwide vitamin cartel.'[23] More recently, the DOJ reported that its 'Leniency Program is the Division's most effective generator of international cartel cases' and that 'cooperation from amnesty applications has resulted in scores of convictions and more than $2 billion in criminal fines' since 1997.[24]

Moreover, the average jail sentence for HCC conduct in the US 'has more than doubled over the past five years, rising to an average of 18 months,' with 'more than 40 defendants receiving jail sentences of one year or longer including nine defendants in FY 2005'.[25]

In Canada, the total value of fines obtained under the basic conspiracy and bid-rigging provisions of the Competition Act was over $ 185 million during the period 1992 to 2000, in comparison with a total of $ 3.3 million over the period 1980 to 1991 (the year that the Competition Bureau first adopted an immunity policy).[26]

[22] Scott Hammond, 'Caught in the Act: Inside an International Cartel', Presentation to the OECD Competition Committee Working Party No. 3, Public Prosecutors Program, Paris, 18 October 2005, available at http://www.usdoj.gov/atr/public/speeches/212266.htm.

[23] Scott Hammond, 'Fighting Cartels—Why and How? Lessons Common to Detecting and Deterring Cartel Activity', Presented at Modern Museum, Stockholm, Sweden, 12 September 2000, at 3–4, available at http://www.usdoj.gov/atr/public/speeches/6487.htm.

[24] Scott Hammond supra, n. 21, at 13.

[25] Ibid., at 3–4.

[26] Harry Chandler and Robert Jackson, 'Beyond Merriment and Diversion: the Treatment of Conspiracies under Canada's Competition Act', presented at the Roundtable on Competition Act Amendments, Insight Conferences, Toronto, Ontario, 25 May 2000, at Appendix 1, available at http://www.competitionbureau.gc.ca/internet/index.cfm?itemID=1197&lg=e.

In turn, the striking levels of fines and other sanctions that increasingly are being imposed in jurisdictions with effective leniency programmes is attracting the attention of the mainstream press and is raising public awareness of both the harm associated with HCC conduct as well as the harsh penalties that may be imposed. Together with the increasing stigma associated with such conduct in society at large, this has no doubt helped to deter future HCC conduct by others.

The Elements of an Effective Leniency Programme

Before discussing the elements of an effective leniency programme, it bears underscoring that no such programme, no matter how well crafted, can be successful unless it is accompanied by a serious commitment on the part of the enforcement agency to take vigorous action against HCC behaviour. In the absence of such a commitment, it is increasingly recognized that those who may be inclined to participate in HCC conduct will not perceive that there is a real risk of detection and the initiation of enforcement proceedings against them.

A second prerequisite to a successful leniency programme is the existence of strong sanctions for engaging in HCC conduct.[27] In the absence of such sanctions, the international experience has demonstrated that cartel participants will have little incentive to disclose the existence of the car tel. A simple comparison between the achievements of leniency programmes in jurisdictions that impose strong sanctions (for example, the US and EU) and the achievements of leniency programmes in jurisdictions with weak sanctions will suffice to demonstrate this point.

Where these two important prerequisites exist, a leniency programme can be an enormously helpful enforcement tool. However, to be effective, experience has taught that these programmes must (a) provide a high degree of certainty to potential applicants regarding the reward for being the first to disclose the existence of a cartel or the first to cooperate after the commencement of an investigation, (b) articulate clearly defined conditions that must be met to obtain leniency, (c) be transparent and predictable in all other respects, (d) provide strong assurances regarding confidentiality, (e) provide incentives to disclose the existence of other prohibited conduct, and (f) offer individuals the prospect of obtaining leniency.

Where the programme also addresses partial leniency, the foregoing key elements need to be reflected in that aspect of the programme as well, for

[27] See ICN supra, n. 5, at paragraph 2.3; and OECD supra, n. 4, at 25.

example, by providing a high degree of clarity and certainty as to the rewards for cooperation for those who are not the 'first in the door' of the enforcement agency.

Certainty Regarding the Reward for Being 'First In'

To be effective, a leniency programme must provide a high degree of certainty regarding the reward for being the first to disclose the existence of the cartel, or the first to cooperate after the initiation of an investigation. The importance of this was first recognized in the US, after the DOJ's initial leniency programme, adopted in 1978, failed to generate much interest. That policy was based on giving 'serious consideration' to refraining from prosecuting a company that confessed its wrongdoing before the DOJ began investigating the cartel. It appears that in developing that policy, the DOJ expressly decided not to limit its prosecutorial discretion in any way, for example, by making full leniency automatic for the first to disclose the existence of the cartel.[28] Moreover, the policy was not written, a fact that added to the uncertainty for potential applicants. A further deficiency was that full leniency was not available once an investigation had begun. As a result of these shortcomings, the DOJ only received 'roughly one amnesty application per year from 1978 until the policy was revised in 1993'.[29]

Under the DOJ's revised policy, which is written and available on the DOJ's website,[30] full leniency is automatic for an applicant that meets six criteria, including being the first to disclose the existence of the cartel to the DOJ. Where the DOJ has already commenced an investigation, full leniency is still guaranteed to the first person to come forward and meet seven conditions (one of which is that the person is the first to come forward).[31]

The success that the DOJ achieved by offering certainty for applicants that are either the first to disclose the existence of a cartel or the first to come forward and begin to cooperate after the commencement of an investigation but before sufficient evidence has been obtained to move forward with the case, has led several other jurisdictions to embrace this aspect of the US

[28] R. Hewitt Pate, 'International Anti-Cartel Enforcement', Presentation to the 2004 ICN Cartels Workshop, Sydney, Australia, 21 November 2004, at 4, available at http://www.usdoj.gov/atr/public/speeches/206428.htm.

[29] Ibid.

[30] See US Department of Justice, Antitrust Division, Corporate Leniency Policy, available at http://www.usdoj.gov/atr/public/guidelines/0091.htm; and Individual Leniency Policy, available at http://www.usdoj.gov/atr/public/guidelines/0092.htm.

[31] Corporate Leniency Policy, ibid., part B.

leniency programme. For example, the revised leniency programme of the European Commission, adopted in February 2002, incorporates this element of certainty, both with respect to the situation where there is no pre-existing investigation and the situation where there is such an investigation but the Commission does not yet have sufficient information to enable it to find an infringement.[32] The same is true of the revised Canadian leniency programme[33] and the new programmes in Australia,[34] Ireland,[35] and Korea.[36]

By comparison, in the UK,[37] and Japan,[38] this certainty is provided only where there is no pre-existing investigation.

Prior to revising its programme, the European Commission's pre-existing 1996 policy was widely considered to be unattractive to potential applicants because one of the requirements of the programme was that an applicant be the first to adduce 'decisive evidence of the cartel's existence', and the determination of whether such evidence had been provided was not made until the very end of the case.[39] Moreover, full leniency was not available after the Commission became aware of a cartel.

[32] Supra, n. 14, at paragraphs 8–10.

[33] Supra, n. 1, at paragraph 13.

[34] Australia Competition and Consumer Commission, ACCC Immunity Policy for Cartel Conduct (26 August 2005), available at http://www.accc.gov.au/content/item.phtml?itemId=708758&nodeId=file434c43b10e343&fn=Immunity%20policy.pdf. See also ACCC Immunity Policy, Interpretation Guidelines, available at the same URL. This policy replaced the June 2003 policy entitled ACCC leniency policy for cartel conduct.

[35] Irish Competition Authority, Cartel Immunity Programme, 20 December 2001, available at http://www.tca.ie), at paragraph 12.

[36] See Arquit and Buhart supra, n. 7, at 104.

[37] Where there is a pre-existing investigation, the first applicant to come forward to apply for immunity must provide '"added value" to the OFT's investigation, i.e., information which genuinely advances the OFT's investigation.' See Office of Fair Trading, Leniency and no-action, interim note on the handling of applications (July 2005) (the 'Interim Note'), at paragraph 2.29, available at http://www.oft.gov.uk/NR/rdonlyres/FE4F98BF-D8C5-48FB-9F7E-D6133F907538/0/oft803.pdf.

[38] See The Fair Trade Commission's Policy on Criminal Accusation and Compulsory Investigation of Criminal Cases Regarding Antimonopoly Violations, (Tentative translation), at paragraph 2(a), available at http://www.jftc.go.jp/e-page/legislation/ama/policy_on_criminalaccusation.pdf.

[39] See part B(b) of the Commission Notice on the non-imposition or reduction of fines in cartel cases, OJC 207, 18 July 1996, available at http://europa.eu.int/comm/ competition/antitrust/legislation/96c207_en.html.

Clearly Defined Pre-conditions

Following the lead of the US leniency programme, it is increasingly common for other leniency programmes to distinguish between the situation where the enforcement authority has not commenced an investigation (the 'Type A Situation') and the situation where an investigation has already been commenced but the agency has not yet obtained sufficient evidence to move forward[40] with the case (the 'Type B Situation'). In Type A situations, the following conditions are commonly required:[41]

1. The provision of full, frank, continuing, and complete cooperation throughout the investigation;[42]
2. The company was not *the* (as opposed to simply 'a') ringleader;[43]
3. The company terminates its involvement in the cartel;[44] and
4. The company did not coerce anyone else to participate in the cartel. Additional conditions that are required in Type A situations in one or more of the jurisdictions with effective immunity programmes include:

[40] In the US, the threshold is sufficient evidence to be likely to result in a sustainable conviction. Supra n. 30, at paragraph B(2). In Europe, the threshold is sufficient evidence to find an infringement. Supra n. 14, at paragraph 10. In Canada, the threshold is sufficient evidence to warrant a referral to the Attorney General. Supra n. 1, at paragraph 13(b). In Australia, the threshold is sufficient evidence to institute proceedings. Supra n. 34, at paragraph 4(b). In the UK, the threshold is sufficient evidence to issue a statement of objections. Supra n. 37, at paragraph 3.11.

[41] As to the conditions required under the Canadian programme, see generally Crampton supra, n. 10, at 25–9.

[42] There can be important nuances in the specific language used in the leniency programmes of a particular jurisdiction. See the US policy supra, n. 30, at paragraph A(2); the European Commission's policy supra, n. 14, at paragraph 11(a); the Canadian policy supra, n. 1, at paragraph 16; the Australian policy supra, n. 34, at paragraph 6 (see also the ACCC's *Interpretation Guidelines* supra, n. 34, at paragraphs 52–7); and the UK policy supra, n. 37, at paragraphs 3.9(a) and (b).

[43] This is a requirement of the US, Canadian, and Australian policies, which make it clear that if a party is merely a co-leader of a conspiracy it will still be eligible for immunity. Note that the US policy also precludes immunity for a party that is the 'originator of' the cartel. Supra n. 30, at paragraph A(6).

[44] See generally OECD (2002) supra, n. 4, at 17, where the important differences in the US, European Commission, UK, Canadian, and Korean programmes are briefly discussed. See also Gary Spratling, 'The Corporate Leniency Policy: Answers to Recurring Questions', Remarks to the 1998 Spring Meeting of the Antitrust Section of the American Bar Association, Washington, 1 April 1998, at 3, where the more strict requirements of the US policy are discussed in detail, available at http://www.usdoj.gov/atr/public/speeches/1626.htm.

5. Providing restitution to victims, where possible;[45]
6. Disclosing other competition law offences in which the company was involved;[46] and
7. The confession is truly a corporate act, as opposed to isolated confessions of individual executives or officials.[47]

In most of the jurisdictions with effective immunity policies, there is no difference between the conditions required in Type A and Type B situations, except those relating to the definition of the two situations.[48] However, in the US, there is an additional important difference. Instead of requiring that the corporation 'did not coerce another party to participate in the illegal activity and clearly was not the leader in, or originator of, the activity', the corresponding Type B condition is as follows: 'The Division determines that granting leniency would not be unfair to others, considering the nature of the illegal activity, the confessing corporation's role in it, and when the corporation comes forward.'[49] The DOJ's Programme then states:

In applying condition 7, the primary considerations will be how early the corporation comes forward and whether the corporation coerced another party to participate in the illegal activity or clearly was the leader in, or originator of, the activity. The burden of satisfying condition 7 will be low if the corporation comes forward before the Division has begun an investigation into the illegal activity. That burden will increase the closer the Division comes to having evidence that is likely to result in a sustainable conviction.

It may be noted that in some jurisdictions, such as Canada[50] and Australia,[51] the leniency policy explicitly provides that if the first person to approach the

[45] This condition is required in the US and Canada. The nuances of the US approach are discussed in detail by Spratling, ibid. With respect to Canada's approach, see Crampton supra, n. 10, at 28–9.

[46] This is a condition in the Canadian and Irish programmes supra, n. 1 and 35, respectively. The US DOJ employs a well-known 'omnibus question' technique at the end of its oral examination of witnesses under the leniency programme. See Gary R. Spratling and D. Jarrett Arp, 'The Continuing Transformation of International Cartel Enforcement', paper delivered to the American Bar Association, Section of Antitrust Law, International Cartel Workshop, New York, 5–6 February 2004, at 8–9.

[47] This is a requirement of the US, Irish, and Australian programmes. As to the US programme, this condition is discussed in detail in Spratling supra, n. 44, at 5–6. See also OECD supra, n. 7, at 23.

[48] See, for example, the policies in Canada, Australia, the UK, and the European Union.

[49] Supra n. 30, at B(7).

[50] Supra n. 1, at paragraph 18.

[51] Supra n. 34, at paragraph 51.

enforcement authority is not eligible for immunity another participant in the cartel may be granted immunity.

Transparency and Predictability

In addition to being clear and precise as to the conditions that must be satisfied before leniency will be granted and the rewards for those who satisfy the conditions, an effective leniency programme should be transparent and predictable with respect to (a) how the conditions are interpreted, (b) the agency's policy regarding confidentiality, (c) the precise circumstances in which information provided by an applicant may later be used against the applicant, (d) how discretion is exercised with respect to any potentially ambiguous or unaddressed aspects of the programme, (e) the agency's policies, practices, and expectations in relation to each stage of the process, and (f) other aspects of how the programme is applied in practice.

How this transparency is achieved can vary. For example, in the US, it is achieved to a large degree through speeches by senior enforcement officials, typically the Deputy Assistant Attorney General for Criminal Enforcement at the DOJ, which are then made available to the general public on the DOJ's website.[52] In Canada, the Competition Bureau has issued responses to frequently asked questions[53] and has on occasion refined its position in speeches. In the UK, the Office of Fair Trading has issued a number of guides[54] and, recently a fairly comprehensive 'interim note'.[55] The US DOJ and the UK OFT also have prepared and uploaded on their websites model plea agreements[56] and 'no action' letters,[57] respectively, which provide even greater certainty and clarity to potential applicants regarding the terms and conditions of the leniency that they will receive.

[52] See http://www.usdoj.gov/atr/public/criminal.htm.

[53] See, for example, Competition Bureau Revises Responses to Frequently Asked Questions on Immunity Programme (hereinafter the 'FAQs'), available at http:// www.competitionbureau.gc.ca/inter net/index.cfm?itemID=1980&lg=e. This document superseded a document entitled Immunity Program—Frequently Asked Questions, issued in 2003, which is no longer available on the Bureau's website.

[54] See, for example, the documents and links available at http://www.oft.gov.uk/Business/Cartels/default.htm.

[55] Supra n. 37.

[56] See the appendices to Spratling supra, n. 19.

[57] See the Annexe to the OFT's guide entitled 'The Cartel Offence—Guidance on the issue of no-action letters for individuals', (April 2003), available at http:// www.oft.gov.uk/nr/rdonlyres/c6b72edf-ea6a-42f4-9f44-e8fed8268458/0/oft513.pdf.

Most importantly, however, transparency is achieved by minimizing the degree of discretion in the leniency programme. As the current Deputy Assistant General for Criminal Enforcement at the US DOJ has observed: '[I]n order for an Amnesty Program to work, you need to do more than just publicize your policies and educate the public. You have to be willing to make the ultimate sacrifice for transparency—the abdication of prosecutorial discretion.'[58] A similar observation recently was made by the Korea Fair Trade Commission.[59]

Confidentiality

A critically important consideration for potential leniency applicants is the extent to which the fact of their application and any information provided in support of their application and as part of their cooperation obligations will remain confidential.[60] In recognition of this, enforcement agencies increasingly are making their leniency programmes more attractive to potential applicants by guaranteeing the maximum degree of confidentiality possible under their laws.

Importantly, this includes a guarantee that none of the above-described information will be shared with enforcement authorities in other jurisdictions. This policy was first embraced by the US DOJ in early 1999, when the DOJ acknowledged that concerns regarding the potential disclosure of information to foreign enforcement agencies had been identified by a number of potential applicants for leniency as giving rise to a 'strong disincentive to self report and cooperate'. Essentially the same position has now been taken by the Canadian Competition Bureau,[61] the ACCC,[62] and, with one important exception, the UK's OFT.[63]

However, it appears that leniency applicants 'routinely consent ... to the sharing of information among jurisdictions in which they have obtained conditional amnesty, so that those jurisdictions may conduct coordinated investigations'.[64]

[58] Hammond supra, n. 23, at 7.

[59] Supra n. 20, at paragraph 17 ('The KFTC looked into the success of other jurisdictions and found that the removal of discretion and adoption of automatic immunity have been important factors for the success' of the KFTC's leniency programme).

[60] See generally OECD supra, n. 7, at 22.

[61] See the Competition Bureau's revised FAQs supra, n. 53, at paragraph 33.

[62] See the ACCC's *Interpretation Guidelines* supra, n. 34, at paragraph 44.

[63] See the OFT's Interim Note supra, n. 37, at paragraphs 5.5 (dealing with individual immunity) and 5.6 (dealing with corporate immunity).

[64] Pate supra, n. 28, at 6.

In some jurisdictions, such as the US[65] and Canada,[66] this non-disclosure policy is also extended to other domestic enforcement agencies. This has been recognized within the ICN as removing a significant disincentive for potential applicants to apply for leniency.[67]

It is important to note that these policies of not disclosing to other enforcement authorities information received from applicants for full leniency typically does not apply to subsequent cooperating parties, that is, those seeking partial leniency who don't qualify for full leniency.

Also, broader assurances provided by enforcement authorities regarding the preservation of the confidentiality of information provided pursuant to an application for full leniency, as well as the confidentiality of the identity of the applicants, typically are subject to any legal requirements that may override the enforcement agency's policy.[68]

Another step that some enforcement authorities (for example, in the US, Canada, and Europe) have been taking to reduce potential applicants' concerns about confidentiality is to provide assurances that information submitted under the leniency programme will not be disclosed to private plaintiffs or other third parties. In addition, these authorities have begun to permit companies to submit their application orally, to minimize the possibility that they subsequently may be forced (by a court, for instance) to disclose the contents of that application to plaintiffs in private enforcement proceedings, either in that jurisdiction or abroad. As the current Director General of the European Commission's DG Competition has observed:[69]

> [W]hile the Commission certainly does not want to hinder civil litigation, neither does it believe that plaintiffs in civil litigation should gratuitously benefit from the entirely unrelated and autonomous procedure of the Commission's leniency program, thereby undermining the latter program in the process. By adopting this approach, the Commission is following a similar line on this issue as that set out by the US Department of Justice.

[65] See OECD supra, n. 4, at 24.

[66] See the Competition Bureau's FAQs supra, n. 53, at paragraph 32.

[67] See supra, n. 5, at paragraph 2.5.

[68] See, for example, paragraph 32 of the Canadian Competition Bureau's Immunity Program supra, n. 1.

[69] Lowe supra, n. 13, at 4. In addition to the US and the European Union, other jurisdictions that permit oral applications to be made include Canada, Korea, and the UK.

Incentives to Disclose Other Illegal Conduct ('Amnesty Plus' and 'Penalty Plus')

Experience has established that the effectiveness of leniency programmes can be substantially strengthened by including incentives to disclose other illegal conduct. These incentives broadly fall into two mutually reinforcing groups that have become known as 'amnesty plus' and 'penalty plus'.

'Amnesty plus' creates a strong incentive to disclose other illegal conduct, usually participation in one or more other cartels, by allowing participants in the initial cartel the opportunity to obtain amnesty in respect of their participation in the other cartel(s) while obtaining an additional reduction, over and above what they otherwise would receive, in connection with the initial cartel. For example, if a participant (company X) in cartel A was ineligible for full leniency in respect of cartel A, an 'amnesty plus' element of a leniency programme would enable company X to obtain a further reduction in the sanctions to which it otherwise would be subject in respect of its participation in cartel A, in return for being the first to disclose the existence of cartel B. This reduction would be over and above the reduction to which it would be already entitled by virtue of its cooperation in respect of cartel A. Of course, company X and its officers, directors, and employees also would receive full leniency in respect of cartel B.[70]

The contribution that 'amnesty plus' can make to a leniency programme is perhaps most strikingly demonstrated by the experience in the US, where it has been reported that 'amnesty plus' is responsible for 'nearly half' of the 56 grand jury investigations into international cartel activity that were on going in November 2005.[71] As a result of the success that the US has had with 'amnesty plus', it has been embraced in several other jurisdictions.[72]

Turning to 'penalty plus', in Canada and the US if an applicant for leniency fails to report its involvement in other cartel activity it likely will suffer harsh consequences. In Canada, a condition of the Competition Bureau's leniency policy is that the applicant 'must reveal any and all offences in which it may have been involved'.[73] Therefore, the Bureau 'will recommend that the Attorney General revoke any grant of immunity and take appropriate

[70] At least one enforcement authority has gone so far as to provide detailed guidance regarding how it ascertains whether there is one versus multiple cartels. See the OFT's Interim Note supra, n. 37, at paragraphs 6.8–6.11.

[71] Scott Hammond supra, n. 21, at 11.

[72] For example, 'amnesty plus' has been incorporated into the leniency programmes of competition agencies in Canada, the UK, Australia, and Korea.

[73] Supra n. 1, at paragraph 16(a). The Bureau recently has clarified that this provision is confined to criminal competition offences under the Competition Act and that

action against the party concerned' if it fails to disclose the existence of other cartel conduct.[74]

In the US, companies failing to take advantage of the 'amnesty plus' opportunity 'risk potentially harsh consequences' that include the likelihood that the DOJ 'will urge the sentencing court to consider the company's and any culpable executives' failure to report the conduct voluntarily as an aggravating sentencing factor'.[75]

Leniency for Individuals

In jurisdictions where individuals face independent liability for having participated in cartel conduct, leniency programmes typically provide that any leniency granted to a corporation will also be extended to *current* directors, officers, and employees of the corporation. The practice with respect to former directors, officers, and employees varies by jurisdiction, with some (such as the UK[76] and Ireland[77]) guaranteeing the same treatment to former employees while others (such as the US,[78] Canada,[79] and Australia[80]) retaining discretion to determine whether to extend full leniency to former employees on a case-by-case basis. However, in each of these jurisdictions, it is possible for individuals to separately apply for leniency.

---

applicants will be expected to exercise reasonable due diligence in determining whether they have been involved in other criminal competition offences. The Bureau has added:

> Applicants should also anticipate that the Attorney General will ask them about any criminal activity, under any legislation, that can reasonably be expected to impact their credibility as a witness. Before offering immunity it is essential that Crown counsel be satisfied that the applicant has disclosed all the information likely to affect its credibility. Such disclosure may relate to criminal activity in Canada or abroad.

See supra n. 53, at paragraph 30.

[74] Ibid., at paragraphs 26 and 27.

[75] Hammond supra, n. 21, at 11. The Canadian Competition Bureau is considering adopting a similar policy. See Competition Bureau Canada, 'Immunity Program Review Consultation Paper' (February 2006) at paragraph 25, available at http://www.competitionbureau.ac.ca/internet/index.cfm?itemID=2022+1g=e.

[76] See *Interim Note* supra, n. 37, at paragraphs 4.10–4.11 and 4.16.

[77] See supra n. 35, at paragraph 19.

[78] See Spratling supra, n. 44, at 7.

[79] See the Competition Bureau's Immunity Bulletin supra, n. 1, at paragraph 19. For a more detailed discussion, see generally Crampton supra, n. 10, at 30. The bureau is currently reviewing this and other aspects of its programme. See supra n. 75.

[80] See the ACCC's Interpretation Guidelines supra, n. 34, at paragraphs 46–7.

An obvious benefit associated with allowing for the possibility of individuals to obtain full leniency is that it expands the universe of potential applicants, thereby exercising an additional destabilizing influence on cartels. More importantly, knowledge of the possibility for employees and past employees to seek full leniency often prompts corporations to apply for leniency in circumstances where they otherwise may not have done so; or in any event to do so more quickly.

Of course, the benefits associated with extending a leniency programme to individuals are directly proportional to the severity of the potential sanctions to which individuals are exposed. If those potential sanctions are not material or are easy to circumvent (for example, if it is easy for corporations to reimburse its officers, directors, or employees for any fines they may have to pay), individuals are not likely to be as motivated to report illegal conduct as they would be in circumstances where such circumvention is more difficult, or where they face the prospect of a significant jail sentence. By contrast, where individuals are exposed to potential significant sanctions that they are not likely to be able to recoup from the company, they are much more likely to seriously consider applying separately for leniency, particularly in circumstances where the company has decided not to do so or is still in the process of deciding what to do. This view has been advocated by the US Congress, which recently passed legislation substantially increasing the maximum sanctions available for individuals (and corporations) under the Sherman Act.[81]

The OECD has noted that the combination of personal liability and personal leniency can give rise to another important benefit for an anti-cartel enforcement programme. Specifically: 'The prospect of personal liability may also secure the co-operation of former employees, particularly if they are now working for a competitor.'[82]

Given the difficulties associated with preventing firms from indirectly reimbursing employees, and given the much more harsh individual consequences associated with imprisonment, the US DOJ 'has long supported the belief that the most effective way to deter and punish cartel activity is to hold the most culpable individuals accountable by seeking jail sentences'.[83] As a

[81] See the Antitrust Criminal Penalty Enhancement and Reforms Act of 2004, Pub. L. No. 108–237, 118 Stat. 661, 665–9. Amongst others, it increases the imprisonment for individuals convicted of violating Section 1 of the Sherman Act from 3–10 years. See generally, Scott Hammond, 'An Overview of Recent Developments in the Antitrust Division's Criminal Enforcement Program', Remarks to the American Bar Association Midwinter Leadership Meeting, Kona, Hawaii, 10 January 2005, at 10–11.

[82] Supra n. 4, at 26.

[83] Hammond supra, n. 21, at 3.

result, the DOJ has been an active advocate, domestically[84] and in international fora such as the OECD and the ICN, for significant jail sentences and increased financial penalties for individuals.

The Process of Obtaining Full Leniency

Precise mechanisms for obtaining full leniency vary across jurisdictions. Generally speaking, the process is characterized by three essential steps:

1. applying for a 'marker' or 'place-holder' from the enforcement agency;
2. supplying further information to the agency by means of a 'proffer' or other process, which commonly results in a grant of provisional or conditional leniency; and
3. co-operating with the agency's investigation in accordance with the terms of the conditional leniency agreement, and ultimately obtaining a final grant of leniency or immunity.[85]

An application for full leniency is normally preceded by an internal investigation (usually conducted by in-house or outside legal counsel) to confirm the existence of potentially illegal cartel conduct. Even before such an investigation has been fully completed, companies and individuals considering applying for full leniency will quickly need to know whether any of the other cartel participants have already come forward with an application, thereby precluding the possibility of further conditional grants of full leniency. For these reasons, enforcement agencies in several jurisdictions will permit an oral request to be made for a 'marker' or 'place-holder', which may be made on an anonymous and hypothetical basis,[86] to enable to applicant to ascertain whether full leniency is still available and to preserve its 'first in' status while it completes its internal investigation and gathers the information required to make a formal proffer for full leniency.

In order to obtain a marker, most jurisdictions will require only basic information about the product or product sector together with a generic

[84] See generally, Hammond supra, n. 81, at 10–11. See also Arquit and Buhart supra, n. 7, at 178–9.

[85] Certain jurisdictions, notably Japan and South Korea, appear to collapse the provisional and final immunity processes by not offering the possibility to obtain a formal grant of conditional immunity.

[86] These include the US (see Arquit and Buhart supra, n. 7, at 172); Canada (supra n. 53, at paragraphs 1–5); the UK (supra n. 37, at paragraph 52.3–2.3.7); Ireland (supra n. 35, at paragraph 23); and Australia (supra n. 34, at paragraph 5).

description of the type of activity involved (for example, price fixing, bid rigging, market or customer allocation). This generally is considered to be sufficient for the agency to determine whether it has already granted a marker to another participant or, in any event to determine whether there is an on-going investigation into the matter. If full leniency is still available, fulfilment of the agency's marker requirements will result in confirmation that the applicant has secured 'first place status' in the queue.

In the last few years, several jurisdictions, including Canada,[87] the US,[88] the UK,[89] and Australia[90] have begun to permit purely oral leniency application processes.[91] This is because the broad reach of civil production and discovery regimes in the US and elsewhere creates a potentially huge disincentive to applying for leniency for companies and individuals having civil liability exposure.

Some agencies have now suggested time limits during which an applicant must 'perfect' the marker or place-holder.[92] However, enforcement agencies in the US, the UK, and the EC have not embraced such limits, in recognition of the fact that in complex and/or international matters more flexibility typically would be warranted, for example, to enable the holder of a marker to complete an internal investigation and/or gather the evidence required to make the proffer.

The second phase of the process involves 'perfecting' the marker, by providing a sufficient level of detail to permit the agency to assess whether a violation has likely occurred and whether there is sufficient evidence to proceed with a formal investigation.

After sufficient information is provided to the agency, an applicant will, in most jurisdictions, be entitled to receive a conditional or provisional grant of immunity or full leniency, which normally operates as a good faith confirmation by the agency that, subject to further co-operation, a grant of final

[87] Supra n. 53, at paragraph 20.

[88] Supra n. 7, at paragraph 169.

[89] Supra n. 37, at paragraph 2.17.

[90] Supra n. 34, at paragraph 40.

[91] Korea has now followed suit. See amendment of notification on implementation of the leniency programme, available at http://www.ftc.go.kr/eng. By contrast, Japan continues to require the process to be launched in writing.

[92] For example, the ACCC has suggested a 28-day period (see the agency's Interpretation Guidelines supra, n. 34, at paragraph 28), while the Canadian Competition Bureau has established a 30-day period (see supra n. 1, at paragraph 15). Both of these jurisdictions allow some flexibility depending upon complexity and other factors.

immunity or full leniency will be provided. The conditional grant of leniency will normally be in written form and will specify terms under which final immunity may be granted.[93] Although rare, leniency has been revoked in the EC[94] and the US.[95]

In the third phase, the applicant will be required to continue to provide full, frank, continuing, and complete cooperation.

Partial Leniency

Partial leniency typically refers to offering non-immunized cartel participants a reduction of the penalty that otherwise would be imposed on them in return for cooperation. This is something that has been a feature of law enforcement in other areas of the world for a very long time, often in the context of what is colloquially known as 'plea-bargaining'.

As noted at the outset of this chapter,[96] in some jurisdictions, such as the US, Australia, and Ireland, the leniency or amnesty programme technically applies only to full amnesty or immunity. Partial leniency is available pursuant to other policies of the enforcement agency or the prosecuting agency. In other jurisdictions, the leniency programme explicitly covers both full and partial leniency. In the end, it is not particularly important that partial leniency be offered as part of the same policy as full leniency. What is important is that partial leniency be available and that the agencies' policies, practices, and procedures regarding partial leniency be fully transparent and predictable.

The obvious benefit that partial leniency offers for enforcement agencies is the opportunity to avoid lengthy and unpredictable costly legal proceedings against the cooperating entity or entities. An additional benefit is that, by extending partial leniency to one or more cartel participants, the case against remaining participants can be substantially strengthened to the point where the balance of negotiating leverage tilts to a degree that they also agree to cooperate.

[93] Canada's Competition Bureau has pledged that the final immunity terms will be 'on the table' at the time of negotiation of the provisional grant of immunity. Supra n. 53, at paragraph 25.

[94] See R.O. http://europa.eu.int/rapid/pressReleasesAction.do?reference=IP/05/1315&format=HTML&aged=0&language=EN&guiLanguage=en.

[95] See *Stolt-Nielsen S.A., Stolt-Nielsen Transportation Group Ltd. and Richard B. Wingfield* v. *U.S.*, Court of Appeals for the Third Circuit (Action No. 04-CV-537), opinion filed 23 March 2006, available at http://www.usdoj.gov/atr/cases/215600/215681.htm.

[96] Supra n. 1.

In some jurisdictions, the degree of partial leniency granted varies directly with the order in which cartel participants approach the enforcement agency. In other words, the most favourable partial leniency treatment is provided to the second party to begin to cooperate with the agency (assuming that the first party to do so has obtained conditional full leniency); the second most favourable partial leniency is provided to the third party to begin to cooperate with the agency, and so on.[97] This approach promotes a 'race to the agency' dynamic. However, it arguably does not allow for an appropriate balancing of aggravating and mitigating factors.

[97] See, for example, supra n. 14, at paragraph 23, where it is stated that the first company to fulfil the conditions of the EC's partial leniency policy will receive a reduction of 30–50 per cent of the fine which would otherwise have been imposed, the second successful applicant 20–30 per cent, and subsequent successful applicants will receive a reduction of up to 20 per cent. See also the description of Japan's similar policy supra, n. 7, at 91; and the description of South Korea's policy of allowing up to a 30 per cent reduction in surcharges for the second party to begin cooperating with the KFTC supra, n. 7, at 102–3, and supra n. 23, at paragraph 17. Cf. the European Competition Authorities' Principles for Leniency Programmes supra, n. 6, at paragraph 6, which suggests that members of the European Competition Network 'offer significant but substantially smaller reductions in sanction to second and subsequent applicants'.

5

Competition Law and Intellectual Property Rights*

Valentine Korah

Tension between Competition and Intellectual Property Rights (IPRs)

Intellectual property rights (IPRs) are rights to exclude others from exploiting a non-corporeal asset. They include patents, design rights, copyright, trademarks, and other items. They may lead to significant market power when there are no substitutes on either the demand or supply side of the market. In other words, they may amount to entry barriers and make it harder for new competitors to enter the market. Nevertheless, this is relatively unusual. Patents, for instance, cover only the inventions and applications claimed and, unless these are important, patents are of little value. Patents holders rarely extend their protection to other countries within the year of first application under

* Reproduced from 'Competition Law and Intellectual Property Rights', published in Dhall, V. (ed.). 2007. *Competition Law Today: Concepts, Issues, and the Law in Practice* (first ed.), Oxford University Press, New Delhi.

I, Valentine Korah, am indebted, for help in providing me with information and thoughts, to two experts in competition and IP, Shamnad Basheer of George Washington University and Thomas Cheng of the University of Hong Kong. The remaining errors are, of course, mine.

the Paris Convention[1] because the cost of making further applications, including translations, exceeds the expected value of the patent for further countries. Nevertheless, some patents are immensely valuable and the question arises whether competition law should intervene to limit their scope, or whether this should be left to the legislator when it defines the scope of the right.

Functions of IPRs

There are several reasons for granting IPRs: firstly, they may encourage various kinds of investment. Patents may be justified on the ground that without the prospect of an exclusive right, few firms would invest large resources in research and development (R&D). The inventor would meet competition from those who have not made a similar investment and are able to sell more cheaply. There would be no incentive to perform the original R&D if others could take a free ride on it. Secondly, national patent offices publish patent applications and claims and, even before the patent expires, the protected invention can legally be used by others for R&D, although not for commercial manufacture or sale. Consequently, the exclusive right can be perceived as the price of publication. Thirdly, as Arrow argues,[2] patents facilitate the negotiation of licences. The licensee is unlikely to agree to pay a licence fee or accept other restrictions on its conduct unless it has been able to test the technology, but that would be difficult to arrange if the licensee were then free to exploit the invention without infringing the law.

In this chapter, I write mainly of patents and copyright, but many of the arguments apply to other kinds of IPRs. Some have different justifications. Trademarks encourage the holder to invest in the reputation of the product, as consumers will be able to identify it by reference to the trademark. It saves consumers from confusion. Since marks are valuable and the holder will want to maintain its reputation they are indirectly a guarantee of quality, but only to this extent. In civil law systems, traditional artistic copyright gives effect to the natural law right to exploit the fruits of one's artistic endeavour and to restrain conduct that might harm the artists' reputation. The Anglo-American tradition, however, stresses the incentive to artistic endeavour.

[1] The Paris Union Convention for the Protection of Industrial Property of 20 March 1883, *United Nations Treaty Series*, vol. 828, No. 11851.

[2] Nelson, R. (ed.) (1962), 'Economic Welfare and the Allocation of Resources for Innovation', *The Rate and Direction of Incentive Activity*, Princeton: Princeton University Press.

There are many kinds of IPRs, but most of them encourage some kind of investment thought to be useful and which would not be made, or not be so well or frequently made, without the prospect of being able to exclude others from exploiting it. Most patents and other IPRs are limited nationally. The holder of an Indian patent cannot restrain anyone from exploiting the patented invention in Thailand, unless it also holds a patent granted in that country. Firms owning important rights may have to apply for protection in many countries, but this can be very expensive, because twenty to thirty pages of translation of technical claims and specifications are required in each language.[3]

Perceived ex post, after the investment is made, IPRs may operate as barriers to entry by third parties. There is a trade-off between providing the incentive to invest in innovation and the liberty of others to exploit the protected product. The trade-off is, however, theoretical rather than practical as neither side of the balance can be quantified. Competition in innovation, however, is widely thought to be more important than competition from someone providing the same product in the same way. Joseph Schumpeter[4] said that 'competition that counts [is] competition from the new commodity, the new competition the new sources of supply, the new type of organisation...competition which commands a decisive cost or quality advantage and which strikes not at the margins of the profits and the outputs of the existing firms but at their foundations and their very lives'.

He argued that 'to survive in capitalist competition, incumbents must withstand a perennial gale of competition in the form of the new consumer goods, the new methods of production or transportation, the new markets, the new forms of industrial organization'.

This is why dynamic competition in innovation is considered by many to be more important than static competition between suppliers of similar products.[5]

Most IPRs are limited in various ways by the legislation granting them to encourage competition. They do not last for ever. Even trademarks last only so long as they are used. There are exceptions to copyright protection for fair use, or to patent protection for research purposes. Compulsory licences

[3] Although there are regional systems which enable the translated application to be postponed until after grant, by which time it may be easier to tell whether it is worthwhile to extend the right.

[4] Schumpeter, J.A. (1943), *Capitalism, Socialism and Democracy*, London: George, Allen and Unwin Ltd, 84.

[5] See also, Korah, V. (2005), 'The Interface between Intellectual Property Rights and Competition in Developed Countries', 2:4 SCRIPT-ed 462, available at http://www.law.ed.ac.uk/ahrb/script-ed/vol2–4/korah.asp.

may be granted by the Patent office. The question arises whether such limitations should be provided for ex ante, before the commitment to invest is undertaken, by legislation, or whether they should be imposed ex post by competition law.

After an important technological breakthrough, such as the internal combustion engine, patent examiners may not realize how wide the exclusive right they are granting will be. In the US, many wide patents, such as the one click on the Amazon website, have been granted and many dubious ones have been upheld by the Federal Circuit for the District of Columbia, which hears all patent appeals in the US. In Europe, the requirements of novelty and inventive step[6] are probably stricter than in the US, but the EC extended copyright from life plus 50 years to life plus 70 to avoid a German constitutional crisis.[7] It might have been better to have allowed longer protection in Germany than elsewhere. At least the rest of us could have enjoyed the copyright works free of royalty sooner.

Public Goods

It is difficult to know how to reward those investing in public goods—those which were expensive to create but can be exploited at virtually no cost once they have been created. It takes resources to build a bridge but, once built, it costs very little to permit people to use it. This is often true of technology, which is expensive to develop, but can be used at little cost. Technology would be used most efficiently if access was granted at average variable cost—often almost nil—but then there would be no incentive to make the original investment. The option of leaving the government to fund R&D is not satisfactory, as civil servants have not been good at spotting winners. The decision has therefore been taken in most developed countries to let the market decide the worth of the investment. This is done by giving an exclusive right to the

[6] Patents, these days, are usually granted only if the invention is not published, not obvious to someone skilled in the art, and is likely to serve an industrial purpose.

[7] The term of copyright in Germany was life plus 70 years, whereas in other member states it was life plus 50. Consequently, works that were in free circulation in most Member States after 50 years could still be prevented from coming into Germany. This was considered to be inconsistent with the fundamental principle of the Common Market free movement. So, the Commission proposed a directive to the Council (Council Directive 93/98/EEC-Term of protection of copyright, OJ 1993, L290/9) requiring member states to protect copyright for life plus 70 years. The only reason for lengthening the term in most member states was to save the Germans from having to shorten the term in that country.

person whose application first reaches the patent office.[8] It can then obtain the value of the invention by using it itself or assigning or licensing its IPRs at a price.

Functions of Competition Law

There is considerable dispute about the function of competition law. Is it desired in order to *protect competitors* from being kept out of the markets they wish to enter? Is it to increase efficiency and *consumer welfare* or is to increase efficiency and *total welfare*, including that of the firm with market power? At first in the EC, competition was perceived by many as protecting competitors, especially small and medium sized firms. In the last decade, however, it is clear that the enforcement agency sees it as protecting consumer welfare.[9] The US went through similar stages at earlier periods[10] and the enforcement agencies there state that they intend to protect consumers. Most economists, however, would prefer to protect total welfare and the Canadian case law has adopted that test. Efficiencies are relevant in Canada even if the cost savings and other benefits they generate are not passed on, whereas anticompetitive conduct is not acceptable in the US and EC unless part of the benefit is passed on to consumers.

Other functions of competition law may be to protect small firms because 'small is beautiful'. Where there are substantial economies of scale in relation to demand, however, that might be an expensive option. In many industries, factories could not be built on an efficient scale and used to the full. Other possible functions are to produce a level playing field so that the situation is

[8] In the US, it used to be to the first to invent, but that had the drawback of not being transparent: a firm might spend resources on inventing something of which only one firm knew, only to find that the latter was entitled to the patent, although the second inventor might be allowed to use its own invention.

[9] For example, Commission notice, Guidelines on the Application of Article 81(3) of the Treaty, OJ 2004, C101/97: 13. The objective of Article 81 is to protect competition on the market as a means of enhancing consumer welfare and of ensuring an efficient allocation of resources. Competition and market integration serve these ends since the creation and preservation of an open single market promotes an efficient allocation of resources throughout the Community for the benefit of consumers.

[10] See, for example, Jones, Clifford A. (2006), 'Foundations of Competition Policy in EU and USA: Conflict, Convergence and Beyond', in Hanns Ullrich (ed.), *The Evolution of European Competition Law—Whose Regulation, Which Competition*?, Chapter 2, Edward Elgar, 2006.

seen to be fair for all and freedom to enter a market. Some countries like to protect national champions to compete worldwide. These possible functions will not be considered in this chapter.

Conditions in Developing Countries

Conditions in developing countries are very different from those in developed countries.[11] Barriers to entry tend to be higher. This results in some important industries being concentrated. Local firms with better access to cheap labour (skilled and unskilled) must not be restrained from cooperating with multinational firms that are large enough to invest heavily in R&D and have cheaper access to capital. The economy may not have sufficient financial resources to be able to pay for sophisticated products. Tariffs and quotas for goods have been reduced by the various WTO rounds, and even for services there has been movement under GATS, but they still exist.[12]

Where, in a particular sector, entry barriers are high any market power conferred by an IPRs is likely to last longer than in a large developed country. This may tilt the balance some way towards granting compulsory licences where this would not be done in a more developed country. The need for access is likely to be more important and to last longer.

[11] For India, see Basant, Rakesh and Sebastian Morris (2000), 'Competition Policy in India, Issues for a Globalising Economy', *Economic and Political Weekly*, 29 July. This was the time when thought was being given to devising the Competition Act, 2002. The authors discuss the invasive regulation of earlier times and the liberalization being carried out; the increasing reliance of the Indian corporate sector on buying foreign technology; the importance of integrating the cheaper capital of multinational companies, and the lower costs of other kinds available to Indian firms.

[12] Mukhopadhyay, Sukumar (2002), in 'Excise and Customs Duty Reform', *Economic and Political Weekly*, 37(4) 26 January, pp. 285–8, criticizes the complexity of the Indian excise and customs duties. There are many levels of duty and many exceptions. Even if duties are not high, the complexity creates additional work, delays imports and exports, and adds to the cost.

See also US Trade Representative Reports, 'Foreign Trade Barriers', 213, available at http://www.ustr.gov/Document_Library/Reports_Publications/Section_Index.html, where it is said that 'India's economy is one of the most closed in the world. Thus India's tariffs remain among the highest in the world'. India has abolished the need for an import licence on most consumer goods, but they are needed for sensitive goods and are almost unobtainable for motor cycles (p. 214).

Where few local firms can afford the investment in R&D done by multinationals, strong patent rights to encourage innovation are less desirable than in developed countries. Few important patents are owned by nationals.

Under the Agreement for Trade Related IP (TRIPs), all members of the WTO were required to make product patents generally available even for medicines. This must be contrary to the interests of many developing countries but they are allowed to provide for compulsory licences.

Compulsory Licensing by Dominant Firms under the Competition Act, 2002 (India)

The Competition Act does not impose an obligation on dominant firms to supply or license, but Section 4 provides that

1. No enterprise shall abuse its dominant position.
2. There shall be an abuse of dominant position under Sub-section (1), if an enterprise,
   - (a) directly or indirectly, imposes unfair or discriminatory
     - (i) condition in purchase or sale of goods or service; or
     - (ii) price in purchase or sale (including predatory price) of goods or service
   - (b) limits or restricts
     - (i) production of goods or provision of services or markets thereof; or
     - (ii) technical or scientific development relating to goods or services to the prejudice of consumers; or
   - (c) indulges in practice or practices resulting in denial of market access; or
   - (d) makes conclusion of contracts subject to acceptance by other parties of supplementary obligations which, by their nature or according to commercial usage, have no connection with the subject of such contracts; or[13]

[13] This language is similar to that in Article 82(EC). The Commission and ECJ have been hostile to tying, which was perceived as extending market power from one market to another. The Commission now accepts that tying may lead to many kinds of efficiency. There is a group exemption for technology transfer which applies to licences of many kinds of IPRs with tying provisions (but not of trademarks) provided that if the parties could have competed without the licence their combined market share does not exceed 20 per cent of the relevant product or technology market and if they could not have competed without the agreement and its tie, 30 per cent each.

(e) uses its dominant position in one relevant market to enter into, or protect, other relevant markets.

The abuse of a dominant position has been analysed by Alberto Heimler and Robert Anderson above and I will not consider it here, save to say that in the absence of any express provision, the US and EC courts have developed a duty in exceptional circumstances for dominant firms to supply or license, which illustrates the tension between property rights given to induce investment and competition which requires the possibility of access to markets.

The doctrine of essential facilities was developed in the US to limit property rights and was first applied to physical assets rather than IPRs in circumstances where it was not so difficult to determine the compensation for the property owner. In *US* v. *Terminal Railroad of St. Louis Association*,[14] a joint venture between the railroads that had started to go west but found themselves barred by the Mississippi at St. Louis acquired the only two bridges across the river there as well as the St. Louis Railway station. Another bridge would be a very expensive project as, not only is the river broad, its course shifts naturally and there were no other sites where such a bridge was technically feasible for many miles. Access was vital to the railroads that arrived after the bridge was built and the development of the railroads across the continent was an important activity.

The Supreme Court ordered that new railroads be given access to the bridge on terms similar to those agreed between the original members of the association. Some adjustments should be made to provide for the greater risk incurred by the original members and to leave them with a reward for their investment that would act as an incentive to further investments of any kind by others. That would have been more manageable than determining that the level of remuneration should be somewhere between the cost of permitting entry (building lines to connect the new railroad's lines to those on the bridge, employing lawyers to draft the contracts, negotiating the compensation, and so on), on the one hand, and the opportunity cost, the loss of

---

It is hoped that with the Commission's more economic approach these days, ties by dominant firms will not always be held to infringe Article 82.

The whole attitude of the Commission and courts has altered since the early cases on Article 82. Both institutions are more receptive towards economic arguments. Commission officials have issued a discussion paper for consultation and are expected to adopt guidelines in 2007. The Indian Authority should be advised not to follow old EC cases on Article 82 as the underlying philosophy may change.

The attitude to tying in the USA has also become less hostile.

[14] 224 US 383, 32 S.Ct.507, 56 L Ed 810 (1912).

the monopoly profit enjoyed by members of the association. More recently, economists have suggested long run incremental costs (LRIC), but that is not easy to determine.

After a period when lower courts extended the doctrine to more dubious cases, its growth was constrained by the classic article of Philip Areeda.[15]

Recently, it was further narrowed by the Supreme Court in *Verizon Communications Inc.* v. *Trinko, LLP*[16] and by the Court of Appeals for the Federal Circuit in *Covad Communication Company et al.* v. *Bell Atlantic Corp et al.*[17]

In *Commercial Solvents*,[18] the Court of Justice of the European Communities (ECJ), confirmed a decision by the Commission[19] that a refusal by a world monopolist to supply Zoja, a former customer with whom it competed downstream, amounted to the abuse of a dominant position contrary to Article 82 (EC). Commercial Solvents' patents had expired, but only it had the know-how to make the raw material on a commercial scale. Within the common market only two firms would make the finished product, an important drug for treating tuberculosis,[20] if Zoja were refused supplies.

[15] 'Essential Facilities: an Epithet in Need of Limiting Principles' (1989) 58 *Antitrust Law Journal*, 841.

[16] 540 US 398 (2004).

[17] 1 March 2005, 540 US 398 (2004).

[18] *Istituto Chemioterapico Italiano SpA and Commercial Solvents Corp* v. *Commission* (6 & 7/73), 6 March 1974, [1974] ECR 223, [1974] 1 CMLR 309, CMR 8209.

[19] The administrative body of the EC, which is charged with enforcing competition law.

[20] The Court said:

> [25] However, an undertaking being in a dominant position as regards the production of raw material and therefore able to control the supply to manufacturers of derivatives cannot, just because it decides to start manufacturing these derivatives (in competition with its former customers), act in such a way as to eliminate their competition which, in the case in question, would have amounted to eliminating one of the principal manufacturers of ethambutol in the Common Market. Since such conduct is contrary to the objectives expressed in Article 3(1)(g) of the Treaty and set out in greater detail in Articles 81 and 82, it follows that an undertaking which has a dominant position in the market in raw materials and which, with the object of reserving such raw material for manufacturing its own derivatives, refuses to supply a customer, which is itself a manufacturer of these derivatives, and therefore risks eliminating all competition on the part of this customer, is abusing its dominant position within the meaning of Article 86. In this context it does not matter that the undertaking ceased to supply in the spring of 1970 because of the cancellation of the

It is unclear whether the ECJ was protecting those paying for the treatment of tubercular patients or a small or medium sized firm. The Court did not say the case was exceptional, but the Advocate General focussed on the stranglehold downstream.

In *Volvo*,[21] the Court drew back and ruled that the right to exclude was 'the very subject matter' of copyright in spare parts. It was entitled to sue for copyright infringement those who had imported a spare part from a country where Volvo enjoyed no protection. The Court added, however, that in three circumstances a refusal by a dominant firm to supply a dealer on fair terms might be abusive: charging unfair prices, refusing to supply spare parts to dealers to whom they refused a licence, and failing to supply spare parts for old models, when there were a significant number of them on the road. These examples of abuse have been treated as extending the doctrine of refusing to supply to new customers in those circumstances.

In the *Magill* case[22] the ECJ confirmed that in special circumstances, a refusal by a dominant firm to supply might be abusive. The only three TV stations authorized to transmit in Eire and Northern Ireland (separate member states) refused to supply advance notice of their programmes to Magill, which wanted to produce a comprehensive guide to the programmes of all three stations. They each successfully sued Magill for copyright infringement and obtained injunctions. The Court confirmed (para 47) that the stations were each dominant over the lists of their own programmes. At para 50 it added that 'in exceptional circumstances' the exercise of its exclusive right may amount to an abuse and continued:

> 54. The appellants' refusal to provide basic information by relying on national copyright provisions thus prevented the appearance of a new product, a

---

> purchases by Zoja, because it appears from the applicants own statement that when the supplies provided for in the contract had been completed, the sale of aminobutanol would have stopped in any case.

[26] It is also unnecessary to examine, as the applicants have asked, whether Zoja had an urgent need for aminobutanol in 1970 and 1971 or whether this company still had large quantities of this product which would enable it to reorganise its production in good time, since that question is not relevant to the consideration of the conduct of the applicants'.

[21] *Volvo AB* v. *Erik Veng (UK) Ltd* (238/87), 5 October 1988, [1988] ECR 6211, [1989] 4 CMLR 122, CMR 14498, paras 8–11.

[22] *Radio Telefis Eireann and Others* v. *Commission* (C-241 & 242/91 P), 6 April 1995, [1995] ECR I-743, [1995] 4 CMLR 718, [1995] 1 CEC 400 (ECJ).

comprehensive weekly guide to television programmes, which the appellants did not offer and for which there was a potential consumer demand. Such refusal constitutes an abuse under heading (b) of the second paragraph of Article 82 of the Treaty.

55. Second, there was no justification for such refusal either in the activity of television broadcasting, or in that of publishing television magazines....

56. Third, and finally, as the Court of First Instance also held, the appellants, by their conduct, reserved to themselves the secondary market of weekly television guides by excluding all competition on that market (see the judgment in Joined Cases 6/73 and 7/73 *Commercial Solvents* v. *Commission* [1974] ECR 223, paragraph 25) since they denied access to the basic information which is the raw material indispensable for the compilation of such a guide.

The judgment has been criticized and any obligation to license has been limited by the opinion of AG Jacobs and the judgment of the ECJ in *Oscar Bronner*.[23] The drawbacks of requiring supply to an essential facility were well set out by AG Jacobs:[24] compulsory access reduces the incentive to invest in the original facility, or its duplication where that is practicable, and leads to detailed regulation to determine the amount of compensation payable. In his view, access should be granted only when there is an insuperable obstacle to enter an adjoining market. It should, however, be easier to claim compulsory access where the original facility was created by a firm in the public sector. I would go further and, if there was a stranglehold in an important neighbouring market, require a licence to an essential facility that was created when the state had granted special or exclusive rights so that the inventor had not been subject to competitive constraints when creating the object of the exclusive right.

The judgment in *Magill* was largely confirmed by that in *NDCH* v. *IMS*.[25]

The Commission objected to Microsoft's refusal to give its competitors full interoperability information that would enable them to design workgroup

[23] *Oscar Bronner GmbH & Co KG* v. *Mediaprint Zeitungs—und Zeitschriftenverlag GmbH & Co KG and Others* (C-7/97), 26 November 1998, [1998] ECR I-7817, [1999] 4 CMLR 112, [1999] CEC 53.

[24] The ECJ is assisted in each case by the opinion of an Advocate General. They are full members of the Court with the same status as the judges. Their opinions are a little like the judgment of the court below, but are not at all binding, although some have been very influential.

[25] *IMS Health GmbH & Co KG* v. *NDC Health* (C-418/01), 29 April 2004, [2004] 4 CMLR1543 (there have been several judgments involving IMS. This was the preliminary ruling on the injunction against infringing copyright). I have explained the case law more fully, in Korah V. (2006), *Intellectual Property Rights and the EC Competition Rules*, Oxford: Hart Publishing, 2006, Chapter 8.

server operating systems on which Microsoft Windows would work satisfactorily. The decision[26] is controversial[27] and is on appeal to the Court of First Instance.[28]

The European Obligation for a Dominant Firm to Supply or License

In *Magill*, the ECJ did not rely on copyright, but on the stations being the only source of information about their programmes. In *IMS*, the ECJ did rely on the injunction not to infringe copyright. In many judgments including *Magill*, it has been made clear that IPRs do not necessarily confer a dominant position: it depends on whether there are adequate substitutes.

Instead of saying that the circumstances were special because the new entrant's product was new, the ECJ in *Magill* and *IMS* might more sensibly have considered whether the market downstream was important. Novelty may be relevant to the importance of a licence, but should not be a general condition. Not only is novelty an imprecise concept, the parts in *Volvo* that had to fit a specific model of car would be useless if they were entirely new.

In my view, the judgments were right to consider that a duty to supply new customers may arise.[29] It is worse for consumers if no one supplies than if only the firm dominant upstream does so but some scholars are more worried about discrimination when the dominant firm supplies its downstream activity more cheaply than it supplies its competitors.[30] It should, however,

[26] *Microsoft* decision, 24 March 2004 [2005] 4 CMLR 965.

[27] Microsoft had invested vast sums in developing operating systems for client PCs. Incentives for such investment should not lightly be removed.

On the other hand Microsoft was exceptionally dominant in a network industry where barriers to entry are very high. If it were to extend its dominance into one neighbouring market after another, it might become impossible for any firm successfully to attack its original monopoly over operating systems for client PCs. The arguments are set out at length by the Commission in its decision.

[28] *Microsoft* v. *Commission*, T-201/04 [2005] 4 CMLR 406, (CFI interim order, refusing to suspend remedies granted by the Commission, IP (04)382), [2004] 4 CMLR 1231. Judgment on the substance is expected early in 2007.

[29] *Queensland Wire Industries Pty Ltd* v. *Broken Hill Pty Ltd* (1988) 83 ALR 577, comment Korah (2000) 32 *Victoria University of Wellington Law Rev* 231, 233 et seq, Hanks and Williams (1990) 17 Melbourne ULR 437.

[30] This view is formalistic when the entity downstream is wholly owned by the firm dominant upstream. A transfer price within a group of companies is not constrained by any market.

be possible to refuse supply if sufficient evidence is adduced that the new customer would not treat the products properly and would harm the reputation of the product. This would be more difficult where the customer had formerly been supplied voluntarily.

None of the cases have considered generally how the compensation to the holder of an IPRs should be fixed. In *Microsoft*,[31] the Commission required the parties to agree, but no criteria were prescribed and the parties could not agree. It said that the complainant should not have to compensate for the loss of the monopoly profit. In *Bronner*, AG Jacobs said there must be compensation, but did not consider how this should be fixed, except to say that doing so would be regulatory and have to be revised continuously. This is a strong reason for rarely requiring compulsory access.

Given the importance for India of acquiring foreign technology, however, the balance of advantage may have shifted towards requiring access to patented technology.

Compulsory Licensing under Indian Patent Act

By virtue of the Indian Patents Amendment Act, 2002, Chapter XVI, it is possible to apply to the Controller for a compulsory licence once three years have expired from the date the patent was sealed.

S. 84(1) At any time after the expiration of three years from the date of the sealing of a patent, any person interested may make an application to the Controller for grant of compulsory licence on patent on any of the following grounds, namely:

(a) that the reasonable requirements of the public with respect to the patented invention have not been satisfied, or
(b) that the patented invention is not available to the public at a reasonable affordable price, or
(c) that the patented invention is not worked in the territory of India....

Compulsory licences were available under the previous patent law, but in narrower circumstances. When the WTO required members to grant product patents even for medicines, the Indian legislator may have looked to ways of reducing legally the power of foreign pharmaceutical firms large enough to be able to invest in considerable R&D. Smaller Indian firms with better access

[31] *Microsoft* 24 March 2004, [2005] 4 CMLR 965 (not reported in the OJ. It takes over 300 pages on the Commission's website).

to cheap labour would want to take a licence to make medicines before the patents expired and combine the complementary advantages.

Since the most valuable IPRs are held by large multinational companies, the incentive to invest is not greatly increased by an exclusive right to exploit in India. The incentive comes mainly from the developed world.

In view of the possibility of compulsory licences it may not be necessary to invoke the provisions of the Competition Act to impose an obligation on a patentee to license. Nevertheless, the grant of a licence under the Patents Act is the discretion of the Controller of patents and may be subject to conditions and the payment of a reasonable royalty. A new entrant might welcome direct access to the Competition Commission of India under the competition legislation.

A doctrine of essential facilities may be developed in relation to other kinds of assets, such as transport facilities and the telecommunications local loop and, if so, the doctrine might be extended by the Competition Commission of India to products protected by patents.

Moreover, there are other kinds of IPRs, such as copyright, which is not covered by the provisions in the patent legislation. Software is broadly protected by copyright in India. The decision of the EC Commission in *Microsoft*[32] shows how important a duty to disclose interface information may be.

Importance of Access in Developing Countries

There are various reasons why compulsory licensing may be more desirable in developing countries than in developed ones.

Invasive Indian Regulation

In many developing countries there may be invasive regulation of all the kinds mentioned by Allan Fels in the beginning of his chapter. That used to be the case in India,[33] but there has been significant liberalization in India since 1991[34] and the economy has blossomed. Invasive regulation may also prolong any market power the holder of an IPRs enjoys and again may tip the balance towards granting compulsory licences.

In developing countries much investment is made by the state or by private undertakings that enjoy special or exclusive rights. At para 66 of

[32] 24 March 2004, [2005] 4 CMLR 965. The order requiring disclosure is subject to appeal and the judgment of the Court of First Instance in Luxembourg is expected early in 2007.

[33] See chapter below.

[34] See chapter by Kumar in this book. See also n. 11 above.

his opinion in *Oscar Bronner*, AG Jacobs observed that where the original investment was made at public expense it would be particularly difficult for a new entrant to compete. The same may be said about sectors where a private company enjoyed special or exclusive rights and suffered little competition at the time the investment was made. Such a company would have been less constrained by competitive pressures and the incentive to invest might not be unduly reduced by a requirement to license. Nevertheless, the problem of deciding the amount of compensation remains when there is no market for comparison. Cost plus is a poor criterion of price that encourages escalation in cost. Comparisons with prices elsewhere are likely to be unsatisfactory because conditions elsewhere are usually different; the price of labour is likely to be low in a developing country. The legislature is to be congratulated for extending the Competition Act to the commercial activities of government and for making the authority independent and autonomous.

Where a state activity is privatized, a regulator may be appointed to control excessive exploitation. Then the compensation may be fixed by the regulation on an arbitrary formula and avoid the uncertainty leading to much costly litigation.

Access to Patented Medicines

In most developing countries, few people have access to expensive medicines and in India, there is no universal health insurance. Nevertheless, I wonder how far a duty to make technology available would help. Licences or the production and distribution of the medicines themselves are likely to cost the pharmaceutical companies amounts that are unlikely to be affordable by most of the population. Even medicines for treating AIDS, which are made available more cheaply than in developed countries, are usually available only to a tiny proportion of the population. Even if only average avoidable costs were charged, how many people could afford them? A duty to supply would almost certainly have to allow the holder of the IPRs to recover its average avoidable cost, or the pharmaceutical companies would leave the country, where their competition is so important.

Moreover, if general public interests are to be furthered under competition law, there will be great uncertainty. The legislation providing the possibility of compulsory licences, inter alia on grounds of health, was enacted around the same time as the new Competition Act. The Indian government chose to protect various policies by legislation. In my view it is better to provide, ex ante and in legislation, any limitations to IPRs necessary to make new entry possible than for the authority to have to work out whether circumstances are sufficiently special to require access after the investment in technology has been made. The differing policies are usually not commensurable. Other public interest policies are better pursued under separate rules.[35]

The decision on the amount of compensation to be paid by the compulsory licensee will not be easy in the absence of criteria as to what royalty is reasonable, but the Controller may develop criteria, which will reduce the level of uncertainty under the Competition Act.

Importance of Advocacy

As stated by Kumar and Dhall in their chapters, advocacy is one of the most important activities[36] of the Competition Commission of India, which has not yet started to enforce the Act. It is important that the Commission should regularly be heard whenever new IPRs are being created or when their duration or extent in other directions is being considered. Should antitrust limit IPRs that are wider than is necessary to induce sufficient innovation? Even with hindsight, it is hard to determine whether a right is palpably too broad. If the extent of protection is determined case by case, the resulting uncertainty may fail to induce sufficient investment. Has the competition authority, the economists and lawyers appearing before them, got better training or sources of information to decide the amount of protection required to induce the optimal level of investment than has the legislature, the Patent Controller, or examiners?

While the legislation provides the possibility of compulsory licences, the decision on the amount of compensation to be paid to the patentee will not be easy in the absence of criteria as to what royalty is reasonable, but the Controller may develop criteria, which will reduce the level of uncertainty under the Competition Act. Limitations in legislation seem to me more practical and far more certain than an action for the abuse of a dominant position contrary to the Competition Act. The same arguments apply if state monopolies' functions are expanded or new special and exclusive rights are created.

Copyright law reform by analogy has been adopted in Europe. Legislators have found it easier because they do not have to think, for instance, about what is the proper scope of copyright in software. They can just take over the existing rules for literary copyright and the political onus is on the objectors

[35] Bork, Robert H. (1993), *The Antitrust Paradox, A Policy at War with Itself*, New York: Free Press, Chapter 2.

[36] As considered by the Raghavan Committee. See also chapter, 'India's Competition Act, 2002' by Vinod Dhall in the 2007 edition of *Competition Law Today*, text after n. 107.

to disagree. The result has been wide IPRs, extended to the highest level of protection anywhere in the European Common Market.[37]

In my view it would be much more sensible for those advising the legislator to think how much protection is likely to produce sufficient amounts of software. Unlike literary and artistic copyright it is likely to be held by a company rather than an individual. So, protection lasting as long as the creator's family may need help is inappropriate.

The competition authority might do well to help define the appropriate extent of the right when new rights are being granted or old ones extended. The answers may not be clear, but to leave the issues open will certainly increase the need for litigation which few IPRs holders or infringers can afford, and is no more likely to be right than some arbitrary formula for a compulsory license set in the legislation.

Licences

The other main aspect of competition law relevant to IPRs is the terms that may be written into a voluntary licence. No one disputes that granting a non-reciprocal licence is unlikely to restrict competition appreciably when neither party is dominant. Exclusivity either way does no harm to competition if other firms are available with whom to cooperate. The pooling of patents by most of the patentees in a particular sphere can, however, exclude new entrants, especially when industry standards are protected by IPRs. Most debateable issues, however, concern the other terms of the licence. If they infringe S. 3(1), S. 3(2) renders them void. Section 3(1) prohibits agreements which cause or are likely to cause an appreciable adverse effect on competition within India.

Presumptions

Section 3(3) imposes a presumption of illegality for agreements between competitors fixing prices, etc. A vertical agreement between firms that compete only in a quite different market does not come within Section 3(3).

It was sensible not to impose a presumption against vertical agreements. Unlike horizontal agreements, each party to a vertical agreement has an interest in ensuring that the other is operating on the minimal margin necessary to persuade it to collaborate. Each party has an interest in controlling the market decisions of the other. Anyone alleging illegality of a vertical agreement should

[37] See n. 7 above.

have to establish that the agreement 'causes or is likely to cause an appreciable adverse effect on competition within India' contrary to Section 3(1).

The strength of the presumptions is considered by Vinod Dhall in the final chapter of the 2007 edition of *Competition Law Today* and will be very important. All other agreements, including those falling within Section 3(4)[38] are capable of being pro-competitive, although they could be anticompetitive in specific circumstances if one of the parties has significant market power.

In the US, the enforcement Agencies[39] accept that licensing intellectual property is often pro-competitive. So does the EC Commission, which in its latest group exemption for technology transfer[40] covered, up to a 30 per cent market share, vertical agreements including tying and some exclusivity in production, although resale price maintenance is not allowed.

Currently in India, licensors may be multinational companies with great negotiating power. As the economy develops, however, a typical licensee may come to be much larger than the licensor. It is usually expensive to set up a production line and produce commercial quantities, far more so than to invent the product and even the machinery to produce it. Often firms are unwilling to invest in organizing production and distribution unless assured that other firms will not take a free ride on their work in perfecting the technology and making a market. For them, exclusive distribution ('I will license only you to exploit the IPRs in your territory') may be necessary to induce the investment. Resale price maintenance, unless part of an agreement between competitors, may also induce investment by the licensee, which is assured that licensees for other areas will not be able to undercut it. Neither clause can protect the licensee from competition from rival technology.

Exclusive supply agreements ('you will buy all or most of your requirement from me') may enable a licensor to maintain the confidentiality of any know-how it discloses to the licensee. If the licensee is using several sources of technology, it is difficult to ensure that the owner of the other technology does not discover the licensed know-how. It may also help the licensor to collect

[38] (a) tie-in arrangement;
(b) exclusive supply agreement;
(c) exclusive distribution agreement;
(d) refusal to deal; and
(e) resale price maintenance.

[39] Antitrust Guidelines for the Licensing of Intellectual Property, 6 April 1995, at 2.3.

[40] Regulation 772/2004, on the application of Article 81(3) of the Treaty to categories of technology transfer agreements, OJ 2004, L123/11.

royalties, in that the licensee cannot credibly say that he made the product without the licensed technology. Especially if the licence provides an exclusive territory, it may be important to ensure that the technology is not stultified. Without an exclusive supply clause, the licensor might not have invested in developing the original technology. Many exclusive supply agreements do not foreclose, for example, if there are many other actual or potential licensees.

Tying may be necessary to ensure that products are technically compatible. There may be economies of scope in dealing with more than one item. Often tying is a mechanism making it easier to discriminate, possibly in favour of a firm that uses the process less.

On the other hand, all these practices can restrict competition, if the party protected has significant market power. Section 4 (abuse of a dominant position), is relevant when one of the parties has significant market power. Where none of them has such power and the agreement is vertical there is no presumption either way. The person alleging illegality will have to show that the agreement causes or is likely to cause an appreciable adverse effect contrary to Section 3(1). Under the US rule of reason, few victims can establish an infringement. I hope it proves easier to do so under the Indian legislation.

Section 3(5)

Section 3(5) provides that nothing in Section 3 shall restrict: '(i) the right of any person to restrain any infringement of, or to impose reasonable conditions, as may be necessary for protecting any of his rights which have been conferred upon him under various Indian statutes conferring IPRs.'

In so far as this permits suing for infringement, this provision is sensible. The section applies only to agreements, not to the unilateral abuse of a dominant position. So this does not make refusals to deal legal or prevent compulsory licences. It seems, however, to go further and to cover the imposition of unfair or discriminatory conditions by the licensor. It does not cover unfair terms imposed on the licensor. I assume that the burden is on the licensor to establish that any conditions are reasonable.

As the Indian economy develops and invents its own technology, it may be the licensee, not the licensor, which has negotiating power[41] and the licensor may need contractual protection against being exploited by the licensee.

[41] Large firms can often exploit their own technology, and often it is more profitable to do so when possible than to license it. Small inventors cannot always finance setting up a production line and making a market and may license a large firm. In the case of a developing country, however, it may be necessary for smaller firms to exploit the technology created by large foreign companies.

Requiring the licensee to use only the licensor's technology in order to ensure the confidentiality of the accompanying know-how is probably reasonable and allowed, but is it reasonable to ensure that the licensor's technology is exploited rather than that of a third party in order to increase the operations that generate royalties?[42] I hope that Article 3(5) is not interpreted so widely as to discourage small IPRs holders from granting licences to larger and more powerful firms. Perhaps this is not the most likely scenario in a developing country.

There is much to praise in the new Indian Competition Act in relation to IPRs. Compulsory patent licensing is to be done under the Patents Act, and the essential facilities doctrine remains for other kinds of IPRs. The doctrine may be wider than in the US and than on my interpretation of the EC law, but that may be right for a developing economy, more likely to be dependent on R&D carried out by large firms in developed countries. Moreover, barriers to entry tend to be higher in developing countries. So it is more difficult to enter markets where only a few firms have market power. Access is likely to be more important and remain so for longer than in a developed country.

Compulsory licences under the patent legislation are probably better than the application of the essential facilities doctrine. The Controller may have little idea what a reasonable royalty should be, but (s)he can develop criteria known before a commitment to invest is accepted, no less well than the competition authority and the uncertainty may be alleviated. This reduces the mischief while leaving the relief in exceptional cases.

I very much hope that the Competition Commission will set up mechanisms for reviewing what it has done. Introducing competitive thinking to business that has been used to invasive regulation is not easy and mistakes will inevitably be made. It will need professional economists in its staff, some in senior positions. It should put in place the review of the outcomes of its decisions. Has the market become freer or have firms with market power found ways round the decree?

We live in interesting times.

[42] See some of the provisions that have been considered unreasonable in other countries in the text to n. 48 in the chapter by Vinod Dhall in the 2007 edition of *Competition Law Today*. Many of those may be required if smaller firms are to be induced to invest in R&D and license it to someone in a better position to exploit it.

6

Exemptions, Exceptions, and Differential Application under Competition (Antitrust) Law*

R. Shyam Khemani

'Best practice' advice recommends that competition (antitrust) law should be a *general law of general application*. That is, the law should apply to *all sectors* and *all economic agents* in an economy engaged in the *commercial* production and supply of goods and services. In this regard, both private and public (namely state) owned and operated enterprises should be subject to the same treatment.

However, as this chapter discusses, exemptions and exceptions are at times warranted and granted to industries and certain types of economic activities and/or business transactions. An *exemption* refers to being 'excused or

* The views expressed in this chapter are those of the author and do not necessarily reflect the views held by the staff, management, or directors of the World Bank Group or any of his present or past institutional affiliations. This chapter recasts and extensively draws on an earlier paper written by the author on this subject for UNCTAD ('Application of Competition Law: Exemptions and Exceptions', UNCTAD/DITC/CLP/Misc. 25, March 2003).

free from some obligation to which others are subject'. An *exception* is to be 'excluded from or not conforming to a general class, principle, rule, etc'.[1]

While the terms exemption and exception (also exclusion) have specific meanings within the context of particular national legal systems, it may be noted that these terms are often used interchangeably.[2] In addition to exemptions and exceptions, there often occurs *differential* application of competition law-policy principles to certain sectors or firms. This is distinct from exemptions or exclusions and implies that a different set of standards and procedures are applied to competition related matters than may be the general case.

For greater clarity, some examples may be useful. In some countries, state-owned and state-operated enterprises are exempted from the purview of competition law while private sector firms are not. Similarly, in some jurisdictions mergers and acquisitions (M&A) by firms that lead to market dominance or substantial lessening of competition may be prohibited whereas in certain other cases and/or jurisdictions exceptions for selected M&A transactions may be made if there are efficiencies or other offsetting benefits. In addition, the exemptions may be sector-specific in nature and cover certain industries such as telecommunications and electricity supply or that these industries are subject to sector-specific laws with very different provisions relating to competition matters. The exemptions may also be non-sector specific and cover certain functional types of economic arrangements such as specialization and rationalization agreements, and cooperation between firms for the exchange of information and development of product standards.[3] Generally speaking, exemptions tend to be broader in scope, as is the case with sector-specific or industry examples whereas exceptions tend to be more narrowly focused, often determined on a case by case basis, applying a 'rule of reason' approach such as in selected

[1] These definitions are based on *Funk & Wagnalls Standard Dictionary*, 1991.

[2] See World Trade Organization, 'Exceptions, Exemptions, and Exclusions Contained in Members' National Competition Legislation', Document WT/ WGTCP/ W/172 (2001). This document contains a useful summary table which provides a 'birds-eye' view of various country and sectoral exemptions and exceptions to competition law in the different jurisdictions. See also Barry E. Hawk 'OECD Trade Committee Study of the Sectoral Coverage (and Limitations) of Competition Laws and Policies', Mimeo. OECD (1996).

[3] See UNCTAD Consultations, 'Competition Law and Policy: The Scope, Coverage and Enforcement of Competition Law and Policies and Analysis of the Provisions of the Uruguay Round Agreements Relevant to Competition Policy, and their Implications for Developing Countries', Document TD/B/COM.2/ EM/2 (1996).

M&A transactions and specialization agreements which, while resulting in the lessening of competition may still be on balance in the public or consumer interest.

While 'best practice' advice suggests that competition law-policy should apply to all sectors and firms in the economy engaged in commercial economic activity, in practice various types of exemptions and exceptions are granted for social, economic, and political reasons. The granting of exemptions and exceptions does not necessarily imply the weakening of competition law enforcement. Indeed, it may well be that such instances are necessary for furthering the objectives of competition law-policy. For example, virtually all competition laws strictly prohibit horizontal price agreements between competitors, as they tend to lessen competition. However, various forms of non-price horizontal agreements do not necessarily have the same effect and may be in the public interest if inter-firm cooperation results in standardization of products, improved quality, and increased information so that consumers have better choices. A review and analysis of such exemptions and exceptions, and the underlying rationale is useful for re-evaluating the coverage of competition laws, and can also serve as a guide for countries such as India which is still at the early stage of implementing the Competition Act (2002, as amended).

In this context the main questions that often arise and are worth reviewing include:

- What is the rationale for the exemptions and exceptions from the application of competition law-policy?
- Are there any guiding principles that should be borne in mind when granting such exemptions and exceptions?
- What are the examples of such exemptions and exceptions in different jurisdictions that could serve as a guide?

The remaining sections of the chapter are organized as follows. The next section presents a brief overview of the general nature and scope of competition law-policy, and the extent to which exemptions and exceptions from its application may or may not be desirable. The following section discusses some of the underlying economic or other rationale(s) for exemptions and exceptions that have been commonly granted across a number of countries and extracts some general guidelines. The subsequent section describes the coverage of competition laws in a selected sample of countries, including India, and suggests some general policy recommendations. Annexure I gives a brief 'tour de monde' of various economies' exemptions and exceptions.

The Nature and Scope of Competition Law-Policy

The Interdependent Nature of Economic Activity

There are fundamental legal and economic reasons for advancing the proposition that competition law-policy should be generally applicable to all sectors of the economy where commercial transactions take place. Entities engaged in the same or similar lines of activity should be subject to the same set of legal principles and standards to ensure fairness, equality, and non-discriminatory treatment under the law. Such an approach will result in greater predictability and consistency in the interpretation and application of the law, and promote more transparency, accountability, and confidence in the legal and other institutions responsible for the implementation of the law. It would foster 'due process' under the law.

However, the economic reasons for adopting such a policy approach relate not so much to equity and fairness, but to the interdependent nature of economic activities conducted in different markets, and the promotion of allocative efficiency. Conditions prevailing in one market can affect prices and outputs in other markets either because one good or service is an input in the production of other goods and/or services, or because the goods and services substitute or complement each other. Exemptions from the application of competition principles in one sector may perpetuate or induce distortions that can affect the efficiency of economic activity conducted in other sectors. Indeed, various industries and markets for goods and services tend to be 'seamlessly' interconnected even when the linkages are not directly obvious because of the role price and profit signals play in the redeployment of resources across different lines of economic activity.

An important function of competition law-policy is to prevent private restrictive business practices and public policies that may unnecessarily impede the redeployment of scarce resources from lower to higher valued uses. For example, a policy of insulating specific industries from competitive pressures may enable incumbent firms to restrict output, charge higher prices, and earn greater profits, which in turn, can result in several direct and indirect adverse economic effects. For consumers, there may be less choice, and transfer of income to producers in the form of higher prices paid. For industries that rely on the particular goods or service as an input in their own production processes, the higher prices charged will lead to higher costs and undermine the relative competitive position of the firms in the markets they serve. These markets need not be solely domestic in nature. They could be markets for exports or markets in which the firms compete against imported products, and foreign-exchange earnings or savings may be foregone. The higher prices and profits that generally result from restricting competition, may also take away resources, create shortages, and/or redirect resources from the production of other goods and services. Even if the production and sale of a given product has no demand or substitution linkages with the production and sale of another product, there may be linkages through the common pool of resources (such as labour and capital) that firms in both industries may be reliant on. Distortions in one market may 'ripple' through to other sectors of the economy. For example, insulating the domestic steel producer from competitive pressures may result in higher steel prices which may in turn result in higher automobile, construction, and other product costs which use steel as an input. Due to the artificially higher profits earned in the steel industry, the firms may be more willing to pay higher wage rates, and bid away labour from other industries, creating labour shortages or resulting in higher costs of production for other goods and services. Moreover, the steel companies having the comfort of assured domestic markets for their products will have lower incentives to be innovative unless other offsetting measures are imposed upon them. Thus, it should be recognized that the granting of exemptions and/or policies insulating any given sector (or firms) from competition, is likely to have other direct and indirect adverse effects on the economic system as a whole. Whether the costs of such exemptions and exceptions or policies are outweighed by the benefits need to be carefully assessed.[4]

Competition Law-Policy and Other Economic Policies

Although the process of competition pressures firms to become efficient, and offer a greater choice of products and services at lower prices and higher

[4] The concept of the interdependent relationship between different sectors, firms, and/or economic agents (basically referred to as 'general equilibrium' analyses in standard micro-economic theory) dates back to the late eighteenth-century writings of F. Quesnay (*Tableau economique et maximes generales du gouvernment economique,* Paris, 1758) and the subsequent writings of economists such as Walras, Pareto, and Leontif. In a general equilibrium framework, overall efficiency and total economic welfare of society is maximized when conditions of 'perfect competition' prevail in each and every area of economic activity conducted in the economy—a theoretical proposition which in the real world does not exist. Alternative theories of the 'second best' by economists R.G. Lipsey and K. Lancaster ('The General Theory of Second Best', *Review of Economic Studies*, XXIV, 1956–7) have been put forward, recognizing that distortions may prevail in some sectors of the economy. In economic policy-decision making, it is not easy to apply a general equilibrium framework in the matter of dealing with exemptions and it is more practical to assess, on a case-by-case basis, the exemptions in such a way as to avoid unnecessary restrictions on the process of competition.

quality, these may not be the sole reasons for governments to enact competition legislation. Competition law-policy in several countries is based on a multiple set of values that are neither easily quantifiable nor reduced to a single economic objective. These values may reflect the society's wishes, culture, history, institutions, and other factors that cannot nor should necessarily be ignored.

A brief survey would indicate that the objectives and scope of competition law-policy tend to vary across countries and over time. For example, in countries such as Canada and New Zealand, the primary objective of the competition legislation is to maintain and encourage competition with emphasis being placed on the promotion of economic efficiency. In the United Kingdom, while the objectives include 'public interest'—a broader concept than that of competition alone, the administration of the Competition Act (1998) and the Enterprise Act (2002) has evolved to include consumer welfare and economic efficiency among its primary objectives. In the United States, the enforcement of competition laws has increasingly focused on consumer welfare and economic efficiency. However, this has not always been the case. When the United States' Sherman Act was first enacted in 1890 (and for much of the twentieth century), there was explicit preference for 'pluralism' in terms of diffusion of economic power. There was also a tendency for protection of small businesses and local economies. In the European Union, priority is given to economic or market integration and prevention of dominance by large firms. In Germany, as in several other Member States of the European Union, preserving or ensuring freedom of individual action and economic freedom are viewed as being important among the objectives of competition law-policy.[5] In several developing countries, the spectrum of different objectives of competition law can be observed. For example, Colombia, being a small open economy, places emphasis on economic efficiency. In Indonesia and Russia, the law includes concerns regarding fairness, diffusion of economic power, and safeguarding small- and medium-sized enterprises. In several former centrally planned economies of Central and Eastern Europe, the competition laws have objectives and approaches which emulate that of the European Union—in part because of aspirations of these countries to become members of the European Union. In India, the objectives of the Competition Act are '... keeping in view the economic development of the country ... to prevent practices having an adverse effect on competition, to promote and sustain

[5] For further discussion of the objectives of competition law, see Chapter I of the World Bank and OECD, 'A Framework for the Design and Implementation of Competition Law and Policy' (1999).

competition in markets, to protect the interests of consumers and to ensure freedom of trade....' (Preamble, Competition Act, 2002).

In addition to the differences in objectives and weights assigned to various economic and societal goals in different countries, the general nature of competition laws gives rise to extensive interface with other government policies. The nature of this interface may be such that the aims of different government policies can be complementary to, or in conflict with, promoting competition. In areas such as privatization, international trade, investment, and regional development policies, there are often conflicts with the objectives of competition law-policy. In several countries, governments have privatized state-owned enterprises with exclusive or monopoly rights so as to obtain a higher sale price and/or attract foreign investment. Also import controls or investment restrictions have been instituted in order to protect domestic firms, which deters new entrants and foreign investment.[6] The differences in the goals of various government policies give rise to tensions regarding the priority assigned to competition law-policy vis-à-vis the government's other economic policies and objectives. These differences may not be easy to resolve and the parameters governing the application of competition law-policy may require judicial interpretation and/or decisions at a higher level of government.

The Rationale and Major Types of Exemptions

The brief overview of competition legislation of various countries discussed in the preceding section, however, suggests that there are more similarities than differences in the general approach towards exemptions. While some

[6] Until the economic–financial crisis in the late 1990s, Korea, for example, had various restrictions on foreign ownership. In non-strategic companies, foreign ownership was previously restricted to a maximum of 10 per cent. This was changed to 33 1/3 per cent of stock without approval of the company's board of directors, and subsequently completely removed. Restrictions on foreign participation in state-owned enterprises have also been relaxed. As a result of these various policy changes, including stepped up application of its competition law, gross foreign direct investment on a disbursement basis increased in Korea from nearly $3 billion in 1997 to $5 billion in 1998. Foreign direct investment commitments for 1999 reached nearly $15 billion. In the *decade* prior to the crisis, foreign investment in Korea totalled at best $4 billion! In the Czech Republic, the privatization and sale of Skoda automobile works to Volkswagen was allegedly accompanied by demands for tariff and non-tariff protection. In Jamaica, the privatization of the telephone company included a 25-year exclusive monopoly on international long-distance telephone services.

economies such as the European Union describe the general conditions for granting exemptions, others tend to be more specific by listing particular sectors or activities such as Canada and the United States (see Annexure I). Nonetheless, the economic activities that are generally granted or eligible for exemptions fall into at least four types of categories:

- Exemptions aimed at balancing unequal economic or bargaining power,
- Exemptions aimed at addressing information, transaction costs, and 'collective action' problems,
- Exemptions that reduce risk and uncertainty, and
- Special sector or interest group demands.

Balancing Unequal Economic or Bargaining Power

Collective Bargaining

Several jurisdictions exempt collective bargaining activities of workers to form unions or group together to negotiate wages and other employment conditions. Such an exemption is aimed at counter- balancing the superior economic power and bargaining position most firms/employers have vis-à-vis individual workers, and to prevent exploitation of labour. While the increased wage costs of collective bargaining activity will increase costs of production, firms will not necessarily be able to pass on these costs in the form of higher prices for the goods produced if there is effective competition prevailing in the market(s). Moreover, firms will tend to have incentives to adopt more efficient methods of production. However, some tensions with the broader objectives of competition policy can arise, if as a result of labour demands, the adoption of new machinery, technology, and organizational methods are prevented or delayed. Economic efficiency, innovation, and dynamic change may be impeded. These tensions are likely to be more prevalent in developing and transition market countries where less capital-intensive techniques and production processes are used. The collective bargaining exemption can also be abused if labour unions engage in secondary boycotts such as preventing the purchase of inputs from or selling products to firms with different labour union membership, 'feather-bedding' of jobs which require less time or workers, and/or unreasonably preventing the necessary employment of workers and independent contractors. It may be noted in passing that not in all situations are workers and employers necessarily in conflict with each other. Various economic studies point to the fact that wage rates paid by entrenched monopolists tend to be high, and make it difficult for new entrants to hire workers on a competitive cost basis. Unions are aware of this and share in the monopoly profits of the incumbent firms. Competition authorities need to be cognizant of such risks and prevent the misuse of the collective bargaining exemptions.

Agriculture, Dairy, Fishing, and Forestry

Exemptions for these sectors have been generally introduced in various countries in order to assist farmers, fishermen, and forestry workers, get 'fair' and 'stable' prices for their products and labour. The seasonal nature of these activities, the cycles in production or harvesting, and the social objectives of ensuring viable farming, fishing, and forestry communities are also among the reasons for the exemptions. In addition, with the advent of large processing firms in these sectors, the relative weak bargaining position of individuals engaged in these activities could be exploited. The formation and exemption of cooperatives and marketing boards have been seen as possible measures to correct this. The cooperatives can enable its members to bargain more effectively for higher prices for their products, and cooperate in areas such as processing, transportation, storage, standards, and marketing to exploit available synergies and efficiencies not likely to be attained on an individual basis. However, this should not be construed as implying that cooperatives are not forms of business for commercial gains. Competition law provisions should still apply if cooperative members collude amongst themselves and/or with non-members to restrain trade to monopolize markets.

Small- and Medium-Size Firms, Purchasing, or Buying Groups

The increased concentration in several types of industries has given rise to 'monopsonistic' market power by large firms. This can be countered by permitting the formation of purchasing or buying groups, which generally consist of small- and medium-sized firms. Under such arrangements, the members can have countervailing bargaining power and obtain lower prices. By consolidating purchasing decisions, transaction costs of doing business as well as potential economies of scale and scope in purchasing by the buying firms, and also in production by the sellers, could be exploited. For these reasons, purchasing or buying groups do not necessarily contravene competition law provisions unless they are used as a vehicle to engage in collusion and other anticompetitive business practices in downstream markets.

Addressing Information, Transaction Costs, and 'Collective Action' Problems

Collection and Exchange of Statistics, Credit Information, Development and Adoption of Standards

Information is an important factor in facilitating efficient trade and exchange. So is the development, adoption, and marketing of products of given standards of size, quality, and other such attributes. Without information, higher costs of doing business, mistakes, and unnecessary risk and uncertainty can occur. The lack of standardization can adversely affect interchangeability in use of products, economies of scale and scope, and expanding the market demand. There are few if any incentives for individual firms to engage in such activities, which serve the common good, because of high individual costs and 'free-rider' problems. Exempting trade associations and firms engaged in collecting and disseminating relevant information, and promoting standards, with the proviso that they will not result in the violation of the other provisions of competition law, can thus serve to enhance economic efficiency and consumer welfare.

Intellectual Property Rights (IPR)

The exemption accorded to intellectual property rights (IPR) is one of the more complex areas of competition law and policy. Protecting and conferring statutory monopoly rights over patent, trademark, and copyright products, is aimed at creating not only incentives for inventive activity but also for the early disclosure of inventions, and the diffusion of new ideas, products, and production methods. Through such incentives, technological change and progress can be fostered and can result in dynamic economic efficiencies. However, a careful balance has to be struck. Since exemptions in this area grant statutory monopoly rights to firms over the IPR-protected product(s), and exclude coverage of such matters as the prices that can be charged, the licensing of the product, geographic markets, and exclusive dealing, the firms can potentially abuse their dominant market position. In such cases, provisions need to be in place for withdrawing or limiting the exemptions. Many jurisdictions have published guidelines and legal provisions that delineate permissible and prohibited practices under the competition law.[7]

[7] See UNCTAD (1996) ibid., and the UNCTAD secretariat report 'Competition Policy and the Exercise of Intellectual Property Rights' (TD/B/COM.2/CLP/22) for further discussion of IPR exemptions.

Learned Professions

Exemptions for various professional occupations such as law, medicine, and accounting, are granted on the grounds of ensuring qualified and ethical services. However, experience demonstrates that professional bodies frequently limit competition by erecting barriers to entry such as setting preferential standards and qualifications, preventing even informational advertising, and fixing fees. Often, self-regulation results in setting higher standards than are necessary. Given that most professional services are non-tradeable and in the case of medical services, entail non-discretionary expenditures, the consumer welfare consequences can be quite significant. Except for ensuring minimal qualifications and standards of services, exemptions for professional bodies are not justifiable on economic grounds.

Exemptions that Reduce Risk and Uncertainty

Insurance, Investment Brokerage, and Banking Services

The exemptions granted for underwriting insurance and securities, and other selected activities of financial institutions such as consortium lending, are granted so as to reduce risk and uncertainty. However, these exemptions do not extend to pricing of insurance or security brokerage services, or to setting of interest rates and service charges by banks. Although in many jurisdictions, financial institutions are completely exempted from the purview of competition legislation on the arguments of 'systemic stability' or 'specialized nature of the industry', there are no sound economic reasons for doing so. Given the central role played by financial intermediation, savings, and investment in the economic development process, it is important to ensure a competitive financial services industry.

R&D Cooperatives

R&D activity can be highly uncertain, risky, and require large investments over extended periods of time. Moreover, such activity, essential for technological progress and economic development, may not take place if firms fear antitrust actions against cooperative R&D joint ventures. Exemptions for such type of R&D activities are therefore, generally speaking, justifiable. Cooperation and competition between firms are not necessarily in conflict with each other. In several industries such as pharmaceuticals and electronics, firms cooperate in R&D but compete vigorously against each other in the pricing and sale of their respective products. In most instances, the exemptions are time-limited and necessary only as long as the cooperative or joint venture activity is envisaged. As in other situations, the exemptions can be withdrawn and member firms be prosecuted if the R&D cooperative has served to engage in illegal activities in violation of the competition laws.

Special Sectors and Interest Group Demands

In a number of jurisdictions, exemptions are granted for 'special' sectors such as energy, liner shipping, air, trucking, professional sports, small business, and government enterprises. In most of these cases there are no credible economic bases for exempting these sectors or types of economic activities from competitive pressures. This view also holds for many 'natural monopolies', which, while being regulated by separate bodies, are insulated from or adopt different principles in the application of competition law. Recently, for example, in an investigation of 'Abuse of Dominant Market Position', the Indian Ministry of Railways advanced a claim that running of the railways was a 'sovereign function' and therefore not subject to the Competition Act. However, the claim was rejected by the Delhi Court which noted that in a welfare state, the state carries out many activities through what may be monopolies but that does not make them sovereign. Except for administration of justice, maintenance of law and order, etc., that are considered as inalienable functions of government, in other areas such as providing cheap transport for people and goods, which amounts to carrying on a business activity by the state, does not convert it into a sovereign body. Claims have been advanced by other enterprises and ministries such as Coal India Ltd and the Ministry of Telecommunications among others.

Developments in technology, organizational methods, and applied economics, suggest alternative pro-competition approaches towards these sectors are feasible. For example, privatization, deregulation, structural changes, and the introduction of competition in several countries in the airline, power, and telecommunication sectors have increased productivity, lowered prices, and improved services. Arguments advanced for exemptions by specific industry groups (as against generic types of business arrangements) should almost always be treated with suspicion.

Recommendations

This overview of exemptions granted to specific types of economic activities and sectors under the competition laws of various countries suggests that there are more similarities than differences between jurisdictions. In almost all of the economies reviewed, the competition laws apply to both public and private sector enterprises, and exempt areas that are covered by other government legislation and regulations. India's Competition Act (2002) in essence adopts a similar approach though as yet no sectors are explicitly exempted.

Exemptions from the application of competition laws may be justified on various grounds such as reducing risk and uncertainty, facilitating innovation, collection and dissemination of information, and counterbalancing unequal bargaining power. However, as governments need to respond to such needs, it may be useful to adopt certain basic procedures and principles in the granting of exemptions. In this regard, it is suggested that:

1. Exemptions should be granted on a limited-time basis with a 'sun-set' clause and provisions for periodic review.
2. Review of exemptions should include analysis of their impact on economic efficiency and consumer welfare, and in a cost-benefit framework identify the 'winners' and 'losers', and whether indeed there are overriding benefits that serve the consumer or broader economic interests.
3. Exemptions should be granted after public hearings with participation of the interested and affected parties.
4. Exemptions should be least restrictive of competition. In many areas, where particular exemptions and/or exceptions are granted, such as infrastructure industry dealing with power, telecommunications, and transportation; alternative, less anticompetitive approaches are feasible.
5. Exemptions should be generic in nature, relating to types of economic activities or arrangements, and be less industry- or sector-specific.

The application of these principles will tend to avoid rent-seeking behaviour and limit the number, nature, and scope of the exemptions and exceptions, and the differential application of competition law-policy. It will also ensure that the procedures for granting exemptions and exceptions are more accountable and transparent, and foster greater policy and economic coherence.

Annexure I

Exemptions and Exceptions

Selected Country-Specific Examples

Many competition laws either exempt specific sectors and/or types of economic activity, and/or have provisions for the granting of such exemptions in given situations. It is worth observing that there generally tend to be fewer exemptions in countries which have recently adopted competition laws (mainly developing and transition market economies) as compared with more industrialized nations. However, this could be reflective of the fact that in many of the less-developed countries, effective implementation of competition law has yet to take place. Also various businesses are likely to be still unaware of the potential impact competition law can have on their economic activities, and lobbying for exclusions from the application of competition law has yet to take place. In more advanced industrial countries, exemptions granted from competition law have generally tended to evolve and expand over time due to specific issues and cases confronted in the application of the law, and the resulting lobbying by businesses. In addition to legal and economic reasons, various historical, cultural, and political factors have also played a role.

A brief review of different competition laws suggests that a wide range of exemptions and exceptions have been granted by various jurisdictions. The most common exemptions relate to labour, agriculture, and transportation, mainly for reasons discussed earlier. There are also exclusions from competition law in sectors such as financial services, energy, telecommunications (including postal services), and media/publishing. In some of these latter cases, different sector-specific laws containing provisions relating to competition matters such as prices, entry, and ownership restrictions have been adopted. These are discussed in greater detail later in the chapter.

Industrialized Country Competition Laws

Canada and the United States were among the first nations to enact specific competition legislation dealing with anticompetitive business practices (in 1889 and 1890, respectively). Over time, the scope of the competition laws in these two countries has been broadened significantly and with it special exemptions have been carved out in response to changing economic conditions and/or lobbying by special interest groups. For example, in Canada, as late as 1976, the competition law provisions did not apply to the services sector of the economy, or to Crown (state-owned) corporations. Until the competition law was amended, regulations governing the activities of commercial banks, airlines, professional bodies (such as lawyers, doctors, accountants), and infrastructure services (such as electricity and telephone) did not explicitly address competition concerns. In sectors such as airlines and commercial banks, separate provisions have been adopted in enabling legislation.

As the law stands in Canada, the provisions of the Competition Act have exemptions for:

- collective bargaining which permits employees to form unions or groups to negotiate wages, and other conditions of employment;

- associations of fishermen to negotiate terms regarding buying and processing of fish; and travel agents to negotiate prices and commissions paid for domestic flights (to counter the monopoly or near-monopoly position of the domestic airline);
- underwriting of insurance and securities;
- amateur sport to form leagues, and teams.

Provisions also exist for trade associations and business firms to exchange statistics, develop product standards, define terminology, engage in cooperative R&D, restrict advertising expenditures, adopt common weights and measures, packaging, etc.

In addition, with notification and prior clearance, firms are permitted to form export cartels with the objective of increasing exports, or also enter into specialization and rationalization agreements in order to achieve economic efficiency.

In all the aforementioned areas, the exemptions only apply if they do not lead to violation of other provisions of the law. For example, if the trade association exchanges statistics that allows price fixing agreements amongst its members, it would be considered illegal use of the exemption and the firms would be subject to prosecution under the relevant provisions of the law.

Limited exemptions are also provided for professional sports, financial institutions' activities, and products covered by intellectual property laws (patents, copyrights, and trademarks). However, as in the case of the aforementioned examples, these exemptions cannot be used to violate specific provisions of the Competition Act. For example, financial institutions cannot get together and set the deposit/loan interest rates and other service charges to customers (except for transactions outside Canada); professional sports organizations cannot impose unreasonable terms and conditions or limit the opportunities of individual players, but can form leagues and enter into franchise agreements that may be necessary to maintain reasonable balance among teams, and participate in international agreements to that effect. In a similar vein, the statutory monopoly position granted to products under the patent law may be withdrawn or amended if a firm engages in illegal business practices.

Economic activities permitted or covered by regulations/laws of other federal and provincial bodies (namely, state actions) are also generally exempt from the application of competition law. Competition law does not take precedence over other government-enacted legislation. However, the exemption(s) is subject to the interpretation as to whether or not the practices in question are or were intended to be specifically permitted. For example, if professional bodies such as lawyers, accountants, et al., are permitted to engage in self-regulation of their business affairs, the enabling law delegating this authority must be clear that it permits setting of fees, restricting entry, and the like. If this is not the case, the competition law provisions apply, and there is no protection accorded to illegal business practices.

The basic thrust of these exemptions is to facilitate legitimate exchange of information, reduce risk, counter-balance uneven bargaining or economic power, permit cooperation, and foster innovation so that the market can function better and more efficiently.

Canada's competition law also contained an 'exception' for M&A which may result in substantial lessening of competition but also have *offsetting* economic efficiencies, and/or factors such as including increase in the real value of exports, that may benefit the economy as a whole.

In the United States, while the Sherman Act (1890), Clayton Act (1914), and other legislation do not list specific sectors or economic activities, the exemptions have been defined over time by court and congressional actions. The areas cover agriculture, defence mobilization, energy, export trade associations, government enterprises, insurance, labour, learned professions, marine insurance, newspaper joint operations, resale price maintenance, small business concerns, sports, state actions, transportation by air, ocean, and surface. In addition, various measures, regulations and laws permit the formation of trade associations, exchange of statistics, development of product standards, and cooperation in R&D (the latter under the National Research Cooperative Act, 1984). Exemptions are also provided for selected aspects of IPR dealing with products covered by patents, copyrights, and trademarks. In addition, actions by State governments may be immune from federal antitrust laws if there are specific provisions in state laws and regulations that permit such actions. In a recent case, *FTC* v. *Phoebe Putney* (2013), the US Supreme Court ruled that the acquisition of a hospital in Georgia which post-merger would have resulted in 86% market share in the provision of acute-care hospital services was not subject to state action immunity as the State had not clearly articulated and affirmatively expressed a policy allowing the hospital authority to make acquisitions that substantially lessen competition.

A report of the United States Department of Justice published in 1977 identified 16 separate areas which were exempted from the antitrust laws, covering such diverse economic activities as agriculture, energy, transportation, banking and insurance, newspapers, learned professions, and baseball. While the overall 'patchwork' of exemptions was recognized as arising from 'history and political chance', in many areas the report questioned their continued justification and credibility. In most cases the exemptions were found to have a 'special interest flavour ... and tends to be of direct concern only to the interests protected by it from competition that would otherwise exist'.[8]

The issues relating to immunities and exemptions from US antitrust laws was revisited by the United States Antitrust Modernization Commission's Report (2007).[9] The Report generally dis-favoured immunities and exemptions and called for their re-evaluation. It also recommended creation of public record on any existing or proposed immunity being considered by Congress, consultation with the Federal Trade Commission and the Department of Justice, and other measures for increased transparency and accountability.

A detailed discussion of all the exemptions under United States antitrust policy falls outside of the scope of this chapter.[10] However, the reasons for some of the exemptions that appear unique to the United States are discussed ahead.

Newspaper Joint Operating Arrangements

'Pluralism' and diversity of views is a hallmark of a well-functioning democracy, and in the United States, various laws and regulations have been instituted to prevent undue concentration in the media industry. M&A between and amongst newspaper publishers and broadcast companies are scrutinized not only under the antitrust laws but also under laws and regulations dealing with television and radio. However, in 1970, the Newspaper Preservation Act was passed which exempted certain joint operations of newspapers, in order to foster the survival of (generally smaller) newspapers in economic distress by permitting the combination of printing and other business operations while maintaining independent editorial and reportage functions. It should be noted, however, that this exemption does not extend to pricing of newspapers, advertising rates, distribution, and other such activities where antitrust law provisions would normally apply. Recently, there have been various proposals, mainly by large conglomerate firms, to change the cross-media ownership restrictions, especially in larger markets.

Professional (Baseball) Sports and Broadcasting

A Supreme Court decision during the 1920s, ruled that professional baseball did not fall within the scope of the federal antitrust laws as it was not 'trade

[8] See 'Report of the Task Group on Antitrust Immunities', US Department of Justice, January 1977. Quotes are from pp. 4–8.

[9] See www.govinfo.library.unt.edu/amc/.

[10] Moreover, this ground has already been covered by the Department of Justice's Report supra, n. 8.

or commerce' and the inter-state nature of ball games and movement of ball clubs/players was merely an incidental part of the sport. Other professional sports such as football and basketball are similarly exempted by this court interpretation. During the 1960s, The Sports Broadcasting Act granted antitrust immunity to certain joint agreements among professional football, baseball, basketball, and hockey leagues concerning the selling of rights for the telecasting of their games. Critics have questioned these exemptions for which there are no cogent economic arguments or evidence presented. In recent years, the congressional authorities have raised the issue of removing these exemptions, especially during the strike by baseball players over salaries (which tend to be very high by any comparative standard), share of stadium gate and broadcasting revenues, and when local team games are 'blacked-out' from television.

Horizontal Mergers and Acquisitions

The United States antitrust enforcement policies allow for a 'defence' (exceptions) to be made for horizontal M&A, which while resulting in substantial lessening of competition have significant efficiency gains that cannot be realized otherwise through less anticompetitive means such as a joint venture. The United States enforcement policy and court cases in this regard have interpreted this exception very strictly. Generally speaking, the merger cannot result in lower output and the efficiency gains must not only be credible but of a magnitude that prices are not likely to increase. Moreover, the efficiency gains must be passed on to the consumer in the form of lower prices and/or improved quality and choices.[11] Till date, there has been no case where the efficiency defence in an M&A transaction has been accepted.[12]

The European Union, under Article 81(3) of the Treaty of Rome can grant exemptions to certain agreements and practices if they have significant countervailing benefits, either on their individual merit or through the application of a 'block exemption'. A block exemption relates to certain categories

[11] See Federal Trade Commission and Antitrust Division, Department of Justice: 'Horizontal Merger Enforcement Guidelines' (1997) which can be downloaded from the website www.usdoj.gov or www.ftc.gov.

[12] The 'efficiency defence' came into play in a recent case: *FTC* v. *H.J. Heinz Co.* et al. (US Court of Appeals, District of Columbia, 2001) relating to the acquisition of another baby food manufacturing company, namely Beech-Nut. However, while the lower court refused the FTC's request for a preliminary injunction against the merger, and significant efficiencies arising from the merger were identified, the appeals court disallowed the merger on competition grounds. Available at www.ftc.gov/ftc/antitrust and www.11.georgetown.edu/Fed-Ct/dc/opinions for further information.

of agreements and to agreements in specified sectors. Only the European Commission can issue exemptions, which must be notified for clearance (except in the case of those matters covered by block exemptions). If an agreement or practice is not notified and authorized, it is subject to investigation and prosecution under the competition provisions of the Treaty.

Individual Exemptions

There are two positive and two negative conditions that must be met in order for an individual exemption to be granted.

The positive conditions require that the agreement:

- contribute to improving the production or distribution of goods or to promoting technical or economic progress; and
- allow consumers a fair share of the resulting benefits.

The negative conditions are that the agreement:

- not impose restrictions on firms that are not indispensable to the attainment of the aforementioned objectives; or
- give rise to the possible elimination of competition in a substantial part of the market of the products in question.

Block Exemptions

The European Commission has issued a series of block exemptions for certain types of business practices and economic sectors in order to reduce the number of notifications, and the regulatory burden imposed on both the Commission staff and business firms. The block exemptions that have been granted cover exclusive distribution and purchasing arrangements, R&D cooperatives, patent and know-how licensing, and specialization agreements.

In each of the exempt areas, clauses are listed that define what may be legally incorporated or prohibited in the agreements. For example, a joint-venture agreement between firms may contain a 'non-competition clause' if it is 'indispensable' to the success of the venture, otherwise it may be viewed as collusion to limit competition. Similarly, a block exemption may permit territorial restrictions of sales by firms for a period of time but not allow any other restrictions of competition.

The Commission has issued a number of exemptions covering transportation (road, inland waterways, air, and marine), insurance, and agricultural sectors, and also computer reservation systems and motor vehicle distribution and licensing. Export cartels are also exempted insofar as they do not restrict exports and/or competition in the common market.

In contrast to the Canadian and United States approach, where exemptions are based either on specific laws and legal provisions, and/or court rulings, the European Commission approach towards granting exemptions is through administrative actions. The exemptions can be time-bound and can be reviewed and amended by the Commission itself. The European Union does not have provisions for granting exceptions to M&A transactions that may result in dominance on the grounds of economic efficiencies.

The United Kingdom's Competition Act (1998) has provisions for granting exemptions on similar basis as contained in Article 81(3) of the Treaty of Rome. The Director General of Fair Trading may also impose conditions on a parallel exemption or vary or cancel the parallel exemptions that may be granted by the European Commission. The exemptions are time-limited, and can have effect earlier than the date on which it is granted.

The provisions of UK's Competition Act apply to public bodies or undertakings insofar as they engage in commercial economic activities. Enterprises or sectors covered by specific legislation may not be subject to the provisions of the Competition Act if certain activities are explicitly permitted which may tend to restrict competition. However, the Director General may make representations or call for the review and amendment of such laws in the interest of promoting competition. In this connection, it is noteworthy that even though the recently privatized and deregulated economic activities such as the provision of water, power, and telecommunications services are subject to oversight by different regulatory bodies, the provisions of the Competition Act still apply. The Competition Act continues to exempt certain medicaments and books from the resale price maintenance (RPM) provisions. The law does not contain an exception for mergers on efficiency grounds. However, the Minister of Trade and Industry may override the decision of the competition authority if an M&A transaction is considered to be in the public interest.

Australia's competition legislation: The Competition and Consumer Act (CCA) provides the Australian Competition and Consumer Council (ACCC) extensive powers for maintaining and promoting competition. Aside from the exemptions granted in areas similar to those prevailing in many other countries such as international liner cargo shipping, collective bargaining agreements, etc., the ACCC has extensive oversight responsibilities for competition matters in the provision of telecommunication and other infrastructure services, which as noted earlier, do not always fall under competition laws of other jurisdictions. The application of the Act has been extended to cover certain operations of the previously exempted government's postal services monopoly.

Some 'Commonwealth'/territory Acts permit conduct that would normally contravene the CCA, but may be permitted if it is specifically authorized under those other Acts. The CCA is otherwise generally binding on Crown (government) agents. A distinguishing feature of Australia's competition regime is that the ACCC also has oversight of competition matters in various infrastructure services such as telecommunications, electricity, etc. In other words, common competition principles apply whereas in many other jurisdictions, there are sector-specific laws and regulations for the provision of such services.

Japan's Antimonopoly Act (namely Act on Prohibition of Private Monopolization and Maintenance of Fair Trade) applies to all industries. However, it has exemptions covering natural monopolies/infrastructure industries relating to '... railways, electricity, gas, or any other business constituting a monopoly by the inherent nature of the said business' (Article 21) and IPR and cooperatives for agricultural and consumer products that are governed by other laws or regulations. In addition, there are provisions for exempting cartels for exports, depressed industries, and small- and medium-sized enterprises. Japan also exempts some pharmaceutical and cosmetic items from the prohibition of the resale price maintenance provisions. The exemptions require notification and authorization by Japan's Fair Trade Commission (JFTC) or the relevant authorities established under other laws. The cartels currently exempted from the Antimonopoly Act are being reviewed by the relevant ministries and agencies, from the stand-point of abolishing them in principle, under Japan's regulatory reform programme. With respect to M&A transactions, Japan's competition law-policy does not contain an efficiency exception.

Developing and Transition Market Economies' Laws

Since the 1990s, more than 40 developing and transition market economies have revised or adopted competition laws for the first time. A synoptic overview of the nature and scope of the laws and the exempt areas specified, in a selected sample of these countries is presented ahead.[13]

Algeria and Morocco: In both these countries the competition laws apply to all spheres of economic activity in both the private and public sectors. In Algeria, the Competition Board may not take action against agreements that are not designed to hamper free competition and/or constitute a violation

[13] This material is drawn from different issues of a recurrent publication of the UNCTAD secretariat entitled the 'Handbook on Competition Legislation' which contains the texts of, and commentaries upon, competition legislation provided by UNCTAD Member States.

of other provisions of the law. This would cover agreements relating to professional bodies, exchange of information, cooperatives, trade associations, and the like. Morocco has a similar general approach in defining the scope of application of its legislation. However, natural monopolies established under other laws and regulations, including areas subject to price controls are exempt. Also special situations requiring government interventions due to natural or other crises (both domestic and international) are exempt for a period up to six months. Such interventions must be justified and authorized by the Competition Council.

Bulgaria, Croatia, Czech Republic, Lithuania, Poland, Romania, Slovakia, and Ukraine: These former centrally planned economies have, in varying degrees, similar approaches towards competition policy, which in some cases explicitly reflect Articles 85 and 86 of the Treaty of Rome. For example, these clauses have been incorporated in Croatian Competition Law. The laws apply to all enterprises with provisions for granting exemptions for specific types of activities or matters covered by other legislation. However, the Bulgarian law states that the Law on Protection of Competition is neither subordinated to, nor limited by, intergovernmental agreements. Hungary's competition law, which also extends to state enterprises and regulated industries, requires in the instance of agricultural products, the Minister of Agriculture to ensure that the economic advantages outweigh the disadvantages resulting from restrictive practices. Subject to market share thresholds, exemptions are also given to temporary acquisitions of control or ownership by financial institutions, insurance companies, financial holdings, and investment companies or property managing organizations. The Czech Republic, Lithuania, Poland, Romania, Slovakia, and Ukraine tend to more generally exempt economic activities mandated by other laws and regulations.

Chile, Colombia and Venezuela: Chile's Antimonopoly Law (Decree-Law No. 211, 1973) applies to all kinds of goods and services, without exception, regardless of the entities being large, small, or medium-sized enterprises in the private or public sector. However, restrictions maintained and authorized by pre-existing laws on aspects of business in areas such as banking services, intellectual and industrial property, production and trade in saltpetre, iodine, copper, petroleum, transport, charting, and coastal traffic continue to be respected. Colombia's competition law provisions (Decree no. 2153, 1992), similarly apply to all commercial economic activity, without prejudice to the powers assigned in current legislation to other authorities. In this respect, exemptions are provided for R&D cooperatives, public infrastructure services, and the financial sector, among others. In addition, Colombia's competition law allows for exceptions to be made for M&A that may have overriding efficiency and other public interest benefits. Venezuela's competition law also applies to all sectors and enterprises in the economy. As in other jurisdictions, it contains provisions for authorizing exemptions but requires that they benefit consumers or users, and be least restrictive of competition. Under Venezuela's law, the president of the Republic and/or the Ministerial Council can, after hearing representations made by the superintendent for the Defense of Free Competition, override or authorize a particular business practice.

The approach towards exemptions in several other developing countries such as *Ivory Coast, Jamaica, South Africa, Turkey, and Zambia, among others* surveyed for this chapter tend to be very similar. In essence, economic activities or arrangements permitted under other enabling laws and regulations are largely exempt, as are areas such as collective bargaining, agricultural marketing cooperatives, liner shipping, insurance and other financial sector activity, and export cartels.

India's Competition Act (2002, as amended): Section 54 specifies the Central Government's power to exempt:

54. The Central Government may, by notification, exempt from application of this Act, or any provision thereof, and for such period as it may specify in such notification—

any class of enterprises if such exemption is necessary in the interest of security of the State or public interest;

any practice or agreement arising out of and in accordance with any obligation assumed by India under any treaty, agreement, or convention with any other country or countries;

any enterprise which performs a sovereign function on behalf of the Central Government or a State Government:

Provided that in case an enterprise is engaged in any activity including the activity relatable to the sovereign functions of the Government, the Central Government may grant exemption only in respect of activity relatable to the sovereign functions.

In addition, Section 62 refers to the application of other laws not being barred (implying differential application of competition law-policy):

62. The provisions of this Act shall be in addition to, and not in derogation of, the provisions of any other law for the time being in force.[14]

Section 3 sub-clause 5 indicates that:

Nothing contained in this section shall restrict—

The right of any person to restrain any infringement of, or to impose reasonable conditions, as may be necessary for protecting any of his rights which have been or may be conferred upon him under—

the Copyright Act, 1957 (14 of 1957);

[14] It is not clear as to whether this provision refers only to central government laws or also to those enacted by the state governments.

the Patents Act, 1970 (39 of 1970);
the Trade and Merchandise Marks Act, 1958 (43 of 1958); or the Trade Marks Act, 1999;
the Geographical Indications of Goods (Registration and Protection) Act, 1999 (48 of 1999);
the Designs Act, 2000 (16 of 2000);
the Semi-conductor Integrated Circuits Lay-out Design act, 2000 (37 of 2000);
(ii) The right of any person to export goods from India to the extent to which the agreement relates exclusively to the production, supply, distribution or control of goods or provision of services for such export.

In essence, the approach being adopted by India is similar to that of various other countries. However, the determination of exemptions rests with the central government. The provisions relating to IPR appear to imply that the restrictions from application of the competition law provisions may be removed if the conditions imposed by firms tend to be unreasonable. However, this would presumably have to be determined through judicial interpretation as to what constitutes to be reasonable or unreasonable. The Competition Act itself does not define this. Also, at this point in time, the interface between the Competition Act and other laws and regulations, especially those relating to specific sectors such as telecommunication, energy, and other services have yet to be clearly delineated.

7

Competition Advocacy and Interface with Government*

Philip Lowe and Geraldine Emberger

Role of Competition Advocacy

Competition Advocacy

Competition advocacy is, together with competition law enforcement in individual infringement cases, a very important pillar relied upon by competition agencies around the world when promoting effective competition. A commonly accepted definition of competition advocacy is that it includes all activities of a competition agency that are intended to promote competition apart from those that involve enforcement of the competition law.[1] Competition advocacy in broad terms can be understood to comprise all activities pursued by competition authorities to spread a competition culture. The addressees of advocacy measures can be public stakeholders, like legislators, regulators, or judges but also the business and legal community or the public at large.

* Reproduced from 'Competition Advocacy and Interface with Government', published in Dhall, V. (ed.). 2007. *Competition Law Today: Concepts, Issues, and the Law in Practice* (1st ed.), Oxford University Press, New Delhi.

[1] See ICN Report 'Advocacy and Competition Policy', 2002, available at http://www.internationalcompetitionnetwork.org/.

The content of competition advocacy measures varies depending on the legal and administrative framework and the degree of importance policy makers attach to the benefits of a sound competition policy at large. It also varies according to the concrete objective pursued. One objective can, for example, consist in the raising of general awareness of competition issues with regulators, academia, the judiciary, and other public and private stakeholders. Another objective can be the participation of competition agencies in the formulation of a country's economic policies, which may affect competitive market structures, business conduct, and economic performance at large.

Depending on the objectives, competition advocacy measures may take the form of publications of guidance aimed at improving the understanding and acceptance of the competition rules by the addressees. They may further consist in the active involvement of competition agencies in the regulatory impact assessment (RIA) process leading to the adoption of new laws and regulations or in the involvement of competition agencies in hearings before sector regulators or parliamentary committees, or as amicus curiae in court proceedings.

Interface between Advocacy and Competition Law Enforcement

Advocacy and enforcement have a common aim, that is, to ensure that competition is not distorted. They are complementary since fighting private restrictions can only be successful when supported by advocacy removing or preventing public restrictions. By way of example, pursuing price fixing by private operators can only be effective in the long term if the regulatory framework does not facilitate this kind of behaviour. Similarly, a competition authority may succeed in using enforcement to increase competition in a market. But if industry participants succeed in lobbying policy makers, inducing them to introduce restrictive laws, these efforts will be frustrated in the long run. The removal of public barriers to competition is thus at least as important as the elimination of private barriers created by companies.

Advocacy and enforcement are further, mutually enhancing activities. The experience and market knowledge obtained by a competition agency through the handling of merger or antitrust cases may support its advocacy efforts and make them more credible.[2] In some cases concurrent enforcement action may

[2] The sector know-how gained in large merger cases is particularly relevant in this respect. Competition authorities have to analyse competition impacts ex ante, which is also required in the assessment of draft legislation.

lead policy makers to abstain from restricting competition through regulatory or administrative intervention[3] or to remove restrictive regulations.[4]

Why Competition Advocacy Is So Important

It is widely recognized that the removal of competition restrictions created by regulation and legislation is at least as important as the removal of private restrictions, particularly in regulated sectors. As Tim Muris, the former chairman of the FTC, puts it, '[a]ttempting to protect competition by focusing solely on private restraints is like trying to stop the flow of water at a fork in a stream by blocking only one of the channels'.[5]

The most evident example demonstrating the importance of competition advocacy is the process of liberalization experienced by developing and developed countries all over the world. The gradual opening to competition of traditionally regulated sectors, which often used to be monopolized and where incumbents often retain a fair degree of market power, revealed the need to also adapt the regulatory framework governing the different sectors (for example, energy, telecom, public transport, and so on). The experience of liberalization shows that it is harder to remove competitive restrictions than avoiding them from the outset, especially if businesses benefiting from them defend their well-established privileges. Reforms usually take a long time to be implemented. Public restrictions can thus even be more harmful than private ones.

Public restrictions on competition occur not only in transition economies and developing countries but also in established market economies. Of particular concern are over regulated markets with restrictions on competition which are disproportionate in that their cost is not outweighed by the benefits

[3] One example is the merger between the Spanish bank, Banco Santander and A. Champalimaud (Case COMP/M.1724) which was blocked by the Portuguese government although it had been approved under the EC merger rules. After the European Commission opened an accelerated infringement procedure against Portugal before the European Court of Justice, the Portuguese government revoked its earlier decision.

[4] See, for example, the decision of the European Commission on a German postal law of 2004 discriminating against commercial mail preparation providers and preventing them from competing effectively. The German government has to report to the Commission on the measures taken to end the competition law infringement; see Decision of the Commission of 20 October 2004 in case COMP/38.745 BdKEP/ Germany.

[5] See remarks of Tim Muris before the Fordham Annual Conference on 24 October 2003.

they bring about. Competition advocacy is a core instrument to address those types of restrictions and to promote competitive markets.

This chapter therefore focuses in particular on competition advocacy measures, which are directed towards promoting competition-friendly legislation with public stakeholders, mainly regulators and legislators, at international, regional, and national level. These measures mainly target economic legislation having an important impact on the behaviour of businesses or on market structures. This chapter next deals with the interface between competition and regulation and then looks into ways of integrating competition assessment in the drafting of economic regulation and solutions proposed at international and national level. Finally, it provides an overview of recent developments at EU level, in particular the competition test which has been introduced in the 2005 Impact Assessment Guidelines applied to Community (EC) legislation. Chapter VI tries to draw some conclusions on the crucial elements of successful advocacy work as carried out by competition agencies.

Interface between Regulation and Competition

How Regulation Can Influence Competition

There are several ways how regulation can impact competition.[6] First, regulation can contradict competition policy objectives if it encourages or even requires conduct, or establish conditions contrary to competition law principles. For example, regulations may permit price coordination or require territorial market division.[7] Second, regulation can be designed as to substitute for competition policy. This is, for example, the case in respect to natural monopolies, where regulation is directed towards controlling market power directly by setting price caps or controlling access to infrastructure. This kind of public intervention may be justified at a certain moment and later on become obsolete due, for example, to technological change or to changes in the market structure.

Third, regulation can incorporate competition law and policy concepts, for example, by introducing rules and standards of fair competition or tendering

[6] The different scenarios are also described in a submission by UNCTAD of 31 January 2003 to the OECD Global Forum on Competition; see page 8 of document CCNM/GF/COMP/WD(2003)31.

[7] See, for example, certain elements of the Common Market Organisations (CMOs) introduced at EC level for agricultural products such as sugar or tobacco, containing sales quota and price restrictions, thus eliminating competition.

rules to ensure competitive bidding.[8] Fourth, regulation can use competition institutions' methods, for example, by using incentive-based instead of prescriptive methods, or relying on the competitive dynamics of the market, by using tradeable emissions rights or tax incentives. These two forms are often combined in one regulation. While the former (for example, bidding rules) prescribes a certain behaviour, which is assumed to increase competition or avoid undue restrictions,[9] the latter (for example, emissions trading) introduces mechanisms creating an economic incentive for the industry to obtain the legislative objective pursued (for example, the incentive to reduce greenhouse gas emissions in order to sell unused allowances on the market, generating competitive—in this case financial—advantages).

Potential Conflicts between Competition and Regulation

Conflicts usually arise if regulation directly or indirectly restricts competition in the market. The most evident kind of restriction is represented by direct restrictions or even eliminations of competition, which may arise if regulations exempt a whole sector from the application of the competition rules. Examples are rules excluding the defence industry from the application of the competition regime for reasons of national security or rules imposing retail price maintenance. A further prominent example is that of professional services, such as services provided by architects, lawyers, notaries, engineers, and so on. In a large number of countries such professional services are subject to regulations such as fee scales and rules limiting inter-professional competition. Some (self) regulations, for example, reserve real estate transactions or out-of-court legal advice to members of the bar, either ban all forms of comparative advertising or prohibit advertising by certain professions. Those rules may discriminate against new entrants, who cannot use certain important marketing tools to introduce their products.[10]

Second, in addition to direct restrictions, there are rules which indirectly restrict competition by determining certain parameters of the competitive

[8] One problem which may arise with broad competition principles (for example, in Commission directives) is that different regulators may apply different standards, which lead to discrimination of certain market players.

[9] For example, in a bidding process tendering rules seek to ensure that all viable offers are considered and that the award decision is based on objective, non-discriminatory, and transparent principles.

[10] Although aimed at protecting consumers, the net effect may be a loss in consumer welfare, if consumers cannot easily compare different offers or if they are deprived of alternative choices.

process, for example, by setting minimum quality standards for certain products or services. These rules may reduce the degree of differentiation between suppliers and decrease their incentives to compete vigorously as competitors align their offer towards the minimum quality. Third, the regulatory framework may also contain provisions allowing state subsidies which distort competition.

Potential Adverse Effects of Conflicts

The adverse effects resulting from the conflicts between competition and regulation as described above may take various forms. Restrictive regulation may, for example, cause higher market concentration, for example, if it leads to asymmetric costs faced by businesses leading to the exit of certain players. Regulation may also increase entry or exit costs with the effect that new entrants may take too long to achieve the minimum efficient scale to operate on the market. Furthermore, certain types of regulation may reduce the vigour of competition or even induce competitors to collude, for example, through increased transparency. National regulation may also grant 'advantages' to certain companies, which may not legally qualify as State aid, but have the same effect. Finally, regulation may reduce consumers' or suppliers' choice, for example, by rising switching costs or by affecting innovation, or diminish the offer of new products, for example, by too stringent product standards.

Addressing the Adverse Effects

One particular effective means to influence economic regulation and legislation is the participation of competition authorities in the drafting of legislative proposals, in particular through RIA. This form of competition advocacy is sometimes also referred to as 'competition screening'. As part of their screening activities competition agencies typically provide comments, opinions, and suggestions on draft bills or the conditions of projects. The aim of competition screening is not to prevent regulation but to avoid or mitigate the effects of unnecessary or excessive restrictions of competition.

The need to screen regulation as to its impact on competition has been widely discussed at the international level. Some of the research carried out on this topic by international organizations and networks concerned with competition policy will be summarized in the following section.

Competition Screening: Work Achieved Internationally

OECD

The OECD Council, on 15 March 2005, adopted the 'OECD Guiding Principles on Regulatory Quality and Performance',[11] replacing the 1997 Recommendations.[12] They promote some very essential principles on the relationship between regulatory and competition policy. The guidelines start by recommending that new and existing regulation should be systematically reviewed with reference to competition and that RIAs should be used to assess the effects of regulation on competition objectives and market openness. The guidelines further suggest that competition authorities be provided with the authority and capacity to advocate reform, and support public awareness of the role and benefits of competition. It further advises to design regulations in all sectors as to stimulate competition and that policy makers at all levels join forces internationally to eliminate unnecessary regulatory barriers to trade and investment. Finally, it suggests that non-regulatory policies (mainly subsidies) be reviewed and adjusted if they unnecessarily distort competition.

These principles are of a general nature and do not contain any specific indications or guidance for governments and regulators as to their implementation in practice. However, they can be seen as an important basis for further progress in the field of competition advocacy, and screening in particular. The content of these principles is, for example, reflected in some key policy documents recently drafted by the European Community while reviewing its Competitiveness and Growth Agenda,[13] such as the Commission's 'Communication on Better Regulation' of 16 March 2005 or the 'Broad

[11] See http://www.oecd.org/dataoecd/24/6/34976533.pdf.

[12] OECD Ministers requested in 1995 that the OECD examine the significance, direction, and means of reform in regulatory regimes in member countries. The 1995 Recommendations for Improving the Quality of Government Regulation were the first-ever international statement of regulatory principles common to member countries. Building on this fundamental text, and broadening it to embrace market openness, competition policy, and micro-economic principles in a multidisciplinary framework, in 1997, the OECD produced a Report to Ministers on Regulatory Reform. The 1997 Report is available at http://www.oecd.org/dataoecd/17/25/2391768.pdf.

[13] The Lisbon Agenda for Growth and Jobs. Its core strategic objectives and initiatives are summarized in the 'Community Lisbon Programme: Common Actions for Growth and Employment', adopted by the Commission on 20 July 2005, available at http://europa.eu.int/growthandjobs/pdf/COM2005_330_en.pdf.

Economy and Policy Guidelines' (or 'Integrated Guidelines')[14] adopted by the Council on 12 April 2005, which are meant to govern the economic and regulatory policies at European level and at the level of the Member States of the European Union. The OECD principles are also reflected in the recently revised Impact Assessment Guidelines applying to EC legislative and policy proposals.[15]

ICN

Important research into competition screening has also been undertaken by the International Competition Network (ICN), a virtual network of competition authorities with almost 100 members around the world, which regularly exchange information and develop mechanisms of cooperation enhancing effectiveness and efficiency of competition law enforcement and policy measures. The Advocacy Working Group of the ICN at the 2002 Annual Conference in Naples presented a report concluding that 'a more systematic consultation, possibly enshrined in law as early in the process as possible, is considered by many to produce the best results. A certain degree of bindingness of the opinions issued to policy makers, enhances significantly the effectiveness of advocacy.' Another option proposed was the 'comply or explain' approach which forces policy makers to account for the reasons not to adopt the advice of the competition authority.

The work of the Advocacy WG was subsequently continued by the Capacity Building and Competition Policy Implementation subgroup (CBCPI), which two years later presented a report to the Annual Conference in Seoul on 'Competition Advocacy in Regulated Sectors: Examples of Success'.[16] The report evaluated the degree of success of specific competition advocacy initiatives in six different sectors: electricity, gas, telecommunications, railways, air services, and maritime transport. The most effective advocacy tools used by competition authorities were found to be their advice to regulators on, for example, market definition and specific competition impacts, their ability to issue binding or non-binding opinions on draft laws and to authorize

[14] See in particular, Guideline No. 8 which stipulates that 'priority be given to … selective screening of markets and regulations by competition and regulatory authorities in order to identify and remove obstacles to competition …', available at http://europa.eu.int/growthandjobs/pdf/integrated_guidelines_en.pdf.

[15] SEC(2005) 791, available at http://intracomm.sg.cec.eu.int/i/impact/index.php?lang=en&page=guidel.

[16] See http://www.internationalcompetitionnetwork.org/capacitybuild_sg4_seoul.pdf.

participants in the bidding process (for example, in the context of privatization). The Seoul report also recognizes the importance of other forms of competition advocacy with a more long-term perspective, such as the organization of seminars and workshops or regular meetings with regulators or the organization of regular staff exchanges.

UNCTAD

The UN Set of Multilaterally Agreed Equitable Principles and Rules for the Control of Restrictive Business Practices adopted by the General Assembly in 1980 is to date the only multilateral document on competition policy which contains rules on anticompetitive practices and structures and provides a cooperation framework between developing and developed countries. Its Section E contains broad principles and rules to be followed by states at national, regional, and sub-regional level. States are inter alia called upon to base their legislation primarily on the principle of competition. The UN Model Law on Competition[17] which is based on the UN Set in Chapter VII refers to the relationship between competition authorities and regulatory bodies including sector regulators. The advocacy role of competition authorities is circumscribed by their influence on the drafting of economic regulation, especially in infrastructure industries (see point 1 of Chapter VII). The Model Law recommends that such legislation be subject to an ex-ante screening by competition authorities, in particular if such proposed legislation limits the independence and liberty of action of economic agents or if it may result in restrictions of competition. The definition of competition-relevant regulation is rather broad, including all instruments used by governments to determine the behaviour of economic operators, including not only legislation but also administrative guidance and rules adopted by self-regulatory bodies (such as interest groups and professional associations) to which governments have delegated certain regulatory powers (see point 2 of Chapter VII). The definition of regulatory barriers to competition includes acts performed by governmental executive authorities or local self-government bodies giving rise to administrative barriers to entry, exclusive rights, certificates, licences, and other permits restricting the start of business operations (see point 3 of Chapter VII).

The commentary on Chapter VII of the UN Model Law concludes that the relationship between competition authorities and regulators is particularly relevant in industries such as public utilities or public services, which require government intervention to secure universal service. While

[17] See http://r0.unctad.org/en/subsites/cpolicy/docs/Modelaw04.pdf.

the principal need to intervene in these sectors (especially for developing countries) is not questioned, it is recommended that consultations should be held between the competition authority and the regulatory body, which should be independent of government and separated from regulated firms or entities to assume obligations regarding accountability. The commentary concludes that there is no unique model for cooperation between regulators and competition authorities although the mandate-driven division of labour approach seems to be the most frequent variant. The following section seeks to describe some of the various models applied by competition authorities around the world.

Competition Screening Methods

Many national competition authorities are active in the field of competition advocacy while some have a particularly strong record of using that tool to open up heavily regulated markets. The Irish[18] and the Finish competition authorities,[19] for example, played an important role in driving liberalization of network industries in these countries.

The Danish Competition Authority (DCA) regularly screens markets to identify dysfunctional (black) ones. The DCA has developed a set of competition indicators involving a benchmarking across industries identifying dysfunctional markets. One important benchmark for the level of competition is the regulatory framework in a given market. The DCA observes that '[p]ublic regulation can possibly limit competition in a market through limitations on marketing, restricting the number of companies in a given market, controlling prices, allowing binding resale prices etc. These regulating mechanisms are often implemented in order to solve specific problems but at the same time they may reduce competition potentially

[18] For the Irish Competition Authority, see John Fingleton's speech, 'Enforcement and Advocacy in Regulated Markets', at the Italian Competition Day in Rome on 9 December 2003.

[19] The advocacy role of the Finnish Competition Authority (FCA) was significant in making initiatives to deregulate the closed Finnish markets during 1988–95, in particular in telecommunications. Before membership in the EU, the FCA primarily took structural initiatives to open up markets such as liberalizing imports, abolishing licences, and reforming technical standards; other initiatives focused on abolishing monopolies and restructuring state-owned enterprises. See for example, the 2004 ICN Report on interrelations between antitrust and regulatory authorities, addressed to the third annual conference in Seoul, available at http://www.internationalcompetitionnetwork.org/seoul/aers_sg3_seoul.pdf.

leading to consumer detriment.'[20] Every year the DCA, after consultations with the relevant sector ministries, publishes detailed recommendations on some selected markets on how regulation could be better designed to enhance competition.[21]

The UK in 2002, introduced a system obliging all government offices to assess the impact of legislative acts they propose on competition. The UK competition authority, the Office of Fair Trading (OFT) together with the UK Cabinet Office provides advice to regulators and central government not only on how to avoid possible restrictions of competition but also on how to design new laws with a view to making them more pro-competitive. The competition assessment section of RIAs requires policy teams in other government departments to work through a two-stage process. In the first stage, policy teams identify the economic market(s) affected by the proposal in question. Policy teams then apply a filter of nine questions which are all answered with a 'yes' or 'no'. This is known as the 'competition filter'. This identifies those proposals where there is a risk of a substantial effect on competition. Where the answers to the nine questions are mostly 'no' then this suggests that the proposal has a lower risk of generating a substantial effect on competition. Policy teams then have to explain the answers to their questions (that is, why the majority are 'no' answers). This is known as a *simple assessment*. Where the answers to the nine questions are mostly 'yes', then policy teams need to explore the potential impacts on competition in much more detail. This is known as a *detailed assessment*. A recent example of a detailed assessment is contained in the Regulatory Impact Assessment published for the Gambling Bill.[22]

The US FTC has a competition advocacy programme in place since the early 80s and has actively intervened in a number of sectors including

[20] See also the OECD contribution by DK to the October 2004 session of the Joint Consumer and Competition Policy Committee.

[21] See, for example, their 2004 report on the telecommunications sector and liberal professions, legal counselling, etc. at http://www.ks.dk/english/publications/2004/kr2004/.

[22] Sources of information available for policy teams include the Cabinet Office guidance, available on its website at http://www.cabinetoffice.gov.uk/and the OFT guidance, available on the OFT website at http://www.nao.org.uk/r ia/ria_introduction.htm. In the financial year 2004–5 the OFT responded to more than 140 requests for advice. The majority of these were for new regulatory proposals but about 20 per cent were repeat requests as proposals moved through the policy development process.

legislation on airlines, rail transportation, telecommunications, food labelling, restructuring of the electricity industry,[23] and the financial services market.[24]

Deborah Platt Majoras, the FTC Chairman, stated in one of her recent speeches: 'If we prompt decision makers to think harder about what they are trying to accomplish and whether it can be done in a way that is less restrictive of competition, we likely have provided some benefit.'[25] The US carries out competition screening by using competitive assessments within a broad cost-benefit framework which considers many different effects of alternative regulatory options. The Office of Budget and Management (OMB) has published guidance on regulatory analysis,[26] which alerts drafters of regulations to the risk of unintended harms and side-effects which impede market efficiency. The OMB guide even contains a presumption against certain types of regulatory action, which cannot easily be rebutted, such as price controls in competitive markets, production or sales quotas in competitive markets, or mandatory uniform quality standards for goods and services, if the potential problem addressed by the proposed regulation can be adequately resolved through voluntary standards or by informing consumers.

In Australia, the key driver of competition advocacy has been the implementation of the National Competition Policy (NCP)[27] in 1995. The NCP was responsible for bringing to the forefront of the thinking of regulators, policy makers, and government, firstly the importance of competition and secondly the question of how competition can bring about economic gains and efficiencies.[28]

[23] The FTC argued successfully that open access to transmission grids would only work if sellers can rely on the independence of the grid operator.

[24] FTC successfully argued before the Commodities Futures Trading Commission (CFTC) to allow Eurex to set up an all-electronic operation in the US, a request which was heavily opposed by the incumbents who claimed that the new entrant could engage in predatory pricing. According to reports from business, the incumbents lowered their trading fees upon entry of Eurex (see CTFC Release, available at http://www.cftc.gov/opa/press04/opausferemarks.htm).

[25] See keynote address to CRA on 8 February 2005 on 'Applying a Cost/Benefit Analysis to the FTC4s Advocacy Program'.

[26] See http://www.whitehouse.gov/omb/inforeg/riaguide.html.

[27] The objectives of the NCP are the creation of an economy-wide competition law, competitive neutrality between government and private enterprises, the removal of regulatory restrictions to competition, structural reform of public monopolies, access to essential facilities, and prices oversight to constrain monopoly pricing.

[28] One of the major achievements of the NCP is competition neutrality. Many government business activities were able to obtain certain advantages over their

It is mandatory for Australian Government departments, agencies, statutory authorities, and boards to prepare a regulatory impact statement (RIS) for all reviews of existing regulation, proposed new or amended regulation, quasi-regulation, and proposed treaties involving regulation, which will directly or indirectly affect business, or restrict competition. The Australian Government's RIS requirements are explained in 'A Guide to Regulation (1998)'.[29] The RIS process seeks to assist officials to move towards 'best practice' regulatory design and implementation. For proposals which maintain or establish restrictions on competition (such as barriers to entry for new businesses or restrictions on the quality of goods and services available), it must be established that the benefits to the community outweigh the costs and that the government's objective can be achieved only by restricting competition.

The Canadian Competition Act of 1986 provides the Commissioner of the Competition Bureau (CB) with authority to advocate competition before regulatory bodies. Under Section 125 of the Act, the Commissioner is authorized to make representations and call evidence before any federal board in respect of competition. Under Section 126, the Commissioner at the request of any provincial board or on his own initiative with the consent of the provincial authority in question, may make representations and call evidence in respect of competition. The Commissioner also participates at high level officials' groups and makes representations to Parliament committees on matters relating to the Competition Act or any matter relevant to competition policy (and has done so, for example, in the airline sector). The CB may also review and comment on draft bills. Its opinions are not binding upon the regulatory bodies. However, the CB has carried out important research in certain industries and initiated studies, the results of which were published in anticipation of a change in government policy, thus speeding up the necessary reform process (for example, in the field of electricity).

The Turkish Competition Act in Article 27(g) empowers the Board of the Turkish Competition Authority (TCA) to provide its opinion on competition policy aspects of government legislation and regulations. A communiqué issued by the Prime Minister in 1998 urges other government agencies and ministries to consult with the TCA in advance about proposed regulations and

---

private sector rivals as a result of their public ownership (such as exemption from taxes, lower costs of finance due to government guarantees, and exemption from regulations affecting private sector activity). The NCP removed this impediment to efficient resource allocation and ensured that public businesses face the same costs and commercial pressures that face their private sector competitors.

[29] See http://www.pc.gov.au/orr/reports/guide/reguide2/index.html.

decisions that may have implications for competition policy. In this regard, the TCA has assumed a role of consultant to the government and the sector regulators. In the course of the current privatization process, the TCA provides advice on privatization plans and in particular on the tender conditions, before they are announced to the public. The TCA was inter alia successfully involved in the adoption of a framework for the regulation of distribution and services in the natural gas market and in the privatization of Turk Telekom, the former monopoly provider of telephone services in Turkey.[30]

The Indian Competition Act 2002 in its Chapter VII, Article 49(1), provides that '[i]n formulating a policy on competition (including review of laws relating to competition) the Central Government may make a reference to the Commission for its opinion on possible effect of such policy on competition... .' The Commission is required to answer within 60 days from such a request. Section 49(2) provides that the opinion of the Commission is not binding upon the government while Section 49(3) calls upon the former to take suitable measures to promote competition advocacy, create awareness, and impart training on competition issues.

Since the sections of the Indian Competition Act relating to enforcement work have not yet been brought into force due to pending amendments following court proceedings,[31] the effectiveness of its competition advocacy provisions cannot be assessed. The government has also reserved the right to put in place more detailed rules on the promotion of competition advocacy (see Article 63(2)(j) of the Competition Act). It can, however, be observed that the Indian Competition Act seems to explicitly recognize the need for dialogue in formulating crucial aspects of policy and the corresponding obligations of the parties to this dialogue. Although the opinion by the Competition Commission does not oblige the government, this procedure involves an active dialogue between the central government and the Competition Commission.

In conclusion, there seems to be broad support at national and international level for the integration of competition assessment into the regulatory

[30] See in particular Turkey's submission to the 5th UNCTAD conference, 14–18 November 2005 in Antalya.

[31] The Indian Competition Act has been challenged before the Supreme Court and some of its provisions are now proposed to be amended through an amendment bill that has been introduced in Parliament. The Competition Commission is not for the time being able to undertake inquiries into anticompetitive agreements and abuse of dominant position and regulation of combinations. It does, however, engage in advocacy activities, for example, through organizing regular seminars on competition law, bringing out advocacy literature, undertaking market studies, giving its views to government on competition issues, and advising on competition policy.

process. By way of example, at least 23 OECD governments have chosen to include competitive effects within the process of regulatory impact assessment. As described above, there are various models regarding the exact modalities (such as, for example, the exact powers of the competition authorities or the type of legislation to be screened). These modalities can be decisive for the failure or success of the competition screening exercise. The following chapter will give a short overview of the legal framework and the practical approach applied by the European Commission.

The EC Approach

Legal Framework

Apart from its enforcement role, advocacy is the core tool available to the European Commission to promote competitive markets, or in the words of Art. 4.1 of the Treaty on the European Community (ECT), 'an open market economy with free competition'. With respect to competition policy Article 3(g), ECT gives the Community a clear mandate to ensure that competition in the internal market (the territories of the 25 EU Member States) is not distorted and to promote competitive markets. There is thus no doubt that competition policy aspects have to be considered when drafting new EU legislation. At a national level this means that Member States must not adopt any legislation which requires, favours, or reinforces the effects of agreements, decisions, or concerted practices contrary to Article 81–7[32] of the ECT (or secondary law based on these provisions).[33] This limitation may also be understood as a minimum requirement for EU legislative proposals rendering ineffective the rules on competition.

Consorzio Industrie Fiammiferi (CIF)

The European Court of Justice (ECJ) has recently encouraged competition authorities in the European Union to take a critical approach towards legislation which frustrates the objectives of the European competition rules.

In the CIF case, the Italian competition authority (Autorità Garante della Concorrenza e del Mercato or AGCM) had sanctioned, for breach of

[32] These Articles of the EC Treaty contain rules on anticompetitive practices and agreements, the abuse of a dominant position, and on state aid.

[33] See Case 267/86 *Van Eycke* [1988] ECR 4769, paragraph 16, and, most recently, Case C-198/01 *Consorzio Industrie Fiammiferi* [2003] ECR I-0000, paragraphs 45 and 46.

Article 81 ECT, the members of a consortium of Italian manufacturers of matches, Consorzio Industrie Fiammiferi (CIF), on the basis that it had engaged in price fixing and market sharing activities on behalf of its members. The fine was imposed although, at the time of the infringement, an Italian law not only allowed but even encouraged the manufacturers to form a consortium and enter into the described anticompetitive behaviour. The ECJ confirmed the AGCM's position and even stated a duty by a national authority to disapply the Italian legislation requiring or favouring infringements of Article 81 ECT,[34] or reinforcing the effects of the anticompetitive conduct. Moreover, the Court confirmed that the AGCM was entitled to impose penalties vis-à-vis the companies liable for the infringement provided that they were not obliged to adopt the anticompetitive behaviour (but simply encouraged to do so or benefited from measures that made it easier to adopt such behaviour).

With respect to competition screening and advocacy by competition authorities, this judgment is important since it confirms earlier statements by the Court that there is a duty to disapply national legislation that is in contradiction to Community law and which applies not only for national courts but also for all organs of the state, including national competition authorities. This certainly gives a signal to national competition authorities encouraging them to step up competition advocacy efforts.

Competition Screening through Regulatory Impact Assessment (RIA)

Impact Assessment (IA) in the EU is applied to all initiatives set out in the Commission's Legislative and Work Programme (CLWP).[35] The revised Impact Assessment Guidelines for EC legislation endorsed by the Commission on 15 June 2005[36] replace the previous single-sector type assessments (business, gender, environment, etc.) by an integrated assessment of the

[34] Article 81 prohibits agreements between undertakings and concerted practices, which may affect trade between Member States, and which have as their object or effect the prevention, restriction, or distortion of competition within the common market.

[35] The 2005 Work Programme can be accessed at http://europa.eu.int/eur-lex/lex/LexUriServ/site/en/com/2005/com2005_0015en01.pdf; Acts falling under the executive power of the Commission (for example, Commission Block Exemption Regulations, enforcement decisions), Commission internal guidelines, best practices, and Green Papers (since the latter are a basis for discussions rather than policy documents) are not subject to IA.

[36] SEC(2005)791, available at http://europa.eu.int/comm/secretariat_general/impact/docs/SEC2005_791_IA%20guidelines-main.pdf.

underlying issue or problem, the possible options for public intervention and their likely economic, social, and environmental impacts. Upon the initiative of DG Competition, the new IA Guidelines for the first time include a specific test used to assess competition impacts as part of the overall economic assessment. The drafters of Community legislative and policy proposals (that is, the Commission services proposing new legislation or modifications to existing laws and policy initiatives) are asked to consider competition goals when explaining the reasons justifying the proposed intervention and also when comparing the different legislative options with a view to finding the optimal solution.

In considering whether public intervention at European level is appropriate, drafters of legislation have to examine whether the proposed regulation does not create more harm for consumers than benefits. For example, a consumer protection regulation which is meant to make up for market failures such as information asymmetries or lack of buyer power may interfere directly with the ways companies compete. Some of these rules (for example maximum prices or minimum quality standards) may have unintended side-effects as they reduce the variety of innovative goods and services and create entry barriers, excluding certain providers from the market. The question has to be asked whether the intended consumer protection level can also be achieved by alternative means other than regulation (for example voluntary information requirements for suppliers of certain goods or services).

Once the decision to regulate has been taken, the drafters of the proposal have to assess the overall economic impacts including competition impacts. The particular questions, which they have to consider in this context are:

> Does the (legislative) option affect EU competition policy and the functioning of the internal market? For example, will it lead to a reduction in consumer choice, higher prices due to less competition, the creation of barriers for new suppliers and service providers, the facilitation of anti-competitive behaviour or emergence of monopolies, market segmentation, etc.? (see Table I on page 29 of the IA Guidelines).

In short, drafters of legislation are asked to consider what restrictions of competition may directly or indirectly result from the proposal (for example, restrictions on entry, limiting the use of competition parameters, etc.) and whether there are less restrictive means available to achieve the same legislative objective. Annexure IX to the Guidelines[37] in Chapter 9.2 describes

[37] See http://europa.eu.int/comm/secretaria t_general/impact/docs/ SEC2005_ 791_IA%20guidelines-anx.pdf.

different impacts on competition in the internal market (the EU 25), pointing drafters of legislation to rules which have the potential to cause the greatest distortions of competition. The emphasis is on sectors relevant for the economic growth and competitiveness, that is, high value-added sectors and network utilities, such as financial services, energy sector, and innovation. The following types of regulation are considered to be particularly relevant for competition screening (non-exhaustive list):

- Legislation on liberalization, industrial policy, and internal market measures.
- Legislation introducing special commercial rights (for example, IPRs) or exempting certain activities from the application of the competition regime.
- Legislation on sectors pursuing environmental, industrial, or regional policy goals having an effect on economic activities.
- General regulation (for example, corporate law) having a commercial impact, notably by limiting the number of under takings in a certain sector.

Within these types of regulations there are three main categories of rules which may potentially impact on the competitive process:

1. Rules providing for a non-application of the competition rules.
2. Rules which directly interfere with companies' commercial conduct.
3. Rules which indirectly impact on various competitive parameters.

The possible content of these three categories of rules, their potential negative impact on competition, as well as examples for possible alternative options are further explained in a guidance paper published on DG Competition's website.[38]

An example of the first category (non-application of the competition rules) is the implementation by the 25 Member States of the EU of three recently adopted directives on waste management, introducing an obligation for companies to recycle their waste observing specific conditions. The Commission recently published on its website a comprehensive guidance paper to advocate competition-enhancing implementation by Member States.[39] The guidance paper does not prescribe a particular form of implementation but simply explains the competition effects of the different options, advocating against

[38] 'A Guide to Competition Screening', available at http://europa.eu.int/comm/competition/publications/advocacy/legis_test.pdf.

[39] See http://europa.eu.int/comm/competition/antitrust/others/waste.pdf.

solutions which would induce market sharing or price fixing, and in favour of allowing competition between several waste management systems. The example shows that it is possible to implement competition and environmental policies in a mutually reinforcing way.

Examples of the second category (direct interference with business conduct) are rules restricting the business conduct of services providers, such as television operators, including quantitative restrictions on TV advertising or contain content quotas. These rules pursue legitimate objectives such as the protection of minors or cultural diversity. However, if applied without distinction to all service providers, they risk having a chilling effect on new business models such as pay-per-view or digital TV, reducing the ability for newcomers to compete with established players. Newcomers which have a reduced coverage of geographic areas or clients could have difficulties to meet the strict quota obligations. A diversified application of these rules could avoid competition restrictions while still assuring protection of viewers.

The third category (indirect interference with business conduct) refers to regulation, which unduly restricts access by competitors to important resources in concentrated markets (for example, raw materials, land, IPRs, or know-how on production methods) or favours incumbent suppliers at the expense of new entrants (for example, by requiring the fulfilment of certain environmental performance targets in the energy field, which can only be met by incumbents). These rules may raise entry barriers and reduce the number of potential players, thus leading to a limitation of offerings and higher prices. These rules may also run counter to the efforts of liberalization. In order to avoid these conflicts, it is recommended to avoid regulation which *de facto* favours established providers. Especially in the liberalized sectors such as telecoms, postal services, or public transport, regulation should provide that suppliers are selected on the basis of transparent, non-discriminatory, and objective procedures.

In addition to competition screening through regulatory impact assessment, the Commission is also using other instruments allowing it to analyse the influence of regulation on competition. One particularly effective instrument is the conduct of sector inquiries.

Competition Advocacy through Sector Investigations

The recently reviewed EU antitrust rules[40] empower the Commission to use comprehensive investigative powers (similar to the ones used in individual infringement proceedings) to open inquiries into a market or sector if trade patterns, price rigidities, or other circumstances suggest that competition may be

[40] Article 17 of Regulation 1/2003, which applies since 1 May 2004.

distorted. Companies are under a legal obligation to answer to the written and oral information requests of the Commission. The aim of these sector inquiries is to obtain a better understanding of the reasons for the observed anticompetitive features. Sector inquiries can thus help to proactively identify all significant barriers to competition, including barriers created by existing sector regulation.

In June 2005 the Commission launched comprehensive inquiries into two key sectors, financial services and energy. These sectors were chosen because they are highly relevant for the competitiveness of European businesses and they are also areas where consumers are increasingly dissatisfied with the services provided.[41] In the electricity and gas sectors, the focus is on the functioning of wholesale supply markets and other issues that have a European dimension, such as cross-border energy networks. The inquiries are being carried out in close cooperation with national energy regulators and national competition authorities. In carrying out the financial services inquiries, the Commission is working closely with market participants and Member State authorities to examine whether markets are providing low prices and high quality financial products and services to end-users, in particular, consumers and SMEs.

Where the sector inquiries identify concrete cases of distortion of competition, DG Competition or the competent national competition authority may intervene with appropriate legal instruments, including the opening of individual infringement proceedings against certain companies. But the results of these inquiries, which can be expected in the course of 2006, may also show that government regulations hamper effective competition. In this case, the results of the inquiry may be used by competition authorities as a basis to launch a discussion with regulators and governments to advocate for the removal of competition restrictions.[42]

Outlook

General Observations

In the light of the preceding remarks, there are several basic observations which can be made on the relationship between competition and

[41] In the energy sector, for example, it was observed that energy prices paid are too high in the EU due to a high degree of concentration, vertical foreclosure, lack of international market integration, lack of transparency, and insufficient trust in price formation.

[42] The Commission has previously undertaken similar investigations into the liberal professions and is currently leading this dialogue with Member States and professional associations to advocate the removal of unnecessary barriers to entry; see report of 5 September 2005.

regulation. First, it can be observed that most regulation relevant for commercial activities is driven by objectives which do not directly address competition issues. Still, almost any change in the regulatory framework will normally have a direct or indirect impact on competition.[43] Regulators should, wherever possible, favour options, which do not unnecessarily or excessively restrict competition.

It is fair to say that, both at national and international levels, there is broad consensus that regulation should be based on the principles of competition, market openness, and non-discrimination. Competition authorities should advise governments and regulators how best to achieve this aim. As to the practical implementation of this principle, there exist a wide variety of different models, ranging from the integration of competition assessments in the regulatory impact assessment process (see EU approach) to the adoption of national competition review programmes leading to the systematic review of legislation (approach chosen by Australia and Denmark). Some jurisdictions have introduced a separate competition test for new legislation consisting of several stages (see, for example, the UK filter test) while others examine competition effects within a broad cost-benefit framework (see, for example, the US approach). But independently from the model applied, there are in the authors' view certain general elements which merit special attention as they are crucial for the success of competition advocacy activities.

Crucial Elements

The first challenge competition authorities are usually faced with is to identify the regulatory restrictions, which may affect competition in a certain market/sector. The competition authority should be given a clear mandate as competition advocate and its rights and duties in this respect should be laid down in competition law and—if appropriate—also in sector legislation. As a rule, competition authorities should be involved in the drafting and design of economic legislation at a very early stage in the procedure to ensure that its comments can be appreciated and taken into account. Ideally, the Competition Act or other relevant legislation ensures that the competition

[43] There are of course regulations which are neutral to competition because the adverse effects are evened out by positive ones. Take the example of a new rule applied to all gas suppliers to install modern (expensive) equipment for environmental/safety reasons. Such a rule could at first sight be seen as favouring existing suppliers if the latter get a transition period while new entrants must buy the modern equipment immediately. However, this effect is neutralized if one considers that existing players still have to amortize the costs of their original investment.

agency's opinions are duly considered (if not binding) and that any deviation from important competition policy principles has to be explained by the legislator (see, for example, the US system which contains even a presumption against certain regulations which are considered to be anticompetitive, as explained earlier). The early involvement of competition experts combined with the fact that impact assessments are made public at certain stages of the procedure will increase pressure on policy makers to take important comments by competition agencies into account (see, for example, the new impact assessment rules applied by the European Commission).

If unnecessary regulatory restrictions have been identified, competition agencies have to be able to propose alternative solutions, which meet the purported legislative objectives. In this context it is important that competition agencies are provided with the resources necessary to engage in competition advocacy *in addition* to competition law enforcement. It may also be required to appoint specific contact persons concentrating on advocacy in certain sectors to allow the development of a specific 'advocacy' expertise inside the competition agency. This expertise is crucial for the success of competition advocacy initiatives since regulators will only be inclined to cooperate if competition agencies are able to make constructive comments and propose realistic alternatives. This requires a sound knowledge of the sector at stake. Competition authorities should thus be equipped with the necessary powers to acquire the market knowledge needed to engage in advocacy activities.[44]

Furthermore, given that resources are usually limited, it is decisive that competition agencies set clear priorities when engaging in competition advocacy. This involves, as a first step, the identification of certain types of rules, which typically impact on competitive conduct or market structures (see, for example, the list provided in DG Competition's guidance paper on competition screening). In a second step, the agency will select certain sectors, which it wants to monitor, because they display a high degree of concentration, or because they are in a critical stage of liberalization. The planning of advocacy activities is greatly facilitated by the availability of work plans indicating the legislative and policy proposals, which are meant to be adopted over a given legislative period (see, for example, the Commission's Annual Legislative and Work Programmes, which are published on the internet), although planning should be flexible enough to allow authorities to react on new initiatives. The competition agency is usually well advised to choose a balanced mix between

[44] This knowledge may be derived from the handling of individual infringement cases but also by other means (see for example, the European Commission's powers to carry out sector inquiries on its own initiative).

interventions on uncontroversial legislative projects ('easy victories') and such which are politically highly sensitive and difficult to influence.

There will certainly be political resistance faced by competition authorities when advocating competition-friendly legislation. Two factors may help to overcome this resistance. The first one is the backing of competition policy goals and advocacy measures at central government level (prime minister's office, federal chancellery, etc.). In the UK, for example, the competition agency works side-by-side with the Cabinet Office's Better Regulation Task Force to screen national and EC legislative proposals. In Denmark, the government initiated the systematic screening of existing national legislation with a view to revealing its adverse impact on competition and competitiveness. Each ministry was asked to contribute and propose legislation for review while the whole process was coordinated by the prime minister's office together with the ministry for finance and economic affairs and the Danish competition agency. A second decisive factor, which improves acceptance of competition advocacy is the ownership factor. The competition assessment is normally carried out by the respective government office or ministry proposing legislation. The competition agency should not only offer general guidance and individual advice on legislative projects but also expert knowledge on competition law and policy to the drafters of legislation, for example, through specialized training sessions or staff exchanges (for example, the French DGCCRF engages in this type of competition advocacy activities aimed at spreading specific skills across a range of governmental ministries and departments). This is a more long-term goal and will take time but is worth pursuing. Legislators and regulators are often reluctant to accept comments from external sources but will be more prepared to consider competition aspects if presented by their own staff.

Finally, the greatest challenge competition agencies face is to convince their governments that competition policy principles and other legislative objectives, such as consumer protection or environmental goals, can not only be compatible but even mutually enhancing. Therefore, it is very important that competition agencies and governments continue to exchange views and share their experiences on competition advocacy in international organizations and networks, such as the OECD or the ICN. Competition-friendly legislation can indeed make a significant contribution to economic growth, enhance the competitiveness of businesses, and deliver benefits to consumers.

Future Developments

Recent developments at international level show that competition advocacy is still on top of the agenda. The OECD, for example, has recently published a report on competition in public services which deals specifically with regulation of natural monopolies, in particular transport infrastructure (ports, railways infrastructure, pipelines, etc.).[45] The report analyses different possibilities of granting access to essential facilities if competition from other modes of transport is limited. Furthermore, the OECD is working on a report evaluating different methods of including competition as part of regulatory impact analysis, the follow-up of which will be discussed in the course of 2006. In addition, the Fifth UNCTAD Conference on Competition Policy has recently decided that in 2006, a group of intergovernmental competition experts will look into the special relationship between competition authorities and sector regulators.[46]

This continuing interest is based on the firm conviction of many policy makers and competition experts that competition advocacy, and competition screening in particular, can make a difference. The authors share this conviction. Competition advocacy clearly has been an important driver of liberalization of former monopolies in many countries across the world. A recent OECD report on the benefits of liberalizing product markets[47] concludes that the further reduction of competition restraining regulation, tariff barriers, and the ease of restrictions of FDI to OECD best practice levels would lead to significant gains in GDP per capita in OECD countries of up to 5 per cent. The report also finds that product market reforms that stimulate competition would provide the largest part of these overall gains in OECD. Aligning the stance of domestic regulations on that in the least restraining country could lead to an increase in GDP of 1¾ to 3 per cent in the OECD area with the highest gains in countries with the highest regulatory barriers to competition.[48]

It is thus fundamental to engage in competition advocacy, not only for developed countries but also for competition agencies in developing countries

[45] SG/SGR(2005)6; Report of 16 November 2005 of the Special Group on Regulatory Policy called 'Competition in public services: Ensuring access to key capacity for new entrants'.

[46] This topic will form one of four priorities for 2006; Resolution adopted at the 5th Review Conference on 18 November 2005; Document TD/RBP/CONF.6/14, available at http://www.unctad.org/en/docs/tdrbpconf6d14_en.pdf.

[47] See Report of 2 December 2005, ECO/WKP(2005)50; 'The Benefits of Liberalising Product Markets and reducing barriers to International Trade and Investment in the OECD'.

[48] The OECD study does not cover regulation on health and safety standards or environmental protection but focuses on barriers in the service and agricultural sectors, which are most acute in the OECD countries. The sectors which are most restricted by regulation are postal services, rail transport, and gas supply.

and countries in transition. Economic policies in these countries often undergo fundamental changes with respect to market opening, the establishment of new regulatory institutions, and the privatization of state-owned enterprises. The spread of market reforms is giving rise to an intensive-rule making process. Dialogue between the competition authority and other rule makers at an early stage is vital to ensure that competition provides the foundation of legislation.[49]

If competition agencies succeed in spreading the message that competition advocacy enhances economic growth and benefits consumers without impairing other legislative objectives (such as social policy or universal service obligations), they should be able to gradually strengthen their impact on new and existing regulation. This will hopefully lead governments to create the necessary conditions for competition agencies to contribute their expertise to the legislative process, resulting in more competition-enhancing regulation and the spread of a competition culture at large.

[49] A 2002 ICN survey showed that most developed and developing countries seem to spend less than 20 per cent of their total resources on that activity. In particular, agencies in developing countries often lack the technical expertise necessary for meaningful participation in many proceedings. See ICN Report 'Advocacy and Competition Policy' 2002, available at http://www.internationalcompetitionnetwork.org/.

8

Competition and Regulation

Allan Fels

There are several dimensions to any discussion of the relationship between competition and regulation. First, there is the question of relationship of competition policy to regulation in the most general sense of that term, which refers to government laws, regulations, and other edicts. In the modern economy many regulations affect the state of competition, quite often negatively.

Second, there is the question of competition and regulated industries. In most Organization for Economic Cooperation and Development (OECD) countries this refers to industries, most often public utilities such as in energy, telecommunications, and transport. Such industries are usually the subject of economic regulation. Key questions concern how exactly these industries are regulated and by whom and what the effect on competition is.

Third, there is a related question of how does competition law apply in regulated industries, who applies it, and, to the extent that it does apply, what are the special issues?

In this chapter we will briefly discuss each of these dimensions.

A recurring issue in each dimension is whether competition and regulatory policies complement one another, or whether they are in conflict with one another.

General Regulation

A vast number of laws, regulations, and government policies affect the state of competition. These regulations apply at all levels of government including local, regional, state or provincial, national, and international; and they cover all sectors and apply in all fields of government activity. Their effect on competition may be positive or negative. No analysis of competition policy in the modern economy is complete without considering the effects of regulations on competition. Indeed many economists argue that the effects on competition of anticompetitive regulations are greater than the effects of anticompetitive practices in the private sector. They also claim that where there is a lack of competition in any industry most often the fundamental cause is government laws that affect competition, for example, by restricting entry.

It is this consideration which has given rise to the concept of a comprehensive competition policy. Such a policy involves not only antitrust or competition law (which basically applies to behaviour by business) but it also includes a wide range of government laws and policies that affect competition.

A *comprehensive* competition policy includes all government policies that affect the state of competition in any sector of the economy including policies that restrict, as well as those that promote, competition.

A *national* comprehensive competition policy in a federation includes laws and regulations at all levels of government, federal, state, and local, that affect the state of competition. A national comprehensive competition policy includes:

- prohibition of anticompetitive conduct (traditional competition or antitrust laws);
- liberal international trade and investment policies;
- free movement of all factors of production (labour, capital, and so on) across internal borders;
- removing government regulation that unjustifiably limits competition, for example, legislated entry barriers of all kinds, professional licences, minimum price laws, restrictions on advertising;
- the reform of inappropriate monopoly structures, especially those created by governments;
- appropriate access to essential facilities;
- a level playing field for all participants, including competitive neutrality for government businesses and an absence of state subsidies that distort competition;
- separation of industry regulation from industry operations, for example, dominant firms should not set technical standards for new entrants.

A comprehensive competition policy therefore includes policy concerning amongst other subjects: international and interstate trade; intellectual property; foreign ownership and investment; tax; small business; the legal system; public and private ownership; licensing; contracting out; bidding for monopoly franchises; and a range of other policies. Some of the aforementioned policies have a very direct effect on competition, whilst others affect the general economic environment and the general climate of competition of the country, for example, foreign ownership and investment restrictions.

A comprehensive competition policy therefore goes far beyond the application of conventional competition law. Conventional competition law prohibits anticompetitive conduct by business enterprises. It prohibits cartel behaviour, monopolization, anticompetitive mergers, other anticompetitive practices, and on the demand side may extend to prohibitions on false advertising and misleading and deceptive conduct. Typically it applies to private sector behaviour and, in most countries these days to government businesses. It does not, however, generally apply to government laws that restrict competition, for example, by restricting entry, setting minimum prices, exempting businesses or sectors from the reach of competition law and so on, although in some cases in some countries laws that seek to override competition law directly (for example, by purporting to legitimize a cartel) may be invalid.

The medical profession provides an example of how the law can be used to restrict competition ostensibly in the public interest. It is argued, not unreasonably, that there should be restrictions on who can practice medicine. We do not want any citizen to be able to practice brain surgery without professional qualifications (although Milton Friedman has claimed that there should be no restrictions other than that medical practitioners be required to display their qualifications so that consumers know what they are buying). Economic theory provides some support for the establishment of consumer protection in regard to the medical profession. The economic argument is that there is information asymmetry between the consumer (or patient) and the medical practitioner (whether doctor or specialist). The consumer in particular has no way of judging the quality of the service being provided. There is also the possibility of considerable harm from unqualified practitioners. On this basis it is argued that there should be some regulation of the medical profession.

However, when one examines the nature of regulation, it is apparent that there are major restrictive effects on competition. First, the practice of medical work is restricted to qualified practitioners. Moreover, within the medical profession and medical workforce there are sharp demarcations in many countries that may prevent paramedics, for example, nurses from performing elementary medical operations (for example, giving injections) because performing them is reserved for doctors. In short, medical regulation establishes monopoly and thereby prevents entry both by unqualified persons and by persons who may well be qualified to carry out certain medical tasks competently. This limits supply and competition and allows higher prices.

Second, entry to the profession and/or the workforce is severely limited in most countries, by pressure from the medical profession wishing to restrict supply in the name of protecting standards but equally often with the purpose of restricting supply in order to raise income. Often this is supported by governments wishing to restrict supply in the belief that this will reduce medical bills. The basis for this government behaviour is usually the belief that an increase in the supply of doctors will lead to an increase in the amount of treatment and, in turn, an increase in cost to the public sector and to the community. Whilst it is imaginable that the restrictions on supply are solely aimed at preserving standards, a more realistic view in most countries is that they have an additional substantial anticompetitive purpose.

Third, in many countries there are restrictions on competitive behaviour by medical practitioners. Sometimes there are price-agreements, agreed fees, prohibitions on advertising, and so on. These may be authorized by the law or simply exempted from the application of competition law. Alternatively, they may not be protected by statute in which case they may be open to prosecution under competition law.

Fourth, there are often special restrictions on entry by foreign qualified practitioners.

Taking these four restrictions together, it becomes apparent that the benefits of regulation could be outweighed by the costs.

Regulation of the medical profession provides an example of competing theories of regulation. One theory is that regulation operates essentially in the public interest, usually to protect the public from harm. The other theory is that regulation generally serves the purposes of those being regulated and operates against the public interest generally by restricting competition.

Deregulation Policies

The economic deregulation movement tries to remove as much regulation of economic activity as possible. In most OECD countries there has been a wave of deregulation but many areas requiring significant regulation remain. Moreover, for every act of deregulation there is often a new form of regulation, often with anticompetitive effects. The Business Council of Australia has demonstrated that in Australia for each week that the national parliament sits several hundred pages of new laws are enacted and that the amount of new laws enacted in the last 5 years equals in volume to the amount enacted in the previous 90 years. One difficulty with deregulation policies is that they often focus in an ad hoc manner on selected cases.

The most serious attempt at a systematic comprehensive national competition policy comes from Australia. In 1991 the national, state, and territory governments agreed that a national competition policy should give effect to the following principles:

1. No participant in the market should be able to engage in anticompetitive conduct against the public interest;
2. As far as possible, universal and uniformly applied rules of market conduct should apply to all market participants regardless of the form of business ownership;
3. Conduct with anticompetitive potential said to be in the public interest should be assessed by an appropriate transparent assessment process, with provision for review, to demonstrate the nature and incidence of the public costs and benefits claimed;

In order to give effect to these principles, the governments agreed to establish in October 1992 an independent review of national competition policy headed by Professor Fred Hilmer, director of the Australian Graduate School of Management.

Following the publication of the report in August 1993 a number of meetings between all the governments were held. Although some difficulties arose, eventually in April 1995 the Council of Australian Governments (COAG), consisting of the Commonwealth, state and territory governments, agreed to a national competition policy based on the Hilmer Report.

There are six main elements in the comprehensive national competition policy. They are:

1. *A competition law applicable to all forms of business virtually without exception.* The Trade Practices Act (now renamed and known as the Australian Competition and Consumer Act) was amended so that, with State and Territory application legislation, the prohibitions of anticompetitive conduct contained in Part IV were applied to all businesses in Australia; hence federal constitutional limitations were removed. Moreover, 'Shield of the Crown' immunity for State and Territory government businesses was removed.

   Although the applications legislation was the product of State and Territory legislatures the enactments conferred exclusive public enforcement jurisdiction upon the Australian Competition and Consumer Commission (ACCC). No State enforcement agencies were established.

The broad effect of these changes was that the Trade Practices Act now covers public utilities, government businesses, health, energy, communications, transport, education, sport, agriculture sectors, and so on.

There is a general labour market exemption for employer/employee collective bargaining regarding remuneration and terms and conditions of employment. Intellectual property exemptions remain but are to be cut back.

The National Competition Policy reforms do not entirely remove the ability of governments to exempt specific conduct from the competitive conduct rules in the process of establishing regulatory arrangements for particular industries. However, the reforms restrict the manner in which exemptions may be made.

2. *A process for the review and reform of all laws in Australia at all levels of government that restrict competition to determine if they are in the public interest.* Each government agreed to develop a timetable for the review and, where appropriate, reform of all existing legislation that restricts competition. All legislation was then to be reviewed at least once every 10 years.

   The guiding principle in reviews was that legislation should not restrict competition unless it could be demonstrated that:
   (a) the benefits of the restriction to the community as a whole outweigh the costs; and
   (b) the objectives of the legislation can only be achieved by restricting competition.

   Each government would also ensure that proposals for new legislation that restricted competition were accompanied by evidence that the legislation was consistent with the aforementioned principle and would publish an annual report on its progress towards achieving its timetable for review.

   An interesting byproduct was that the agreement on legislation review made it easier to achieve reviews which would not otherwise have happened.

3. *A process for the review and reform of public utility monopoly structures.* Each government agreed to abide by various principles in the reform of public monopolies.

   Before introducing competition into a sector traditionally supplied by a public monopoly, governments agreed to remove from the public monopoly any responsibility for industry regulation, and to relocate industry regulation functions so as to prevent the former monopolist enjoying a regulatory advantage over its rivals.

Also, before introducing competition into a market traditionally supplied by a public monopoly, and before privatizing a public monopoly, governments would undertake a review into a range of matters, including: the appropriate commercial objectives of the business; the merits of separating any natural monopoly elements from potentially competitive elements of the public monopoly; the merits of separating potentially competitive elements of the public monopoly, and the community service obligations undertaken by the public monopoly; regulation to be applied to the industry; and ongoing financial relationships between the owner and the public monopoly.

4. *A competitive neutrality policy putting government business operations on the same level as competing private sector business operations*. Each government agreed to abide by principles of competitive neutrality. The objective of competitive neutrality policy is the elimination of resource allocation distortions arising out of the public ownership of entities engaged in significant business activities: government businesses should not enjoy any net competitive advantage simply as a result of their public sector ownership.

   These principles:

   (a) apply to significant government businesses or business activities undertaken by government for profit and in competition with other firms; and

   (b) require the neutralization of any net competitive advantage arising from public sector ownership.

   In order to neutralize this advantage, the agreement sets out a number of measures—corporatization, imposition of full taxes (or tax equivalents), debt guarantee fees, and imposition of regulation on an equivalent basis to the private sector. In some instances, pricing principles can be used instead of these measures. Each government had to (and did) publish a policy statement on competitive neutrality. The policy statement includes an implementation timetable and a complaints mechanism. Each government would also publish an annual report on the implementation of this principle. The issue of state aids to industry is less important in Australia than in Europe. However, a report on this subject was subsequently commissioned from Australia's Productivity Commission.

5. *A generic law regarding regulating access to 'essential facilities'*. This is discussed in further detail later in the article.

6. *A prices surveillance regime*. This is discussed in further detail later in the article.

These principles recognized that competition was not an end in itself but rather a means for improving welfare. With this in mind, the Competition Principles Agreement adopted a holistic approach, setting out other factors (including ecologically sustainable development, social welfare, consumer interests, and efficient resource allocation) which must, where relevant, be taken into account in implementing the principles.

Regulation of Utilities

There are a range of utilities that are covered by economic regulation—energy, telecommunications (and other forms of telecommunications), transport, water, and so on.

Sometimes the list is wider especially in developing countries. Even in developed countries there are a range of competitive or potentially competitive industries which over the years have been regulated, for example, airlines and trucking for many years in the United States prior to deregulation; the professions; much of agriculture; the energy sector. In many of these areas the broad policy need has been for deregulation.

More complex is the case of utilities which are natural monopolies—or arguably that—or which are monopolies by virtue of existing protective laws. Most often the policy approach is regulation—but in fact there is a range of possibilities for dealing with them.

Take electricity and gas as examples. Most often gas and electricity utilities have been publicly owned, highly vertically integrated from production or generation through to retail. They have usually been monopolies at each horizontal level. Rather than simply regulating them or ensuring through public ownership that there is public control, some governments have adopted a range of policies to introduce more competition and efficiency. This range of policies has included:

- Ownership and control policies. This has included moving public utilities, from full public ownership and control governments through stages such as commercialization, separation, and privatization. The aim here has been to separate them as much as possible from governments, to put them on a more commercial footing, sometimes to reduce union influence by separating them from political control, and sometimes to raise revenue by selling them.
- Exposure to increased interstate, interregional and international trade, and competition.

- Structural break-up. This has involved both vertical and horizontal break-up of utilities in the interests of generating competition. Horizontal break-up usually promotes competition. There is sometimes a case against this based on the loss of economies of scale. Vertical break-up can also be important for competition. At some stages of the production chain there is obvious scope for competition whilst at other stages there may be a pure monopoly situation, for example, in some cases at transmission or gas pipeline level. Incumbent utilities typically control monopoly facilities such as the above and may use them to hinder competition when they also operate in potentially competitive parts of the industry. The problems can often be best overcome by vertical separation.
- Application of competition law.
- Access laws.
- A variety of other government policies intended to promote competition, for example, competitive bidding to own or manage monopoly facilities.

There are similar questions regarding telecommunications. There is much to be said for the view that the best way of introducing competition into former monopoly telecommunications areas is through divestiture either on a horizontal or vertical basis. The advantage of this is that it avoids the need for subsequent regulation and provides a competitive market-based solution to resource allocation and production problems in a particular sector. However, when this has not been possible, direct regulation has been chosen as the policy instrument typically involving regulation of access to essential facilities.

Regulation of water is another important policy area. Most often the policy issue of principal concern has been the failure to price realistically in relation to supply and demand factors.

Access Laws

Telecommunications is the best known field in which access laws apply. Generally the field is characterized (or believed to be characterized) by natural monopoly in some activities and competitive conditions in others. Policy in most countries has been driven by a general belief that 'the last mile' is uncompetitive. This refers to the fact that the copper wires that carry phone calls from the home to telephone exchanges are a natural monopoly. It would involve uneconomic duplication to 'dig up the streets' (in fact with improved technology not a great deal of street digging is required these days) to install competing wires. This is generally thought to be an area of natural monopoly (although in the longer term it is gradually being eroded by new technology, for example, mobile phones and other forms of non-wire communication). However, in most countries the assumption of natural monopoly has been made and has driven policy. Without access by competitors to the use of such lines owned by the monopolist it is very difficult to compete. Supposing someone wants to compete at other levels of the industry, say on long distance calls. Competitive conditions would apply in that dimension of a telephone call even if the call from the home to the exchange which transmits long distance calls is a monopoly. Competition in other sectors would not occur without there being access to the home or small business via the 'last mile'.

The answer then is access laws. Under them the 'new' entrants are allowed access to the use of the monopolist's facilities to compete with it. These are sometimes called 'essential facilities'. These are facilities which are essential as inputs at some point in the production process whether downstream or upstream for there to be productive operations at other levels of the production process. An ability to carry calls from the home or business to the relevant local or other relevant exchange using the incumbent's facilities is essential if there is to be say competition in the market which say covers long distance calls (which is a contestable market). The other element of essential facilities doctrine is that the facility is a monopoly (or perhaps part of a small group of firms which could be seen as a collective monopoly by virtue of closely coordinated behaviour).

In Australia for there to be access under the law, there are three necessary criteria:

- The use of the facility is a necessary input in a production process.
- It would be uneconomic to duplicate or develop that facility, or, more simply, that it is a natural monopoly.
- It would be in the public interest to give access as it would promote competition and efficiency.

If access is granted under these laws then the further question remains as to the terms and conditions, especially the price at which access is given. There has been a vigorous debate over pricing criteria over the years. The most popular form of control is so called long-run incremental cost (LRIC). The regulator sets a price which covers the costs including the capital costs of the facility being used by the access seeker and includes in it a reasonable profit.

The Australian Competition Policy Reform Act 1995 inserted a new generic legal regime providing for third party access to services from a range of facilities of national importance.

This is a somewhat complex piece of law. It balances a number of policy variables. These include the benefits to competition of granting access; the probable detriments to investments if new entrants can use the facilities of an established player, possibly with ultimate detrimental effects on 'facilities based competition'; property rights issues (requiring appeal processes and the involvement of the Courts and Tribunals); federalism issues; and issues about the role of governments (reflected in the role of designated minister).

Retail Price Control

Utilities are usually also subject to control of their prices to consumers and small business. For many years regulation was conducted on the basis of setting prices that covered the costs of the utilities and which also provided for a 'reasonable' rate of return on investment. This form of regulation was seen as providing few incentives for efficiency since all costs could be passed on. Indeed some argued that in certain cases price regulation actually provided an incentive to overspend on capital facilities in order to maximize profit. An alternative approach developed in the 1980s was dubbed 'incentive based price regulation'. This took the form of 'CPI-X' pricing. A firm would be given a formula for several years in advance under which it was allowed to raise its prices by the increase in the consumer price index minus an allowance for improved productivity. This was seen as giving firms maximum encouragement in keeping costs down and to operate efficiently. If their productivity performance was better than the X-factor all the profits could go to themselves.

The other general pricing issue which invariably arises in this area is the role of cross subsidies. Numerous public utility monopolies are expected to set prices that provide cross subsides to parts of the population, for example, the rural population or sometimes to consumers, or sometimes to small business have distorting effects on competition and resource allocation.

The Interaction between Competition Policy and Regulation

There has been significant debate in many countries as to the most appropriate framework for administering economic, technical, and competition regulation. Among the issues debated have been the merits of general versus industry specific competition regulators and of integrated versus separate administration of economic, technical, and competition regulation. There has also been debate about the role of national and state regulation.

Australia has broadly adopted the approach of incorporating as many economic regulatory functions as possible in its national competition regulator, chiefly on the grounds that a competitive culture should drive regulatory decisions.

However, competition law and regulatory institutions have generally been kept separate in most OECD countries, with provisions making it clear where the boundaries between the activities are, and providing for some degree of coordination.

Applying Competition Law to Regulated Industries

Most deregulation has been brought about by a wish to remove restrictions on competition. However, deregulation can give rise to various concerns and questions. Often the pre-deregulatory situation involves the establishment and protection of a monopoly. Deregulation entailed open entry by small players into fields dominated by former monopolies or dominant firms. What was often required was not only the application of competition law but also some additional laws, for example, access laws (see ahead). Also if deregulation includes the break-up of monopolies on a horizontal or vertical basis, special attention to the application of competition law is usually required on the part of the regulator. One cause is merger pressure, the other reason is the possibility of collusion between entities and people that were formerly in one organization.

***

In regards to the several topics discussed in this chapter, there is a recurring theme. Do competition and regulatory polices complement one another? Or are they in conflict with one another? On the first view, competition law and policy is applied in particular areas to bring about competitive, efficient markets. In some situations, however, it is not possible to have a competitive solution either because there is some kind of natural monopoly situation, or because legislation itself restricts competition. Given then the existence of market power there is the possibility of such outcomes as monopoly pricing and resulting inefficient resource allocation. The role of regulation then is to bring about efficient outcomes by, for example, setting prices at levels that would apply if there were competition. Such an outcome would mean that competition and regulatory policies complement one another. Likewise, there may be instances where regulation is needed to achieve desirable social outcomes such as enhanced safety or environmental protection. Once again, the ideal policy is to promote as much competition as possible whilst having safety or environmental regulation that achieves objectives that cannot be achieved by competition policy alone. Again, there is complementarity.

However, in practice there is often a different outcome—conflict. Regulation obstructs the promotion of competition and economic efficiency.

Regulation may limit entry into an industry in the name of protecting safety, environment, or consumers. It may apply prices in such a way as to discourage competition. It may, for example, set a low price for the incumbent which discourages new entry. It may impose cross subsidies under which, for example, high profits are made in one area and used to subsidize low prices in another area—not only does this distort market forces but it may also inhibit competition in low prices areas. Also laws may have to be enacted to protect the high priced activity from new entry that seeks to engage in 'cherry picking' by only supplying in the profitable area of activity. Much regulation, in fact, hinders competition and economic efficient outcomes.

Accordingly, the relationship of competition and regulation is a complex one, varying from one situation to the next, and not capable of easy generalization.

9

The Efficient and Effective Competition Authority

Lennart Göranson

The current globalization process has seen an impressive number of economies around the world setting up the institutions needed in an open market economy—including competition authorities—and most likely this trend will continue in the foreseeable future. Establishing a first body in charge of competition policy, and gradually developing that organization into a full-fledged enforcer of competition law and advocate for pro-competitive reform is not a simple exercise. And here, like in other areas of policy development, dialogue, sharing of experience, and learning from both good and bad examples will help.

The international dialogue on competition law and policy traditionally had a strong focus on legal and economic analysis. Application of competition law on individual cases is one area where such analysis is applied. Pro-competitive regulatory reform is another. There has also been much discussion on processes, like international cooperation, sanctions, and leniency. And another area that in recent years attracted much attention is competition advocacy.

This chapter will approach a different theme, namely the performance of competition authorities. Although this topic has by no means been totally ignored, it seems that the dominance of the legal and economic disciplines in competition policy has somewhat put back organizational and managerial issues. However, having the best legal and analytical tools is not enough for bringing the best out of competition policy. These tools must also be handled efficiently and effectively by the agency in charge. And that is a concern not only of competition authorities in their infancy. No organization, whatever its age and record, can afford being lax about the search for organizational perfection.

The object of the article is the competition authority, also known as antitrust agency. This term will be used to designate a public body or branch of government having main responsibility for enforcing national competition law together with other tasks in the competition policy area. This delimitation does not exclude that the discussion may also be relevant for supra- or sub-national competition institutions, as well as national bodies in charge of competition law and policy in a specific sector, which in some countries is the case with sector regulators.

The article will initially discuss how performance could be understood in the public sector, and what a competition authority is expected to do. Some competition authorities are obviously doing better than others. Among the multitude of criteria of good performance, four core principles characterizing the successful competition authority will then be suggested. Enhancing the performance of a competition authority is a matter of organization and management, and the article will touch upon some of the available techniques for doing that. Finally the concluding remarks will focus upon measurement as key to organizational improvement.

Competition Authority Performance

Anyone who has spent part of his or her career in the public sector knows how difficult it is to define its performance as compared to recording the success of a private enterprise. A company strives for profit maximization, at least in theory. In real life it may seem that other goals may also play a role, like total business volume, market coverage, financial strength, or quite simply the establishment of a business empire. On the other hand, it could be argued that the latter kind of goals are not ends in themselves, but merely means to achieve long-term maximum profit. In any case, performance in trade and industry is normally easy to quantify and measure. That is not the case for a public body in charge of competition law and policy.

The fact that defining public service performance is difficult does not mean that we should give up trying. On the contrary, huge efforts have been made to that end, not least as a result of the ambitious programmes to enhance efficiency in the public sector that many countries launched in the latter part of the twentieth century.

Today, it is common for a public agency to produce and publish an annual report. In such reports we normally find data and facts that describe the authority's performance. Four approaches to that end will be discussed: (a) input, (b) action, (c) output, and (d) outcome.

Input

The starting point in describing what a competition authority does is often a summary of the inputs. In the annual report we expect to find hard numbers on staff and budget. We also find legislation and other rules that the authority has competence to apply, as well as the powers it may exercise when doing that. However, information on inputs tells what the competition authority can do, but not what it actually does.

Action

The next level is enumerating the activities that the authority is performing. Typical actions of a competition authority include monitoring markets, analysing market behaviour, or enforcing competition law. Still, an organization may devote much time and money on various activities without evidence of any result of these efforts. Obviously, a description of what the agency is doing remains insufficient as evidence of its performance.

Output

Only when looking at outputs do we approach real, tangible performance. Some examples of outputs of a competition authority are; a decision to impose a fine, a ruling on the legality of a business practice, a report on the state of competition in a sector, or a submission to the government to act against anticompetitive regulation. Such outputs are the evidence that action—with the use of available inputs—has produced a result.

Outcome

But the output remains useless if it has no effect. A more advanced approach in defining performance is focusing on the outcomes. What happened as a result of the competition authority's intervention? What were the effects on competition in the market of the authority's decision? How has the world become different from what it would have been if there were no competition authority?

These four levels of performance will help us define the concepts of efficiency and effectiveness, and the difference between them. Without going into semantics, the term 'efficient' as used in this article refers to the relation between output and input. More output with the use of the same amount of resources increases efficiency. The same is the case when the output is kept constant, but input is reduced through savings, maybe as a result of austerity programmes in the public sector. There are several ways to increase efficiency, like (a) letting machines take over manual work, (b) organizing work in a more rational way, or (c) by enhanced knowledge and experience.

Effectiveness, on the other hand, is related to the outcome rather than the output. The performance of a competition authority is effective when the intended impact is achieved. Consequently, the successful competition authority must be both efficient and effective; it must use the available resources in a way that maximizes the products it delivers, but it must also see to it that these products lead to the overarching goals of the country's competition policy.

What Competition Authorities Do

Among the world's competition authorities, there is a broad variety ranging from those with a narrow scope—be it enforcement of a Competition Act or competition advocacy—to multi-purpose agencies adding consumer protection, state aid monitoring, sector regulation, public procurement, or other policy areas to the core competition policy tasks.[1]

The OECD Global Forum on Competition in February 2003 wanted to take a closer look at what competition authorities actually and typically do.[2] In order to gather information related to the design of national competition authorities, the OECD Secretariat had in advance sent out a questionnaire to participants. The focus of the survey was on the place of the competition authority in the administrative structure, its relation to other bodies—horizontally and vertically—and its competences.

[1] The German competition authority, Bundeskartellamt, provided an example of an agency with a fairly narrow scope, only adding public procurement to the core area of competition law enforcement and involvement in legal reform. In contrast, the Australian Competition and Consumer Commission had a wider variety of tasks, including the application of competition, fair trading, and consumer protection laws, and regulation of infrastructure services.

[2] The OECD Secretariat note CCNM/GF/COMP(2003)2 'Optimal Design of a Competition Agency', available at http://www.oecd.org/dataoecd/58/29/2485827.pdf.

As could be expected, almost all competition authorities replied that they investigate infringements of competition law. The share of the competition authority's resources engaged in investigations varied widely, from 20 per cent to 94 per cent, with an average over 40 per cent of total resources.

Other tasks performed by close to all responding competition authorities were decision-making in individual cases of competition law enforcement, and general sector investigations or economic studies. This high share for decision-making would of course not imply that those authorities have the power of taking all kinds of decisions on a case. For instance, a competition authority may have powers to grant an individual exemption but would have to bring the case to court for a ruling on sanctions. Decision-making took, on average, a more important share of the competition authorities' resources (above 25 per cent), as compared to sector investigations and economic studies (10 per cent). More than 85 per cent of the competition authorities replied that they have competition advocacy as one of their tasks. The share of total resources devoted to competition advocacy, where this task was included in the competition authority's responsibilities, was reported normally to stay in the interval of 10–20 per cent.

No other individual task was performed by as many as one-third of the competition authorities replying to the questionnaire. The most common tasks outside the core competition law and policy area were, in falling order, consumer protection, sectoral regulation, price control, state aid control, and public procurement control. The share of responses indicating those tasks ranged from 30 per cent for consumer protection down to 20 per cent for public procurement control. One response indicated more than 40 per cent of total resources being devoted to consumer protection. For other respondents this share stayed within the interval of 5–15 per cent. Telecommunications was the sector most commonly regulated by competition authorities, followed by the energy sector. No authority reported that more than 20 per cent of total resources were spent on sector regulation.

Successful Competition Authority

What is a successful competition authority like? Some may claim that it—like the anecdotal elephant—is difficult to define but you recognize it when you see one. Still, waiting for that moment to come does not provide much guidance in our efforts to improve the authority's performance.

Quite naturally, there is a multitude of factors that may be perceived as indicators of a successful competition authority. But in order to make this long list operative and manageable there is a need for structure and limitation.

To this end, it is suggested that the successful competition authority be characterized by four core principles, namely (a) professionalism, (b) integrity, (c) impact, and (d) presence. For each of these principles, three key indicators will specify in more detail selected characteristics of a successful competition authority.

Professionalism

Doing the Right Things

The professional competition authority focuses on substance and not on process. It sets priorities guided by objective and agreed criteria. In the law enforcement area, active case screening is used for giving priority to most important cases. But in addition to an objective and systematic approach, a sense of mission may help a competition authority find the most successful way ahead. Conversely, the professional authority is not wasting resources on issues of minor importance.

Doing Things Right

The authority has procedures in place ensuring correct handling of cases, respecting high standards of due process and legal certainty. Internal control mechanisms are actively applied already at early steps of the process—and continually—in order to prevent it from going wrong.

Knowing the Game

The competition authority has access to top-ranking expertise in competition law and competition economics. Such expertise may be part of the regular staff on a permanent basis. Alternatively, external experts may be engaged temporarily when most needed. In addition to legal and economic competency, competition officials should have a good understanding of the functioning of enterprises. Finally, knowing the game also means having a correct perception of the role of the competition authority. A visionary leadership may have an important role to play for raising such awareness in the organization.

Integrity

Above Suspicion of Sleaze

Like Caesar's wife, competition authority leaders and staff must keep a broad safety margin to any behaviour in pursuit of personal interest. Routines and practices are applied that build public confidence in the impartiality of the agency's officials.[3]

Untouched by Undue Influence

There is no attempt from the political level or other stakeholders to influence the competition authority's action in individual law enforcement cases or advocacy initiatives. Should such attempts nevertheless occur, the authority will firmly reject them.

Proactive Where Competition Is at Threat

The competition authority does not hesitate to take action when needed, even when powerful interests are challenged. Safeguarding the integrity of the authority also means being prepared to take risks. In fact, the role as leader of a competition authority is a high-risk profession. No competition authority can expect to be liked by everyone all the time, and if it is, it could probably just as well be closed down. On the other hand, risk-taking may raise the credibility of the competition authority in the public mind.

Impact

Winning Cases Brought to Court

A decision on a case may be scored as an output of the authority, and the same goes for bringing a case to a court of justice. However, this output has no impact if the court overrules the decision or rejects the indictment. The successful competition authority mostly wins the cases brought to court. On the other hand, winning 100 per cent of the cases is not ideal, as it may mean playing too safe. A competition authority that wants to improve its performance should be prepared also to test the limits of existing legislation in order to develop jurisprudence.

Imposing Sanctions with True Deterrent Effect

What counts is not first instance decisions on sanctions but the sanctions eventually being enforced. There is massive evidence that the gains of restrictive

[3] Examples of such practices include (a) keeping a register of competition officials' holding of shares, (b) applying 'quarantine' rules when officials are recruited from private enterprises or law firms, and (c) banning competition authority employees from engaging in side-line assignments that may entail conflicts of interest.

behaviour may be colossal.[4] Participants in a cartel conspiracy may cynically count on retrieving more through fixed prices than the amount of fines in case of a possible disclosure. Only fines that are perceived as sufficiently severe to outweigh the gains from anticompetitive behaviour will have a deterrent impact on anticompetitive behaviour.

Competitive Behaviour Is Visibly Affected

The final test of the competition authority's impact is what happens in the market. In order to demonstrate impact we need persuasive evidence that competition in the market would have been less effective, short of the competition authority's action.

Presence

What the Competition Authority Stands For and What It Does Is Well Known

A competition authority living a quiet and anonymous life can never expect to become successful. Successful agencies typically spend most of their time in the searchlight. But being known is not enough—there has to be a reasonably correct perception of the authority and its work in the public mind and among interested parties like big and small business, lawyers, government agencies, NGOs, media, and so on. Pursuing a policy of openness and transparency contributes to a better understanding of the authority's work.

How Competition Works Is Well Known

Promoting and defending effective competition will never gain appreciation if there is a lack of understanding of the competitive process as such, including the functioning of a market economy. In order to score high on presence, the competition authority must make sure that both the general public and other stakeholders know how to benefit from effective competition, and how competition may be threatened.

[4] Estimates of harms caused by cartels have been discussed in 'Hard Core Cartels: Third Report on the Implementation of the 1998 Recommendation' (OECD 2005, available at http://www.oecd.org/dataoecd/58/1/35863307.pdf) and a more comprehensive survey of cartel cases where the harm could be estimated and compared with sanctions imposed was reported in 'Nature and Impact of Hard Core Cartels and Sanctions against Cartels under National Competition Laws' (OECD 2002, available at http://www.oecd.org/dataoecd/16/20/2081831.pdf).

The Competition Authority Has High Status

The views of the competition authority have high credibility and its actions are respected.

Enhancement of Competition Authority Performance

Having identified the characteristics of the efficient and effective competition authority the obvious next question is: How do we get there? As a general observation, the efficient and effective competition authority is, above all, characterized by the review of what it does and how it does it. Measuring, assessing, and evaluating performance in a systematic way is therefore key to improvement.

Sometimes, the argument is heard that a lack of resources does not allow the authority to devote time and staff to evaluation. That operative work has to be given priority. However, follow-up of outcomes is not a luxury, something that draws resources from day-to-day operations. It should, on the contrary, be considered as important as the doctor's examination whether the patient got better or worse after a surgery.

The most obvious motive for evaluating performance is to enhance the quality of the competition authority's work, but there are also other good reasons for engaging in assessment and evaluation.

Experimentation

Competition policy inevitably entails some degree of uncertainty. Questions like 'Is certain behaviour increasing or restricting competition?', 'What is the most effective response?', or 'Are we regulating the market too much or too little?' will never find the ultimate answer. In order to find the right balance, there is a need for feedback through reviews of outcomes.[5]

[5] Two illustrations from the United States underscore the role of experimentation in competition policy. The first is the development over the past half-century of policy against cartels as a series of interrelated experiments with measures that primarily sought to increase the rate of detection for collusive schemes and to boost the punishments for violators. The enhancement by the Department of Justice (DOJ) of its leniency programme in 1993 and 1994 is perhaps the best known and most widely emulated of these experiments, which at the time met much scepticism within and outside DOJ. The only way to know whether stronger assurances about immunity from criminal prosecution would attract more disclosures was to try it out. That the programme would make a genuine difference was not self-evident at

Transparency

In many jurisdictions, cases are increasingly closed through settlements and agreed remedies.[6] Such settlements may be less effective than reasoned formal decisions in providing guidance to other market actors. Indeed, the competition authority and the parties involved may have a common interest in describing the outcome as positive and unproblematic. An independent assessment could on the other hand offer a more critical view.

Multiple Law Enforcement

Some countries have more than one agency enforcing competition law. For instance, federal countries may have agencies on both the national and the regional levels, and some countries, like the United States, even have two agencies enforcing competition law on the national level. There are also examples of competition authorities sharing their powers to enforce competition law with a sector regulator.[7] And as a result of globalization, more and more cases are now being handled by more than one jurisdiction. In all these cases ex-post evaluations of competition law enforcement contribute to convergence.

---

the time. The second example involves the US Federal Trade Commission's decision in 1984 to permit General Motors and Toyota to engage in a production joint venture. The FTC's approval of the transaction reflected an understanding that attaining important efficiency gains and productivity advances promised by the transaction would require the Commission to loosen, at least on an experimental basis, existing antitrust restrictions on collaboration involving major competitors. When the transaction was approved with conditions, some observers contended that the FTC had made a catastrophic policy choice. Subsequent analysis of the GM–Toyota joint venture has suggested that the collaboration gave General Motors valuable experience in implementing lean production and labour management systems that helped inspire the company's design of its Saturn division.

[6] The enforcement of competition laws in a number of jurisdictions, such as the European Union and the United States, today relies significantly upon settlements. One important source of this development is the establishment of mandatory notification mechanisms and waiting periods for merger control. Pre-merger notification systems have expanded recourse to settlements involving divestitures or conduct-related undertakings to resolve competitive concerns with individual transactions.

[7] For instance, in the United Kingdom, the sector regulators for gas, electricity, communications, and water have full power along with the Office of Fair Trading to apply the Competition Act.

Benchmarking

Assessments of the performance of a competition authority may allow it to compare its operational processes with other competition authorities, thereby offering an opportunity to learn from best practices.

Public and Political Support

It is not unusual that stakeholders question the usefulness of competition law enforcement and pro-competitive regulatory reform. Such scepticism may emanate from vested interests that fear the effects of more dynamic competition. But in many cases it is merely a matter of competition culture. The mechanisms and benefits of a competitive market economy are often not fully recognized by the general public, and sometimes the same goes for opinion leaders. Lack of support for the competition agenda is often a major problem in economies in transition, but also in countries where market economy is established since long, similar reactions may be observed. Candid assessments and evaluations of the outcomes of competition law enforcement and pro-competitive regulatory reform—including both positive and negative lessons—are likely to help in building public and political support.

Assessments and evaluations may have different orientation, such as (a) general performance, (b) case-specific, or (c) process-oriented. Assessments that aim at a general improvement of the competition authority's performance are normally not stand-alone activities, but are part of a more comprehensive and systematic approach. As an example, an elaborate planning process for a competition authority may include the following elements:

- Comprehensive inventory, measurement, and analysis of internal and external factors
- Identifying or setting the vision, goal, or rationale of the competition authority
- Setting specific targets or objectives
- Designing activities needed to reach targets
- Planning the use of resources needed for these activities
- Measuring outputs, assessing outcomes, and evaluating the state of internal and external factors.
- Analysing deviations from the plan, and planning for the following period.

In this example, measurements are made both in the initial phase—to provide a base—and towards the end, in order to establish developments. Planning models may obviously be designed in a number of ways, but the underlying general philosophy is mostly the same. As a common denominator, four steps in the process to enhance performance may be identified: (a) where we are, (b) where we want to go, (c) how to get there, and (d) where we eventually arrived.

Where We Are

Any exercise aiming at the improvement of the authority's performance must take its start in a thorough assessment of the current situation. One approach for doing this is the so-called SWOT analysis, which includes both the positive and negative aspects of the organization and its environment.

	Positive	Negative
Internal	STRENGTHS	WEAKNESSES
External	OPPORTUNITIES	THREATS

Alternatively, approaches may be used that are more competition authority-specific, focusing on the dimensions or principles that have been identified as most important indicators of the authority's performance.[8]

Where We Want to Go

'Would you tell me, please, which way I ought to go from here?' 'That depends a good deal on where you want to get to,' said the Cat. 'I don't much care where ...' said Alice. 'Then it doesn't matter which way you go,' said the Cat. Lewis Carroll, *Alice's Adventures in Wonderland.*

Knowing where you are is not enough. In order to find the best way ahead we also have to decide where we want to go. Management by objectives is a widely used technique for setting performance targets, for both individuals, units of an organization, and the organization as a whole.

Ideally, this approach will release energy by focusing on outcomes, rather than prescribing activities in detail. A classical example is the announcement made before Congress by US President John F. Kennedy in 1961: 'I

[8] An example of the latter approach is the OECD model for performance assessment. Based on advice from a panel of prominent competition leaders, this model identifies nine organizational dimensions specific for competition authorities. A first assessment was carried out with the Portuguese competition authority in Spring 2005 in order to help the authority develop an improvement plan.

believe this nation should commit itself to achieving the goal, before this decade is out, of landing a man on the moon and returning him safely to the Earth.'[9]

Looking back, we can see how this simple statement released massive efforts in many parts of society, which eventually allowed the US to take a lead over the Soviet Union in the space race.

Thus, this process starts with identifying objectives that are perceived as relevant indicators of good performance. Objectives may, of course, be more or less sophisticated: They may specify an action (what we do), an output (what we deliver), or an outcome (what happens as a result). In order to effectively trigger good performance, objectives should meet certain criteria. The so-called SMARTT criteria suggest that an objective should meet the following standards:

- Specific: if the objective is too vague, we will either be unable to tell whether we achieved it, or we could too easily claim it was achieved,
- Measurable: measurement is indispensable in order to assess whether we achieved the objective fully, partially, or not at all,
- Agreed: setting an objective should be seen as a contract between the individual or organization and the body he/she/it is reporting to,
- Realistic: objectives that we know cannot be achieved are likely to be disregarded,
- Time bound: 'as soon as possible' is often equal to 'never'—only a fixed dead-line will trigger the efforts desired, and
- Tough: an objective should be a challenge, and if there is no risk of failing, there will be no additional effort to achieve it.

Objectives that define actions seldom meet these criteria. 'The Competition Authority will reinforce its efforts to fight hard-core cartels' may sound proactive. However, it does not tell more precisely what the authority will do (not specific), it is hardly measurable, we have no indication when this will happen or be finalized (not time bound), and above all—the authority could get away with very limited action and still claim that it, to some extent, has reinforced its efforts (not tough). Setting 'SMARTT' objectives may be an art, but efforts to apply more sophisticated objectives are rewarded by enhanced momentum and commitment.

[9] Special Message to the Congress on Urgent National Needs delivered by President John F. Kennedy before a joint session of the US Congress on 25 May 1961.

How to Get There

When people start making plans for an organization, the first thing they often ask themselves is 'what shall we do?' This may be a natural reaction, and holding back the desire to approach the 'doing' as quickly as possible is indeed not always easy. However, discussing which way to go before we have clearly established where we are and where we want to reach is a futile exercise.

But once these pre-requisites are in place, the next step is to establish an action plan. Such a plan typically includes the following elements:

- *What* activities will we run?
- *Who* is in charge of running each action?
- *When* will the activity take place and/or be finalized?
- *How* is the activity performed, what resources are needed and how will they be organized?
- *How* is the fulfilment and/or outcome of the action measured?

Where We Eventually Arrived

The process of enhancing competition authority performance starts with measurement and it will also end with measurement. Thereby the circle is closed, setting the baseline for the following stage.

Assessing outcomes may provide much more useful information than a simple yes/no to the question whether an objective was achieved. Depending upon how the objective was defined, there may also be situations where we came more or less close to the target but did not hit the bull's eye. And where such a deviation was found, the obvious next question is 'why?' Analysing the reasons behind failure fully to achieve objectives may well be one of the most important sources for organizational improvement.

There are three important steps in making information useful and operational: (a) receiving the information, (b) reflecting upon what it tells us, and (c) acting in an appropriate way.

Receiving information means more than the information being technically available. Especially when information is perceived as negative, maybe even threatening, psychological barriers may prevent people from taking in the message or believing in its accuracy. There may also be organizational barriers to receiving correct information. If you work for someone who kills messengers who bring bad news, you soon learn always to deliver good news—or no news at all.

Information may sometimes speak for itself, but in most cases further reflection is needed to interpret its true meaning. And based upon such reflection, the appropriate response can be designed and carried out.

Consequently, information that leads to no action, or to misdirected action, has no value. Much has been written about the attack on Pearl Harbour in 1941, and it seems that information on a massive movement of aircraft was available in advance at some level of the US defence system. But it led to no action, possibly because it was not believed to be correct, not forwarded at the right instances, or its implications not correctly understood.

The Art of Measurement

Once we decide to measure performance in order to create a baseline for action and/or to assess achievement of objectives, there is a multitude of approaches and techniques to select among. Finding the most appropriate measurement method is related to the way we prefer to define performance and to the design of our objectives. Key issues are what, how, and who.

What Should We Measure?

Selecting criteria just because they are easy to measure may be wrong and give counter-productive incentives. We have a tendency to behave as we are measured. A famous cartoon in *Krokodil*, once the most popular weekly of the Soviet Union, showed the entire staff of a steel plant carrying a single giant nail out of the factory. The factory director, speaking to his chief engineer, says, 'Well, comrade, I see that our plan is in tons again this month.'

Competition authorities do not produce nails, but there are other examples of measurement criteria that may direct efforts the wrong way. For instance, a focus on the number of notifications could result in initiatives to increase that number by lowering thresholds. This will lead to more administrative work but will most likely have no impact on competition in the market. On the contrary, resources may as a result be shifted from productive to unproductive work.

If measurement is case-centred, putting an emphasis on the number of decisions, the obvious way to score better in this dimension is to speed up the investigation, which may result in bad analytical quality. The same thing may happen if reducing the total time for handling a case is given priority before all other concerns.

And if figures on fines collected are highlighted, we may run risks of disregarding legal certainty in order to improve the score.

Of course, these examples should not discourage any competition authority from keeping track of the development of notifications, decisions, handling times and fines, and so on. But measurement should also include other dimensions that are more relevant as indicators of efficient and effective performance. These are some examples of what to measure:

- *Input*: Most annual reports cover inputs like financial and human resources, complaints, and notifications received.
- *Output*: Statistics on issues like the number of decisions or rulings, amount of fines, and published reports are mostly found in annual reports. However, too much emphasis on a case-centric approach may entail risks, like measuring airlines quality by the number and size of departing flights—without caring about how, where and when they return to earth.
- *Attitudes and knowledge*: What do lawyers think of the competition authority's analytical skills? Do small businesses know the contents of the Competition Act? Do economic journalists feel that the competition authority has weight in deregulation matters? Such indirect indicators of performance do often tell more than naked case statistics.
- *Effects of the competition authority's action*: What happened after the decision on a notified merger? Did competition increase in a sector where the competition authority busted a cartel? Did Government and Parliament act in accordance with the competition authority's regulatory reform proposals?
- *Organizational performance*: Does the competition authority have mechanisms, procedures, and structures in place allowing it to perform efficiently and effectively—and to improve its performance?

How Do We Measure and Who Makes the Measuring?

Some measurements could obviously best be done by the competition authority itself. This is normally the case with the kind of data on inputs and outputs that we find in annual reports. More advanced evaluations and assessments could be done by the authority itself. For instance, many competition authorities perform ex-post analyses of closed cases. Performance of specific functions may be evaluated through polls to staff being 'customers' of that service.

There are, on the other hand, many advantages with having an external body carry out an assessment, like (a) less burden on the authority's staff resources, (b) access to know-how on measurement methodology, (c) more candid replies from interviewees, and (d) results perceived as more credible in the public mind. These are some examples of external assessments that competition authorities have used as part of their performance evaluation:

- Studies made by individual researchers or research teams.
- Evaluations made by other government institutions.
- Opinion polls made by Gallup institutes.
- Assessments by international organizations like the OECD, UNCTAD, and ICN.

Many competition authorities have found it useful to develop their co-operation with academia. The benefits go two ways: the competition authority may provide materials and practical insight in the functioning of markets that help academic researchers in their work. Conversely, better access to the front-line of legal and economic research may help the authority to fine-tune its approach to various competition issues. Engaging researchers in studies of the outcomes of competition law enforcement and pro-competitive regulatory reform is one of several ways to strengthen the links with the academic world.

A second category consists of evaluations made by government bodies outside the competition authority. The most noteworthy of these works have been prepared by national authorities with responsibility for auditing government agencies.[10] Due to their status as government institutions and by reason of their information gathering powers, these auditing authorities typically have extensive access to the internal records and personnel of the competition agency in performing their research.

One category of measurements deals with knowledge and attitudes among stakeholders and interest groups. When designing such studies, access to expertise on interview techniques and sampling methodology is a clear advantage. And in carrying out the poll, the likelihood of getting unbiased answers is evidently greater if a neutral person conducts the interview.

International organizations active in the field of competition law and policy perform many activities that provide feedback to competition authorities on their performance. Case study seminars, needs assessment workshops, and country or regional studies are some examples. Peer reviews may be the most ambitious model for assessing the performance of the competition regime of a country. And another example, launched by the OECD, is the performance

[10] One example of such studies is the evaluation made by the US General Accountability Office of the effects of a competition agency's interventions, published in 2004. In this study based on econometric models, the audit authority sought to measure the competitive effects of eight petroleum industry mergers completed between 1997 and 2000. The study concluded that six of the mergers resulted in price increases, while two caused petrol prices to fall.

assessment of national competition authorities that focuses on the quality of internal management and procedures.

Competition is a phenomenon that can be found not only in goods and services markets, but also in the political market. Competing ideologies fight for support among stakeholders and the general public, and the organizing principles based on the competition model are challenged by proponents of protectionism or anticompetitive regulation.

Also, competition authorities as such face competition. A lack of support may result in resources being shifted over to authorities in charge of other policy areas. Alternatively, more successful public agencies may acquire powers in the area of competition law and policy at the expense of the competition authority.

In order to effectively further the policy area assigned to it, the competition authority needs to be successful in the organizational sense. Having the best possible legal and analytical tools is a pre-requisite that is necessary but not sufficient. The successful competition authority must also see to its performance and use appropriate management tools to enhance the efficiency and effectiveness of that performance.

Measurement is a key element of such tools. The efficient and effective competition authority is above all characterized by the review of what it does and how it does it. This measurement is done not only for enhancing its internal performance, but also for giving legitimacy to the policy area it handles, and for adjusting the way competition policy is implemented so that it results in maximum value and minimal harm.

Thus, by adopting a process of systematic and repeated measurement, the competition authority will foster the culture of a true learning organization.

10

World Competition Law

Conflicts, Convergence, Cooperation

Eleanor M. Fox

One hundred and thirty nations have enacted competition laws. Increasingly, the acts and transactions that fall within the purview of these laws are in international commerce. Laws are national, but markets do not stop at national borders. Conflicts predictably occur and international dimensions naturally emerge. This chapter describes national and multi-national responses to this phenomenon. Responses include the exercise of jurisdiction over offshore acts, efforts of nations to coordinate and cooperate, and consideration of a possible global framework for global problems. This chapter argues that responses should also take account of special needs of developing countries.

The story starts with the adjustment of national law to deal with offshore and international problems. It proceeds to cooperative efforts of nations through bilateral and regional arrangements, the development of consciousness about legal and procedural convergence, and the emergence of international fora for discussion and solutions to transnational problems. The story includes efforts, particularly by the European Union, to obtain a competition competence in the World Trade Organization, and the sidelining of those efforts in the course of trade negotiations. It includes attention to the special needs of developing countries, efforts at coordination by jurisdictions, and better understanding of one another through various organizations and networks including the Organization of Economic Cooperation and Development (OECD), the United Nations Conference on Trade and Development (UNCTAD), and the newest international organization, the International Competition Network (ICN).

Extraterritoriality and the 'Effects' Doctrine

United States' antitrust law is the oldest actively enforced antitrust law in the world. US cases pioneered the doctrine of jurisdiction to reprehend acts taken abroad that harm the regulating nation's citizens. The effects doctrine at first touched the raw nerves of sovereignty and received a hostile reception. 'Effects' jurisdiction is now accepted in some form by most antitrust jurisdictions. Those raw nerves continue to be touched when one nation's actions impact its neighbours in unwelcome ways; but the controversy has been much tempered by the now recognized shared interests of nations in a competitive environment that facilitates world economic integration, fosters efficient business responses, and increases world economic welfare.

We begin with the history and evolution of the effects doctrine.

United States v. *Aluminum Corporation of America (Alcoa)*[1] gave birth to the effects doctrine, which holds that a nation has jurisdiction to reprehend conduct that has direct effects, especially intended effects, within its borders. *Alcoa* fell at the cusp of the era in which the United States recognized the need to control offshore cartels to protect Americans. At that time, competition was not widely embraced as the rule of trade, and most cartels were legal abroad. The home nations of the cartelists complained about American unilateralism. The United States held its ground, and was exonerated some 40 years later when most of the world accepted the paradigm of markets and competition and realized that they, too, needed effects jurisdiction to protect themselves. From the vantage of the twenty-first century, the utility and indeed inevitability of the doctrine is clear. Were there not an effects doctrine, either the whole world would now be cartelized or we would long since have adopted an international law against cartels.

The 1960s and 1970s brought other efforts and concerns. On the one hand, antitrust was seen as a moral imperative in America and US courts were not reluctant to require American firms to behave abroad as they were required to behave at home. Some courts held that the US antitrust laws followed US

1 *United States* v. *Aluminum Co. of America*, 148 F.2d 416 (2d Cir. 1945).

firms in foreign markets.[2] This was a view applied—but erratically—to out-bound commerce. As for in-bound commerce, there was continued resistance by trading partners to the application of US law to condemn acts done on their home territories that were lawful where performed. The voices of resistance, often led by the United Kingdom, produced US court decisions that seemed to soften the unbending US position that US law applies to foreigners that directly, substantially, and foreseeably hurt the American market. *Timberlane*[3] and *Mannington Mills*[4] heralded negative comity. This was the notion that if foreign concerns outbalance US interests, a US court might either declare that it had no jurisdiction,[5] or exercise discretion to dismiss the case. The softening, however, was almost entirely rhetorical. In not one instance, in which there was in fact antitrust harm in the United States, did a court dismiss a case on grounds of comity or lack of subject matter jurisdiction.

The US *Alcoa* doctrine was adapted to European Community law in 1988. Suppliers of wood pulp from the United States, Finland, Sweden, and Canada allegedly cartelized to raise the price of wood pulp supplied to Europe. In many cases, the sellers did not have subsidiaries or agents in Europe. The European Court of Justice found jurisdiction of the Commission to apply the Treaty of Rome. The effect of the conspiracy in Europe was substantial and direct, and the cartel was 'implemented' in Europe.[6]

In the United States, the line of cases led, in 1993, to *Hartford Fire*,[7] in which Lloyds of London reinsurance firms were accused of conspiring to cut back reinsurance coverage in the United States and of using a boycott to pressure the cutback. The UK defendants moved for dismissal on the basis of comity, noting that the UK gave the power of self-regulation to Lloyds of London to assure the financial soundness of the 'London market', and arguing that, in consequence, UK/Lloyds of London maintained a pervasive system of regulation; that the challenged acts of the UK firms were legal in the UK; and that conflict between US and UK law required dismissal. The US Supreme Court disagreed, stating simply that the defendants intended

[2] *Industria Siciliana Asfalti, Bitumi, S.p.A.* v. *Exxon Research & Engineering Co.*, 1977 WL 1353 (S.D.N.Y. 18 January 1977).

[3] *Timberlane Lumber Co.* v. *Bank of America*, 549 F.2d 597 (9th Cir. 1976).

[4] *Mannington Mills, Inc.* v. *Congoleum Corp.*, 595 F.2d 1287 (3d Cir. 1979).

[5] See Fox, E. 1987. 'Extraterritoriality, Antitrust, and the New Restatement: Is Reasonableness the Answer?', *New York University Journal of International Law and Politics* 19 (565).

[6] *A. Ahlström Osakeyhtio* v. *Commission*, [1998] ECR 5193.

[7] *Hartford Fire Ins. Co.* v. *California* (*Hartford*), 509 U.S. 764 (1993).

to affect and did affect the US market, and no conflict warranted dismissal because the UK firms could follow the Sherman Act without violating the UK law.

Before *Hartford*, although ultimately deemed not applicable to *Hartford*, the US Congress laid down a marker. American business was complaining that US antitrust law followed them into foreign markets, and that it handicapped them at a time (the early 1980s) when they particularly needed to hone their efficiencies and become more competitive in world markets. In response, Congress enacted the Foreign Trade Antitrust Improvements Act of 1982 (FTAIA).[8] The Act, no model of clarity, accomplished one thing clearly: to the extent that the US law held American firms accountable for their harms in foreign markets, it no longer did so. When in Rome, or when selling into Rome, it was fine to do what the Romans did (to Romans). It was not necessary for US firms to comply, also, with the US law.[9]

The FTAIA eventually gave rise to the famous *Empagran* case,[10] in which direct purchasers from firms that fixed the price of vitamins in the world market sued for treble damages in a US court under the US law. The victims who had made their purchases in the United States had already sued and settled. The plaintiffs in *Empagran* were from Ecuador, Panama, Australia, and the Ukraine, and they had bought their price-fixed vitamins outside of the United States. Defendants moved to dismiss their suit on grounds that the FTAIA ruled out suits by purchasers who bought in foreign markets. The

[8] The Foreign Trade Antitrust Improvements Act provides as follows:

Sections 1 to 7 of this title [the Sherman Act] shall not apply to conduct involving trade or commerce (other than import trade or import commerce) with foreign nations unless:

(1) such conduct has a direct, substantial, and reasonably foreseeable effect:
  (A) on trade or commerce which is not trade or commerce with foreign nations, or on import trade or import commerce with foreign nations; or
  (B) on export trade or export commerce with foreign nations, of a person engaged in such trade or commerce in the United States; and
(2) such effect gives rise to a claim under the provisions of sections 1 to 7 of this title, other than this section.

If sections 1 to 7 of this title apply to such conduct only because of the operation of paragraph (1) (B), then sections 1 to 7 of this title shall apply to such conduct only for injury to export business in the United States.

[9] See supra n. 5.

[10] On remand, the court found that plaintiffs had preserved a claim that the markets were linked but that plaintiffs' harm was not proximately caused by the US effects, and it dismissed the case. *Empagran S.A.* v. *F. Hoffmann-LaRoche Ltd.*, 417 F.3d 1267 (D.C. Cir. 2005), cert. denied, 546 U.S. 1092 (2006).

US Supreme Court assumed that the foreign markets in which they bought were not linked to the US market, and on this assumption it agreed with the defendants that the US courts lacked jurisdiction. The Court took the opportunity to stress the importance of comity. It noted trading partners' claims that America's hosting of foreign plaintiff lawsuits would undercut the trading partners' development of their own private damage systems and would undercut their leniency programmes by raising the stakes involved in reporting a cartel and seeking amnesty. In order not to 'interfere with a foreign nation's ability independently to regulate its own commercial affairs', the Court said, it would apply principles of prescriptive comity and construe the statute to allow only a narrow reach of the Sherman Act.

Empagran has since been invoked as the start of a new era of negative comity. In a world of global markets, multitudinous enforcers, and increasing potential for overlaps and conflicts, it is argued, deference is increasingly important in order to minimize the disharmony of laws.

The virtues of negative comity have been invoked (unsuccessfully) in the merger cases of *Boeing/McDonnell Douglas*[11] and *GE/Honeywell,*[12] in the cartel case of *Hartford Fire,*[13] and in the monopoly cases against Microsoft and Intel.[14] But negative comity is not a panacea for advancing competition in the interests of the people of the world. Not atypically, a dominant enterprise prevails upon its home nation to ask the enforcing nation to bend its rules to accommodate a national champion.[15]

Global Problems—Global Solutions?

The global dimension of competition problems is increasingly salient. In the 1970s and 1980s, IBM's use of its dominant market power had direct effects worldwide. In the 1990s and 2000s, Microsoft's use of its dominant market

[11] Case IV/M 877, O.J. L 336/16, European Commission decision of 8 December 1997; US FTC Statement, [Transfer Binder] Trade Reg. Rep. 24, 295 (1 July 1997).

[12] See *General Electric Co.* v. *Commission*, Case T-210/01 (Ct. of First Instance 14 December 2005). Available at http://www.curia.eu.int/en/content/juris/index.htm.

[13] See supra n. 7.

[14] See, for example, Goldman, C., C. Hersh, and C. Witterick. 2005. 'Comity After Empagran and Intel', *Antitrust* 19 (Summer): 6. C. E. Fox. 2005. 'Remedies and the Courage of Convictions in a Globalized World: How Globalization Corrupts Relief', *Tulane Law Review* 80 (571). See, for the European General Court's statement of law regarding jurisdiction over global strategies that harm Europe, *Intel Corp.* v. *Commission*, Case T-286/09, 2014 ECR II (12 June 2014), para. 231 et seq.

[15] See *Hartford* supra, n. 7.

power had direct effects worldwide. Boeing/McDonnell Douglas, Exxon/Mobil, Sandos/Ceiba-Geigy (Novartis), Gencor/Lonrho, British Oxygen/Air Liquide, WorldCom/Sprint, and GE/Honeywell were all actual or proposed mergers of firms doing business in world markets. In the 2010s, China had raised its antitrust profile by enforcement against global mergers cleared by the West.[16]

Global mergers present a special problem. Global mergers may have harmful effects in nations that constitute separate markets and lack the power to protect themselves. This is particularly true for developing countries, whose voices are not heard and as a practical matter must live with whatever the industrialized countries decide is good for them (the industrialized countries).[17]

Mannesmann/Italimpianti[18] highlights the problems. An Italian company and a German company, the only makers of specialized pipes for oil drilling operations, suitable only for developing countries, merged. China was the principal buyer of this stage of technology. The merger did not fall within European merger control. Germany allowed the merger because the German market—like the Italian market—was not hurt. Unusually, Italy conditioned merger clearance on the firms' acceptance of licensing obligations that could ease China's monopoly problem. While Italy reached out to benefit China in

[16] See, for example, Evrard, Sebastian J. and Baohui Zhang. 2014. 'Merger Control in China: Understanding MOFCOM's Unique Approach, Competition Policy International', 29 May 2014. Available at https://www.competitionpolicyinternational.com/merger-control-in-china-understanding-mofcom-s-unique-approach/.

[17] This may have been the case in *Kimberly-Clark/Scott* and in *Union Pacific/Southern Pacific Railroad*, both of which impacted Mexico. *Kimberly-Clark/Scott Paper*, Case IV/M623 (16 January 1996), [1996] O.J. (L 183) 1; *Union Pacific Corp.*, Finance Docket No. 32760, Decision No. 44, 1996 WL 467636 (S.T.B. 12 August 1996), aff'd, *Western Coal Traffic League* v. *Surface Transp. Board*, 169 F.3d 775 (D.C. Cir.1999).

The dilemma is illustrated by the merger of the two largest cement and construction material producers in the world—Lafarge, based in Paris, and Holcim, based near Zurich. The Western competition authorities cleared the merger subject to spin offs of competitively overlapping assets in their jurisdictions. However, these are the only significant cement producers in small, developing countries such as Mauritius, which had to live with whatever second best solutions they had the practical power to order.

[18] See Case No. 3622 (C2227), Fiatimpresit-Mannesmann Demag-Techint/Italimpianti, Bolletino della Autorita Garante della Concorrenza e del Mercado, 4 March 1996, pp. 15–16, 70–1, 130 (Italian Antitrust Auth. 15 February 1996).

this case, developing countries in similar circumstances cannot count on any protection at all. They must simply bear the consequences of global market power. Multinational mergers may increasingly impact developing nations with no voice.

Similar problems are posed by world cartels. World cartels are being uncovered with increasing frequency. Vitamins and lysine are but two of the notorious examples.[19] For cartels, a principal gap within the current system of national (only) enforcement and nation-to-nation cooperation concerns price fixing by firms in developed countries targeted at developing countries. A second gap may exist if no nation with a mature antitrust system is sufficiently impacted by a world cartel to take action or exercise jurisdiction, as may have been the case in the alleged Thai rubber thread cartel[20] and East of Burma steel cartel.[21] Third, where nations whose consumers are harmed exercise restraint out of respect for the sovereignty of the cartelists' home nation, or the harmed nation's hands are tied by dim prospects for effective enforcement, the gap may be great, as in the case of OPEC, marketing boards, and national commodity cartels.

In addition to these gaps in effective competition law, problems stem from perceived illegitimacy of enforcement by one jurisdiction against prominent firms domiciled in another jurisdiction. US politicians called it illegitimate for the European Union to enjoin the merger of GE and Honeywell.[22] Charles James, then an Assistant Attorney General in Charge of Antitrust, warned Europe not to reprehend Microsoft for conduct allowed under US law.[23] William Baxter, when Assistant Attorney General, having withdrawn the US monopoly case against IBM, told the European Commission

[19] See Connor, John M. 2001. Global Price Fixing: Our Customers are the Enemy, New York: Springer; Harry First, 'The Vitamins Case: Cartel Prosecutions and the Coming of International Competition Law', *Antitrust Law Journal* 68 (711).

[20] *Dee-K Enterprises, Inc.* v. *Heveafil Sdn. Bhd.*, 299 F. 3d 281 (4th Cir. 2002), cert. denied, 539 U.S. 969 (2003).

[21] See Jenny, Frédéric. 'A Tale of Three Cartels', Luncheon Remarks at the ABA Antitrust Section's 2003 Forum on International Competition Law (5 February 2003). Available at apps.americanbar.org/antitrust/at-committees/at-ic/ppt/spring/03/jenny-1.ppt.

[22] See 'US Intervenes Over Stalled Honeywell Deal', *Financial Times*, 16 June 2001, p. 1; Editorial. 2001. 'Europe to GE: Go Home', *Wall Street Journal*, A14.

[23] See 'DOJ's James warns EC against use of 'monopoly leveraging' argument in Microsoft', Global Competition Review, 20 May 2002. Available at http://www.globalcompetitionreview.com/news/news_item.cfm?item_id=264.

that its plan to order IBM to disclose interface changes was illegitimate.[24] When Korea found Microsoft guilty of abusing its dominant position in the Korean market and imposed a multi-million dollar fine and ordered the unbundling of Media Player and instant messaging software from the operating system, the US deputy assistant attorney general declared that Korea was chilling competition; that regulators should avoid substituting their judgment for the market's, and, in effect, that the Koreans should not do what the Americans (arguably) would not do.[25]

If in the matter of Boeing/McDonnell Douglas the airlines (the customers) had sued in a US court and the court had enjoined the merger,[26] that result would surely have been accepted as legitimate. The decision of the Federal Trade Commission to close the investigation would have been irrelevant (or just another view).[27] There was, however, no US court case, and Americans treated the merger as not Europe's business.[28]

The perception of illegitimacy is understandable. No one has elected the United States or the European Union or any other jurisdiction to be enforcer for the world. Moreover, when the action of one nation's antitrust agency coincides with that nation's economic interest (as in *Boeing/McDonnell Douglas*), observers abroad do not lightly shake the suspicion that the decision was based on industrial policy, not on the purity of antitrust.[29] When

[24] See DOJ Oversight: *US* v. *A.T.&T.:* Hearing Before the Senate Comm. On the Judiciary, 97th Cong., 56–130 (1982) (statement of William F. Baxter, Assistant Att'y Gen., Antitrust Division, Department of Justice). See also E. Fox, 1986. 'Monopolization and Dominance in the United States and the European Community: Efficiency, Opportunity, and Fairness', *Notre Dame Law Review* 61(981): 1014–15.

[25] J. Bruce McDonald, Deputy Assistant Attorney General for Antitrust. Press Release, 7 December 2005.

[26] Lexecon, the Chicago-based economic consulting firm, had studied the merger and concluded that it was price-raising. See *Boeing/McDonnell Douglas*, Case No. IV/M.877, 1997 O.J. (L336) 16 (8 December 1997) (McDonnell Douglas's competition had put a seven per cent lid on price).

[27] See *State of California* v. *American Stores Co.*, 495 U.S. 271 (1990) (holding that a state may sue for an antitrust violation and obtain further divestiture after an FTC consent decree). See also *Consolidated Gold Fields PLC* v. *Minorco, S.A.*, 871 F.2d 252 (2d Cir. 1989), cert. dismissed, 492 U.S. 939 (1989) (upholding an injunction against a world merger that the EU, British, and US agencies had cleared).

[28] See Tyson, Laura D'Andrea. 1997. 'McBoeing Should Be Cleared for Takeoff', *Wall Street Journal*, 22 July 1997, A14.

[29] See Fox, E. 1998. 'The United States of Boeing Versus the European Union of Airbus', 16 *The Brookings Review* 16(30).

jurisdictions reach contrary conclusions on the competitive effects of the same global merger or international conduct, neither agency commands the trust of the world. Deep cooperation among national authorities, which is currently practiced, and cross-fertilization that tends to narrow the margin of substantive difference, averts some clashes, but not all.

The whole is not the sum of the national-interest parts. Optimizing two, three, four, or five national interests does not add up to world welfare. For example, in *Boeing/McDonnell Douglas*, the European Commission imposed conditions rather than a prohibition, apparently to appease the United States, even though an injunction seemed to some Europeans to be the correct solution. In *Institut Merieux/Connaught*,[30] the Federal Trade Commission ordered licensing rather than an injunction against the merger, perhaps for the same reason, avoiding clash by a suboptimal solution. Furthermore, in *Mannesmann/Italimpianti*,[31] Italy not only did not abort the merger to monopoly (which threatened no consumer harm in Italy), but the competitor-beneficiaries of the relief it ordered—rights to technology licenses—were only Europeans.[32] Global problems find suboptimal solutions in a world without law or concepts that surmount national borders.

Multilateral, Regional, and Bilateral Agreements

Since at least the 1940s, in the context of trade negotiations, some policy makers have argued that a liberal world trading system implies rules against private as well as public restraints of trade. The Havana Charter, negotiated in 1947–8 as the blueprint for the then proposed International Trade Organization (ITO),[33] would have required nations to take appropriate measures against transnational restrictive business practices, including price-fixing, market division, and restraints limiting market access and triggering monopolistic control. The Havana Charter would have authorized the ITO to request an offending member nation 'to take every possible remedial action'

[30] Docket No. C-3301 (23 August 1990, FTC Consent Order) (1990 FTC Lexis 291).

[31] Supra n. 18.

[32] See generally, Bhala, Raj. 1996. *International Trade Law, Cases and Materials*, Virginia, US: Michie Co. 1095, 1125–32, Chapter 11; in particular, Bhala's discussion of the resolution of the U.S./Japan semi-conductor dispute.

[33] Havana Charter for an International Trade Organization, 24 March 1948 (E-Conf. 2/78). See Lowenfeld, A. 2002. International Economic Law (2002), New York: Matthew Bender & Co, Chapter 3, Sec. 3.2.

to cure such private restraints.[34] The US government withdrew its support for the ITO, however, and the Havana Charter was never adopted.[35]

In the decades that followed, many large corporations based in the United States and elsewhere expanded multinationally, and sentiment rose to control the behaviour of the multinational firms.[36] In 1976, the Organization for Economic Cooperation and Development, an organization of the industrialized countries, issued Guidelines on Conduct for Multinational Enterprises.[37] The OECD Guidelines, which principally concerned investment, contained a detailed section on restrictive business practices, which was replaced by a more general statement in 2000.[38]

Meanwhile, the United Nations Conference on Trade and Development had become a forum for consideration of world antitrust principles, to be negotiated among the industrialized countries, the socialist bloc countries, and the less developed and developing countries (Group of 77). The resulting Set of Multilaterally Agreed Equitable Principles and Rules for the Control of Restrictive Business Practices ('RBP rules' or 'UNCTAD Code') was presented to the UN General Assembly and accepted by consensus resolution as a non-binding recommendation in 1980.[39] The RBP rules state that they should be interpreted in favour of developing countries and that they are intended to provide fair and equitable control of business practices for the benefit of the trade and welfare of developing countries.

Beginning in 1981, however, just after the adoption of this voluntary code, US antitrust law made a U-turn. US antitrust law—which had favoured pluralism and the underdog, became rules in the interests of efficient allocation of resources as seen through the eyes (and pocketbooks) of US consumers. If the United States had once desired or tolerated a world antitrust scheme sympathetic to distributional concerns for the less well off, it did not do so any

[34] Ibid., at Art. 48(7).

[35] See Lowenfeld, Chapter 3. Sec. 3.2.

[36] See ibid., Chapter 13, Sec. 13.4(b).

[37] 1976 OECD Declaration on International Investment and Multinational Enterprises, revised in 'OECD Guidelines for Multinational Enterprises', adopted 27 June 2000.

[38] The current guidelines, last updated in 2011, can be found at http://dx.doi.org/10.1787/9789264115415-en. Similarly, a 1967 OECD competition recommendation against restrictive business practices was replaced in 1995 by a Revised Recommendation of the Council concerning Cooperation between Member Countries on Anticompetitive Practices affecting International Trade, 27 and 28 July 1995—C(95)130/FINAL.

[39] UN Doc. A/Res/35/63 (5 December 1980).

more.[40] The United States participates with many other nations in helping to advance the interests of less developed nations in suppressing anticompetitive acts; but it sees 'advancement' through the prism of efficiency defined in terms of aggregate wealth (meaning that if winners—including those in the developed world—win more than losers lose, the problem is solved) and with the default assumptions of robust markets, feasible entry, and the ability of even powerless firms to manoeuvre around restraints. This framework does not usually align with the economic context of developing countries.

Bilateral Cooperation

Even while the UNCTAD RBP code was being negotiated, jurisdictional clashes were occurring as a result of aggressive US antitrust enforcement against foreign actors. The antitrust clashes of the 1970s, and particularly the claim of trading partners that the US agencies and courts had exceeded jurisdictional bounds and were treading on their sovereignty, led to the adoption of three memoranda of understanding (MOUs). Agreements were signed by the United States and Germany (1976), the United States and Australia (1982), and the United States and Canada (1984, revised 1995).[41]

These agreements provide for notification by one authority of its actions that may affect the important interests of the other party, consultations if there is a conflict of interest, and cooperation in gathering and sharing information of mutual benefit. The major purpose of the MOUs was to resolve or modulate conflicts of interest by the exercise of restraint, for example, by deciding not to challenge the neighbour's cartel.

A second generation of bilateral agreements came into being at the end of the 1980s and particularly in the 1990s when so many nations adopted

[40] See Fox, E. and L. Sullivan 1987. 'Antitrust—Retrospective and Prospective: Where Are We Coming From? Where Are We Going?' *New York University Law Review* 62(936). Negotiation of a code of conduct on the transfer of technology was in progress in 1980 but was never completed.

[41] Agreement between the Government of the United States of America and the Government of the Federal Republic of Germany, 23 June 1976, *CCH Trade Regulation Reporter* 4(para 13): 501; Agreement between the Government of the United States and the Government of Australia Relating to Cooperation on Antitrust Matters, 27 April 1999, US–Australia, in *CCH Trade Regulation Reporter Combined* 4(para 13): 502; Agreement between the Government of the United States of America and the Government of Canada Regarding the Application of their Competition and Deceptive Marketing Practices Laws, 3 August 1995, US–Can., *CCH Trade Regulation Reporter* 4(para 13): 503.

market systems and competition laws. The new agreements were designed principally to enhance positive cooperation, such as assistance in investigation and enforcement.

The United States has entered into a number of Mutual Legal Assistance Treaties (MLATs) whereby nations agree to assist one another in the enforcement of criminal law. The United States entered into an MLAT with Canada in 1988 which expressly includes criminal antitrust enforcement.

In the year 1991, a new phrase came into the lexicon—'positive comity.' The United States and the European Commission signed a Cooperation Agreement Regarding the Application of their Competition Laws.[42] The most innovative article (Article V) lays the groundwork for one party to take action to protect market access for the firms of the other, as follows: If one party believes that anticompetitive acts taken on the territory of the other are adversely affecting its important interests, it may request the other to initiate enforcement activities. The notified party will consider the request and advise the notifying party of its decision, and of developments.

The 1991 Cooperation Agreement also provides for notification of enforcement activities that may affect the other's important interests. It contemplates that notification would be given far enough in advance of a complaint or settlement for the enforcing party to take the views of the other party into account. The parties agree to exchange information in order to promote understanding, to assist enforcement and coordination of parallel enforcement, and, based on comity factors, to avoid conflicts.

In 1994, the US Congress passed the International Antitrust Enforcement Assistance Act,[43] allowing the United States to enter into bilateral agreements for enhanced cooperation with foreign antitrust authorities, including sharing certain confidential information with foreign antitrust authorities and gathering evidence on their behalf. Australia alone has entered into such an agreement with the United States.

In 1998, the United States and the EU strengthened Article V of the 1991 agreement.[44] The 1998 agreement contemplates that, when one nation believes it is harmed by anticompetitive activities directed principally towards

[42] 'Agreement between the Government of the United States of America and the European Communities Regarding the Application of Their Competition Laws', 23 September 1991, *CCH Trade Regulation Reporter* 4 (para 13): 504.

[43] 15 U.S.C. §§ 6201–12.

[44] Agreement between the Government of the United States of America and the European Communities on the Application of Positive Comity Principles in the Enforcement of Their Competition Laws, 4 June 1998, *CCH Trade Regulation Reporter* 4 (para 13): 504A.

the territory of the other, the first jurisdiction agrees that it will turn over information and normally suspend its own enforcement activities against the conduct until the second jurisdiction has proceeded to grant relief. The Agreement provides:

1. This Agreement applies where a Party satisfies the other that there is reason to believe that the following circumstances are present:
   (a) Anti-competitive activities are occurring in whole or in substantial part in the territory of one of the Parties and are adversely affecting the interests of the other Party; and
   (b) The activities in question are impermissible under the competition laws of the Party in the territory of which the activities are occurring.
2. The purposes of this Agreement are to:
   (a) Help ensure that trade and investment flows between the Parties and competition and consumer welfare within the territories of the Parties are not impeded by anticompetitive activities for which the competition laws of one or both Parties can provide a remedy; and
   (b) Establish cooperative procedures to achieve the most effective and efficient enforcement of competition law, whereby the competition authorities of each Party will normally avoid allocating enforcement resources to dealing with anticompetitive activities that occur principally in and are directed principally towards the other Party's territory, where the competition authorities of the other Party are able and prepared to examine and take effective sanctions under their law to deal with those activities.

Under the 1998 agreement, a party may request enforcement, and the two parties may then agree that the requesting party will suspend its contemplated enforcement. The agreement states that the requesting party will normally suspend its enforcement if:

1. the challenged acts 'do not have a direct, substantial and reasonably foreseeable impact on consumers in the Requesting Party's territory,' or the acts 'occur principally in and are directed principally towards the other Party's territory;'
2. the adverse effects on the Requesting Party are likely to be adequately remedied in the Requested Party's jurisdiction; and
3. the Requested Party agrees to devote adequate resources, use best efforts, and notify the Requesting Party of intentions and status and take into account its views.[45]

[45] Mergers are excluded from the 1998 agreement, apparently in response to the concerns of US businesses about the sharing and leakage of confidential information.

The United States made one referral to the European Commission in anticipation of the 1998 agreement: the claim that SABRE, a US-based airline computer reservation system, was blocked from effective competition in the French, German, and Spanish markets for airline computer reservation services by anticompetitive refusals to provide it with accurate up-to-date scheduling information by the French, German, and Spanish airlines that owned the competing (and dominant) computer reservation system, Amadeus. After two years and much pressure from the US political sources, the European Competition Directorate-General opened an investigation and subsequently entered into a settlement with Air France.[46]

The United States has entered into bilateral cooperation agreements with the following jurisdictions or their competition authorities: Australia, Brazil, Canada, Chile, China, EU, Germany, India, Israel, Japan, Mexico, and Russia. The European Union, Canada, Australia, and Japan are developing similar networks of bilateral agreements. The European Union is exploring new generation arguments that would allow sharing of important confidential information without consent of the parties but with protections.

Despite interest in positive comity, however, no positive comity referral has ever been made at or after the date of the 1998 agreement (SABRE having been referred before that date). This lack of track record may indicate that the nation against which the anticompetitive acts are directed will normally want to open proceedings in any event, to protect its citizens. Moreover, the referring nation in these cases is normally not threatened with harm to competition but rather with harm to competitors.

Regional Cooperation

In addition to the various cooperation agreements noted earlier, nations in a number of regions of the world have formed free-trade areas, and their commitments often contemplate increasing economic integration of the area and in some cases coordination of competition policies.

The European Union is by far the most tightly integrated community of nations short of a federation. It has a common competition policy. There are numerous looser variations. In the North American Free Trade Agreement, Canada, Mexico, and the United States each agreed that it would adopt

[46] See 'Report of the International Competition Policy Advisory Committee to the Attorney General and Assistant Attorney General for Antitrust' (ICPAC Report). 2000. pp. 232–4. Available on *justice.gov* under Antitrust Division, Public Documents, International Documents.

or maintain national measures to proscribe anticompetitive conduct, take appropriate action, and consult with the other member states when their interests are affected.[47] Canada has a free trade agreement with Chile with a similar provision, and which, going notably farther than NAFTA, precludes application of anti-dumping laws in the free trade area.[48] Australia and New Zealand have created the Australia New Zealand Closer Economic Relations Trade Agreement (CER),[49] which establishes a common abuse-of-dominance law and prohibits application of anti-dumping laws in the free trade area. In South America, nations have joined together in the Andean Pact and MERCOSUR.[50] In Africa, they have joined together in COMESA (Common Market for Eastern and Southern Africa) and in separate agreements for southern, western, and eastern Africa, such as the West African Economic and Monetary Union (WAEMU) and the Economic Community of West African States (ECOWAS). In the Caribbean, nations have formed CARICOM. Asian Pacific countries maintain a loose cooperation forum (APEC), at which members discuss competition principles, and ASEAN (Association of Southeast Asian Nations), which aspires to a common market including obligations of Member States to adopt competition laws. Europe itself has concentric circles of free trade agreements, including EFTA (all but three of whose members have now joined the European Union), and the EEA (the European Economic Area), which includes the EU Member States and the EFTA states and, like EFTA, provides for application of European competition law in the broader area. Moreover, within Europe, since 2004 when powers of enforcement of EU competition law devolved to Member States, the Member States and the Competition Directorate-General of the European Commission have formed a uniquely well-functioning network for coordination of actions called the European Competition Network (ECN).

Competition principles are being negotiated in the context of two other proposed free trade areas—the Trans-Pacific Partnership (TPP), comprising a broad swath of countries from the United States and Canada to Peru,

[47] See North American Free Trade Agreement signed at Mexico City, Ottawa, and Washington December 1992, entered into force 1 January 1994, Chapter 15.

[48] Canada–Chile Free Trade Agreement entered into force 1997, Chapter J. Available at http://international.gc.ca/trade-commerce/trade-agreements-accords-commerciaux/agr-acc/chile-chili/fta-ale/background-contexte.aspx?lang=eng.

[49] Adopted in 1983. See Allan Fels. 2000. 'Administrative/Prosecutorial Discretion of Antitrust Authorities', in B. Hawk (ed.), in 1999. Fordham Corp. Law Inst. Yonkers, New York: Juris Publishing, Chapter 27, pp. 587–606.

[50] See Treaty Establishing the Southern Common Market, 26 March 1991, signed at Asuncion. *International Legal Materials* 30, p. 1041.

Brunei, Japan and Vietnam, and the Trans-Atlantic Trade and Investment Partnership (T-TIP), which is being negotiated between the United States and the European Union.

These regions vary in their consideration and treatment of competition principles. Only in Europe and to a lesser extent in Australia/New Zealand is competition law one of the organizing and central policies of the free trade area.[51]

Substantive Law—Convergences and Divergences

The antitrust laws of nations normally have three main components. They prohibit anticompetitive agreements, including joint ventures, monopolization or abuse of dominance, and anticompetitive mergers. In the category of anticompetitive agreements, jurisdictions normally prohibit cartels, which are agreements among competitors not to compete on terms of trade such as price or output and agreements to divide markets. In a significant number of jurisdictions, the law enables the competition authorities to identify or limit anticompetitive practices of state or local government.[52]

While all antitrust laws have some prohibitions against cartels, the laws diverge on whether cartels are prohibited per se or only when unreasonable, and on the extent of exceptions and exemptions. For most other acts, practices, contracts, and transactions, laws may differ both on the conception of what 'anticompetitive' means, and whether and to what extent anticompetitive measures may be justified by efficiencies or by non-market values, such as health and safety, ethics, and industrial policy (for example, protecting jobs, creating national champions). The debate on what is anticompetitive reflects a significant divergence. Working assumptions are often involved; for example, the assumptions that markets tend to work well and that government antitrust intervention tends to be inefficient and impose costs, or the counter-assumptions that private power tends to impair the working of markets and government intervention is helpful in removing the impediments. US case law developed the distinction between protecting competition (and

[51] See Capobianco, Antonio, John Davies, and Sean Ennis, 'Implication of Globalisation for Competition Policy: The Need for International Co-operation in Merger and Cartel Enforcement', 20 June 2014, SSRN.com, http://ssrn.com/abstract=2450137, for an excellent analysis of the need for, and state of, competition cooperation in the world today, bilateral, regional, and multilateral.

[52] See Fox, E. and D. Healey. 2014. 'When the State Harms Competition—The Role for Competition Law', *Antitrust Law Journal* 79.

consumers' interests in best goods and services at lowest prices), and protecting competitors from efficient competition. Most—but not all—nations accept the mandate to protect efficient competition and disavow a goal to protect competitors; but even so, nations disagree about how to reach this goal. The controversy is well illustrated by jurisprudence of the United States and the European Union on the law of monopolization and abuse of dominance regarding exclusionary practices and duties to deal. The United States applies a strong principle, subject to few exceptions, that even a monopoly firm can choose to deal or not with competitors that need its product or service. US case law reflects the presumption that freedom to deal or not aligns with the interests of consumers.[53] European Union case law presumes that openness of and access to markets align with the interests of consumers, and, unlike US law, it imposes duties of special responsibility on dominant firms not to exclude rivals unnecessarily.[54]

The US and the EU models are the two principal antitrust models in the world. Nations, especially newer antitrust jurisdictions, tend to gravitate towards one or the other. In any event, the antitrust law of these two jurisdictions is constantly, incrementally converging. The law, including the framework for analysis, regarding mergers of competitors is quite similar or identical.[55] But the law on exclusionary practices and on vertical (distribution) restraints remains distinct in important respects;[56] and conglomerate effects, while now subjected to a higher standard of proof in the EU than was previously the case, are regarded more seriously in the EU than in the United States.[57]

[53] *Verizon Communications Inc.* v. *Law Offices of Curtis V. Trinko*, 540 U.S. 398 (2004).

[54] See Fox, E. 2014. 'Monopolization and Abuse of Dominance: Why Europe is Different', *The Antitrust Bulletin* 59(129): Fox, E. 2002. 'What Is Harm to Competition?—Exclusionary Practices and Anticompetitive Effect', *Antitrust Law Journal* 70(371).

[55] See *Airtours* v. *Commission*, [2002] ECR II-2585; Oracle/PeopleSoft, Case COMP/ M. 3216 (European Commission 2004); *United States* v. *Oracle Corp.*, 331 F. Supp. 2d 1098 (N.D. Cal. 2004). But see *General Electric Co.* v. *Commission* supra, n. 12.

[56] Differences in the law of vertical restraints are sometimes attributed to the EU objective of market integration. This is not a complete explanation; the prohibition of certain vertical restraints does not tend to integrate the market.

[57] See Fox, E. 2006. 'The European Court's Judgment in *GE/Honeywell*—Not a Poster Child for Comity or Convergence', *Antitrust* (ABA Antitrust Section, Spring), 20(2): 77.

It is often asserted that developing countries have special needs and interests that may influence the shape of their antitrust laws. These 'special and differential' needs are seldom articulated, except that the claim is made that if an international regime should be adopted, developing countries should not be subjected to the same obligations as developed countries (for example, to open their markets to incoming trade), and that the effective date of obligations should be delayed.

To enlighten the inquiry whether developing countries would be better off with antitrust rules and standards that differ from developed country norms, we must identify particular characteristics of developing countries' economies and capacities that may point in this direction, and particular goals that may be specially suited to developing countries. We must consider what is different about developing countries that might warrant differences in the formulation of competition law rules and standards, and what those differences would be.

Special characteristics of developing countries include: systemic poverty and great disparity of wealth, lack of infrastructure and other indicia of economic handicaps, lack of universal education, deficient education for the poorer population, capital market failures and high costs of capital, a large informal sector of the economy, dominance of agriculture and cottage industry markets as a source of livelihood, years of government controls and monopolistic state-owned enterprise, scarcity of enforcement resources, and more than usual pervasiveness of corruption combined with excessive and rigid licensing and other regulatory barriers. In many cases, where the nation has a comparative advantage, it is in natural resources or cottage-industry markets such as textiles; for exports, it sells into highly competitive markets, and for imports, it buys from oligopolistic industries.

Do these characteristics suggest differential antitrust rules, and in what direction? In particular, do they suggest that developing countries' antitrust laws should contain more exemptions? Do they suggest a need for rules of fairness to protect entrepreneurs and small business from 'too much' competition? Do they suggest a need and a right to discriminate against powerful foreign firms that threaten to overrun their markets? Do they suggest that developing countries should take account of distribution of wealth; that their law should not be blind to who gets the gains? In considering what is harm to competition, should developing countries prefer a European model that has an eye to openness and access to markets, and that values lost incentives by handicapped rivals? Or should it prefer an American model that places its bets on freedom of firms, even dominant firms, to act in the interests of consumers? In formulating their rules and standards, should they lean towards adoption of bright-line rules so as to minimize discretion of enforcement authorities, and if so, should they generalize in a way that yields more, or less, antitrust enforcement? These are difficult questions. I shall offer several comments and a general suggestion.

I assume that developing countries want what is good for efficient economic development. Hard competition rather than protection is generally good for economic development, with derogations cautiously made in clear view of the trade-offs. One should bear in mind that many, if not most, egregious anticompetitive practices that harm developing countries—for example, cartels and boycotts in aid of cartels and hard core acts of monopolization—are prohibited by universal norms and for these there is no reason for different rules. As to many other possibly prohibited acts, such as those that arguably amount to abuse of dominance, economic context is always relevant; that special standards are not needed just because barriers are high. Certain rules, however, such as the US predatory pricing and price-squeeze rules, assume robust markets and relative ease of re-entry and build these assumptions into a rule of law. Developing countries might consider whether they would draw the line differently.

Bright-line rules, where not economically unwise, can be especially helpful to developing countries, to avoid exercises of discretion influenced by politics, privilege, and corruption.

A final principle may lean away from differential rules: Developing countries almost by definition lack capacity. It would surely be very difficult for them to develop rules of their own, and so much simpler simply to adopt an existing body of law. This factor may counsel reluctance in reformulating and redesigning the law; even though clear and precise exceptions from developed country models may be workable.

My general suggestion is the following. There is currently intense world debate on issues involving the correct or best standard for competition law. Much of the action is occurring within the International Competition Network. At present, antitrust law is tending to converge towards the EU and US paradigms. The US may be the most tolerant in the world of dominant firm conduct. Developing countries should be part of this debate, before the enterprise of convergence has moved in a direction they would not choose. The questions posed above should be addressed by many voices in the developing world, and developing countries should decide among themselves what is good for them.

Global Antitrust?

A number of scholars and policy makers have proposed a global framework for competition law, arguing that the law should be as broad as the markets and that national-only law may tend towards nationalism and leave unfilled gaps.[58] Others have opposed a global framework, arguing that it may lead to lowest-common denominator rules and unaccountable decision-makers.[59]

In this Section I consider proposals for a world framework. Most proponents of global antitrust conclude that the appropriate forum would logically and practically be the WTO.[60] It is the only existing global economic body to which antitrust law could be incrementally added, and sympathetically so, to its current mandate, and it has a framework for dispute resolution.

If we should embrace a system of global governance for antitrust, what form should it take? The various proposals can be grouped into three forms, more or less, although the choices may be seen as points along a continuum. First, the strong form would establish a complete antitrust regime for matters significantly affecting world commerce, possibly even encompassing a world antitrust enforcement system and court.[61] This regime might be integrated with the trade regime, or it might be antitrust 'on its own bottom'.

[58] See notes 60, 61, and 62 infra.

[59] See Klein, Joel I., 'Anticipating the Millennium: International Antitrust Enforcement at the End of the Twentieth Century', in 1997 Fordham Corp. Law Institute 1, 9–10, [Barry E. Hawk (ed.), 1998] Yonkers, New York: Juris Publishing; Tarullo, Daniel K. 2000. 'Norms and Institutions in Global Competition Policy', 94 *American Journal of International Law* 478; Diane P. Wood. 2003. 'Soft Harmonization and Competition Laws: Track Record and Prospects', 48 *The Antitrust Bulletin* 305.

[60] See, for example, Guzman, Andrew T. 2001. 'Antitrust and International Regulatory Federalism', 76 *New York University Law Review* 76(1142); Robert D. Anderson and Peter Holmes. 2002. 'Competition Policy and the Future of the Multilateral Trading System', *Journal of International Economic Law* 5(531); Frédéric, Jenny. 2002. 'Globalization, Competition and Trade Policy: Convergence, Divergence and Cooperation', in Clifford A. Jones and Mitsuo Matsushita (eds), *Competition Policy in the Global Trading System: Perspectives from the EU, Japan and the USA*, Hague/London/New York: Kluwer Law International, pp. 295–334; Philip Marsden, 2003. *A Competition Policy for the World Trade Organization*. London: Cameron, May.

[61] See Munich Working Group, Draft International Antitrust Code, World Trade Materials 5(126), September 1993, reprinted in 64 BNA Antitrust & Trade Reg. Rep., Special Supp. 10 July 1993. A minority of the Munich Working Group proposed an alternative approach that would have incorporated most of what was later contained in the antitrust sections of the Doha agenda. See S–8–9 at part VIII, and see Fox, E. 2013. 'A Liberal Competition Code for the World Whose Time Has Not Yet Come', *Concurrences Review*, No. 1.

See also Anderson, Robert D. and Frèdèric Jenny. 2005. 'Competition Policy, Economic Development and the Role of a Possible Multilateral Framework

A second model would envision a framework measure sensitive to the trade-and-competition context. By utilizing the trade law concepts that discipline government acts in restraint of trade, it would focus on the most critical problems of private and public/private transnational restraints that cannot be solved horizontally because of national interests.[62]

A third approach is a minimal form of the second model combined with certain on-the-ground tasks such as technical assistance and peer review. This approach is reflected in a proposal of the European Union submitted in the Spring of 2002 to the WTO Working Group on the interaction between Trade and Competition Policy. The proposal calls for a protocol requiring that every member country of the WTO must adopt a measure prohibiting hard-core cartels. The competition law regime (national or regional) could include other provisions, and exemptions as well. Additionally, the competition laws of the regime must meet the WTO standards of transparency, non-discrimination, and procedural fairness. The nations must establish a mechanism for mandatory consultation and cooperation on hard-core cartel offenses. Cooperation on other matters would be voluntary. A WTO Competition Policy Committee would be established to monitor the agreement, facilitate cooperation, conduct voluntary peer reviews, and facilitate exchanges of information. An integrated approach to technical assistance would be offered to developing countries.[63]

This proposal formed the basis for the competition item that initially appeared on the WTO Doha Development agenda. The competition item was, however, a casualty of failed trade negotiations on subsidies, and was

---

on Competition Policy: Insights from the WTO Working Group on Trade and Competition Policy', in E. Medalla (ed.), *Competition Policy in East Asia*, Chapter 4.

[62] See infra. For scholarship sympathetic to this model, see Graham, Edward M. and J. David Richardson (eds). 1997. 'Issue Overview', in *Global Competition Policy* 3: 3–46; Anderson and Holmes supra, n. 60; Jenny supra, n. 60.

Philip Marsden, in *A Competition Policy for the World Trade Organization*, would focus on one of the most critical problems at the intersection of trade and competition: anticompetitive business arrangements that substantially impede market access. See Marsden supra, n. 60.

[63] WTO Working Group on the Interaction between Trade and Competition Policy, 'Communication from the European Community and Its Member States', WTO Doc. WT/WGTCP/W/184 (22 April 2002). Much of the proposal tracks the Doha mandate. See E. Fox, 'Competition Law', in Lowenfeld supra, n. 33, at 340. The United States lost interest in the Charter, and it was never adopted. See Lowenfeld supra, at 151, 181–3.

removed from the Doha round agenda (while the Doha round itself faltered and nearly failed). The proposal is nonetheless important, reflecting as it does the distillation of much thinking about a feasible world framework that would benefit developing as well as developed countries.

The strong-form (first) proposal above-mentioned is generally regarded as neither practical nor acceptable to the nations of the world. Even the task of reaching agreement on the terms of a substantive antitrust law for the world would be a daunting one, especially as the terms of antitrust prohibitions become more precise and therefore more meaningful. Some industrialized countries fear that such a comprehensive agreement, with rules and standards and a system for enforcement, would straight-jacket nations into a single set of rules and could create an unaccountable and rigid bureaucracy.[64] Some developing countries fear that such an agreement would be, to them, a Trojan horse, housing the interests of the industrialized world.

The second and third models could address certain problems that are not fully solvable horizontally. They are: (a) Developing countries cannot protect themselves from world cartels, and those harms spill over to the rest of the world. (b) Discovery and information problems abound; information needed for enforcement is beyond reach. While industrialized countries can ease the problems by bilateral agreements, developing countries do not have the clout to obtain such cooperation. (c) Exploitative and protectionist national industrial policies often trump antitrust. Restraints by states themselves slip through the cracks of the WTO as states 'privatize protection'.[65] (d) Nations do not have enforcement incentives commensurate with world welfare, and nation-to-nation reciprocity can lead to welfare-reducing solutions.

The second model, building upon and working synergistically with horizontal networks of deep cooperation, could address each of these problems.

[64] See n. 59 supra.

[65] This is the language used in Eastman Kodak Company's complaint against Japan to the US Trade Representative, complaining that outsiders were shut out of the Japanese consumer photographic film and paper markets. Japan was required by WTO disciplines to lower its state barriers to market access. Kodak argued that Japan had no intention of lowering barriers to its market; it merely handed over the reins to Fuji Film. Memorandum from Dewey Ballantine to Eastman Kodak Company, Composed in Support of a Petition Filed Pursuant to Section 301 of the Trade Act of 1974, as amended May 1995 (on file with author).

The WTO telecom agreements helpfully address mixed state/private restraints. See Fox, E. 2006. 'The WTO's First Antitrust Case—Mexican Telecom: A Sleeping Victory for Trade and Competition' ('Mexican Telecom'), in *Journal of International Economic Law* 9(271).

This track would incorporate the basic consensus substantive antitrust principles into a framework directive. Principles would prohibit hard-core cartels, including both import and export cartels,[66] and also market-blocking, unjustified monopolistic practices. Nations would be invited to implement the directive by adopting national law formulated in their own terms.[67]

This model would provide a pathway for addressing system clashes. Protocols for resolving clashes (for example, divergent conclusions on whether a global merger is anticompetitive) would be adopted. For example, although several nations' laws could be applicable to one global transaction, stylized choice-of-law principles could be developed on the basis of most meaningful contacts and most extensive threatened harm.

For purposes of determining the legality of the transaction in the world market, the chosen formulation of law would be applied to the entire affected geographic area as if the entire affected area were within the borders of the nation whose law is applied.[68] No discrimination based on nationality of consumers or producers would be allowed.

Important questions of interface between competition policy and anti-competitive state action would be placed on an agenda for discussion and resolution, so that, for example, the mix between public and private action as alleged by the United States and Kodak with regard to Japan and Fuji Film could be treated as a coherent, indivisible problem.[69] Furthermore, principles

[66] Allowable justifications could be worked out, possibly starting with and tightening the OECD Hard Core Cartel Recommendation. Developing countries' claims for exemptions for commodity cartels and marketing boards could be considered, but within a developed framework requiring justification, transparency, and proportionality.

[67] Thus, nations would be free to make their own choices of formulation and application, within the range of world-accepted principles, as long as those choices were transparent and non-discriminatory. See Fox, E. 1996. 'Trade, Competition, and Intellectual Property—TRIPS and its Antitrust Counterparts', *Vanderbilt Journal of Transnational Law* 29(481) (suggesting such an approach for a TRIPS-acceptable intellectual property/antitrust interface). See also Fox, E. 1998. 'International Antitrust: Against Minimum Rules; For Cosmopolitan Principles', *The Antitrust Bulletin* 43(5): 9 (point 8 on p. 9 of this article suggests such an approach for blocked market access).

[68] See Fox, E. 2002. 'Mergers in Global Markets: GE/Honeywell and the Future of Merger Control', in *University of Pennsylvania Journal of International Economic Law* 23(457) (suggesting such an approach for merger law clashes).

[69] Kodak complained that it was denied access to the Japanese market by a mix of public and private restraints. Allegedly, Fuji Film (among other things) cornered all

would be developed to determine the appropriate standard or rule to govern situations such as the uranium and aluminium cartels and the New Zealand dairy marketing board, where governments played a significant role in facilitating firm cooperation under the rubric of the 'public interest' but did not order the next stage of cartelization.[70]

Meanwhile, a synergistic relation with and among horizontal networks would be nurtured. For example, through the International Competition Network (ICN), national antitrust officials would be encouraged to work out the terms of a voluntary multilateral cooperation agreement on information exchanges and on positive comity. With the advice of the bar, academia, and

---

important film distributors, and made it nearly impossible for an outsider to nurture a fledgling distributor within a reasonable time frame. An aggressive challenger would turn to other methods of piercing the market, but all other natural means were foreclosed by other restraints. The Japanese law allowed resale price maintenance, which Fuji Film fostered, so Kodak could not compete by enlisting retailers to discount its product. Japanese law banned premiums, so Kodak could not compete by offering a free roll of film with each sale. The Large Scale Retail Store Act allowed smaller firms in a neighbourhood to veto the establishment of large stores and condition their operating hours, so Kodak lost the option of aggressive sales through large retail stores. According to Kodak, it was the *combination* of public and private restraints that marginalized Kodak in Japan. Yet there was no forum within which to challenge the symbiotic combination, and Kodak was relegated to isolating the parts of an integral public/private restraint. See 'Japan Measures Affecting Consumer Photographic Film and Paper', WT/DS44/R 31 March 1998. See also Section 304 Determinations: Barriers to Access to the Japanese Market for Consumer Photographic Film and Paper, Fed. Reg. 61(30): 929 (18 June 1996).

A WTO panel decided *Mexico—Measures Affecting Telecommunications Services, WT/DS204/R,* 2 April 2004, finding that Mexico violated its obligations under the General Agreement on Trade in Services (GATS), and antitrust obligations in the Reference Paper to the Annex thereto, whereby Mexico undertook to open its market to international calls terminated in Mexico. The violative conduct was an integral combination of public and private restraints. This is the first finding of an antitrust offense in the context of the WTO. See Fox, E. Mexican Telecom supra, n. 65.

[70] In the case of aluminium, governments agreed to orderly marketing after Russian stocks flooded the world market. See Norton, Erle and Martin du Bois. 1994. 'Foiled Competition: Don't Call It a Cartel, But World Aluminum Has Forged New Order', *Wall Street Journal*, 9 June 1994, A1. US producers fell into line and held back their production. A lawsuit against the five major US aluminium companies was dismissed on grounds of political question, act of state and the Noerr-Pennington doctrine (right to lobby government). *Hammons* v. *Alcan Aluminum Corp.*, 132 F.3d 39 (9th Cir. 1997), cert. denied, 525 U.S. 949 (1998).

consumer organizations, agency officials would be encouraged to continue to work out principles and practices for pre-merger notification and filing, and the process of merger analysis. They would recommend modalities pursuant to which the home jurisdiction of alleged violators would cooperate with harmed jurisdictions in discovery and possibly enforcement. Networking participants would also draft protocols for priorities and rules of non-discrimination in the event of clash. These voluntary agreements, or at least some of them, might ultimately be adopted on the world level. Others—where the prospect of commitment threatens to produce watered-down rules—might remain horizontal and voluntary.

Principles of non-discrimination, transparency, and due process and protocols for clash resolution would be incorporated into a binding agreement. So too would principles requiring aid in discovery by the nations in the best position to undertake the discovery.[71] On the other hand, the coordination and rendering of technical assistance by mature antitrust jurisdictions to new and developing agencies and by more mature jurisdictions to their younger neighbours, and voluntary peer reviews, which transfer knowledge in a specially tailored way, might be seen as particularly fitting horizontal tasks. Technical assistance regimes could be monitored and coordinated by ICN. Peer reviews could continue to be offered by the OECD and the UNCTAD.

Dispute resolution would be reserved for clear and objective violations of obligations by nations, such as failing to adopt an anti-cartel law or failing to provide transparency in derogations from the cartel law. Dispute resolution by specialized panels could eventually be available in other instances as well. For example, a specialized panel might be needed to resolve disputes concerning which jurisdiction's formulation of law should be accorded priority in the case of an international merger. A specialized panel may be needed, also, to determine whether one nation has credibly applied its law (the standard in NAFTA Article 19 anti-dumping cases). Experience is likely to reveal where

[71] See Agreement on Trade Related Aspects of Intellectual Property Rights (TRIPS), § 8, Art. 40(3), 15 April 1994, Marrakech Agreement Establishing the World Trade Organization, Annex 1C, Legal Instruments—Results of the Uruguay Round. 1994. *International Legal Materials* 31 (33): 81 (Section 8, Art. 40(3) treats the issue of control of anticompetitive practices in licenses); Report of the Task Force on the Competition Dimensions of NAFTA (E. Fox, Chair), Ch. 4, § III (ABA Antitrust Section 1994) [hereinafter 'NAFTA Report']. The principle against export and import cartels was one of the eight framework principles of the NAFTA Report specifically adopted by the Antitrust Section and by the ABA. Specific details on mechanisms for enforcement and implementation of a rule against import and export cartels may be found in both reports. See NAFTA Report at 111–12.

these specialized panels will be most critically needed to make the system more nearly seamless.

The third model is a cooperative protocol. It is less ambitious than model two. Although it would require commitments on transparency, non-discrimination, and due process, and a law against cartels, it does not address the most challenging gaps and illegitimacies—state-related restraints emanating from state action, national industrial policies, and hard core export cartels and other nationalistic behaviour. Thus, it does not address the core problem of creating a more nearly seamless, less parochial world.[72] Model three does not treat the free-trade/free competition problem as an integrated whole. It does not seek to solve the Kodak/Fuji Film-type problem, in which combined state and private restraints create barriers.

The limits and omissions of model three are not an oversight. Model two makes a frontal challenge; it takes on the 'impossible' task of economically democratizing a still balkanized world in a global economy. Model three is more pragmatic, and its goals are within reach.

Those who resist internationalization of antitrust oppose both models two and three as well as model one. They argue that pure antitrust law will be compromised by impure trade law.[73] The contrary may be true: an embrace of international competition principles does not threaten the integrity of antitrust. Rather, the real barrier to nations' willingness to embrace an international framework is the political attachment of nations to their anti-dumping laws and other instruments of selective protectionism, and the accompanying fear that under a serious international competition regime, markets will truly be open to forces of trade and competition beyond the control of the state.

Two tasks must ultimately be recognized as the sine qua non of world economic community: addressing the public half of public/private restraints, and addressing public/private restraints as a coherent whole. Advocacy through national channels can lay vital groundwork. Optimizing competition within its existing space can do deceptively little if state restraints crowd out the room for free competition on the merits.[74] A sensible world policy on trade

[72] This model addresses other elements as well, many of which are ancillary to model 2 also and some of which overlap with ongoing initiatives of ICN (technical assistance) and OECD and UNCTAD (peer review).

[73] See Klein supra, n. 59.

[74] ICN addresses the problem by urging competition advocacy by antitrust agencies against excessively anticompetitive measures in their own nations. See, for example, Timothy J. Muris, Creating a Culture of Competition: The Essential Role of Competition Advocacy, at http://internationalcompetitionnetwork.org/muris-naples.pdf. There is, however, no world ombudsman standing the ground against

and competition would begin to address the legitimate, and illegitimate, justifications for state restraints on trade, much as does the Treaty on the Functioning of the European Union. Bringing competition policy and its free competition values frontally into the world trading system by advocating a strong anti-cartel rule and a strong stance of hospitality towards sustained low pricing may ultimately put pressure on the community of nations to confront and appreciate their mutual interest in disciplining undue state restraints. This is what nations that resist a WTO competition initiative fear the most: not that protectionist trade law will compromise antitrust, but that free-market antitrust will endanger protectionist trade measures. For this reason, model two is both critical to world well-being and not easily embraced by nations.

While we await acceptance of model two, we can embrace model three, sorting out what can best be done at the horizontal level and how this groundwork can feed into a more nearly coherent world antitrust system.

---

nations' excessive restraints. To the contrary, there appears to be a Faustian, oligopolistic pact regarding national measures that harm world competition; for example, each nation knows that if it criticizes the others' anti-dumping laws too vigorously it may be forced to relinquish its own.

See, for the extent to which competition laws do and could usefully reprehend state anticompetitive restraints, E. Fox and D. Healey. 2014. 'When the State Harms Competition—The Role for Competition Law', *Antitrust Law Journal* 79, p. 769.

PART II

COMPETITION LAW IN SELECT JURISDICTIONS

11

Competition Law in Australia*

Sitesh Bhojani

Australia is a federation of six states and two territories. By international standards, it is a small market economy with a population of 20 million people. Under the Australian constitution the Federal Parliament has the main revenue powers. The Federal Parliament and Government have broad responsibility for regulation and management of the national economy and national markets. State/Territory legislatures and thus their governments have power to regulate markets within their jurisdictions. The Council of Australian Governments (COAG—a council of all governments: federal/state/territory) coordinates market regulation across jurisdictions.

From 1900 to 1960, Australia was among the top three nations in the world in terms of per capita income. From 1960 to 1992, its rank slid to number 15. With significant primary produce exports, this was partly due to declines in world primary produce prices. But many domestic markets were protected from international competition by tariffs and other barriers and/or from new local competition by either statutory regulation or anticompetitive agreements between incumbent producers.

* Reproduced from 'Competition Law in Australia', published in Dhall, V. (ed.). 2007. *Competition Law Today: Concepts, Issues, and the Law in Practice* (first ed.), Oxford University Press, New Delhi.

Significant removal of these breaks on productivity growth commenced in the 1970s. At the same time, improvements in consumer protection regulation greatly assisted consumers themselves to make markets work better through better-informed choices. By regulating product and information standards, consumer protection regulation also contributed significantly to increasing the capacity of Australian firms to compete internationally on quality.

The Trade Practices Act 1974 (Cth) is the principal Federal legislation dealing with promoting both competition and consumer protection. The legislation as a whole has been characterized as 'remedial' by the High Court of Australia, Australia's highest appellate court.[1]

This chapter endeavours to highlight the development of competition law in Australia in the context of a unique comprehensive national competition policy setting. It includes some details of key concepts, issues, and distinguishing features of Australia's competition laws. Case examples are used to illustrate the role of public and private enforcement in creating a competitive and compliance oriented culture within the Australian business community; and the range of sectors of the economy which is the subject of competition law enforcement action. In particular, application and enforcement of Competition law to Federal, State, and Territory governments insofar as they carry on a business, and to the professions are a noteworthy development of the impact and reach of Australia's Competition laws.[2] The cases also provide an insight into the Australian judiciary's approach to interpretation and application of Australian competition law.

Australia's National Competition Policy Reforms

April 1995 saw a historic, unanimous agreement between Australia's Commonwealth, State and Territory governments to adopt a National Competition Policy (NCP) for Australia. The agreement was reached at a meeting of the COAG—comprising the Prime Minister, State Premiers, and Territory Chief Ministers. The NCP reforms are an example of cooperative Federalism in action in Australia. The NCP represents one of the most extensive, nationally coordinated economic reform programmes in Australia's history. Its foundation is recognition that competitive forces drive economic growth by

[1] See *NT Power Generation Pty Ltd* v. *Power and Water Authority* (2004) 219 CLR 90 at p. 116 par [66] per McHugh A-C.J., Gummow, Callinan and Heydon J.J.

[2] See, for example, *NT Power Generation Pty Ltd* v. *Power and Water Authority* (2004) 219 CLR 90 and *ACCC* v. *Australian Medical Association (WA Branch) Inc* [2001] FCA 1471 (http://www.austlii.edu.au/au/cases/cth/federal_ct/2001/1471.html) and (2003) 199 ALR 423.

providing strong incentives for suppliers to be cost-conscious, price-competitive, and innovative. The objective of NCP was to enhance the living standards of Australians. So whilst NCP reforms promote competition to encourage businesses to use resources more effectively, reduce prices, and respond better to consumer needs, NCP is not about competition for its own sake. NCP recognizes that promoting competition in every activity or circumstance is not practical or desirable—its processes provide for social, environmental, equity, regional, and adjustment objectives to be recognized in implementation.

The COAG emphasized that the competition policy reform package would enhance the national economic interest by improving Australia's international competitiveness as well as enhancing the interests of Australian consumers.

Specifically, the three inter-governmental general agreements comprising NCP:

- Extended the anticompetitive conduct provisions of the Trade Practices Act to unincorporated enterprises and all government businesses.
- Provided for structural reform of public monopolies and other government businesses including the merits of separating:
  - regulatory from commercial functions;
  - natural monopoly from potentially contestable service elements; and
  - contestable elements into smaller independent businesses.
- Required adoption of competitive neutrality policies by each government to ensure that government businesses do not enjoy any competitive advantages over private companies as a result of their public ownership (including independent mechanisms to assess complaints alleging breach of these requirements).
- Required creation of independent authorities to set, administer, or oversee prices for monopoly service providers.
- Introduced a national access regime to provide third-party access on reasonable terms and conditions to essential infrastructure such as telecommunications networks, gas pipelines, ports, and electricity transmission services.
- Introduced a Legislation Review Programme to assess whether (existing or future) regulatory restrictions on competition are in the public interest. COAG's guiding principle is that legislation (including Acts, enactments, Ordinances, or regulations) should not restrict competition unless it can be demonstrated that:
  - the benefits of the restriction to the community as a whole outweigh the costs; and
  - the objectives of the legislation can only be achieved by restricting competition.
- Created two new bodies—the Australian Competition and Consumer Commission (ACCC) responsible for the enforcement of the competition

and consumer protection provisions of the Trade Practices Act, making determinations under the access regime, and prices surveillance. The National Competition Council (NCC) exercises recommendatory powers on access and price surveillance issues and has advisory powers on matters determined by governments, including compliance with NCP reforms.

- Required the Commonwealth to provide financial incentives known as competition payments to the States and Territories. The per capita element had an estimated annual cost to the Commonwealth of A$2.4 billion by 2005–6. The Competition Payments are dependent on the States and Territories meeting agreed reform objectives as assessed by the NCC. These financial incentives recognized the fiscal dividend from implementation of agreed reform commitments.

NCP was augmented by other sector-specific intergovernmental agreements on electricity, gas, water resource policy, and road transport.

After a decade of implementing NCP reforms, Australia's central government asked an independent body, the Productivity Commission, to conduct an inquiry into the impacts of NCP to date, and report on future areas 'offering opportunities for significant gains to the Australian economy from removing impediments to efficiency and enhancing competition'. The Productivity Commission's Report was intended to inform the COAG's review of NCP and possible future reforms. In April 2005, whilst releasing the Productivity Commission's Report, the Commonwealth Treasurer noted that the Report estimated that the observed productivity and price changes in key infrastructure sectors (electricity, gas, urban water, telecommunications, urban transport, ports, and rail freight) in the 1990s to which NCP and related reforms have directly contributed, have served to increase Australia's GDP by 2.5 per cent, or A$20 billion. In its Report of 28 February 2005, the Productivity Commission acknowledged NCP as a landmark achievement in economic reform. It also acknowledged that NCP cannot be said to have been an unqualified success because not all reforms have delivered and there have been transitional costs. However, the Commission said that NCP has brought substantial benefits to the Australian community, which overall have greatly outweighed its costs. NCP has:

- Contributed to the productivity surge that has underpinned strong growth in average household incomes over the last decade, including:
  - the lowest unemployment rate for about 23 years and labour force participation at its highest level since World War I; and
  - a substantial increase in taxation revenue as anticipated by the NCP agreement on competition payments, increasing the capacity of all gov-

ernments to fund a range of services of benefit to the community such as health and education.

- Reduced the prices of some goods and services, especially for business users (such as a 19 per cent drop in average real electricity prices; a drop in rail freight rates ranging from 8 per cent for wheat to 42 per cent for coal; a drop in port charges of up to 50 per cent; a drop in average telecommunications charges of more than 20 per cent; a drop in the average retail price of drinking milk of 5 per cent—despite an 11 cents/litre levy to fund an assistance package for dairy farmers);
- Expanded the range of products available to consumers (for example, a wider range of service packages and new technologies in the telecommunications sector); and
- Helped meet some environmental and social goals (for example, some road and rail transport reforms have enhanced road safety).

Australia was at the crossroads after its decade of NCP reforms. Would it take the road that lets Australians relax and enjoy the dividends of a reform task that is largely complete? Or would it take the road that recognizes various international and domestic challenges to the Australian economy calling for further effective reforms—and higher living standards across Australia?

The 17th COAG meeting was held on 10 February 2006 in Canberra.[3] All governments seized the opportunity to work together to deliver a substantial new National Reform Agenda embracing human capital, competition, and regulatory reform streams. COAG said that, 'As national demographic trends begin to bite and global competition intensifies, it is vital that all governments work together to deliver the best possible reform outcomes for Australia. Complacency is not an option.'[4]

COAG decided to build on the highly successful National Competition Policy reforms.

> COAG endorsed a new National Competition Policy (NCP) reform agenda aimed at providing a supportive market and regulatory framework for productive investment in energy, transport and other export-oriented infrastructure, and its efficient use, by improving pricing and investment signals and establishing competitive markets. COAG noted the Productivity Commission's conclusion that NCP has delivered substantial net benefits to the Australian economy and across the community, and all governments recommitted to the principles

[3] See the Communiqué of that meeting at http://www.coag.gov.au/meetings/100206/index.htm.

[4] COAG Communiqué at p. 1.

contained in the Competition Principles Agreement [being one of the three general inter-governmental agreements forming NCP].[5]

Australia's Competition Laws

The Australian Constitution places restrictions on the extent to which the Federal Parliament can make laws to cover all trade within the states by unincorporated businesses and also regarding the business activities of State or Territory government business enterprises.

The first three federal Acts dealing with restrictive trade practices in Australia were the Australian Industries Preservation Act, 1906 (Cth); the Trade Practices Act, 1965 (Cth); and the Restrictive Trade Practices Act, 1971 (Cth).

Essentially, Australia's competition laws now comprise the provisions in Part IV of the Commonwealth Trade Practices Act 1974 (TPA) and State and Territory counterpart laws known as Competition Code of [the State or Territory] and Competition Policy Reform Act. The Competition Codes 'mirror' the provisions in Part IV of the TPA but apply them to natural persons rather than just corporations. So the Competition Codes extend the competition laws to unincorporated businesses (particularly the professions). The State and Territory Competition Policy Reform Acts extend the competition laws to State and Territory governments insofar as those governments carry on a business either directly or through an authority of the government.

The object of the TPA is 'to enhance the welfare of Australians through the promotion of competition and fair trading and provision for consumer protection'.[6] It proscribes certain forms of conduct and has detailed provisions for enforcement and providing remedies for past or proposed contraventions.

It should be noted that the TPA also covers:

- Price monitoring and the regulation of particular industries such as telecommunications, gas, electricity, shipping, and airports;
- Telecommunications-specific regimes dealing with anticompetitive conduct and for regulated access to carriage; and
- Consumer protection provisions to deal with information asymmetry issues, unfair market practices, and product safety matters.

[5] COAG Communiqué at p. 5. A full set of recommendations agreed by COAG are at Attachment B to the COAG Communiqué.

[6] See Section 2 TPA.

The key provisions of Part IV of the TPA dealing with restrictive trade practices (other than the provisions dealing with anticompetitive mergers) are considered to be:[7]

- Contracts, arrangements, or understandings that have the purpose, effect, or likely effect of substantially lessening competition (Section 45);
- Contracts, arrangements, or understandings that restrict dealings or affect competition through exclusionary provisions (Sections 45 and 4D);
- Contracts, arrangements, or understandings in relation to prices (Section 45A);
- Secondary Boycotts (Sections 45D, 45DA, 45DB, 45DC, 45DD, 45E, 45EA, and 45EB);
- Misuse of market power (Section 46);
- Exclusive dealing (Section 47); and
- Resale price maintenance (Sections 48 and 96).

The subject matter of each of those provisions of Australian competition law could easily form the subject matter for separate chapters. For present purposes, some of the key issues, concepts, and judicial approaches will be set out below to highlight the Australian approach to competition law.

A unique and important aspect of Australian competition law is the power granted by the Parliaments to the national competition regulator, the ACCC to confer immunity, on a case by case basis, to certain forms of restrictive trade practices. The provisions in Part VII of the TPA provide for the power and the role of the ACCC. The State and Territory Competition Codes incorporate these provisions and apply them to persons who are not corporations. There are two options available for obtaining immunity. The first is known as 'Authorization' and the second as 'Notification'.[8]

Authorizations may only be granted prospectively and are available to persons for entry into or giving effect to contracts, arrangements, or understandings that are anticompetitive; engaging in Secondary Boycott conduct; engaging in exclusive dealing conduct; engaging in resale price maintenance; and also for effecting an anticompetitive merger. The statutory test that the ACCC is required to apply in assessing an application for authorization is essentially whether the public benefits of the conduct sought to be engaged in

[7] The terms of the relevant provisions of the Trade Practices Act 1974 (Cth) can be accessed at http://www.austlii.edu.au/au/legis/cth/consol_act/tpa1974149/.

[8] See the ACCC website at http://www.accc.gov.au/content/index.phtml/itemId/142.

outweighs the anticompetitive detriment of that conduct. Only if the ACCC is so satisfied can it grant the authorization. The process is a public process that is open and transparent. The ACCC is required to publish draft reasons for its proposed decision and also final reasons for its decision.

The Notification option for obtaining immunity is currently only available for exclusive dealing conduct. For exclusive dealing conduct other than third line forcing immunity is conferred by the TPA immediately on lodging the notification. For third line forcing, the immunity is obtained automatically 14 days after the notification is lodged. The onus in this process is on the ACCC to take steps to remove the immunity provided by the notification if it is satisfied that the public benefit from the notified conduct would not outweigh the likely detriment to the public resulting from the conduct or the lessening of competition.

An appeal by way of rehearing on the merits, to a specialist administrative Tribunal known as the Australian Competition Tribunal, is available from ACCC decisions regarding Authorizations and Notifications.

By virtue of the Australian Constitution, the judicial power of the Commonwealth of Australia vests in the High Court of Australia, and any other federal court which the Federal Parliament creates or in such other courts as it invests with federal jurisdiction. Competition law matters in Australia are regarded as 'Special Federal matters' and are adjudicated upon exclusively in the Federal Court of Australia or on appeal by the High Court of Australia. This has meant that a substantial degree of expertise has developed in relation to such matters within the Federal Court of Australia.

The specialist administrative review body for some ACCC and some other competition law related decisions, the Australian Competition Tribunal (formerly known as the Trade Practices Tribunal), has no staff or physical resources of its own. The Tribunal is established under the TPA. The funds appropriated by Parliament for the purposes of the Tribunal are managed by the Federal Court. Registry services and administrative support for the Tribunal are provided by the staff of the Federal Court of Australia. The Tribunal consists of a President and Deputy Presidents and other members appointed by the Governor-General. A presidential member must be a judge of a federal court. Other members must have knowledge of or experience in industry, commerce, economics, law, or public administration. For the purpose of hearing and determining proceedings, the Tribunal is constituted by a presidential member and two non-presidential members. Currently, all presidential members are Judges of the Federal Court of Australia.[9]

[9] See the Tribunal website at http://www.fedcour t.gov.au/aboutct/aboutct_admin_other_act.html.

Australia's Substantive Competition Law Provisions

Competition

Competition is only defined in the TPA as *including* competition from imported goods and services rendered by persons not resident in or carrying on business in Australia. In the Australian context the following comments by the Trade Practices Tribunal have been approved by the Courts:[10]

> 'Competition' is such a very rich concept (containing within it numbers of ideas) that we should not wish to attempt any final definition which might, in some market settings, prove misleading or which might, in respect of some future application, be unduly restrictive. Instead we explore some of the connotations of the term. Competition may be valued for many reasons as serving economic, social, and political goals. But in identifying the existence of competition in particular industries or markets, we must focus upon its economic role as a device for controlling the disposition of society's resources. Thus we think of competition as a mechanism for discovery of market information and for enforcement of business decisions in the light of this information. It is a mechanism, first for firms discovering the kinds of goods and services the community wants and the manner in which these may be supplied in the cheapest possible way. Prices and profits are the signals which register the play of these forces of demand and supply. At the same time, competition is a mechanism of enforcement: firms disregard these signals at their peril, being fully aware that there are other firms, whether currently in existence or as yet unborn, which would be only too willing to encroach upon their market share and ultimately supplant them.
>
> This does not mean that we view competition as a series of passive mechanical responses to 'imperfect market forces'. There is of course a creative role for firms in devising the new product, the new technology, the more effective service or improved cost efficiency. And there are opportunities and rewards as well as punishments. Competition is a dynamic process: but that process is generated by the market pressure from alternative sources of supply and the desire to keep ahead.

And:

> Competition expresses itself as rivalrous market behaviour. In the course of these proceedings, two rather different emphases were placed upon the most useful for m such rivalry can take.

[10] See *Re Queensland Co-operative Milling Association Ltd; Re Defiance Holdings Ltd* (1976) 8 ALR 481 at 514–16.

On the one hand it was put to us that price competition is the most valuable and desirable form of competition. On the other hand it was said that if there is rivalry in other dimensions of business conduct—in service, in technology, in quality and consistency of product, an absence of price competition need not be of great concern.

In our view, effective competition requires both that prices should be flexible, reflecting the forces of demand and supply, and that there should be independent rivalry in all dimensions of the price-product-service packages offered to consumers and customers.

Competition is a process rather than a situation. Nevertheless, whether firms compete is very much a matter of the structure of the markets in which they operate.

Contract, Arrangement, or Understanding

Contract is not defined in the TPA and carries its normal common law meaning of a legally binding agreement. The terms, 'arrangement' and 'understanding' describe something less than a binding contract or agreement. The following summary by Sackville J. provides a useful summary of what is required:

> An arrangement or understanding for the purposes of ... [the TPA] is apt to describe something less than a binding contract or agreement: ... However, in order for there to be an arrangement or understanding ... there must be a meeting of the minds of those said to be parties to the arrangement or understanding. There must be a consensus as to what is to be done and not merely a hope as to what might be done or happen: ... Ordinarily, an arrangement or understanding involves communication between the parties arousing expectations in each that the other will act in a particular way: ... There is no necessity for an element of mutual commitment between the parties to an arrangement or understanding, although in practice such an arrangement or understanding would ordinarily involve reciprocity of obligation.[11]

The distinction between an 'arrangement' and an 'understanding' for the purposes of the TPA has not yet been fully explored. Parliament has used three words in descending order of formality but the cases to date seem to have equated 'arrangement' with 'understanding' and apparently required a

[11] See *Australian Competition & Consumer Commission* v. *Amcor Printing Papers Group Ltd* [2000] FCA 17 (19 January 2000) at para [75].

plaintiff to establish 'commitment' with discussion on whether the commitment needs to be mutual.[12]

Exclusionary Provision

As defined in the TPA,[13] it is essentially, a provision of a contract, arrangement, or understanding between two or more competitors which has the purpose of limiting supply to or acquisition from particular persons or classes of persons. It is often referred to as the 'primary boycott provision'. However the High Court of Australia has ruled that the section is not limited to 'boycotts'. In particular the High court has said that the term 'boycott' has not been used by the Parliament, lacks a precise meaning, may tend to distract inquiry towards seeking the meaning of that term rather than the statutory language, and may foster the incorrect assumption that the section only applies when there is some form of animus towards the object or objects of the exclusion (the particular persons or classes of persons). It is sufficient if the purpose of the provision is 'directed toward' a particular person or class of persons rather than 'aimed at' or 'targeting' the person or class. That avoids the connotations of aggression or the inducement of harm, found in judicial discussions of boycotts.[14]

Market

For the purposes of the TPA, market has both a descriptive role and a purposive role. It 'means a market in Australia and, when used in relation to any goods or services, includes a market for those goods or services and other goods or services that are substitutable for, or otherwise competitive with, the first-mentioned goods or services'.[15] For the purposes of Australian competition law the following explanation of the concept of a market by the Trade Practices Tribunal is regarded as the authoritative view and has been referred to with approval by the High Court of Australia:

[12] The High Court of Australia rejected the opportunity to clarify these issues in refusing the ACCC's Application for Special Leave to Appeal on 2 June 2006 in *ACCC* v. *Apco Service Stations Pty Ltd & Anor* [2006] HCATrans 272. Essentially the Court considered that the way that the case was pleaded and run below rendered it an inappropriate case for the grant of Special Leave to Appeal.

[13] See Section 4D.

[14] See *News Limited* v. *South Sydney District Rugby League Football Club Ltd* (2003) 215 CLR 563 and *Rural Press Ltd* v. *ACCC* (2003) 216 CLR 53.

[15] See Section 4E of the TPA.

We take the concept of a market to be basically a very simple idea. A market is the area of close competition between firms, or putting it a little differently, the field of rivalry between them ... Within the bounds of a market there is substitution—substitution between one product and another, and between one source of supply and another, in response to changing prices. So a market is the field of actual and potential transactions between buyers and sellers amongst whom there can be strong substitution, at least in the long run, if given a sufficient price incentive. Let us suppose that the price of one supplier goes up. Then on the demand side buyers may switch their patronage from this firm's product to another or from this geographic source of supply to another. As well, on the supply side, sellers can adjust their production plans, substituting one product for another in their output mix, or substituting one geographic source of supply for another. Whether such substitution is feasible or likely depends ultimately on consumer attitudes, technology, distance, and cost and price incentives.

It is the possibilities of such substitution which sets the limits upon a fir m's ability to 'give less and charge more'. Accordingly, in determining the outer boundaries of the market we ask a quite simple but fundamental question: if the firm were to 'give less and charge more' would there be, to put the matter colloquially, much of a reaction? And if so, from whom? In the language of economics the question is this: From which products and which activities could we expect a relatively high demand or supply response to price change, ie, a relatively high cross-elasticity of demand or cross-elasticity of supply?'[16]

Market Power

For the purposes of the TPA, the High Court of Australia has made numerous comments on this issue including the following:

Market power can be described as the ability of a firm to raise prices above the supply cost without rivals taking away customers in due time, supply cost being the minimum cost an efficient firm would incur in producing the product ... ';[17] The term 'market power' is ordinarily taken to be a reference to the power to raise price by restricting output in a sustainable manner ... But market power has aspects other than influence upon the market price. It may be manifested by practices directed at excluding competition such as exclusive dealing, tying arrangements, predatory pricing or refusing to deal ... The ability

[16] *Re Queensland Co-operative Milling Association Ltd; Re Defiance Holdings Ltd* (1976) 8 ALR 481 at 517.

[17] *Queensland Wire Industries* v. *BHP Ltd* (1989) 167 CLR 177 at 189 per Mason C.J. and Wilson J.

> to engage persistently in such practices may be as indicative of market power as the ability to influence prices;[18] ... market power means capacity to behave in a certain way (which might include setting prices, granting or refusing supply, arranging systems of distribution), persistently, free from the constraints of competition. This is the generally accepted meaning of the concept, and it is reflected clearly in the provisions of s 46(3). Barriers to entry into a market by competitors are a common reason for the existence of market power. They could exist, as in the present case, because of technological factors, or they might result, for example, from legislation which gives a statutory monopoly.[19] The essence of power is absence of constraint. Market power in a supplier is absence of constraint from the conduct of competitors or customers. This is reflected in the terms of s 46(3). Matters of degree are involved, but when a question of the degree of market power enjoyed by a supplier arises, the statute directs attention to the extent to which the conduct of the firm is constrained by the conduct of its competitors or its customers.[20]

Substantial Lessening of Competition

The High Court of Australia has noted some competing possible interpretations of this phrase particularly the word 'substantial' but has not yet ruled on the correct one for the purposes of the TPA. It accepted that 'substantial in the sense of being meaningful or relevant to the competitive process' expressed the relevant question before the Court.[21]

Relevance of Foreign Competition Law Terms and Concepts

The High Court of Australia has on a number of occasions cautioned against use of terms or concepts from the Competition laws of other countries when interpreting or applying the Competition laws in Australia as enacted by the

[18] Ibid., at p. 200 per Dawson J and approved in *Melways Publishing Pty Ltd* v. *Robert Hicks Pty Ltd* (2001) 205 CLR 1 at p. 27 par[67] per Gleeson C.J., Gummow, Hayne and Callinan J.J.

[19] *Melways Publishing Pty Ltd* v. *Robert Hicks Pty Ltd* (2001) 205 CLR 1 at p. 27 par[67] per Gleeson CJ, Gummow, Hayne and Callinan JJ.

[20] *Boral Besser Masonry Limited (now Boral Masonry Ltd)* v. *Australian Competition and Consumer Commission* (2003) 215 CLR 374 at p. 420 par [121] per Gleeson C.J. and Callinan J.

[21] *Rural Press Ltd* v. *ACCC* (2003) 216 CLR 53 at 71 par [41] including footnote (67) per Gummow, Hayne, and Heydon J.J. with whom Gleeson C.J. and Callinan J. agreed.

Parliament. For example, in *Boral Besser Masonry Limited (now Boral Masonry Ltd)* v. *Australian Competition and Consumer Commission*:[22]

> Section 46 does not refer specifically to predatory pricing, or recoupment, or selling below variable or avoidable cost. These are concepts that may, or may not, be useful tools of analysis in a particular case where pricing behaviour is alleged to contravene s 46. Care needs to be exercised in their importation from different legislative contexts. In the United States, for example, predatory pricing is often discussed in the context of monopolisation, or attempts to monopolise, in contravention of the Sherman Act 1890. In Europe, Art 86 of the Treaty of Rome prohibits conduct which amounts to an abuse of a dominant position in a market. We are concerned with the language of s 46. We are principally concerned with whether BBM had a substantial degree of power in a market, and whether, in its pricing behaviour, and its upgrading of its production facilities, it took advantage of that power.
>
> Predatory pricing is a concept that was examined in the evidence of economists, and in the judgments in the Federal Court. Ultimately, however, it is the language of the [TPA] that must be construed and applied. The expression was used by Dawson J in *Queensland Wire Industries Pty Ltd* v. *Broken Hill Proprietary Co Ltd* as an example of a practice that may manifest market power, but his Honour had no occasion to explain what he meant by it. One of the most important features of the decision in that case was a rejection of the argument that the concept of 'taking advantage' in s 46 involves some form of predatory behaviour or abuse of power going beyond that which follows from the terms of the statute itself.
>
> There is a danger that a term such as predatory pricing may take on a life of its own, independent of the statute, and distract attention from the language of s 46. There is also a danger that principles relevant to the laws of other countries may be adopted uncritically and without regard to the context in which they were developed.
>
> Finkelstein J, in his reasons for judgment, pointed out that the context in which predatory pricing has been considered in the United States is materially different from that of s 46, and that an expectation of recoupment of monopoly prices at the end of a period of illegal pricing behaviour is not a statutory requirement for the application of s 46.'

And:

> We were referred in submissions to many decisions and commentaries in a number of jurisdictions which touch upon the practice of 'predatory pricing'.

[22] (2003) 215 CLR 374 at p. 421 pars [124] to [127] per Gleeson C.J. and Callinan J.

However, the question whether the Full Court erred in overruling the dismissal by Heerey J of the ACCC's case against BBM is to be considered not by looking to what has been said respecting the practice of 'predatory pricing' and then reviewing the factual findings made by Heerey J. It is necessary to look first to the text and structure of the [TPA], particularly s 46. (References omitted)[23]

In *Visy Paper Pty Ltd* v. *ACCC*:[24]

In identifying the operation to be given to s 45(6), it is not useful to adopt a description of the relevant arrangement as 'horizontal' or 'vertical'. There are at least three related reasons why that is so.

First, the [TPA] does not adopt a classification which uses those terms. Adopting them confuses the task of construing the [TPA's] provisions. It is necessary to pay attention to the text of applicable statutes in preference to judicial or other glosses on that language. Not only does adopting these terms distract attention from the language of the [TPA], it does so by introducing terms which are, so it seems, intended to convey value or other judgments about the social or economic consequences that are assumed or expected to follow from the making of or giving effect to the arrangement to which one of these descriptions is applied. Much turns, therefore, on both the content given to the terms and the validity of the assumptions about consequences that their use entails.

Secondly, and no less importantly, employing the descriptions of 'horizontal' and 'vertical' appears intended to adopt, or at least runs a serious risk of inviting the adoption of, the usage of such terms in the wholly different statutory context of United States antitrust law. In particular, the use of these terms invites attention to the distinction drawn in the antitrust law of that country between arrangements which are to be condemned as 'per se' violations of antitrust law and arrangements which are to be tested against the so-called 'Rule of Reason'. As Judge Posner rightly has written, '[t]hese are not illuminating terms. What they *gesture at* is the distinction, fundamental in law, between a rule and a standard' (emphasis added). It is unhelpful to use the language of gesture in preference to construing the statute.

Even in the United States, 'horizontal' and 'vertical' are not terms having agreed or fixed meanings. They are jargon, used as shorthand descriptions, sometimes conveying different meanings to different readers. Moreover, it is not accepted in that country that their use necessarily entails any conclusion about the economic consequences of the arrangement. As Professor

[23] (2003) 215 CLR 374 at p. 430 para [165] per Gaudron, Gummow, and Hayne J.J.

[24] (2003) 216 CLR 1 at pp. 10–1 paras [23]–[7] per Gleeson, C.J., McHugh, Gummow and Hayne J.J. and see pp. 18–20 at paras [52]–[7] per Kirby J.

> Hovenkamp points out, '[s]imply to conclude that an agreement is horizontal establishes nothing about whether it is competitive or anticompetitive'.
>
> These are reasons enough to conclude that the adoption of these terms is not useful in the present context. There is, however, a third point of particular application to this case. The non-competition provisions proposed restricted the acquisition of goods and restricted the supply of services. They can, therefore, be said to reflect a dual and composite relationship. Describing the effect of those provisions as a 'horizontal' or a 'vertical' restraint states a conclusion which masks that dual character. Moreover, it inverts the proper order of inquiry because the argument proceeds from classification to a conclusion about the application of the [TPA], rather than beginning with the proper construction and application of the relevant provisions. (References omitted)

In Australia, the approach to statutory construction of the TPA is governed by the general approach to that issue as provided in the High Court's decision in *Project Blue Sky* v. *Australian Broadcasting Authority*.[25] That case is authority for the following propositions:

- The primary object of statutory construction is to construe the relevant provision so that it is consistent with the language and purpose of all the provisions of the statute.
- The meaning of the provision must be determined by reference to the language of the instrument viewed as a whole.
- The process of construction must begin by examining the context of the provision that is being construed.
- A legislative instrument must be construed on the prima facie basis that its provisions are intended to give effect to harmonious goals.
- Where conflict appears to arise from the language of particular provisions, the conflict must be alleviated, so far as possible, by adjusting the meaning of the competing provisions to achieve that result which will best give effect to the purpose and language of those provisions while maintaining the unity of all the statutory provisions.
- A court construing a statutory provision must strive to give meaning to every word of the provision.
- The duty of a court is to give the words of a statutory provision the meaning the legislature is taken to have intended them to have. Ordinarily, that meaning (the legal meaning) will correspond with the grammatical meaning of the

[25] [1998] HCA 28 at paras [69]–[71] and [78]; (1998) 194 CLR 355 at pp. 381–2, 384 paras [69]–[71] and [78] per McHugh, Gummow, Kirby, and Hayne J.J. (references omitted).

> provision. But not always. The context of the words, the consequences of a literal or grammatical construction, the purpose of the statute or the canons of construction may require the words of a legislative provision to be read in a way that does not correspond with the literal or grammatical meaning.

The latest illustration of this approach and differing views resulting from it is the High Court's decision regarding construction of a provision of the TPA dealing with severability (s 4L of the TPA) and its interaction with the exclusive dealing provisions of the TPA (s 47) particularly dealing with third line forcing.[26] The High Court found that s 4L of the TPA is 'engaged (a) only if there is a contract (as distinct from an arrangement or understanding), (b) only if the *making* of that contract contravenes the [TPA], and (c) only if the making of the contract contravenes the [TPA] by reason of the inclusion of a particular provision in the contract. It follows that s 4L cannot be engaged in respect of a number of kinds of contravention of the [TPA] because it cannot be said that they turn on the making of a contract which contravened the [TPA] by reason of the inclusion of a particular provision.' The majority of the Court[27] went on to hold that on its proper constructions 4L *requires* severance rather than *permits* severance of the offending condition of the contract. Justice Kirby in the minority held that severability was to be an exceptional solution and said '[i]t would be remarkable if, in the language of s 4L, the exceptional cases of severability were given such predominance as to undermine the important work of the exclusive dealing provisions in protecting competition and fair trade practices.'[28]

Australian Competition Law Compliance

Compliance with competition law in Australia is achieved through both public and private enforcement. As can be seen from the case examples below, both forms of enforcement action have contributed significantly to the development of Australian Competition law jurisprudence, awareness, and compliance. A valuable and insightful account of the role and impact of the competition regulator in the Australian community under the leadership of Allan Fels as its Chairman is provided in the book by Fred Brenchley,

[26] *SST Consulting Services Pty Ltd* v. *Rieson & Anor* [2006] HCA 31 (15 June 2006).

[27] Gleeson C.J., and Gummow, Hayne, Heydon, and Crennan J.J.

[28] *SST Consulting Services Pty Ltd* v. *Rieson & Anor* [2006] HCA 31 (15 June 2006) at para [108].

Allan Fels—A Portrait of Power (Wiley 2003). In addition, as a public enforcement agency, the ACCC launched for consultation a draft Leniency Policy to break 'Hard-Core Cartels' in July 2002[29] and in June 2003, launched its Leniency Policy for Cartel Conduct.[30] In November 2004, the ACCC announced a review of its Leniency Policy for Cartel Conduct.[31] On 26 August 2005, the ACCC issued its revised policy.[32]

Examples of some key Competition cases taken by ACCC.

Cartel Cases

- *TPC* v. *TNT Australia Pty Ltd and Others*[33]—Freight industry. Penalties of about A$12 million were imposed against three large freight companies and nearly twenty executives.
- *TPC* v. *Pioneer Concrete (Qld) Pty Ltd and Others*[34]—Pre-mixed Concrete industry. Penalties of over A$20 million were imposed against three premixed concrete suppliers and some of their executives.
- *ACCC* v. *ABB Power Transformers and Others;*[35] *and ACCC* v. *ABB Distribution Transformers Ltd and Others*[36]—Electrical Transformers

[29] See http://www.accc.gov.au/content/index.phtml/itemId/88120.

[30] See http://www.accc.gov.au/content/index.phtml/itemId/346231 and http://www.accc.gov.au/content/index.phtml/itemId/454181.

[31] See http://www.accc.gov.au/content/index.phtml/itemId/550606/fromItemId/2332 and see http://www.accc.gov.au/content/item.phtml?itemId=529200&nodeId= file41d9fa6b8a0da&fn=Leniency%20Discussion%20Paper.pdf for the discussion paper about the Review.

[32] See http://www.accc.gov.au/content/index.phtml/itemId/706275/fromItemId/620299 and http://www.accc.gov.au/content/index.phtml/itemId/706268.

[33] See http://www.austlii.edu.au/au/cases/cth/federal_ct/unrep7321.html. Also see (1995) ATPR 41–375.

[34] See http://www.accc.gov.au/content/index.phtml/itemId/86962/fromItemId/472035.

[35] Proceedings instituted in October 1999—for summary of allegations see http://www.accc.gov.au/content/index.phtml/itemId/322766.

Also see http://www.austlii.edu.au/au/cases/cth/federal_ct/2003/626.html and cases cited in para 2 of the reasons for judgment, and http://www.austlii.edu.au/ au/cases/cth/federal_ct/2004/819.html.

[36] Proceedings instituted in November 2000—for summary of allegations see http://www.accc.gov.au/content/index.phtml/itemId/87555.

Also see http://www.austlii.edu.au/au/cases/cth/federal_ct/2003/626.html and cases cited therein.

industry. Penalties of over A$35 million were imposed against six electrical transformer companies and nine executives.

- *ACCC* v. *Roche Vitamins Australia and Others*[37]—Animal Vitamins industry. Penalties totalling A$26 million were imposed on three animal vitamin suppliers.
- *ACCC* v. *Rural Press Ltd*[38] Regional Newspaper industry. The High Court of Australia upheld ACCC claim of arrangement with purpose or effect of substantially lessening competition and breaching exclusionary conduct provision but not a misuse of market power.
- *ACCC* v. *Leahy Petroleum Pty Ltd and Others*[39]—Retail Petrol industry. Court upheld ACCC claim of price fixing following contested hearing.
- *ACCC* v. *Woolworths Ltd and Liquorland (Australia) Pty Ltd*[40]—Retail Liquor industry. Liquorland and the ACCC settled their proceeding. In the settlement, Liquorland and the ACCC agreed that Liquorland had contravened the TPA in that the relevant provisions of the deeds contained exclusionary provisions—provisions between two or more persons who were competitive with each other and the provisions had the purpose of preventing, restricting, or limiting the supply of goods to particular persons or classes or persons. Liquorland refused to accede to the proposition consensually that there had been a contravention by it of s 45 (2) of the TPA by the provisions having the purpose of substantially lessening competition. Penalties of $4.75 million were imposed on Liquorland. Woolworths did not participate in that settlement. It denied any contravention of the TPA. The matter was heard by the Court over thirty-four days concluding on

[37] Proceedings instituted in about December 2000—for summary of allegations see http://www.accc.gov.au/content/index.phtml/itemId/87582.

Also see http://www.austlii.edu.au/au/cases/cth/federal_ct/2001/150.html and http://www.accc.gov.au/content/index.phtml/itemId/87653.

[38] Proceedings instituted in July 1999—for summary of allegations see http://www.accc.gov.au/content/index.phtml/itemId/322960/fromItemId/2332/pageDefinitionItemId/16940. Also see *Rural Press Limited* v. *Australian Competition and Consumer Commission*; [2003] HCA 75 (11 December 2003) and http://www.accc.gov.au/content/index.phtml/itemId/420243/fromItemId/378016.

[39] Proceedings instituted in May 2002—for summary of allegations see http://www.accc.gov.au/content/index.phtml/itemId/88078. Also see *ACCC* v. *Leahy Petroleum* [2004] FCA 1678 (17 December 2004).

[40] Proceedings instituted in June 2003—for summary of allegations see http://www.accc.gov.au/content/index.phtml/itemId/346179/and regarding the outcome see http://www.accc.gov.au/content/index.phtml/itemId/750980/fromItemId/2332 and http://www.austlii.edu.au/au/cases/cth/federal_ct/2006/826.html.

20 July 2005. On 30 June 2006, the Court concluded that in respect of two of the four provisions there was a contravention by Woolworths of s 45 (2) of the TPA in respect of the exclusionary provision case. The Court also concluded that Woolworths contravened s 45 (2) in respect of the purpose of substantially lessening competition case in respect of all four episodes. This conclusion was based on the assessment of all the evidence, including the evidence of officers of Woolworths responsible for the events in question and after concluding that the relevant markets in which to assess the conduct of Woolworths for the sale of takeaway packaged liquor, were in these circumstances, and for this analysis, the local markets as pleaded by the ACCC.

Misuse of Market Power Cases

- *TPC* v. *CSR Ltd*[41]—Plasterboard and Related Products industry. Misuse of market power by reason of a constructive refusal to supply plasterboard and related products. Penalty of A$220,000 imposed (from a maximum penalty then of A$250,000).
- *ACCC* v. *Commonwealth of Australia*[42]—Meteorological services industry. The ACCC alleged that the Commonwealth of Australia through the Bureau of Meteorology breached Section 46 of the Trade Practices Act because it refused to supply basic meteorological information to a competitor for the purpose of deterring the entry of that competitor into the market for enhanced meteorological services. It also alleged that the Bureau provided specialized meteorological services on a non-commercial basis for the purpose of deterring competitive conduct. The matter was settled prior to trial.

  Boral Besser Masonry Limited (now Boral Masonry Ltd) v. *ACCC*[43]—Masonry Products industry. The High Court of Australia by a 6:1 majority overturned a unanimous decision of the Full Court of the Federal Court,

[41] See (1991) ATPR 52,135.

[42] Proceedings instituted in December1995—for summary of allegations see http://www.accc.gov.au/content/index.phtml/itemId/86959/fromItemId/472035. The proceedings were settled in May 1997 before going to trial see http://www.accc.gov.au/content/index.phtml/itemId/87108.

[43] Proceedings instituted in March 1998—for summary of allegations see http://www.accc.gov.au/content/index.phtml/itemId/322775/fromItemId/2332 and http://www.austlii.edu.au/au/cases/cth/federal_ct/1999/1318.html Also see http://www.austlii.edu.au/au/cases/cth/federal_ct/2001/30.html http://www.accc.gov.au/content/index.phtml/itemId/87651/fromItemId/378012/pageDefinitionItemId/16940

and held that Boral Masonry Ltd did not misuse its market power in the market for concrete masonry products in Melbourne because it did not have a substantial degree of market power to trigger the threshold required by s46 of the Trade Practices Act. The decision was the first consideration by Australia's highest Court of below cost pricing and the misuse of market power provision in the Trade Practices Act.

- *ACCC* v. *Universal Music, Sony Music and Warner Music and Others*[44]—Importation and Retailing of Compact Discs industry. The ACCC alleged the defendants had taken unlawful action (threatening to withdraw significant trading benefits from retailers and cutting off supply to retailers who stocked parallel imports of compact discs) in order to discourage or prevent Australian businesses from selling competitively priced parallel imports of compact discs. The conduct was alleged to constitute a misuse of market power and exclusive dealing prohibited by the Trade Practices Act. Senior executives were alleged to have been involved in the conduct. The Full Court of the Federal Court upheld an appeal by Universal and Warner that their conduct did not breach the misuse of market power provision but confirmed that the conduct did breach the exclusive dealing provisions. The Full Court also upheld the ACCC's appeal on penalty increasing the total penalties from about A$1 million to over A$2 million.
- *ACCC* v. *Australian Safeway Stores Pty Ltd and Others*[45]—Bread industry. The allegations concerned the supply of bread by Tip Top Bakeries to retailers who discounted the price of the bread. The ACCC alleged that Safeway took action against Tip Top Bakeries and other bread manufac-

---

http://www.austlii.edu.au/au/cases/cth/high_ct/2003/5.html and http://www.accc.gov.au/content/index.phtml/itemId/88315.

[44] Proceedings instituted in September 1999—for summary of allegations see http://www.accc.gov.au/content/index.phtml/itemId/322787. Also see http://accc.gov.au/content/index.phtml/itemId/87686 http://www.austlii.edu.au/au/cases/cth/federal_ct/2001/1800.html http://www.accc.gov.au/content/index.phtml/itemId/87931; http://www.austlii.edu.au/au/cases/cth/federal_ct/2002/192.html.

http://www.accc.gov.au/content/index.phtml/itemId/357338 and http://www.austlii.edu.au/au/cases/cth/FCAFC/2003/193.html.

[45] Proceedings instituted in December 1996—for summary of allegations see http://www.accc. gov. au/content/index.phtml/itemId/86770 and http://www.accc.gov.au/content/index.phtml/itemId/87102.

Also see http://www.accc.gov.au/content/index.phtml/itemId/87980 http://www.austlii.edu.au/au/cases/cth/FCAFC/2003/149.htmlhttp://www.accc.gov.au/content/index.phtml/itemId/346156 and http://www.austlii.edu.au/au/other/HCATrans/2004/344.html.

turers to induce them, or attempt to induce them, to take action to have the discounting cease. It alleged that Safeway refused to accept further supplies of bread from Tip Top Bakeries, and the other major bread manufacturers, who were supplying retailers who were discounting the price of bread. Safeway recommenced purchasing bread from the manufacturer concerned once the discounter had ceased discounting.

The Full Court of the Federal Court partially upheld the ACCC's appeal and held that Safeway had, on four of the nine instances alleged, misused its market power and had also engaged in price fixing as alleged in one instance. Applications by Safeway and the ACCC for special leave to appeal to the High Court of Australia were each dismissed. On 31 January 2006, the trial judge imposed penalties totalling A$8.9 million for the breaches found by the Full Court.

- *ACCC* v. *Baxter Healthcare Pty Ltd*[46]—Medical products industry. It was alleged that Baxter Healthcare Pty Ltd misused its market power and engaged in exclusive dealing in the supply of medical products to certain Australian State and Territory health purchasing authorities in contravention of the TPA. The TPA generally applies to Governments when those Governments are carrying on a business. The Federal Court found that because Baxter was supplying state purchasing authorities which were not carrying on a business and therefore entitled to Crown immunity, the Crown immunity extended to protect Baxter from the proceedings brought by the ACCC. Without this protection, the Federal Court would have held that Baxter had breached the exclusive dealing provisions of the TPA in relation to its offers to supply sterile fluids which were tied to the sale of peritoneal dialysis products. Further, without this protection Baxter also would have contravened the misuse of market power provisions of the TPA. The ACCC had appealed the decision. On 24 August 2006, the Full Court of the Federal Court dismissed the ACCC's appeal. It agreed with the trial judge that because Baxter was supplying state purchasing authorities which were not carrying on business and therefore entitled to immunity from the TPA, Baxter was also immune from the provisions of the TPA because of a principle of derivative immunity. On 22 September 2006, the ACCC announced that it was seeking Special Leave to Appeal to the

[46] Proceedings instituted in November 2002—for summary of allegations see http://www.accc.gov.au/content/index.phtml/itemId/88219. Trial completed second half of 2004 for outcome see http://www.accc.gov.au/content/index.phtml/itemId/692184/fromItemId/620299 and http://www.austlii.edu.au/au/cases/cth/federal_ct/2005/581.html.

High Court of Australia. That application is likely to be heard in the first quarter of 2007.

Competition Cases by the Private Sector

- *Queensland Wire Industries* v. *BHP Ltd*[47] (February 1989). Refusal by BHP to supply Y bar (an intermediary fencing product) to QWI. Held by High Court of Australia to constitute a misuse of market power.
- *Melway Publishing Pty Ltd* v. *Robert Hicks Pty Ltd*[48] (March 2001)—Refusal to supply street directories for distribution and to maintain its exclusive distribution system was held, by the High Court of Australia, not to constitute a misuse of market power by Melway.
- *News Limited* v. *South Sydney District Rugby League Football Club Limited*[49] (August 2003). Merger of competing sporting competitions. Provision that no more than a certain number of teams participate in new competition. Whether provision included for purpose of preventing, restricting, or limiting supply of goods or services to, or acquisition of goods or services from, particular persons or classes of persons in contravention of the exclusionary provisions of the *Trade Practices Act*. High Court of Australia held alleged conduct did not constitute a breach.
- *NT Power Generation Pty Ltd* v. *Power and Water Authority*[50] (October 2004). PAWA, a statutory authority, had a monopoly in the markets for electricity transmission and distribution services and for electricity supply in the Northern Territory. It owned the transmission and distribution infrastructure. No transactions occurred in the transmission and distribution services market. Issues on appeal before the High Court of Australia included:
  - Crown in right of the Northern Territory—Carrying on a business for the purposes of the Trade Practices Act;
  - Whether authority's exclusive use of the infrastructure was part of carrying on a business;
  - Whether PAWA's control of the infrastructure gave it market power in both markets;
  - Whether PAWA's refusal of access to its infrastructure involved taking advantage of its market power or only of its proprietary rights;
  - Whether refusal was due to a 'direction' from the Minister;

[47] See http://www.austlii.edu.au/au/cases/cth/high_ct/167clr177.html.

[48] See http://www.austlii.edu.au/au/cases/cth/high_ct/2001/13.html.

[49] See http://www.austlii.edu.au/au/cases/cth/high_ct/2003/45.html.

[50] See http://www.austlii.edu.au/au/cases/cth/high_ct/2004/48.html.

- Whether Minister's purpose in giving direction meant authority's refusal was not for a proscribed purpose; and
- Whether authority's regulatory role meant refusal was not for a proscribed purpose;

The High Court held that the TPA did apply to the conduct of PAWA and that its conduct in refusing NT Power's request for access to its infrastructure constituted a misuse of market power.

Proposed Amendments to TPA

In response to the recommendations of the Dawson Review[51] of the competition provisions of the TPA and some Parliamentary inquiries[52] on the subject, the Australian government announced[53] that it would be amending the TPA by introducing criminal sanctions for serious cartel conduct; amending the merger provisions to enable businesses to have a choice of going directly to the Australian Competition Tribunal regarding some merger matters or using the current option of going to the ACCC first and then if required, to the Tribunal on appeal and providing for a more formalized merger clearance process; and clarifying the meaning and application of the misuse of market power provisions. The proposed amendments were caught up in the political process for a year. On 19 October 2006, the first round of the amendments were passed. These amendments provide—a simplified notification process for collective bargaining by small businesses; businesses to go directly to the Australian Competition Tribunal (rather than the ACCC first) for authorization of a merger; search warrant evidence seizure powers for the ACCC; maximum civil penalties for corporations to be the greater of A$10 million or three times the gain from the contravention or where the gain cannot be readily ascertained, 10 per cent of the turnover of the body corporate and any related bodies corporate; and retain the per se prohibition on third line

[51] Review of the Competition Provisions of the Trade Practices Act, January 2003 Chaired by Sir Daryl Dawson, AC KBE CB.

[52] The Effectiveness of the Trade Practices Act 1974 in protecting small business, Senate Economics Committee 2003.

[53] See, for example, the Commonwealth Treasurer's press release and government response of 16 April 2003: http://www.treasurer.gov.au/tsr/content/pressreleases/2003/021.asp and http://www.treasurer.gov.au/tsr/content/publications/tparesponse.asp.

forcing conduct. The reforms to clarify the misuse of market power provisions and criminalize cartels are still to come.

It should be noted that as part of Australia's National Competition Policy, state and territory governments must be consulted regarding proposed amendments to the TPA and a majority approval to the proposed changes has to be obtained by the Federal government. The state and territory governments would then amend their Competition Codes to mirror the changes to the TPA and maintain a uniform set of provisions.

Federal enactments dealing with restrictive trade practices in Australia can be traced back to the Australian Industries Preservation Act 1906 (Cth), the Trade Practices Act 1965 (Cth), and the Restrictive Trade Practices Act 1971 (Cth). However the 1974 enactment of the TPA is generally regarded as the coming of age of competition law in Australia. Steady implementation and enforcement of the TPA saw a changing of the Australian business culture from one often regarded as being characterized by 'orderly marketing arrangements' to a more competitive culture.

To accelerate Australia's competitive performance, the 1992 appointment by the COAG of the Hilmer Committee to advise the COAG on the implementation of a National Competition Policy and its subsequent report of August 1993 and the adoption and implementation by the COAG and by all Australian Parliaments of National Competition Policy reforms in the 1994–6 period stands out as a landmark achievement, even on an international basis, of economic reforms. For over a decade, the reforms have boosted the competitiveness of the Australian economy with consequent impact on efficiency and productivity and provided benefits of enhanced welfare and growth.

A key aspect of the reforms was the universal application of the competition laws to all businesses in Australia (including all government businesses and unincorporated businesses). Continued provision of extensive education and compliance material and vigorous enforcement of Australia's competition laws by the ACCC have contributed significantly to an ongoing change in Australian business towards a more competitive culture with enhanced understanding of and focus on compliance with Australia's competition laws. Improved private sector awareness and enforcement of Australia's competition laws have also contributed significantly to those outcomes.

Further proposed reforms of Australia's competition laws (including criminalization of serious cartel behaviour) will further refine and highlight the Australian focus on promoting fair and competitive markets in Australia. As markets continue to go global and free trade agreements between Australia and various trading partners continue to increase, the message from Australian parliaments that Australia is open for business but will not tolerate anticompetitive conduct is being strengthened.

12

EC Competition Law*

The First Experiences of Modernization

Michael J. Reynolds

Background

The European Economic Community was established by the Treaty of Rome in 1957. It has been known as the European Community (EC) since the Maastricht Treaty of 1992, reflecting its move towards a more political rather than a purely economic community. The original treaty was amended and consolidated by the Amsterdam Treaty (the Treaty) of 1999. As of May 2004, the European Community comprises 25 Member States.[1]

At the heart of the Treaty is the establishment of a common market and economic and monetary union, and the implementation of common policies

* Reproduced from 'EC Competition Law: The First Experiences of Modernization', published in Dhall, V. (ed.). 2007. *Competition Law Today: Concepts, Issues, and the Law in Practice* (first ed.), Oxford University Press, New Delhi.

[1] Austria, Belgium, Cyprus, the Czech Republic, Denmark, Estonia, Finland, France, Germany, Greece, Hungary, Ireland, Italy, Latvia, Lithuania, Luxembourg, Malta, the Netherlands, Poland, Portugal, The Slovak Republic, Slovenia, Spain, Sweden, and the United Kingdom.

to promote development of the community. The main aims of competition policy are the protection of consumers and competition, as opposed to the protection of competitors. In order to achieve these aims, it is important that the internal market of the community should not be distorted, and that the principle of an open market with free competition should be adhered to. Thus, single market integration is a key principle of competition policy. The Treaty is concerned with other aspects of the promotion of competition within Europe. Thus, the elimination of obstacles to the free movement of goods, services, persons, and capital are given high priority. Further, the setting up of a public procurement regime to govern the buying procedures of public authorities or utilities for goods, works, and services introduces the twin goals of Europe-wide competition and cost efficiency. The creation of the Euro was another important step in allowing price transparency, and price competition, and contributed substantially to the competitiveness of the European economy.

The Competition chapter of the Treaty is to be found at Title V. The rules which apply to undertakings are found at Articles 81 to 86; those which deal with aids granted by states are at Articles 87 to 89.

The principal provisions relating to undertakings are to be found at Articles 81 and 82. These key Articles set the framework within which business activities are subject to intervention by the European Commission ('Commission'). Articles 87 to 89 provide rules for preventing the market distorting effect of State aid to enterprises. A brief overview of all of these provisions is set out below.

The Treaty does not contain any specific provisions relating to mergers. Historically, mergers were dealt with by the application of Articles 81 and 82. However, this was considered to be an inadequate way of governing mergers and so, in 1989, the EC Merger Regulation (ECMR) was introduced. The current rules are contained in Council Regulation (EC) 139/2004. A brief overview of the ECMR is given below.

EC competition law underwent a major overhaul and significant changes were brought about to procedure since 1 May 2004. These are discussed in the main body of the text which follows.

Article 81 EC Treaty

Article 81(1) of the EC Treaty prohibits agreements, decisions by associations of undertakings, and concerted practices between undertakings which may affect trade between Member States and which have as their object or effect the prevention, restriction, or distortion of competition within the Community. Article 81(2) provides that such agreements are void unless and until exemption[2] is granted by the European Commission under Article 81(3).[3]

An 'agreement' implies that two parties have knowingly entered into or adopted a particular course of action. The agreement need not be in writing nor need it be an express oral agreement. The notion of a 'concerted practice' has been interpreted by the European Courts very widely. A concerted practice exists where a form of 'coordination between undertakings which, without having reached the stage where an agreement properly so-called has been concluded, knowingly substitutes practical cooperation between them for the risks of competition'.

There must be two or more undertakings. Consequently, agreements that are purely intra-company, for example, between parents and subsidiaries or affiliates in the same economic group, are not caught by Article 81.

The agreement, decision, or concerted practice must affect trade between Member States, Conduct in only one Member State may also infringe Article 81(1) if it has an appreciable effect on trade between Member States.

Examples of practices which have been held to be contrary to Article 81(1) have included the following: the exchange of information about the level of prices and quantities of goods delivered; agreement by suppliers to notify their prices to other suppliers who are members of an association; the adoption of common rules on the computation of costs; and exchange of information concerning exports.

Prior to 1 May 2004, there was a system, created by Regulation 17/62,[4] which required parties to notify their agreements, decisions, or concerted

[2] Categories of agreements may be granted exemption, in advance if they satisfy the four criteria set out in Article 81(3): that the agreement (i) results in an improvement to the production or distribution of goods and promotes economic or technical progress; (ii) provides consumers with a fair share of the economic benefits; (iii) only contain restrictions that are indispensable to the achievement of the economic benefits that are the objectives of the agreement; and (iv) do not eliminate competition in respect of a substantial part of the products concerned. This has resulted in a series of block exemptions. Agreements falling within the terms of the block exemption do not need to be notified to the Commission and are valid without specific authorization. The system of block exemptions survived the Commission's modernization package.

[3] Since 1 May 2004, National Competition Authorities have parallel competence with the European Commission to apply Article 82(3) EC, and are required to apply Articles 81 and 82 to all activities falling within their scope (rather than national laws).

[4] OJ 1962 62/204: Regulation as last amended by Regulation (EC) No 1216/1999 (OJ 1999 LI 148/5).

practices to the Commission in order to apply for, and obtain, an exemption under Article 81(3). The notification process was an extremely time-consuming and burdensome one, for companies and for the Commission alike.

It is Article 81 (EC) which is particularly applicable in the context of cartel investigations. The Commission now has a dedicated Cartels Unit with specialists in anti-cartel work. As part of the Commission's drive to flush out cartels, it introduced, in 1996, a 'Leniency Notice', which has since been amended. The current notice[5] came into force on 19 February 2002, and has been a significant factor in encouraging whistle-blowing and thus the detection and punishment of cartel behaviour throughout Europe.

Article 82 EC Treaty

Article 82 of the EC Treaty addresses a different type of anticompetitive behaviour, namely the abuse by one or more undertakings of a dominant market position. Whilst dominance in a market is not of itself unlawful, a dominant undertaking will infringe Article 82 if it abuses its dominant position and there is an effect on trade between EC Member States.

In determining whether a dominant position exists, the Commission will consider a number of factors, including the market share of the undertaking(s) and its competitors and its customers' market power as well as other characteristics of the market. The classic definition of dominance is the extent to which an undertaking has the power to 'behave, either individually or jointly, to an appreciable extent independently of competitors, customers, and ultimately consumers'.[6] A market share of 50 per cent or greater, in the absence of exceptional circumstances, generally gives rise to a presumption of dominance.[7]

A company with a high market share, or which may be considered to have a position of joint or collective dominance in an oligopolistic market, must take particular care in its behaviour.

Simply acquiring or maintaining a dominant position does not violate Article 82. There must be an abuse of that position. The most common examples of abusive behaviour include: long-term supply contracts for a large proportion of a customer's needs; buying and selling at unfairly low or high prices; charging discriminatory prices; refusing to supply a customer without

[5] Commission Notice on immunity from fines and reduction of fines in cartel cases (2002/C 45/03).

[6] Case 27/76 United Brands.

[7] Case C62/86 AKZO.

good reason; tying; and attempting to induce customer loyalty by granting fidelity rebates or discounts. It is not possible to apply for an individual exemption for conduct falling within the scope of this Article.

At the time of this writing, the Commission is conducting a public consultation on a staff discussion paper, which looks at ways in which the regime for dealing with Article 82 could be changed. The review is a mechanism for setting out in a clear and consistent manner theories of harm underlying the application of Article 82 on the basis of sound economic assessment and to develop practical and workable rules, which take into account the reality of the market. The results of the review are not expected before the end of 2006.

Enforcement of Articles 81 and 82 EC Treaty

The Commission and national competition authorities have joint competition to apply and enforce Articles 81 and 82. In addition, the Court of First Instance, the European Court of Justice and national courts have jurisdiction to determine the applicability of Articles 81 and 82.

Agreements that infringe Article 81(1) are void and unenforceable unless they qualify for an exemption under Article 81(3). Moreover, the Commission has the power to impose the following sanctions for violations of Articles 81 and 82:

- fines of up to 10 per cent of an infringing firm's previous year's group turnover;
- orders requiring an undertaking to terminate infringements; and
- interim measures.

Furthermore, private parties may bring a cause of action for damages or injunctive relief relating to alleged infringements of the EU competition rules, although issues relating to standing, procedure, and the amount of damages are governed by national law.

Mergers

Under the ECMR, the Commission has, subject to limited exceptions, exclusive jurisdiction within the EU over 'concentrations' having a 'Community dimension' (the so-called 'one-stop shop' principle). Such transactions require prior notification to and clearance by the Commission. In the case of public bids, the normal procedures of the ECMR apply, subject to the operation of certain specific provisions. Where the ECMR does not apply, the transaction is subject to the merger control rules of the EU Member States. There are specific rules for determining whether a 'concentration' exists, and specific thresholds to determine whether such a concentration would have a 'community dimension'.

Under the ECMR, a concentration with a Community dimension should be notified to the Commission prior to its implementation and following the conclusion of the agreement; the announcement of the public bid; or the acquisition of a controlling interest. In addition, parties will be able to make notification prior to the normal triggering events, if they can demonstrate to the Commission a 'good faith' intention to conclude an agreement (or in the case of a public bid, where they have publicly announced an intention to make such a bid), providing that the agreement or bid would result in a concentration with a Community dimension. A concentration may not be put into effect until the Commission has concluded its investigation and reached a decision.

The ECMR requires the Commission to prohibit transactions which would 'significantly impede effective competition' in the common market or in a substantial part of it, in particular as a result of the creation or strengthening of a dominant position. A dominant position is one which would enable the merged entity to behave to an appreciable extent independently of its competitors, customers and, ultimately, of its consumers.

The Commission will also examine vertical links between the parties to ensure that the transaction will not have any significant foreclosure effects in any relevant market, either upstream or downstream, and, in conglomerate transactions, it will examine the extent to which the combined financial resources or the pooling of technical and commercial expertise might give cause for concern.

State Aid

State aid that distorts competition in the Common Market is prohibited by Article 87 EC. By giving certain firms or products favoured treatment to the detriment of other firms or products, state aid seriously disrupts normal competitive forces. Whether or not there had been state aid depends then on whether there has been an advantage granted by a member state or through State resources which distorts competition, favours certain undertakings or the production of certain goods, and which has an effect on trade between member states. There are certain *de minimis* rules which are beyond the scope of this chapter.

Broadly speaking, aid which has not been notified is unlawful and the undertaking in receipt of the state aid may be required to pay it back. It is for the member state to notify the Commission. Article 87(2) sets out the grounds on which aid may be compatible with the Common Market.

Modernization

The modernization of European competition law was launched on 1 May 2004, when Council Regulation (EC) 1/2003[8] (the 'Regulation') came into force. Much debate, consultation, and negotiation had taken place during the five years preceding the adoption of the Regulation which was heralded as a bright new age for the Directorate General for Competition (DG Comp) of the European Commission. The Regulation was flanked by Commission Regulation (EC) 773/2004[9] on the conduct of the Commission for the application of Articles 81 and 82 (the 'Implementing Regulation') and a further six notices[10] comprising the entire modernization package. These changes were in part driven by the need to review the existing framework of competition policy enforcement within the European Union (EU) and to ensure the efficient protection of competition in the enlarged EU. It was also driven by concerns that the existing centralized process of enforcement was cumbersome, inefficient, and overly burdensome.

The reform aimed to enhance enforcement by simplifying procedures, transferring additional powers to the member states, and strengthening the Commission's existing powers of investigation. Companies would no longer need to notify their individual arrangements or agreements in order to obtain clearance or exemption under the antitrust rules. The reasoning behind this major sea-change was that the previous notification regime diverted substantial Commission resources from the investigation of the most anticompetitive agreements and had resulted in legal uncertainty in relation to many other agreements, as cases were often cleared by the administrative 'comfort

[8] OJ [2003] L1/1.

[9] OJ [2004] L123/18.

[10] Commission notice on cooperation within the Network of Competition Authorities OJ [2004] C 101/43; Commission notice on the cooperation between the Commission and the courts of the EU Member States in the application of Articles 81 and 82 EC OJ [2004] C 101/54; Commission notice on the handling of complaints by the Commission under Articles 81 and 82 of the EC Treaty OJ [2004] C 101/65; Commission notice on informal guidance relating to novel questions concerning Articles 81 and 82 of the EC Treaty that arise in individual cases (guidance letters) OJ [2004] C 101/78; Guidelines on the effect on trade concept contained in Articles 81and 82 of the Treaty OJ [2004] C 101/81; Guidelines on the application of Article 81(3) of the Treaty OJ [2004] C 101/97.

letter'-route rather than by way of a formal decision. The Regulation aimed to reduce bureaucracy, with the Commission relinquishing its monopoly over the grant of exemptions under Article 81(3), and national competition authorities or courts being empowered to rule on the application of Article 81(3). At the same time, the Regulation established the European Competition Network (ECN) to provide for greater cooperation between national competition authorities (NCAs) and the Commission.

As mentioned above, the package comprises not only hard law, in the form of the Regulation and Implementing Regulation, but also 'soft' law in the guise of the six notices. These latter instruments, according to Mario Monti 'provide further clarification on aspects of the new antitrust rules ... [and] constitute a valuable instrument which provides guidance in the application of Articles 81 and 82'.[11] Thus, while the Regulation and Implementing Regulation define the structure and legal basis for the new regime, it is noteworthy that the shift to a more notice-based system allows for differences of interpretation which could potentially impact upon the validity or otherwise of an agreement.

This chapter proposes to reflect upon certain aspects of the package which were hailed as innovative and comment, to the extent discernible or possible, upon the extent to which the stated aims have been achieved. There is a paucity of published hard data concerning the preliminary results of modernization but this chapter will be considering:

1. The European Competition Network;
2. Leniency; and
3. Private enforcement.

European Competition Network

The ECN's purpose, as stipulated in the recitals[12] of the Commission notice on cooperation within the network of competition authorities (the 'Notice') is to be both practical and efficient as increased cooperation should ensure that agreements and practices brought to the attention of an NCA will also be made known to the Commission and vice-versa. The NCAs forming part

[11] Foreword to 'Modernization of EC Antitrust Enforcement Rules: Council Regulation (EC) no 1/2003 and the Modernization Package' published by the European Commission, Directorate-General for Competition, Brussels-Luxembourg 2004.

[12] OJ [2004] C 101/43 at paragraph 3.

of the ECN have signed a statement as set out in the annex[13] to the Notice. However, it is at present unclear whether the ECN is intended to become an institution, but it is understood that NCA officials do attend meetings in Brussels to discuss policy and cases. It is further believed that the Commission intends to set up a joint confidential website to facilitate exchange of information with the NCAs.

The aim is to ensure both an effective division of work and an effective and consistent application of EC competition rules by the best placed authority. According to the Notice, the NCA will be the best placed authority when:

- The agreement or practice has substantial direct actual or foreseeable effects on competition within its territory.
- The authority is able to effectively bring to an end the entire infringement.
- It can gather (with or without assistance of other competition authorities) the evidence required to prove the infringement.

However, where a complainant has lodged multiple complaints with several NCAs or when several of them have opened a case on their own initiative, the NCAs must decide, as early as possible, which member is the best placed authority. The Notice provides for parallel action by NCAs but also points out that the NCAs 'may find it useful to designate one of them as a lead authority'.[14] An example of this designation can be found in the Dutch shrimp cartel case[15] (detailed below).

Following the terms of the Notice, the Commission will be the best placed authority when:

- All the criteria applicable to NCAs in Section 2.3 apply; and the alleged infringement affects competition in more than three Member States which constitute either one single cross-border market or several national markets.
- Community interest requires the adoption of a Commission decision either because the case raises a novel issue or because enforcement will be more effective;[16] or
- It initiates an investigation for the adoption of a decision to prohibit an anticompetitive conduct; to adopt interim measures; or to make commitments binding on the companies.

[13] OJ [2004] C 101/43 at p. 53.
[14] OJ [2004] C 101/43 at paragraph 13.
[15] Dutch Competition Authority decision of 14 January 2003 in case 2269/32.
[16] OJ [2004] C 101/43 at paragraphs 14–15.

Substance

As can be seen above, the Commission clearly has greater scope for intervention than NCAs and rightly so. However, one of the major concerns has been ensuring the consistent application of the EC competition rules under the new modernization package. In other words, can the new regime ensure that the competition rules are applied uniformly across the Member States and if not, how much margin exists?

NCAs and national courts of 25 Member States are faced with a challenge of not taking decisions running counter to those already taken and those contemplated by the Commission while at the same time assuming full responsibility for their decisions in the light of their national legislation. Further, although Member States' national competition legislation has either been modelled on or been amended to reflect Articles 81 and 82 of the Treaty, there are national differences in relation to procedural issues during investigations, levels of fines, the types of civil and criminal sanctions and issues surrounding an agreement's severability.

There is therefore a real risk that so-called 'forum shoppers' can exploit this decentralized system in order to seek to have their case reviewed by the NCA which is perceived to be the most sympathetic to their case. This puts an even greater pressure on NCAs to apply competition law correctly and for the Commission to ensure that it is applied uniformly throughout the Member States. One of the safeguards contained in the Notice is that NCAs are therefore required to send the Commission a draft decision 30 days prior to the adoption of a final decision. This allows the Commission to identify any inconsistent application of the rules as well as to take over the investigation if necessary. This obviously may lead to the Commission stepping on NCA's toes which could prove a highly explosive battleground especially with Member States with long established national competition regimes. To remedy this, the Commission has to 'consult'[17] that NCA before it can relieve it of its competence. In addition, the Commission promises that it will inform the ECN in due time of its intention to apply Article 11(6), so that ECN members can ask for a meeting of the advisory committee on the matter before the Commission initiates proceedings.[18]

In the context of civil procedure, there are also concerns about equality of treatment and the new powers of national courts to enforce Article 81(3) of the Treaty. The Regulation and the Notice attempt to foster coherence by allowing courts to request information or an opinion from the Commission

[17] Council Regulation (EC) 1/2003, Article 11(6), second sentence.

[18] OJ [2004] C 101/43 at paragraph 56.

on questions relating to EC competition rules. They must also forward copies of all judgments regarding Articles 81 and 82 to the Commission for inclusion in the National Court Cases Database. In addition, NCAs can submit observations to the national courts of their Member State on issues relating to the application of Articles 81 and 82, and the Commission may also submit such observations to national courts on the facts of the case. In this regard, the ability of national courts to obtain advice on matters of fact is a welcome development as the contentious points in relation to disputes concerning Articles 81(3) and 82 are often issues of fact.

The ECN currently has 16 cases on the National Court Database: Belgium: 3; Ireland: 1; France: 2; Netherlands: 4; Germany: 4; Denmark: 1; and United Kingdom: 1. It remains to be seen how efficiently this database will work in practice since all judgments are published in their national language and some judgments are confidential (for example, all four German cases) and thus not available from this website to practitioners at large. The impact of the UK case is discussed below.

Leniency

In the context of cartels, consistent application of EC competition rules may prove particularly difficult. Under the leniency notice for immunity or reduction of fines (the 'Leniency Notice'),[19] leniency applicants volunteer self-incriminating information concerning a cartel in which they have participated. In exchange they receive full immunity or a reduction in the penalties which would otherwise have been imposed. It is therefore vital that sensitive information which has been volunteered is not disclosed. The role of the ECN is therefore worrying for leniency applicants for two reasons:

1. A leniency application to the Commission or an NCA may trigger an investigation by another NCA or the Commission (Article 11 of the Regulation: Cooperation between NCA and Commission); and
2. Information shared with one authority may be transmitted to another NCA (Article 12 of the Regulation: Exchange of Information).

Under Article 11(3) of the Regulation, an NCA must inform the Commission before or without delay after commencing the first formal investigative measure. This information may also be made available to other NCAs. However,

[19] Commission notice on immunity from fines and reduction of fines in cartel cases OJ [2002] C45/03.

under the Notice the information submitted by one leniency applicant may not be used by another NCA as the basis for starting an investigation.[20] It has to be noted that this provision does not preclude an NCA from initiating an investigation as long as the information relating to the leniency applicant has been received from a different source.[21]

Equally, under Article 12 of the Regulation, an NCA may ask another NCA, to which a leniency application was made, to provide it with information irrespective of whether it has received information from a different source. To deal with this potential concern to applicants, the Notice applies the provisions to information received from an applicant which was voluntarily submitted to the NCA or information obtained by the NCA following an inspection. Under the Notice,[22] this information may only be transmitted to another NCA where:

1. The leniency applicant has given his non-revocable consent;
2. The NCA requesting the information has received a separate application to the same infringement and from the same applicant; or
3. The NCA providing the information also gives written commitments as to the information's use.

Practitioners have to bear in mind that the Notice is merely a notice, thus it is not binding on the NCAs and leniency applicants should look at these guidelines as best practice rather than the black letter law of how the leniency procedure is regulated. Time will tell whether the Notice provisions are adhered to strictly or whether certain circumstances allow for discrepancy. Nevertheless, the NCAs that have signed a statement[23] regarding the Notice to acknowledge the principles set out, declare that they will abide by them.[24]

A further development introduced by the Regulation is the extended power of the Commission to relieve an NCA from applying Articles 81 and 82 of the Treaty by virtue of Article 11(6) of the Regulation. Should this coincide with an investigation which the NCA has already started, the Commission may only do so after having consulted the NCA. From the point

20 OJ [2004] C 101/43 at paragraph 38.

21 OJ [2004] C 101/43 at paragraph 39.

22 OJ [2004] C 101/43 at paragraph 40–1.

23 OJ [2004] C 101/43 at page 53.

24 For a current list of NCAs, see http://www.europa.eu.int/comm/competition/antitrust/legislation/list_of_authorities_joint_statement.pdf.

of view of the leniency applicant this does not mean that, by applying to the Commission for leniency, he can avoid the risk of being sanctioned by an NCA. The Commission may not initiate proceedings (due to its limited resources or national scope of the cartel) and/or another cartel member may decide to apply to the NCA instead.

The Dutch shrimp cartel[25] is a good example of cartel allocation within the ECN. It involved four large Dutch producer organizations as well as eight Dutch wholesale traders but also some smaller German and Danish producer organizations for entering into prohibited agreements on catch quotas and prices for North-Sea shrimps. Since the centre of gravity of the cartel was situated in the Netherlands, the Commission referred the case to the Dutch NCA. This NCA then sought and obtained assistance from the German and Danish NCAs during the fact-finding stage and finally adopted a decision imposing fines for the effects of the cartel in the Netherlands. The two other NCAs did not pursue the case although they could have imposed fines on the parties for the effects of the cartel on their territory.

Under the terms of the Notice it is therefore the applicant's responsibility[26] to consider to which authority a leniency application should be made. Some considerations to bear in mind are:

1. The applicant's cartel scope: Does the cartel occur in more than three Member States? If so, the Commission is likely to take jurisdiction.[27]
2. Does the Member State in which the cartel operates have a leniency programme? What are the provisions on immunity, penalties, and costs of the programmes?
3. Are other cartel members operating in different jurisdictions? Where would they apply for leniency?
4. Would it be advisable to apply outside the EU, for example, in the US?

Since the Leniency Notice came into force in 2002, leniency applications have risen to about 20 in the first year alone, compared to 16 between 1996 and 2002. However, the increased cooperation and flexibility of allocation may make the leniency applications complex, and more uncertain as to their outcome. As procedures have not been harmonized among the Member States (19 out of 25 member states operate their own leniency programmes), practitioners may be faced with more parallel leniency applications, that is,

25 Dutch Competition Authority decision of 14 January 2003 in case 2269/32.
26 OJ [2004] C 101/43 at paragraph 38.
27 OJ [2004] C 101/43 at paragraph 14.

to the Commission and one or more NCAs which will inevitably add to the existing procedural complexity.

Recent practice has also raised questions of uncertainty for the applicant in assessing jurisdiction between the NCA and/or Commission. Although the NCAs must inform the Commission when an investigation has been opened, it is not clear what this actually means. For example, when an undertaking blows the whistle on a cartel in a Member State and the NCA does not immediately start investigating because its procedures do not require it to do so or due to heavy or prioritized workload, when does it need to inform the Commission or ECN? Is the onus entirely on the party blowing the whistle to alert the Commission and/or the 24 other NCAs? In one case, a leniency application was made in one Member State by a party and covered a large number of products in a range. The NCA decided to pick off the products one by one and launch proceedings accordingly. In a series of unfortunate events, the whistle was blown by another party at the Commission for the same geographic market but in one of the product lines not yet investigated by the NCA referred to above; the Commission commenced a proceeding on the basis of a narrow geographic market, ignoring the application for leniency, about which it said it did not know; and another NCA started an infringement proceeding for the same product but in its own territory!

Another jurisdictional issue relates to members of the ECN. It is assumed that, if as is believed, officials attend ECN meetings in Brussels they would be all from NCAs that signed a statement as set out in the annex of the Notice. In the case of the Advisory Committee, for example, Article 14(2) of the Regulation and the Notice[28] stipulate that additional representatives who do not belong to an NCA may be appointed where there is a discussion on horizontal issues. It would be interesting to know whether such an option is open to the ECN and whether in the telecoms sector, for example, UK's Office of Communications would sit in or not? There may be much divergence of views between the various NCAs and it would seem that, in the interest of transparency, undertakings should have a better view of the new 'institution' that has been created in Brussels.

Indeed, even within the Commission, not everybody seems to be invited to the ECN table. Does the hearing officer get to join in, for example, when important procedural decisions are made? Is the Commission's Legal Service consulted about the decisions taken during the process? It is important to point out that EC modernization of antitrust legislation does not aim to redress the differences in procedural rules between the various Member

[28] Footnote 23 of OJ [2004] C 101/43 at paragraph 58.

States. Therefore it is inevitable that private action litigants involved in multi-jurisdictional cases seek to find the court which either provides them with the highest award in damages or greatest prospect of success.

Provimi[29] involved an action for damages for breach of a statutory duty (to comply with Article 81) brought by three companies (two English and one German) which had purchased vitamins from subsidiaries within the Roche and Aventis groups which were involved in a vitamins price fixing cartel. The claimants wanted their claim to be dealt with in the English courts because of the more advantageous UK discovery rules which require the parties to disclose documents which support as well as hinder their case. Thus in this case, the claimants were hoping to benefit from the defendants disclosure of possible incriminating documents which would support the claimants' case. However, the claimants had to show that the English courts had jurisdiction despite the fact that the underlying contracts stipulated foreign jurisdiction clauses (Germany) and the claimants as well as defendants were not exclusively domiciled in the UK. The court held that, irrespective of where the alleged loss was suffered, the claim for the entire loss could be brought in England on the grounds of the Brussels and Lugano Convention, provided that an English subsidiary of Roche or Aventis implemented the anticompetitive conduct irrespective of whether the claimants had purchased the vitamins from the English subsidiary.

From a US perspective, this issue of forum shopping in cross-border transaction has also been recently decided in the courts. In the *Empagran*[30] case, the US Supreme Court had to decide whether the Foreign Trade Antitrust Improvements Act (FTAIA) permitted purchasers that purchased outside the US to bring an antitrust action in the US courts. The court held that US courts did not have jurisdiction unless there is a US domestic anticompetitive effect on US commerce resulting from a non-US anticompetitive conduct. However, the decision went only as far as addressing the US and non-foreign market relation. It did not address whether the US courts would apply the same principle to global markets with global prices.

Private Enforcement

Prior to modernization, a defendant could delay an action for breach of Article 81 by notifying the offending agreement, rule, or practice for exemption and/

[29] *Provimi Ltd* v. *Aventis Animal Nutrition SA* et al., and other cases [2003] EWHC 961 (Comm).

[30] *Hoffman-La Roche* v. *Empragran* SA542 US (2004).

or clearance. The national court had little option but to stay proceedings until the Commission had ruled on the application of Article 81, and any appeal rights on that decision to the European Courts had been exhausted, a process which could take many years and deter all but the most determined litigants (for example, Crehan decision took 12 years).Whether parallel investigation by the Commission and/or the NCA are speedier remains to be seen. In addition, claimants still have to overcome substantial evidential difficulties in proving an infringement, particularly in Member States with less liberal discovery rules.

There will inevitably be circumstances where the law is unclear. There is always the possibility of an Article 234 reference to the ECJ, and Article 15 also expressly preserves the national courts' option of requesting assistance from the Commission in a specific case. However, both these options rely on the national court itself taking the initiative. The Commission has therefore reserved to itself the right to lodge observations in cases before national courts where there is a need for consistent application of Articles 81 and 82.

These observations are not binding on the national courts and usually will be used in appeal cases. However, taking the legal enforceability of a Commission observation aside, its sheer weight in terms of symbolic influence may have a considerable impact on the overall prosecution of any case. How the national courts will react to these observations is an area of great uncertainty.

Crehan Effect

To date the only case from the UK to be submitted to the National Court Database is *Crehan*.[31] Although this case was started under the old antitrust regime, the judgment is nevertheless the first award of damages in English law for breach of competition law. Reports suggest that there are about eight damages claims pending in national courts across the EU, and one would imagine the number of claims currently being pursued in one forum or another to be considerably higher.

Although a landmark judgment, this case has raised a series of issues in relation to the private enforcement of competition law in the national courts. The right to a remedy stems from the direct effectiveness of Articles 81 and 82 and the court held that any remedy for breach of Articles 81 and 82 must comply with the principles of effectiveness and equivalence. In other words,

[31] *Bernard Crehan* v. *Inntrepreneur Pub Company CPC* [2004] EWCA 637.

the conditions for obtaining a remedy for breach of EC competition law must not be excessively difficult or practically impossible to achieve, nor must they be less favourable than those relating to similar domestic claims. However, in the absence of Community law rules governing the matter, these principles are to be applied through national law, by the national courts following national procedural rules.

What does that mean in practice and how does that fit in with national rules on standing, causation of loss, the availability of defences, or indeed whether a court is permitted to rule on competition issues?

Ashurst Report Summary

As regards the status quo in the EU, the Commission has published a comparative study on the conditions across the European Union of claims for damages in the case of infringement of EC competition rules (the 'Report'). The Report provides a comparative analysis of the different legal systems in the EU, and attempts to identify the essential obstacles to private enforcement of competition law. In particular, the study contains an analysis of economic models for the calculation of damages, identifies potential victims of competition infringements, and, albeit hypothetically, ways in which private enforcement claims could be facilitated.

The words of the Report's opening sentence sets the tone: 'the picture that emerges from the study is one of astonishing diversity and total underdevelopment'.[32] Below is a summary of the main obstacles raised in the Report together with some specific examples of 'astonishing diversity' throughout the Member States.

First of all, it appears that there is a lack of clarity in bringing a claim for damages for infringement of EC competition law as only 3 Member States (Finland, Lithuania, and Sweden) have a specific legal basis for EC-based damages claims and only 11 Member States[33] have national legal basis damages claims (Cyprus, Estonia, Ireland, Italy, Latvia, Slovenia, Spain, and the UK). The Report suggests that although the absence of a specific legal basis does not create in itself a hindrance to bringing a claim, public knowledge of such a basis may provide more of an incentive.

[32] Commission study on the conditions of claims for damages in case of infringement of EC competition rules, Comparative Report, executive summary, p. 1.

[33] Germany has been omitted from this list due to the recent proposed changes as stipulated in the 7th amendment to the German Act against Restraints of Competition law (GRC).

Coupled with this is the issue of standing. To obtain standing, a claimant has to prove some kind of interest in bringing the action. This is a common requirement and exists in most Member States although its scope varies. For example, in the case of *Max Bögl Bauunternehmen*[34] the court held that purchasers of cement at cartel prices could not claim damages unless they had been individually targeted by a market-sharing cartel. Thus, merely proving that one had purchased cement in a market by which the prices as a whole were affected by cartel would not suffice. However, in *Provimi* the English High Court held that the claimants had standing to sue the subsidiary of a cartel even where the subsidiary was unaware of the cartel price arrangements and the claimants actually made no purchase from the subsidiary.

These differences on standing clearly affect the options available to indirect purchasers in bringing a claim. Although the Report did not find national or EC case law on indirect purchasers bringing a claim for damages for breach of competition law, the possibility of it, from a theoretical point of view, was not dismissed by Member States albeit with foreseeable problems. In particular, the Report finds that the lack of causal link between the indirect purchaser (as the claimant) and the defendant due to the existence of a middleman, that is, a party that originally purchased the goods from the defendant, will be the main hurdle for indirect purchasers bringing a claim.

The difficulty in establishing causation was seen in a recent English case, *Arkin*.[35] The claimant brought an action for damages for breach of Articles 81 and 82 based on losses incurred from what he alleged to be predatory pricing by a competitor in breach of Article 82. The claim did not succeed because the claimant could not establish infringement of either provision of the EC Treaty. The court held that the losses claimed were caused primarily by the claimant's failure to withdraw from the market and the decision instead to cut his rates to unsustainably low levels. In the court's view, this behaviour broke the chain of causation.

If a claimant has established a legal basis and standing, he also needs to consider how he can discharge his burden of proof. Clearly, if it is too high it will deter him from starting his action since the volume of evidence required may be too difficult to obtain. The Report shows that Member States approach this issue differently by either shifting the burden onto the defendant (Germany)[36] or providing means for a minister to submit observations

[34] Max Bögl Bauunternehmen et al./Hanson Germany AZ 102 O 134/02 Kart (2003).

[35] *Arkin* v. *Bochard Lines Ltd* [2003] EWHC 687.

[36] Section 20(5) GRC.

which may assist the claimant discharging the burden of proof (France).[37] In contrast, in Sweden, the claimant undertaking can only obtain standing if it has a contractual relationship with the infringing party.

However, there is a gulf of difference in relation to the form, discovery, and production of evidence between the Member States. In common law legal systems, the claimant is under an obligation to disclose evidence which both supports and hinders his case. In civil law jurisdictions, claimants are not required to disclose evidence which hinders their case subject to direction from the court. In addition, most national courts of the Member States do not have the same powers for pre-trial disclosure which, if you are a claimant from a civil law system, may burden you more as you would not be able to rely on disclosure from the defendant (as under the common law system) and you may be subject to a limited amount and form of documents a civil judge could order to be disclosed.

A further deterrent in bringing a claim is the passing on defence, that is, the claimant did not suffer loss from anticompetitive behaviour (for example, by being overcharged due to a cartel) since he passed it on to the end consumer. The Report establishes that there is very little case law on this defence (Demark, Germany, and Italy) but that in the 22 other Member States (with the exception of Cyprus) the defence could be used.

In contrast, in the United States, many antitrust damages claims (90 per cent of which are private actions) involve companies, rather than end-consumers, claiming damages for having been 'overcharged' for some input due to anticompetitive behaviour caused by cartels. Such claims may be fruitful since US federal law has disallowed the passing on defence in the *Hanover Shoe* judgment.[38] Ultimately, US federal law does not permit the defence that these firms ultimately passed on the overcharge to their own customers through higher prices.

At EU level, Italy has accepted the passing on defence in proceedings for damages for breach of national competition law.[39] However, in Germany, a district court ruled[40] against a compensation claim brought by a food manufacturer against a supplier of vitamin products which had been found to have participated in one of the global vitamin price-fixing cartels on the basis of the passing on defence. The court dismissed the case due to the fact that the undertaking was capable of passing on the increased price to its customers

[37] Article L470–5 Com. Code.

[38] *Hanover Shoe Inc* v. *United Shoe Machinery Corp* 395 US 481(1968).

[39] *VIH Srl* v. *Juventus FC SpA*, Turin Court of Appeal decision, 6 July 2000.

[40] NJW [2004] 6 U 183/03—Karlsruhe district court.

by raising its sales prices accordingly. The court also refused to grant punitive damages as compensation claims under German law do not generally have a punitive dimension.

The Report establishes that throughout the Member States there is no uniform procedure of class actions (as known in the US) which might provide an incentive for claimants to pool their efforts together, especially in light of the evidential obstacles and difficulties of bringing a claim as outlined above. However, most Member States have various forms of collective or representative actions, although only Austria and the Netherlands have collective claims seeking damages. Unlike in the EU, the US has a long established system of class action, whereby a lawyer can bring a claim on behalf of an unidentified group of plaintiffs. This is difficult to implement in the European jurisdictions since a lawyer requires the identity of his client in order to act in the client's best interests and the Member States therefore tend to favour representative actions brought by consumer associations. For example, in the UK, consumer associations specified by the Secretary of State can bring actions for damages on behalf of two individual consumers before the Competition Appeal Tribunal, the UK's specialized competition court, based on a decision by the Office of Fair Trading or the European Commission.[41] In addition the UK civil procedure system allows for group litigation order mechanisms where 'there is a common or related issue of fact or law'.[42] In contrast, Sweden has in 2003[43] enacted The Act on Class Actions which allows for different types of collective action, including actions brought by non-profit organizations and individuals.

As far as damages are concerned most Member States see damages actions as a means for restitution. Few Member States apply punitive or exemplary damages. According to the Report, interest rates vary from 2–14 per cent which may also have a considerable impact on the overall award and half of the Member States do not distinguish between ex ante and ex post calculation models:

1. In *Crehan*, the High Court assessed the quantum of damages on an ex post basis (damages for loss of profits as between the date of the injury[44] and the time of the judgment). This amounted to £1,300,000. Unfortunately for Mr Crehan, the Court of Appeal applied an ex ante approach and assessed

[41] See Section 47B of the Competition Act 1998, as inserted by Section 19 of the Enterprise Act 2002.

[42] Civil Procedure Rule 19.10.

[43] The Act on Class Actions, 2002:599, which entered into force on 1 January 2003.

[44] When Mr Crehan surrendered the lease of the pub he was running.

damages as at the time of the injury and thus did not award damages for lost profits between the time of injury and the date of the judgment. Mr Crehan was awarded £130,000 for 12 years of litigation.
2. In Italy, damages are calculated by experts at a later hearing.[45]
3. In France, defendants are ordered to pay interim damages until the assessment of the damages after reference to the relevant court.[46]

Ashurst Report Summary—Improving Private Enforcement

The Report considers a number of areas in which action can be taken to facilitate private enforcement, including access to courts, the level of risk and uncertainty, facilitating proof, and reducing costs. A number of the issues which emerge from the study might well be resolved at a national level. The report does suggest that an option to removing at least some of the obstacles referred to above might be through further community legislation, although recognizing that this would constitute a substantial inroad into the principle of national procedural autonomy. Below is a summary of suggestions taken from the Report:

Facilitating access to the courts by:

1. removing limitations to standing to facilitate access to the courts;
2. introducing US style class actions/consumer actions/public representatives; and
3. clarifying the law to ensure standing or creating special rights for indirect purchasers.

Reducing risks by:

1. clarifying the law to achieve legal certainty in the outcome of cases;
2. creating a single specific legal basis for EC and national competition law based claims;
3. creating specialized courts for competition based actions;
4. training national judges in the enforcement of competition law;
5. creating greater communication between NCAs and their national courts (for example, references); and
6. appointing experts.

[45] *Telsystem/SIP-Telecom* Court of Appeal of Milan decision 18 June 1996.

[46] *Mors/Labinal* CA Paris, 13 May 1993.

Facilitating proof by:

1. lowering the standard of proof;
2. reversing the burden of proof;
3. facilitating access to documents for courts, parties, and NCAs;
4. introducing expert evidence; and
5. publishing guidelines on the calculation of damages in competition cases.

Reducing costs by:

1. creation of specialized courts; and
2. allowing for early settlement

Increasing awareness of consumer's competition rights.

The Commission is currently working on a Green Paper on private enforcement of the EC Competition Rules, which was adopted on 19 December 2005. The purpose of the Green Paper, which sets out a number of possible options to facilitate private enforcement, is to stimulate debate and facilitate feedback from the industry.

In Closing

It is still early days in the application both of the Regulation and the many accompanying notices issued by the Commission. However, the mere fact that most of the explanatory law is 'soft' law means that the Commission, the NCAs, the National Courts, and the ECJ will have much scope in applying the Regulation. As discussed above, the new system does not necessarily foster improvement in the rights of defence nor does it make it any more attractive for undertakings to apply for leniency in cartel cases. The credo seems still to be that when an undertaking believes that the alleged infringement has in any way a Community dimension, then it is best to go to the Commission for immunity. Given that the Commission has in recent cases adopted very narrow geographic market definitions, it is quite likely that it will be tempted to take on the proceeding.

The second issue which is really worrying is the lack of hard law governing the ECN's procedures and the apparent lack of transparency in its working. With so many jurisdictions being able to come forward and take a case, would it not be advisable to set up a proper procedure and a much tighter regulatory procedural framework? No one who has any experience of the Advisory Committee under old Regulation 17 can have any doubt as to the opaque way in which such bodies work and the need for a more strict set of rules seems self-evident, particularly as the same national officials might sit at the Advisory Committee and indeed, at the hearing.

In one field of course, the Regulation is yet to find its rightful place and that is in the area of leniency. The Commission published on 29 September 2006, a Draft Commission Notice on immunity from fines and reduction of fines in cartel cases.[47] However, the main focus of the review is on the introduction of the American-style 'marker system' and the inclusion of rules relating to the so-called 'paperless procedure' and not an improved rules of procedure.

The rights of defence of undertakings also seem to need more protection under the new system. In this light, it might be useful to strengthen the hearing officer mandate and give the hearing officers a role to play in making sure that the ECN properly abides by the rules. Indeed, the hearing officer interfaces with the NCAs during the hearing procedure and would therefore be in an ideal situation to see that the ECN functions correctly upstream from the hearing. It has often been the case that to involve the hearing officer early in an issue of conflict of jurisdiction or confidentiality has resulted in the Commission reassessing its position and it would be useful to give the hearing officer the actual right to become involved in proceedings before a Statement of Objections is sent. Giving it a role within the ECN would seem to be the answer in achieving greater protection for the parties to a proceeding.

Finally, as the new Commissioner has stated that she wishes to make sure that competition rules are relevant to the consumer, this is a good time to make a real effort in the area of private enforcement. It is unfortunately naïve to think that it would be possible to harmonize 25 different sets of civil procedure systems, so why not use Commission notices to move things along? Another way might be for individual governments to take a lead and offer class actions as a means to an end. The French President Jacques Chirac, recently launched an initiative[48] to introduce class actions into French law and this might give many consumers the foothold they would need to encourage reform on a national level and then benefit from their very own 'forum shopping'.

[47] See http://ec.europa.eu/comm/competition/cartels/legislation/draft_revised_notice_en.pdg.

[48] See the French president's speech of 4 January 2005 'a l'occasion des voeux aux forces vives' (in French) http://www.elysee.fr/magazine/actualite/ sommaire.php?doc=/documents/discours/2005/05VXFV.html.

Of course, it is also fortunate that under the European Constitution, competition reform remains outside the ambit of the co-decision procedure so it is also to be expected that ever more 'soft' law will come tumbling out from DG Comp. Some even expect Commissioner Kroes to undertake another reform of antitrust procedure during her tenure and start negotiations for another regulation, which would give more guarantees to consumers and undertakings alike in the field of cartel law.

13

Competition Law in Germany*

Ulf Böge

The Need for a Competition Law

There is one question which arises time and again: Is a competition law necessary and if so, why? And remarkably, it is not only the transition and developing countries which are about to introduce a competition law system that raise this question but also the industrialized countries. At least in Germany, it often seems that politics and apparently also many companies have less confidence in market forces than they have in regulation. An argument that is often raised is that there is a need for national champions to be able to withstand international competition. Yet, companies who make such demands act against their own medium and long-term interests.

The question of the necessity of competition law raises the further question 'Why exactly do we need competition?' The answer to the latter question is rooted in the functioning of a free market economy. In a market economy, the activities of manufacturers and consumers are not planned by a central body but individually by economic agents. Competition is responsible for coordinating these plans. It enables prices to be determined in markets by the

* Reproduced from 'Competition Law in Germany', published in Dhall, V. (ed.). 2007. *Competition Law Today: Concepts, Issues, and the Law in Practice* (first ed.), Oxford University Press, New Delhi.

free interaction of supply and demand. These prices have an important control function for the trade in goods and services. The prices show the suppliers the areas in which they can use their production factors most efficiently. For consumers, they are also an indication as to where they can satisfy their demand as economically as possible. By encouraging companies to compete for customers, a competition system brings about price reductions and improvements in quality. Competition makes companies perform better. Through innovations and technical advancement, companies increase their chances of making a bigger profit (positive sanction). Poor performance is penalized by losses and if a company fails permanently it will be forced to withdraw from the competitive process (negative sanction). Competition is therefore not an end in itself but a means to safeguard and defend freedom and prosperity.

Competition is at the same time a complex matter: On the one hand, it undoubtedly produces the best results for all market participants down to the consumer. On the other hand, it constantly poses companies with new challenges and is thus often uncomfortable. In order to avoid competitive pressure, companies are inclined to impede, distort, or eliminate competition by agreements, mergers, or abusive practices. These restraints of competition harm the economy. A legislative framework is required to counter such distortions of competition[1] and to give companies the basic freedom to make decisions, subject to the proviso that competitive structures and the individual's freedom of action are maintained.

History of Competition Law in Germany

Germany has had a competition law since 1923. Until then the legal control of competition restraints was confined to general civil law provisions. Here the principle of freedom of contract overrode the negative effects of competition restraints on market partners and the economy. As a consequence, Germany was known as the land of cartels. Cartels were legitimate and enforceable. In 1905, the number of cartels in various sectors in Germany was 385. But even the competition law system introduced in 1923, which focused on abuse control, was largely unsuccessful. In 1929, the Cartel Office of the Reich Association of German Industry estimated the number of cartels at 1543.

After the Second World War, the victorious powers, especially the US, called for the cartels to be banned and for extensive deconcentration. The

[1] There are several additional requirements that need to be fulfilled before competition can develop. These are, inter alia, a legal system that grants private persons rights of disposal over goods and services, that allows for entrepreneurial activities (freedom of trade), the free choice of a party to a contract (freedom of contract), and that guarantees a well-functioning monetary system.

initial aim was to break up the industrial conglomerates, which had often played a significant role, also during the War. The focus of this policy was later to change. The aim was to turn Germany into an economically stable ally. Competition was seen as a means to achieve this.

At the request of the Allies, deliberations started in Germany on the introduction of a competition law. Here, Germany developed its own ideas and schools of competition doctrine which, despite this keen desire, were fiercely contested. As a result these discussions took considerable time. It took eight years from the first draft of an Act against Restraints of Competition (ARC) to its passing into law in 1958. In Germany the ARC is considered to be the 'constitution of the free market economy'.

The ARC has been amended seven times since its entry into force. The 7th and latest amendment to the ARC only came into force on 1 July 2005.[2] Its aim was in particular to adapt German competition law to European competition law. With the latest amendment the current system of notification and authorization of anticompetitive agreements is replaced by the principle of legal exception. The 7th Amendment to the ARC also creates preconditions for improved cooperation between the Bundeskartellamt and other competition authorities worldwide, especially within the European Competition Network (ECN); this applies, for example, in the area of information exchange and mutual assistance with investigations.

Competition Authorities

The Bundeskartellamt took up its work with the coming into force of the ARC in 1958. In addition to the Bundeskartellamt, several other institutions fulfil the function of a competition authority, namely: the competition authorities of the *Länder*, the German Federal Minister of Economics and Technology, and the European Commission.

Competencies of the Different Competition Authorities

The competencies of the individual competition authorities can be summarized as follows:

- The Bundeskartellamt has sole competence for merger control proceedings. In abuse and cartel proceedings it is the competent authority if the effect of the anticompetitive or discriminatory conduct in question extends beyond

[2] An unofficial English translation of the current version of the ARC may be found at http://www.Bundeskartellamt.de/wEnglisch/download/pdf/GWB_ 7_ e.pdf.

the territory of a federal state. Since 1999, the Bundeskartellamt has also served as the first instance of appeal in review proceedings concerning the awarding of public contracts, that is, if a company applies for the review of a public award procedure.

- The co-existence of the Bundeskartellamt and the *Land* Competition Authorities reflects the federal structure of the Federal Republic of Germany which allocates state authority also to the individual *Länder*.

  The *Land* competition authorities are competent for abuse and cartel proceedings whose impact is confined to the territory of one *Land* only. With the 7th Amendment to the ARC it is now possible to refer cartel proceedings from the Bundeskartellamt to *Land* competition authorities and vice versa.
- The Federal Minister of Economics and Technology is the competent authority if companies apply for a ministerial authorization after their merger has been prohibited by the Bundeskartellamt. In that case the Minister has to decide whether the restraint of competition resulting from the planned merger is outweighed by advantages to the economy as a whole or is justified by an overriding public interest. The opinion of the Monopolies Commission has to be obtained before a decision is reached in the ministerial authorization proceedings. The Monopolies Commission is an independent body of experts consisting of two university professors and three representatives from the business sector. The Commission has its own secretariat. It is not an independent competition authority in itself, nor has it any decision power, but its expert opinion plays a significant role.
- The European Commission is the competent authority for merger control if the participating companies achieve certain turnover thresholds. Furthermore, it is competent for abuse and cartel proceedings where trade between Member States is affected and when no national competition authority is competent according to EC Reg. 1/2003.[3]

Independence of the Bundeskartellamt

A crucial feature of the Bundeskartellamt's work is its independence. Decisions on mergers, cartels, and abusive conduct are taken by eleven Decision Divisions. The areas of responsibility are organized according to economic sectors, but one Decision Division is exclusively dedicated to the prosecution of hard-core cartels. The Decision Divisions' method of operation resembles that of a court. A collegiate body consisting of the chairman and two associate

[3] Council Regulation (EC) No. 1/2003 of 16 December 2002 on the implementation of the rules on competition laid down in Articles 81 and 82 of the Treaty, OJ L1 of 4.1.2003, p. 1.

Organization Chart of the Bundeskartellamt

1 November 2006

Responsibilities of Decision Divisions: All decisions in administrative and administrative fine cases; Participation in proceedings of the supreme *Land* authorities

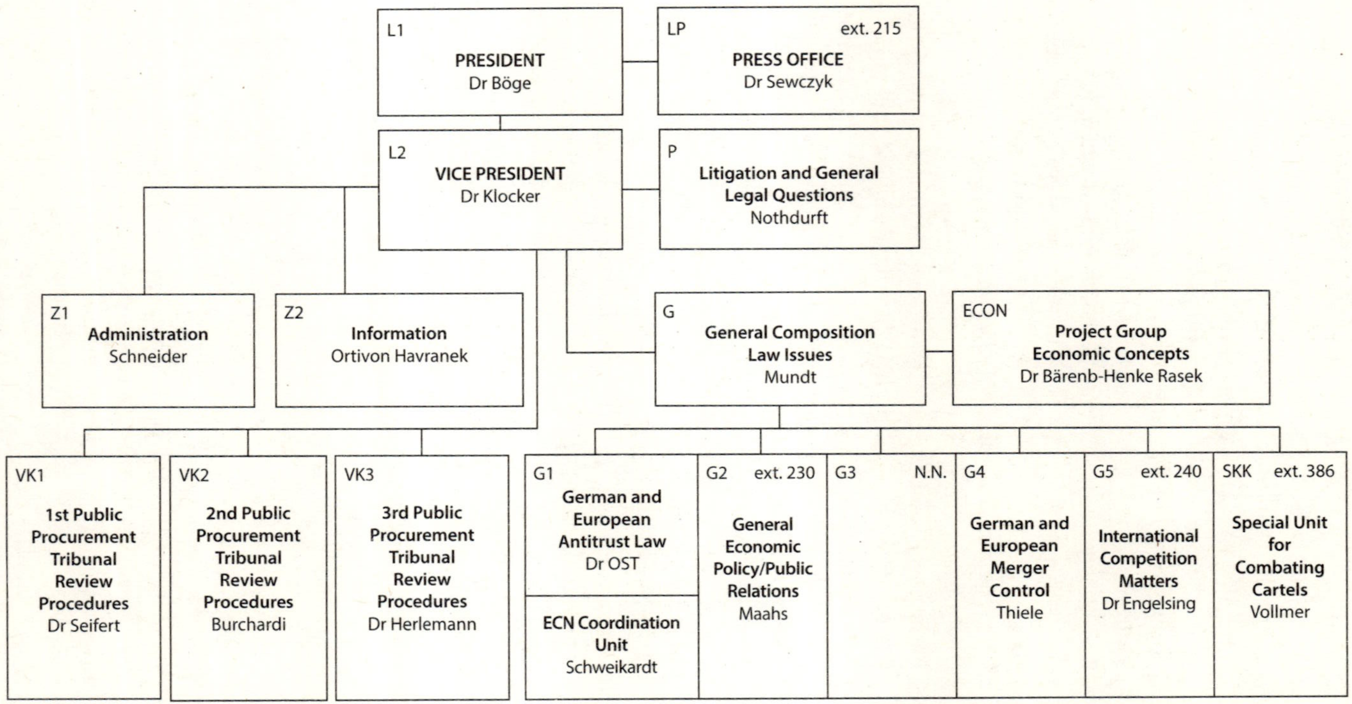

B 1	B 2	B 3	B 4	B 5	B 6	B 7	B 8	B 9	B 10	B 11
1st Decision Division	**2nd Decision Division**	**3rd Decision Division**	**4th Decision Division**	**5th Decision Division**	**6th Decision Division**	**7th Decision Division**	**8th Decision Division**	**9th Decision Division**	**10th Decision Division**	**11th Decision Division**
Temme	Reh	Heistermann	Hossenfelder	Fehrmann	Paetow	Topel	Dr Becker	Dr Ruppelt	N.N.	Dr Wagemann
basic and extractive industries construction industry and related services	agriculture and forestry food industry textile industry wood products other consumer goods automative industry	health sector chemical industry	waste management industry financial services business-related services	mechanical and plant engineering metal industry patents and licences	paper industry media culture, sports, entertain-ment	broadcast engineering telecommunic ations EDP	energy, water mineral oil	transport postal services trade		Prosecution of administrative offences in conjunction with violations of Sec. 1 ARC and Art. 81 EC

members of the relevant Decision Division decides by majority vote. The decisions are taken independently of internal or external instructions, a fact that is of paramount importance for the Bundeskartellamt's work. Consequently, decisions are based solely on competitive criteria.

The Bundeskartellamt's independence from political influence is so important because competition is by no means a self-sustaining system. On the contrary, competition is constantly threatened with restriction or even elimination by sectional interests. The general public benefits from competition. However, especially in times of economic crises, individual companies find reasons to avoid competition. If in such situations politicians—justifiably concerned about, for example, preserving jobs—were to put pressure on the Bundeskartellamt to base its decisions on criteria other than competition, the competitive system would be in danger of being undermined.

Another highly significant feature of the German system is that the Bundeskartellamt's decisions do not need to be confirmed by a judge. This not only strengthens its independence, it also improves the situation for companies with regard to the time span until a definite decision is taken. In Germany, for example, in merger cases it is possible to obtain a definite decision within a month after notification. Moreover, the Bundeskartellamt has far-reaching investigatory powers and significantly larger human resources than the courts to deal with factual issues. The Bundeskartellamt '... may conduct any investigations and collect any evidence required' (Section 57 of the ARC). This includes in particular, market surveys by requesting information from market participants and other forms of market investigations. Further investigative methods are: taking of evidence by inspection, testimony of witnesses and experts, seizure of evidence, etc. Because of its highly specialized work, the Bundeskartellamt has gained profound market know-how over the years.

The Three Pillars of German Competition Law

Prohibition of Cartels

Section 1 of the ARC is the basic norm of German competition law; it provides for a general prohibition of cartels. In a cartel, several companies coordinate their market conduct by means of an agreement in order to exclude competition between them. Classic examples are agreements between companies:

- on uniform prices they intend to charge (price cartel),
- on the quantities each company may offer (quota cartel), and
- on the territory reserved for each of them (market allocation agreement).

Hard-core cartels are deadly sins against competition. They bring the dynamic competition process to a standstill and thus cause enormous damage to the national economy. Under German law, exceptions from the prohibition of cartels are therefore only applicable if certain cooperations are desired or tolerated by competition policy. The 7th Amendment to the ARC surrendered most of the individual exemptions in favour of a general clause modelled on European law. Under this general clause cartels can be exempted which '... while allowing consumers a fair share of the resulting benefit, contribute to improving the production or distribution of goods or to promoting technical or economic progress, ...' (cf. Section 2 of the ARC). Only the special exemption for cartels of small or medium-sized enterprises was maintained. The previous exemption areas, with the exception of agriculture and retail price maintenance for newspapers and magazines, have been erased as well.

Recent Developments in Combating Cartels

An area of focus of German competition policy in recent years has been the intensified prosecution of hard-core cartels.

Leniency Programme

In 2000, the Bundeskartellamt for the first time introduced a leniency programme. With its leniency programme the Bundeskartellamt assures those cartel members wishing to leave a cartel and cooperate with the Bundeskartellamt in its uncovering, immunity from or a reduction of their fines. The German leniency programme was amended and much improved in 2006.[4] Of particular importance was the introduction of a marker system. According to this, it is initially sufficient for the cartel member to declare his willingness to cooperate and provide information on the type and duration of the cartel law infringement, the product and geographical markets affected, and the identity of those involved. He then has eight weeks to provide the necessary additional information. Another aspect to be emphasized is the possibility of an oral application for leniency and the heightened protection against file inspection by third parties linked to it. This may gain particular importance in the context of private enforcement, where a written application for leniency could be used as evidence against the applicant in a damage suit.[5]

[4] An English translation of the new Leniency Programme, available at http://www.Bundeskartellamt.de/wEnglisch/download/pdf/06_Bonusregelung_e.pdf. Cf. also Dirk Schroeder, Die neue Bonusregelung des Bundeskartellamts—ein großer Schritt in die richtige Richtung, WuW 2006, p. 575.

[5] Cf. ICN Report Interaction of Public and Private Enforcement in Cartel Cases, available at http:/www.internationalcompetitionnetwork.org/capetown2006/ICN-private-enforcement-final-version pdf, p. 39 ff.

Special Unit for Combating Cartels (SKK) and Cartel Decision Division

In order to increase the quota of uncovered cartel agreements and to speed up proceedings, the Bundeskartellamt set up a Special Unit for Combating Cartels (SKK) in March 2002 and since June 2005 the 11th Decision Division has dealt specifically with cartel prosecution. The SKK and the Cartel Decision Division work hand in hand in the prosecution of cartels. The SKK is the central contact point for all those wishing to avail themselves of the leniency programme. It is also a central task of the SKK to provide the personnel and material resources for preparing and carrying out searches. The Cartel Decision Division, on the other hand, deals with the whole proceedings from a legal point of view, that is, from the initial suspicion to the termination of the proceedings, namely the imposition of fines. The decision to establish a Decision Division to deal exclusively with the prosecution of cartels was taken in order to pool resources and know-how in this area.

Sanctioning of Cartel Law Violations

Under the ARC illegal cartel agreements constitute administrative offences. Generally, however, it is within the Bundeskartellamt's discretion to decide whether to initiate administrative offence proceedings or merely administrative proceedings in a cartel case.

Administrative Proceedings

The legal consequence of administrative proceedings is a mere prohibition decision under which the respective anticompetitive behaviour is to be ceased. The 7th Amendment to the ARC, however, considerably extended the Bundeskartellamt's powers under administrative law. For example, the authority may now also order interim measures in administrative proceedings. In addition, a new instrument has been introduced with the possibility of submitting commitments. It enables companies to avoid a competition authority's decision by committing themselves to adopt a certain conduct.

Administrative Offence Proceedings

The legal consequence of administrative offence proceedings is the imposition of a fine. In these proceedings the provisions of the law of criminal procedure are predominantly applicable. However, the proceedings are not criminal proceedings. This means that, other than, for example, under US law, criminal sanctions, and in particular prison sentences, cannot be imposed. The sole exception from this general rule are submission agreements which constitute a criminal offence under German law as well and for which the maximum penalty is imprisonment for up to five years.

Level of Sanctions

Until July 2005 an offence was punishable by a general fine of up to 500,000 Euros. For offences where the additional proceeds obtained as a result of the cartel agreement exceeded 500,000 Euros, a fine could be imposed of up to three times the additional proceeds gained. The calculation of additional proceeds poses a problem for the competition authorities as they must prove that a cartel generated additional proceeds and state their amount. Comparative markets are considered in order to calculate a hypothetical competitive price for the market affected by the cartel. In some cases this may cause severe problems of proof.

Since the 7th Amendment to the ARC came into effect, the calculation of fines has been based on the total turnover achieved by the companies participating in the cartel (again modelled on European law). Under this system, the maximum level of fines is 10 per cent of the companies' total turnover. Although this eliminates the problem of proof with regard to the calculation of additional proceeds, guidelines are still required to stipulate the criteria under which fines are to be calculated within this broad legal framework. In September 2006, the Bundeskartellamt published its guidelines on the setting of fines.[6]

Cement cartel

The largest cartel case in the history of the Bundeskartellamt was without doubt the cement cartel which was uncovered in 2002–3. In this cartel proceeding, the Bundeskartellamt imposed fines totalling approximately €660 million.

The accused companies operated anticompetitive market allocation and quota agreements, some of them since the 1970s, and continued to do so until 2002. The geographic markets affected were the four regional cement markets in eastern Germany, Westphalia, northern Germany, and southern Germany. Due to the agreements between the German cement manufacturers, which had been in place for decades, competition was almost completely excluded in this market. Prices could thus be raised to a level that would have been unattainable under competitive conditions. Buyers of cement and consumers were thus massively harmed.

The successful break-up of the cartel could be mainly attributed to the leniency programme and the establishment of the Special Unit for Combating Cartels. Following information obtained from the construction industry, the Bundeskartellamt carried out a nation-wide search of more than 30 cement companies. The evidence seized during the searches and the confessions by the large manufacturers, some of which fully confessed, confirmed the existing suspicions.

[6] The English translation of the guidelines, available at http:// www.bundeskartellamt.de/wEnglisch/download/pdf/Bussgeldleitlien-E.pdf.

Private Enforcement

Another fundamental element in the fight against cartels is private enforcement. Private enforcement involves the granting of claims for injunctions and damages. By asserting these claims, in addition to the competition authorities the affected market participants themselves can ensure that competition law is observed by taking legal action in civil law proceedings. The affected parties are all competitors or other market participants that are restricted by the violation in question. Accordingly, consumers can also be entitled to claims, for example, if they were forced to pay excessive prices due to a cartel agreement.

Private antitrust enforcement plays an important role in Germany, particularly in abuse and discrimination cases. The 7th Amendment to the ARC has now also improved the possibilities to seek compensation through private actions. In those cases the principal difficulty lies in the challenge for a private plaintiff to develop evidence against cartel members.[7] To overcome these difficulties, a decision by a competition authority which has ascertained a competition violation now has a binding effect for the courts. With regard to the passing-on defence[8] it has been clarified that the damaging party has to bear the burden of proof with regard to the passing on of the damage sustained to the next market level. The burden of proof has thus been shifted to the cartel members.

This and other improvements will further strengthen private enforcement in Germany and thus also increase efficiency in the fight against cartels.[9] From the competition authorities' point of view, private antitrust enforcement complements the competition authorities' activities in several respects. The competition authorities are able to concentrate their relatively limited resources on cases which are of general significance for competition. Furthermore, the Bundeskartellamt can participate as *amicus curiae* in the civil proceedings resulting from private enforcement activities, and thus safeguard a coherent development in the public and private enforcement of competition law. The Bundeskartellamt is to be informed by the courts of all illegal actions arising

[7] Cf. the ICN Report Interaction of Public and Private Enforcement in Cartel Cases, available at http://www.internationalcompetitionnetwork.org/capetown2006/ICN-private-enforcement-final-version.pdf, p. 36f.

[8] The passing-on defence constitutes a defence raised by the defendant, claiming that the plaintiff has been able to pass the damage wholly or partly on to his customers by raising prices correspondingly, and that he has therefore not suffered any damage himself.

[9] 'On the Dangers of an Over-extensive Private Antitrust Enforcement' cf. Böge/Ost, 'Up and Running, or is it? Private enforcement—The Situation in Germany and Policy Perspectives', ECLR 2006, p. 197.

in connection with cartel agreements and upon request be sent all briefs, records, orders, and decisions. Members of staff of the Bundeskartellamt are allowed to take an active part in the court proceedings. The Bundeskartellamt takes its role as amicus curiae very seriously with regard to its possibility of influencing the interpretation of the Competition Act in civil proceedings. In every proceeding before the Federal Court of Justice, it participates by way of oral statements and in leading cases it also provides a written opinion. In the lower courts, the Bundeskartellamt participates by way of written statements in leading cases, in cases connected to ongoing cases of the Bundeskartellamt, or upon request of the court. Altogether, the Bundeskartellamt participates as amicus curiae in about 5 per cent of all the cases. At first glance, this does not seem a lot. But it has to be taken into account that each year there are more than 400 competition-related cases in civil proceedings.

International Cooperation in Combating Cartels

One consequence of the increasing globalization of the economy is that many cartel agreements not only cover a single state's territory but the territories of several states. This development calls for international cooperation between the competition authorities.

ECN

The combating of cartels in Europe reached a new dimension with the establishment of the ECN in May 2004.[10] As the name already suggests, the ECN is a network of European competition authorities. The ECN's membership is made up of the competition authorities of the Member States of the European Union.

Cooperation within the ECN covers all phases of cartel proceedings, where trade between Member States is affected and therefore Art. 81 EC is applicable instead of national competition law. At the beginning of proceedings under European competition law, each authority informs the other network members on the institution of proceedings by way of a notice. Further essential elements of this network are the rules on case allocation,

[10] The legal basis of the ECN is the Council Regulation (EC) No. 1/2003 of 16 December 2002 on the implementation of the rules on competition laid down in Articles 81 and 82 of the Treaty, OJ L1 of 4.1.2003, p. 1. The basic provisions for the functioning of the ECN are laid down in detail in the 'Joint Statement of the Council and the Commission on the Functioning of the Network of Competition Authorities' and in the 'Commission Notice on cooperation within the Network of Competition Authorities', OJ. C 101 of 27.4.2004, p. 43.

the ensuring of information flows between the competition authorities, the processing of information obtained from leniency applications and mutual official assistance.

Use has also already been made of the new competences in the exchange of information and official assistance. For example, in July 2005, the Italian competition authority asked the Bundeskartellamt to conduct a search operation, as comprehensive market investigations had led the authority to suspect price agreements and a foreclosure of the Italian market for baby milk. Apart from the Bundeskartellamt, four other competition authorities simultaneously participated in this search. In another case, the Bundeskartellamt received official assistance from the Austrian competition authority. In both constellations, that is, in cases where the Bundeskartellamt provided or received official assistance, the searches could be coordinated, prepared, and carried out smoothly within a short period of time.

OECD, ICN

Currently the ECN provides for the most intensive form of international cooperation between competition authorities. Further impulses for an international cooperation between the competition authorities are also provided by the OECD and the International Competition Network (ICN).

The OECD has addressed competition law issues since 1967 via its Competition Law and Policy Committee (Competition Committee). It has now published *Recommendations Concerning Effective Action against Hard Core Cartels*,[11] and in addition, *Recommended Practices for the Formal Exchange of Information between Competition Authorities in Hard Core Cartels Investigations*,[12] with the aim of facilitating and improving international cooperation between competition authorities in cross-border cartel prosecution.

The ICN established its Cartels Working Group in 2004.[13] The mandate of the Cartels Working Group is to address the challenges of anti-cartel enforcement, both domestically and internationally, across the entire range of ICN members and amongst agencies with differing levels of experience. It is currently preparing an *Enforcement Techniques Manual* and so-called

[11] Recommendations of the Council concerning Effective Action against Hard Core Cartels of 13.5. 1998, OECD Doc C(98)35, available at http://ww.oecd.org/dataoecd/39/4/2350130.pdf.

[12] See http:/www.oecd.org./dataoecd/1/33/35590548.pdf.

[13] Further information about the ICN can be found at www.internationalnetwork.org.

Anti-Cartel Enforcement Templates which offer a quick overview of the cartel provisions and principles of different jurisdictions.[14] Once a year the ICN hosts an International Cartels Workshop.

Abuse Control

It is the aim of abuse control to safeguard the freedom of competition. This aim justifies the subjection of dominant companies to a special control of conduct, especially since the German law does not provide for the possibility to divest large companies. Abuse control under German law covers:

- abuse of a dominant position (Section 19 ARC),
- prohibition of discrimination and unfair hindrance (Section 20 ARC), and
- prohibition of boycott and other restrictive practices (Section 21 ARC).

The key term in abuse control is market dominance. The level of dominance is assessed on the basis of whether a company has no competitors (monopoly) or is not exposed to any substantial competition, or whether it has a paramount market position in relation to its competitors. The criteria to be considered include the competitive conditions in the relevant market and company-related criteria such as financial power, access to supply and sales markets, links with other undertakings, barriers to market entry, actual and potential competition. The law also provides for so-called thresholds for assuming dominance which are based on the companies' market shares (cf. Section 19 ARC). For individual companies the relevant threshold is a market share of 33.3 per cent, for oligopolies of up to three companies a market share of 50 per cent, and for oligopolies of four or five companies a market share of 66.67 per cent. However, if the respective thresholds are exceeded, the Bundeskartellamt does not apply this method automatically and does not assume dominance without examining the actual effects on the market concerned.

Types of Abusive Market Behaviour

The individual abuse practices are categorized in German law as follows:

Exclusionary Abuse

Exclusionary abuse exists in cases in which dominant companies impede other companies' competitive opportunities without any objective justification. A

[14] See http:/www.internationalcompetitionnetwork.org/cartels/index.html.

typical example is cut-price strategies, that is, prices which are below the average avoidable costs, or rebate systems with a 'loyalty effect' (incremental and retroactive rebates).

Exploitative Abuse

In the case of an exploitative abuse the dominant company charges significantly higher prices than it would have been able to charge if effective competition existed in the market affected (abusive pricing). The comparative market principle is a method to ascertain this. Apart from abusive pricing, exploitative abuse can also take the form of structural abuse. This means that the dominant company sets different prices or business terms for comparable purchasers in comparable markets without any objective justification.

Refusal of Access to Essential Facilities

This type of abuse exists in cases where a dominant company refuses to allow another company access to its networks or other infrastructure facilities against adequate remuneration, provided that without such concurrent use the other company is unable for legal or factual reasons to operate as a competitor of the dominant company on the upstream or downstream market. This basically corresponds to the essential facilities doctrine, which is a type of exclusionary abuse.

Discrimination

Other forms of abuse of a dominant position are the unfair hindrance of business activities and the different treatment of similar companies without any objective justification (cf. Section 20 of the ARC). These do not only apply to dominant companies but also to companies that are superior in relation to other companies dependent on them. Typical examples are the granting of loyalty rebates to retailers to induce them not to purchase from other competitors or the refusal to supply retailers because of their pricing policy.

Boycott

The prohibition of boycott (Section 21 ARC) is a general prohibition and not linked to market power. A boycott exists where a company requests another company to refuse to sell to or purchase from a third company.

Abuse Control Sanctions

Abuse control basically provides for the same sanctions as applied to violations of the prohibition of cartels. Just like illegal cartel agreements, a violation of the prohibitions of abuse of a dominant position, discrimination, and boycott constitutes an administrative offence. Therefore, it is within the competition authority's discretion to decide whether to initiate administrative offence proceedings or administrative proceedings.

The legal consequence of administrative offence proceedings is the imposition of a fine according to the principles described above. In administrative proceedings the competition authority may issue a prohibition decision, order interim measures, or request commitments from the companies involved.

Germania/Deutsche Lufthansa

Deutsche Lufthansa is Germany's biggest air carrier and Germania was a newcomer to the market. The Bundeskartellamt saw the pricing strategy of Deutsche Lufthansa as an attempt to squeeze its new competitor Germania out of the market.

Germania started operating scheduled flight services between Berlin and Frankfurt. The company offered tickets at €99 for a one-way, fully flexible, and rebookable flight. The conditions essentially corresponded to Lufthansa's economy tariffs for business travellers. Lufthansa reacted to this by also introducing a fully flexible economy tariff of a total of €200 for an outward and return flight to be booked separately, that is, at an average of €100 per single journey (including fees). Compared with the exclusively fully flexible economy tariffs Lufthansa previously offered, this constituted a price reduction from €485 to €200, (including fees), that is, of almost 60 per cent.

With this price Lufthansa had in effect clearly undercut Germania's price of €99 as it included services which were not offered by Germania. These included catering and a 'miles&more' bonus programme for frequent fliers with Lufthansa. The fact that Lufthansa offered three times as many flights was another considerable incentive for business travellers to fly with Lufthansa and not Germania. Other advantages of flying with Lufthansa were its access to travel agencies and its substantial participation in a specific reservation system, its integration in the Star Alliance network as well as the reputation it enjoyed among long-standing business travellers. Even on conservative estimates the Bundeskartellamt assumed a price advantage of approximately €35 one-way.

The price Lufthansa was asking was set clearly below its average operating costs per passenger. The only rational explanation for this pricing strategy was that it was an attempt to force Germania out of this route and to recoup resulting losses at a later stage by discontinuing this price tariff and resorting to previous ones. Consequently the Bundeskartellamt prohibited Lufthansa from demanding a price (including passenger fees) for a one-way ticket per passenger on the Frankfurt-Berlin route which was not at least €35 above Germania's price, as long as Lufthansa did not have to charge more than €134 as a result.

Long-Term Gas Supply Contracts

A current example of the Bundeskartellamt's decision-making practice regarding abusive dominance is the problem of long-term gas supply contracts between gas transmission companies and distributors. A survey has shown that almost three quarters of the contracts concerned cover 100 per cent of the gas distributor's requirements or at least quantities of between 80 per cent and 100 per cent of the distributor's requirements. Almost all of these contracts run for more than four years, in some cases up to twenty years. This combination of long contract periods on the one hand and a high degree of requirement satisfaction on the other leads to considerable foreclosure effects. The Bundeskartellamt considers these long-term gas supply contracts to be one of the major reasons for the unsatisfactory competitive situation in the gas sector.

The Bundeskartellamt initially tried to achieve a consensus-based solution in order to counteract this restraint of competition. It took up the problem of long-term gas supply contracts ex officio without immediately initiating prohibition proceedings against the companies. Instead the authority conducted numerous discussions with the gas transmission companies, trading companies, and distributors. The purpose of these discussions was to find a solution which served the interests of effective competition and provided both the established and new gas suppliers with a clear schedule for their planning processes. However, the attempt to open up long-term gas supply contracts by consensus failed, in particular due to the fact that the market leader, E.ON/Ruhrgas, was not prepared to sign the formal obligation required. The Bundeskartellamt now tackles long-term gas supply contracts in formal prohibition proceedings. It has released its first decision against E.ON/Ruhrgas. The Bundeskartellamt has prohibited E.ON Ruhrgas' existing long-term contracts with distributors which cover more than 80 per cent of their actual gas requirements. These contracts are to be terminated at the latest by the end of the then current gas year. As regards the conclusion of new contracts with regional and local gas companies, those contracts are to be prohibited which run for more than four years and which cover more than 50 per cent of actual gas requirements, or which run for more than two years and cover more than 80 per cent of requirements. Tacit extension clauses are also prohibited. E.ON Ruhrgas has appealed against this decision. The case is still pending.

International Trends in Abuse Control

Cooperation within the ECN not only covers cartel proceedings, but also abuse control proceedings, when trade between Member States of the European Union is affected. Moreover, at international level much interest is focused these days on the review of abuse control policy. It seems to be one of the 'hottest' areas in international competition policy at the moment.

Already in 2003, the European Commission started to review its policy on the abuse of a dominant position with the aim of modernizing it with a more economic approach. In 2006, the US initiated a review of its unilateral conduct policy and the ICN set up a new working group on unilateral conduct recently, which is co-chaired by the US Federal Trade Commission and the Bundeskartellamt.

Merger Control

The ARC's third area of focus is merger control (cf. Sections 35 ff.) which was introduced in 1973. It is the aim of merger control to maintain competitive market structures and to prevent concentration, also with the objective of diminishing the need for selective intervention by the state in the form of abuse proceedings.

Unlike cartel agreements or other restraints of competition where the participating enterprises remain legally independent, mergers between companies are characterized by the fact that, through the acquisition of shares or assets, formerly independent companies are either merged into one uniform enterprise or at least capital links are created. The restraints of competition that are associated with mergers become evident in a scenario—which is by no means merely hypothetical—where all competitors in a particular market merge and thereby obtain a monopoly position.

Types of Merger Transactions

The following transactions are deemed to be mergers within the meaning of the ARC (cf. Section 37 of the ARC):

- the acquisition of all or of a substantial part of the assets of another undertaking (acquisition of assets),
- the acquisition of direct or indirect control by one or several undertakings (acquisition of control), whereas control denotes the possibility of exercising decisive influence on the activities of an undertaking, for example, through granting veto rights on company-related key decisions (economic and investment planning, the appointment of CEOs, etc.),
- the acquisition of 50 per cent of the shares, or the acquisition of 25 per cent of the capital or voting rights of another undertaking (acquisition of shares),
- any other combination of under takings enabling one or several undertakings to directly or indirectly exert a competitively significant influence on another undertaking; this definition is meant to deter attempts to

circumvent merger control (such as the acquisition of shares of less than 25 per cent coupled with a contractual granting of rights that go beyond the rights associated with minority protection).

Turnover Thresholds and Merger Control Proceedings

The Bundeskartellamt does not examine every merger, but only those where the participating undertakings reach certain turnover thresholds. More precisely, these are mergers where the combined aggregate worldwide turnover of all participating undertaking is more than €500 million and the domestic turnover of at least one participating undertaking is more than 25 million (cf. Section 35 ARC).[15]

Where the relevant turnover thresholds are reached, the participating companies have a general obligation to notify the merger. The merger may not be put into effect before it has been cleared by the Bundeskartellamt. A violation of this obligation to suspend until clearance constitutes an administrative offence and may be punished by a fine.

After a merger project has been notified, the responsible Decision Division has one month to take a decision in the case. Where a case requires a more detailed examination the Bundeskartellamt may initiate so-called main examination proceedings. A decision has then to be taken within four months of receipt of the complete notification.

Decision-Making Powers of the Bundeskartellamt

The Bundeskartellamt decides whether or not to clear a merger project. Clearance may be granted subject to conditions and obligations. However, these must not result in a control of the companies' conduct.

The Bundeskartellamt will prohibit a concentration which is expected to create or strengthen a dominant position unless the participating undertakings prove that the concentration will also lead to improvements in the conditions of competition, and that these improvements will outweigh the disadvantages of dominance (cf. Section 36 of the ARC). Market dominance is examined under the same criteria as are applied to abuse control. In more than 30 years of merger control practice, the Bundeskartellamt has examined more than 30,000 mergers and has prohibited well over 100 mergers. At first sight this may not

[15] For press and broadcasting concentrations, the turnover thresholds that trigger merger control are lower (cf. Section 38 (3), Section 35 (2) Sentence 2 ARC). This is due to the special role diversity of opinion is considered to play in safeguarding democracy.

seem a lot. However, to get the whole picture one would have to add those merger projects where the participating undertakings gave up their intention to merge, modified, or revoked the project in the informal stage of the proceedings due to concerns expressed by the Bundeskartellamt. These amount to approximately 400 additional cases (so-called pre-notification cases).

Axel Springer/ProSiebenSat.1

The merger proceedings attracting most attention recently concerned the planned merger between Axel Springer AG ('Springer') and ProSiebenSat.1 Media AG ('ProSiebenSat.1'). Springer is one of the largest German newspaper and magazine publishing houses, ProSiebenSat.1 is a private broadcasting channel. The Bundeskartellamt has prohibited the merger because it assumed that the merger would lead to a degree of market power which was unacceptable under competition law on the TV advertising market, the reader market for over-the-counter newspapers, and the national advertising market for newspapers.

According to the Bundeskartellamt's findings, ProSiebenSat.1 and the RTL TV group, which belongs to the Bertelsmann group, together hold a dominant position in the TV advertising market with a constant market share of approximately 40 per cent over the last years (a so-called 'uncompetitive duopoly' without any substantial competition from outsiders). The merger would have led to a further assimilation of the corporate structures of the two conglomerates in the neighbouring markets for newspapers and magazines and would have resulted in a number of interlocks between Springer/ProSiebenSat.1 and Bertelsmann. This would have further secured and strengthened the duopoly. The interlocks would have resulted from mutual minority shareholdings of Springer and Bertelsmann in several private radio stations and in press distribution companies; in addition, Springer and Bertelsmann mutually control a rotogravure company.

The merger would also have led to a strengthening of Springer's dominant position in the national reader market for over-the-counter newspapers. With its newspaper BILD, Springer holds a market share of approximately 80 per cent in this market. The merger would have enabled Springer to further secure and strengthen BILD'S position through cross-media promotional and editorial measures (cross-media promotion).

Finally the merger would also have led to a strengthening of Springer's market position in the national advertising market for newspapers. With its newspapers, BILD and Die Welt, the Springer publishing house already holds a paramount market position with a share of approximately 40 per cent. The merger would have enabled Springer to offer from one source coordinated product advertising campaigns in several media and to launch cross-media advertising campaigns for third parties. Thus Springer's market dominance in the advertising market for newspapers would have been further secured. The parties have appealed against the decision. The case is still pending.

Ministerial Authorization

As already mentioned above, the decisions of the Bundeskartellamt are based solely on competitive criteria. This notwithstanding, especially in merger cases, there are of course often enough other important economic policy objectives apart from competition. However, it is not the task of the Bundeskartellamt to articulate and implement these. If in individual merger cases, restraints of competition are outweighed by advantages to the economy as a whole, or are justified by an overriding public interest, they can be given exceptional approval by the Federal Ministry of Economics and Technology, the so-called ministerial authorization. However, by no means should the impression arise that approval by ministerial authorization is common practice in Germany. In fact, the figures confirm its exceptional status: In more than 30 years of merger control practice in Germany there have only been a total of 18 applications for ministerial authorization. In seven cases authorization was granted, in five of these seven it was granted only subject to conditions.

Competencies of the European Commission

Cooperation between the Bundeskartellamt and the European Commission also plays a significant role in merger control proceedings. The competencies of the European Commission in the field of merger control are laid down in the EC Merger Regulation (ECMR).[16] Where the conditions of Article 1(2) and (3) are fulfilled, the European Commission, not the Bundeskartellamt, is the competent authority, even if all undertakings participating in the merger are German. These are mainly cases where the combined aggregate worldwide turnover of the participating undertakings is more than 5 billion and the aggregate EU-wide turnover of each of at least two of the undertakings concerned is more than 250 million.

In addition, there are certain factual criteria under which referrals from Member State competition authorities to the European Commission and vice versa are also possible. Referrals may either be requested by the undertakings concerned prior to notification, or by the Member States after notification (cf. Articles 4, 9, and 22 ECMR). These referral possibilities were introduced for efficiency reasons. They reflect the conviction that the authority best placed to deal with a case should be the one responsible for it.

[16] Council Regulation (EC) no. 139/2004 of 20 January 2004 on the control of concentrations between undertakings, OJ L 24/1 of 29 January 2004.

International Cooperation in Merger Control

The increasing internationalization of markets has led to enhanced cooperation between the competition authorities, not only in the EU but also at international level. The OECD has published its *Council Recommendation* on Merger Review,[17] the ICN Mergers Working Group has inter alia published *Guiding Principles and Recommended Practices for Merger Notification and Review Procedures* and also so-called *Merger Templates*.[18] The following case provides a good example of how such cooperation in merger proceedings might look in practice.

In Vision/General Electric

The Bundeskartellamt in Bonn has cleared the planned acquisition of InVision Technologies, Inc., Newark (USA) by General Electric Company, Fairfield (USA) subject to conditions. The merger was also examined by other competition authorities in Europe and America and was dealt with by the Bundeskartellamt in close cooperation with the US Federal Trade Commission (FTC) in particular.

The case raised competition concerns in the field of x-ray systems for non-destructive testing (NDT). Such systems are used to detect material defects in all kinds of different products without destroying the product or reducing its quality. Since General Electric and InVision would have gained a dominant position in this market in Germany through the merger, the Bundeskartellamt only cleared the project under the condition that the InVision subsidiaries that are active in the same area be sold.

In the course of the US merger control proceedings the parties themselves had offered to sell the respective InVision subsidiaries. In close cooperation, the Bundeskartellamt and the FTC reached an agreement not only on the respective conditions and time limits but also on the nomination of a security trustee to prevent potentially conflicting provisions from the start.

This case is an excellent example for successful international cooperation between competition authorities. It was also in the interest of the undertakings concerned to ensure smooth negotiations between the competition authorities leading to an agreement on the clearance conditions; therefore they decisively supported this process by waiving their right to demand confidentiality of business secrets and documents in the information exchange at an early stage.

[17] The Council Recommendation on Merger Review, available at http:// webdomino1.oecd.org/horizontal/oecdacts.nsf/linkto/c(2005)34.

[18] Available at http://www.internationalcompetitionnetwork.org/mergers/index.html.

In conclusion it can be said that the German competition law has now been in place for almost 50 years, which makes it the oldest competition regime in Europe. In the course of these 50 years it has undergone many modifications and it is subject to constant change even to this day. One of the reasons for this is that economic theories, on which competition law is ultimately based, are constantly developing. For example, research in the field of industrial and institutional economics has in the recent past revolutionized existing approaches also, in methodical terms. However, it is also the developments in the markets that add a new dimension to the dynamics of economic life. In recent decades, the most significant development in this respect has been globalization. It is our task to meet these challenges. Just as in a free competition system, where established economic positions of power are challenged by new, better offers of other competitors, established theories and practices must be subject to constant review and criticism. Here, too, 'creative destruction'—to quote Joseph A. Schumpeter[19]—is the driving force behind a development process whose end is indefinite.

[19] Joseph A. Schumpeter. 1980. *Kapitalismus, Sozialismus und Demokratie*, 5th ed., p. 140.

14

Competition Law in Mexico*

Eduardo Pérez Motta

Competition Policy and Law

The 1992 exposition of motives for Mexico's competition law[1] noted that fostering competition and free market access was a necessary and natural complement to the economic changes that the country had embarked on. This document, which preceded the presentation of the Bill that would become the Federal Law of Economic Competition (LFCE), remarked that in a monopolized market, both the quantity and quality of goods and services was inferior to those produced under competition. Hence, monopoly was inefficient and led to losses in social welfare, as it hampered the country's chances to develop towards its full economic possibilities and permanently reduced its economic wealth.[2] With this as a starting point, competition policy in Mexico has been chiefly concerned with efficiency.

* Reproduced from 'Competition Law in Mexico', published in Dhall, V. (ed.). 2007. *Competition Law Today: Concepts, Issues, and the Law in Practice* (first ed.), Oxford University Press, New Delhi.

[1] The preamble to the law, outlining its content, legal basis, spirit, and intent.

[2] *Exposición de motivos de la LFCE*, available in the Commission's website: http://sp.cfc.gob.mx:8080/cfc01/Documentos/Esp/Nor matividad/Exposición%20de%20motivos%20de%20la%20LFCE/index.htm.

Background

Mexico's competition policy was introduced in 1993 as part of a decade-long reform initiative to end central government control and protection of domestic economic activity and to develop a market-based economy. This initiative included a cease of most domestic price controls, a reduction in entry constraints, as well as the opening of the economy to foreign trade and investment. The opening of the economy was achieved through the signing of free trade agreements (FTAs) starting with the North American Free Trade Agreement (NAFTA) in 1994, which was followed by other FTAs, including one with the European Union.

The government also privatized hundreds of state-owned commercial enterprises and instituted regulatory regimes to deal with market defects in some of the privatized sectors that exhibited natural monopoly characteristics. Since removing trade barriers could not assure competition if private barriers sprang up instead and import liberalization could not ensure rivalry in non-traded sectors, a key element in the government's economic reform was the adoption of a general competition law. Mexico's NAFTA commitments included the adoption of measures proscribing anticompetitive business conduct and in 1993, Mexico adopted the Federal Law of Economic Competition (LFCE) and created the Federal Competition Commission (CFC) to enforce it. The Regulations implementing the LFCE (RLFCE), published in March 1998, develop more specific substantive and procedural aspects of the law's provisions.

The CFC, which has sole responsibility for applying the LFCE, is established as an independent agency that is 'technically and operatively autonomous',[3] although attached to the Economics Ministry for purposes of budgetary administration. The President of Mexico appoints a chairman and four commissioners, who constitute the Plenum, and are vested with the CFC's decision-making authority. They are appointed for staggered ten-year terms and can be removed only for grave cause. The Plenum makes determinations by majority vote and is presided by the Chairman who also directs the CFC's work, represents the CFC publicly, and can appoint and remove personnel.

Scope and Exemptions

The law is designed to give operative force to the anti-monopoly provisions set out under Article 28 of the Mexican Constitution, which opens with

[3] Article 23 of the LFCE.

a broad prohibition of 'monopolies, monopolistic practices, [and] State monopolies'. The prohibition is subsequently narrowed when the article clarifies that functions exercised exclusively by the State in specified 'strategic areas' will not constitute monopolies; also excluded from the prohibition are exclusionary privileges accorded to copyright and patent holders as well as labour associations and export trade associations. The 'strategic areas' currently include postal services, telegraph and radiotelegraphy, petroleum and other hydrocarbons, basic petrochemicals, radioactive minerals, nuclear energy, electric power, and the functions of the central bank in producing coins and paper currency.

The LFCE reflects and further details the boundaries of the constitutional exemptions. Article 4 restates the strategic area exclusion, but clarifies that State-owned enterprises are subject to the law with respect to activities that are not explicitly exempted by the Constitution. Articles 5 and 6 repeat that legally constituted labour associations and export trade associations, respectively, do not constitute monopolies. However, the law adds several requirements for the latter exception, including that association membership must be fully voluntary and that organization of the association must be in compliance with the law of the association's domiciliary state.

Save for these exceptions, the LFCE is applicable, by its terms, to 'all economic agents', expressly including government agencies (Article 3), and to 'all sectors of economic activity' (Article 1). Thus, the state, its agencies, and all state-owned commercial enterprises operating outside the strategic areas are subject to the law. Nevertheless, the CFC ordinarily has no law enforcement jurisdiction when a government agency is acting as a regulatory authority and not as an economic agent, even if the government entity is engaging in regulatory conduct that inappropriately restricts competition. In these cases, the Commission may issue an opinion to the agency in question, but this order has no legally binding effect.

Although the statute does not make any distinction between foreign and domestic actors and the law 'applies to all agents whose actions impact markets in the Mexican territory', the CFC recognizes that enforcement based on an 'effects' test faces a range of difficulties. The Commission has addressed transnational enforcement issues by voluntary submission of the parties, through cooperative agreements with foreign antitrust enforcement authorities, and by adopting regulations designed to exempt certain foreign transactions from its pre-merger notification requirements.

The Federal Law of Economic Competition and Its Code of Regulations

Current Provisions

Control of Cartels and Other Anticompetitive Agreements[4]

Under the LFCE, practices are classified as either absolute (Article 9) or relative (Article 10). 'Absolute' monopolistic practices are prohibited *per se* and agreements to undertake them are legally void. Such practices cannot be defended by claiming that they are efficient, as their inefficiency is presumed conclusively by the law. In contrast, 'relative' monopolistic practices may not be illegal unless the respondent is found to have 'substantial power' in a defined relevant market and fails to prove any efficiency gains derived from the practice.

The absolute monopolistic practices that are subject to the *per se* prohibition under Article 9 include four categories of hard-core cartels: price fixing, output restriction, market division, and bid rigging. The LFCE's absolute prohibition of hard-core horizontal agreements has been a critical weapon in the elimination of publicly sanctioned, but privately arranged, price constraints. In the CFC's early years, much of its enforcement work with respect to absolute practices was focused on rooting out anticompetitive conducts that the system of business chambers and price controls had encouraged. The March 1998 LFCE Regulations include provisions that specifically address these conducts.

Control of Abuse of Dominance or Monopolization[5]

Vertical agreements and unilateral behaviours (abuse of dominance or monopolization) are treated as relative monopolistic practices under the law. Article 10 specifically identifies five types of vertical conduct: (i) vertical market division, (ii) resale price maintenance, (iii) tied sales, (iv) exclusive dealing, and (v) refusals to deal. The sixth and final category specified is the collusive boycott, a horizontal behaviour with a common vertical component. Other types of vertical agreements are meant to fall under the catch-all provision of Article 10, section VII. The regulations implement the catch-all provision by characterizing five additional relative practices under Article 7: (i) predatory pricing, (ii) exclusive dealing in exchange for special discounts,

[4] Articles 8 and 9 of the law, 5 of the regulations.

[5] Articles 8, 10–13 of the law, 6, 7, 9–13 of the regulations.

(iii) cross-subsidisation, (iv) discrimination in price or conditions of sale, and (v) raising rivals' costs.

It should be noted that the LFCE does not address abusive (high) pricing. Unlawful conduct is defined solely in terms of exclusionary practices at the expense of competitors or other firms in the chain of distribution, and not in terms of exploitative practices at the expense of consumers. Exploitation of market power by charging supra-competitive prices to consumers is expected to be self-correcting, as it will normally attract new entrants. The possibility that new entry is prevented by intrinsic market conditions is not addressed by the LFCE, but by provisions in specialized sectoral laws.

Relative monopolistic practices are illegal only if they demonstrably harm competition in the case at issue. The language of Article 10, states that practices must 'improperly displace other agents from the market, substantially limit their access, or establish exclusive advantages in favour of certain persons'. More importantly, a relative monopolistic practice is unlawful under the LFCE only if the responsible party has substantial market power in the relevant market. The Regulations clarify the criteria applied both for defining the relevant market and for determining the existence of market power, and also provide that a respondent may offer a defence on the grounds of efficiency.

Merger Control[6]

Article 16 of the LFCE prohibits mergers whose object or effect is to reduce, distort, or hinder competition. Article 17 requires that, in assessing mergers, the CFC consider whether the merging parties would be able to fix prices unilaterally, substantially restrict supply, impede competitors' access to the market, or engage in unlawful monopolistic conduct. Article 18 adds the requirement that, in analysing mergers, the Commission must identify the relevant market and determine market power. The CFC's March 1998 Regulations include a treatment of relevant market definition and market power determination, as well as language permitting merging parties to defend a merger by proving the existence of efficiencies. The LFCE empowers the Commission to sanction an unlawful merger by ordering partial or full divestiture, as well as other conduct relief and a fine of up to 225,000 minimum daily wages (MDW), equivalent to US $1,035,000.

LFCE Article 20 establishes pre-merger notification requirements that are indexed to the minimum daily wage (MDW). Notification is required if a

[6] Articles 16–22 of the law, and 9–22 of the regulations.

transaction exceeds 12 million MDW (US $56 million), or if it results in a party holding more than 35 per cent of the shares or assets of a firm with sales or assets exceeding that amount. Notification is also required if the parties' assets or annual sales total more than 48 million MDW (US $221 million) and the transaction involves an additional accumulation of assets or shares of over 4.8 million MDW (US $22.1 million). Article 20 of the RLFCE provides for filing a short form notification if the parties certify the transaction's 'plainly manifest' lack of anticompetitive potential. RLFCE Article 21, Section II permits an even shorter notification to be filed within five days following consummation of restructuring transactions, provided that the parent entity has held or controlled at least 98 per cent of the merging subsidiaries' shares for the preceding three years. Foreign mergers must, in principle, be notified to the CFC if they produce effects within Mexico, but section I of the same article waives notification for transactions involving shares of foreign entities in which the acquirer obtains no new Mexican assets or shares.

All notified transactions are subject to CFC examination, a process for which the statute establishes strict deadlines. Notified transactions that receive CFC clearance cannot be attacked thereafter (unless the clearance was based on false information), and although the CFC may contest a merger for which notification was not required, it may do so only within one year after the transaction is completed. The LFCE does not, by its terms, prohibit completion of a notified merger during its review period. It does, however, invoke LFCE Article 19 to order that suspect transactions be held in abeyance until the Commission reaches a final resolution.

Competition Advocacy[7]

A key concern for Mexico's competition authority is to ensure that competition policy becomes a core element that will contribute towards implementing sound regulatory and trade policies. As a result, the CFC has adopted a permanent programme for competition advocacy, which broadly covers its actions aimed at promoting a better understanding of competition policy and is implemented in two broad categories. The first comprises advocacy activities directed at other public entities or private parties whose aim is to influence the development of a structural and regulatory framework that is competition-friendly. The second covers all the actions aimed at raising public awareness about the benefits of competition. Both categories are briefly described below.

[7] Article 24 of the law, 49–51 of the regulations.

Activities Aimed at Lobbying for Competition Friendly Structural and Regulatory Reforms

The competition legislation vests the CFC with authority to issue non-binding opinions: (a) on competitive implications of new laws and regulations as well as of proposed changes to federal programmes and policies at the request of the Federal Executive; (b) regarding existing or draft laws, regulations, agreements, and other governmental acts on its own initiative; and (c) any opinions in response to a request from any private party or governmental agency. In practice, its advocacy efforts have played an important role in discouraging and preventing anticompetitive practices. In regulated sectors, for example, the CFC has sought that legislation and regulations grant it faculties to evaluate economic agents participating in public procurement processes, and grant its determinations on competition conditions a binding character. Through its actions the Commission has been able to influence the design of privatization and concession granting schemes, and prevented excessive concentration that would limit or harm competition.[8]

Initiatives to Foster and Strengthen a Competition Culture

The CFC has undertaken numerous initiatives to make its decisions transparent by making them public through its website, press releases, newsletters, and international fora.[9] In addition, it disseminates competition-related activities within the government and throughout society, including media campaigns, publications, participation in courses and seminars, as well as in working group discussions with different government bodies. These activities rely on the premise that a society informed about the benefits of a competitive marketplace and the impact of the CFC's resolutions and opinions, will be more willing to recognize and support the Commission's enforcement actions.

Distinguishing Features of the Law

In its 2004 report on Competition Law and Policy in Mexico, the OECD noted that: 'The law treats aggressively the most harmful competitive constraints and applies an economically sensitive analysis to the more ambiguous

[8] In recent years, the CFC has used this power in processes relating to the privatization of the government's insurance company and the allocation of radioelectric spectrum for mobile telephony. Both are detailed in the next section.

[9] Sensitive or confidential information is obviously not included and is protected by law.

forms of conduct by using a market power screen and permitting an efficiency defence. The law's elegant organisation and clear conceptualisation reveal its origin as a product of technical expertise, rather than populist adventurism or political compromise.'[10]

LFCE Article 2 states that '[t]he purpose of this law is to protect the competition process and free market access, by preventing monopolies, monopolistic practices and other restrictions that deter the efficient operation of goods and services markets' [emphasis added]. Hence, market efficiency is at the heart of the competition legislation.

Article 6 of the Rulings allows a dominant agent to present an efficiency defence for its allegedly anticompetitive conduct, and establishes that the Commission will consider the following elements, amongst others:

- The practice achieves resource savings, which permits the allegedly responsible agent, to produce the same quantity of the good at a lower cost, or to produce a greater quantity of the good at the same cost, on a permanent basis.
- The actions achieve lower costs if two or more goods or services are produced jointly as opposed to separately.
- The conduct in question lowers administrative costs significantly.
- The conduct in question transfers production technology or market know-how.
- These actions lower production or trade costs arising from an expansion of infrastructure or a distribution network.

The law also makes explicit that a determination of market power will consider the existence of entry barriers and lists some of the elements that the Commission will consider in its assessment of these barriers: capital requirements, that is, 'financial costs or the costs of developing alternative channels'; the relative efficiency of financial markets, that is, whether conditions of 'limited access to financing' exist (Index I); adjustment costs, or '[the] term for recouping the required investment', and whether costs are effectively sunk, '[the] return for alternative uses of infrastructure and equipment' (Index II); fixed costs such as advertising and investments in brands or trademarks as barriers to entry (Index IV); marketing and business practices, such as exclusive arrangements, lie within the definition of barriers provided in index VI; and indexes III, V, and VII consider normative barriers, that is, regulation and regulators' actions, including the use of intellectual and industrial property as a barrier to entry, and regulation relating to international trade as a special case of barriers to entry.

[10] Page 11 of the report. Accessible through the OECD's website: http://www.oecd.org/dataoecd/57/9/31430869.pdf.

Shortcomings Detected in LFCE's Enforcement

In its 2004, the OECD noted a number of shortcomings in the enforcement of the competition law:

> The problem of producing demonstrable results still persists, however, especially because the shower of judicial challenges that the CFC faced in 1998 has grown into a thunderstorm. The CFC has won virtually every case that has risen to the Mexican Supreme Court, which has found numerous portions of the LFCE to be constitutional and has not rendered any definitive decisions finding constitutional defects. Nonetheless, the lower courts have not been so supportive, and the CFC is seen as an easy target for litigious delay at the hands of its prosecutorial targets. This problem extends not only to judicial review of the CFC's procedures and case determinations, but also to the collection of the fines imposed by the CFC for unlawful conduct.[11]

The CFC believes that it needs better tools to detect and attack cartels, such as authority to conduct onsite searches for business records, and a leniency programme. It also needs to avail itself of structural remedies to attack and dismantle structural monopoly. In addition, the CFC believes that some of its opinions should be legally binding, specially those related to the introduction of competition principles in regulated sectors.

In addition, the Supreme Court has declared several articles of the LFCE to be unconstitutional. In November 2003, it issued a decision in the Warner Lambert case[12] declaring unconstitutional the catch-all provision of the law (Article 10, Section VII) on which the CFC had based its regulation against predatory pricing, cross-subsidization, raising rivals' costs, discrimination in price or conditions of sale, and exclusive dealings in exchange for special discounts. Additionally, on 6 January 2004, the Supreme Court declared Articles 14 and 15 as unconstitutional, which deal with the Commission's authority to declare void any state or local authorities' actions that restrict interstate or foreign commerce.

Foreseen Changes to Its Legal Framework

Based on its more than ten years' experience with the upholding of the law, the CFC is currently working on a package of reforms that will allow it to become a more effective enforcer. It includes a leniency programme that will enable it to more successfully prosecute hard-core cartels.

[11] P. 13 OECD Report.

[12] File DE-11–94.

Bill to Introduce Changes to Its Law

There are three specific aims behind the proposed changes to the law:

1. To guarantee that competition principles are taken into account in the drafting of rulings, standards, and public policies,
2. To strengthen the powers of the CFC to prevent and remedy anticompetitive conduct, and
3. To resolve CFC procedural deficiencies underscored in some of the decisions made by the judiciary and identified by the Commission in its more than ten-year experience.

Proposed overall changes include:

- Establishing a comprehensive, whole-of-government approach to competition policy, particularly during the policy-making process, by allowing the CFC to issue binding opinions to the Federal Public Administration, public opinions on bills for laws, rulings, and decrees relating to competition and free market access, and empowering it to determine the existence of barriers to interstate commerce, so that the Executive Branch can bring cases before the Supreme Court against state and local authorities.
- Strengthening the CFC's powers by expanding anticompetitive practices typified under the law and possible remedies available to the CFC.
- Simplifying procedures for increased CFC effectiveness to reduce economic agents' incentives to prolong litigation and abuse the *amparo* proceedings.[13]
- Adopting a leniency programme as an effective tool to combat per se prohibited absolute monopolistic practices.

Enforcement Practices

Control of Cartels

Horizontal Price Fixing in the Liquefied Petroleum Gas (LP Gas) Retail Market[14]

A local organization of a national political party filed a complaint against three gas companies in the metropolitan area of Toluca for agreeing to fix the

[13] An *amparo* is a proceeding established in Articles 103 and 107 of the Mexican Constitution to provide all persons with protection against unconstitutional acts by government. It is available to any party who can raise a claim that he/she is being subjected to an unconstitutional law or that his/her due process rights are being infringed. Due process, in this context, can attack the merits of an agency's decision.

[14] File DE-03–96.

retail price of LP gas. In its investigation, the CFC found that these companies had simultaneously raised the price of LP gas from 1.42 to 1.80 pesos/kg in January 1996.The price of 1.42 pesos/kg had been the regulated price to the final consumer authorized by the Federal Government and the 30 per cent price increase, agreed upon by the companies, had taken place under the new deregulated price policy. The agreement had been supported and facilitated by a coordination mechanism used until then by the responsible parties to negotiate LP gas controlled prices with the regulatory authority. Based on its investigation, the CFC decided to impose fines on each economic agent involved in the horizontal price fixing agreement.[15]

Setting Minimum Distances between Tortilla-Makers and Other Food Sellers[16]

During 2004, the Commission investigated three cases where municipal authorities and trade associations set minimum distances between businesses. The conduct violated Article 9, index III of the LFCE, which bans market allocation agreements among competitors. In addition, the Supreme Court has established that any regulation setting distance requirements between similar businesses is unconstitutional, since it is contrary to the individual right of freedom of work, contained in Article 28, and interferes with free market access. In all cases the Commission issued an opinion to the municipal authority involved expressing the need to modify or eliminate articles in local regulation which obstructed free market access and unreasonably favoured established businesses. As to the local trade associations, the Commission ordered these to immediately suppress their anticompetitive conduct, and in some cases warned them that if it did not do so, it could result in criminal prosecution.

Price Fixing in the Pasteurized Milk Industry[17]

In October 2000, the price of pasteurized milk was raised nationwide with the increase ranging between 6.7 and 7.3 percent depending on the brand. The CFC opened an ex officio investigation to analyse potentially collusive behaviour among economic agents participating in the processed milk market to fix sale prices. The investigation revealed that a number of the largest pasteurized milk producers had entered into contracts and agreements aimed at fixing, raising, concerting, or manipulating the sales price of industrialized

[15] The parties subsequently challenged the decision but the lack of sound legal arguments by the defendants, led the CFC to confirm its decision.

[16] Files IO-09–2003, IO-12–2003, IO-09–2004, and DE-03–2003.

[17] File IO-25–2000.

milk nationwide. Based on Article 41 of the regulations the parties presented written compromises to terminate the legal procedure in advance. They agreed to cease the practice, pledged not to undertake any anticompetitive practice in violation of the LFCE, and agreed to submit to the CFC price information over three years. The proposed commitments, with some additions imposed by the CFC, were considered convenient and the information feasible to survey the operation of the affected market during the following three years.

Control of Abuse of Dominance

Boycott[18]

Harinera Seis Hermanos (HSH) filed a complaint charging *Cargill de México* and a civil association of agriculture product suppliers, *Asociación de Proveedores de Productos Agropecuarios* (APPAMEX), with blocking its access to imported wheat supplies. The CFC initial inquiry provided evidence of a boycott, led by Cargill against HSH whose object or effect was to displace HSH from the market. Although no evidence was found regarding APPAMEX members' refusal to sell imported wheat to HSH, the CFC considered the intent to displace HSH from the market as a violation to the LFCE and noted that pressure was exerted at the request of Cargill through the association. Furthermore, mainly on the basis of its market share, Cargill was found to wield substantial market power in the relevant market for commercialization of US and Canadian hard wheat imports. The CFC resolved that both Cargill and APPAMEX, were responsible for implementing a boycott against HSH and imposed fines on them. In addition, it ordered APPAMEX to modify its regulations given that they facilitated relative monopolistic practices.[19]

Tied Sales and Other Practices in Telecommunications[20]

Long distance operators, Avantel, S.A. and Alestra S. de R.L., filed complaints against Telmex, the privatized state monopoly in telecommunications, alleging practices in violation of the LFCE. Through its investigations the CFC found Telmex responsible for anticompetitive practices derived from charging public telephone users $0.50 per minute for long distance calls when using '800' numbers (traditionally used to provide customers with free communication), for requiring the use of Telmex's pre-paid cards (Ladatel) in order

[18] File DE-52–98.

[19] The CFC's decision was challenged through the filing of an appeal for review. However, the final judgment confirmed the original decision in all its terms.

[20] File DE-07–98.

to access those numbers, and for applying a $0.50 per minute access fee to competitors' clients when calling '800' numbers offered by Telmex. Among the potentially illegal practices uncovered during the investigations were: tied sales, refusal to deal, discrimination, and raising rivals' costs. The object and effect of the conduct was to offset Telmex's main competitors, Alestra and Avantel. Taking into account the harm posed on competition, the effect on firms and consumers and Telmex's market share, the CFC resolved to sanction Telmex with the highest applicable fine for each of the practices indulged.

Imposing Sales Conditions and an Efficiency Defence[21]

In 2002, the CFC initiated an ex officio investigation into large self-service chain stores. One of the principal motivations was a concern that some multi-product self-service retailers were forcing their suppliers to charge higher resale prices to other competing stores under the threat of suspending their purchases. The CFC first began by investigating whether the alleged anticompetitive behaviour consisted of relative monopolistic practices whose aim or effect was, or could be, to unduly displace other economic agents from the market, impede their access, or establish exclusive advantages, by imposing conditions on distributors or suppliers, that is, of violating Article 10, index II of the law. The Commission found the claim unsubstantiated by the facts.

Furthermore, the CFC noted that Wal-Mart Mexico (Walmex) had exhibited accelerated growth following its 2000 strategy of 'low prices everyday', and that this growth had continued amid a slowdown in private spending. In fact, its market participation had increased while that of its principal competitors had decreased. It noted that Walmex's procurement system has introduced important efficiencies into Mexico's distribution markets leading to increases in productivity and profit margins that translated into a greater ability by Walmex to invest its own resources without resorting to debt. The Commission therefore concluded that Walmex's conduct did not violate Article 10 index II of the law.

Merger Review

The Coca Cola Company/Cadbury Schweppes, plc[22]

The Coca Cola Company (TCCC) and Cadbury Schweppes, plc (CS) notified their interest in merging. The transaction involved the purchase of several brands of carbonated drinks and bottled natural water property

[21] File IO-02–2002.
[22] File CNT-166–98.

of CS. In its resolution, the CFC determined that the merger would affect two nationwide markets: the carbonated drinks market (including refreshments, carbonated mineral water, and carbonated drinks) and the market of bottled natural water. To assess TCCC's market power in the carbonated drinks market, the CFC considered, among other elements, that the imported carbonated drinks have, in fact, very little presence in the country; the carbonated drinks market is highly concentrated and that TCCC's market share of 64.4 per cent would increase to 71 per cent as a result of the transaction; PepsiCo, the closest competitor of TCCC had a market share of 18 per cent while the remaining market was divided among small and medium size firms; TCCC brand portfolio has high market value; TCCC's distribution network is the largest in the country; in addition, TCCC's market position is considerably reinforced by its remarkable capacity to advertise its brands.

In the bottled natural water market, the CFC considered the joint market share of TCCC and SC as being negligible. Nevertheless, based on these findings, the CFC determined that the TCCC/CS merger would substantially diminish competition in the carbonated drinks market. Thus, the merger would allow TCCC: (a) to unilaterally fix prices and restrict supply; (b) to foreclose competitors from the market of carbonated drinks and (c) to engage in monopolistic practices. On these grounds, the CFC decided to block the acquisition.

Cintra[23]

In the early 1990s, Aerovías de México (Aeromexico) and Mexicana de Aviación (Mexicana), the two largest air carriers in Mexico went into bankruptcy due to high operational costs and debt. In 1994, creditor banks took over both airlines. In May 1995, these banking institutions requested the CFC authorization to create Cintra, a holding company that would serve as a temporary financial vehicle to improve the financial situation of both airlines. The CFC authorized the creation of Cintra, subject to measures aimed at preventing abuses of market power and ensuring the separate operation of the airlines so that, once the financial and operative restructuring process ended, they could be sold off separately. The CFC reserved itself the power to impose fines and order partial or total divestiture of the airlines if there was substantial damage to competition.

[23] Files CNT-25–95, CNT-119–97, CNT-181–97, CNT-123–99, CON-01–2003, CON-32–2004 and CON-02–2005.

Changes in ownership since 1995, led to the government holding a controlling interest in Cintra.[24] In September 2000, Cintra's shareholders submitted a consultation with the CFC noting that the separate operation of the airlines was not feasible. In its response, the CFC concluded that the merger of Aeromexico and Mexicana would substantially increase concentration in all of the most important routes in the country in a definite and irreversible manner and impose economic and legal barriers that would hinder access to both national and foreign competitors. In 2004 and 2005, shareholders submitted consultations to the CFC presenting different schemes to divest Aeromexico and Mexicana's assets. In 2005, Cintra made public its intention to sell both airlines and their subsidiaries separately. The public auction process considers the CFC's participation in assessing and issuing opinions on the auction call and each prospective bidder.

Regulated Sectors

Privatization of AHISA[25]

In 2000, for example, the CFC objected to a government plan to privatize Aseguradora Hidalgo (AHISA), an insurance company that held the exclusive right to sell policies to government employees through payroll deductions. The Commission concluded that the exclusivity provision was anticompetitive. The privatization plan was thereafter revised by limiting the exclusivity provision to a two-year transitional period. The CFC raised no objection to the revised plan or to the participation by any of the four prospective bidders in the subsequent 2002 auction for AHISA.

Spectrum Allocation for Personal Communications Services[26]

In July 2004, Cofetel called for an auction to allocate available spectrum for broadband Personal Communications Services (PCS). The auction call required prospective bidders to obtain favourable opinion from the CFC. The spectrum being offered was divided into four 2×5 paired Mhz blocks in each of the nine regions covering the national territory and one 2×15 paired Mhz block in two of these regions. Licenses were to be awarded for 20 years,

[24] The transactions to transfer Cintra's shares to government funds were authorized by the CFC, subject to the accomplishment of the conditions imposed in the previous resolution.

[25] Files CNT-LI-22–99 and LI-13–2001.

[26] File LI-10–2004.

renewable for a similar period after directly applying to Cofetel and without the need for CFC intervention.

The auction call imposed a 65 MHz spectrum cap on the combined cellular and PCS frequencies for a (new or incumbent) license holder. This cap takes into account the spectrum owned, leased, or otherwise exploited by the applicant, their affiliates and subsidiaries, and all shareholders (direct/indirect and major/minor). In October 2004, the CFC assessed seven different economic agents: four incumbents and three entrants. Prospective bidders revealed that intended spectrum acquisitions exceeded the available spectrum auctioned, in fact, only the demand of incumbents exceeded the amount of spectrum being auctioned, without surpassing the spectrum cap of 65 Mhz.

The Commission reasoned that since spectrum is a scarce resource, carriers with higher marginal valuations, that is incumbents, have incentives to deter the entry of new competitors and to limit the growth of smaller incumbents by hoarding spectrum. Incumbent carriers also have the deepest pockets, making it highly probable that their bids would win spectrum auctions. In addition, the CFC took into account that the market is highly concentrated as measured by subscribers and earnings, with H concentration indexes of 9,232 and 7,988 for pre- and post-paid markets, respectively. As a result, one of the CFC's chief concerns was that the auction would increase spectrum concentration, impede the entry of new carriers and diminish the prospects of long-term competition among incumbents.

The CFC's goal was to encourage the entry of new participants to the mobile telephony market. Accordingly, it determined that it was necessary to strengthen spectrum caps in the 1.9 Ghz auction to enhance participation so that the process would not lead to increased concentration of spectrum. On January 2005, it gave conditional clearance to prospective bidders to participate in the 1.9 Ghz auction by limiting any agent's acquisition of spectrum to no more than 35 Mhz at the 1.9 Ghz band in all regions. Incumbents challenged the CFC decision in court and a definitive resolution is still pending.

Advocacy Practices

Structural Reform

The CFC has played an increasing role in designing privatization procedures[27] and regulatory frameworks.[28] In the majority of recent cases, the Commission

[27] Examples include satellite communications, ports, airports, and railroads.

[28] Examples include railroads, natural gas, LP gas, transport, telecommunications, broadcasting, and electricity.

has provided its opinion and technical assistance in designing the structure and regulation of key infrastructure sectors. The following example illustrates some of its work in this area.

Railroads Reform[29]

In 1995, the Constitution was amended to open the railroad sector to private participation. In 1996, the Railway Service Law (RSL) was enacted and followed by a programme to divest the vertically integrated state firm, Ferrocarriles de Mexico (FNM); the CFC offered opinions for both. The structural arrangement chosen was to split FNM into three regional or main lines, several short lines, and a Mexico City Terminal, the major node in the system. For each line and its terminals, a single firm controls all the infrastructure facilities and rail operations, but vertical integration is allowed subject to a mandatory access regime. The Mexico City Terminal is a joint ownership with the three companies and the government on equal shares, to guarantee non-discriminatory access. Among other competition-friendly provisions, sectoral regulation specifies access obligations and establishes that prospective bidders and buyers of a concession from other agents must fulfil an application before the SCT, which among other things requires the CFC's favourable opinion on its participation. Authority to review mergers in the railroad sector is held currently by the SCT and the CFC.

Once in place, however, sectoral law enforcement has revealed that current access rights were addressed in a very broad manner and do not provide clear and objective rules that give certainty to market participants when defining rights of way or interconnection services. While the regulator has tried to reduce the problem through the drafting of norms and the issuing of emergency norms, this has not reduced the uncertainty surrounding access rights and interconnection services. Instead, railroad operators have successfully challenged these norms in court and obtained suspensions because, the courts have reasoned, there are no clear criteria that allow the regulator to issue its resolutions. At present, private, public, and legislative representatives

[29] Plan Nacional de Desarrollo 1995–2000 (PND-1995–2000 National Development Plan); *Federal Gazzette* (1995) 'Los Lineamientos Generales para la Apertura a la Inversión en el Sistema Ferroviario Mexicano'. Mexico City, Mexico, 13 November; OECD (2004), 'Mexico: Progress in Implementing Regulatory Reform'; OECD (2004), 'Structural Reform in the Rail Industry: Should Train Operations be Separated from the Provision of Track Infrastructure?', DAF/COMP/WP2(2004)6; CFC files DE-57–2001 and RA-50–2003, IO-05–2002, DC-01–2002 and RA-11–2004.

have demanded amendments to the sectoral law, which would provide a new opportunity for competition advocacy efforts aimed at strengthening access conditions at the sectoral level.

Regulatory Reform

In 2000, the Federal Regulatory Improvement Commission (COFEMER) established a formal procedural mechanism by which the CFC can identify and comment upon regulations proposed by agencies of the Federal Executive. Federal agencies in Mexico are required by statute to submit all their proposed regulations to COFEMER, accompanied by a regulatory impact statement. COFEMER posts the regulations and the impact statement for comment by interested parties, and thereafter issues an assessment of the proposal to the originating agency. The agency then files a response to the assessment, and COFEMER issues a final opinion either approving the proposal or stating its objections. All comments exchanged between the CFC and COFEMER appear on the public record and are considered by the President's Legal Counsel.

In identifying and opposing anticompetitive features of proposed legislation, the Commission routinely reviews legislative activities and, at the request of the Ministry of Economy and the Ministry of Interior, it issues opinions on any competition effects of the proposals during the early stages of the legislative process. To a lesser extent, the Commission is invited to participate in reviewing proposals by Congress and executive branch agencies.

Annexure: Facts and Figures

Enforcement: cases concluded 1993–2004
Total number of cases: 4,770*

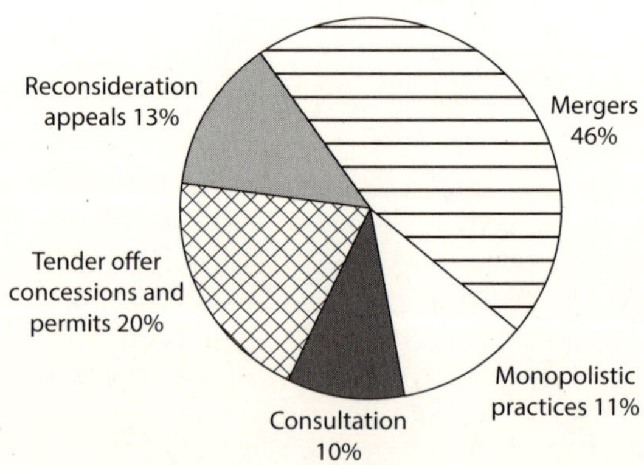

Note: *Does not include 2,334 affairs related with LP gas permits solved in the 2001–4 period.

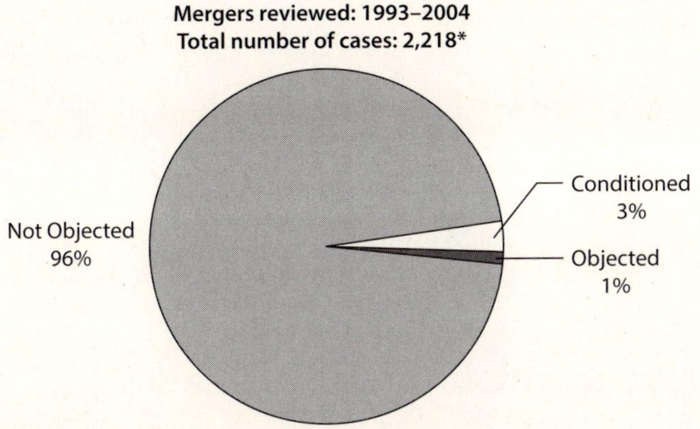

Note: *Includes notified mergers, notices and investigations of allegedly prohibited mergers.

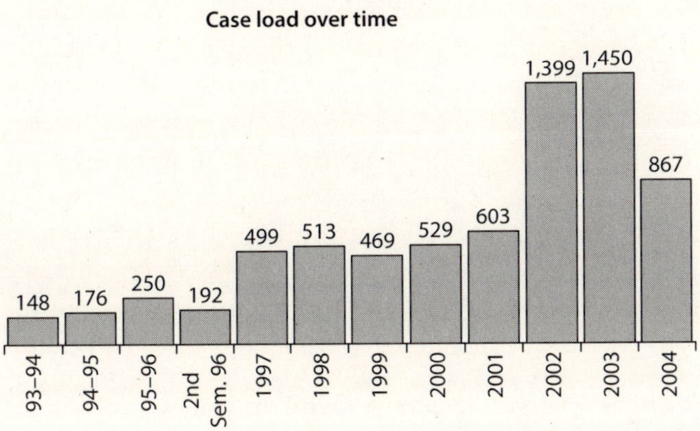

15

South African Competition Law*

Origins, Content, and Impact

David Lewis

Origins

The most casual observer of developments in competition or anti-trust law since the beginning of the 1990s cannot but be struck by two outstanding developments. First, is the mushrooming of national competition authorities across the globe. Whereas in 1990, there were said to be less than 14 functioning national competition authorities, by 2006, there were over 100 such institutions, with much of this proliferation accounted for by developing and transition economies. Second, is the growing contact between these authorities manifest in countless international conferences and journals but, also, in a burgeoning number of bilateral, regional, and multilateral agreements and organizations representing the first fruits of efforts to harmonize the approach

* Reproduced from 'South African Competition Law: Origins, Content, and Impact', published in Dhall, V. (ed.). 2007. *Competition Law Today: Concepts, Issues, and the Law in Practice* (first ed.), Oxford University Press, New Delhi.

The author is grateful to Malanee Murugan-Modise for her assistance in the preparation of this chapter.

to competition law across diverse national jurisdictions and to regulate the conduct of participants in international markets.

While each national competition law responds to particular domestic imperatives—and more will be said on this score—the extent of the proliferation of competition law across so many national economies and societies suggests the existence of some common basis. Clearly, this is to be found in the widespread reduction of direct state involvement in the conduct of economic life. The state's role as a producer of goods and services has diminished significantly, most dramatically, although by no means exclusively, in the countries formally aligned to the Soviet bloc. An equally noteworthy feature of this period is the significant reduction in barriers to international trade.

Policymakers soon recognized that while the retrenchment of the state from direct participation in the economy portended a *smaller* state, it equally required a *smarter* state, a state capable of setting clear rules governing participation in the myriad markets that make up the national and international economies and establishing the legal and institutional framework for securing compliance with those rules. The policy framework that guides this rule-making is competition policy. The various competition statutes and the competition authorities are the legal and institutional representation of these rules.

Recent developments in competition policy and law in South Africa are deeply rooted in these global developments. Here too, the democratic government embarked on a major repositioning of state-owned enterprises and the opening of the economy to international markets. However, major policy initiatives always derive their strength and urgency from domestic social imperatives, and, in South Africa, these strongly predisposed to the introduction of robust competition policy and law.

It is important to appreciate that apartheid represented minority control of the economy, every bit as much as it represented minority rule over political and civic life. By way of pertinent example, a mere listing of the exclusions that straitjacketed black business people would occupy a volume many times greater than this brief review. Black consumers were equally voiceless, although their raw power, manifest in ubiquitous consumer boycotts, played a major role in mass mobilization against the apartheid regime.

In addition to the race-based exclusion that characterized apartheid, the South African government was an enthusiastic adherent of the autarkic, inward oriented policies that dominated development thinking in the post Second World War era. Tariff barriers, exchange controls, and the development of highly subsidized national champions, which were, more often than not, state-owned, were characteristic features of industrial policy. These were all significantly distorted by the existence of apartheid—indeed many received the unquestioning endorsement of government precisely because they were intended to forestall the economic sanctions and general isolation from the international community and markets that accompanied South Africa's pariah status.

Note too that the domination of deep level gold mining with its massive capital requirements also accounted for the phenomenon of the 'mining house', very large, highly centralized corporations that dominated the economic landscape. With growing isolation, manifest in diminishing investment opportunities for South African corporations abroad and in opportunities to invest their significant returns in lucrative non-mining markets as international corporations reduced their presence in South Africa, these mining companies transformed themselves into widely diversified conglomerates, active in mining, manufacturing, and a wide array of services, notably financial services.

The predictable consequences of this combination of racial exclusion, inward oriented industrial policy, and national champions are highly centralized control over the economy by a small number of large corporations, which are in turn controlled by a small grouping of white families and individuals, increasingly high levels of concentration in most major markets, and an underdeveloped small business sector. This combination of protection from international and domestic competition accounted for the inefficiencies that bedevilled South African manufacturing, in particular as it thrived on a diet of subsidy and protection, including of course protection from the judgments of their own customers.

It is little wonder then that the first democratic government came to power strongly committed to the introduction of robust competition law—it was viewed as an instrument for enhancing economic efficiency and consumer well-being and, closely related to these objectives, as a mechanism for easing access to the economy of those whom apartheid had long excluded. Hence, the 1992 Policy Guidelines for a Democratic South Africa drawn up by the African National Congress (ANC), soon to become the governing party of the first democratic government, made a commitment to introduce 'anti-monopoly, anti-trust and merger policies in accordance with international norms and practices, to curb monopolies and continued domination of the economy by a minority within the white minority, and to promote greater efficiency in the private sector'. This commitment then found echo in the democratic government's earliest economic policy blueprints, namely the Reconstruction and Development Programme and the Growth, Employment and Redistribution policy.

The point to emphasize here is that competition law in South Africa, in contrast with many developing economies in which it has recently been introduced, is not simply a product of economic liberalization and so bears little of the burdensome political baggage often associated with that process. It was, and, to a significant extent, still is, viewed as an instrument for redressing the wrongs of the past and this has lent it strong popular support. There are some disadvantages inherent in popular support—as we shall see it has given rise to a statute that, in some of its content, has decidedly populist overtones. It is also responsible for generating a number of unrealistic expectations. But these shortcomings are trivial compared to the advantages of building a competition authority in what is a generally supportive social and political environment.

It may come as some surprise to learn that there was, in the hostile environment of apartheid and protection, already a competition law in place. Indeed, South Africa has had some form of competition regulation on the statute book since the 1950s beginning with the enactment of the Regulation of Monopolistic Conditions Act, No. 24 of 1955. This was repealed by the Maintenance and Promotion of Competition Act, No. 96 of 1979. However, these prior competition regimes were notoriously ineffective. They were poorly resourced and institutionally subordinate—the competition authority was essentially an advisory body whose decisions were, for the most part, subject to ministerial override.[1]

And overridden they were—one notorious example was a market sharing agreement concluded in the 1980s between the country's brewing monopoly and the largest producer of wines and spirits which ensured that these liquor giants stayed out of each other's markets. This agreement was opposed by the competition authority of the time but the recommendation was rejected by a government anxious to lend its support to

[1] As we elaborate below this statute has been replaced by a new piece of legislation. The two statutes differ so significantly that little point is served by a detailed comparison. Suffice to say that the competition authority established under the previous statutory regime constituted a section of a department of state whose powers were, for the most part, confined to providing advice and recommendations to the responsible minister. Moreover, should the investigations of the authority—for which ministerial authority was a jurisdictional prerequisite—have revealed the possible existence of a limited range of restrictive practices, responsibility for further investigation and prosecution had to be handed to the police and the criminal prosecutorial authority. These features alone serve to illustrate the gulf between the approaches embodied in the two pieces of legislation. As we outline below, the current Act establishes an independent agency with separate investigatory and adjudicative agencies including a dedicated appeal court.

a major political ally in the Western Cape, the centre of the wine and spirits industry.[2] The effects of this agreement are predictably present in the contemporary structure of these large markets. In the nearly twenty years' experience of the Promotion and Maintenance of Competition Act—the present statute's predecessor—not one instance of anticompetitive conduct was prosecuted.

Instead of attempting to amend existing legislation, the new government elected to wipe the slate clean. It resolved to introduce a new competition statute, providing, inter alia, for an entirely new institutional structure imbued with significantly greater powers. In conformity with the governance style of the new democracy, the decision to strengthen the application of competition law in South Africa was preceded by wide-ranging public debate. The initial response of many of South Africa's key corporations was decidedly hostile. However, government pressed on over these objections and produced a policy paper outlining its position in support of a new competition law. This constituted the policy framework which guided a legal drafting team appointed by the Minister of Trade and Industry. The drafting team engaged extensively with experts from a range of mature competition jurisdictions.

The drafting team and the Department of Trade and Industry held detailed discussions in the National Economic Development and Labour Council, the statutory multi-partite policy forum, with government's counterparts in organized business and labour. On the basis of these discussions, a draft bill was submitted to the cabinet and then to the legislative process. The trade and industry parliamentary committee convened public hearings to which a range of interest groups made submissions and which were keenly followed in the media. Finally in 1999, after this exhaustive series of public conversations, the President assented to the bill and the Competition Act No. 89 of 1998 became part of the law of the land.

This chapter will describe—in the barest outline—the key provisions of the Act and will then attempt to draw some lessons from the still brief experience of implementing this law. It is—I should declare at the outset—an insider's view, one whose author was involved in the preparation of the earliest policy documents, in the drafting of the Act, and in the process of piloting it through parliament, and who has chaired the Tribunal since its establishment in 1999. I trust that if this compromises the objectivity of some of the

[2] This agreement is extensively referenced in a decision of the present Tribunal regarding the proposed merger of two large firms active in various alcoholic beverages markets. See *Distiller Corporation (SA) Limited and Stellenbosch Farmers Winery Group Limited* (08/LM//Feb02).

assessments—and I would hope that it does not—then this will be compensated for by a 'hands-on' perspective on the lessons, positive and negative, to be learned from an always interesting attempt to enforce competition law in an industrialized, middle-income economy.

The Competition Act No. 89 of 1998

The South African competition statute, is, as one might expect, clearly a product of its environment and of the manner of its drafting. It is an eclectic statute, drawing on the experiences of a range of other jurisdictions. These include the European Union, the USA, Australia, and Canada. However, while clearly reflecting contemporary competition law's overriding concern with efficiency, the South African legislation also attempts to filter these international 'best practices' through the lens of South Africa's national characteristics and requirements. These are particularly reflected in the provisions dealing with 'public interest'—which incorporate both social and industrial policy concerns and objectives—as well as in the design of the institutional structure responsible for administering the Act which reflects the rigorous standards of administrative fairness and due process that characterized the young constitutional democracy.

The Act, in common with its counterparts in most other jurisdictions, is principally concerned to regulate mergers[3] and to enforce the prohibitions against anticompetitive conduct.[4] There are a number of other important functions and powers provided for in the Act—for example, responsibility for competition 'advocacy'[5] and for granting exemptions from the Act[6]—but the core tasks of the competition authorities are undoubtedly those related to merger regulation and anticompetitive conduct.

While this wide-ranging jurisdiction has allowed the competition authorities to assume jurisdiction over international mergers and potentially anticompetitive agreements concluded beyond South Africa's borders, it has not resolved the vexed question of the Act's application to several important regulated sectors. Certain of the statutes establishing the sectoral regulators—for example, the statute governing the telecommunications regulator—predate the Competition Act. These sectoral statutes frequently extend an ambiguous and ill-defined jurisdiction over competition matters to the sectoral

[3] Section 21 (1)(e).
[4] Section 21 (1)(c).
[5] Section 21 (1)(b).
[6] Section 21 (1)(d) read with Section 10.

regulators. This overlapping jurisdiction has allowed important producers and service providers in some vital sectors to 'forum shop' thereby evading regulation of their market conduct altogether. A recent amendment to the Act requires the Commission and the sector regulators to negotiate agreements harmonizing the exercise of jurisdiction in these cases. However, these agreements themselves afford the opportunity for diversionary litigation. Clearly, a permanent solution of this serious problem lies in amending the sectoral statutes so as to remove competition matters from their jurisdiction. But this, involving as it does technical grey areas and, possibly more problematic, regulatory turf, is more easily said than done, although official policy does favour the vesting of exclusive jurisdiction over competition matters with the competition authorities.

The Institutional Structure

The Act establishes a hierarchy of three institutions. These are the Competition Commission, the Competition Tribunal, and the Competition Appeal Court. The Commission is the investigative and prosecutorial body. The Tribunal is the decision-making body, although in limited instances it acts as the first stage of appeal from decisions of the Commission. The Appeal Court hears appeals from decisions of the Tribunal.

The institutional architecture established by the Act embodies several noteworthy features.

Firstly, it provides for the strict separation of prosecutorial and adjudicative functions. Although creatures of the same statute, the functions of the Commission and the Tribunal are strictly separated and they are independently managed and budgeted.

Secondly, the adjudicative body—effectively a court of first instance—is an administrative tribunal. This enables procedures that are more flexible and informal than a court of law and it expedites decision-making in an area where time is often of the essence. It also means that 'lay persons' (that is, persons who are not judges) are able to serve on the Tribunal, so as to cater for the interface between law and economics that is a hallmark of competition enquiries. The Chairperson and members of the Tribunal and the Commissioner, the highest official of the Commission, are appointed by the President of the Republic acting on the advice of cabinet.

Thirdly, the Act establishes a dedicated court of appeal. The Competition Appeal Court is a special division of High Court and, as such, is composed of judges serving on one or other of the provincial benches. This too expedites decision-making and is intended to enable a small group of judges to develop expertise in an unusual and highly specialized branch of the law.

Finally, in a far-sighted departure from past South African practice—and, indeed, from the practice of many other jurisdictions—the Competition Act, with one exception, makes no provision for ministerial veto of any of the decisions of the competition authorities.[7] Section 20 of the Act provides that the Commission and the Tribunal are 'independent and subject only to the Constitution and the law' and that they must be 'impartial and must perform (their) functions without fear, favour, or prejudice.' Specific provisions of the Act facilitate executive participation in both Commission and Tribunal proceedings. But this remains a 'right' to make submissions to the Commission's investigators and to appear before the Tribunal—decision-making authority on all matters within their jurisdiction vests exclusively with the competition authorities.

Prohibited Practices

The Commission is required to investigate all complaints of anticompetitive conduct submitted to it. It may also initiate investigations of anticompetitive conduct. On completion of its investigations, it may refer the complaint to the Tribunal, in other words, prosecute the complaint. Or, if it concludes that the complaint does not establish the basis for a successful prosecution under the Act, it may refuse to refer the complaint. In that event, the complainant is entitled to approach the Tribunal directly. Private complainants are also entitled to approach the Tribunal directly for interim relief pending the final adjudication of a complaint.

The Act prohibits restrictive horizontal[8] and vertical[9] practices as well as abuses of a dominant position.[10] It also prohibits price discrimination by a dominant firm.[11] Certain of these practices are prohibited per se. These cover horizontal agreements to fix price, allocate markets, and rig bids as well as minimum resale price maintenance.[12] Although there is, in respect of

[7] The single potential exception is in respect of banking mergers. See Section 18(2).

[8] Section 4.

[9] Section 5.

[10] Section 8.

[11] Section 9.

[12] In January 2004, the Commission announced a Corporate Leniency Policy to assist it in the detection and prevention of cartel activities in South Africa. This policy provides incentive for firms participating in a cartel to come forward and disclose information on cartel conduct in return for immunity from prosecution. In terms of the leniency policy the Commission has full discretion to grant a self-confessing cartel

agreements of this kind, no possibility of a pro-competitive defence, the Supreme Court of Appeal has recently held that a prior 'characterization' of an agreement that is alleged to contravene the Act is necessary in order to establish that the arrangement complained of does indeed conform to the genus of a horizontal restrictive practice.[13]

Section 7 of the Act provides that a firm with a market share of 45 per cent or greater is presumptively dominant. A market share of between 35 per cent and 45 per cent is considered dominant unless the firm in question can show that it does not have market power. A firm with a market share below 35 per cent is dominant only if it can be shown that it possesses market power.

Section 8 specifies two instances of abuse of a dominant position that are prohibited per se. These are provisions prohibiting the charging of an 'excessive price'. A refusal on the part of a dominant firm to grant competitors access to an essential facility is also prohibited per se. 'Exclusionary acts' in general are prohibited if the complainant or the Commission can show that 'the anti-competitive effect of that act outweighs its technological, efficiency, or other pro-competitive gain'. And finally, a number of particular exclusionary abuses are listed—for example, inducing a supplier or customer not to deal with a competitor, a refusal to supply, bundling, and predatory pricing. These are prohibited unless the firm concerned is able to show pro-competitive consequences that outweigh the anticompetitive effect of the practice in question. That is, in respect of certain named abuses the onus for establishing that pro-competitive gains outweigh the anticompetitive effect shifts from the complainant or the Commission to the alleged perpetrator of the abuse.

Section 10 provides that an agreement or practice may—on application to the Commission—be exempted from the application of Chapter 2 of the Act, that is, the chapter dealing with prohibited practices, if it can be shown

---

member, who is first to approach the Commission and subject to specific conditions, immunity, or indemnity for its participation in cartel activity. Accordingly, only a firm that is 'first to the door' to confess and provide information to the Commission in respect of cartel activity would qualify for immunity under the leniency policy. If other members of the cartel wish to come clean on their involvement in a cartel to which the applicant has already confessed, the Commission may explore other processes outside the policy, which may result in the reduction of a fine, a settlement agreement or a consent order. In the event that the matter is referred for adjudication in the Tribunal, the Commission may consider asking the Tribunal for favourable treatment of the applicants who were not first to come forward.

[13] See *American Natural Soda Ash Corporation & CHC Global (Pty) Ltd and Competition Commission of SA, Botswana Ash (Pty) Ltd, Chemserve Technical Products (Pty) Ltd & Minister of Trade and Industry* Supreme Court of Appeal Case No: 554/03.

that the practice or agreement in question is necessary for the attainment of specified objectives. These objectives include the promotion of exports, promoting the ability of small businesses or firms controlled by historically disadvantaged persons to become competitive and bringing about changes in productive capacity that are necessary to halt the decline of an industry. Decisions of the Commission in respect of exemptions may be appealed to the Tribunal.

The Commission's powers of investigation[14] are considerable as are the remedial powers of the Tribunal.[15] The Tribunal may order declaratory[16] or interdictory relief.[17] It may void an anticompetitive agreement.[18] It may order access to an essential facility[19] and it may require that a firm supply a good or service.[20] It may impose an administrative penalty equivalent to 10 per cent of the offending firm's turnover[21] and, under particular conditions, it may order divestiture.[22] Armed with a finding by the Tribunal confirming the existence of prohibited conduct, a private party may approach a civil court in order to prosecute a claim for damages.[23]

Mergers

Merging firms are required to notify all transactions above a specified threshold to the Commission.[24] This notification must be accompanied by specified

[14] Chapter 5 (Section 46–49A).

[15] Note too that, in contrast, with the conduct of adjudication in South Africa generally, the Competition Act specifically vests the Competition Tribunal with 'inquisitorial' powers. This enables the Tribunal to supplement the record of any proceeding with additional documentary evidence. It also enables the Tribunal to identify witnesses or experts. This power enabling the adjudicator to 'enter the ring' has been widely and productively used, especially in merger evaluations.

[16] Section 58(1)(a)(v).

[17] Section 58(1)(a)(i).

[18] Section 58(1)(a)(vi).

[19] Section 58(1)(a)(vii).

[20] Section 58(1)(a)(ii).

[21] Section 58(1)(a)(iii) read with Section 59.

[22] Section 58(1)(a)(iv) subject to Section 60.

[23] Section 65(6).

[24] A 'Small Merger' is one where the combined annual turnover or assets fall below R200 million and/or target firm below R30 million. (USD1 = approximately ZAR6). Parties are not obliged to notify these transactions but may do so voluntarily. The Commission may, within 6 months of such merger taking place, require notification

information designed to enable the competition authorities to evaluate the transaction's impact on competition and on a number of public interests factors, these being the impact on a particular sector or region, on employment, on the ability of small businesses or firms controlled by historically disadvantaged persons to become competitive, and on the ability of national industries to compete in international markets. Merging parties are also required to serve notice of their merger on the Minister of Trade and Industry and on any trades union representative of the employees in the affected firms.[25]

The Commission is required to investigate all mergers submitted to it. In respect of mergers that fall below a second, higher threshold—designated 'intermediate mergers'—the Commission must, within a strictly specified time period, approve the merger with or without conditions, or prohibit the merger. This decision may be appealed to the Tribunal. In respect of mergers above this second threshold—'large mergers'—the Commission must submit a detailed recommendation to the Tribunal which convenes a public hearing at which the Commission, the merging parties, and other parties who establish an interest in the outcome of the transaction (these may include suppliers, competitors, or customers) are given an opportunity to submit evidence and fully ventilate their arguments. The Tribunal must then, within a strictly delimited timeframe, decide to approve the merger, with or without conditions, or prohibit the merger. These decisions may be appealed to the Competition Appeal Court.[26]

Section 12A(2) specifies a non-exhaustive list of factors that must be considered in determining whether or not a merger is likely to result in a substantial lessening of competition. These reflect the standard criteria adopted in merger analysis, for example, the actual and potential level of import competition, barriers to entry, levels of concentration and history of

---

of small mergers if it believes that there are competition or public interest concerns. For an 'Intermediate Merger', the combined annual turnover or assets are at or above R200 million but below R3.5 billion—target firm at or above R30 million, but less than R100 million. For a 'Large Merger' the combined annual turnover or assets are at or above R3.5 billion—target firm at or above R100 million.

[25] We emphasize that the requirement to notify the Minister is to enable him to prepare submissions for consideration of the Commission investigators and the panel of the Tribunal. It does not, however, cede or imply that any decision-making authority vests with the Minister.

[26] The Supreme Court of Appeal, the apex court for all matters other than constitutional matters, has decided that it is the final court of appeal in competition matters, although leave to appeal to this court would have to be received from the Competition Appeal Court.

collusion, the degree of countervailing power, the prospect of firm failure, levels of innovation and product differentiation, and the prospect that the merger will result in the removal of an effective competitor.

If it is established that the merger is indeed likely to compromise competition, the Commission (in the case of a small or inter mediate merger) and the Tribunal (in the case of a large merger) must—in terms of Section 12(A)(1)—determine whether there are any likely pro-competitive gains from the merger that will counter-weight the negative impact on competition.

Finally, the Commission or Tribunal must establish the impact of the merger on the public interest. This controversial provision is elaborated below.

Some Important Lessons

The practice of competition law is, on any reckoning, a high-stakes game. It constitutes a direct intervention in the manner in which private property is used. It also inevitably confronts the exercise of public power, an important source of anticompetitive conduct. However, its interventions are not designed to preserve an obvious public heritage (as with environmental regulation) or blood-and-flesh human beings (as with labour regulation). It intervenes in the name of preserving and promoting competition, a seemingly abstract cause, and one rendered only slightly less rarefied when translated into categories like 'ensuring access' or 'promoting economic efficiency' or 'enhancing consumer welfare'. Nor are efforts to popularize the work of the competition authorities eased by the inordinate technical complexity of the subject matter. It is not surprising then that there are no counterparts to trade unions or environmental activists in the field of competition policy. Consumers, the natural allies of competition authorities, are generally poorly organized.

On the other hand, there is no end of well-resourced opposition. Hence, while many business people would concede that competitive markets and the competition authorities necessary to secure them are a pre-condition for a thriving economy, most would steadfastly resist their incursion into their own backyards. As already suggested, South Africa is not a society with a strong 'culture' of competition—protectionism, rather, has been the order of the day.

The interventions of the competition authorities have accordingly been resolutely opposed from the first day. A new statute—particularly one implicating property rights—in a new constitutional environment will inevitably be subject to rigorous legal scrutiny. And so it has been with the Competition Act. The powers and procedures of each of the authorities established by the Act have been the subject of lengthy and complex proceedings before the Tribunal, the Competition Appeal Court, and various divisions of the High Court, as those at the receiving end of a competition investigation have sought to limit the powers and sap the resources of the authorities.

The Act and the authorities have survived this scrutiny. In fact, at the end of their first six years of existence, many of the procedural and administrative law hurdles that inevitably confront administrative bodies have been cleared. The competition authorities' rules and procedures have generally won the approval of the courts or, where they have been found wanting, the appropriate lessons have been drawn and, where necessary, amendments made.

However, important lessons have been learned, frequently as a result of mistakes made. Although we insist—and this is, in itself, an important lesson—that laws, institutions, and enforcement and adjudicative practices must respond to the particular conditions of the jurisdiction in which they are rooted, there are lessons of general application from which others may benefit. We will conclude then with an attempt to synthesize the most pertinent and generally applicable of these lessons. In particular, we will focus on two general lessons, both of which refer to aspects of our legislation and of our practice that have generated widespread comment, much of it critical. The first refers to the selection of strategic priorities amongst the functions traditionally undertaken by competition authorities. The second concerns the place of public interest considerations in competition analysis.

These are by no means the only lessons to be drawn from our experience. Hence, we could say much about the vexed question of the relationship between sector regulators and competition authorities; we have learned much about the value—and some of the shortcomings—of independence; our procedures are, it appears, unusually transparent and accessible and we believe that there are important lessons to be drawn from this, particularly around the positive advocacy role played by these features of our practice. However, we will here focus on the questions of selecting strategic priorities and the role of public interest.

Selecting Strategic Priorities: Mergers, Prohibited Practices, and Advocacy

Commentators on the practice of South African competition law have remarked—usually critically—on the extent to which merger regulation rather than enforcement appears to dominate the work of the authorities. It is by no means clear that this criticism is empirically valid. Firstly, restrictive practices invariably involve lengthy and complex investigations. It would be interesting to measure the average time that elapses between the point at which a complaint first comes to the notice of any competition authority, anywhere, and the point at which the court or tribunal make its final decisions—there can be little doubt that, even in the most mature jurisdictions, this will be measured in years rather than months. This is exacerbated in a new competition law regime and a new constitutional regime where the powers and procedures of the authority will inevitably be tested in a process that inevitably involves lengthy high court reviews.

Secondly, restrictive practices investigations have begun to bear fruit. Significant fines have been levied on the state-owned airline operator whose rebates to travel agents were found to contravene the Act's abuse of dominance provisions[27] as well as, in the form of a consent order agreed between the Commission and the firms and confirmed by the Tribunal, on firms in the auto assembly sectors. A large auto component supplier's practice of resale price maintenance was found to contravene Section 5 of the Act which proscribes vertical restrictive practices.[28] Pharmaceutical manufacturers have been subject to the attention of the Commission—in one case a far-reaching settlement between the Commission and several pharmaceutical companies has not only resulted in a significant administrative fine, but, more importantly, has seen the manufacturer of an important anti-retroviral drug license production of this vital product to a number of local generic manufacturers. In the agricultural sector, agreements between producers and packers and export agents have been voided as co-operatives have attempted to transform themselves into private companies whilst simultaneously attempting to maintain the privileges granted them by their previous status.[29]

However, our purpose here is to examine the strategic roots of the concern that too many resources have been occupied by merger review. It stems from a strongly held view that insists that newly established competition agencies should eschew or, at the very least, de-emphasize a role in merger regulation. Our experience leads us to diametrically opposed conclusions. At the heart of these arguments are important strategic questions that face most newly established competition authorities.

There are two variants of the argument that discourages emphasis on merger review in developing countries.

[27] *The Competition Commission* v. *South African Airways (Pty) Ltd.* (18/CR/Mar01).

[28] *Competition Commission* v. *Federal Mogul Aftermarket Southern Africa (pty) Ltd and Others* (08/CR/Feb01).

[29] *The Competition Commission and Patensie Sitrus Beherend Beperk* and *Jakobus Johannes Petrus Bezuidenhout Jan Daniel du Preez and Patensie Sitrus Beherend Beperk* (37/CR/Jun01).

The first, and the argument that is most commonly ventilated within the new competition jurisdictions themselves, observes that the fledgling competition authorities are generally located in small markets that do not allow competing firms to achieve scale economies. Mergers, the argument continues, are mechanisms for achieving these economies and, even if they give rise to anticompetitive structures, they should be tolerated, even welcomed, for the efficiencies and 'international competitiveness' to which they allegedly give rise.

However, this argument is easily countered:

- There are many developing and emerging country markets that do not conform to the small market stereotype.
- Much important merger activity takes place in markets in internationally non-tradable goods and services and that, in any event, truly seamless global markets remain the exception.
- This largely discredited argument for 'national champions' is driven by a heavy dose of self-interest which is why it is as frequently heard in the mature as in the new competition jurisdictions.
- To the limited extent that the argument is valid, it should be, and for the most part is, reflected in the merger evaluation criteria rather than in an attempt to downplay the necessity for merger review in general. Certainly, the South African competition statute requires that we evaluate efficiencies as well as the merger's impact on international competitiveness.

In summary, there is no valid general argument based on economies of scale for de-emphasizing merger review in developing countries. Nor is it an argument that is much supported by the competition authorities themselves. Particular circumstances can be accommodated by the inclusion of an efficiency defence or by obliging the competition authorities to consider the impact of a merger on international competitiveness. The South African statute requires both, with the latter, that is, the impact on international competitiveness, part of the public interest evaluation.

An argument that has found greater favour is one that asserts that, given scarce resources and relative inexperience, emerging competition authorities are better advised to focus on competition advocacy and anti-cartel enforcement than merger regulation. The proponents of this view insist that 'building a competition culture' and chasing down cartels is a more important activity than evaluating mergers, the vast majority of which clearly portend no dangers for competition at all.

While this latter argument appears, on the face of it, to have the interests of effective competition enforcement at heart, our experience establishes that the interests of new competition agencies are not well-served by limiting their role in merger evaluation. On the contrary, merger review builds reputation and learning and, not least, is of particularly substantive competition significance in liberalizing developing and emerging economies.

Let us then examine the advice that favours a phased approach—advocacy first; second, enforcement, particularly that directed at hard-core cartels; and, finally, merger review. Many agencies have accepted this advice—in fact this is precisely the sequencing that is formally provided for in the recently adopted Indian competition statute. This advice, however, well intentioned, is quite wrong.

It is suggested that advocacy is prioritized because it answers the requirement to build a 'competition culture' and because it is often portrayed as the 'soft' end of competition enforcement. In fact, advocacy imposes extravagant demands on new agencies. Effective advocacy requires, at the very least, a well-established reputation and technical competence. It also presupposes a well-developed and sophisticated media strategy.

Instead, fledgling competition authorities with no reputation to speak of are being advised to take on long established producer interests armed with nothing other than the eloquence of their inexperienced advocates. Not only are these producer interests well-versed in the technical complexities of their sectors, they are also usually politically well connected. In fact, many of the targets of the competition advocates are, or have been, state-owned enterprises. And advocacy frequently takes the form of contestation over the direction of government policy or the content of legislation or regulation.

This is not to say that the Competition Commission has failed to engage in advocacy. Indeed, in a number of instances—involving, for example, legislation concerning the regulation of telecommunications as well as a proposed Bill dealing with distribution arrangements in the liquor industry—the Commission has, on its own initiative, appeared before parliamentary committees and articulated well-reasoned arguments in opposition to positions favoured by the executive. At present, Section 21—detailing the functions of the Commission—provides that the Commission is responsible for developing public awareness of the Act[30] and for reviewing legislation and regulations that permit anticompetitive behaviour.[31] The reputation of the authorities has developed to the point where the strengthening of the Commission's advocacy powers—particularly the power to review legislation—should be contemplated. However, and we shall elaborate this view below, the most

[30] Section 21(1)(b).

[31] Section 21(1)(k).

effective advocacy has probably occurred as a result of the transparency of the Tribunal's procedures, which afford members of the media and of the public the opportunity to witness the competition authorities at work.

Similar considerations apply to enforcement. Most enforcement actions presuppose lengthy and complex investigation followed by equally complex and resource-consuming litigation. Because the competition legislation in the new competition jurisdictions is untested, most enforcement actions will inevitably be accompanied by challenges designed to test the powers and jurisdictional scope of the new authorities. The capacity in the early years of competition enforcement for defendants to engage in administrative and procedural diversion makes even the fruit that appears relatively low-hanging difficult to pluck. For all these reasons, by focusing on enforcement, the competition authorities risk engendering the perception that their investigations take inordinately long to conclude and that much of their time and resources are devoted to fighting battles in distant courts over arcane issues in administrative law.

Moreover, the costs of failure and error in the areas of advocacy and enforcement are severe. A loser's reputation is difficult to shake off, particularly when the process of losing exposes political weakness. Most disturbing is the very real prospect of a judiciary, inexperienced in anti-trust and inevitably sceptical, sanctioning genuinely anticompetitive conduct—and thereby establishing precedent that is difficult to reverse—simply because a complex case was mounted before the competition authority possessed the requisite investigative and prosecutorial experience.

This cautionary tale is certainly not meant to discourage advocacy and enforcement activity in the first years of a competition enforcer's life. It simply suggests that a strategy aimed at building a new competition authority should not rest on advocacy or enforcement because both draw heavily on experience and technical competence. And they require the reserves of political capital that enable even the most powerful anti-trust authorities to absorb the inevitable setbacks associated with these activities. New anti-trust authorities are possessed of neither experience, nor wide-ranging technical competence, nor bountiful reserves of political capital.

Merger regulation, by contrast, affords a solid basis for building both technical competence and a reputation for robust enforcement, precisely the attributes necessary for effective competition enforcement and advocacy.

Firstly, merger investigation and analysis does not, generally, involve complex law. Moreover, because merging firms have a positive interest in concluding the competition evaluation as expeditiously as possible, they have, in contrast with investigation of alleged anticompetitive practices, no incentive to use diversionary legal procedures in order to delay the investigation.

On the other hand, merger analysis does involve detailed economic analysis. Again, because the parties are effectively incentivized to cooperate with the process, information is made available relatively easily. For all these reasons, merger analysis is an effective basis for gaining knowledge of the fundamentals of competition economics and experience in applying this learning. In this vein, I believe strongly that pre-merger notification is an essential element of a new competition regime. The alternative would effectively compel new authorities to unwind already consummated mergers thus inevitably introducing legal and political complexity into an activity that is, for the most part, mercifully devoid of these obstacles.

Secondly, it is widely accepted that mergers frequently *destroy* value for the shareholders of the acquiring firm. While we know of no research that examines the impact of mergers on dynamic efficiency—the impact on firm-level costs of production, innovation, etc.—there is, on the face it, little reason for imagining why mergers should perform any better on this measure. While these considerations do not, for the most part, feature in merger analysis, they do suggest that the commercial and economic consequences of erroneously prohibiting a merger are slight at most.

On the other hand, the costs of allowing an anticompetitive merger may be considerable. The introduction of the new competition laws tends to coincide, in many countries, with a period of general liberalization. Certainly, the South African experience suggests—for obvious reasons—that this, in turn, coincides with a shake-up of corporate ownership structures as the diversified conglomerates which characterize many relatively small, inwardly focused economies attempt to focus their activities on their core areas of competence. Mergers are the principal means for affecting this corporate restructuring and this period is, accordingly, a very important moment in the development of the competitive structure of many key markets. It is thus important that an effective merger regime be in place from the commencement of a new competition regime. The Tribunal has, in the six years of its existence, only prohibited seven mergers—although conditions have been imposed on many others—but these prohibitions have come in, for example, the petroleum refining and marketing sectors, in the provision of managed health care, in sugar, and in retail furniture, all responsible for the production and distribution of basic goods and services.

Thirdly, merger review, conducted efficiently and professionally, will have the sort of positive impact on the competition authorities' reputation that is precisely a pre-condition for effective enforcement and, particularly, effective advocacy. Our merger review regime is highly transparent. Although adequate measures are in place to protect confidential information, large mergers are adjudicated by the Tribunal in open session. The Act and the Tribunal have adopted a liberal approach towards allowing interventions by customers, suppliers, and competitors. The media have responded enthusiastically to this opportunity to learn something of the thinking and strategies of what has, hitherto, been a particularly secretive corporate sector. Ordinary people have witnessed powerful corporations called to account for their actions before a public authority. And it has allowed the Commission and the Tribunal to showcase their skills and abilities in the best of circumstances, that is, in circumstances where information is relatively easily accessible and where the prospect for legal challenge is limited.

This is not to advocate for a capricious, highly interventionist merger review regime. The new competition regimes are well advised to measure the length of time that their merger reviews take and their ratio of approvals to refusal or to conditional approvals against their more experienced counterparts. There may be reasons for a degree of divergence in these measures—for example, the South African experience suggests that, in the early days of merger review, while the complex investigations take no longer than similar investigations in the developed country regimes, the approval times for the 'no-brainers' may not compare as favourably. However, a little experience and growing confidence soon leads to the development of effective filtering mechanisms that cure this problem—these may be based on formal 'quick look' procedures which the Commission has recently introduced or they may simply develop in consequence of the growing experience of the Commission's merger investigators. It is possible that precisely because of the relatively small size of some of their markets, the new regimes should expect a slightly higher rate of prohibition than in their developed country counterparts. In general, though, as long as these measures are in the same 'ballpark', there is no reason for fearing that relative inexperience has spawned an unduly onerous merger review regime.

In short, an effective merger regime is relatively easy to implement, it is a powerful learning platform, the costs of error—at least in erroneously prohibiting a merger—are small, and will make a substantively important, pro-competitive contribution to the structure of many important markets. For all these reasons, merger regulation offers competition authorities an opportunity for establishing a reputation for competence, for engaging robustly at the highest levels of the corporate economy and, most importantly, for making an immediate impact on fulfilling their core mandate, the promotion of competitive markets. This has certainly been the experience of the South African competition authorities and one that we readily commend to other new authorities.

Public Interest

As we have already emphasized, a national competition statute—by any measure, a critical piece of economic legislation—will reflect the particular concerns and norms of the society from which it emanates. These—the 'public interest' concerns—are provided for in the preamble and purposes of the Act.

The preamble to the South African Competition Act clearly specifies the society's overriding concern that the economy be made more accessible to all South Africans, the vast majority of whom had been effectively excluded by the operation of apartheid. These and other social and industrial policy concerns are further elaborated in Section 2 which outlines the purposes of the Act. Among the specified purposes of the Act are 'to promote employment and advance the social and economic welfare of all South Africans';[32] 'to expand opportunities for South African participation in world markets ...'[33]; 'to ensure that small- and medium-sized enterprises have an equitable opportunity to participate in the economy'[34]; and, 'to promote a greater spread of ownership, in particular to increase the ownership stakes of historically disadvantaged persons'.[35] Note that Sections 2(a) and (b) specify the more orthodox objectives of competition law, namely, 'to promote the efficiency, adaptability and development of the economy' and 'to provide consumers with competitive prices and product choices'. However, the emphasis in the objectives on small business and black economic empowerment in particular highlights a powerful popular conception of competition law as an instrument for promoting the market access of hither to disadvantaged and excluded communities. Many of the other 'public interest' criteria reflect industrial policy's traditional preoccupation with 'competitiveness' and export performance.

These concerns are operationalized in the Act's treatment of mergers and exemptions. Section 10 of the Act provides that practices and agreements between firms that would otherwise fall foul of the Act may be exempted from prosecution if the competition authorities can be persuaded that the practice promotes exports, small business, black economic empowerment, or prevents the decline of an industry.

Section 12A of the Act requires the authorities to undertake an analysis of the impact of the merger in question with a view to establishing whether or not it gives rise to the likelihood of a substantial lessening of competition.[36]

[32] Section 2(c).

[33] Section 2(d).

[34] Section 2(e).

[35] Section 2(f).

[36] Section 12A (1).

If this likelihood is established, then the competition authorities must determine whether or not there are countervailing efficiency gains[37] *and* also 'whether the merger can or cannot be justified on substantial public interest grounds by assessing the factors set out in subsection (3)'.[38] If the competition analysis establishes that there is no likelihood of a substantial lessening of competition, the authorities must still proceed to determine whether or not the merger can be justified on public interest grounds.[39] In other words, a merger that fails the competition test may nevertheless be approved if a positive impact on the public interest outweighs the substantial lessening of competition; and a merger which passes the competition test may nevertheless be prohibited if it impacts negatively on the public interest.

The specified public interest grounds are the effect that the merger will have on a particular industrial sector or region,[40] on employment,[41] on the ability of small businesses or firms controlled by historically disadvantaged persons to become competitive,[42] and on international competitiveness.[43]

In practice, the public interest grounds most often invoked are employment and black economic empowerment, that is, the impact on the spread of ownership and on the competitiveness of firms controlled by historically disadvantaged persons. The form that this characteristically takes is a plea to the effect that a particular merger, though neutral or even positive from a competition perspective should be prohibited because of its negative impact on employment. Or it is argued that a merger, albeit likely to substantially lessen competition, should nevertheless be permitted because the merging parties have agreed, as part of the merger deal, to sell a significant shareholding to historically disadvantaged persons.

The inclusion of these public interest considerations reflects the concerns of the society and they also reflect the outcome of a legislative process that ensured that the views of a wide range of interest groups were taken into account. We readily concede that public interest considerations weigh more heavily in developing countries than they do in developed countries. The reasons for this are instructive: first, it is widely accepted that there is a greater role for industrial policy, for targeting support at strategically selected sectors

[37] Section 12A (1)(a)(i).

[38] Section 12A (1)(a)(ii).

[39] Section 12A (1)(b).

[40] Section 12A (3)(a).

[41] Section 12A (3)(b).

[42] Section 12A (3)(c).

[43] Section 12A (3)(d).

or interest groups, in developing than in developed countries; secondly, developing country competition authorities are still engaged in a very basic struggle to achieve credibility and legitimacy in their countries. While credibility will certainly not be achieved by bending to the whim of every interest group, nor will it be secured by a competition authority that refuses to take direct account of major national economic problems and aspirations. Hence, while, in a country like South Africa, the competition authorities may well understand the pitfalls in balancing competition and public interest, it is equally recognized that a competition statute that simply ignored the impact of its decisions on employment or on securing a greater spread of black ownership, would consign itself and the authorities that it creates to the scrap heap.

Have these public interest insertions into the South African statute turned the competition authorities into subordinate instruments of industrial and social policy? Do they inhibit the ability of the Competition Act to defend the market against anticompetitive practices and transactions? Experience would suggest not and that for a number of reasons.

Firstly, our act is structured to ensure that any decision regarding a merger or an exemption is taken after consideration of the impact of the transaction or the practice on competition. The uncertainty that a public interest evaluation introduces is significantly ameliorated by the specific content that the Act gives to public interest—it is not, as it often is, an infinitely elastic concept but is specifically limited by the Act's definition. Moreover, the primacy of the competition evaluation is secured by the structure of the Act which provides that the competition evaluation is completed as the prior step in the decision-making process and, hence, that the public interest test is conducted through the filter of a completed competition finding. This structure accordingly underpins a developing jurisprudence that tends to have the principal decision—to prohibit or allow a merger—taken on competition grounds with the public interest considerations occasionally accounting for the imposition of conditions carefully crafted to ameliorate the negative public interest impact. Also, the Competition Tribunal has held quite explicitly that the protection that the Competition Act gives to the specified categories of public interest is ancillary to the protection offered by other legislation specifically directed at protecting those elements of public interest. Hence, employees threatened by a merger are well advised to show that they have sought the protection of the Labour Relations Act before invoking the Competition Act in their defence. By the same token, employers who have ignored these obligations are likely to be reminded of them when appearing before the Competition Tribunal. It is a matter of record that in merger evaluations a pro-competitive merger has never been prohibited on public interest grounds alone; and an anticompetitive merger has never been approved on public interest grounds alone.

Secondly, in each instance it is the competition authority that takes the decision, that balances competition, on the one hand, and social and industrial policy, on the other. The difficulty entailed in making the balance is not to be denied. And yet it was, in the drafting of the Act, relatively easily decided that this balance would have to be made—that is, that public interest considerations would have to be incorporated into the Act. The very credibility of the Act and the competition system required that it be sensitive to major societal concerns and objectives such as employment creation and black economic empowerment. Indeed, in the drafting of the Competition Act, the question of *who* was to make the balance, rather than whether or not a balance was required, was much the most difficult decision. As already elaborated, the legislature decided that this should be the responsibility of the competition authorities rather than handed over to a minister of state or some other cabinet committee.

Given competition law's intrinsic vulnerability to powerful producer lobbies—and included here are worker and provincial lobbies—our experience establishes that the balance between competition and industrial policy is better secured by making the competition authorities responsible for the balancing decision. This is due, in no small measure, to the unusual degree of independence that the competition authorities possess—independence ensures that the competition authorities are well set up to defend their terrain and to carry out their competition mandate.

South African competition law is not unique in its incorporation of public interest considerations. When, for example, an executive or congressional decision in the US can prevent the acquisition of a domestic firm on grounds no better than the foreign domicile of the acquiring firm, we have a major public interest intervention. That this public interest intervention was not made at the behest of the anti-trust authority acting in terms of the relevant competition statutes, is neither here nor there—what is clear is that a business decision driven by market considerations was effectively blocked, not because it threatened the future interplay of market forces, but because it was deemed inimical to the US public interest. The same may be said of the EU farming subsidies.[44] The South African competition law is rather unique

[44] It should be added that not only are these all-clear examples of public interest trumping competition considerations, but they represent a significantly greater distortion of *international* trade than any developing country interventions. Indeed, the South African public interest tests apply to firms regardless of their national origin

in the transparency of its treatment of public interest, in the candour with which it acknowledges that no major piece of social and economic legislation can muster public support and credibility if it does not take heed of popular concerns and objectives.

In summary then, we should take a pragmatic view of the introduction of public interest factors into a competition analysis. It is not evidence of a fatally compromised competition regime. In one way or another it is a feature of most regimes and, in those regimes where it is a particularly strong feature, serious consideration of the public interest by the competition authorities is likely to underpin the credibility of fledgling authorities. Moreover, it is possible to structure the evaluation in such a way that competition considerations occupy pride of place in the ultimate decision, indeed, in such a way that the competition authorities are able to use the public interest investigation to educate key public stakeholders about competition, rather than have them massively constrain the application of competition law.

***

The democratic government that acquired power in 1994 was committed to the introduction of a revitalized competition law. This stemmed, in part, from the process of liberalization of domestic and international markets, but also from the desire to redress past discrimination reflected in ownership centralization and the weakness of small- and medium-sized enterprises. This commitment was honoured with the passing of the Competition Act 89 of 1998.The new statute drew on best practices from many of the world's leading and most experienced jurisdictions, but it is also careful to reflect the concerns and aspirations of the society in which it is rooted.

The Competition Act has been in operation for the past six years. The requirements of the Act have, in this period, become a firmly entrenched feature of the overall governance framework of the economy. This is particularly clear with respect to merger regulation although enforcement

---

and so are neutral with respect to international trade. Many of the public sector considerations that apply in the developed economies effectively discriminate in favour of domestic producers against producers and consumers in other countries and so represent significant distortions of international trade and investment. See, David Lewis (2005). *Harmonisation and Its Limits*, Barry E. Hawk (ed.), in *International Antitrust Law & Policy*.

of the proscription of anticompetitive conduct has also made considerable progress. Despite predictions to the contrary, the public interest provisions of the Act—notably the inclusion of these criteria in the conduct of merger analysis—have not compromised the ability of the authorities to uphold their core mandate, namely the maintenance and promotion of competition. On the contrary, they have enhanced the credibility of the Act and the gradual development of a supportive culture of competition.

16

Korean Competition Law*

Policies and Developments

Youngjin Jung[1]

Korean competition law, concurrent with Korea's economy, has experienced incredible growth and restructuring in recent years. A glaring example of the ascendancy of Korean competition law is a landmark decision rendered by the Korean Fair Trade Commission (KFTC) against the Microsoft Corporation. On 24 February 2006, the KFTC found the Microsoft Corporation guilty of abusing its market dominant position and levied a $30 million dollar fine upon the company and corrective measures more stringent than those made by the EU Commission.[2] With the increase in globalization, the KFTC has widened its jurisdictional scope to include overseas anticompetitive practices that cause harm to the welfare of Korean consumers.[3] Within competition

* Reproduced from 'Korean Competition Law: Policies and Developments', published in Dhall, V. (ed.). 2007. *Competition Law Today: Concepts, Issues, and the Law in Practice* (first ed.), Oxford University Press, New Delhi.

[1] A great deal has been derived from Youngjin Jung and Seung Wha Chang, 'Korea's Competition Law and Polices in Perspective', 26 *Nw. J. Int'l L. Bus.* 687 (2006).

[2] KFTC decision No. 2006–42 before the Seoul High Court.

[3] Article 2–2 of the Monopoly Regulations and Fair Trade Act (MRFTA).

law, especially regarding such traditional areas as cartel investigation, merger review, and the regulatory measures over abuse of market dominance, Korea has increased its enforcement activities.

Korean competition law has been influenced greatly by the country's distinct history, in which the systematic formation of Korean business conglomerates, the *chaebol*, made competition laws an incredibly challenging and important aspect of Korean law. Current Korean competition policies claim to curb such conglomerates and overhaul corporate governance. Additionally, Korea has dealt with a myriad of political and socioeconomic challenges, including the 1997–8 financial crisis that swept over Asia, ultimately compelling policymakers to realize the need for restructuring. Korea in particular realized the need to restructure its economy into one based upon market competition. As such, Korea has been working towards a market-based economy, departing from its previously government-led economy. In addition to reforming expensive and inefficient government structures, Korea has also taken measures to eradicate government intervention, entry barriers to markets, and other anticompetitive elements from its markets.

This article examines the influence of Korea's economic development over its competition law and policies. Included is a brief historical survey of Korea's competition laws and policies as well as an explanation of how the country's perpetually evolving economic shifts and policy changes eventually moulded Korean competition law. It then outlines the major components of the law and evaluates the Korean antitrust authority's enforcement of such laws, comparing Korea's competition law to US and European models, as well as an exploration of the way in which Korea's distinctive economy has sculpted Korean competition law. While overviewing major competition related laws and enforcement activities, traditional areas of competition law enforcement such as abuses of market dominance, cartel and business combination review are explained. Unique characteristics of Korean competition law—regulations on economic concentration are discussed and outreach of Korean competition law is explained before concluding with some suggestions.

Evolution of Competition Policy in Korea

The 1960s and 1970s—Early History of Competition Policy

In the early 1960s, after serious political turbulence ending in a military coup, Korea's new government launched its first five-year economic development plan. To promote the growth of selected labour-intensive, export-oriented industries, the government provided strong financial and tax incentives for companies engaged in export businesses, while enforcing tight control on imports. By the time the second five-year economic development plan came to an end in 1971, the economy was recording annual economic growth of approximately 10 per cent.

In the late 1960s, concerned about growing protectionism among major trading partners and the international competitiveness of Korea's labour-intensive light manufacturing industries, which were under threat from other emerging economies, the government enacted a series of legislations to shift the focus to heavy manufacturing industries. The changed government policy encouraged a handful of companies that had performed well under the first two five-year economic development plans to enter major heavy and chemical industry (HCI) selected by the government.

Korea recorded annual growth of 9.6 per cent throughout the 1970s, but this high rate of economic growth coincided with deepening macroeconomic imbalances and microeconomic inefficiencies. The first and second oil shocks took a heavy toll on the economy, which was reliant on foreign raw materials. Excessive investment and persistent government policy throughout the 1960s and 1970s of setting high entry and exit barriers for strategic industrial sectors solidified monopolistic and oligopolistic market structures and caused an inefficient allocation of resources. The selective economic strategy pursued in this era also propelled the formation of the chaebol—Korea's family-owned industrial conglomerates, including global giants like Samsung, Hyundai, LG, and SK—further accelerating the concentration of economic power. The share of the ten largest chaebol rose from 5.1 per cent of GDP at the beginning of the HCI drive to over 10 per cent by the end.

Against this backdrop, the government believed that to maintain economic growth in an expanding market, it needed to create a more competitive industrial environment. Its initial attempts to diffuse criticism of the country's monopolistic and oligopolistic markets were formulated during the course of rapid economic development in the 1960s. In 1963, the *Sambun* case stirred a public outcry, leading to a public consensus on the need to contain monopolistic and oligopolistic behaviour. This case involved several large producers of wheat flour, sugar, and cement for the domestic market who were able to charge three to four times the listed price for goods by sustaining chronic shortages of supply. Not only were they earning excessive profits, they were also practising widespread tax evasion.

In response to this public outcry, in 1964 the government announced a draft competition law consisting of 29 articles. The law proposed the formation of a competition-regulating body that would oversee prices and contract terms. The Economic and Planning Board, an influential bureaucratic agency overseeing economic development throughout the 1960s and 1970s, took charge of this new agency. However, because objections from businesses prevented the bill from entering the cabinet agenda, it could not reach the National Assembly. The government made a second attempt by submitting a new bill defining the competition-regulating body solely as an advisor. Yet, the National Assembly still chose not to consider the bill, despite the significant reduction in the powers of the proposed regulatory body. The government reintroduced the bill in August 1967, but failed once again to overcome intense lobbying from businesses.

One of the arguments made by businesses was that any sort of market competition regulations would ultimately be premature, considering that the goal at that time in Korea was to accumulate industrial capital. This argument worked against another competition law bill submitted by the government in 1971, which was ultimately rejected by the National Assembly. This bill was submitted as a consequence of a 1968 National Assembly investigation regarding misuse of foreign capital, consumer exploitation, and excessive profits. The National Assembly had alleged that Sinjin, a monopolistic automobile manufacturer that had obtained a commercial loan from a foreign entity, sold its *Korona* cars in the domestic market at approximately four times the overseas price. Regardless of the obvious need for regulation, the businesses continued to prevail against governmental efforts.

Finally, as Korea suffered widespread inflation in the 1970s, triggered by a worldwide oversupply of the dollar, the first oil shock, and rampant cartelization around the globe, the government enacted the Price Stabilization and Fair Trade Act in late 1975.While this act aimed to ensure fair trade and stabilize prices, in practice it focused more on the stabilization of prices and failed to accomplish the creation of fair markets.

In late 1979, Korea faced a progression of unprecedented political events, including the assassination of President Park Chung Hee. The military coup that followed initiated a new government run by ruling elites who aimed to create new goals for Korean society. The government enacted numerous social and economic reforms, one of which was the enactment of the Monopoly Regulation and Fair Trade Act (MRFTA) in 1980. This was a significant achievement considering the fierce lobbying it faced from businesses and the objections raised by other government agencies also charged with industrial policy. The passage of the MRFTA heralded a new phase in the regulation of monopolistic and oligopolistic behaviour and represented a major step on the path to a more balanced and equitable society. The MRFTA garnered overwhelming support from the media and consumer organizations, if not from businesses.

The Early 1980s to 1997

The enactment of the MRFTA, which had been intended to control traditional anticompetitive behaviours such as competition-restricting mergers and to regulate market-dominant behaviour, failed to diffuse the economic concentration of the chaebol. Instead, the market share in terms of turnover of the 30 largest chaebol in the mining and manufacturing sector increased from 34.1 per cent in 1977 to 40.8 per cent in 1985.[4] The cross-shareholdings and cross-debt guarantees of the chaebol continued to expand like the tentacles of an octopus.

By the early 1980s, the growth-first strategy of the previous two decades had greatly alleviated poverty for the mass population, the public was becoming interested in wealth distribution and equity issues, and negative public opinion of the chaebol began to rise considerably. Workers, intellectuals, and other organizations, including the ruling Democratic Justice Party—which was plagued by the political legitimacy crisis—began to hold the opinion that the chaebol had been exploiting the Korean people and had gained their wealth and prominence through unfair means, supported by the government. The chaebol's dominance of the markets and their predisposition for nepotistic hiring decisions ultimately led to public distrust over the entire economic system along with doubting the political system.

Plagued by questions about its legitimacy, the government instituted a new legal system seeking to regulate the chaebol. Chapter 3 of the MRFTA, created in 1986 and entitled 'Regulation of Economic Concentration', contained a series of provisions to regulate large-scale companies. However, in 1989 there were 43 chaebol with assets of more than KRW 400 billion—eleven more than in 1987. Over the same two-year period, the number of chaebol-affiliated companies increased from 509 to 673. To account for 28.1 per cent of the net asset value of the 43 chaebol, the total amount of mutual investment among affiliates surged from KRW 3.3 trillion to KRW 16.97 trillion. The share of total turnover of the 30 largest chaebol in the mining and manufacturing sector was 39.6 per cent in 1994, again revealing no sign of a slowdown in economic concentration.

Until the financial crisis of 1997–8, the government continued to tighten its regulations on the chaebol. In 1992, a provision tightening the restrictions on debt guarantees among chaebol affiliates aimed to prevent them from excessive debt financing that could undermine their financial structure. In

[4] Development of Foreign Affairs and Trade, 'Korea Rebuilds: From Crisis to Opportunity' (1999), available at www.dfat.gov.au/publications/Korea_Rebuilds/Korea.pdf.

1996, a new provision was added to the MRFTA to curb inside transactions among affiliated companies that were not based on arm's-length valuations. However, these attempts to stem the tide of economic concentration were not met with much success.

1997 to the Present: A Restructured Economy and Competition Policies

The 1997–8 financial crisis that hit Korea caused the IMF to pressure the government into amending the MRFTA to facilitate economic and corporate restructuring, thereby lifting regulation of the total amount of investment and easing restrictions on holding companies. This removed regulation was reinstated after the financial crisis and since 1999, the economy has recovered well, yet the chaebol continue to be an undeniable presence. The top 30 chaebol supply businesses within 20 or so major industries and have more than 600 affiliates. Their total assets comprise over 45 per cent of all corporate assets in Korea. While there remains a strong need for competitive markets for healthier economic growth and consumer protection, the government cannot blindly impose extreme restrictions on the chaebol, given that the country's economy depends on them. The government also needs to ensure that the Korean companies have the financial ability to compete with foreign entities that may not be subject to the same strict rules of competition law in their domicile countries.

Of late, the government appears to view economic concentration as being closely interwoven with issues of corporate governance, therefore arguably taking a more flexible stance under the MRFTA towards regulation of economic concentration. In other words, the government seems to be working under the notion that these regulations could be gradually eliminated if the corporate governance of the chaebol sufficiently improves. The government has undertaken 'the Three Years' Roadmap for Market Reform', under which it would lift most of the restrictions relating to economic concentration, once certain conditions were met, such as transparency in corporate governance. However, such idiosyncratic regulations on economic concentration are unlikely to be dismantled in the foreseeable future.

Overview of Korean Competition Law

Major Legislations

The MRFTA encompasses all the traditional aspects of competition policy that are the subject of competition law in other countries: anticompetitive mergers (Art. 7), cartels (Art. 19), monopolization (Art. 3–2), resale price maintenance (Art. 29), and exclusive dealing arrangement (Art. 23–5). As the central legislation designed exclusively to deal with competition law and policy, the Act also addresses aspects of economic concentration in the Korean economy by regulating undue subsidies (Art. 23–7), debt guarantees (Art. 10–2), and equity investment (Art. 9, 10) among chaebol affiliates.

Korean competition law in a broader sense is composed of various other legislative acts such as the Telecommunications Business Act (amended on 10 August 1991) and the Act on the Structural Improvement of the Financial Industry (amended on 13 January 1997), which regulate merger and acquisition (M&A) activity in the telecommunications and financial industries. Additionally, the Unfair Competition Prevention Act (1961) regulates competition in the area of intellectual property, especially trademarks.[5] The Consumer Protection Act (1979) provides for a Consumer Protection Agency to enforce its provisions.

Significantly, the KFTC devotes resources to administering several companion statutes governing specific areas concerning antitrust. First, the Fair Subcontract Transactions Act (established on 31 December 1984) aims to establish fair subcontracting practices. This act seeks to create a competitive environment for small and medium-sized subcontractors by prohibiting large companies from unjustifiably reducing payments to such subcontractors. Second, the Adhesion Contract Act (established on 31 December 1986) aims to eliminate biased contracts, written and circulated by businesses, which preclude the consumer's right to choose the terms of a transaction. It sets out higher standards for businesses when issuing formal contracts. Third, the Fair Labelling and Advertising Act (established on 5 February 1999) aims to ensure that consumers are given accurate information that enables them to make informed choices. Fourth, the Door-to-Door Sales Act (amended on 29 December 1995) aims to protect consumers and secure a smooth flow of goods and services in door-to-door sales and pyramid selling schemes, requiring businesses to take pre-emptive measures to prevent consumer exploitation. Fifth, the Installment Transactions Act (established on 31 December 1991) aims to protect consumers when signing instalment contracts. Sixth, the Fair Franchise Transactions Act (established on 13 May 2002) aims to establish a fair trade system for franchise businesses and ensure the mutually beneficial and balanced development of franchisers and franchisees. Finally, the Consumer Protection in Electronic Commerce Act (established on 30 March 2002) stipulates that protection measures are required against consumer errors and personal information.

[5] The Act has been revised several times. It was renamed the Unfair Competition Prevention and Trade Secret Protection Act in 1998.

Competition Policy in Practice

The Functions of the KFTC

The KFTC is the principal governmental agency in charge of enforcing the MRFTA. It operates at a ministerial level under the umbrella of the Prime Minister and functions as a quasi-judicial body. The KFTC consists of a committee made up of nine members (the decision-making body) and a secretariat (the working body). It has more than 400 employees and a budget of over 250 million Korean Won. The role of the courts in enforcing competition law in Korea is relatively limited because the system of private lawsuits does not allow for treble damages, class actions, and effective pre-trial discovery processes as in the United States. Administrative proceedings conducted by the KFTC therefore play a central role in the enforcement of the act.

About 80–90 per cent of the tasks performed by the KFTC are the traditional ones of cartel regulation, business combination reviews, regulation of abuse of market dominance, and monitoring of unfair trade practices.[6] In addition, as mentioned earlier, the KFTC pursues policies dealing with economic concentration. The regulations set out in Chapter 3 of the MRFTA differ from traditional competition law in that they apply without regard to the concept of a relevant market—the cardinal element of competition policy in most jurisdictions. The philosophy that financial capital must be kept separate from industrial capital in order to prevent the chaebol from dominating the national economy is also reflected in the provisions of the MRFTA.[7]

Apart from its unique authority to deal with general concentration of ownership, the KFTC is endowed with the capability to conduct competition advocacy among other government agencies.[8] As a competition advocate, it seeks to prevent laws and regulations that would restrict competition from being enacted and to have existing regulations that impede competition removed. It does this by consulting with other government agencies to identify anticompetitive regulations and suggesting possible remedies to the Regulatory Reform Committee in the Prime Minister's Office.[9] In 2000, the KFTC considered 481 cases of legislation brought to it for prior consultation.[10]

[6] So Mee Sung and Kwangshik Shin, *Twenty Years of Competition Policy* (2001), p. 6.

[7] K.U. Lee, 'Economic Development and Competition Law in Korea', 1 *Wash. U. Global Stud. L. Rev.* (2002) p. 67 at pp. 69–70.

[8] Ibid., at 72.

[9] Korea Fair Trade Commission, 2001 Fair Trade White Paper 496 (2001), (Hereafter, 'KFTC White Paper').

[10] Ibid.

The agency is also consulted on matters relating to the privatization of state-owned enterprises, where its job is to come up with measures to facilitate competition during the privatization process, so that public monopolies are not simply transformed into private monopolies.[11]

In light of the foregoing discussion, it is apparent that concerns may legitimately be raised about the conflict between the KFTC's extensive powers—over the chaebol in particular—and its traditional antitrust mandate, which would normally require it to pursue an efficiency maximization policy. Although there is a need to restrain the chaebol from abusing market-dominant positions in certain markets, it is difficult to justify a strict anti-chaebol policy that might decrease consumer welfare. This is more so in light of the present global economy, where the chaebol themselves face strong competition from foreign companies that are not bound by the same disciplines.

Enforcement of Competition Law

As mentioned, private lawsuits based on MRFTA provisions are rare because aggrieved individuals can only file a suit before the courts after the corrective measures imposed by the KFTC have been finalized. Individuals could conceivably lodge a tort claim under the Civil Code, but due to the difficulty of gathering evidence this would be a rare occurrence. The prosecutor's office also plays a very limited role in enforcing the MRFTA because, in most cases, it can prosecute offenders only if the KFTC has referred the matter to it. It is therefore safe to say that the KFTC plays the dominant role in enforcing the MRFTA. In this sense, Korea's competition regime is closer to the European than the American system: in Europe administrative agencies play a central role in enforcement whereas in the United States multiple actors are involved in the enforcement of antitrust law. Moreover, the courts have a much greater role to play in the United States than in Korea.

To enhance the role of individuals in the enforcement of antitrust law, a new legislative bill was introduced early this year to allow aggrieved individuals to file damages claims with the courts without waiting for the KFTC's corrective measure to be finalized. The government expects this and some other, yet to be announced, improvements to the system to spur the number of private lawsuits in Korea. While it is too soon to tell whether such legislative changes will bring a dramatic increase in private lawsuits in Korea, the record of private lawsuits as of now is not encouraging. On the other hand, an increasing

[11] KFTC, *History of the Development of a Market Orientation Economy*, (2001), pp. 187–90, (hereafter 'History').

number of enterprises have been challenging the corrective measures imposed on them by bringing administrative suits before the Seoul High Court, which exercises exclusive jurisdiction over administrative antitrust suits. About 40 such cases have been filed annually over the past several years.

A study of the KFTC's enforcement history reveals that it has tended to emphasize behavioural over structural regulation. In particular, it has expended a great deal of resources on regulating unfair trade practices to correct imbalances in markets where the par ties have an unequal position. This interest of the KFTC can be attributed in part to the strong legacy of the industrial policies of the 1980s.[12] During the period between 1981 and 2000, the KFTC issued a total of 5,521 corrective notices in connection with unfair trade practices, including cases of resale price maintenance.[13]

Most of these involved issues of vertical restraint arising from transactions between manufacturers, wholesale dealers, and retailers. Between 1981 and1992, the KFTC issued only 94 corrective notices in connection with violations of cartel regulations. However, from 1993 to 2000 it markedly stepped up its level of enforcement, imposing as many as 238 corrective notices in connection with collusive behaviour—a coveted record even compared with that of developed countries. In respect of meagrey controls, one of the premier structural instruments, the KFTC has only a meagre record of enforcement. During the 20 years from 1981 to 2000, it issued corrective measures in only 12 cases. Despite some positive signs in recent years, out of 600 or so corporate combination filings recorded each year in 2001, 2002, and 2003, the KFTC has taken corrective action only in a very small number of cases.[14] Arguably, the primary legal instrument to deal with Korea's entrenched monopolistic and oligopolistic market conditions is a set of MRFTA provisions on abuse of a market dominant position. However, cases involving the aforementioned have been scarce.

The KFTC has a unique set of tools to alleviate the evidentiary difficulties in enforcing the MRFTA. The three so-called 'statutory presumption' provisions apply in the context of identifying market-dominant enterprises, determining substantial restraint of competition resulting from mergers, and identifying collusive behaviour that restrains competition. Another of the extraordinary powers of the KFTC concerns the collection of evidence from

[12] Supra n. 7, at 3.

[13] Ibid., at 26.

[14] Yong Seok Ahn and Youngjin Jung, 'Merger Control in Korea', *Asia Pac. Antitrust Rev.* (2004), p. 62 at 64. Supra n. 96.

financial institutions.[15] To facilitate the investigation of internal transactions among chaebol affiliates with respect to funds, assets, and personnel, for a limited duration the KFTC has the power to ask their financial institutions to provide relevant financial information.[16]

Finally, it would be remiss not to stress the importance of administrative surcharges in ensuring compliance with the law. Surcharges are being imposed in an increasing number of cases of anticompetitive behaviour, and the ceiling on these surcharges is rising.[17] Moreover, the KFTC is able to impose administrative surcharges without resorting to the courts.[18] This unique enforcement tool is considered very effective, mostly due to the size of the surcharges; from April 2005 companies taking part in cartels may be subject to surcharges amounting to as much as 10 per cent of their total sales volume.[19] Although strong and effective as an enforcement tool, the surcharge system also faces criticism because of the KFTC's overly wide discretion in setting the amount of the surcharges.

All countries maintain articles of law that partially or entirely exempt certain sectors from the application of competition law. Common examples are utility industries such as telecommunications and electricity, which are often government-owned or regulated in the belief that they have natural monopolistic aspects. In Korea, the range of such exemptions is gradually being reduced as regulatory and technological developments in areas where corporations had previously enjoyed a monopoly position have increased the scope for competition.[20] Recently, the KFTC has attached special emphasis to combating monopolistic and oligopolistic structures in markets where public enterprises are dominant.[21]

Regulating Abuse of Market Dominance

Emboldened by the successful prosecution of the Microsoft Corporation, the KFTC has noticeably strengthened its enforcement activities against domestic and foreign companies alike that have engaged in abuse of market dominant position. The way market dominance is regulated in MRFTA is similar to that

15 MRFTA, Art. 50(5).
16 Ibid.
17 History, at 685–95.
18 Ibid.
19 KFTC White Paper, 55, at 65–7.
20 History, at 282–99.
21 Ibid.

of Article 82 of EC Treaty, which codifies abuses of market dominance. It is a general understanding that with respect to abuse of market dominance, Korea follows the European model rather than the American model since at least the statutory language set forth in Article 3–2 of MRFTA does not regulate an enterprise with a dominant market power only, unless the enterprise abuses its dominance.[22] As showcased in the latest Microsoft case, the KFTC places great emphasis in regulating abuse of market dominant position, especially in 'new economy' industries as opposed to smoke-stack industry.[23]

MRFTA prohibits a dominant enterprise from abusing its dominant position. The dominance provision under the MRFTA may apply equally to a market-dominant foreign enterprise where activities take place in a foreign country, to the extent that such activities affect the Korean market.

The MRFTA defines a market-dominant enterprise to be in a position, as a supplier or customer in a particular area of business, to determine, maintain, or change the prices, quantity, or quality of the commodities that are the subject of a deal, services, or other terms and conditions of a deal, individually or jointly with other entities. In particular, to determine whether an entity is dominant in the relevant market, factors such as its market share, the existence of any entry barriers, the extent to which the barriers have been entrenched, and the relative size of its competitors in the relevant market are to be considered as a whole.

Pursuant to the MRFTA, an entity whose market share in the relevant market meets either of the following criteria is presumed to be dominant: (a) the market share of the enterprise is 50 per cent or more; or (b) the total market share of no fewer than three enterprises is 75 per cent or more; provided that an entity whose market share in the relevant market constitutes less than 10 per cent is to be excluded from the application of the dominance control law.

The MRFTA defines the following five types of acts as being abusive of market-dominant position and more detailed types and criteria thereof are determined in the Presidential Decree and accompanying public announcements:

> Article 3–2(1) of the MRFTA defines abuse as follows: (i) an act unreasonably determining, maintaining, or changing the price of commodities or services;

[22] In practice, even US antitrust law does not condemn a monopoly *per se*. Despite the language of Section 2 of the Sherman Act, the judicial gloss on the section indicates that for there to be a violation of the said Section, a company must not only possess monopoly power, but should also commit a certain exclusionary act. See US v. *Grinnell Corp.*, 384 U.S. 563, 570–1 (1966).

[23] Press Release, Korea Fair Trade Commission, 'The Findings of the Microsoft Case' (7 December 2005), available at http://www.ftc.go.kr/eng/.

(ii) an act unreasonably controlling the sale of commodities or provision of services; (iii) an act unreasonably interfering with the business activities of other entities; (iv) an act unreasonably hampering the participation of new competitors; and (v) an act unfairly excluding competitive enterprises, or which might considerably harm the interests of consumers.

Where a market-dominant entity engages in an abusive act in violation of the MRFTA, the KFTC is empowered by the law to order the market-dominant entity to reduce its prices, to cease and desist the unlawful act, to publicly announce the receipt of a corrective order from the KFTC, and/or to take other measures necessary for correction. The most prominent case involving the market-dominance provision concerns Microsoft's abuse of its market-dominant position in the PC and server operating system market through the unlawful tying of Windows Media Player, Windows Instant Messenger and Windows Media Service. On 24 February 2006, the KFTC sent its final decision to Microsoft that ordered Microsoft Corporation and Microsoft Korea, (a) to unbundle the tied Windows Media Player/instant messenger programme from their dominant Widows PC operation system and the tied Windows Media Server from their dominant Windows Server operation system, and (b) to offer a Windows PC operation system with 'Media Player Centre' and 'Messenger Centre' that will contain links to webpages which allow consumers to download competing media players and instant messengers, should Microsoft continue to sell a bundled version of Windows Media Player and Instant Messenger.

Another prominent case is POSCO's Refusal to Deal with Hyundai HYSCO (2001), a case in which POSCO refused to supply Hyundai-HYSCO, the largest Korean manufacturer of pipe and steel used in automobiles, with cold-rolled sheets. The KFTC decided to order POSCO not to interfere with the business activities of competitors by refusing to supply the cold-rolled sheets. The Seoul High Court confirmed the KFTC's decision and the case is pending before the Supreme Court.

Since the enactment of the MRFTA in 1980 and until 2005, the KFTC has handled about 30 cases in the area of regulating abusive behaviours of market-dominant entities, which is perhaps a small figure. The reason for this small figure may be found in the relatively strict standard required to find a market-dominant enterprise.

Accordingly, the KFTC has extensively invoked the provision that proscribes 'unfair trade practices' as an alternative to the provision of abuse of market dominant position. Under unfair trade practices provision, the KFTC does not need to prove an alleged violator to be a market-dominant enterprise. In fact, arguably, most of the acts that constitute abusive behaviours of market-dominant companies also fall under those that constitute unfair trade practices. Therefore, the above-referenced relatively small number of cases does not necessarily indicate that the KFTC has been oblivious to the abusive acts of market-dominant entities—particularly so, in light of the fact that it has aggressively enforced the provision on unfair trade practices, which would fall under the ambit of abusive acts of a market-dominant company.

Cartel Regulations

The MRFTA aims to prohibit and prevent enterprises from taking part in cartel agreements, which include the fixing of the price of goods or services, transaction volume, and transaction conditions; but it is difficult to prove that there is a cartel agreement because most cartel activity happens behind closed doors. The MRFTA has been amended to make clear that even if the actual performance of the concerted activity is disregarded, if there is a cartel agreement, it may violate the MRFTA. Article 19–5 of the MRFTA has a unique presumption clause that infers the existence of an agreement if parallel behaviours are ascertained in the market. This provision has instigated controversy, in particular concerning whether there is a need to investigate 'plus factors' in cases of 'conscious parallelism'.[24] In what could be seen as at least a technical victory for the KFTC in cartel enforcement, recently the Supreme Court confirmed that it is not necessary to show a 'plus factor' in interpreting the presumption provision on collusive behaviour.[25]

Generally, the KFTC has spent increasing resources on the regulation of international cartels. For the first time in 2002, the KFTC applied the MRFTA extra-territorially. The KFTC imposed a $9.2 million surcharge on an international cartel in graphite electrodes. Additionally, in 2003, the KFTC imposed a $3.3 million surcharge on the foreign companies involved in an international vitamin cartel.

As the KFTC strengthens its investigation of cartels, it has faced challenges in its relationship with other governmental authorities and legal systems. Like other jurisdictions, Korea has a number of regulations reflecting industrial policy. Even though many enterprises under KFTC's investigation have argued that they acted in accordance with the regulations and the guidelines set out by the relevant administrative agencies, the KFTC has adhered to its position that such excuses cannot justify cartel activity. For instance, in 2005,

[24] Andrew I. Gavil, et al., *Antitrust Law in Perspective*, (2002), pp. 255–6.

[25] Supreme Court, 15 March 2002, 98Doo6514, 6521, 28 May 2002, 2000Doo1386.

the KFTC widened its enforcement activities to include regulatory sectors such as telecommunications and financial industries, such as in the Korea Telecom (KT) investigation, which involved agreements reached on telephone service subscription rates between KT and Hanarotelecom. The two companies had reached an agreement to reduce the difference in the two companies' service subscription rates. Despite vigorous objections to the application by the KFTC of cartel regulations without regard to telecommunications sector regulations, the KFTC imposed administrative fines on both KT and Hanarotelecom.

The amended MRFTA, effective as of 1 April 2005, and the subsequent enforcement decree, have introduced major changes to the leniency programme as it applies to collusive behaviour. The enforcement decree under the amended act provides for an 'automatic' leniency policy for the first individual who reports the cartel to the KFTC. If the informant is the first and sole provider of evidence necessary to prove the existence of the cartel, the informant provides a full report and cooperates fully with the KFTC throughout its investigation; and if the informant has ended its involvement in illegal activity, this informant will receive neither an administrative fine nor any corrective measures which would usually be imposed by the KFTC.

The first informant receives complete amnesty from administrative penalty, and is 'practically' free from criminal penalty.

Unlike the US leniency programme a second individual who reports to the KFTC before its investigation will also receive a reduction in fines and more lenient corrective measures. This informant must be the second sole provider of evidence necessary to prove the existence of a cartel which has ceased its illegal cartel activity.

'Amnesty plus' is a new feature under the amended decree. Under this feature, if an entity that cooperates in a cartel investigation reveals a company's involvement in a second cartel in a different product/service market, this entity becomes eligible for additional reductions or exemptions in fines as applicable to the first investigation.

The number of leniency applications are on the rise in Korea. Also, to facilitate international leniency applications, Korea has introduced a 'paperless or oral' leniency application procedure taking account of the implications for US discovery procedure.

M&A Review

The MRFTA prohibits business combinations that substantially restrict competition in the relevant market, and the KFTC has the authority to issue a corrective order to an enterprise that violates or is likely to violate such regulation.

Recently, the KFTC made attempts to bolster its investigative reach and strength within business combinations. In September 2004, the KFTC prevented a major Korean piano maker, SAMICK Musical Instrument Co., Ltd. (SAMICK), from acquiring Young Chang Co., Ltd. (Young Chang), another piano making enterprise. The KFTC reasoned that SAMICK's acquisition of Young Chang would result in an abuse of market power and subsequent damage to consumers' interest, because the predicted market share of the combined companies would reach up to 92 per cent in the Korean domestic market and result in a de facto monopoly. Some criticized this decision as they argued that current piano makers have weak competition power as compared to foreign companies, and the combination of the two still would not outweigh the dominant powers of overseas imports. Therefore, they argued that such an acquisition cannot be deemed to restrict competition. The case went to Seoul High Court[26] which decided in favour of the KFTC and is currently pending before the Supreme Court.

The KFTC also determined that conglomerate integration would restrict competition within the acquisition of Jinro Co., Ltd, a soju (Korean wine) manufacturer, by Hite Co., Ltd., a beer manufacturer. The main questions concerning competition within this case were (a) whether soju and beer were substitutable products and (b) whether there would be an anticompetitive effect due to the fact that the two products utilized the same distribution channel (liquor wholesalers). The KFTC ultimately found that soju and beer were not in the same product market. However, the KFTC also found that the combination of the two dominant companies would potentially restrict competition because the conglomerate companies have the ability to abuse their dominant power in downstream sales to consumers as well as in upstream wholesale markets. It can be said that the KFTC accepted the controversial 'portfolio effects' of conglomerate business combinations. While the KFTC approved the combination, it also simultaneously adopted corrective measures to address any potential anticompetitive effects. The countermeasures set in place included a provision that for the next five years, Hite would be unable to raise the retail price of soju and beer beyond the consumer price inflation rate and that the two companies' sales divisions would have to be managed separately. For this case, the KFTC utilized its authority and power in order to conduct intensive market research to investigate the two issues mentioned above and in order to hand out ideal corrective measures.

[26] Seoul High Court 15 March 2006 (2005 NU 3174).

Generally, if the KFTC finds that the business combination would substantially restrain competition, then this transaction would be prohibited under the MRFTA, except if: (a) the enhancement of efficiency related to such Business Combination outweighs the anticompetitive effect, or (b) if such a business combination is necessary for the revitalization of a financially distressed company (Art. 7). Accordingly, Korean law stipulates an 'efficiency defence' and a 'failing company defence' which follow the merger guidelines of the United States.

According to the KFTC's horizontal merger section in its Business Combinations Examination Guidelines, a business combination may be regarded as having anticompetitive effects if (i) the aggregate market share of the combining companies in the relevant market is 50 per cent or greater or (ii) the aggregate market share of the top three companies including the combining companies in the relevant market is 70 per cent or greater.

Special Regulatory Regime on Concentration of Economic Power

Total Investment

The MRFTA restrains the concentration of economic power by limiting the total investment amounts. As of early 2006, the total value of all the assets of companies belonging to any business group has an upper limit of KRW 6 trillion. A company subject to the limitation on total investment amount cannot acquire or hold stocks within domestic companies in excess of 25 per cent of its net asset amount.[27] Debatably, this provision is intended for the chaebol and aims to set a ceiling on its total investment size in order to regulate market dominance. However, this limitation rule does not apply to a holding company,[28] a financial or insurance company, a company under insolvency, restructuring or similar proceedings, or a company belonging to any business group whose debt-to-equity ratio (the ratio of debt to total assets

[27] The net asset amount of a company, for the purposes of this limitation, is equal to the larger of the total capital or equity (or paid-in) capital *less* the amount of any equity investment in that company held by its affiliates (valued at par). The stock of other domestic companies held by a company subject to the limitation is valued at acquisition cost. Also, stock of overseas companies and treasury stock do not count toward the total investment amount.

[28] A holding company is a company that satisfies two conditions: It must have at least one hundred billion won in assets and the value of the shares it holds in its subsidiaries must account for at least 50 per cent of the value of its assets.

less debts) is less than 100 per cent as shown on the consolidated financial statement.

Regulation of Holding Companies

A holding company may hold shares in its subsidiaries beyond the limitation on the gross investment amount (as described above). However, it is subject to other restrictions. A holding company may have only financial or insurance companies as subsidiaries or only companies that are not financial or insurance companies. That is, a holding company may not have both kinds of subsidiaries. A holding company may not hold less than a certain minimum equity interest in a subsidiary and may not have a debt-to-equity ratio exceeding 100 per cent. The government's policy of separating financial and industrial capital therefore is upheld by the regulations on holding companies and the restrictions on voting rights by financial or insurance companies.

Regulation of Unfair Subsidization

The MRFTA introduced the regulation of unfair subsidization in December 1996 through an amendment to the MRFTA. This amendment prevents a company from providing economic interest to its affiliates by trading the fund, asset, and labour force on the considerably favourable terms compared to the normal market price. This regulation is very unique to the MRFTA. The regulation of unfair subsidization is based on the economic and legal theory that, if the fund, asset, or labour force are traded at a more favourable price than the normal market price among the companies belonging to the business group, other independent companies not belonging to the business group will have an unfavourable position compared to the affiliates in the business group. Therefore these independent companies that do not belong to the business group will be deprived of fair competition opportunities in the market, resulting in encouraging the concentration of economic power. An example of the strong regulation of unfair subsidization is that the surcharge on general unfair trade practices may be imposed to the extent of 2 per cent of the relevant turnover, while the surcharges on unfair subsidization may be imposed within 5 per cent of the relevant turnover. Thus, more surcharges may be imposed and the KFTC may request financial institutions to submit the financial transaction information in order to investigate unfair subsidization. This regulation was enforced from April 1997 and was actively applied to the inside transaction of chaebol during the economic crisis in Korea from the end of 1997 until around 1999. The KFTC decided on 35 unfair subsidization cases for 2 years from 1998 to 1999 and particularly imposed surcharges of approximately KRW232.2 billion (about USD232 million) on the top five chaebols. However, as the internal control system of companies has recently been strengthened, unfair subsidization has decreased and the number of cases regulated by the KFTC as unfair subsidization has also decreased considerably. For the years 2004 and 2005, the KFTC decided on 13 unfair subsidization cases and the contents and the scale of the relevant unfair subsidization activities were dramatically more reduced than before. Notwithstanding the above, unfair subsidization is reviewed as the important issue in the transaction among the affiliates belonging to the business group.

Other Regulations

Cross-Shareholding Regulation and Prohibition of Debt Guarantees

Generally, a financial or insurance company belonging to a business group with at least KRW2 trillion in assets may not exercise voting powers based on any shares of stock it holds in a domestic affiliate or another domestic company belonging to the same business group (Art. 11). Certain exceptions apply, under the reasoning that financial capital should be separated from industrial capital (Proviso of Art. 11).

With approval under the Insurance Business Act and other laws, a financial or insurance company may exercise voting rights based on the shares it holds for the purpose of carrying on financial or insurance business. (Items 1 and 2 in Proviso of Art. 11). If the agendum is the appointment or dismissal of a director or officer, an amendment of the articles of incorporation, or a merger or transfer of the whole or a substantial part of the business or if the amount of shares it holds in the affiliated company does not exceed 30 per cent of the company's total shares as of the end of 2005, which will be gradually reduced up to 15 per cent, then a financial or insurance company may exercise voting rights based on its shares in a listed or registered domestic affiliate (that is, listed with the Korea Stock Exchange or registered with Kosdaq) (Item 3 in Proviso of Art. 11).

While this limitation soundly restricts financial and insurance companies' voting rights on an affiliated company within the chaebol group, the exceptions allow for efficient operation of the financial and insurance companies of the group. Companies, however, took a different view of the restriction. Some of Samsung's financial affiliates filed a suit with Korea's Constitutional Court to invalidate this provision on the grounds that the limitation abridges their property rights and does not support equal or fair treatment within Korea's Constitution. There is a continuing struggle between the government which wishes to regulate the economic concentration and the chaebol which desires to loosen the limitations in order to have more commercial freedom.

Market Reform Roadmap

On 30 December 2003, the KFTC announced 'The Three Year Market Reform Roadmap', which included three measures introduced by the government: strengthening the transparency and accountability of business management, improving corporate ownership and the governance structure of large business conglomerates, and enhancing market competition. This reform aimed to improve the internal and external monitoring system of companies and business groups by enhancing transparency, fairness, and competition in market transactions.

As mentioned earlier, however, the regulations on economic concentration are unlikely to be abolished in the foreseeable future as the KFTC is reluctant to give up its role in regulating large business conglomerates while public sentiment in Korea remains very much against such large businesses.

Korean Competition Law Goes Global[29]

On 4 April 2002, the KFTC took the unprecedented step of applying Korean antitrust law extra-territorially to six foreign manufacturers of graphite electrodes. It imposed a total fine of $9.2 million on the manufacturers for price fixing.[30] On 29 April 2003, the KFTC concluded a sweeping investigation into an alleged international cartel by six foreign vitamin manufacturers, levying a total fine of $3.3 million.[31] On 24 March 2006, the Supreme Court finally affirmed the KFTC's extra-territorial application of Korea's cartel regulations.[32] Apart from these court proceedings, in 2005 an amendment was made to the MRFTA to empower the KFTC to exercise it extraterritorially.[33]

The six graphite electrode manufacturers investigated by the KFTC together account for about 80 per cent of worldwide production. On 21 May 1992, these manufacturers met in London to settle on some basic principles that would govern their product pricing and production amounts for years

[29] Youngjin Jung, 'Korean Competition Law: First Step towards Globalization', *Journal of Korean Law*, Vol. 4, no. 2 (2005), pp. 177–99.

[30] KFTC Decision, 4 April 2002: Case 02–77.

[31] KFTC Decision, 29 April 2003: Case 03–98.

[32] Supreme Court's decision, 2004 DU 11275.

[33] MRFTA, Article 2–2.

to come. They agreed to raise their prices whenever any of them raised their prices in a country where there was a domestic manufacturer of graphite electrodes—the 'respect for home market' principle. They also agreed to set the prices and quantities of products to be exported to a country where there was no domestic manufacturer—the 'respect for non-home market' principle.

Graphite electrodes are an essential component in steel production. In the absence of a domestic manufacturer to supply the steel industry, Korea must import all its graphite electrodes from abroad. With 90 per cent of its imports supplied by six manufacturers operating as a cartel, the KFTC recognized that Korea was suffering significant economic losses. During the period of the cartel the six manufacturers sold about $553 million worth of graphite electrodes to Korean steel producers at prices that increased by approximately 48.9 per cent between 1992 and 1997, from $2,255 to $3,356 per tonne.

The case of the vitamin cartel investigated by the KFTC follows a similar pattern. In September 1989, six vitamin manufacturers agreed to fix their market shares at the level prevailing in 1988, both in the world market and in regional markets such as Asia. To ensure that the market share allocated to each company remained the same regardless of changes in the overall market, they regularly exchanged information on their allocated and actual sales amounts. With 'price before volume' as the guiding principle for their collective behaviour, the manufacturers decided that when one of them raised its prices, the others would follow suit.

At the time, only Vitamin H was produced in Korea, and the raw materials for other vitamins, such as beta carotene and vitamins A, E, and D3, were imported from abroad. During the cartel period, Korea imported approximately $185 million worth of vitamin raw materials from the six manufacturers, with prices rising during the period and declining afterwards. For example, the price of Vitamin A (0.5 miu/gm cwd) for animals rose from $26.50 per kilogram in 1989 to $31.27 per kilogram in 1998 then declined to $19.06 per kilogram in 2001 after the expiry of the cartel. Both importers and consumers clearly sustained significant economic losses due to the actions of the cartel.

The KFTC's investigation into the vitamin cartel was greatly aided by the findings of competition authorities in other countries such as the United States, Japan, and Canada. Bilateral cooperation with these countries to break the vitamin cartel helped the KFTC gain valuable experience in regulating international cartels.

Also, as for business combination notification, on 1 July 2003, the KFTC adopted a notification requirement for foreign-to-foreign mergers. Under the revised rules, a report must be filed with the KFTC if (a) a foreign company with total assets or turnover of W100 billion or more acquires or is acquired by another company, and (b) sales in the domestic market of the acquiring or the acquired company exceed W3 billion (about $2.5 million).

One may conclude that Korean competition law is a prime example of the way that competition law is intrinsically interrelated with political, social, economic, and cultural surroundings. Up until the early 1960s, Korea faced devastating poverty and a stagnant economy. The Korean government therefore implemented an aggressive growth strategy throughout the 1960s and 1970s, which relied heavily on industrial policy while greatly neglecting competition policies, eventually leading to phenomenal economic growth, but at substantial political and social costs. In 1981, the Korean government addressed this problem with attempts to strengthen market competition through the establishment of competition law.

Even though less developed countries might be tempted to follow the Korean model by focusing their attentions and resources on industrial policy while denying competition policy, such a pursuit would be misguided. As can be seen by this study, disregarding competition policy in order to unrestrictedly pursue an aggressive industrial policy will eventually lead to considerable political and social costs. It would be wiser for developing countries to adopt a well-planned mix of industrial policy and competition policy at an early stage of economic development, perhaps in a similar process as that taken within Korea's development of the broadband Internet market.

Currently, the 'excessive' KFTC exercises its authority to achieve multiple objectives in addition to promoting economic efficiency and consumer welfare. Arguably, the KFTC holds 'excessive' regulatory power. A practice that is unique to Korea (and debatably Japan) is the regulation of economic concentration. This may exemplify typical ex ante government interventions, which do not support the dynamics of a global economy in which the chaebol are confronted by unfettered international competition in world markets. It is possible that the KFTC's pursuit of broader social goals could also lead to an inefficient allocation of resources, which would undermine the very purpose of competition policy. It would be advisable for the KFTC's role and mission to be defined more clearly in order to minimize the negative effects of pursuing policies as defined by Korea's economic circumstances or other considerations.

Because of globalization, countries cannot pursue competition policy without considering and being influenced by international trade and investment. As globalization continues to spread, the economic interdependence among nations has become more prevalent while economic sovereignty continues to lose its standing. At present, one country's competition policy most often influences the welfare of consumers in other countries. Tremendous efforts have been exerted at such forums as the ICN, WTO, and OECD in order to try to resolve conflicts that result from incongruous competition policies among trading partners. As a result of increased globalization, governments need to fully analyse and prepare for the way in which their competition policies interact with international trade and investment policies.

Considering its previous successes, Korea's competition law and policy will surely continue to evolve and develop in order to face the new challenges within Korea's economic infrastructural development.

17

The Competition Regime in the United Kingdom

Christopher Bellamy

From 1 April 2014, as part of a series of wide-ranging reforms to the competition regime in the UK, the UK's two main competition bodies, the Office of Fair Trading (OFT) and the Competition Commission (CC), were replaced by the new, single Competition and Markets Authority (CMA). The CMA took over the competition (and some consumer) law functions of the OFT and all of the functions of the CC. The competition law regime in the UK is set out, for the most part, in two statutes: the Competition Act, 1998 (the 1998 Act) and the Enterprise Act, 2002 (the 2002 Act), both as amended by the Enterprise and Regulatory Reform Act, 2013 (the 2013 Act).

The 1998 Act sets out two key prohibitions against anticompetitive agreements or concerted practices (the Chapter I prohibition) and abuses of dominance (the Chapter II prohibition), which are closely modelled on the equivalent provisions contained in Articles 101 and 102 of the Treaty on the Functioning of the European Union (TFEU). The 1998 Act also gives the CMA the power to impose penalties of up to 10 per cent of turnover, and powers of investigation including the power to conduct unannounced inspections called dawn raids.

The 2002 Act includes the rules on merger control and market investigations. The merger control framework in the UK is voluntary, in the sense that it does not require the merging parties to seek clearance prior to completing a merger. A market investigation is an examination into whether there is an adverse effect on competition in any market(s) for goods or services in the UK and, if so, what remedies may be appropriate. Recent examples include inquiries into private healthcare, energy, and retail banking.

In addition, the 2002 Act contains a criminal offence, which may be committed by individuals responsible for agreeing to enter into serious cartel arrangements. The 2002 Act also includes a power to disqualify individuals from acting as directors of a company which has been found guilty of infringing competition law.[1]

To complicate matters, companies operating in the UK are subject to both UK-specific competition law and European competition law, as set out in the TFEU. Under Regulation 1/2003, which decentralized the enforcement of EU competition law, the CMA is responsible for the application of Articles 101 and 102 of the TFEU in the UK. If the CMA applies Chapter I in relation to an agreement that may appreciably affect trade between EU Member States, it is obliged to apply the EU competition rules at the same time, and such an agreement may only be prohibited under Chapter I if it is also prohibited under the TFEU.

Development of UK Competition Law

Prior to 1998, competition law had developed in a piecemeal fashion in the UK. Historically, the common law did, in some narrow circumstances, prevent parties from enforcing anticompetitive agreements. For example, the doctrine of restraint of trade allowed a party to an agreement to avoid certain types of anticompetitive restrictions.[2] The doctrine was conventionally of particular relevance to certain types of contracts, for example, employer/employee contracts and contracts for the sale/purchase of a business.

There was also a network of technical statutory provisions which applied to certain agreements and in certain circumstances, including the Restrictive Trade Practices Acts 1976 and 1977 and the Resale Prices Act 1976. The

[1] For example, a breach of the Chapter I or Chapter II prohibition under the 1998 Act, or a breach of Article 101 or 102 of the TFEU: see Section 9A of the Company Directors Disqualification Act 1986 which was inserted into the 2002 Act.

[2] The doctrine of restraint of trade still applies in the UK but its sphere of application is narrowed in contexts where EU competition law could also be applied to the contract in question. In the case of *Days Medical Aids* v. *Pihsiang* [2004] EWCH 44 (Comm), Langley J held that where an agreement would not be prohibited by EU competition law, it was not possible to apply the doctrine of restraint of trade in order to strike down part of the agreement.

resulting system was complex, formalistic, and difficult to apply, and failed to catch some agreements which were seriously anticompetitive while applying to other agreements which were insignificant. Certain agreements could be justified on public interest grounds, but few cases were brought. Furthermore, the system lacked an effective means of enforcement.

In addition, monopolies were controlled under the Fair Trading Act 1973 using a public interest test applied by the Monopolies and Mergers Commission (MMC), the predecessor of the CC. Where there were found to be practices operating against the public interest, it was for the Secretary of State to decide whether or not enforcement action should be taken. In relation to the control of mergers under the Fair Trading Act 1973, there were fewer concerns, but it was up to the Secretary of State to decide whether a merger should be investigated by the MMC on 'public interest' (including, but not limited to, competition) grounds and to decide whether to uphold the MMC's decision.

The fundamental changes introduced by the 1998 and 2002 Acts were designed, in particular, to rationalize the control of anticompetitive agreements and abuses of dominance, to harmonize the UK regime with EU law, to strengthen the powers of competition authorities, to distance competition law enforcement from the possibility of political influence, and to replace tests based on public interest with clearer, more economic, concepts of competition.

However, there were concerns that there was unnecessary duplication between the OFT and the CC, and that competition cases were taking too long to be completed. The UK competition regime was reformed by the 2013 Act, which came into force on 1 April 2014. The stated aims of these reforms, billed as 'evolution rather than revolution', were to strengthen and improve the regime, enable the new CMA to take forward high impact cases, and improve speed and predictability for businesses, while building on the strengths of the previous regime.

Framework for Administrative Enforcement

The CMA is responsible for enforcing the law against anticompetitive agreements and concerted practices, and against abuses of dominance. This includes a responsibility, shared with the Serious Fraud Office, for prosecuting individuals considered to be guilty of the criminal cartel offence.[3] The CMA also carries out reviews of mergers and identifies those which merit

[3] Section 190 of the 2002 Act.

a more in-depth review.[4] In addition, the CMA has more general powers to review markets[5] and may trigger a market investigation into particular markets.[6] As well as its competition functions, the CMA also has a number of consumer protection functions.

The CMA is a body corporate. Its primary duty is to seek to promote competition both within and outside the UK for the benefit of consumers. The CMA's governance structure, designed to reflect the two phases of decision-making in merger and markets cases, comprises the CMA Chair, the CMA Board (responsible for strategy and performance and for decisions in phase I merger and markets cases, as well as antitrust cases), an independent CMA panel (responsible for phase II decisions), and staff (including the Chief Executive).

The CMA is obliged to prepare and publish general advice and information about the application and enforcement of UK and EU competition law and the procedures that it will follow.[7] Numerous and detailed guidance notes, which are available on the CMA website,[8] provide a very useful resource.

The CMA has wide-ranging powers of investigation and enforcement. Under the 2002 Act, the CMA has powers to require the production of evidence and documents and attendance at interviews and meetings, and to impose financial penalties for failure to comply. Under the 1998 Act, the CMA has powers to investigate suspected anticompetitive agreements or abuses of dominance, whether under UK or EU law.[9] These include powers to launch dawn raids, require companies to produce information and documents,[10] compel interviews,[11] and impose financial and individual criminal penalties for failure to cooperate.[12] The CMA operates a leniency scheme to encourage companies who uncover evidence of a cartel to disclose the cartel to the CMA. In return for this disclosure, companies and individuals who have participated in cartel activity can benefit from immunity from financial penalties and criminal prosecution. Where a company is the first to

[4] See Sections 22 and 33 of the 2002 Act.

[5] For example, under Sections 5 and 6 of the 2002 Act.

[6] Section 131 of the 2002 Act.

[7] Section 52 of the 1998 Act.

[8] See https://www.gov.uk/government/organisations/competition-and-markets-authority.

[9] These powers are set out in Sections 25 et seq. of the 1998 Act.

[10] Section 26 of the 1998 Act.

[11] Section 26A of the 1998 Act.

[12] Section 42 of the 1998 Act.

disclose a cartel which was previously unknown to the CMA, it will (according to CMA guidelines) usually be offered 100 per cent immunity as long as it complies with certain conditions. Given that fines are potentially very significant, up to 10 per cent of the worldwide turnover of a company, it is unsurprising that many of the cartel decisions taken under the 1998 Act have involved leniency applicants.

In addition, specialist regulators responsible for regulated sectors, such as telecommunications, water, and energy, are also empowered to enforce the 1998 Act in their particular sector.[13] They hold these powers concurrently with the CMA although, in practice, it is unlikely that the CMA would proceed to investigate a matter which fell within the potential jurisdiction of one of the regulators. In some instances, sector-specific regulatory powers permit the regulator to refer issues such as pricing to the CMA. To encourage the sectoral regulators to exercise their concurrent powers, the 2013 Act requires sectoral regulators to consider using their 1998 Act powers before using their sector-specific powers. There is also a duty on the CMA and sectoral regulators to cooperate, and they have formed a UK Competition Network as a forum to facilitate this.

The UK also has the benefit of a specialist judicial tribunal with jurisdiction over competition law matters. The Competition Appeal Tribunal (the Tribunal) was established under the 2002 Act as a fully independent judicial body having the power to review administrative decisions taken in competition cases.[14]

The Tribunal hears appeals from decisions of the CMA and the regulators relating to the application of the prohibitions set out in the 1998 Act or the TFEU.[15] Appeals may be brought, for example, against decisions that the prohibition has or has not been infringed and decisions as to the amount of

[13] The sector regulators include the Office of Communications (OFCOM), the Gas and Electricity Markets Authority (OFGEM), the Water Services Regulatory Authority (OFWAT), the Office of Rail and Road Regulation (ORR), the Civil Aviation Authority (CAA), Monitor (now part of NHS Improvement) and the Northern Ireland Authority for Utility Regulation (NIAUR), the Financial Conduct Authority (FCA), and the Payment Systems Regulator (PSR). The duties imposed on Monitor (in relation to healthcare services in England) differ from those imposed on other concurrent regulators, resulting in differences in the application of the concurrency regime in this area.

[14] Section 12 of the 2002 Act.

[15] The Tribunal also has the jurisdiction to hear appeals from decisions of the telecommunications regulator under the Communications Act 2003.

any penalty.[16] These appeals are full appeals on the merits of the case, and the Tribunal must either uphold or set aside all or part of the disputed decision—where it does this, the Tribunal may either refer the matter back to the CMA to take a new decision or, in an appropriate case, take a decision itself.[17]

The Tribunal also has jurisdiction to decide applications on a judicial review basis in respect of decisions taken by the CMA relating to mergers or market investigations under the 2002 Act.[18] Because these cases must be decided according to judicial review principles, the Tribunal is not empowered to take its own decision on the facts. If a flaw at the administrative stage is sufficiently serious, the matter must be remitted to the CMA.

Finally, breaches of the 1998 Act or of Article 101 or 102 of the TFEU can give rise to an action for civil damages or an injunction. These claims may be heard by either the High Court or the Tribunal. Previously, the Tribunal's jurisdiction was limited to claims for damages in 'follow on' actions where the CMA had already taken a decision that the relevant prohibition had been infringed. However, from 1 October 2015, when the Consumer Rights Act 2015 entered into force, the Tribunal has had the jurisdiction to hear claims for damages in 'standalone' actions, where an infringement decision has not yet been taken. The 2002 Act makes provision for the Lord Chancellor to adopt regulations for the transfer of cases to and from the Tribunal.[19] Two cases have been transferred from the Tribunal to another court to date.

The Tribunal is presided over by a president, who must be a senior legally qualified person with appropriate experience and knowledge. In addition, the Tribunal has a panel of Chairmen (who must also be senior lawyers) and a panel of ordinary members. Judges of the Chancery Division of the High Court are also members of the panel of Chairmen.

[16] Sections 46 and 47 of the 1998 Act. The one exception to the Tribunal's merits jurisdiction in appeals brought under the 1998 Act relates to decisions of the CMA to accept binding commitments pursuant to Section 31A of the 1998 Act in lieu of proceeding to a final decision in a matter; appeals against such decisions are to be determined by reference to judicial review principles.

[17] Under Schedule 8, Sections 3(2)(d) and 3(2)(e) of the 1998 Act, the Tribunal is empowered to give such directions or take such steps as the CMA could itself have given or taken and to make any other decision which the CMA itself could have made.

[18] The Tribunal can also hear appeals against penalties imposed for a failure to cooperate with an investigation by the CMA.

[19] Claims which may be made under Sections 47A and 47B of the 1998 Act may be transferred between the civil courts and the Tribunal under Rules 71 and 72 of the Competition Appeal Tribunal Rules 2015.

The Tribunal's rules of procedure are set out in the Competition Appeal Tribunal Rules 2015 which are available on the Tribunal's website.[20] Each case is heard by a panel of three judges: a Chairman (who may be the President or one of the other designated Chairmen) and two additional members.

The Secretary of State for Business, Innovation and Skills, the UK government minister responsible for the departments which enforce competition law, has an overall rule-making and approval function under the 1998 Act. Under the 2002 Act, the role of the Secretary of State was greatly reduced, and only in a very small minority of cases does he have any decision-making power. The 2013 Act gave the Secretary of State some new powers, including the power to request that the CMA investigate public interest issues alongside competition issues following a market investigation reference.

The Influence of European Competition Law

Much of the competition law currently applicable within the UK has been inspired by EU law. The substantive prohibitions set out in Chapter I and Chapter II of the 1998 Act very closely mirror the equivalent EU law prohibitions set out in Articles 101 and 102 of the TFEU.

Furthermore, a specific provision set out in Section 60 of the 1998 Act is intended to ensure that, as far as is possible, the 1998 Act is applied in a manner which is consistent with the equivalent European provisions. Thus the CMA, the specialist sector regulators and the Tribunal, so far as possible, must avoid taking decisions which are inconsistent with either the principles of EU law or EU jurisprudence. Decisions taken by the European Union Courts (the Court of Justice and the General Court) therefore have a very important influence on the interpretation of equivalent UK laws.

The UK authorities also have the power to directly enforce European competition law relating to cartels, anticompetitive agreements and abuse of dominance set out in Articles 101 and 102 of the TFEU. Article 5 of Regulation 1/2003 directly empowers national competition authorities to take certain decisions: (a) requiring that an infringement be brought to an end; (b) ordering interim measures; (c) accepting commitments; and (d) imposing fines, periodic penalty payments, or any other penalty provided for in their national law.

Indeed, the UK authorities and courts, along with other national authorities and courts, are obliged to apply European law in addition to or even in place of national law in certain circumstances. For instance, the CMA is

[20] See http://www.catribunal.org.uk/240/Rules-and-Guidance.html.

required to apply and enforce Article 101 whenever it applies national competition law (that is, the Chapter I prohibition set out in the 1998 Act) to anticompetitive agreements which may affect trade between Member States and therefore potentially fall within the scope of EU law as well as UK law. In this situation, Article 3(2) of Regulation 1/2003 provides that national competition law cannot prohibit agreements which may affect trade between Member States but which do not restrict competition within the meaning of Article 101(1) or which fulfil the conditions for exemption set out in Article 101(3) of the TFEU (or benefit from a block exemption)—that is, if an agreement would have escaped sanction under EU law, it cannot be sanctioned by a stricter national law. However, there is nothing under Regulation 1/2003 to prevent the UK authorities and courts taking a stricter approach to unilateral conduct under the Chapter II prohibition than that taken under Article 102 of the TFEU.

Following the UK's EU membership referendum in June 2016, there has been much debate over how the 'Brexit' process will evolve. The implications for competition law could be far-reaching, including, for example, in relation to Section 60 of the 1998 Act and the potential loss of the EU one-stop-shop for merger control. A Select Committee of the UK Parliament's House of Lords has launched an inquiry into Brexit and competition policy. Information about the scope of the inquiry and evidence from various stakeholders is available on the Parliament website.

A Brief Outline of the Substantive Law

Cartels and Anticompetitive Agreements

As mentioned earlier, rules prohibiting anticompetitive agreements and concerted practices are set out in Chapter I of the 1998 Act and the equivalent EU rules are set out in Article 101 of the TFEU. Article 101 applies to any agreement which may affect trade between Member States, and Chapter I applies to any agreement which may affect trade in the UK. A particular agreement may well affect trade at both levels.

Section 2 of the 1998 Act prohibits 'agreements between undertakings, decisions by associations of undertakings, or concerted practices' which 'have as their object or effect the prevention, restriction or distortion of competition within the UK'. The law thus prohibits not only formal agreements between companies (undertakings), which would include, for example, hard-core cartels where companies agree to fix prices or share markets, but also anticompetitive terms in ordinary commercial contracts and more informal agreements such as 'gentleman's agreements'.

An agreement which contravenes Section 2 is automatically void unless it falls within an exemption set out in Section 9 of the 1998 Act, which applies to certain agreements which have countervailing benefits for consumers, for example, improving production or distribution or promoting technical or economic progress. The equivalent European exemption is set out in Article 101(3) of the TFEU. An important change brought about by Regulation 1/2003 was to make the provisions of Article 101(3) of the TFEU directly enforceable by the national competition authorities and courts, rather than subject only to administrative action by the European Commission.

There are a wide variety of agreements which might potentially prevent, restrict, or distort competition. Section 2 of the 1998 Act lists the types of agreements which are 'in particular' prohibited (reflecting an equivalent list set out in Article 101(1) of the TFEU). Agreements listed include: price-fixing agreements; market-sharing agreements; agreements to limit or control production, markets, technical development, or investment; and agreements which apply dissimilar conditions to equivalent transactions with other trading parties, thereby placing them at a competitive disadvantage.

Given the potentially wide scope of the Article 101 of the TFEU prohibition (reflected in Chapter I of the 1998 Act), a key feature of EU law has been the existence of 'block exemptions' contained in European Regulations which set out the conditions under which particular classes of agreements will be exempted. For example, there are block exemptions which apply to vertical agreements, to technology transfer agreements, and to specialization agreements. Agreements which would fall within the scope of a block exemption regulation benefit from a parallel exemption from the application of the Chapter I prohibition in the UK.[21]

A company which has been found guilty of breaching Article 101 or Chapter I can face very significant penalties. The CMA has the power to impose fines of up to 10 per cent of the worldwide turnover of an undertaking.[22] When calculating fines, the CMA will consider aspects such as the seriousness of the infringement, the size of the undertaking involved, the duration of the infringement, the desirability of deterring both the undertaking on whom the penalty is to be imposed and others from breaching the prohibition, and the involvement of senior management in the infringement. In practice, higher levels of fines will be reserved for certain categories of infringements, known as 'hard-core' infringements, rather than, for example, agreements which narrowly fall outside the scope of a block exemption.

[21] Sections 10(1) and 10(2) of the 1998 Act.

[22] Section 36(8) of the 1998 Act.

The Criminal Cartel Offence

The cartel offence applies in relation to certain types of seriously anti-competitive agreements, including agreements relating to at least two competing companies fixing prices, sharing markets, limiting production or supply, or rigging bids.[23] The offence only applies to agreements in relation to undertakings operating at the same level of the supply chain[24] and to agreements which are implemented in whole or in part in the UK.[25] In all cases, a nexus to the UK is required (that is, the arrangements, operating as intended, would affect production or supply within the UK).[26] Prosecutors are required to show that an individual agreed with one or more other persons that two or more undertakings will engage in one of the seriously anticompetitive types of arrangements mentioned earlier. The cartel offence originally required the individual to have acted dishonestly. However, since 1 April 2014, dishonesty is no longer a necessary element of the offence.

The offence is subject to certain exclusions and defences. Parties to arrangements that would otherwise fall within the offence may bring the arrangements outside the scope of the offence by ensuring that customers are given relevant information about the arrangements (the 'notification exclusion'), that relevant information about the arrangements is published in a specified manner (the 'publication exclusion') or, in the case of bid-rigging arrangements, that the person requesting the bids is given relevant information (the 'bid-rigging notification exclusion').[27]

There are also three defences to the cartel offence. First, it will be a defence (where the arrangements would take effect in the UK) that, at the time of making the agreement, the defendant did not intend that the nature of the arrangements would be concealed from customers.[28] A second defence exists if an individual is able to show that, at the time of making the agreement, he or she did not intend that the agreement would be concealed from the CMA.[29] Finally, it will also be a defence for the defendant to show that, before making the agreement, he or she took reasonable steps to ensure that the nature of the arrangements would be disclosed to professional legal

[23] Section 188 of the 2002 Act.

[24] Section 189 of the 2002 Act.

[25] Section 190(3) of the 2002 Act.

[26] Sections 188(3) and 188(4) of the 2002 Act.

[27] Section 188A of the 2002 Act.

[28] Section 188B(1) of the 2002 Act.

[29] Section 188B(2) of the 2002 Act.

advisors for the purpose of obtaining advice before their making or their implementation.[30]

An individual found guilty of the cartel offence can be liable to imprisonment for a term of up to five years or to an unlimited fine, or both.[31] Proceedings can only be brought by or with the consent of the CMA or by the director of the Serious Fraud Office. Since the introduction of the criminal cartel offence, only five individuals have been convicted.

The first prosecutions under the cartel offence were announced by the OFT in December 2007. Three individuals pleaded guilty to dishonestly participating in a cartel to allocate markets and customers, fix prices, and rig bids for the supply of marine hoses and were sentenced to between two and a half and three and a half years in prison (although this was subsequently reduced on appeal).[32] However, the high-profile collapse of the first contested prosecution in the *BA/Virgin* case[33] in 2010 prompted a review of the OFT's decisions, policies, and procedures that had led up to the collapse of the trial.[34] In the year following the publication of this report, the OFT announced that it was closing a handful of other criminal cartel investigations that it had been pursuing, on the basis that there was insufficient evidence to prosecute. At the time of writing, the CMA has no open criminal cartel cases in the public domain. No cases have yet been brought under the revised criminal cartel offence, which came into force on 1 April 2014.

Abuse of Dominance

The abuse by a company of a dominant position in any market is prohibited by Chapter II of the 1998 Act and Article 102 of the TFEU. Abusive conduct is prohibited if it may affect trade within the UK[35] or between Member States of the EU, respectively. Article 102 of the TFEU and Section 18(2) of the 1998 Act set out examples of conduct that may, in particular, constitute an abuse. Such conduct includes, for example, directly or indirectly imposing unfair purchase or selling prices or other unfair trading conditions and limiting production, markets, or technical developments to the prejudice of consumers.

[30] Section 188B(3) of the 2002 Act.

[31] Section 190 of the 2002 Act.

[32] *R* v. *Whittle and Others* [2008] EWCA Crim 2560.

[33] *R* v. *George, Crawley, and Others* [2010] EWCA Crim. 1148.

[34] OFT, Project Condor Board Review (December 2010).

[35] Section 18(1) of the 1998 Act. The prohibition applies to undertakings holding a dominant position in the UK or any part of it (Section 18(3) of the 1998 Act).

For undertakings found guilty of an abuse of dominance, the same penalties apply as in relation to anticompetitive agreements, that is, fines can be imposed of up to 10 per cent of worldwide turnover.

Mergers

The UK has a two-stage merger control procedure. The first phase is conducted by a case team comprising members of the CMA's Mergers Unit, with decisions taken by a director of the Mergers Unit in cases that raise no serious competition issues and by the senior director of Mergers (or another senior member of CMA staff) in cases that raise more complex or material issues. The second phase, if the CMA believes a case warrants a detailed review, is conducted by an inquiry group of at least three people selected from the CMA's panel of independent experts. The independent inquiry group acts as the decision-maker in a phase II investigation, which ensures a distinct process from phase I.

As previously mentioned, merger control in the UK is relatively unusual in that companies are not obliged to notify the CMA prior to completing transactions which fall within the scope of the UK merger review laws, and mergers may be closed without notification or clearance. However, if a transaction meets the jurisdictional thresholds, the CMA can open an investigation on its own initiative. Further, regardless of whether the transaction has been notified, the CMA has powers to make an interim order, including at phase I, to prevent the parties taking steps that could affect the CMA's ability to take remedial action. In completed mergers, the CMA is able to reverse integration steps that have already taken place. In mergers that have not yet completed, the CMA is able to suspend all integration steps before clearance and may prevent parties from closing in exceptional cases.

Transactions are caught where:

- two or more enterprises cease to be distinct, or will cease to be distinct, as a result of being brought under common ownership or control;
- either: (a) the UK turnover of the target undertaking exceeds £70 million; or (b) a combined share of supply of goods or services of at least 25 per cent is created or strengthened; and
- either the merger has not yet taken place, or it has taken place not more than four months before a phase II referral is made (unless the merger took place and was not made public, without the CMA being informed of it).

Two enterprises cease to be distinct when they come under common ownership or control. Common control here includes each of: legal control (over 50 per cent of voting rights); a controlling interest; and the ability to exercise material influence over the commercial policy of a company. There are no statutory criteria for material influence but, as a broad rule of thumb, material influence may arise with shareholdings of 15 per cent. A shareholding below 15 per cent may exceptionally attract scrutiny, where other factors indicating an ability to exercise material influence over commercial policy are present.

The CMA is obliged to refer a merger for an in-depth phase II review if it believes that it is or may be the case that a merger has resulted, or may be expected to result, in a substantial lessening of competition within any market or markets in the UK for goods or services.[36] The scope of the CMA's duty to refer has been clarified by the Court of Appeal in the *IBA Health* case.[37] The Court ruled that the OFT (now the CMA) must refer if, on reasonably based analysis, having investigated the matter, it believes that it may be the case that, as a result of the merger, competition will be substantially lessened. The use of 'may' here means less than a 50 per cent likelihood but more than fanciful and is a matter for the CMA's judgment on all the facts of the case.

The important point is that the Court of Appeal expressly ruled that the role of the phase I investigation as a first screen is not simply to identify problematic cases and refer them for a phase II investigation. On the contrary, its judgment means that in an apparently difficult case the CMA can decide not to refer if, despite high shares or other grounds for competition concern, it has enough evidence reasonably to conclude that competition would not be substantially lessened.

The 'substantial lessening of competition' test is likely to be satisfied where a merger is expected to reduce market rivalry to such an extent that the competitive process would no longer deliver a similar level of consumer benefits over time as would occur in the absence of the merger. This entails a comparison of the prospects for competition with and without the merger, as well as other factors, such as the likelihood of new entry, buyer power, and efficiency gains. The Tribunal has held that the term 'substantial' in 'substantial lessening of competition' does not require that the lessening of competition be 'large' in absolute terms. Rather, a significant lessening of competition should suffice, regardless of whether the lessening of competition was large in absolute terms.[38]

This duty to refer does not apply if the merger proposals are insufficiently advanced to warrant referral, if the market is not of sufficient importance,

[36] Sections 22(1) and 33(1) of the 2002 Act.

[37] *Office of Fair Trading and Others* v. *IBA Health Limited* [2004] EWCA Civ 142.

[38] *Case 1214/4/8/13 Global Radio Holdings Limited* v. *Competition Commission* [2013] CAT 26, paras 18–25.

or if there are obvious countervailing consumer benefits. The exceptions are likely to be applied only very rarely at phase I.

At phase I, the CMA must make a decision on whether its duty to refer applies within a statutory 40 working day timetable, which begins from the working day after the CMA confirms receipt of sufficient information to enable it to begin its investigation.

Where the duty to refer does apply, the CMA may, instead of referring the transaction for a phase II investigation, accept from the parties undertakings to remedy, mitigate, or prevent the substantial lessening of competition or any adverse effects of the substantial lessening of competition, known as undertakings in lieu of reference. The undertakings must achieve as comprehensive a solution as is reasonable and practicable, and will generally only be appropriate where the competition concerns raised by the merger and the remedies proposed to address them are clear-cut, effective, and capable of ready implementation. The CMA is highly unlikely to accept behavioural remedies at phase I, and undertakings will therefore usually be structural in nature (that is, divestments).

Where a merger is referred for a phase II investigation, it then falls to the CMA's panel of independent experts to decide whether the merger has resulted, or may be expected to result, in such a substantial lessening of competition. If it decides that there will be an anticompetitive outcome, the CMA must consider whether action should be taken to remedy, mitigate, or prevent the substantial lessening of competition. The CMA inquiry group has 24 weeks, from the date of the reference, to prepare and publish its report. One extension of no more than eight weeks is allowed where there are special reasons justifying an extension. The CMA has extensive powers to remedy adverse effects where a merger has been implemented. These include the power to order divestment, thus causing the referred acquirer to become a forced seller some months after the financial close of an acquisition.

Market Investigations

Investigations into the functioning of a particular market have long been a feature of the UK competition law. The European Commission is also able to carry out investigations into particular market sectors, and in recent years it has launched a wide-ranging investigation into pharmaceuticals. The European Commission, however, has no powers to intervene in a market unless it identifies an infringement of Article 101 or 102 of the TFEU or other relevant legislation (for example, telecoms regulation).

In the UK, the CMA has much wider powers to deal with any perceived problems with the functioning of a particular market at the end of a market investigation.[39] These include, for example, requiring the supply of goods or services, regulating prices to be charged, or even ordering the break-up of a business.

The 2013 Act introduced a number of reforms to the markets regime to strengthen it and improve its functioning. These include giving the CMA the power to investigate practices across markets (rather than just within a market), as well as giving the Secretary of State the power to request the CMA to investigate public interest issues alongside competition issues during a market investigation reference. This enables the CMA to consider competition and public interest issues holistically.

The CMA follows a two-phase decision-making process in relation to the markets regime. A CMA case team will first conduct a market study (a preliminary investigation into the workings of a market) either on its own initiative or in response to a so-called 'super-complaint'. Super-complaints can be brought by certain designated consumer bodies, such as the Consumers' Association and the National Association of Citizens Advice Bureaux. The CMA Board will then take a phase I decision, within 12 months of the formal launch of the phase I investigation, as to whether or not to refer a market for a more in-depth phase II market investigation (the 'market investigation reference').

The CMA Board has the power to refer a case for a market investigation where it has reasonable grounds for suspecting that any feature or combination of features of a market or markets in the UK for goods or services prevents, restricts, or distorts competition in connection with the supply or acquisition of any goods or services in the UK.[40] A feature of a market is broadly defined in the 2002 Act, and can include an aspect of the structure of the market or the conduct of suppliers or customers or those active in the market.[41] In practice, these provisions confer a very broad discretion on the CMA to trigger an in-depth review of the functioning of a particular market.

The Secretary of State has the power to make a market investigation reference and to intervene in cases which involve public interest issues. The only public interest issue so far identified is national security, although the Secretary of State may, by order, introduce new public interest considerations. In common with other competition provisions, the CMA exercises

[39] Set out in Schedule 8 of the 2002 Act.

[40] Section 131(1) of the 2002 Act.

[41] Section 131(3) of the 2002 Act.

concurrent jurisdiction with the relevant sectoral regulators to make market investigation references in relation to goods or services connected with their statutory responsibilities.

If a market investigation reference is made, the CMA will appoint an inquiry group from a panel of specialist members who will conduct a detailed public investigation and will conclude on whether there is an adverse effect on competition in the referred market(s). During its investigation, the CMA has wide powers to call witnesses and require the production of documents.[42] An administrative timetable will be published in relation to each investigation, indicating expected dates for each stage of the investigation. These stages are likely to include: initial questionnaires; oral hearings; the publication of a statement of issues; the publication of the CMA's emerging thinking; the notification of the CMA's provisional findings; and the notification of possible remedies. The CMA inquiry group must publish a report setting out its findings and the action (if any) it proposes to take within 18 months of the date of the reference (extendable once by 6 months in complex cases).

Both the CMA's initial decision to refer or not to refer a case for a market investigation and any decision made by the CMA in the course of a market investigation may be appealed to the Tribunal. In conducting a review, the Tribunal will apply the same principles as would be applied by a court in judicial review proceedings.

[42] Sections 109–16 of the 2002 Act.

18

Competition Law in the United States of America*

Stephen Calkins

In one sense, US competition law is very easy. US antitrust lawyers, as they are known (this chapter will use 'competition law' and 'antitrust law' interchangeably), usually worry about only three statutory provisions: Sherman Act Section 1, 15 U.S.C. § 1; Sherman Act Section 2, 15 U.S.C. § 2; and Clayton Act Section 7, 15 U.S.C. § 18. The first prohibits agreements in restraint of trade, the second monopolization and attempts and conspiracies to monopolize, and the last mergers and acquisitions that may substantially lessen competition. With a few exceptions, that is all the statutory law one needs to know.

In another sense, US competition law is very hard. Those few important statutory provisions are easy to note but answer few questions. Seemingly simple rules often prove challenging in their application to complex facts. The courts treat competition law as a kind of common law, freely changing legal standards from time to time without Congressional guidance. Legal

* This commentary reflects only the author's individual views. Of necessity, this is only an overview of US competition law. For a longer introduction, the reader is referred to Ernest Gellhorn, William Kovacic, and Stephen Calkins. 2004. *Antitrust Law and Economics in a Nutshell* (5th ed.) ("Nutshell") and to *ABA Antitrust Section, Antitrust Law Developments* (7th ed., 2012).

standards are informed by economics, moreover, so as economics evolves the law may evolve with it. Two federal enforcement agencies and numerous state attorneys general enforce the law and participate actively in trying to shape its evolution, while the strong majority of lawsuits are filed by private parties. Confusion about legal standards can be created when, for instance, government enforcers refrain from bringing certain kinds of cases but old cases remain on the books, available to be invoked by private litigants.

A Brief History

US competition law is commonly traced to the passage of the Sherman Act in 1890, although a few state antitrust laws preceded it and the act itself was something of a codification of the common law. This was an era of limited federal government, and early interpretations struggled to decide what kind of actions should be subject to federal control. The early 1900s saw sweeping rhetorical and legal attacks on the 'trusts' as they were called, culminating in the Supreme Court's ordering the dismemberment of the Standard Oil trust. *Standard Oil Co.* v. *United States*, 221 U.S. 1 (1911). Competition policy played a starring role in the 1912 presidential campaign, leading to the election of Woodrow Wilson and the enactment in 1914 of the Clayton Act, 15 U.S.C. § 12 et seq., and the Federal Trade Commission Act, 15 U.S.C. § 41 et seq.[1] The Clayton Act provided for private enforcement of the antitrust laws and substantively addressed price discrimination (Section 2), tying and exclusive dealing (Section 3), mergers and acquisitions (Section 7), and interlocking directorates (Section 8). The most important of those provisions today are Section 7 (as amended in 1950 by the Celler–Kefauver Act, through which Congress expressed concern about increasing concentration), and Section 2 (as amended in 1936 by the Robinson–Patman Act). The Federal Trade Commission Act created a new, independent agency and charged it with preventing 'unfair methods of competition' and, thanks to a 1938 amendment, 'unfair or deceptive acts or practices'.

No brief review of more than a century of legal and economic tumult can do more than mention highlights.[2] Even the briefest review, however, would mention the critical role played by Thurman Arnold, the longest-serving Assistant Attorney General for Antitrust (AAG). Arnold served under

[1] See Doris Kearns Goodwin. 2014. *The Bully Pulpit, Theodore Roosevelt, William Howard Taft, and the Golden Age of Journalism*, Simon & Schuster, New York, N.Y.

[2] A leading antitrust history is Rudolph J.R. Peritz. 2001 (revised ed.). *Competition Policy in America*, Oxford University Press, Oxford.

President Franklin Roosevelt from March 1938 to March 1943. By relentless energy and promotion, he made competition a centrepiece of national economic policy and helped resist the lure of collective action. One of the cases he brought, *United States* v. *Socony-Vacuum Oil Co.*, 310 U.S. 150 (1940), was a seminal case establishing the per se illegality of price-fixing; another, *United States* v. *Aluminum Co. of America*, 148 F.2d 416 (2d Cir. 1945), reigned for decades as the leading case condemning monopolization (which it interpreted expansively).

Thurman Arnold's tenure started a long period of US competition law marked by ever-expanding use of the per se rule and great emphasis on market shares and market structure. The Supreme Court viewed competition law in part as a way to advance social values and protect the small producer from the big. Doctrinally, the Court sought to achieve clear rules specifying conduct that was illegal.

The high water mark of the concern about concentration is marked by the 1968 submission of the 'Neal Report', a task force report commissioned by President Lyndon Johnson. Report of the White House Task Force on Antitrust Policy, *reprinted at* Cong. Rec., 27 May 1969, at 13890 (although submitted in 1968, it did not become public until 1969).[3] It recommended enactment of a 'Concentrated Industries Act' and a 'Merger Act' which would mandate deconcentration of any 'oligopoly industry' and limit conglomerate mergers.

Although Congressional hearings developed these themes, no legislative solution emerged. The lasting effect of this part of the Neal Report was through reactions stimulated by it. Robert Bork wrote a blistering dissent that foreshadowed his influential book, *The Antitrust Paradox* (1978). The Neal Report itself was quickly countered by the Report of the Task Force on Productivity and Competition (1969), known as the 'Stigler Report,' 115 Cong. Rec., 16 June 1969, at 15933 et seq. Richard Posner, who participated in that project, developed themes from that report into *his* influential book, *Antitrust Law: An Economic Perspective* (1976) (now in a 2001 second edition). More generally, the ferment about concentration led to the singularly influential 1974 Airlie House Conference on Industrial Concentration,[4] which helped bring forth a new paradigm that was notably less concerned about moderate levels of market share and concentration.

[3] For the story of this and other competition task force reports, see Stephen Calkins. 2006. Antitrust Modernization: Looking Backwards, *The Journal of Corporation Law*, 31(2) (symposium issue): 421–52.

[4] Harvey J. Goldschmid, H. Michael Mann, and J. Fred Weston (eds). 1974. *Industrial Concentration: The New Learning*. Little, Brown & Company, Boston.

What came to be known as the Chicago School approach to antitrust began its rise to ascendency.

The courts eagerly followed where the academics led. President Richard Nixon played a critically important role in this change. Between June 1969 and January 1972, he appointed four new Supreme Court Justices: Chief Justice Warren Burger and Justices Blackmun, Powell, and Rehnquist, replacing Chief Justice Warren and Justices Fortas, Black, and Harlan. In 1975 President Ford appointed Justice Stevens to replace Justice Douglas, and the Court had become notably more conservative. A long series of government wins in merger cases ended in *United States* v. *General Dynamics Corp.*, 415 U.S. 486 (1974) (5-4). Expansive readings of price discrimination law ended in *Great Atlantic & Pac. Tea Co.* v. *FTC*, 440 U.S. 69 (1979). A quietly subversive opinion introduced the concept of 'antitrust injury,' which would serve to constrain much future private antitrust enforcement and spotlight the purposes of the antitrust laws. *Brunswick Corp.* v. *Pueblo Bowl-O-Mat, Inc.*, 429 U.S. 477 (1977). The ascendency of per se rules was halted by *Broadcast Music, Inc.* v. *CBS, Inc.*, 441 U.S. 1 (1979), which can be read to say that only some arrangements influencing price deserve to be condemned as price fixing. And, most important, *Continental T.V., Inc.* v. *GTE Sylvania, Inc.*, 433 U.S. 36 (1977), aggressively reversed an existing Supreme Court precedent and boldly enshrined economics as the centrepiece of US competition law.

Another critical step in the path towards modern US competition law was the appointment by President Reagan of AAG William Baxter. During Baxter's service, from March 1981 to the end of 1983, he did much to change the way practitioners and judges thought about competition law. To this day, revised versions of his 1982 Merger Guidelines are the starting point for thinking about market definition, market power, concentration, and merger policy.

Although we usually think about the evolution in competition law in terms of substantive rules and doctrines, procedural changes can play critically important roles. Here, three years stand out: 1976, 1993, and 2007. The American Bicentennial year saw enactment of the Hart–Scott–Rodino Act's premerger notification programme, which fundamentally changed the way that merger law was practiced by requiring advance notice of significant mergers and acquisitions (see 15 U.S.C. § 18a). That same Act deliberately invigorated state antitrust enforcement by authorizing state attorneys general to enforce the Sherman Act with parens patriae treble damages actions on behalf of state residents, 15 U.S.C. § 15c, while another 1976 statute, the Crime Control Act, sent seed money for antitrust enforcement to the states. The second year listed earlier, 1993, was the year the Department of Justice

Antitrust Division (Division) expanded its Leniency Policy into a guaranteed amnesty programme if certain criteria were met.[5] The result was an international cartel programme that continues vibrant to this day. The third year, 2007, marked the Supreme Court's important decision in *Bell Atlantic Corp.* v. *Twombly*, 550 U.S. 544 (2007). The courts had become very tough on plaintiffs trying to withstand motions for summary judgment where there was ambiguous evidence concerning an alleged agreement. *Twombly* transposed this rigor earlier into the judicial process, to the motion to dismiss, which has the important effect of denying discovery to plaintiffs whose ability to prove an agreement is not already reasonably well advanced.

Enforcement of Competition Law

For better or worse, a hallmark of US competition law is the way it is enforced. In particular, firms engaging in an anticompetitive practice could find themselves sued by one or more of the Antitrust Division, the Federal Trade Commission (FTC), any of the 51 state attorneys general (counting the District of Columbia), or lawyers representing individual or classes of customers, competitors, suppliers, or possibly other injured private parties. Consequences could include criminal penalties (including incarceration and massive fines), injunctions, treble damages, and, in rare cases, disgorgement or consumer redress.

Department of Justice Antitrust Division

The Antitrust Division is headed by an Assistant Attorney General nominated by the President and confirmed by the Senate. The AAG is, frequently, someone appointed directly or indirectly from the private sector who serves typically for two or three years. The AAG is supported (currently) by five Deputy Assistant Attorneys General, four Directors of Enforcement, a General Counsel, and an Office of Operations.[6] The work of the Division is done in eleven 'sections,' each headed by a chief, three field offices, and the Economic Analysis Group.

The crown jewel of the division's work is its cartel programme. These are extremely serious prosecutions because price fixing and related offenses such as bid rigging are felonies, and full constitutional protections apply. Criminal

[5] The Division's Leniency Program can be found at http://www.justice.gov/atr/public/criminal/leniency.html.

[6] See http://www.justice.gov/atr/about/sections.html.

enforcement tools, such as search warrants and electronic surveillance, are regularly used. Grand juries collect evidence and vote indictments, and conviction can result in draconian penalties. Those penalties have increased steadily over time.[7] For offenses committed on or after 22 June 2004, corporations can be fined up to $100 million per offense or possibly even more, and individuals can be sentenced to up to 10 years in prison and fined up to $1 million (or possibly even more) per offense (15 U.S.C. § 1). These penalties are supplemented by penalties for obstruction of justice, perjury, and mail and wire fraud.

The bottom line of all this has been a triumphantly successful programme. In the five most recent fiscal years, 158 individuals—many of them foreign nationals—have been sentenced to prison.[8] Fifty or more criminal cases are filed each year; annual fines total between $500 million and a $1.3 billion dollars, and average jail time is now 25 months.[9]

When the Antitrust Division proceeds civilly, it files lawsuits in federal district court and is subject to the normal rules of civil procedure. Some of the most important civil cases are merger cases, which are discussed separately later in the chapter. The Division uses civil discovery tools to build a case and the court enjoins the wrongful conduct, usually by consent and usually without imposition of any penalty. (The government may sue to recover its damages as a purchaser, but this authority rarely plays an important role.)[10]

The Federal Trade Commission

In 1914, Congress, dissatisfied with the course of competition enforcement during the first two decades, supplemented the Justice Department's role

[7] See Stephen Calkins. 1997. Corporate compliance and the Antitrust Agencies' Bi-Modal Penalties, *Law & Contemporary Problems*, 60 (127): 131–2.

[8] See Antitrust Division Workload Statistics FY 2004–2013, available at http://www.justice.gov/atr/public/workload-statistics.html.

[9] Criminal Enforcement Fine and Jail Charts Through Fiscal Year 2014, available at http://www.justice.gov/atr/public/criminal/264101.html#a

[10] In *United States* v. *Keyspan Corp.*, 763 F. Supp. 2d 633 (S.D.N.Y. 2011), the court for the first time approved the use of disgorgement as an additional remedy—there, in a consent order. Since then, the Division has successfully sought disgorgement several times, see *Depriving Wrongdoers of Ill-Gotten Gain,* Division Update, *Spring* 2015, at http://www.justice.gov/atr/division-update/2015/depriving-wrongdoers-ill-gotten-gain.

by creating the FTC.[11] The vision for the FTC was as a guide to business, pointing the way towards fair methods of competition. From the start is was a collective body, with five commissioners nominated by the President and confirmed by the Senate. Whereas the Justice Department could invoke the power of criminal penalties, the Commission was limited to ordering firms to cease engaging in what were found to be 'unfair methods of competition'—without any penalty being imposed.

The classic FTC case involves administrative adjudication. The Commission has broad powers to order pre-complaint investigations. When a majority of the Commission has 'reason to believe' that a firm (called a 'respondent') is engaging in an 'unfair method of competition', the Commission issues a complaint. Thereafter a trial is held before an Administrative Law Judge, who issues an opinion that is inevitably appealed (by one side or the other, or both) to the full Commission. The Commission typically hears oral argument and issues an opinion and final order. If (and only if) it is adverse to the respondent, the respondent may appeal to its choice of almost any court of appeals (15 U.S.C. § 45(c)).

Although that is the classic procedure, it little accords with modern practice. Most FTC competition law cases are settled by consent orders. A majority of the FTC's competition cases involve mergers and acquisitions, which are discussed later in the chapter. For the rest of the competition law docket (the Commission has a very active consumer protection programme), the Commission tries to identify situations where individuals or forms are engaging in anticompetitive practices not sufficiently egregious to deserve criminal penalties. In recent years, the Commission's competition enforcers have occasionally borrowed from its consumer protection programme the idea of filing cases in federal court and seeking 'disgorgement' or 'consumer redress' under special authority enacted in 1976.[12]

In principle, 'unfair methods of competition' can encompass more than the generally enforceable antitrust laws, but in practice the FTC usually applies general antitrust principles. Many Commission non-merger competition cases concern the business of health care, where criminal laws are only very rarely applied. Recent FTC Supreme Court cases include *FTC* v. *Actavis, Inc.*,

[11] The birth of the FTC is wonderfully chronicled in Marc Winerman. 2003. *The Origins of the FTC: Concentration, Cooperation, Control, and Competition*, *Antitrust Law Journal* 71(1): 1–97.

[12] See Stephen Calkins. 2006. *Civil Monetary Remedies Available to the Federal Government*, *University of San Francisco Law Review* 40(SF)(3): 567–99 (symposium issue) (in part discussing the Commission's 2003 Policy Statement on monetary penalties in competition cases, which was withdrawn in 2012).

133 S. Ct. 2233 (17 June 2013) (reverse payments) and *North Carolina Bd. of Dental Examiners* v. *FTC*, No. 13-534 (25 February 2015) (state action).

Much of the Commission's work in competition law does not involve filing cases at all. The Commission has a robust programme of non-litigation competition work, which includes doing studies, conducting hearing and workshops, widely advocating competition principles, giving advice as to the legality of various arrangements, and filing amicus briefs in state and federal courts. (The Division does some of this as well.)

Merger Enforcement

Merger enforcement was fundamentally changed in 1976, when the Hart–Scott–Rodino (HSR) Act mandated that substantial mergers and acquisitions (mergers) be reported in advance to the two federal antitrust agencies (15 U.S.C. § 18a).[13] Ever since then, the key decisions about most mergers have taken place before consummation. The HSR gave the agencies the ability to investigate mergers using the club of delayed consummation to enforce compliance with discovery requests made through the HSR process. Although in theory HSR was going to apply only to the very largest mergers and delay their closing only minimally, in fact it applied to up to almost 5,000 transactions a year until Congress changed and inflation adjusted the thresholds; recently it has applied to 13–1400 a year,[14] and parties to complicated transactions often find it sensible to delay closing—sometimes for many months—while trying to resolve agency concerns. Partly as a result of this, the vast majority of mergers challenges are settled in advance of closing.

When settlement does not prove possible (maybe once or twice a year), litigation ensues. Both agencies file most of their cases in federal district court, seeking to enjoin the proposed merger. These hearings are often extended and result in publication of quite detailed opinions. The agencies have been on a winning streak of late, but they have also experienced losing streaks. The FTC nominally reserves the right to proceed with administrative adjudication even after a court denies injunctive relief, but this almost never happens. Both agencies also have the authority to challenge, post-closing, a merger that they did not challenge in advance (for instance, because they were unaware

[13] For guidance on whether an HSR filing is needed, see FTC's helpful website dedicated to the premerger notification programme at http://www.ftc.gov/enforcement/premerger-notification-program.

[14] Annual HSR Report to Congress Fiscal Year 2013, Figure 1, available at http://www.ftc.gov/system/files/documents/reports/36th-report-fy2013/140521hsrreport.pdf.

of it). This is unusual but becoming more common, especially now that the notification thresholds have been raised.

State Enforcement

Particularly during the 1980s, after the Hart–Scott–Rodino Act encouraged state antitrust enforcement and when state attorneys general perceived that the Reagan Administration was being insufficiently aggressive, state antitrust enforcement became a force with which to be reckoned.[15] Today every state has its own competition law. State attorneys general can file actions either under those laws or under federal law, including (since 1976) as parens patriae to seek treble damages on behalf of state residents (15 U.S.C. § 15c, 15f). States coordinate actions with the federal enforcers (one typical model would see the federal government obtaining an injunction and the states monetary relief) and with each other. The latter is accomplished through the National Association of Attorneys General Antitrust Multistate Task Force, which coordinates multistate litigation through task forces (see http://naag.org/antitrust.php). In addition to litigating (and sometimes winning quite substantial recoveries), state attorneys general have issued guidelines and file amicus briefs and other comments expressing their views.

Private Enforcement

In numerical terms, government antitrust enforcement is just the tip of the iceberg. The vast majority of antitrust lawsuits are private. The Clayton Act broadly provides that 'any person who shall be injured in his business or property by reason of anything forbidden in the antitrust laws may sue therefor' and recover treble damages, costs, and attorneys fees (15 U.S.C. § 15a). Private parties also may seek injunctive relief (15 U.S.C. § 26). Although on the surface this is a sweeping authorization, over the years it has been limited by court-created doctrines. In particular, courts have been quite demanding about which persons have standing to bring an antitrust case, tending to favour injured persons in close proximity to the wrongdoing. See *Associated General Contractors of California, Inc.* v. *California State Council of Carpenters*, 459 U.S. 519 (1983). A related doctrine provides that although direct purchasers can recover for the entire overcharge they paid (even if they passed it on to others), indirect purchasers usually cannot recover anything at all as a matter of federal law (many state laws are more permissive). The

[15] See Stephen Calkins. 2003. *Perspectives on State and Federal Antitrust Enforcement, Duke Law Journal* 53(2): 673–735.

latter principle is known as the '*Illinois Brick* doctrine', after *Illinois Brick Co.* v. *Illinois*, 431 U.S. 720 (1977). Perhaps even more important, the Supreme Court has held that '[p]laintiffs must prove *antitrust* injury, which is to say injury of the type the antitrust laws were intended to prevent and that flows from that which makes defendants' acts unlawful'. *Brunswick Corp.* v. *Pueblo Bowl-O-Mat, Inc.*, 429 U.S. 477, 489 (1977). This inquiry focuses attention narrowly on the purposes of the antitrust laws, and serves both to limit the range of persons who can sue and constrain the theories they can advance. Other procedural trends working against plaintiffs include tougher standards for certifying classes, see *Comcast Corp.* v. *Behrend,* 133 S. Ct. 1426 (2013) (5-4), and robust enforcement of mandatory arbitration clauses in (often form) contracts, *see American Express Co.* v. *Italian Colors Restaurant,* 133 S. Ct. 2304 (2013).

Private enforcement has played a critical role in shaping American competition law. Treble damages provide much of the deterrent effect of US competition law. Much of what we know as US antitrust law is the product of court decisions resolving private litigation. Even where government enforcers play a role, the existence of private litigation drives the antitrust system towards adopting clear principles, such that potential defendants can win not as a matter of government grace but as a matter of law.[16]

Jurisdiction

At one time, the question of federal jurisdiction was terribly important to US competition law, with many leading cases turning on whether a restraint sufficiently affected interstate commerce. Those days are over; today, as a practical matter, US conduct sufficiently harmful otherwise to violate the antitrust laws could rarely, if ever, be defended on grounds that the conduct and its effect were too localized.

Although the question of local versus interstate commerce is rarely an important issue, the international reach of US competition laws is a matter of considerable controversy. US courts initially looked to the situs of the act to decide legality, *American Banana Co.* v. *United Fruit Co.*, 213 U.S. 347 (1909), but the famous 1945 *Alcoa* opinion adopted the 'effects test': agreements made abroad can violate the Sherman Act 'if they were intended to affect imports and did affect them'. *United States* v. *Aluminum Co. of America*, 148 F.2d 416, 444 (2d Cir. 1945). Although the test was controversial at the time, in 1993 the Supreme Court wrote that 'it is well established by now that

[16] See Stephen Calkins, *Corporate Compliance,* supra n. 7, at 149–61.

the Sherman Act applies to foreign conduct that was meant to produce and did in fact produce some substantial effect in the United States'. *Hartford Fire Insurance Co.* v. *California*, 509 U.S. 764, 796 (1993).

Congress unsuccessfully sought to bring clarity to the issue by passing the Foreign Trade Antitrust Improvements Act of 1982 (FTAIA). This Act declares that the Sherman Act 'shall not apply to conduct involving trade or commerce (other than import trade or import commerce) with foreign nations unless—(1) such conduct has a direct, substantial and reasonably foreseeable effect—(A) on [domestic or import commerce], or (B) on export trade or export commerce ... of a person engaged in such commerce in the United States; and (2) such effect gives rise to a claim' under the Sherman Act (15 U.S.C. § 6a). Where the Sherman Act applies to conduct only because of sub-clause (B), the Act shall apply 'only for injury to export business in the United States'. It is uniformly agreed that this is a model of poor drafting, with debate occurring only over whether the solution is to go back to Congress or pray that the courts will wrench clarity out of the confusion. Numerous judicial attempts—the issue arises with regularity—have resulted in some limited progress.

FTAIA poses many issues. Are its limitations substantive (the merits of the case) or jurisdictional (the power of the court)? The clear trend is correctly to the former. See, for example, *United States* v. *Hsiung*, 778 F.3d 738 (9th Cir. 2015). Does the FTAIA apply to import commerce? Clearly not. *Hsiung, supra; Minn-Chem, Inc.* v. *Agrium, Inc.*, 683 F.3d 845, 855 (7th Cir. 2012) (*en banc*). Some uncertainty remains, however, about whether it matters that the defendants imported the goods, and about how to proceed for damages actions and criminal/equitable actions (if different) if some but not all of the goods involved were imported. The Ninth Circuit interpreted the statutorily required 'direct ... effect' to mean 'follows as an immediate consequence', *United States* v. *LSL Biotechnologies*, 379 F.3d 672, 680 (9th Cir. 2004), but the government agencies have been more successful recently in persuading other courts to require only 'a reasonably proximate causal nexus'. See *Lotes Co.* v. *Hon Hai Precision Indus. Co.*, 753 F.3d 395 (2d Cir. 2014). In a case that attracted great attention, the Seventh Circuit rebuffed Motorola Mobility's claim for damages involving allegedly price-fixed LCD panels that were purchased overseas by Motorola's foreign subsidiary and incorporated into mobile phones for shipment to the US and elsewhere—but the Court noted that the result might be different were the government seeking criminal or injunctive remedies. *Motorola Mobility LLC* v. *AU Optronics Corp.*, 775 F.3d 816 (7th Cir. 2015). Addressing similar facts, the Ninth Circuit was able to avoid addressing 'the outer bounds of import trade' because at least some of the transactions involved in a government criminal challenge were directly imported. *Hsiung*, supra.

Determining whether commerce is domestic, import, or foreign non-import is no simple matter. In 2004 the Supreme Court took a start towards resolving another conundrum, ruling that when a global conspiracy causes both US harm and independent harm abroad, a private plaintiff may not recover for that independent foreign harm at least unless it is inextricably linked with domestic harm. *F. Hoffman-La Roche Ltd.* v. *Empagran S.A.*, 542 U.S. 155 (2004), *on remand*, 417 F.3d 1267 (D.C. Cir. 2005) (giving a narrow reading to the 'inextricably linked' exception).

Jurisdictional restraint may also come from judge-made doctrines. In particular, much ink has been spilt about the concept of 'comity'—although the most recent Supreme Court treatment limited its applicability to where US and foreign law truly conflict. *Hartford Fire Insurance Co.* v. *California*, 509 U.S. 763 (1993). The 'act of state' doctrine bars US courts from judging sovereign acts committed in a foreign state by that state's government. See also the Foreign Sovereign Immunities Act, 28 U.S.C. § 1602.

Substantive Law Highlights

US competition law has evolved into a relatively stable equilibrium.[17] The Antitrust Division devotes the vast majority of its resources to bringing criminal cartel cases and challenging mergers. Under Republican presidents the Division has filed very few single-firm cases, and the record under Democratic leadership is not much different (although under President Clinton the Division brought the important *Microsoft* case). Long ago, the Division foreswore bringing price discrimination cases. Lacking criminal enforcement authority, the FTC's principal antitrust interest is merger enforcement, although it also has a meaningful programme of bringing civil challenges to horizontal restraints (particularly in the health care field) and selected abuses of dominance (including involving intellectual property), and occasionally it explores whether Section 5's coverage of 'unfair methods of competition' permits it to do a little more (with the most successful such foray concerning attempted price fixing). The FTC has only rarely filed vertical restraint cases and even more rarely price discrimination ones.

Horizontal Restraints

Sherman Act Section 1 makes illegal '[e]very contract, combination … or conspiracy, in restraint of trade ….' 15 U.S.C. § 1. (Indeed, engaging in such

[17] See William E. Kovacic. 2003. The Modern Evolution of U.S. Competition Policy Enforcement Norms, *Antitrust Law Journal*, 71(2): 377–478.

behaviour is a felony, punishable by $100,000,000 for a corporation or, for an individual, $1,000,000 and up to 10 years imprisonment—although only some violations are treated that harshly.)[18] The challenge, of course, is to make those words mean something. US courts looked to common law traditions and then built upon this to achieve current understandings. As the Supreme Court has explained, the problem is that Section 1 'cannot mean what it says. The statute says that: "every" contract that restrains trade is unlawful. But ... restraint is the very essence of every contract; read literally, § 1 would outlaw the entire body of private contract law."' *National Society of Professional Engineers* v. *United States*, 435 U.S. 679, 687–88 (1978) (footnotes omitted). Only *unreasonable* restraints are unlawful.

The great sin under US antitrust law is price fixing. Whether called cartelization, bid-rigging, or something else, it is automatically unlawful. The same broad condemnation includes all naked horizontal agreements to raise prices or reduce output, or to divide markets. These are said to be unlawful 'per se,' meaning that they cannot be defended on the grounds that the parties lacked market power or did not have any actual impact. *United States* v. *Socony-Vacuum Oil* Co., 310 U.S. 150 (1940); Trenton *Potteries Co.* v. *United States*, 273 U.S. 392 (1927). It is equally illegal for horizontal competitors to fix the prices they will charge and the prices they will pay.

Much of US antitrust history has consisted of establishing these principles, subjecting them to attack, and implementing of them. For instance, *Socony* famously declared: 'Under the Sherman Act a combination formed for the purpose and with the effect of raising, depressing, fixing, pegging, or stabilizing the price ... is illegal *per se*'; 310 U.S. at 224. It even indicated that purpose alone, without ability to effectuate it, was sufficient. But when a group of competitors establish and improve the functioning of a competitive marketplace, they will be intentionally influencing prices by making supply and demand work more efficiently; yet this has long been upheld. *Chicago Board of Trade* v. *United States*, 246 U.S.231 (1918).

A landmark case in this progression is *Broadcast Music, Inc.* v. *CBS*, 441 U.S. 1 (1979). The big music licensing houses (ASCAP and BMI) had created blanket licenses that proved so popular that the vast majority of music licenses were with ASCAP or BMI, not with individual composers. The court of appeals held that this near-complete elimination of price competition was 'price fixing' and illegal per se. The Supreme Court reversed. In the Court's

[18] A 2004 amendment increased these amounts from $10 million, $350,000, and three years, respectively. Especially before this amendment, the government used alternative authority to set corporate fines at twice the company's pecuniary gain or twice the pecuniary loss suffered by victims, whichever is greater. 18 U.S.C. § 3623.

new treatment, 'price fixing' became less a factual assertion that started the analysis, and more the legal conclusion announced *after* the analysis. The inquiry needed in order to characterize conduct is 'whether the practice facially appears to be one that would always or almost always tend to restrict competition and decrease output, … or instead one designed to "increase economic efficiency and render markets more, rather than less, competitive."' 441 U.S. at 19–20 (citations omitted).[19]

Although *BMI* was a setback to per se rules, they continue to play a role. Examples of practices found to be illegal per se include:

A horizontal agreement to eliminate short-term credit for purchasers. *Catalano, Inc.* v. *Target Sales, Inc.*, 446 U.S. 643 (1980).

Horizontal competitors agreeing on list prices. *Plymouth Dealers' Ass'n of Northern California* v. *United States*, 279 F.2d 128 (9th Cir. 1960).

An agreement among competitors to alter product formulas to reduce purchases of an expensive ingredient. *National Macaroni Mfrs Ass'n* v. *FTC*, 345 F.2d 421 (7th Cir. 1965).

An agreement between two competitors to stay in separate territories. *Palmer* v. *BRG of Georgia, Inc.*, 498 U.S. 46 (1990).

An agreement among legal aid attorneys to refrain from working until their compensation was increased. *Superior Court Trial Lawyers Ass'n* v. *FTC*, 493 U.S. 411 (1990).

For a time, it seemed that all agreements not unlawful per se were judged under what was known as the 'rule of reason'. This required the plaintiff to prove anticompetitive effect, after which the defendant could attempt to justify the restriction as necessary to achieving procompetitive benefits, in which event the plaintiff could attempt to show it was not so necessary, and, in any event, that the bad outweighed the good. In practice, many courts expected plaintiffs to define markets and prove market power—not an easy thing to do. [For an example of such a case, see *Texaco Inc.* v. *Dagher*, 547 U.S. 1 (2006), where the Court refused to apply the per se rule to the setting of prices by a fully-integrated joint venture, with the Court noting that it 'presumptively applies rule of reason analysis'.]

In the past 30 years, the courts have struggled to identify a middle category of restraint which could be condemned without proving a full-blown rule of reason case.[20] Identifying and understanding this category, known variously as the 'quick look' or the 'truncated rule of reason' or the addressing of

[19] See Stephen Calkins. 2007. *Broadcast Music, Inc.* v. *Columbia Broadcasting System, Inc.,* Eleanor M. Fox and Daniel A. Crane (eds), in *Antitrust Stories.*

[20] See Stephen Calkins. 2000. California Dental Association: *Not the Quick Look but Not the Full Monty, Antitrust Law Journal* 67: 495.

'inherently suspect' practices, continues to be a work in progress.[21] In *FTC* v. *Actavis, Inc.*, 133 S. Ct. 2223 (2013), the FTC unsuccessfully advocated for application of the 'quick look' in pay-for-delay patent settlement cases—but the Court, rebuffing the respondents' attempt to immunize their conduct, insisted that competition laws should be applied and could be done so without undue difficulty. The Court reiterated a truth that is easier to say than to apply: '"[T]here is always something of a sliding scale in appraising reasonableness," and as such "the quality of proof required should vary with the circumstances."' *Id.* (citations omitted).

One kind of horizontal restraint has received separate attention over the years: group boycotts. Few concepts have caused more confusion. Although it has been said that group boycotts are per se illegal, many lower courts have limited the per se label to one or another form of 'classic' group boycotts, often a group of competitors preventing a rival from obtaining something important to effective competition.[22] Many arrangements that could be called group boycotts are actually better analysed as concerted refusals to deal—which, depending on the facts, might best be considered under the per se rule, the full rule of reason, or, often, something in between.

Vertical Restraints

US vertical restraint law has been on a long odyssey. To oversimplify, courts initially viewed vertical restraints with great suspicion and tended to condemn that which they did not understand. Today, vertical restraints are generally viewed with equanimity, and where courts are uncertain about the effects of a restraint they tend to uphold it.

Non-price Vertical Restraints

One striking change occurred with respect to general non-price vertical restraints, by which (for instance) a manufacturer confines a reseller to a particular geographic territory. This limits intra-brand competition but can enhance inter-brand competition. These post-sale restraints were declared unlawful per se in *United States* v. *Arnold, Schwinn & Co.*, 388 U.S. 365 (1967). That position was squarely rejected in the landmark opinion,

[21] See *California Dental Ass'n* v. *FTC*, 526 U.S. 756 (1999); *North Carolina State Bd. of Dental Examiners* v. *FTC*, 717 F.3d 359 (4th Cir. 2014), *aff'd*, 135 S. Ct. 1101 (2015); *North Texas Specialty Physicians* v. *FTC*, 528 F.3d 346 (5th Cir. 2008).

[22] See, for example, *Full Draw Productions* v. *Easton Sports, Inc.*, 182 F.3d 745 (10th Cir. 1999).

Continental T.V., Inc. GTE Sylvania Inc., 433 U.S. 36 (1977). Since then, general non-price vertical restraints have been judged under the rule of reason—and virtually always upheld, usually on summary judgment for want of market power.

Vertical Price Restraints

GTE Sylvania drew a sharp distinction between vertical non-price and vertical price restraints: the latter had long been considered per se illegal and would continue to be so treated. Protests that it was not always easy to distinguish between price and non-price restraints were ignored. The per se ban on vertical price restraints [often referred to as resale price maintenance (RPM)], was amended in *State Oil Co.* v. *Khan*, 522 U.S. 3 (1997), to apply only to vertical *minimum* price restraints, and then repealed by a five-to-four vote in *Leegin Creative Leather Products, Inc.* v. *PSKS, Inc.*, 551 U.S. 877 (2007). Although the Court stated that 'the potential anticompetitive consequences of vertical price restraints must not be ignored or underestimated', *id.* at 894, and suggested that over time courts would be able to develop structured analyses and even presumptions (the concern most highlighted by the Court was facilitation of a cartel), there have been few such developments. Business counselling concerning RPM is complicated by the existence of state competition laws and the view of many state AG's that under those laws RPM remains per se illegal.

In truth, even when fully in place the RPM ban was more theoretical than real because it applied only when there was a vertical price agreement, and a series of Supreme Court cases had made it exceedingly hard for a plaintiff to prove the necessary agreement. An early Supreme Court case, *United States* v. *Colgate & Co.*, 250 U.S. 300 (1919), recognized a seller's right to choose to whom to sell (or not sell). This right was considerably emasculated in subsequent years, only to be ringingly reaffirmed in *Monsanto Co.* v. *Spray-Rite Service Corp.*, 465 U.S. 752 (1984) and *Business Electronics Corp.* v. *Sharp Electronics Corp.*, 485 U.S. 717 (1988). *Monsanto* held that the classic pattern—complaints from full-price retailers about a discounter followed by termination of that discounter—was insufficient to prevent a defendant winning summary judgment, precisely because such a pattern is so predictable. 'There must be evidence that tends to exclude the possibility that the manufacturer and nonterminated distributors were acting independently', 465 U.S. at 764. Indeed, a plaintiff had to prove agreement on a specific price or price level. Because the law on proving vertical price agreements was so demanding, defendants regularly won summary judgment in spite of suggesting resale prices and encouraging their use, terminating discounters, and conditioning cooperative advertising programmes on refraining from advertising discounts. What remains to be seen is whether, now that the consequences of proving a price agreement are not so draconian, plaintiffs will have an easier time proving the existence of an agreement.

Exclusive Distributorships

It is important to distinguish between exclusive distributorships, whereby a manufacturer promises a reseller that it will not supply rival resellers, and exclusive dealing (discussed ahead), whereby a reseller agrees not to stock rival brands. Even the *Schwinn* opinion recognized that exclusive distributorships are often procompetitive and should be judged under the rule of reason. They are almost invariably upheld.

Tying

Although the per se ban on tying is under assault, it still remains in place—but this is a singularly convoluted per se rule. Proof requires at least (a) two separate products or services, (b) conditioning the sale of one on the purchase of the other, (c) sufficient economic power in the 'tying' product, and (d) an effect on a not insubstantial amount of commerce. *Jefferson Parish Hosp. Dist. No. 2* v. *Hyde*, 466 U.S. 2 (1984). The decision whether there are two products or services is often made ad hoc, although the majority opinion in *Jefferson Parish* said that it should turn 'not on the functional relation between them, but rather on the character of demand for the two items', 466 U.S. at 19. (A four-Justice plurality would have preferred yet a different approach.) Courts disagree about the extent to which proof of the requisite conditioning requires proof of coercion; nor is it clear whether a violation is shown when a customer is forced to take a product it otherwise would not have purchased at all. (*Jefferson Parish* can be read both ways on this point; without much discussion the Court in *Illinois Tool Works Inc.* v. *Independent Ink, Inc.*, 547 U.S. 28 [2006], adopted the more expansive reading) With respect to sufficient economic power, *Jefferson Parish* referred to 'market power' but then defined that concept as any 'special ability … to force a purchaser to do something that he would not do in a competitive market', and included within the concept possession of 'a unique product that competitors are not able to offer', 466 U.S. at 14 and 17. On its facts, the Court found that a firm with a 30 per cent market share lacked sufficient power, and many but not all lower courts have followed this lead. On this issue, the *Illinois Tool Works* Court simply declared that a plaintiff can win a tying case only by proving 'that the defendant has market power in the tying product'—and this time failed to define 'market power' in terms of uniqueness.

As if the above was not sufficiently complicated, there is more. Some lower courts have added other requirements, such as the defendant's having an economic interest in the tied product, or even proof of an economic effect in the tied product market. Unlike true per se rules, moreover, this one seems to recognize a possible quality control defence. *Eastman Kodak Co.* v. *Image Technical Services, Inc.*, 504 U.S. 451 (1992). Finally, the four-Justice concurrence in *Jefferson Parish* called for replacement of the per se rule with the rule of reason, and the D.C. Circuit in *Microsoft* held that the per se rule was so poorly designed to address newly integrated products in markets for innovative technology that it insisted in applying the rule of reason. *United States* v. *Microsoft Corp.*, 253 F.3d 34 (D.C. Cir. 2001). The Supreme Court explained in *Illinois Tool Works* that it has come to appreciate that '[m]any tying arrangements ... are fully consistent with a free, competitive market,' so the per se rule against tying cannot be regarded as on entirely sound footing.

Exclusive Dealing

Exclusive dealing, in which a reseller promises not to stock rival brands, historically, has always been treated more leniently than tying, perhaps because the possible procompetitive benefits were more apparent. The four-Justice plurality in *Jefferson Parish* addressed the issue with sufficient authoritativeness that many lower courts have looked to its teaching (and upheld exclusive dealing arrangements). Application of the rule of reason to exclusive dealing usually requires consideration of the extent of foreclosure, with courts being untroubled by foreclosure of 20 per cent or even sometimes the 30 per cent at issue in *Jefferson Parish*; the duration of the exclusive dealing arrangement, with some courts finding contracts of a year or less, or terminable at will, presumptively lawful[23]; and entry conditions. Where a firm has sufficient market power, however, enforcers continue to view exclusive dealing as a device that can be abused to harm competition. See *McWane, Inc.* v. *FTC*, 783 F.3d 814 (11th Cir. 2015).

Mergers and Acquisitions

Merger standards have changed almost as much as vertical restraint analysis. The original Sherman Act proved a feeble tool with which to resist anticompetitive mergers, prompting Congress specifically to address mergers in 1914

[23] But cf. *United States* v. *Dentsply Int'l, Inc.*, 399 F.3d 181 (3d Cir. 2005) (business realities made contractual freedom to switch suppliers ineffective in preventing maintenance of monopoly power).

in Clayton Act Section 7. Section 7 was further strengthened by an important amendment in 1950, such that today it prohibits mergers and acquisitions 'where in any line of commerce in any section of the country, the effect ... may be substantially to lessen competition', 15 U.S.C. § 18. The amended Section 7 stimulated the Supreme Court to issue a series of decisions so hostile to mergers that Justice Stewart was moved famously to protest that '[t]he sole consistency I can find is that in litigation under § 7, the Government always wins'. *United States* v. *Von's Grocery Co.*, 384 U.S. 270, 301 (1966) (Stewart, J., dissenting).

The Government's record was broken in 1974 when an opinion authored by Justice Stewart signalled a more cautious approach.[24] Then, merger law was changed forever by AAG Baxter's issuance of DOJ's 1982 Merger Guidelines. As revised periodically (most recently in 2010), those Guidelines set out the agencies' approach to merger analysis and have also served to influence court decision-making. (The Guidelines are available at http://www.justice.gov/atr/public/guidelines/hmg-2010.html.)[25]

One important contribution of the Merger Guidelines was to bring focus to market definition. The Guidelines employ a foiling concept: start with a small possible market and ask what would happen were a hypothetical monopolist to raise prices by a non-transitory small but significant (such as 5 per cent) amount. § 4.1. If that increase would be profitable, a market has been identified; if not, broaden the possible market a little and try again. Although theoretically elegant, this concept is not always easy to litigate. Courts struggle to define markets by examining economic evidence (natural experiments are invaluable), evidence of the understandings of the merging firms and their rivals, evidence of customer views (although this has proven controversial), and related factors.

A cousin of market definition is ease of entry. If firms in an adjacent area or selling a related product would enter the instant prices rose, they are effectively in the market already. But if firms would enter not instantly but timely and in sufficient scale as to roll back any price increase, then ease of entry prevents harm to competition. (§ 9).

[24] See *United States* v. *General Dynamics Corp.*, 415 U.S. 486 (1974).

[25] The current guidelines address only horizontal mergers, and this brief overview follows that lead. The vast majority of merger challenges are to horizontal mergers, although complaints sometimes allege threatened harm to potential as well as actual competition. For an overview of an important vertical merger challenge, see William P. Rogerson, *Vertical Mergers in the Video Programming and Distribution Industry: The Case of Comcast and NBCU,* in John E. Kwoka, Jr. and Lawrence J. White. 2013. *The Antitrust Revolution* (6th ed.), Oxford University Press, New York, NY.

Probably the most important contribution of the 1982 Guidelines was to set out with precision why DOJ is concerned about mergers. The sole purpose of merger enforcement—slightly tweaked by now—is to prevent mergers that are likely to 'create, enhance, or entrench market power or to facilitate its exercise'. § 1. Gone was any concern about size, in and of itself. Instead, the Guidelines examine two theories of competitive harm: coordinated effects and unilateral effects.

Coordinated effects played the greater role in the 1982 Guidelines. They used a measure of concentration new to the courts, the Herfindahl–Hirschman Index (HHI), which is calculated by summing the squares of the shares of firms in a market. The 2010 Guidelines characterize post-merger markets as either 'unconcentrated' (HHI's below 1500), 'moderately concentrated' (HHI's between 1500 and 2500), and 'highly concentrated' (HHI's above 2500). § 5.3. The Guidelines are sanguine about mergers that would result in an 'unconcentrated' market or that would increase the HHI by less than 100 points. Mergers that increase the HHI by more than more than 100 points 'potentially raise significant competitive concerns and often warrant scrutiny'. Also warranting such scrutiny are mergers that increase the HHI by 100–200 points and result in 'highly concentrated markets'. Any merger that would increase the HHI by more than 200 points, resulting in a 'highly concentrated market,' 'will be presumed to be likely to enhance market power.' § 5.3. But the Guidelines caution that analysis cannot end with market share statistics; one also must examine factors such as ease of entry and other market conditions affecting coordinated interaction. In practice, a substantial number of merger investigations are closed when the number of competitors would change from 6 to 5 (65 per cent closed), 5 to 4 (36 per cent closed), and 4 to 3 (23 per cent closed). FTC, Horizontal Merger Investigation Data, Fiscal Years 1996–2011, Table 4.1 (January 2013) (also noting importance of 'hot documents' and customer complaints).

Unilateral effects analysis has played expanded roles in more recent iterations of the Guidelines, see § 6, and in agency deliberations and challenges. If a firm with a leading brand in a differentiated products business acquires its closest substitute (the agencies may consider diversion ratios), that acquisition may make possible an anticompetitive price increase). Unilateral effects can also arise in markets with bargaining and auctions, in homogeneous product markets, and through 'diminished innovation or reduced product variety,' *id.*

Also expanded (in 1997) was the Guidelines' treatment of efficiencies. Efficiencies can justify what would otherwise be an unlawful merger if they are 'merger-specific' (unlikely to be accomplished otherwise), verified, and not arising from reductions in competition (§ 10). Normally they can prevent a merger challenge only if they are shown to be so great and so likely to be passed on to consumers as to prevent a post-merger price increase; even then, the Guidelines caution, efficiencies 'almost never justify a merger to monopoly or near-monopoly', *id.*

One consequence of the HSR premerger notification programme is that relatively few merger challenges are litigated, and what litigation occurs is not always pursued to the end. Partly as a result of this, the Supreme Court has not issued a merger opinion since 1975, *United States* v. *Citizens & Southern National Bank*, 422 U.S. 86 (17 June 1975), and even appellate court decisions are few and far between. The result is a little less law, as such, and a little more agency discretion. One important way that that discretion has been used has been to employ rigorous empiricism to predict post-merger results. See Guidelines § 6.1 ('Where sufficient data are available, the Agencies may construct economic models designed to quantify the unilateral price effects resulting from the merger.') In *FTC* v. *Staples, Inc.*, 970 F. Supp. 1066 (D.D.C. 1997), econometric analysis predicted that a merger of two office supply 'superstores' would result in increased prices, which helped bolster a court's grant of a preliminary injunction also based on finding a narrow product market. Sophisticated analysis of switching data was relied upon to block a merger in *United States* v. *H&R Block, Inc.*, 833 F. Supp. 36 (D.D.C. 2011) whereas in *United States* v. *Oracle* Corp., 331 F. Supp. 2d 1098 (N.D. Cal. 2004) the Court found fault with DOJ's predictions as to how the merger would affect competition. For all the increased sophistication in analysis, one still finds courts being concerned about apparently excessive concentration. See *PromMedica Health Sys.* v. *FTC,* 749 F.3d 559, 570 (6th Cir. 2014) ('Even in unilateral-effects cases, at some point the Commission is entitled to take seriously the alarm sounded by a merger's HHI data.'); *United States* v. *Bazaarvoice, Inc.*, No. 13-cv-00133-WHO (N.D. Cal. 8 January 2014).

Dominant Firms

US monopoly law presents a paradox. The black letter law—the enunciated legal standards that begin any analysis—has not changed in decades.[26] Yet no area of law is 'hotter' or more in flux.

[26] The operative statutory language remains unchanged from 1890: It is unlawful to 'monopolize, or attempt to monopolize, or combine or conspire with any other person or persons, to monopolize any part of the trade or commerce among the several States, or with foreign nations … .' (15 U.S.C. § 2). Although the statute declares this conduct to be a felony, in fact it is virtually never enforced criminally. Also of relatively little importance is the third offense (conspiracy to monopolize), which largely duplicates Sherman Act Section 1 and will not be discussed in this brief review.

The basic statement of monopolization was written in 1966 and has never been displaced: 'The offense of monopoly under § 2 of the Sherman Act has two elements: (1) the possession of monopoly power in the relevant market and (2) the willful acquisition or maintenance of that power as distinguished from growth or development as a consequence of a superior product, business acumen, or historic accident'. *United States* v. *Grinnell Corp.*, 384 U.S. 563, 570–1 (1966); see also *Verizon Communications, Inc.* v. *Law Offices of Curtis V. Trinko, LLP*, 540 U.S. 398, 407 (2004). The standard phrasing of the offense of attempted monopolization comes from 1993, when the Supreme Court summarized the lower court holdings: 'Consistent with our cases, it is generally required that to demonstrate attempted monopolization a plaintiff must prove (1) that the defendant has engaged in predatory or anticompetitive conduct with (2) a specific intent to monopolize and (3) a dangerous probability of achieving monopoly power'. *Spectrum Sports, Inc.* v. *McQuillan*, 506 U.S. 447, 456 (1993) (citation omitted).

Venerable black letter law also provides the definition of monopoly power. Thus, a standard text opens its discussion of monopoly power by noting that it has 'traditionally been defined as 'the power to control market prices or exclude competition', *ABA Antitrust Section, Antitrust Law Developments* 223 (8th ed. 2017), quoting *United States* v. *E.I. duPont de Nemours & Co.*, 351 U.S. 377, 391 (1956). As with so much of US competition law, however, the challenge is in applying those vague and largely unchanged commands.

Monopoly Power

Although in principle monopoly power can be proven directly, in practice it is usually inferred from very high market shares in a well-defined product and geographic market and evidence that entry is difficult. Market definition for Section 2 cases is often informed by the Merger Guidelines approach discussed earlier, with the caveat that if a firm is currently charging a monopoly price, considering the consequences of yet a further price increase might suggest that a market is broader than it really is. (This is known as the *Cellophane* fallacy, after the Supreme Court case in which the Court appears to have made that mistake, *United States* v. *E.I. du Pont de Nemours & Co.*, 351 U.S. 377 [1956].) Although generalizations are always imperfect, most courts seem to consider a 70 per cent share sufficient to establish a prima facie case of monopoly power, and most courts regard shares below 50 per cent as insufficient. Between those two numbers lies some uncertainty.

Wilful Acquisition of Maintenance

The widespread agreement on the second part of the test for monopolization conceals the underlying conundrum: what does 'wilful acquisition or maintenance' mean? No single answer has achieved general acceptance. Perhaps the best expression is that found in the leading treatise, which defines exclusionary conduct as acts that

1. are reasonably capable of creating, enlarging, or prolonging monopoly power by impairing the opportunities of rivals; and
2. that either do not benefit consumers at all, or are unnecessary for the particular consumer benefits that the acts produce or produce harms disproportionate to the resulting benefits.

Phillip E. Areeda & Herbert Hovenkamp, Antitrust Law Para 651a, at 72 (2d ed. 2002)

The Supreme Court has given clearest guidance on predatory pricing cases. Modern predatory pricing law commenced in 1975, with publication of the seminal Areeda–Turner article. Phillip Areeda and Donald F. Turner, *Predatory Pricing and Practices under Section 2 of the Sherman Act*, 88 *Harv. L. Rev.* 697 (1975), reformulated in 3 Areeda & Hovenkamp at paras 720–49. They advocated presuming that pricing above marginal cost—or its more easily measured surrogate average variable cost—was lawful. Predatory pricing law was fundamentally changed by that 1975 article, with the result that almost no plaintiff ever won a case thereafter. The new era was enshrined by two Supreme Court cases, *Matsushita Electric Industrial Co.* v. *Zenith Radio Corp.*, 475 U.S. 574 (1986), and *Brooke Group Ltd.* v. *Brown & Williamson Tobacco Corp.*, 509 U.S. 209 (1993). After *Brooke Group*, the law was clear that a plaintiff could win a predatory pricing case only by showing both pricing below cost (the Court reserving on exactly *which* cost) and a dangerous probability of 'recouping its investment in below-cost prices'. Recoupment in turn required showing that 'the structure and conditions of the relevant market' were such as to permit sufficiently 'sustained supracompetitive pricing' to earn back all of the revenues foregone by the low pricing, with interest, 509 U.S. at 224–6. The Court extended this demanding standard to predatory bidding cases in *Weyerhaeuser Co.* v. *Ross-Simmons Hardwood Lumber Co.*, 549 U.S. 312 (2007) and then to the low-price part of a price squeeze analysis in *Pacific Bell Tel. Co.* v. *Linkline Communications, Inc.*, 555 U.S. 438 (2009).

Although that trio of Supreme Court cases establishes quite a bulwark against change, ferment continues in the Academy and it is starting to be reflected in the lower courts. New economics learning has shown that predatory pricing can be more pernicious than the Court recognized. That learning has not yet been enshrined by a court adopting an alternative test, but some courts are uneasy about the status quo. That unease has been manifested in the treatment of bundling, which courts have thus far been unwilling to treat as just another kind of predatory pricing, deserving of being viewed permissively. See *Cascade Health Solutions* v. *Peacehealth,* 515 F.3d 883 (9th Cir. 2008) (discount attribution test); *LePage's, Inc.* v. *3M*, 324 F.3d 141 (3d Cir. 2003) (en banc). Plaintiffs have been less successful in challenging loyalty discounts, see *NicSand, Inc.* v. *3M Co.*, 507 F.3d 442 (6th Cir. 2007); *Concord Boat Corp.* v. *Brunswick Corp.*, 207 F.3d 1039 (8th Cir. 2000), with a notable recent exception where the discounts formed part of a larger pattern, *ZF Meritor, LLC* v. *Eaton Corp.,* 696 F.3d 254 (3d Cir. 2012).

Some observers have attempted to borrow from the Supreme Court predatory pricing cases to craft a generalized test for identifying predatory conduct known as the 'sacrifice' or 'no economic sense' test. It is set out in its broadest form in the US antitrust agencies' amicus brief supporting the granting of certiorari in *Verizon Communications Inc.* v. *Law Offices of Curtis V. Trinko, LLP* (brief filed December 2002). That brief asserted as follows: 'Conduct is "exclusionary" or "predatory" in antitrust jurisprudence if the conduct would not make economic sense for the defendant but for its elimination or softening of competition. For example, exclusionary conduct normally involves the sacrifice of short-term profits or goodwill in order to maintain or obtain long-term monopoly power'. (Amicus brief at 10) (filed Dec. 13, 2002) (citations omitted). The subsequent government *Trinko* merits brief advanced a different 'disproportionality' test: conduct that harms competition can be unlawful when the harm is 'disproportionate to consumer benefits (in terms of providing a superior product, for example) and to the economic benefits to the defendant (aside from benefits that accrue from diminished competition)'. Amicus brief at 14 (filed 23 May 2003).

The leading alternative tests are those of Areeda–Hovenkamp set out earlier and a four-step approach offered by the en banc D.C. Circuit in *Microsoft*:

1. 'First, to be condemned as exclusionary, a monopolist's act must have an "anticompetitive effect". That is, it must harm the competitive *process* and thereby harm consumers. In contrast, harm to one or more *competitors* will not suffice.'

2. 'Second, the plaintiff … must demonstrate that the monopolist's conduct indeed has the requisite anticompetitive effect.'
3. 'Third, if a plaintiff successfully establishes a *prima facie* case under § 2 by demonstrating anticompetitive effect, then the monopolist may proffer a 'pro-competitive justification' for its conduct. If the monopolist asserts a procompetitive justification—a nonpretextual claim that its conduct is indeed a form of competition on the merits because it involves, for example, greater efficiency or enhanced consumer appeal—then the burden shifts back to the plaintiff to rebut the claim.'
4. 'Fourth, if the monopolist's pro-competitive justification stands unrebutted, then the plaintiff must demonstrate that the anticompetitive harm of the conduct outweighs the procompetitive benefit.' 253 F.3d at 58–9 (emphasis in original).

The *Microsoft* court found exclusionary conduct in license restrictions that reduced the use of a rival browser, in Microsoft's making it difficult for consumers to remove Internet Explorer, in exclusive dealing arrangements, and in a campaign of deception and coercion designed to prevent Java from undermining Microsoft's power. Other fact patterns in which the question of exclusionary conduct has been addressed include exclusive dealing (sometimes a serious concern, see *McWane, Inc.* v. *FTC,* 783 F.3d 814 [11th Cir. 2015]; *United States* v. *Dentsply Int'l, Inc.*, 399 F.3d 181 [3d Cir. 2005]); product innovation (courts are generally permissive, see *Berkey Photo, Inc.* v. *Eastman Kodak Co.*, 603 F.2d 263 [2d Cir. 1979]), but not where consumers are coerced and competition impeded, see *New York* v. *Actavis plc,* No. 14-4624 (2d Cir. 22 May 2015) (a 'product hopping' case); refusals to deal (*Verizon Communications Inc.* v. *Law Offices of Curtis V. Trinko, LLP*, 540 U.S. 398 [2004], appears to limit violations to termination of existing arrangements beneficial to consumers); essential facilities (rarely if ever a violation, see *Trinko*); intellectual property abuse (see *Actavis, supra; In re Motorola Mobility* LLC, No. C-4410 [FTC 23 July 2013] [consent order] [breaching commitments to license standard essential patents by seeking injunctions]); and miscellaneous dirty tricks and nefarious practices, see *Conwood Co.* v. *U.S. Tobacco Co.*, 290 F.3d 768 (6th Cir. 2002) (upholding $1.05 billion verdict). As the court wrote in *Caribbean Broadcasting System, Ltd.* v. *Cable & Wireless P.L.C.*, 148 F.3d 1080, 1087 (D.C. Cir. 1998), '"Anticompetitive conduct" can come in too many different forms, and is too dependent upon context, for any court or commentator ever to have enumerated all the varieties.'

Attempted Monopolization

As noted earlier, the offense of attempted monopolization requires proof of anticompetitive conduct, a specific intent to monopolize, and a dangerous probability of success in doing so. Cases rarely turn on the presence or absence of specific intent. The most litigated issue is dangerous probability of success. Results vary in part because courts regularly take market conditions and especially ease of entry into account, but it is unusual for plaintiffs to win where market shares are below 50 per cent, rare where they are below 30 per cent.

Price Discrimination

Clayton Act, Section 2, was amended in 1936 by the Robinson–Patman Act out of a populist concern for small businesses trying to compete with powerful chain stores. In general, it barred price discrimination unless justified by cost savings or the need to meet competition. It is a singularly poorly drafted statute and has been the subject of scorching criticism for its convoluted wording and its anticompetitive tendencies. The Department of Justice has sworn off enforcing it and even the FTC, which once championed it, now brings only token cases. Nor is the Supreme Court a fan, giving the Act only crabbed readings that 'construe the Act "consistently with broader policies of the antitrust laws"'. *Volvo Trucks North America, Inc.* v. *Reeder-Simco GMC, Inc.*, 126 S. Ct. 860, 873 (2006) (quoting earlier cases).

It is in private litigation that the Act retains some vitality. This brief survey cannot carefully parse the intricate words of the statute, let alone do justice to the mountain of case law interpreting it. It is enough to say that Robinson–Patman issues are raised whenever there are sales of commodities of like grade and quality in commerce where different prices are charged and thereby competition may be harmed (15 U.S.C. § 13).[27] The statute recognizes defences for cost justification, meeting competition, and changing market conditions, but each of these has been given narrow readings by the courts. Often the key issue will be the effect on competition.

[27] Other provisions of the act provide for buyer liability for inducing payment of an unlawful price, prohibit furnishing or paying for 'services or facilities' in connection with the resale of commodities unless all competing customers are offered 'proportionately equal terms,' and confusingly prohibit paying or receiving commissions or brokerage 'except for services rendered'. 15 U.S.C. § 13(c)–(f).

For what is known as 'primary line competition' (lawsuits by competitors of the firm charging the different prices) the standard is very similar if not identical to that for predatory pricing, and defendants almost always rebuff cases on summary judgment. For lawsuits by disfavoured buyers (secondary line competition), however, the lower courts continue to be willing to infer competitive injury from sustained, substantial price difference between competing customers. See *Falls City Industries, Inc.* v. *Vanco Beverage, Inc.*, 460 U.S. 428 (1983). What one might otherwise expect to be a torrent of lawsuits by unhappy recipients of higher prices is checked by a critical impediment: plaintiffs cannot recover damages simply by pointing to the higher prices they paid; rather, they 'must make some showing of actual injury attributable to something the antitrust laws were designed to prevent'. *J. Truett Payne Co.* v. *Chrysler Motors Corp.*, 451 U.S. 557, 562 (1981).

Exemptions and Immunities

Unfortunately, there is a very long list of exemptions and immunities from the US antitrust laws. Some provide complete immunity; some partial (for instance, reduction of damages from treble to single); some theoretically none, except to the extent that entrusting enforcement to a regulatory body rather than the antitrust agencies inevitably reduces the primacy of competition values. Some are statutory, some judge-made. Except as a byproduct of deregulation, none have proven easy to remove.

Other than with respect to the difficulty of eliminating exemptions, generalizations are challenging. Statutory exemptions include ones for agricultural cooperatives, insurance, labour, sports broadcasting, and various forms of communication, energy, and transportation. The most important court-made exemptions are those for petitioning government (known as the *Noerr–Pennington* doctrine), and for government action itself and the results thereof (known as the state action doctrine). Both doctrines are complicated and controversial, are frequently the subject of litigation (including at the Supreme Court), and regularly receive special attention from the antitrust agencies. *See North Carolina State Bd. of Dental Examiners* v. *FTC*, 135 S. Ct. 1101 (2015) (state board composed largely of market participants is not protected from competition review).

***

Any antitrust system—indeed, any legal system—is the product of interaction between substance and procedure. One of the glories of the US system, while also one of its challenges, is the leading role played by private enforcement (especially treble damages enforcement). The legal rules that comprise the American antitrust are clearer and more reliable because they have to be.[28] It simply will not do to trust government officials to refrain from bringing unworthy cases. In the end, trust is placed not in government officials but in the rule of law.

This overview has shown that US competition law is the product of legal evolution, informed by changes in economic understanding. The antitrust agencies play critical roles not just by filing lawsuits but also by participating in the 'antitrust conversation' by filing amicus briefs, issuing guidelines, giving speeches, doing studies, and conducting hearings and workshops.[29] That evolution continues to this day and, significantly, is increasingly global. This writer joins an increasing number of Americans in hoping that future evolution will be informed by lessons drawn from foreign competition regimes.

[28] See Stephen Calkins. 1986. 'Summary Judgment, Motions to Dismiss, and Other Examples of Equilibrating Tendencies in the Antitrust System', *Georgetown Law Journal* 74(4): 1065–161.

[29] See Stephen Calkins. 2016. *The Antitrust Conversation (Continued)*, Philip Lowe, Mel Marquis, Giorgio Monti, eds. *European Competition Law Annual* (2013), Chapter VIII.

PART III

COMPETITION LAW, ECONOMICS, AND POLICY

19

Economic Growth and Consumer Welfare*

The Role of Competition Law

Dando B. Cellini

How can governments best secure economic well-being for their citizens? Modern answers to this question have spanned a continuum ranging from centrally controlled economies where the government owns all property, to government regulation of private industries, to a *laissez faire* policy eschewing government intervention in favour of the operation of market forces. The trend in recent years has been to move away from centrally planned systems toward market-oriented systems. Even within market-oriented systems, such as the United States and Great Britain, successful initiatives have been undertaken to deregulate previously regulated industries, so as to enhance the role of market forces in shaping those industries. These changes emanate from a growing global acceptance of 'the premise that the unrestrained interaction of competitive forces will yield the best allocation of our

* Reproduced from 'Economic Growth and Consumer Welfare: The Role of Competition Law', published in Dhall, V. (ed.). 2007. *Competition Law Today: Concepts, Issues, and the Law in Practice* (first ed.), Oxford University Press, New Delhi.

The views expressed herein are the author's own, and do not purport to reflect those of the US Department of Justice.

economic resources, the lowest prices, the highest quality and the greatest material progress'.[1]

As the value of competition has become more broadly recognized, so has the need for effective legal remedies designed to preserve it. While a policy favouring the 'unrestrained interaction of competitive forces' may sound like a laissez faire policy to some, it is actually not at all the same thing. Because 'unrestrained' competition yields the lowest prices and the highest quality, market participants are frequently motivated to find ways to restrain it. Sellers do not naturally prefer to sell at low prices; they would prefer to sell at prices that yield the highest possible profits for them.[2] History is therefore rife with examples of attempts to restrain competition and legal interventions seeking to restore it. One of the most interesting of these is *The Case of the Monopolies*, which was decided in Tudor England. The English Crown had developed a practice of granting a monopolistic license known as 'letters patent' to encourage the introduction of new inventions. But Elizabeth I began issuing letters patent as a means of raising revenue, without regard to the novelty of the product. She awarded patents for such common items as brushes and pots, among other things, and provoked a public outcry.[3] When Parliament threatened legislation to curtail the practice, Elizabeth declared that the validity of the patents should be left to the common law. The issue came before the courts in 1602 when Darcy, who had obtained a monopoly from Elizabeth on the sale of playing cards, sued to enjoin Allen from engaging in the same business.[4] The court refused to do so, and struck down Darcy's patent as a monopoly which violated the common law. The court's opinion is remarkable because, although it was written more than four hundred years ago, the social costs of stifling competition that are enumerated therein mirror those that concern us today. According to the court, 'there are three inseparable incidents to every monopoly'.[5] These are:

[1] *Northern Pacific Railway Co.* v. *United States*, 356 U.S. 1 at 4, 78 S. Ct. 14 at 517 (1958).

[2] Adam Smith, the father of modern economics, who first explained the advantages of allowing the 'invisible hand' of supply and demand to allocate resources, was well aware of this threat to the public welfare. He wrote in *The Wealth of Nations* that 'People of the same trade seldom meet together, even for merriment and diversion, but the conversation ends in a conspiracy against the public, or in some contrivance to raise prices'. Adam Smith, *An Inquiry into the Nature and Causes of the Wealth of Nations*, bk. 1, ch. 10, pt.2 (1776).

[3] Miller, 'The Case of the Monopolies—Some of its Results and Suggestions', 6 MICH.L. REV. 1, 2 (1907).

[4] *Darcy* v. *Allen*, 11 Co. Rep. 846, 77 Eng. Rep. 1260 (K.B. 1602).

[5] Ibid, at 86a–b, 77 Eng. Rep. at 1262–3.

1. That the price of the same commodity will be raised, for he who has the sole selling of any commodity may and will make the price as he pleases.
2. [T]hat after the monopoly granted the commodity is not so good and merchantable as it was before: for the patentee having the sole trade, regards only his private benefit, and not the common wealth.
3. [That] it tends to the impoverishment of divers artificers and others, who before, by the labour of their hands in their art or trade, had maintained themselves and their families, who now will of necessity be constrained to live in idleness and beggary.[6]

Most of the benefits that accrue to society from open competition—lower prices, higher quality, and freedom to enter a trade or business—were therefore as clearly understood and highly valued in Tudor England as they are in our modern world. But it took centuries to develop the legal tools required to implement a broad public policy favouring competition. Although, as *The Case of the Monopolies* illustrates, some relief from anticompetitive conduct was available through English common law principles, no country enacted a comprehensive set of statutes aimed at thwarting monopolization and conspiracies to restrain trade until the United States passed its antitrust laws, known as the Sherman Act, in 1890.[7] The events leading up to the passage of the antitrust laws offer further confirmation of the proposition that, without appropriate legal constraints, businesspeople are quick to embrace opportunities to suppress competition.

The period following the end of the American Civil War was marked by rapid industrial expansion.[8] As the national output of goods increased, so did competition. Producers eager to preserve their profits sought to enter into various combinations with their competitors to limit supply, fix prices, or divide territories. These combinations were difficult to enforce, however, because they were generally regarded as falling outside of the authority granted to corporate entities by the restrictive state corporation laws of that era.[9] To circumvent this problem, the lawyer for oil tycoon John D. Rockefeller devised a means of establishing a combination of competitors using a private common law 'trust agreement'. The competitors placed their

[6] Ibid.

[7] It should be noted that Canada enacted an anti-combines law in 1889, one year before the passage of the Sherman Act, but it has been described as a 'largely symbolic' statute that had an 'insignificant' impact. Doern & Wilks, *Comparative Competition Policy* 69 (1996).

[8] Thorelli, *The Federal Antitrust Policy* 63 (1955).

[9] Kintner, I., *Federal Antitrust Law* 106 (1980).

corporations into the trust and received in return trust certificates representing an equivalent proportionate value of all the properties held by the trust. Employing this contractual instrument, which was thought to be beyond the reach of state corporation laws, a successful trust could dominate an entire industry. The first of these trust combinations, Rockefeller's Standard Oil Trust, did exactly that, bringing under its control approximately 90 to 95 per cent of the nation's refining capacity.[10] The lure of being able to control prices and output for an entire industry was so great that, almost immediately following the formation of the Standard Oil Trust, former competitors in other lines of business joined hands to create the Sugar Trust, the Whiskey Trust, the Lead Trust, the Match Trust, the Copper Trust, the Zinc Trust, the Castor Oil Trust, and many others.[11] The trusts were almost immediately and universally condemned, with both the Democratic Party and the Republican Party vigorously supporting legislation that would make them illegal. In 1890 the Sherman Act, which contained the country's first federal 'antitrust' laws, was passed unanimously by both houses of Congress and signed into law. In sweeping language, the Act delineates two guiding principles for protecting competition, leaving the courts to sort out what conduct violates those principles. Section one of the Act prohibits contracts, combinations, or conspiracies in restraint of trade, and section two of the Act prohibits monopolization and attempts or conspiracies to monopolize.[12]

For many years thereafter, the United States remained the only country with a statutory ban on anticompetitive practices and enforcement mechanisms in place to compel compliance with the ban.[13] After World War II, however, other jurisdictions began to adopt competition laws. Most significantly, a competition policy was incorporated into the Treaty of Rome, which created the European Economic Community in 1958. In general language which correlates with Sections one and two of the Sherman Act, Article 85 of the Treaty prohibited agreements and concerted practices which have as their object or effect the distortion of competition, and Article 86 of the Treaty prohibited the abuse of a dominant position. As member states of the European Economic Community, now known as the European Union or EU, gradually began enacting their own competition laws, the Treaty of Rome's Articles 85 and 86 served as a model for these

[10] Ibid.

[11] Ibid.

[12] 15 U.S.C §§ 1 & 2.

[13] The US Congress first appropriated funds specifically designated for antitrust enforcement in 1903.

laws. For example, Italy's competition law not only generally tracks the language of the Treaty of Rome Articles but also specifically provides that the Italian law 'shall be interpreted in accordance with the principles' of the EU competition law.[14]

The global trend toward adoption of competition law regimes accelerated dramatically after 1990. A comprehensive study on the subject published in 1998 reported that, as of the end of 1996, 70 countries had enacted competition laws, and 61 per cent of these had done so since 1990.[15] The trend has continued unabated, with approximately 30 more jurisdictions enacting competition legislation since then, bringing the total number of countries that now have such laws to over 100.[16] Better than 70 per cent of that total have put their competition laws into effect since 1990. The trend can be accounted for by examining a congeries of events that have influenced political, social, and economic thinking over the last 15 years.

1990 saw the collapse of the Berlin Wall and the reunification of East and West Germany. The two Germanys had emerged together out of the rubble of World War II, one employing a centrally planned economic system and the other employing a market-based economic system. They offered a stark real-world experiment demonstrating the benefits each economic system could produce for its citizens. Reunification put the deficiencies of central planning on display in the harshest light, fuelling demands for reform in other state-controlled economies. Within the next two years, the Soviet Union had disintegrated into 15 newly formed independent countries. These countries as well as others which had relied on central planning began the process of moving toward a market-based orientation. The adoption of a competition law regime became a commonly implemented reform for these economies in transition. The EU was instrumental in encouraging this reform by requiring countries seeking to join the EU or to gain access to the EU's market to adopt a competition law.[17] However, given the political climate of that time, even countries geographically remote from the EU were motivated to take steps toward implementing a market economy. For example, Mexico

[14] Competition and Fair Trading Act (1990) at Section 1.4, available in English at the Italian Competition Authority's website, http://www.agcm.it.

[15] Palim, 'The Worldwide Growth of Competition Law: An Empirical Analysis', XLIII *Antitrust Bull.* 105, 109 (1998).

[16] International Competition Network: A Statement of Mission and Achievement Up until May 2005, p. 2, available at http://www.internationalcompetitionnetwork.org.

[17] Palim supra n. 15, at 120–3.

enacted a Federal Law of Economic Competition in 1992, and India introduced market-oriented reforms in the early 1990s, which eventually led to the enactment of its Competition Act in 2002.

1990 also marked the introduction of new and important ideas about what national policies best promote economic growth and consumer welfare. In that year, Michael Porter published a highly influential treatise called *The Competitive Advantage of Nations*. Porter, an economist and professor at the Harvard Business School, had won international acclaim during the preceding decade for his studies of competitive strategies within industries and firms. In the late 1980s, with the support of the Harvard Business School and other institutions, he launched a massive multinational study which sought to explain why the environments in some nations seemed to be more stimulating to advancement and progress than in other nations. Porter set forth the conclusions he reached as a result of that study in his treatise. He begins by positing that 'The principal economic goal of a nation is to produce a high and rising standard of living for its citizens', and then goes on to examine what governmental policies are likely to promote the achievement of that goal, and what governmental policies are likely to impede it.[18] Porter found that 'Few roles of government are more important to the upgrading of an economy than ensuring vigorous domestic rivalry'.[19] He describes the association between vigorous domestic rivalry and the creation and persistence of competitive advantage as '[a]mong the strongest empirical findings from our research'.[20] As a result, 'The importance of domestic rivalry for national advantage has strong implications for antitrust policy.'[21]

Porter argues that strict enforcement of competition laws encourages the continual improvement and innovation that drive a nation's industries to produce economic growth. His review of more than 100 historical case studies yielded few examples of 'national champions' or firms with unrivalled domestic positions that were internationally competitive, even though such firms were often heavily subsidized by government. On the contrary, he found that nations with leading world positions in successful industries often have a number of strong local rivals.[22] In summarizing the findings of his extensive empirical analysis, Porter unambiguously concludes that 'strict antitrust laws' are 'beneficial', and declares that 'my evidence seriously questions the wisdom

[18] Porter, *The Competitive Advantage of Nations* 6 (1990).

[19] Ibid., at 662.

[20] Ibid., at 117.

[21] Ibid., at 662.

[22] Ibid., at 117.

of … regulation that limits competition'.[23] Over the course of the ensuing years, many other studies, often carried out under the auspices of international organizations, confirmed the linkage Porter perceived between the vigorous enforcement of competition laws and economic growth. A World Bank research project published in 2000 examined data from over 100 countries for the ten-year period from 1989 through 1995 to determine whether higher levels of domestic competition are significantly correlated with faster current and future rates of per capita economic growth, and reached the following conclusion: 'Our findings indicate that the effectiveness of antitrust and competition policy enforcement is positively associated with long-run growth.'[24] By 2002, a report issued by the United Nations Conference on Trade and Development (UNCTAD) could confidently assert that 'the positive interaction between competition, competitiveness, and development seems to be indisputable'.[25]

However, accepting the principle that effective competition law enforcement promotes economic growth does not ensure that its promise will be fulfilled; there remain substantial obstacles that must be overcome. As noted above, more than 70 per cent of the competition law regimes in the world today are of relatively recent vintage, having been adopted within the last 15 years. Many of them are in countries still in the process of evolving away from command and control economies that had long been in place. In such environments, policymakers may be loathe to abandon familiar regulatory structures in favour of the operation of market mechanisms. Indeed, even in the United States, which has the world's longest history of competition law enforcement, it has taken many years to convince policymakers to introduce economic deregulation into key industries such as airlines, trucking, railroads, banking, and natural gas. Yet the gains realized by opening these industries up to competitive forces have been remarkable. One study found that, after deregulation, each of these industries 'has significantly improved its service quality and reduced its real average prices from 30 to 75 per cent'.[26]

[23] Ibid., at Preface, p. xvi.

[24] Dutz and Hayri, 'Does More Intense Competition Lead to Higher Growth?', World Bank, Development Research Group, April 2000, Working Paper #2320, available at http://www.worldbank.org/research/growth.

[25] UNCTAD, 'The Relationship Between Competition, Competitiveness and Development' at 17 (2002), available at UNCTAD Competition Policy website, competition documents page.

[26] Winston, 'U.S. Industry Adjustment to Economic Deregulation', 12 *J. Econ. Persp.* 89 at 100 (1998).

Competition policy advocates will, of course, continue to meet resistance from those who are hostile to the operation of free markets, but circumstances have never been more favourable than they are now for promoting what many have begun to call a 'culture of competition'.[27] The adoption of broadly similar competition laws by legislative bodies all over the world signals an emerging consensus that certain types of economic harm, such as price fixing or abuse of a dominant position, can be dealt with effectively through statutory prohibition. Before these laws were enacted, the available choices would have been to address such harm through government regulation or control, or to leave it unaddressed. Now the proliferation of competition law regimes has created a new paradigm, and those charged with enforcing these laws have become its principal proponents. Under this paradigm, market forces are given free rein to allocate a nation's resources with an efficiency government regulation or control cannot match, thereby maximizing economic growth and consumer welfare. The enforcement authority created by the competition law regime intervenes only when a distortion that impedes the free operation of market forces occurs or is threatened, and then only to the extent necessary to correct the distortion, so competitive vigour can be maintained. Entrusted with the duty of protecting the market mechanism, the competition enforcement authority in each jurisdiction quite naturally assumes the complementary role of chief advocate for the market mechanism in that jurisdiction. The more than 100 competition law regimes currently in place thus have a shared interest in promoting a culture of competition.

Increasingly, international agencies and forums are playing a vital role in contributing to the creation of a competition culture. The Paris-based Organization for Economic Co-Operation and Development (OECD) has a Competition Committee that brings together senior competition law officials from its 30 industrialized country members on a regular basis. The goal of these meetings is to identify best practices in competition law policy and enforcement, foster convergence among national competition policies, and promote increased cooperation among competition enforcement agencies. In 2001, the OECD created a Global Forum on Competition to promote regular discussions on an annual basis between competition officials of OECD members and a large group of developing country non-members. The United Nations Conference on Trade and Development convenes a group of

[27] See, for example, Hon. Timothy J. Muris, 'Creating a Culture of Competition: The Essential Role of Competition Advocacy', speech before International Competition Network (28 September 2002), available at http://www.ftc.gov/speeches/.

competition experts at least once a year to discuss competition policy issues. It also offers technical assistance and conducts studies on competition topics. The World Bank provides financial assistance and expertise to newly-formed national competition agencies. Even the World Trade Organization, which historically has focused only on trade policy issues, formed a Working Group on the Interaction between Trade and Competition Policy, which met actively until 2003. Most notably, in 2001 the International Competition Network (ICN) was established as the first international body comprised exclusively of competition agencies and devoted exclusively to competition law enforcement and advocacy. ICN's membership includes 94 competition authorities from 83 jurisdictions.

Three major factors appear to account for the heightened focus on competition law today at both the national and the international level. The first of these is widespread acceptance of Michael Porter's insight that vigorous domestic competition upgrades a nation's economy, producing prosperity at home while better equipping the nation's industries to compete internationally. Industry rivals engage in a continuous struggle to gain competitive advantage over each other by making countless market-driven adjustments to improve products and services. By offering the least intrusive way to protect this dynamic struggle against economic abuses, competition law maximizes economic growth and consumer welfare.

The second major factor influencing the growing attention being given to competition law is, in a sense, the flip side of the same coin as the first factor: recognizing that competition law is the best way to protect against economic abuses also means recognizing that government regulation or control are less good alternatives. As global competition intensifies, the social costs of maintaining regulatory regimes where decisions are necessarily based upon incomplete and inadequate market information are coming under increasingly close scrutiny. Nations striving to create economically vibrant environments can ill afford manipulated allocations of resources and artificial barriers to entry and exit. Evidence of the benefits of economic deregulation continues to mount, so it can be anticipated that policymakers will face increasing pressure from competition advocates to broaden the scope of competition law regimes at the expense of regulatory regimes.

The last and perhaps the least well-anticipated factor driving the burgeoning national and international interest in competition law is the elimination of time and distance constraints on so many activities in the global marketplace by recent advances in telecommunications. Thomas Friedman observed in a recent best-selling book that 'it is now possible for more people than ever to collaborate and compete in real time with more other people on more different kinds of work from more different corners of the planet and on a more equal footing than at any previous time in the history of the world—using computers, e-mail, networks, teleconferencing, and dynamic new software.'[28] This change has occurred with startling rapidity—really in just the last few years. Today laptop computers are being jointly designed by teams located in Texas and Taiwan.[29] Presentations for the clients of New York investment banking firms are being prepared in Chennai.[30] An Indian employee of an American firm retained by these investment bankers has said that 'In these last years, we've found that New York and Chennai can do the same things—that we almost are the same thing. Already, we are half of the time in New York, just our bodies are left behind.'[31]

Because the new technology is no respecter of national borders, a global common language will have to be developed to discuss business practices that employ it. That common language is competition law. The fundamental tenets adopted by competition law regimes all over the world are largely the same: price fixing, bid rigging, territorial allocation, monopolistic practices, and abuse of dominance are forbidden, and mergers are, for the most part, subject to some sort of review process. International forums are in place that provide venues for improving our understanding of what business practices promote the goals of economic growth and consumer welfare, and what business practices stifle them. The common language of competition law will continue to evolve as the global economy continues to evolve, but a fruitful dialogue is already well underway.

[28] Friedman, *The World Is Flat* 8 (2005).

[29] Ibid., at 415.

[30] Katherine Boo, 'The Best Job in Town', *The New Yorker*, 5 July 2004, p. 54 at 56.

[31] Ibid., at 65.

20

The Economics of Competition Law*

Amit Bubna and Shubhashis Gangopadhyay

Competition law, broadly, relates to efforts at promoting competition through legislative means. In a world increasingly familiar with and favouring laissez-faire economics, the use of non-market methods for promoting competition offers an apparent disconnect with the 'free market' notion. The ostensible purpose of free market is to allow for the operation of market forces rather than non-market methods such as licensing. So how do we justify the existence and, indeed, an increased adoption of competition law by countries, both developed and developing? Might there after all be an economic rationale?

A competition law primarily has three main items on its agenda. First and foremost, it aims to control the formation of oligopolies and cartelization of economic activities. Firms colluding to fix prices would be subject to the terms of competition law. Second, competition law concerns itself with affecting the workings of existing monopolies. For instance, competition law may constrain a natural monopoly (that is, a firm in an industry where the market *naturally* only supports the existence of one firm) attempting to set a price that may be considered 'excessive'. Finally, competition law also aims to prevent firm

* Reproduced from 'The Economics of Competition Law', published in Dhall, V. (ed.). 2007. *Competition Law Today: Concepts, Issues, and the Law in Practice* (first ed.), Oxford University Press, New Delhi.

actions that serve to extend, or move the market towards, a monopoly. Supplier actions, such as offers of exclusive territorial rights to retailers that reduce retailers' incentive to compete, are potentially subject to competition law.

It is amply clear that 'competition' in competition law is a misnomer. It deals not so much with competition but its complement, namely the lack of competition. Economists have traditionally been interested in the workings and effects of competition and how they are blocked by oligopoly or firms with market power. So, the link between economics and competition law is a natural one. However, what are less obvious are the economic arguments behind competition law.

The Objective of Competition Law

Before we explore the economic rationale for competition law, we must briefly investigate the ultimate objective of such a law. Should it be to enhance welfare? Whose welfare or, who is the intended beneficiary?

In the simplest economic model, welfare is maximized under perfectly competitive markets. Suppose there are constant returns to scale, that is, where the cost of producing a unit is independent of the number of units produced. In this case, welfare can be measured simply as consumer surplus. Consumer surplus is the difference between the consumer's valuation of the good (a measure of her willingness to pay for the good) and the price she pays for it. Under constant returns to scale, firms make zero profit and hence, welfare is equated to the surplus available to the consumer from the purchase of the product. In other words, consumer surplus and welfare are equivalent. The lower the price, all else unchanged, the greater is the consumer surplus. Thus, the objective of maximizing consumer surplus would suggest that competition law needs to focus only on reducing the price of a product. However, it would also imply that any action that could create efficiencies in *production* but increase prices for consumers ought to be disallowed under the competition law that seeks to solely increase consumer surplus.[1]

The emphasis on 'consumer' in consumer surplus is based on a distinction between buyers and sellers. However, the difference between these two classes of economic players is more imagined than real, even more so today. With more mature capital markets and increased capital market participation either directly or indirectly through mutual funds, etc., more and more consumers are also owners of firms. Thus, even if the objective of competition law were to

[1] We later discuss other non-redistributive reasons why price may not be the appropriate policy variable for addressing competition issues.

maximize consumer surplus, an exclusive focus on the buyers, or consumers, would only partially fulfil the stated objective. In the extreme case, there would be no difference between buyers and sellers, so that maximizing consumer surplus should imply maximizing both consumer and producer surplus. In fact, the outcome that maximizes the sum of consumer and producer surpluses is what economists refer to as an 'efficient' outcome. Therefore, overall efficiency could be an alternative objective of competition law.

It may be argued that not all consumers are investors, particularly in developing countries with large income disparities. As such, there could be a 'disconnect' between maximizing consumer surplus and total surplus. Yet, it is unclear whether this would justify an objective of maximizing consumer surplus. The exclusive focus on low prices for consumers rather than firm profits effectively serves to redistribute incomes from firms to consumers. To use competition law as a vehicle for income redistribution appears inappropriate. Maximizing the total surplus is a measure of how efficient a given industry is as a whole. So, competition law that focuses on attaining overall efficiency would increase the size of the pie. Thereafter, other mechanisms may be more effective in redistribution between both groups of economic agents such that, at least in theory, both are better off (Pareto superior outcome). Alternative fiscal tools could achieve the redistribution purpose without additionally distorting incentives of economic players, as would likely result under competition law focusing on consumer welfare alone.

In general, for welfare maximization, it is necessary that the price of the product be equal to the cost of producing an additional unit of the product (or, that price equals marginal cost). However, it is not essential that firms make zero profit. Consider, for instance, a pure monopolist who can charge a different price to each of its customers (that is, perfect price discrimination). In fact, the monopolist would set the price to equal the good's value to each consumer. Such a monopolist is able to extract the entire consumer surplus as profit. And yet, production will be at a level where price charged to the marginal consumer equals marginal cost. And, the necessary condition for welfare maximization will be achieved. In other words, maximization of welfare is not the same thing as the maximization of consumer surplus.

So, what has competition got to do with maximizing the welfare of society? For a monopolist to perfectly discriminate among its buyers, it must be the case that it is not possible for one buyer to interact with the other buyers (market segmentation). Otherwise, the buyer who pays the lower price can sell to the buyer who is asked to pay a higher price by the monopolist. Those being asked to pay the higher prices would prefer to not buy from the monopolist but from those buyers who are paying the lower price(s). This will destroy the monopolist's ability to price-discriminate, forcing the monopolist to charge one price to all its buyers. We are back to the case of a standard monopoly where it is optimal for the monopolist not to set price equal to marginal cost. And that destroys efficiency and reduces welfare. A competitive market, on the other hand, gets us efficiency precisely when buyers cannot be segmented.[2]

A related question is—should competition law protect small firms from large firms with deep pockets? Such an (equity-based) objective need not be at odds with the efficiency argument if the law prevents anticompetitive behaviour by large firms, such as predatory pricing. However, if the law goes further and protects or encourages small inefficient firms to continue in existence (through subsidies or a price floor, for instance), it would provide a drain on scarce economic resources and further encourage the growth of an industry with little or no incentive to increase operational efficiency. Even in industries characterized by economies of scale, no firm would have an incentive to grow beyond a certain size. It would prefer to continue to benefit from the shelter competition law offers. While there may be other reasons for supporting small and medium enterprises, it is not clear whether competition law is the appropriate tool and whether competition authority's meagre resources ought to be used for such an objective. Moreover, it seems inappropriate to restrain or put firms, albeit large but possibly efficient, at a disadvantage for reasons unrelated to their actions or market structure.

For the rest of the discussion, we will assume that the objective of competition law is to maximize total surplus rather than to pursue redistributive goals.

The Economics of Monopoly

The economics of competition law has been closely related to that of monopoly. In this section, we explore possible reasons for this association.

A monopoly, by definition, is a market structure with only one seller. Any consumer seeking the product is constrained to buying it from the monopolist. However, this constraint per se would be no basis for competition law. If the monopolist were altruistic, for instance, and offered the product for free, it can hardly justify regulatory intervention. Alternatively, if demand were perfectly elastic, price will always equal marginal cost. Thus, more than

[2] Various other arguments have been forwarded for focusing on consumer welfare. Unlike producers, consumers may be larger in number and more dispersed. Free rider problems may disadvantage consumers from lobbying the legislature while industry organizations lobby for adoption of producer-friendly regulation. But such arguments would apply to all regulations, not just to competition law.

the number of sellers, it is critical to know whether the seller has any market power, that is, the ability to price the product above its marginal cost.

In reality, most economic activities are undertaken with a profit motive. So, a profit-maximizing monopolist chooses a price for its product, constrained in this process only by the demand it faces. In a standard monopoly setting, the monopolist charges a price that the marginal consumer is willing to pay, which exceeds the cost of producing the unit sold to the marginal consumer. The monopolist has market power. As a result, the buying consumer is paying more and hence is worse off. But this in itself need not comprise an argument for competition law. After all, the price a consumer pays is what a firm's owner receives. (Recall the constant returns to scale example and the perfectly discriminating monopolist referred to in the last section.) Regardless of whether the price is high or low, a payment for a product is merely a transfer from one economic agent to another. Surely, controlling such transfers among economic agents cannot be the motive behind competition law.

The alleged inefficiencies lie elsewhere. Since the monopoly price exceeds the cost of producing an extra unit, there are consumers whose value for the product exceeds the cost of producing it but is not high enough to justify paying the price being asked for. Herein lies the inefficiency. Unsatisfied demand could be met by lowering the price while continuing to cover the cost incurred in producing it.[3] A monopolist with market power does not have the incentive to do so. It maximizes its profit by charging a high price, resulting in (allocative) inefficiency or deadweight loss.

There is another source of inefficiency. Monopoly is attractive from a producer's perspective. The ability to price above cost allows supernormal profits, that is, profits over and above the opportunity cost of the inputs used. Each firm, therefore, would have an incentive to acquire such market power. Competition for such access could take place through the use of political influence or lobbying. Existing monopolists too could seek to further their market power to increase the monopoly rents. In these endeavours, firms would be willing to spend real (scarce) resources up to the rent they expect to earn from their monopoly power, if successful. However, even in the extreme case where the monopolist earns zero expected profit after such lobbying activity, society as a whole is worse off. Real resources would have been spent in the firms' rent-seeking activities, without any corresponding benefit to

[3] Imagine a perfectly inelastic demand where consumers are willing to pay up to a certain maximum. The monopolist obviously uses its market power by setting the price at that maximum. Lowering the price will not affect that demand and hence, the production. Thus, in this extreme case, the seller has market power but it does not lead to inefficiency.

society from the use of those resources. The possibility of market power is therefore unproductive.

Finally, an important consequence of competition as against a monopoly is to force firms to operate in the most efficient manner. Efficiency may be thought of in terms of the choice of technology, operation, management, etc.; anything that leads to reducing costs and hence, the conservation of resources. In general, firms that choose an inefficient input-mix will have a higher cost of production. This will have an adverse impact on the bottom-line. Unless all firms in a competitive market are equally inefficient, the firms with higher costs of production will be unable to keep their price low enough compared to the more efficient firms. As a consequence, inefficient firms will be driven out of the market. Such a process does not work in a monopoly since there are no other firms whom the monopolist has to out-sell. Competition ensures that a firm has the incentive to find newer and better ways of reducing cost; otherwise, someone else will reduce their cost of production and take the market away from them. It is this pressure to reduce costs that the monopolist never faces and therefore, does not feel motivated to search for better technologies that conserve scarce resources. This is unacceptable from a societal perspective. Similar arguments may be made with respect to the other aspects, such as managerial incentives and operational efficiency.[4]

Role of Competition Law in Addressing Inefficiencies

Could Lower Price Address Allocative Inefficiency?

How may the inefficiencies be addressed? Given that a high price, under market power of firms, lies at the heart of these inefficiencies, it would appear that a lower price would be a natural resolution. (Note that the objective of a lower price is not driven by considerations of equity or consumer welfare but by the inefficiencies resulting from the existence of market power with the suppliers). One mechanism could be for the competition commission (or any other regulatory authority) to impose a price ceiling. For eliminating the allocative inefficiency, the price would have to be set at a level such that the monopolist has an incentive to produce enough to meet the demand at that price.

[4] It is worth pointing out that there are conditions under which increased competition may also reduce efficiency. For instance, if a firm is already under financial distress, the disciplining role of competition could be lower. See Schmidt, K.S. (1997), 'Managerial Incentives and Product Market Competition', *Review of Economic Studies* 64, pp. 277–84.

However, the task of setting the price is easier said than done. To begin with, it imposes a severe monitoring responsibility on the commission, which could be infeasible. More importantly, price-setting assumes that the regulator knows what the correct price ought to be, which in turn assumes that it has information on the industry cost structure as well as consumer preferences. This can hardly be true. So any price that may be set by a regulator is most likely to be inaccurate. In the face of errors in price-setting, the allocative inefficiencies could actually be aggravated compared to when there is no such intervention. At too low a price, production will be less and, even among the consumers, the benefit will accrue only to those who manage to get the good. The ones who are thereby rationed are worse-off than they would be under a higher price. In fact, rationing itself leads to a waste of resources. Interested buyers may have to waste time in queues or in lobbying to successfully get an allocation of the good. Similar arguments could be used for a policy that fixes the quantity to be produced by a monopolist rather than the price.

Could Increasing the Number of Firms Eliminate Inefficiency?

An important factor driving the inefficiencies is that there is one firm in the market. So, a possible solution to a monopoly is to increase the number of participating firms in the market. After all, classical economics defines a competitive market in terms of a large number of players. However, the premise of having many firms in an industry to eliminate monopoly inefficiencies is questionable.

It could be argued that on occasion, monopoly may be a temporary situation. The determination of market power or lack thereof based on the number of players could be misleading. A monopolist, despite being the only producer in the industry, seldom operates in a vacuum. It must take into account the threat of entry. If a market is seen to be profitable, it is likely to attract other firms. A monopolist must consider this possibility of increased future competition when determining its price. So, the fear of entry could keep a monopolist's market power in check. Indeed, this is the conclusion of the 'Contestable Markets' theory, suggesting that there is little scope for a competition policy that concentrates on the number of firms in an industry.

Another argument questioning the focus on number of participants is based on the role of consumers and the nature of the product rather than of potential entrants. A monopolist may initially charge a higher price for the consumers who value the product more. In the future though, he would be inclined to reduce the price to cater to the lower-valuation consumers. However, knowing this, the higher-valuation consumer would rationally wait to buy until the price has been lowered. Consequently, the monopolist is constrained to sell all its units at a low uniform price. Despite there being only one producer, there is little or no market power. This theory of durable goods is another argument against focusing on the number of participants and their market share as the basis for competition policy.

Increasing the number of firms in a monopoly market may itself promote inefficiencies. A society's welfare depends not just on what may be currently available but also on innovation. Imagine a world without personal computers and airplanes, or for that matter trains. Our lives are defined by innovations—to production processes as well as new products. Dynamic efficiency refers to the benefits that flow from innovation. What is the role of a monopoly in innovation?

Like any other economic decision, a firm would choose to innovate if its resulting profit (X) exceeds profit without innovating (Y). In a competitive market, Y is zero, that is, a firm in a perfectly competitive market earns zero profits (that is, $Y = 0$). Thus, a competitive firm would innovate as long as the resulting profit, X, is positive. However, a monopolist earns supernormal profits, that is, $Y > 0$. Therefore, the profit threshold for the monopolist to be willing to innovate is higher than that for a competitive firm. A monopolist has less to lose from not innovating. Differently put, a competitive firm has more to gain from innovating than a monopolist. Therefore, the absence of competition may lead to dynamic inefficiency as well. This may provide additional justification for competition policy.

In reality, the empirical evidence on the link between monopoly and R&D efforts is mixed. Popular wisdom worldwide would suggest that firms need to be offered a patent to enable them to reap the benefits of innovation. A monopoly, through an ex post patent, serves to provide ex ante incentive for necessary investment. Such incentives are particularly critical for innovations that may be easily replicated.

Last but not the least, no competition commission can increase the number of firms by decree. The most it can do is ensure that whoever wants to enter the market as a producer is able to do so. In other words, competition policy can work towards what is known in the economics literature as 'free entry'. As long as the economy allows free entry, a monopolist faces a threat from potential entrants and, therefore, may be disciplined to keep prices low.

Could Free Entry Provide the Solution?

The theory of contestable markets provides a good rationale for promoting free entry. If the monopolist charges high prices, its profit would be high, encouraging potential entrants to enter the market and compete with the incumbent producer. This will force the monopolist to charge low prices and take in less profits than would have been the case if there were no potential entrants. However, if a monopolist is already unable to exploit its market power, because of a threat of entry, forcing or inducing entry will be sub-optimal. Consequently, a competition commission should not penalize a monopolist firm for charging low prices!

The strength of this approach (promoting free entry) lies in the minimal information burden imposed on the (competition) commission, unlike the other suggestions based on fixing price or quantity. It puts the onus of determining entry decision on individual players who have private information on their costs rather than the commission making guesses about each potential entrant's cost structure and magnitude. While the contestable markets theory is not without its drawbacks (which we discuss later), it points to the important role and benefits of free entry for competition policy.

How does one check whether or not there is free entry in a market? More often than not, free entry per se will be a counterfactual. The starting point itself is that there is a monopoly in the market. So, how easy or difficult it is for other firms to enter cannot be determined by looking at the number of active firms in the market. It becomes necessary to examine whether the decision of potential competitors to stay out of a market is voluntary. If there are factors which force firms to stay out of the monopoly market, then there would be a role for competition policy. In particular, one needs to determine whether there are forces other than contestability that have resulted in a monopoly.

Besides contestability, an important reason for lack of entry could be due to a fundamental asymmetry between the incumbent monopolist and a potential entrant. For instance, the monopolist, by virtue of being 'in' has already expended its setup cost. The entrant, since it is yet to get in, is yet to undertake the setup cost. This allows the monopolist to compete more aggressively with the entrant than what the entrant can do with the monopolist. In particular, it allows the monopolist to consider the following strategy: undercut the entrant and force it to make losses should it enter. The monopolist itself may make losses during this phase of undercutting but in the process it will force out the entrant. At least a part of these losses will be recovered later when it has successfully driven out the entrant and is able to return to monopoly pricing. The monopolist will do this if the resultant profit is higher than what it will get if both firms supply the market. The potential entrant, knowing that this is how the monopolist will behave, stays out. Thus, in this case, lack of entry is achieved through (the threat of) a temporary price reduction followed by monopoly pricing once entry has been successfully deterred.

Therefore, an important role of competition policy would be to remove market features that increase entry costs. This would reduce the ability of the incumbent to credibly commit to an aggressive price war (since, loosely speaking, a low entry cost allows the entrant to fight a longer battle). Second, since entry costs can seldom be brought down to zero, competition policy must also reduce the ability of the monopolist to follow an aggressive price-cutting strategy with the intention of increasing price later.

Alternatively, new entrants could be offered price-based incentives, for example, subsidized credit to cover setup costs. Ignoring a discussion on whether the competition commission can require financial institutions to offer such credit, there remains a bigger issue of whether this is an efficient form of intervention for promoting competition, or rather to increase the number of participants in the market. As before, this assumes that the commission has a fairly good idea of what the optimal number of participants ought to be so as to determine the extent of subsidy to offer. Such an assumption is clearly unrealistic. On the contrary, if there is a belief that firms find it difficult to obtain credit for starting a new venture, then the appropriate policy is not to offer a subsidy to prospective borrowers but to tackle the source of the problem in the capital markets.

While the theory of contestable markets and durable goods offer good reasons for not focusing competition policy on the number of players, they cannot be taken at face value. The role of threat of entry in disciplining a monopolist under the contestable markets theory relies on the monopolist's inability to change its price when there is entry. This need not be the case. A monopolist may be able to commit to reducing prices in case of entry. Commitment could take the form of having excess capacity, for instance, whereby the monopolist would easily increase production in the face of entry, lowering prices and making it unprofitable for the entrant. Such a possibility (discussed earlier) would in turn deter the potential entrant from entering the market to begin with. Thus, free entry is not a sufficient condition for a competitive environment.

In the context of durable goods, the monopolist's above-discussed inability to charge a high price assumes that the monopolist is unable to commit to charging a high price in the future. Such an assumption need not hold. For instance, the seller may offer a price guarantee (enforceable) contract promising to refund the difference to a previous buyer if the seller were to reduce the price later. On the face of it, such an offer may seem innocuous, and in fact, beneficial to consumers. It may actually play a role that may help in monopoly pricing. Under such a scheme, the seller would be reluctant to lower the price for future buyers. Doing so imposes an extra burden, that of compensating the past buyers too. Hence, the monopolist may use a contract to commit to not lowering its future price. Such a commitment will therefore enable the seller to charge a monopoly price. Whether or not a market will have monopoly pricing would depend on, among other factors, the nature of the product and actions of the players.

While ensuring free entry is desirable for competition policy, the task of determining this feature in a market is not a straight-forward one. A necessary ingredient for any chance of success is to distinguish between ex post observations and ex ante incentives.

Ex-Ante versus Ex-Post Market Environment

Anticompetitive rules must consider the exante market environment and incentives rather than focus exclusively on ex post situations. There may exist sound economic reasons for arrangements between participants that may appear ex post anticompetitive. Consider a situation of the producer of automobile spares for a particular car company (or brand). The parts producer is often required by explicit contract to produce for this one car company only. It is not allowed to store, produce, or sell any other company's product. Nor is it allowed to sell its products to anyone but the car company with which it has the contract. And, most often, the price of its spares is pre-determined and seldom open to negotiation at the time of actual sales. Clearly, the spare parts producer has very little flexibility and is completely tied to the 'parent' car company.

Is this anticompetitive behaviour? Ex post, at the time the actual sale of spares takes place, it does look a bit anticompetitive. For instance, even if the spare parts producer has excess capacity and can produce more spares for *other* cars, it is not allowed to do so. However, if the competition policy tries to prevent such contracts, it will be counter-productive in terms of efficiency. Typically, to produce for a particular car company, the spare parts producer needs to make investments specific to the car (or, company). Such specific investments improve the quality of pre-specified spares but make it very costly to use the same investment for producing alternative specifications of similar spares required by other car manufacturers. Exclusivity agreements that limit what the parts producer can do actually enables such investments to be made; without them it can be demonstrated that such investments will not be made. With such restrictive clauses, the quality of spares, and hence of the cars, go up. Thus, what is ex post uncompetitive was ex ante efficient.

Such ex ante and ex post distinctions are also very important when one talks of free exit as a necessary condition for competition. Consider a firm in financial distress—a firm unable to meet its financial obligations. Creditors to the firm will want such a firm to be liquidated so that they can collect their dues. However, it is also true that often, when a firm is liquidated, there is some deadweight loss. Such losses could result from the fact that the skill generated among the workers working in a team is lost. Indeed, the value of a company is usually more than the sum of the market valuation of its resources. Alternatively put, the going concern value is more than the sum of the values of its assets. This has led many to argue that it is not good to allow bankrupt firms to close down. Instead, creditor claims should be restructured (rescheduled or reduced) so that the firm can continue as a producing entity. Even if such a move is ex post efficient, it has serious consequences for ex ante efficiency.

When such restructuring occurs, contracts with creditors are violated. At the time of making the loan, the creditor assumed a risk of default on the loan and imputed a value of the loan at risk. Any attempt at continuing with a firm through a (forcefully) restructured claim schedule means that the value of the loan at risk goes down from the level it was assumed by the creditor at the time of making the loan. Simply put, the ability of the creditor to realize its dues is reduced. If the creditor can predict that this will happen, and it will be able to do so if the bankruptcy policies are such, it will increase the cost of the loans it makes. In a capital scarce economy this will hamper investment, and hence, new entry.

Thus, the effectiveness of any competition policy will have to rely crucially on its ability to separate ex post observations and ex ante incentives.

The upshot of our discussion is that it is difficult to completely codify what constitutes competitive behaviour and what is anticompetitive. There are no rules of thumb. Each industry and each firm has to be dealt with separately. The focus should be on the behaviour of firms under specific situations. An action may be found to be perfectly legitimate in one case but anticompetitive in another. What is certainly clear is that the competition policy must avoid simplistic solutions, such as setting 'competitive' prices of goods, both because it is economically unsound and also since it may do more harm than good.

The most important element is for the competition policy to be 'enabling' rather than 'directive' or interventionist. Consider the pre-nineties Indian policy of not allowing firms to have more than 25 per cent of the market. It was felt that this would ensure the presence of at least four players in the market for any commodity and, hence, prevent market power. How much growth in such market power was actually prevented is moot; what it did do was create huge degrees of inefficiency.

The inefficiencies arose in two ways. First, the restriction of market share meant that economies of scale were not achieved. Second, there was no incentive among the bigger incumbent players to expand their market, since they will not be allowed to take all of the new market. In as far as growing new markets is costly, the restriction on market share meant that a firm with 25 per cent market share will pay the cost of developing markets and wait for the others to take up 75 per cent of it! This severely restricted product and market developments in India. This is not an example of enabling laws.

An enabling policy will instead focus on making it easier for firms to develop markets. Instead of restricting incumbents, it will encourage entrants to challenge the incumbents, cut into the incumbent's profit, forcing it to reduce prices. For this purpose, the competition authority should allow for free contracting between parties but also play the role of a watchdog, collecting information and analysing it to determine whether there is any anti-competitive behaviour by firms. Are all producers colluding and offering the same contracts to their dealers (as in firms colluding to set a common price)? Or, is the exclusive contract being chosen from a number of (potentially) competing contracts because it is the most efficient? The ability to successfully answer such questions will distinguish an effective competition law from an ineffective one.

21

The Return of Industrial Policy*

A Threat to Competition Law?

Simon J. Evenett

In many jurisdictions industrial policy, like a phoenix, has risen from the ashes. One of the many questions that this development raises is whether industrial policy's growing profile constitutes a threat to efficiency-based competition law and enforcement? If so, what is the nature of that threat? Is that threat serious? And, are there any steps that a competition agency, and the supporters of competition law in general, can take to ensure that much of the progress made over the past 10–15 years, in particular in jurisdictions with younger competition agencies, is not undone? In this paper I characterize industrial policy, describe the likely factors behind its resurgence, discuss the principal criticisms of industrial policy measures that restrict competition, and outline five possible steps that competition agencies might take in response to this new development.

It is often argued that the attractiveness of many economic policies is cyclical—waxing for a decade or more, followed by a period of wane. Industrial policy certainly follows this pattern, at least in much of the industrialized world and arguably in part of the developing world too. In

* Reproduced from 'The Return of Industrial Policy: A Threat to Competition Law?', published in Dhall, V. (ed.). 2007. *Competition Law Today: Concepts, Issues, and the Law in Practice* (first ed.), Oxford University Press, New Delhi.

industrialized countries, industrial policy was very much in vogue, influencing how many governments restructured existing industries and sought to promote the industries of tomorrow, from the 1950s through to the 1970s. Industrial policy fared less well there in the 1980s and 1990s as more and more governments put their faith in market forces. For some younger readers, then, the current resurgence of interest in industrial policy may appear novel. Others, no doubt, may be left wondering why the arguments that so discredited industrial policies in the late 1970s and 1980s no longer have the force that they once had. The latter question is not, however, the topic of this chapter. Here, the focus is on the implications of the resurgence of industrial policy for competition law and its enforcement.

In this chapter, the following questions are addressed. In what ways, if any, does industrial policy threaten competition law and its implementation? Can the objectives, and measures taken in the name of, industrial policy be reconciled with those of competition law? If not, what is at stake and what can competition enforcement officials do about it? These questions, then, are partly conceptual in nature and sometimes they refer to the forces of political economy at work. Moreover, to the extent that they refer to potential choices available to competition enforcement officials, pragmatism as well as economic principles may provide elements of the answer. The arguments in this chapter certainly draw on all three aspects of the matter on hand (namely, microeconomic principles, political economy factors, and pragmatic considerations.) No doubt certain aspects of the relationship between industrial policy and competition law can be usefully articulated by reference to one discipline. However, in my view, a complete portrait requires consideration of a number of different perspectives.

There are very good reasons why the competition policy community should take the resurgence of industrial policy seriously. The first is that the argument that competition law will impede or reduce the effectiveness of industrial policies (and, in the eyes of the latter's proponents, thereby slow the pace of economic progress) has been used successfully to delay the enactment of competition laws, as the history of competition legislation in China, India, Malaysia, and Vietnam can attest.[1] A related concern is that industrial policy considerations convince national policymakers to water down national competition legislation. Particularly vulnerable appears to be merger review, as some fear that this may impede the creation of large national firms.

A third reason why this topic is important is that the same political economy forces that have led to a resurgence of interest in industrial policy may

[1] Accounts of discussions over the possible enactment of competition law in these four jurisdictions can be found in Lin (2005), Chakravarthy (2005), Lee (2005), and Huy (2005), respectively.

also be brought to bear on the competition agency in the enforcement of its powers. The political milieu in which competition law is enforced is likely to have changed, and by how much and in what ways may well vary across jurisdictions. This is not to say that national policymakers have completely repudiated markets as a means of allocating resources (although the rhetoric of some of elected leaders in Central and Southern America comes pretty close to this), rather that the relatively market-friendly political environment in much of the world during the years 1980–2000 is evolving. One question that immediately arises from this observation is whether the priority given by a competition agency to competition advocacy needs to be re-evaluated as the political climate becomes more nationalistic and interventionist.

Before developing any more arguments, I think it is important to warn the reader of one rather disturbing feature of the literature on industrial policy, which is also found in the small literature on the relationship between industrial policy and competition law. Without suggesting that every writer on these subjects is guilty of the following, there appears to be a strong ideological bent to some of the contributions to these two streams of literatures.[2] From time to time, there are some pretty extraordinary detours undertaken when sacred cows are under threat and this seems to obscure some important arguments with considerable policy relevance. For example, the argument that competition between firms was a significant contributor to East Asian economic growth during the 1970s and 1980s, neither denies that industrial policy might have had a role in bolstering growth (perhaps through other channels) nor that industrial policy played a role in fostering competition between firms (through, for example, government-arranged contests for scarce investment funds or licenses to produce or to export). Many supporters of industrial policy reject laissez-faire approaches without realizing that advocating greater inter-firm rivalry does not necessarily imply promoting laissez-faire policies. In short, readers will have to keep their wits about them, for discussions over the relationship between industrial policy and competition law appear, from time to time, to be a proxy for debates over states versus markets. Seeing the debate over the former in terms of the latter is likely, however, to obscure important aspects of the problem.

The remainder of this chapter is organized as follows. In the next section industrial policy is characterized (defined is too strong a word as the reader will soon appreciate) and a first set of implications about its relationship to competition law drawn. The following section puts the resurgence of industrial policy

[2] Indeed, in a recent survey of industrial policy, Pack and Saggi (2006) note: 'Few phrases elicit such strong reactions from economists and policymakers as *industrial policy*.' (p. 1, italics in the original.)

in its political context and examines the implications for competition law and its enforcement. Next, the merits of restricting competition so as to pursue certain industrial policy goals are considered, and here reference is made, amongst others, to some thoughtful observations of competition enforcement officials on these matters. The last section describes five potential steps that competition agencies have available to them, should industrial policy's profile increase further. The chapter ends with some concluding remarks and reflects further on the need for fresh thinking in competition agencies, in particular at the most senior levels, as the political environment becomes less and less supportive of economic policies based solely on microeconomics-based efficiency criteria.

Characterizing Industrial Policy

For a policy measure that received so much attention during much of the early postwar era, and which is experiencing something of a comeback, the innocent reader might assume that there was an agreed definition as to what industrial policy is and what its purpose is. Remarkably this is not the case and I have often wondered if one reason for the enduring appeal of industrial policy is precisely because it has not been, and may never be, precisely defined.

Some argue that the objective of industrial policy is to encourage structural change in an economy (Singh 2002), typically towards sectors where there is faster productivity growth (Dervis and Page 1996; Pugel 1984; Pack and Saggi 2006). In principle, identifying which sectors have had higher productivity growth in the past is possible, possibly giving industrial policy a measurable objective. Alas, matters are not so simple as the past may provide an unreliable guide as to which sectors will grow quickly in the future.

Others distinguish between industrial policies that are devised to influence the entire economy[3]—the so-called horizontal measures—from those that seek to influence outcomes in a given sector or sectors. The latter forms of industrial policy involve discrimination in favour of certain economic activities and/or against other activities. Such discrimination is often justified on the grounds that the sector in question is 'strategic', which is often short hand for saying 'of particular importance to the economic prospects of the country' in question. No doubt there are other ways of thinking about what is a strategic economic activity, but an economic perspective might emphasize those activities that have significant knock-on effects to other activities that are not taken fully account of through the normal operation of markets. Whether

[3] Or perhaps more accurately the private sector and, where appropriate, the productive aspects of the state sector.

such knock-on effects can be identified, understood, and quantified in such a way as to guide policymaking is another matter.

Even if the goals of industrial policy are unclear or, if clear, do not have reliable empirical counterparts, then perhaps the set of government measures known as industrial policy is well defined? Unfortunately, this is not the case either. Pangestu (2002) offers perhaps the most exhaustive classification of the different policy instruments that have, at some point or the other, been referred to as industrial policy. The first sign of trouble is that her list is so long that she organizes the dozens of measures into three groups, namely, external market interventions (for policy measures towards international trade but not international investment), product market interventions, and factor market interventions (including measures towards international investments as well as domestic investments and labour). According to Pangestu, policy measures from tariffs to training technicians have been labelled industrial policy. Indeed, Pack and Saggi (2006) note that 'industrial policy means different things to different people' and one reason for this is the wide range of state measures classified as industrial policy. Having reviewed this literature the only succinct characterization that I can come up with for the state measures included under the portmanteau term industrial policy is 'not macroeconomic policy'!

What are the implications for competition law and its enforcement of these characterizations of the objectives of industrial policy and the state measures associated with it? The first implication, perhaps obvious but no less fundamental for that, is that the objectives of competition law tend to be dynamic or intertemporal in nature. Some proponents of industrial policy, notably Singh (2002), seize on this point to criticize competition law as giving too much weight, and in the limit exclusive weight, to static concepts of efficiency. The force of this criticism is muted considerably by the widespread appreciation among the competition law community of the concept of dynamic efficiency and its importance for enforcement in certain situations. (In fact, a fair reading of developments in enforcement practice in the 1990s would show that the competition law community in North America took the lead in considering the consequences for enforcement of corporate acts that might substantially affect market outcomes over time, such as those following a proposed merger between firms where at least one party has a substantial, or potentially important, pipeline of potential innovations that might be brought to the market at a later date.) If all industrial policy amounts to is considering dynamic efficiency, then arguably many modern competition agencies can accommodate the return of industrial policy with ease.

Perhaps more of a concern, however, is that the objectives of industrial policy can be read to give little, less, or no weight to efficiency considerations.

In which case, one cannot rule out that whatever objectives drive industrial policy may lead to state measures being proposed that do not fare well on an efficiency-based metric. Before taking this argument further, however, it is worth recalling that numerous competition agencies have multiple objectives set out for them in their respective national legislation. Whether this is desirable is a good question, but the point I want to make here is that some competition agencies already have experience juggling multiple objectives and for them taking on an industrial policy objective might not be too challenging. (For others, the experiences of agencies that have managed multiple policy objectives may well become of greater interest should industrial policy's profile continue to rise.) Where there is undoubtedly a challenge is for those agencies which purport to see the world entirely through an efficiency lens. They may well find their competition advocacy efforts receiving a less favourable hearing and their enforcement decisions questioned on a more regular basis.

The second implication follows from the fact that, although industrial policy may privilege a non-efficiency objective, this does not necessarily imply the complete repudiation of efficiency considerations. Efficiency may, therefore, become secondary but still important. If this situation arises, then the competition advocacy functions of a competition agency may have to evolve from arguing for state measures that best allocate scarce resources to emphasizing state measures that meet the non-efficiency objectives of industrial policy with the least possible distortion to resource allocation. Again, some competition agencies already have experience with variants on this situation; that is, with offering advice to government bodies whose objectives are not entirely based on efficiency considerations. Consider, for example, a utility regulator that has a mandate to provide universal service to a nation's or region's customers. If, in fact, that mandate is interpreted as providing a certain threshold level of service, then an optimistic scenario arises as the competition agency can offer advice on which measure or measures meets that threshold level at least cost. However, other logical possibilities give rise to more difficult choices on the part of the competition agency. Suppose instead that the stated objective of the regulator is to maximize the number of persons with access to a given service. Furthermore, suppose the regulator is considering two policy proposals. Proposal A promises to deliver 90 per cent coverage and will distort competition causing $5 billion in harm. Proposal B promises 95 per cent coverage at a greater cost in terms of resource misallocation, say $10 billion. Which proposal should the competition agency advocate if it knows that the utility regulator cares about its service coverage mandate as well as efficiency? This dilemma has a direct analogue in the context of industrial policy. In the above example replace the coverage mandate by an objective to maximize export growth and the utility regulator by a trade or industry ministry, and surely one begins to see immediately the challenges facing competition advocacy when government bodies privilege non-efficiency objectives on industrial policy grounds. In short, even though some competition agencies have experience with this type of situation, if the profile of industrial policy continues to grow, then agencies are likely to face the difficulties arising from this type of situation more frequently than in the past.

The third implication is, for the large part, benign for competition agencies. If a nation's industrial policy does in fact cover state measures from training technicians to tariffs, then arguably a lot of industrial policy measures have absolutely no bearing on the rivalry between suppliers, be they in product markets or in factor markets. Moreover, to the extent that an industrial policy intervention raises welfare—as seen on an efficiency metric—this may well be applauded by the competition law community. One implication of this argument is that it is important to identify precisely which industrial policy interventions deliberately seek to influence interfirm rivalry and risk distorting the allocation of resources. For it may well be the case that a government's industry policy in no way unduly seeks to influence competition in domestic markets. For example, offering low-interest loans to students to study engineering is unlikely to distort product market competition. Indeed, for many of the state measures associated with industrial policy, the tension with competition law may in fact be more apparent than real.[4]

[4] The literature on the role of industrial policy in East Asia's phenomenal growth provides an excellent example of the need to differentiate between those state measures that deliberately seek to influence inter-firm rivalry and those that do not. Many heterodox analysts argue that industrial policy played a central role in raising economic growth (and other measures of economic performance, in particular export growth) in this region and some are quick to point out that the countries in question typically had weak or impotent competition agencies or no competition legislation at all during their high growth phase. Elsewhere I have carefully reviewed the leading texts of these analysts, trying to identify the instances where the government deliberately influenced the degree of competition in markets, potentially in a way that those steeped in an efficiency-based mindset would find objectionable (Evenett 2003 and 2005). For sure, there are examples of state measures which could fall into this category (including export and recession cartels in Japan from the 1950s to the mid-1970s, and state-led mergers and consolidations). The overwhelming impression, though, is that the vast number of industrial policy interventions would not face objections from an efficiency-minded competition agency. However, where this literature does identify deliberate attempts to influence inter-firm rivalry, little or

Even though many industrial policy measures are not a concern for competition agencies there are some measures that might be and, of course, this is where tensions can arise. Three types of initiative come specifically to mind. I will describe them here and describe their relative merits later in the section titled, 'Competition—Motivated Criticisms of Selected Industrial Competition Measures'. The first are policies to create national champions by deliberately allowing some firms to merge (or be acquired by other firms) or measures to protect those champions by forbidding other firms to engage in mergers or acquisitions. Here, typically, it is argued that a firm needs scale to be able to effectively compete. The second initiative allows firms, encourages them, or mandates them, to form cartels or other forms of horizontal agreements so as to pursue one or more of the following objectives: increase exports, facilitate restructuring (including exit from the industry in question), and to finance investment. The third initiative involves direct or indirect subsidization of favoured firms. Such subsidies are referred to as state aids in many jurisdictions and can take numerous forms, including the direct subsidization of production costs and guarantees related to undertaking risky activities such as exporting to parties where there is some likelihood of non-payment. Each of these three initiatives could, in principle, affect inter-firm rivalry and so shift resources away from their optimum allocation.

By dwelling on the objectives of industrial policy and the state measures typically associated with it, the goal of this section was to identify various possible implications for competition law and its enforcement of the return of industrial policy. It should be apparent that, in principle, a nation's industrial policy could be formulated in such a way as to pose no threat to a competition

---

no serious empirical evidence is provided to demonstrate that these measures alone actually worked, that is, they attained the government's stated objective and not some other intervening factor or consideration. Nor, to the best of my knowledge, have those who praise such competition-distorting measures bothered to calculate the associated resource misallocation costs, so the reader does not have a well-rounded picture of the pros and cons of the measures taken. (In this respect the literature, which is replete with qualitative accounts, is woefully incomplete.) It is for these reasons that I have been sceptical of any claims of the sort which state or imply that (a) the competition-distorting state measures used in East Asia worked or played a central role in East Asia's spectacular growth performance, (b) that the overall benefits of such measures (after properly taking into account the resource distortion costs) were positive, and (c) that East Asia's spectacular economic development would have been compromised by the enactment and implementation of effective competition law. Overall, the deficiencies of the literature on industrial policy's contribution to East Asia's economic rise do not, in my view, provide a reliable basis for privileging industrial policy over competition law or, for that matter, vice versa.

agency or require no changes in the agency's mode of operation. However, it cannot be said that industrial policy must have benign consequences for competition law, as the discussion over the differences in objectives and the description in the last paragraph of three industrial policy-related measures that could directly influence product market competition makes clear. The precise nature of any threat to competition law and its enforcement bodies will depend on the objectives and form of the industrial policy undertaken, the parties responsible for implementing the industrial policy, and the goals of the competition agency and its modus operandi. As these factors are likely to differ across nations we should not be surprised if the nature of any threat differs too. Even so, it is hoped that discussion in this section has shed light on some of the considerations that ought to be taken into account in an analysis of the implications of the return of industrial policy for competition law enforcement.

Resurgence of Industrial Policy; the Political Environment

The significance of industrial policy is not necessarily its novelty. Rather, it is that after an era in which policymakers were prepared to put considerable weight on market forces and liberalized domestic commerce and international trade—an era in which competition law spread markedly around the world and when many nations took steps to strengthen their competition laws—industrial policy with all its interventionist trappings seems to find favour with more policymakers in a larger number of countries. While the political economy factors underlying industrial policy's resurgence are interesting in their own right, understanding the implications of these factors for the political environment facing competition law and its enforcers is the central purpose of this section.

Four distinct, and somewhat related, factors are responsible for the resurgence of industrial policy.[5] The importance of these factors no doubt varies across jurisdictions and nothing should be inferred from the order in which the following points are made. The first reason is that liberalization of national economies (both internally and with respect to foreign commerce) has created pressures on domestic firms to restructure their operations. Sometimes that restructuring is defensive in nature, that is, to enhance corporate performance against foreign subsidiaries or imports. At other times, the restructuring can be thought of as offensive in motivation, namely, to restructure to take

[5] I use the word 'resurgence' deliberately as some have argued that industrial policy never really went away in certain jurisdictions. And in some cases what was previously called industrial policy may have been relabelled.

commercial advantages brought about by reform. In either case, there appears to be considerable dissatisfaction among policymakers (and sometimes among corporate executives too) with the pace of corporate restructuring, as the recurring discussions on competitiveness in Europe and Latin America can attest. Implicitly, and sometimes explicitly, these policymakers are calling into question whether market forces alone adequately foster restructuring. The temptation to encourage domestic mergers and to create so-called national champions is likely to have direct implications for the conduct of merger reviews. Moreover, governments may resort to market-sharing arrangements to facilitate a more 'orderly' restructuring of a domestic industry under competitive pressure.

A related, and second reason, is that in much of the developing world the market-friendly tenets of the so-called Washington Consensus have been rejected, or at least demoted, over the past 5–10 years. This consensus, which was originally designed to encapsulate the advice given by the International Monetary Fund and the World Bank to Latin American nations in the late 1980s and early 1990s and which was subsequently applied more or less to the rest of the developing world, was one of the biggest casualties of the East Asian financial crisis in 1997 and 1998, a searing event that led many East Asian policymakers to search for an alternative formula for economic development.[6] Once East Asian governments, who after all were the star performers in the development growth stakes, became lukewarm or outright hostile to the Washington Consensus other developing countries became more open about their doubts too.[7] Arguably, the search for another formula for develop-

[6] Whether bad advice from the International Monetary Fund or the World Bank was the principal cause of the origins or the subsequent depth of the East Asian financial crisis is quite another matter. There is considerable debate on this subject which goes well beyond the scope of this chapter. What is particularly unfortunate is that rather than identify which, if any, elements of the Washington Consensus were at fault, the tendency in East Asia (and elsewhere) has been to reject all of its elements. Given that promoting competition is an implied part of that Consensus this has given opponents of competition law and policy another rhetorical weapon.

[7] There is an open question as to how much of the Washington Consensus was actually believed by developing country governments in the first place. For sure, there were some reformist governments who openly supported market-friendly policies (Chile and Mexico come to mind.) However, other governments may have paid lip service to the Washington Consensus, making reforms (which from time to time might have been significant reforms) so as to curry favour with the International Monetary Fund or the World Bank (from whom they may have wanted to secure finance) or with multinational corporations (from whom they may have wanted to secure foreign investment.)

ment has not led to a new consensus and considerable variations in policy have been observed. One approach has been to argue that successful countries have successful large internationally competitive firms. This is the modern-day equivalent of the famous 1953 saying made in the United States that 'What's good for the country is good for General Motors, and vice versa'. China has been particularly enamoured with this line of reasoning and in 1998 Chinese Vice-Premier Wu Bangguo made the following remarks in a speech:

> In reality, international economic confrontations show that if a country has several large companies or groups it will be assured of maintaining a certain market share and a position in the international economic order. America, for example, relies on General Motors, Boeing, Du Pont and a batch of other multinational companies. Japan relies on six large enterprise groups and Korea relies on 10 large commercial groupings. In the same way and in the next century our nation's position in the international economic order will be to a large extent determined by the position of our nation's large enterprises and groups.[8]

True to these words, China has consciously developed a 'national team' of large groups of companies, some of which it hopes will hold their own on world markets. The State Council in China is said to have created 120 groups of companies through state-led consolidation and these groups have also received numerous privileges not available to other firms. This is said to be part of China's 'Grasp the Large' strategy in which the overwhelming majority of the small state-owned enterprises were privatized (or 'let go') and selected large firms nurtured by the state. Nolan (2001) in his extensive analysis of Chinese national team summarizes the situation as follows: 'The national team, therefore, can be considered the "generals" at the vanguard of the current policy to develop the large-scale sector' (p. 76). The creation and evolution of this national team constitutes an important current example of industrial policy in the developing world.

Renewed interest in the sources of East Asia's economic prowess is the third reason why industrial policy has greater prominence today. (The high degree of political stability maintained through this region's economic growth spurt also appears to be an attractive feature to many policymakers outside of East Asia.) Many policymakers seem to have concluded that industrial policy with its interventionist imperatives were important parts of the successful policy mix in East Asia and this has served the current proponents of industrial policy well. Of particular interest in the East Asian context is the relationship

[8] This quotation was reported in *Jingji Ribao* on 1 August 1998 and is reproduced in Nolan (2001: 71).

between the intensity of rivalry between domestic firms and external competitiveness. What one concludes about this relationship is likely to have considerable bearing on one's view of the appropriate role for competition law.

A fourth reason is growing concerns about the nationality of firm ownership in industrialized countries. Whether it is French 'economic patriotism', Polish, Italian, and Spanish opposition to takeovers of large national companies by other European firms, or American concerns about the ownership of US port facilities and high-technology computer companies, the past 18 months have seen a remarkable return to the proposition that 'nationality matters', at least as far as corporate ownership is concerned. Whether this impulse among policymakers spreads to other sectors or other government measures remains to be seen. Even so, parallels have been drawn to an earlier era when certain industrial policy measures were predicated on similar assumptions.

Having described four reasons why industrial policy has made a comeback, it is useful to ask whose interests this comeback serves. This might shed light on the array of interests that could oppose any competition agency's efforts to temper industrial policy initiatives. A range of corporate, bureaucratic, and political interests are arraigned in favour of revitalized industrial policies. One set of proponents are the senior managers and large shareholders of companies which believe that they need to expand their scale of operations so as to effectively compete at home and on world markets. A potentially different set of proponents are the managers and employees at companies under pressure to contract or restructure. Fearing the loss of their jobs and associated benefits, these interests may favour measures that constrain competition during 'orderly restructuring' and the like. Officials in industry ministries, and sometimes in trade ministries, may well favour industrial policy, not least because it might enhance their profile within government, result in higher budgets, and more powers. Finally, an important group of potential supporters are ministers who often feel the need to be seen doing something to advance the economic interests of their country. The activist nature of much industrial policy lends itself nicely to high-profile media announcements and publicity, creating the perception (if not the reality) that ministers are in charge and taking measures that purportedly benefit the national economy. Also, the expected accomplishment of these measures can often be characterized in concrete terms, such as employment and export levels and growth.

What do these political economy factors mean for the enforcement of competition law? The first point is that, assuming the international trading system continues to be relatively open and that some domestic and external reform occurs, pressures for industrial policy measures are likely to continue. Assuming the international trading system remains relatively open and the volume of cross-border mergers and acquisitions stays at current levels or rises, then pressures on firms to adjust will intensify and this may trigger demands for more industrial policy initiatives. Plausible lines of causation pointing to the opposite conclusion, however, are much harder to come by.

The second implication is that, independent of whether any industrial policies are actually implemented, the interests pushing for industrial policies are sure to influence the political environment in which competition agencies operate. Senior officials at competition agencies know they have a certain amount of political goodwill towards them and must decide if and when to use it. Surely the latter decisions will be influenced by an evolving political environment that is more conducive to industry policy interventions.

The third implication concerns appearances. Industrial policy measures could be portrayed as collaborative initiatives between governments and business that concern tangible, easy to understand, and important economic outcomes, such as employment, exports, and (maybe) productivity. In contrast competition law enforcement can appear antagonistic (with an agency seen to be 'attacking' a firm, which might be a national business icon) and is motivated by a metric (efficiency) that may not be readily understood and does not lend itself to instant, independent measurement. That the present European Commissioner for Competition felt compelled to write to the *Financial Times* recently to categorically state that her Directorate-General is not conducting a vendetta against the Microsoft Corporation provides a leading example of how a competition agency's actions can be portrayed negatively. Similar challenges are likely to arise in those jurisdictions where active industrial policies are pursued.

Finally, the perception that industrial policy and competition law are at odds with one another could be exploited by long-standing opponents of competition law. Rather than attack the latter directly, exaggerating the clash between industrial policy and competition law may be more effective. In jurisdictions where industrial policy proponents are making progress, competition agencies may wish to review their competition advocacy activities so as to include more opportunities to stress that there is a wide range of industrial policy measures that do not raise competition-related concerns. With these political economy considerations in mind, the next two sections outline arguments and steps that competition agencies might employ should industrial policies continue to gain ground.

Competition-Motivated Criticisms of Selected Industrial Policy Measures

In this section, two forms of industrial policy intervention that have direct implications for inter-firm rivalry are assessed from a microeconomic efficiency-based perspective. It is important to stress that the arguments advanced here are not a broad-based critique of industrial policy and should not be construed as such.

The first class of interventions considered here are those that economists often refer to as second-best measures to fix a specific market failure or to meet a stated government objective. The use of export cartels, rationalization cartels, and cartels to help firms finance investments are examples of this type of second-best industrial policy intervention. As will be argued below, the principal criticism of these measures is that an alternative policy instrument exists which could fix the market failure or attain the stated government objective with a smaller distortion of resources away from an efficient market outcome. In the limit, if the alternative policy instrument can fix the market failure or attain the stated government objective without distorting resource allocation at all, then this alternative is referred to as a first-best policy instrument. (And so first-best policy instruments are preferable to second-best policy instruments, etc.) More generally, policy instruments can be ranked in terms of the distortions they create in the process of attaining some industrial policy objective. On this argument the economy would be better served by adopting the policy instrument that distorts market outcomes the least while attaining the stated industrial policy objective. Let's apply this approach to the following example.

Suppose a nation has a nascent financial system which tends to lend funds for investment only to the largest firms.[9] As investment is an important determinant of corporate performance over the longer term, and in the aggregate influences national economic growth, does it make sense to fund investment by allowing companies to raise the prices that they charge customers? Moreover, given that no one firm in a competitive market can afford to raise its prices much (in the limit, strictly at all) above rival firms for fear of losing some or all of their customers, then does the government need to step in and solve the collective action problem by allowing (or even mandating) the firms to form a cartel that fixes prices? It should be conceded immediately that, assuming the cartel is stable and the parties to it do not unduly undercut the cartel agreement, such a step is likely to raise the total profits earned by the firms providing, in principle, funds for investment. The concern, of course, is that these funds have to come from somewhere, in this case from the pockets of consumers or the balance sheets of corporate customers. Prices are kept above marginal costs of production and resource allocation is distorted.

[9] Given the complaints from business people running small and medium-sized firms about the inability to obtain loans from the banking system in industrialized countries, this example should not be thought as only referring to developing countries.

Let us now apply the test proposed above. Are there alternative policy instruments that can attain the stated goal—here raising a certain level of funds for investment—without distorting competitive forces? The answer is yes. A first-best policy intervention exists and this would involve the government determining precisely why the nation's financial system will not lend money to smaller and medium-sized firms. If the impediments to the latter are legal measures or anticompetitive behaviour in the financial sector, then the first-best action is to take steps to fix these problems. (It being taken as given, for the purpose of this example, that the investment plans of the small and medium-sized companies are commercially viable.) One implication of the principle of policy design being applied here is that the optimal policy intervention is the one that is the most direct solution to the problem at hand, and not some intervention that attains the objective through indirect means (such as raising investment funds through cartelization).

An inferior alternative to the first-best measure might be for the government to offer interest rate subsidies to the firms when they borrow. This has two disadvantages compared to the first-best solution; namely, that a firm's investment decision may become distorted by the very same interest subsidies (in that a firm may now seek to borrow more) and that the subsidies need to be financed by taxation or government borrowing, both of which can introduce distortions (however small) to other markets. (These two concerns apply even if the government has all the information needed to set the correct interest rate subsidy; a heroic assumption at the best of times. Without accurate information, a third disadvantage then arises.) The advantage, however, of an interest rate subsidy over cartelization is that the former does not distort the prices charged by the firms in question. Another alternative policy, which has similar advantages and disadvantages as the interest subsidy, is for the government to offer grants directly to the firms for investment purposes. Again, the price-raising effects of the cartel are avoided.

A proponent of cartelization might respond to these observations with the following two counterarguments. First, they might argue that fixing national financial systems can take a long time and in the meantime companies will still go without needed investment. In contrast, cartelization can provide funds for investment in the short-term. The force of this argument depends, amongst others, on the nature of the changes required of the financial system. Even if short-term improvements in the financial system are not possible, then the interest rate subsidies and grants described above are alternative measures that do not distort product market competition in the way that cartels do. Therefore, one might complement measures to improve the financial system with a short-term programme to finance investment through the latter two measures.

A second counterargument is that government treasuries cannot afford to pay interest rate subsidies or direct grants, especially in developing countries where (it is often argued) there are many needs competing for resources from state budgets. This argument is not entirely pervasive, for if bolstering investment really is as important for economic growth and long-term economic performance (as the proponents of cartelization often claim) then surely it would be a priority for even a cash-strapped developing country? Another source of doubt is that the reason many developing countries do not have sufficient government revenues to make investment-promoting outlays is because of insufficiently developed, inefficient, and in some cases corrupt, national taxation systems. Again, if funds for investment (public or private) are so important for development then an important priority is to improve the national taxation system and not to resort to indirect means of financing investment, such as allowing the cartelization of product markets.

Another and perhaps more prominent form of industrial policy intervention, that is often at odds with the tenets of modern competition law, concerns so-called national champions. Geroski (2005) characterizes the dilemma as follows:[10]

> Perhaps the clearest expression of this tension comes in debates about national champions particularly when these debates are staged in smaller nation states. The creation of national champions is sometimes seen as the only way for firms based in a particular country to compete in a global market populated by competitive giants based in home markets that are larger or more supportive. Yet, national champions are often national monopolists (or very nearly so), and antitrust authorities tend to be uncomfortable with monopolies even in smaller markets. For proponents of national champions, competition policy can be an obstacle (or worse), while for many competition authorities, the creation of national champions seems like a dangerous form of meddling with markets. (p. 2)

Geroski goes on to analyse forensically (and there is no other word for it) the various assumptions upon which the case for national champions is based. Those assumptions are (a) that national markets are too small for firms to thrive in and so they must expand their scale and operate in regional or global markets, (b) that enterprises need to achieve a certain size to be competitive, and (c) that certain sectors must be nurtured if the nation's economy is to prosper.

[10] Readers are advised that if they read only one contribution on the subject of national champions and competition law, they should give serious consideration to making their choice this excellent, concise, and analytical yet approachable speech by late Professor Paul A. Geroski, chairman of the United Kingdom's Competition Commission.

With respect to the 'need' to operate internationally, apart from truly homogenous goods, Geroski argues that there are few differentiated products sold on a global scale. (He argues that Marlboro cigarettes, a prominent example of a globally-marketed good, is the exception rather than the rule.) He urges business people and policymakers to consider whether products tailored to the specific needs of different sections of national populations (which invariably have smaller production runs) are a viable alternative to selling the same good everywhere.

With respect to the need for critical mass, Geroski does not dismiss this argument out of hand noting that in some industries a certain level of research and development outlay is needed to be a viable competitor. What he questions, however, is how pervasive these circumstances are—especially when many of the advantages of scale in knowledge-based industries can be replicated by the co-location of small rival firms. Average costs may fall as a firm's output level increases, but in locations like Silicon Valley average costs of each firm are thought to fall as the size of the sector increases.[11] Co-location of rival producers, with the information flows between employees and the thick pools of talent and high-quality suppliers that are induced to locate close by, can induce cost reductions and productivity increases. In such sectors, a positive relationship between firm size and productivity is far from obvious. In short, whether critical mass is a necessary condition for corporate success is very much open to question.

The state-encouraged creation of large firms with market power raises another concern for Geroski. Specifically, firms may have the scale to compete but that does not imply that they have the incentive to do so. Good reasons must be advanced as to why a national champion does not 'opt for the easy life', making little effort to keep costs under control and to create new products. In other words, society may get precious little in return for the higher prices that it pays for a national champion's products, prices which result from the latter's market power.

Others have reflected on the case for merging national firms with the goal of creating an internationally competitive national champion. In a thoughtful submission to an OECD Global Forum in 2003, the Government of Ireland notes that there may be no problem from a competition law perspective so long as the newly-created firm faces sufficient competition from remaining domestic firms or international rivals (Government of Ireland 2003). It may well be that the relevant markets for

[11] The former are referred to as internal economies of scale and the latter as external economies.

the champion's products are not national, but are sub-regional, regional, or global instead.[12] In which case, the ability of the national champion to raise prices after the merger could be very limited or non-existent. Under these circumstances a competition agency motivated by efficiency considerations would not find itself in disagreement with proponents of this particular industrial policy intervention.

When a competition agency concerns itself only with domestic welfare, as many do, from an efficiency-based perspective a merger or acquisition that creates a national champion will be problematic if the associated expansion is financed by charging higher prices in domestic markets. (Of course, the problem arises because of the market power of the consolidated company and not because of the champion's size.) Sometimes a variant of this argument is advanced whereby the investment is said to finance an expansion of scale or efficiencies associated with overseas expansion. The former chairman of the US Federal Trade Commission, Robert Pitofsky, eloquently described how he would assess a proposed merger or acquisition defended in those terms, in so doing identifying a number of pertinent competition law-related factors:

> If that argument were advanced, we would consider it but our approach would be skeptical. This is not a strictly chauvinistic interpretation of American merger law. First, it is consistent with the basic premise … that domestic firms are best able to succeed in international markets if required to compete rigorously at home.… Second, balancing anti-competitive effects in a domestic market against efficiencies in a foreign market is unusually difficult. Finally, it is an unattractive proposition to 'tax' United States consumers (as a result of the domestic anti-competitive effect) in order to confer benefits on US exporters and non-US consumers. (Pitofsky 1999)

The purpose of this section has been to review a number of arguments that can be usefully deployed by competition agencies when facing two forms of industrial policy intervention that have achieved a certain amount of prominence in the past. Considerable thought has been given to these matters and many of the arguments described in this section are likely to be applicable in a new era of industrial policy as they were in previous decades.

[12] Government of Ireland (2003) also argues that a nation's distribution system can be an important determinant of whether a national champion will face greater competition should it try to raise prices in domestic markets. One implication of this viewpoint is that a competition agency may wish to give higher priority to tackling anticompetitive practices in national distribution systems, should a policy of actively creating national champions be pursued.

Steps That Can Be Taken by a Competition Agency

Competition agencies need not watch the return of industrial policy silently from the sidelines. In this section, five non-mutually exclusive steps are discussed which have implications for both the enforcement and advocacy functions of competition agencies.

The first option is for the competition agency to argue in its public pronouncements that there is no inherent tension between (efficiency-based) competition law and firm size, or for that matter, firm competitiveness. Put another way, competition agencies are not against large firms per se. It is only when such firms engage in anticompetitive practices, typically because they face too little competition, that generally speaking, competition-related concerns arise. It is important to dispel the impression that competition law and enforcement always stands in the way of state-led or state-encouraged corporate consolidation. If such consolidation occurs, a related but distinct point is that the competition agency may want to step up its efforts to advocate for market opening and in particular, as suggested by Government of Ireland (2003), in those distribution sectors which can shield large incumbent firms from rivals. In general, competition agencies might argue that corporate consolidation ought to be coupled with measures to facilitate entry into the relevant markets. Without such reforms, the agency could argue, how can the government be sure that the national champions will have an incentive to keep costs under control and continue innovating? An aggressive competition agency might argue that such market opening is a pre-requisite for successful state-led corporate consolidation.

The second step is for the competition agency to argue that industrial policy measures should directly target the state objective or market failure in question and that the preferred policy measure is the one which creates the smallest distortion to resource allocation.[13] In general, this will involve a competition agency advocating that a government should consider more than one measure for attaining a given industrial policy objective. In some cases the least distortive measure may take longer to attain the policy objective than another alternative. Moreover, the desire 'for results' in the near term may lead a government to prefer the latter over the former. In such circumstances a competition agency might argue that the government implement both measures (assuming that they are not directly contradictory) and phase out the greater resource-misallocating measure once the other measure has proved

[13] A competition agency has a number of ways of making this point ranging from speeches made by senior officials to undertaking studies of the effects of industrial policy measures and publication of their results.

effective or after a specified period of time. A different but related argument that competition agencies can make is that industrial policy measures, in particular those likely to distort inter-firm rivalry, should be reviewed after a specified period of time to see if they are attaining their objectives at least possible societal cost. Ideally, the competition agency and perhaps experts outside of government should be involved in such reviews. Of course, this is an argument based on the potential cleansing power of 'daylight' (transparency).[14] A more aggressive variant of this proposal is to advocate that industrial policy measures cease after a pre-specified period of time, unless renewed after a review of their effectiveness and consideration given to the benefit of a set of measures to the overall economy.

The third step that competition agencies can take is to document and publicize the contributions of its activities to the industrial policy-related objectives that a government may have. These objectives often include exports (output and employment), growth of so-called strategic sectors, productivity growth, etc. It is important to stress here that I am not advocating that competition agencies abandon efficiency standards. Rather, that they highlight the useful byproducts that follow from the agency's activities. After all, if promoting competition is the right policy prescription (and I think that, as a general proposition, it is) then its consequences ought to manifest itself in terms of certain measures of long-term economic performance,[15] including some probably of interest to industrial policy advocates. Here competition agencies can draw upon plenty of empirical economic research that shows that greater inter-firm rivalry generates economic benefits in aggregate (beyond efficiency). A longstanding example of such research is the hypothesis popularized by Michael Porter that greater domestic firm rivalry enhances export performance.

A far more controversial option available to competition agencies is to allow the government's industrial policy objectives to influence the choice of enforcement cases the agency undertakes. Many factors appear to influence case selection in competition agencies, not just the likely possible harm done by an anticompetitive act or the potential for harm done by a proposed merger or acquisition. Whether it is advisable to add another determinant and how much weight to give it is the matter at hand. Replacing potential

[14] Having said that I am under no illusion that daylight necessarily throws off the proponents of industrial policy measures. Perhaps the most one can expect from such transparency-increasing initiatives is that they increase the political cost of supporting a socially expensive industrial policy instrument.

[15] I would not like to think about the ramifications if this were not the case.

harm done (or some other efficiency-based metric) entirely with an industrial policy-based metric in the selection of cases would eliminate one efficiency-based aspect of competition law and would, quite rightly, be opposed by many observers. However, if the prominence of industrial policy continues to rise, then perhaps there is a pragmatic case for having a few cases in a competition agency's portfolio that could be useful in demonstrating the impact of competition law enforcement on the very metrics that industrial policy advocates put so much weight on. I emphasize the word 'pragmatic' in the last sentence and I am aware that this suggestion is motivated by how a competition agency might respond to a changing political environment and not by a firm adherence to microeconomic principles.

The fifth and final step concerns the objectives and metrics used by competition agencies when assessing corporate acts. I raise this matter more for the sake of completeness than out of any major conviction on my part. As will become clear, these are very difficult matters and one where a competition agency and its senior officials should proceed with caution. The question is whether and on what terms a competition agency should take non-efficiency objectives, such as those relating to industrial policy, into account. This is not a new question (see, for example, a report by the American Bar Association on this subject in 2003, ABA 2003) but it is likely to recur if the profile given to industrial policy attains levels seen in earlier decades.

Suppose for the purpose of exposition that, on industrial policy grounds, a government seeks to increase exports of selected sectors. If a national competition agency wanted to consider the possibility of including export-based considerations into enforcement-related decision making along with an efficiency metric, then what are the possible options? One option is to have separate standards for both exports and efficiency. Questions then arise as to whether both standards have to be met, whether only one standard has to be met, and what happens when one standard is met and the other comprehensively fails.

Another option is to give exports and efficiency consideration in decision making but not in any formal manner (such as requiring equal weight be given to both considerations.) This would allow for trade-offs between efficiency and export objectives, which may sound attractive until one is forced to face the question: how many dollars of domestic customer welfare losses is the agency prepared to acquiesce to in return for a dollar of higher export revenues?[16] The answer to that question requires a value judgment, one that

[16] Recall the quotation from Pitofsky in the last section. It should be said that the same question would arise for an objective other than exports, such as employment.

the competition agency and those in government who support industrial policy may not agree upon. This implies that the incorporation of industrial policy considerations into the agency's decision making need not guarantee the end of criticism from the supporters of industrial policy. Moreover, taking exports into account in an informal manner is likely to generate, at least initially, greater uncertainty about the agency's decision making, which the private sector is likely to take exception to.

The observations above suggest that incorporating industrial policy objectives into an agency's decision-making processes itself involves taking some very difficult decisions. Indeed, a supporter of the exclusive use of efficiency standards might argue that the very difficulties in making these decisions is the strongest argument against incorporating industrial policy considerations in the first place. I have considerable sympathy with this viewpoint and in jurisdictions where industrial policy pressures are not acute, or likely to become acute, perhaps the soundest policy recommendation is for competition agencies to respond in other ways to any industrial policy initiatives that do arise.

However, recent experience in industrialized countries (referred to above) does not make me particularly sanguine about the universality of this policy recommendation. It was not long ago that a leading competition agency in an industrialized country had its decision on an energy-related merger of national significance overturned by elected officials. Elsewhere, there are jurisdictions which have enacted competition laws that allow for similar overrides by a government minister or the cabinet. These institutional arrangements arguably undermine the independence and prestige of the competition agencies in question, and surely the question must arise as to whether governments might seek to introduce more such overrides as a means of addressing perceived tensions between competition law and industrial policy? Competition agencies have a strong incentive to avoid this outcome and should industrial policy pressures mount, then I can understand why senior officials at a competition agency might give more consideration to the (arguably messy) ways of incorporating industrial policy-motivated metrics into agency decision making. A changing political environment may make it impossible for a competition agency to adhere to a purist line on efficiency standards. Moreover, given the prominence attached to industrial policy in the early postwar era it is unclear looking forward that this eventuality can be dismissed out of hand.

The goal of this section was to outline five steps, of varying degrees of controversy, that competition agencies can take when faced with growing pressure from industrial policy advocates. These steps are not to be read as recommendations, but their existence provides some reassurance that competition agencies need not be passive actors. As argued above, whether to take some of these steps is not entirely a technocratic matter. Pragmatic considerations, not least assessments of likely future trends and changes in the political environment facing a competition agency, will play their role and I can understand perfectly reasonable observers having different assessments of them.

The purpose of this chapter has been to identify the possible tensions between industrial policy and competition law and to discuss what, if anything, competition agencies can do in the face of a resurgence of policymakers' interest in industrial policy. By now it should be clear that the approach taken here is one that is very sympathetic to the interests of competition agencies, that deliberately considers both political economy factors and economic principles, and that discusses both pragmatic as well as doctrinal responses on the part of competition agencies.

The first significant finding is that, while there are some areas of tension, there are many aspects of national industrial policy that have no bearing on competition law enforcement or that would be of concern to efficiency-minded competition agencies. In fact, in certain circumstances (such as when a government's industrial policy is to promote competition) there may be strong complementarities with efficiency-based competition law. That is the good news. The bad news is that the tensions that do exist (and that relate, in particular, to the use of horizontal agreements between firms, to state-encouraged corporate consolidation, and to employing state aids as industrial policy measures) and cannot be dismissed out of hand. Moreover, the interest groups behind industrial policy are significant and, quite probably, much stronger than supporters of competition law. As a result, the political terrain upon which the competition agency operates may become a lot rougher as industrial policy gains currency.

The third finding of this chapter is that the prominent industrial policy interventions that have implications for inter-firm rivalry have been analysed before and found wanting. In this respect, competition agencies are on the side of the angels—well, the economic angels at least! Moreover, the argument that promoting competition and market openness should receive greater attention in an era of industrial policy has some force, not least to encourage national champions to keep their costs down and to stimulate innovation.

The fourth major point made in this chapter is that competition agencies need not be passive agents in the face of industrial policy pressures. Five potential steps were outlined and, where appropriate, competing considerations discussed. One implication of this discussion was that competition agencies are quite likely to respond to industrial policy pressures in different ways and quite possibly for perfectly good reasons.

The rediscovery by many governments of industrial policy highlights an important underlying change that senior officials in competition agencies and supporters of efficiency-based competition law ought to give more consideration to. That is, the golden age when many policymakers (in industrialized and developing countries) were prepared to give freer markets more reign and many subscribed to promoting competition almost unconditionally is over. This golden age also saw a remarkable spread of competition law around the world and it is likely that a great many competition enforcement officials' only experience is of a political environment generally favourable to promoting competition. Arguably this golden age lasted from around 1985 until 2000 (perhaps starting a little earlier in certain English-speaking industrialized countries and ending a little earlier in East Asia). The reasons for its end, which probably have little, directly, to do with competition law and its enforcement, are the mirror image of many of the factors accounting for the rise of industrial policy.

In addition to industrial policy, many policy makers now place greater emphasis on meeting non-economic and social goals, such as the eight Millennium Development Goals which are receiving particular attention in developing countries, and expect state bodies including competition agencies to help meet them. Quite what this means for efficiency-based competition law and its enforcement is as yet unclear. However, at a minimum it suggests that the political environment in which competition agencies operate is changing and that appealing merely to efficiency-based arguments is likely to be less persuasive than in the golden age. The task facing senior officials at competition agencies is now to identify means by which pro-competition principles can be advanced and sustained in a less friendly and unsettled[17] political milieu. It may well be that, should active industrial polices be pursued in many jurisdictions for a decade or two, there could be marked changes in the manner in which competition law is enforced and competition advocacy is conducted.

[17] Unsettled because, as noted earlier, the search for alternative formulas for improving long-term economic performance continues.

References

ABA. 2003. *Report on Antitrust Policy Objectives*, Antirust Law Section, 12 February.

Chakravarthy, S. 2005. 'India', in Douglas H. Brooks and Simon J. Evenett (eds), *Competition Law and Development in Asia*. Basingstoke: Palgrave.

Dervis, Kamal and John M. Page. 1996. 'Industrial Policy in Developing Countries', in *Journal of Comparative Economics*, 8, pp. 436–51.

Evenett, Simon J. 2003. *Study on Issues Related to a Possible Multilateral Framework on Competition*. Document number WT/WGTCP/W228. Geneva: World Trade Organization.

———. 2005 'Would Enforcing Competition Law Compromise Industrial Policy Objectives', in Douglas H. Brooks and Simon J. Evenett (eds), *Competition Law and Development in Asia*. Basingstoke: Palgrave.

Geroski, Paul A. 2005. 'Competition Policy and National Champions', available at http://www.competition-commission.org.ur

Huy, Vu Quoc. 2005. 'Vietnam', in Douglas H. Brooks and Simon J. Evenett (eds), *Competition Law and Development in Asia*. Basingstoke: Palgrave.

Government of Ireland. 2003. 'Competition Policy in Small Economies', Submission to the OECD Global Forum on Competition. Document reference number CCNM/GF/COMP/WD(2003)18.

Lee, Cassey. 2005. 'Malaysia', in Douglas H. Brooks and Simon J. Evenett (eds), *Competition Law and Development in Asia*. Basingstoke: Palgrave.

Lin, Ping. 2005. 'China' in Douglas H. Brooks and Simon J. Evenett (eds), *Competition Law and Development in Asia*. Basingstoke: Palgrave.

Nolan, Peter. 2001. *China and the Global Business Revolution*. Palgrave, Basingstoke.

Pack, Howard and Kamal Saggi. 2006. 'Is There a Case for Industrial Policy?' *The World Bank Research Observer*.

Pangestu, Mari. 2002. 'Industrial Policy and Developing Countries', in Bernard Hoekman, Aaditya Mattoo, and Philip English (eds), *Development, Trade and the WTO: A Handbook*. Washington, DC: World Bank.

Pitofsky, Robert. 1999. 'The Effect of Global Trade on United States Competition Law and Enforcement Policies'. Speech given at the Fordham Corporate Law Institute, October 15.

Pugel, T. 1984. 'Japan's Industrial Policy: Instruments, Trends, and Effects', in *Journal of Comparative Economics*, 8(4), pp. 420–35.

Singh, Ajit. 2002. 'Competition and Competition Policy in Emerging Markets: International and Development Dimensions'. G-24 Discussion Paper Series. No. 18, United Nations. 18 September.

PART IV

COMPETITION LAW IN SOUTH ASIA

22

The Evolution of Competition Law in India*

Amitabh Kumar

This chapter traces the history of evolution of competition law in India. The first competition law, the Monopolies & Restrictive Trade Practices Act (MRTP Act), was enacted in 1969 following the recommendations of the Monopolies Inquiry Committee (MIC) and sought to provide structural remedies in its attempt to curb monopolistic behaviour since it presumed size beyond a threshold to affect competition adversely. This was reflected in the enactment.

The Terms of Reference (TOR) of the MIC were restricted to private sector. Public sector was presumed to exhibit acceptable behaviour. Setting up public sector enterprises in sectors having monopolistic private enterprises was expected to bring contestability into the markets. The MIC rejected the idea of introduction of competitive constraints through dismantling of the licence system or import liberalization.

In 1984, a High-Powered Expert Committee (Sachar Committee) was set up to consider and report on changes necessary in the MRTP Act, 1969, so as to make it more effective. The Sachar Committee noticed the small number

* Reproduced from 'The Evolution of Competition Law in India', published in Dhall, V. (ed.). 2007. *Competition Law Today: Concepts, Issues, and the Law in Practice* (first ed.), Oxford University Press, New Delhi.

The views here are the author's own and do not reflect those of the Competition Commission of India.

of references to the Monopolies and Restrictive Trade Practices Commission (MRTPC) under provisions dealing with monopolistic trade practices and recommended that certain types of cases should be compulsorily referred to the MRTPC, which could pass final orders in such cases. But this was not accepted by the government. The Sachar Committee sought to include unfair trade practices like misleading and disparaging advertisement into the existing law since it was convinced that consumers had no protection against such practices. The Committee suggested the introduction of the concept of deemed illegality to a host of specific trade practices.

This paper also touches upon the main provisions of the MRTP Act and points out the weaknesses in the legislation that could have been partly responsible for it falling short of expectation. The economic reforms of 1991 found certain provisions of the MRTP Act obstructive to private investment. This led to deletion of certain provisions. A need was felt for further review of the law. This led to setting up of a High Level Committee on Competition Policy and Law (Raghavan Committee).

The Raghavan Committee was set up in 1999.The existing law (the MRTP Act) was found to lack provisions to deal with anticompetitive practices in an era of globalization and liberalization. The Raghavan Committee declared the MRTP Act to be falling short of squarely addressing competition and anticompetitive practices. Based on its analysis, the Raghavan Committee found it more expedient to have a new competition law. While the Committee presumed some anticompetitive behaviour to be injurious to competition, it recognized the primacy of *rule of reason* test for the rest. The Raghavan Committee laid great emphasis on competition advocacy role for the competition authority. This report gave birth to a modern competition law, the Competition Act, 2002.

Monopolies Inquiry Committee

The Monopolies Inquiry Commission (MIC) submitted its report in 1965. The MIC was appointed under the Commissions of Inquiry Act, 1952, to:

(a) enquire into the extent and effect of concentration of economic power in private hands and the prevalence of monopolistic and restrictive practices in important sectors of economic activity other than agriculture with special reference to
  (i) the factors responsible for such concentration and monopolistic and restrictive practices;
  (ii) their social and economic consequences, and the extent to which they might work to the common detriment; and
(b) suggest such legislation and other measures that might be considered necessary in the light of such enquiry, including, in particular, any new

legislation to protect essential public interests and the procedure and agency for the enforcement of such legislation.

The appointment of MIC was prompted by a report of the Mahalanobis Committee on Distribution of Incomes and Levels of Living in 1960 which had highlighted growing income inequality in India in the post-independence period. The growing income inequality was contrary to unambiguous provisions contained in the Directive Principles of the Constitution against concentration of wealth, which made the government sit up and take notice of the problem of economic concentration. Article 39 of the Constitution states:

39. Certain principles of policy to be followed by the State—The State shall, in particular, direct its policy towards securing:

(b) that the ownership and control of the material resources of the community are so distributed as best to subserve the common good;

(c) that the operation of the economic system does not result in the concentration of wealth and means of production to the common detriment.

The government realized that for political democracy to thrive, economic power must be kept within control. The greater the economic concentration the more likely is the pressure on democratic values. Acquiring market power meant loss of benefits of competition which could ultimately lead to 'cast shadows over political democracy and social values'.[1]

Even though the MIC recognized the ill effects of concentration of market power, it did not find it feasible to define the term beyond generality. It was, however, clear to the MIC that acquisition of market power meant loss of benefits of competition. The MIC considered monopolistic and restrictive practices to be functions of 'economic concentration'.[2]

The TOR of the MIC was rather limited. Public sector and agriculture sector were excluded from its scope. Public sector was presumed to exhibit acceptable behaviour in the market and, as such, there could be no case against it on account of loss of benefits of competition. Those were heady days for the public sector, which was growing in size and importance under the Five Year Plans and the Industrial Policy modelled on Soviet lines. The reasons for leaving out the agriculture sector are not as clear. Probably, the land reform programme was expected to reduce concentration.

The MIC was expected to study some 'important sectors' of the economy, although the sectors were not identified in the TOR itself. It is evident that

[1] p. 1 of MIC Report.

[2] p. 1, read 'economic concentration' as market power.

knowledge of monopolistic and restrictive practices in some sectors was at the back of the mind of the policymakers. It would not be incorrect to assume that the inquiry was primarily into trade practices of the manufacturing sector which had acquired large capacities, relatively speaking.

The adverse social effect of concentration was acknowledged in the TOR and largely echoed the Directive Principles. Assuming a causal relationship between concentration and monopolistic and restrictive trade practices, the MIC was asked to identify factors responsible for concentration. The MIC was asked to suggest legislative remedy with the right kind of institutional mechanism for enforcement. In a nutshell, the MIC was expected to provide a complete solution to the problems associated with economic concentration in the private sector.

Broadly speaking, besides historical reasons, government policies were found to be the chief cause of economic concentration. The managing agency system permitted one entrepreneur to have control over many enterprises, ultimately resulting in higher concentration *de facto*. New technology lent itself to a particular scale of production. This led to the emergence of large enterprises capable of reaping benefits of economies of scale. The birth of equity culture contributed to their rapid increase in size and was responsible for increase in concentration. The war efforts of India (under British rule then) contributed to economic concentration. Political largesse to 'loyal' industrialists was also responsible for increase in concentration in the post-independence period. Some of the causes of concentration identified by the MIC in the sixties exist even today!

Government policy impacts competition. There are lessons to be learnt from the policies prevalent in the sixties that were identified by the MIC to have caused economic concentration. The Industrial Policy Resolution and the Industrial Development and Regulation Act had put entry barriers—both tariff as well as non-tariff, with profound impact on competition. No less was the impact of policy regarding foreign collaboration, which clearly favoured some. The MIC discovered preferential treatment given to big business by banks[3] and financial institutions in matters of lending. Naturally, the big got bigger.

Despite weak laws and lax enforcement, intellectual property rights were found to be one of the causes of economic concentration. Patent law favoured the owners creating monopolies which led to exclusion of potential entrants. Intellectual property rights even today pose the problem of monopolization.

[3] Readers may recall that many banks were owned by big businesses until their nationalization in 1969.

The MIC used concentration ratio to measure the state of competition in various sectors. Concentration ratio is the aggregate of market shares of the top enterprises measured in percentage. The MIC used C3, that is, aggregate of the market shares of the top three enterprises. In the absence of data on both sales and production for these enterprises, either of the two was adopted for calculating the market share. The norms set by the MIC were:

C3 > 75 per cent	high concentration
75 per cent < C3 60 per cent	medium concentration
60 per cent < C3 50 per cent	low concentration
C3 < 50 per cent	no concentration

The MIC found that out of 100 products which were of importance to ordinary consumers in its opinion, 64 exhibited high concentration with C3 exceeding 75 per cent. The list of products includes food articles (for example, infant milk food, biscuits, chocolate, tea, coffee, oil), clothing (for example, dhoti, saree, shirting, suiting), fuel (for example, kerosene, coal, petroleum), household goods (for example, lantern, stove, fan, lamp, batteries, radio, refrigerators, sewing machines, typewriters, pencils, blankets), conventional necessaries (for example, matches, soap, footwear, toothpaste, talcum powder, razor blades, cigarettes), medicines (for example, vitamins, penicillin, hormones), transport goods (for example, cars, jeeps, commercial vehicles, tyres, bicycles, tubes) and building material (for example, cement, sanitaryware, plywood, roofing sheets). The list is interesting for two reasons. First, many items supposed to be of importance to the ordinary consumer were not affordable by the vast majority of Indians at that point of time. The example of car is sufficient to drive home this point. Second, many of the products in this list exhibit high concentration even now. Examples are biscuits, cigarette, toothpaste, and commercial vehicles.

The MIC made a distinction between *industry-wise concentration* and *country-wise concentration*. When an enterprise invested in the same line of business, it was termed industry-wise concentration while investment in another line of business was called country-wise concentration. These concepts roughly correspond to horizontal and vertical concepts found in modern competition literature.

The Industrial Policy Resolution and the Industrial Development and Regulation Act established a system of licensing both for setting up new projects and expansion of existing facilities. Raising funds from the market was also regulated. Newcomers were at a disadvantage since they had limited access to funds, the requirement of which had gone up considerably due to economies of scale based on contemporary technologies. Foreign enterprises and owners of new technologies preferred to deal with established businesses. The odds were in favour of the incumbents. The direct as well as indirect impact of government policy on the state of competition was profound and the outcomes were creation of structures and systems that were not conducive to competition although it would be unfair to say that these were intended.

Monopoly power was defined by the MIC as the ability to dictate price and control the market.[4] The MIC examined monopolistic trade practices (MTPs) and restrictive trade practices (RTPs) prevalent in the economy. A large number of industries either had a single supplier or one supplier having a large share of the market. Monopolistic practices noticed by the MIC prompted it to state that '[e]very monopolistic practice is on the face of it a restrictive practice'.[5] Collusive behaviour was noticed in sectors having few dominant players.[6] The MIC was quite emphatic in declaring creation of entry barrier as the most reprehensible of monopolistic trade practices and acknowledged the existence of many attempts at creating barriers[7] by private players. Evidence of predatory pricing was also brought to their notice by witnesses.

Based on anecdotal evidence, the MIC came up with a list of RTPs prevalent in contemporary India. Hoarding was common, creating artificial shortage in an already short supply situation, which hit the common man most. Re-sale price maintenance and exclusive dealing were common business practices, often in the name of ensuring quality. Fixation of price of automotive tyres and tubes were admitted by the manufacturers themselves. Instances of cartelization, boycott, and price discrimination were also brought to its notice. Many anticompetitive trade practices found in modern competition literature existed in the Indian economy during the early sixties when industry was supposed to be in its infancy. Singh (2002) argues that competition law must be made to suit the stage of economic development.[8] The Indian experience of the fifties and sixties does not support this argument since some restrictive trade practices prevalent in developed economies were found in a low income developing country like India in the sixties. The presence of ills of free economies of developed countries in developing countries calls for similarity in sanctions and remedies.

[4] p. 125 of the report.

[5] p. 126 of the report.

[6] p. 125 of the report.

[7] One approach at shutting out competition was to influence the government not to issue licence or prevent implementation of the licence already issued.

[8] Singh, Ajit (2002). 'Competition and Competition Policy in Emerging Markets: International and Development Dimensions', G-24 Discussion Paper Series, UNCTAD/GDS/MDPB/G24/18, p. 16.

The MIC was unhappy with the consequences of monopolistic and restrictive trade practices, especially exclusionary behaviour. 'Big business by its very "bigness" sometimes succeeds in keeping out competitors'.[9] The 'bigness' factors were financial strength, predatory pricing, and large scale advertising. This led to flow of investment in non-priority sectors that were not conducive to economic growth. The social consequences of increase in concentration were a great divide between the rich and the poor and gave rise to corruption.

Some interesting non-legislative recommendations were made by the MIC. These recommendations do throw light on contemporary thinking in the country. Setting up public sector enterprises in sectors having monopolistic private enterprises was expected to bring contestability into the markets ignoring aspects of efficiency. The MIC reposed similar faith in promoting SMEs and cooperatives to challenge private monopolies. It rejected the introduction of competitive constraints through dismantling of the licence system or import liberalization and settled for structural changes. The recommendation[10] to give preference to small and weak enterprises was clearly anti-competitive. Competition law is all about preserving the competitive process rather than the competitors.

Having noted the special economic conditions prevailing in India at the relevant time, the MIC set out the objectives for the legislative recommendations in terms of achieving the highest possible production with least damage to people at large while securing maximum benefits.[11] In order to achieve these objectives, concentration was to be curbed when it resulted in reduced production or was against fair distribution. An independent watchdog in the form of an autonomous commission headed by a judge was recommended. The proposed commission was to have an investigating arm to detect RTPs. The MIC recommended punitive powers to the proposed commission but not the power to order civil imprisonment for wilful disobedience, which was kept in the domain of the courts. The MIC had a cautious approach to merger control. The scope of merger control was to be limited to mergers involving a dominant enterprise, which was defined as one with at least one-third of share in production, supply, or distribution of goods.[12] All proposals for expansion were to be made to the proposed commission and approval

[9] p. 137 of the report.

[10] p. 144 of the report.

[11] p. 159 of the report.

[12] This recommendation was to apply only when assets exceeded Rupee 10 million. All inter-connected enterprises were to be considered for this purpose (p. 163).

would be deemed to have been given if there was no decision taken within 30 days. Intellectual property rights were recommended to be under the ambit of the proposed law.

The Monopolies and Restrictive Practices Bill (MRTP Bill) made some significant departures from the recommendations of the MIC. All enterprises having Rs 200 million in assets and all dominant enterprises having Rs 10 million in assets were to seek prior approval of the central government for expansion or setting up a new undertaking. It provided civil court powers limited to enforcing attendance of witnesses and calling for documents to the MRTP Commission (MRTPC) but not to the investigating agency. Trial of offences was left to the courts and the Commission, other than passing 'cease and desist' orders, could not take action against wilful disobedience.

Confidentiality of information collected from parties during proceedings was made part of the law, giving relief to businesses against poaching of commercially vital information by rivals through complaints.

The MIC noted the occurrence of public sector monopolistic positions in many sectors but refrained from making recommendations on two counts. First, the TOR did not include public sector. Second, parliamentary oversight on public sector enterprises was taken as sufficient guard against unacceptable behaviour.

High-Powered Expert Committee on Companies and MRTP Acts

A High-Powered Expert Committee on Companies and MRTP Acts was set up[13] in 1977 'to consider and report on what changes are necessary in the Companies Act, 1956' and the MRTP Act, 1969, with particular reference to modifications which are required to be made in the form and structure of the Companies Act, 1956, and the MRTP Act, 1969, so as to simplify them and to make them more effective, wherever necessary'. This committee will be referred to as the Sachar Committee, for sake of convenience, after its Chairman. The Sachar Committee was asked to report inter alia on the following:

(xi) what improvements, if any, are required to be made in the present administration, structures, and proceedings regarding the enforcement of the provisions of the two Acts;
(xii) changes required in the MRTP Act in light of experience gained;

[13] Department of Company Affairs (Ministry of Law, Justice and Company Affairs) Resolution No 7/6/77-CL.V of 23 June 1977.

(xiii) any other matter incidental or ancillary to the administration of ... the MRTP Act having regard to the growth of trade, commerce and industry.[14]

The Sachar Committee looked into the practical difficulties of the operation of the law for the eight years of its existence and found that the role assigned to the MRTPC was limited and mostly advisory. The Sachar Committee felt that, apart from making some changes in law, especially for protection of consumers against unfair trade practices, it was imperative to make the MRTPC more effective and independent.

The definition of dominance was sought to be changed, although the Committee stuck to the mechanical definition. The definitions of dominant enterprise and monopolistic enterprise in the MRTP Act were dependent upon market share: an enterprise having one-third market share was a dominant one while one having one-half was a monopolistic enterprise. The Committee noted smaller threshold in the Fair Trading Act, 1973, of UK and the presumption of illegality on acquisition of such levels of market share, both in the UK and US[15] and sought to amend the definition in the Indian law. Thus, any enterprise having at least one-fourth of the market share was recommended to be termed a dominant enterprise.[16] The Committee also recommended harmonization of definition of 'goods' in the MRTP Act with the Sale of Goods Act since the existing definitions did not include stocks and shares, mining, processing, and so on. The concept of 'inter-connected undertakings', already introduced in the Companies Act, 1956, was also sought to be introduced to the MRTP Act. Government undertakings were recommended to be brought under the purview of the MRTPC except for expansions, setting up of new undertakings, or mergers, since government control and parliamentary oversight were deemed sufficient to guard consumer interests.

While the MRTPC was created with the objective of curbing monopolistic and restrictive trade practices, the powers to deal with monopolistic practices were vested with the government against the recommendations of the MIC. The MRTPC could only advise the government even though it had the authority to take up cases *suo motu*. The Sachar Committee noticed the small number of references to the MRTPC under provisions dealing with

[14] p. 249 of the report.

[15] p. 237 of the report.

[16] This by itself did not attract any presumption of illegality and only growth of such enterprises were sought to be regulated.

monopolistic trade practices. For the period 16 June 1970 to 31 December 1977, only 59 out of 618 effective applications received by the government had been referred to the MRTPC; most of these were referred in the initial years of operation. The Central Government passed 84 orders between 1 January 1977 and 30 June 1978 without seeking advice of the MRTPC. Weak law permitted the government to totally bypass a statutory body created for the specific purpose of giving advice on MTPs. Assets of large business houses increased considerably during this period.[17] Although the Committee was convinced that all MTPs should be referred to the MRTPC whose opinion should be binding, it chose to adopt a middle path and recommended that certain types of cases should be compulsorily referred to the MRTPC, which could pass final orders in such cases.[18] All cases of mergers and amalgamations were to be referred only when the government wanted to do so and the advice of the MRTPC could continue to be non-binding. However, cases of takeover were to be compulsorily referred by the government to the MRTPC for final orders. As regards the power of division of undertakings was concerned, the Committee suggested a minor change, namely, that the government could continue to retain existing powers except when a reference was made to be MRTPC, the latter would pass final orders. The Sachar Committee, realizing the adverse effect of such practices, sought to provide powers to the MRTPC to deal with MTPs similar to its powers to deal with RTPs.

The Sachar Committee sought to include unfair trade practices (UTPs) like misleading advertisements into the existing law since it was convinced that consumers had no protection against such practices. The Committee was categorical in providing power to the MRTPC to compensate against injury on account of unfair trade practices. Power to grant interim injunction sought to be incorporated was to safeguard consumers against irreparable loss during pendency of inquiry. Further, the MRTPC was to be provided with power of contempt as well as power to try offences against itself. These measures were found necessary to provide teeth to the body in order to make it more effective. The Sachar Committee desired to transform the MRTPC from an advisory body into an adjudicating one. The Committee also recommended combining the positions of Registrar and Director into a Director General of Trade with powers to conduct dawn raids and limited civil court powers to summon witnesses as well as documents.

The law was amended in 1984 on the basis of the Sachar Committee report though these amendments also made significant departure from the

[17] p. 249 of the report.

[18] pp. 249–50 of the report.

recommendations. The powers of the central government to deal with monopolistic practices and division of enterprises were not touched. Since the role of the MRTPC remained advisory, it did not bother to take up cases dealing with either monopolistic practices or recommending division of enterprises.

The amendments made to the provisions[19] dealing with RTPs in 1984 brought in the concept of *deemed* illegality to a host of trade practices for which registration was made mandatory. This was to overcome court rulings to the effect that even when a trade practice fell under Section 33(1), the MRTPC had to establish that it was a restrictive trade practice under Section 2(o)[20] of the Act. These trade practices were exclusionary behaviour, tie-in sales, resale price maintenance, bid rigging, allocation of market, boycott, predatory pricing,[21] and so on. The presumption of such practices to be anti-competitive made sanctions by the MRTPC easy. There was no longer the need to prove the harmful effects of a trade practice on competition.

The 1984 amendments introduced provisions relating to UTPs in Section 36A. This dealt with cases of misrepresentation as well as misleading or disparaging advertisements. Injury or harm to the consumer was necessary before it could be taken up by the MRTPC. These provisions became the bread and butter of the MRTPC and numerous cases were brought to it.

Economic Reforms and the MRTP Act

1991 was a watershed year. Financial crisis faced by the government prompted it to usher economic reforms of a magnitude and at a pace not witnessed before. Liberalization became the buzzword. The economy was opened up; privatization, liberalization of international trade, inviting private investment to hitherto closed sectors, and other reforms took centre stage.

The reforms and existence of entry barriers for enterprises coming under the ambit of the MRTP Act were incongruous. While the need of the day was rapid expansion and setting up of new ventures, prior approval of the government for enterprises above the threshold limit slowed this effort. Consequently, the provisions dealing with monopolistic enterprises seeking prior approval were deleted from the statute book.[22] The MRTPC continued dealing with restrictive and unfair trade practices.

[19] Section 33 (1) of the MRTP Act.

[20] Section 2(o) defines restrictive trade practice.

[21] These expressions were not used in the law and have been inserted by the author for easy understanding.

[22] Part A of Chapter III was deleted.

A few court cases had exposed chinks in the armoury of the MRTP Act in dealing effectively with anticompetitive practices. A complaint against a private school of taking interest-free deposits from parents at the time of admission was taken up. The issue revolved around whether this was a restrictive trade practice in terms of the definition in Section 2(o) of the MRTP Act. The Supreme Court did not think so.[23] Extra-territorial powers of the MRTPC also came to be questioned. While the Supreme Court recognized its extra-territorial authority, the case failed since goods being imported had not reached the customs authority and did not fit into the definition of 'goods' in Section 2(e)(iii) of the Act.[24]

The government, not satisfied with a piecemeal approach desired to look into the whole issue of competition law. A high level committee on competition policy and law under the chairmanship of S.V.S. Raghavan was appointed.

The MRTP Act and the MRTP Commission

Before we go to the findings and recommendations of the Raghavan Committee, a brief description of the MRTP Act, as it exists now may be helpful. The MRTP Act did not apply to an undertaking either owned by the government or by a government-owned company until 1991. It also did not apply to an undertaking owned or controlled by a corporation set up under any central or state law. These restrictions were removed by a notification in 1991.[25] The Act excludes specifically the operations of its provision to banking and insurance companies to the extent that these are covered under specific provisions of laws dealing with them.

The MRTPC is empowered to inquire into monopolistic as well as restrictive trade practices. MTP, as defined originally, had inter alia the following elements:

- practice of maintaining price at unreasonable high level by limiting or reducing or controlling production, supply, or distribution of goods (also supply of services),
- unreasonably preventing or lessening competition in production, supply, or distribution, and
- limiting technical development.

[23] AIR 2001 SC 3858 *Apeejay School.*

[24] AIR 2000 SC 2728 *Haridas Exports.*

[25] Notification GSR No. 605(E) dated 27 September 1991.

The definition was enlarged in 1984 by adding unreasonable increase in cost of production or charges for providing services, unreasonable increase in prices or charges or profits and adoption of unfair methods or unfair or deceptive practices.

RTP is defined as a trade practice that has or is likely to prevent, distort or restrict competition in any manner. There is particular mention of obstruction to flow of resources into production and manipulation of prices or delivery conditions so as to impose unjustified costs or conditions on the consumers as constituting an RTP.

The procedures for inquiry have been provided in the law. The MRTPC can inquire into an RTP on the basis of a complaint or reference made by the central or state government or application made by the director general (investigation and registration)[26] or suo motu. Inquiry into an MTP can be made on the basis of reference made by the central government or suo motu.[27] The MRTPC may ask the director general to make a preliminary investigation and report before launching an inquiry. The director general is empowered to make preliminary investigation suo motu or on a complaint made to him.[28] The MRTPC has limited civil court powers to enforce attendance, record statements on oath, and call for documents. However, the director general has no such powers and has to rely on the MRTPC for enforcing attendance and calling records from the respondents.

The power to grant temporary injunction was incorporated by the 1984 amendment. This was further amplified in 1991 to enable granting of injunction without issue of notice to the affected par ties. These amendments were made to make the MRTPC more effective in dealing with anticompetitive practices. It was felt that without the authority to grant injunction, anticompetitive practice would continue until the end of inquiry, by which time it may be too late to intervene.

The MRTPC has power to award compensation for loss or damage due to anticompetitive practice since 1984, but it can be awarded only on an application by the central government, state government, or a party suffering the loss or damage after the nature and extent of loss or damage has been determined through an inquiry. The amendment made to the law in 1984 enabled the MRTPC to enforce its orders granting temporary injunction and compensation through courts of law. The MRTPC can call for a compliance

[26] The investigating arm.

[27] It could also be made on the basis of application by DG(I&R) with effect from 1991.

[28] This power led to allegations of emergence of a parallel power centre.

report of its orders through the director general or any other officer. Its powers relating to compliance were further enhanced by providing it with powers of contempt by amendments made in 1991.

The MRTPC has extra-territorial reach and can pass orders against parties situated outside India to the extent the anticompetitive practices are carried on in India. This has been acknowledged by the Supreme Court in a recent case.[29] IPRs arising out of patents[30] as well as exports are excluded from the ambit of the law.

When it comes to remedies, the powers of the MRTPC are rather restricted. As far as the structural remedy of division of an enterprise is concerned, it has only non-binding recommendatory powers and the central government has the authority to order such division. Behavioural remedies against MTPs fare no better under the MRTP Act. The MRTPC is left with only an advisory role and the remedies can only be sanctioned by the central government. The prescribed remedies would not pass muster under modern competition laws. The central government can regulate production/supply/distribution, fix price, fix standards, regulate profit and quality. The 1984 amendment accepted trade practice authorized by any law or agreement with the central government, or to meet defence requirements or to ensure supply of essential goods and services from being termed MTP.

Chapter V of the MRTP Act deals with RTPs and UTPs.[31] These provisions provide the bread and butter cases to the organization. Twelve kinds of trade practices are deemed to be restrictive. The list of such practices is given below:

(a) any agreement which restricts, or is likely to restrict, by any method the persons or classes of persons to whom goods are sold or from whom goods are bought;
(b) any agreement requiring a purchaser of goods, as a condition of such purchase, to purchase some other goods;
(c) any agreement restricting in any manner the purchaser in the course of his trade from acquiring or otherwise dealing in any goods other than those of the seller or any other person;
(d) any agreement to purchase or sell goods or to tender for the sale or purchase of goods only at prices or on terms or conditions agreed upon between the seller or purchasers;

[29] AIR 2002 SC 2728 *Haridas Exports*.

[30] Only one law affecting IPR is explicitly mentioned in the MRTP Act.

[31] UTPs were inserted in 1984.

(e) any agreement to grant or allow concessions or benefits, including allowances, discount, rebates, or credit in connection with, or by reason of, dealings;
(f) any agreement to sell goods on condition that the process to be charged on re-sale by the purchaser shall be the prices stipulated by the seller unless it is clearly stated that prices lower than those prices may be charged;
(g) any agreement to limit, restrict, or withhold the output or supply of any goods or allocate any area or market for the disposal of the goods;
(h) any agreement not to employ or restrict the employment of any method, machinery, or process in the manufacture of goods;
(i) any agreement for the exclusion from any trade association of any person carrying on or intending to carry on, in good faith the trade in relation to which the trade association is formed;
(j) any agreement to sell goods at such prices as would have the effect of eliminating competition or a competitor;
    (i) any agreement restricting in any manner, the class or number of wholesalers, producers, or suppliers from whom any goods may be bought;
    (ii) any agreement as to the bids which any of the parties thereto may offer at an auction for the sale of goods or any agreement whereby any party thereto agrees to abstain from bidding at any auction for the sale of goods; or
(k) any agreement which the Central Government may, by notification, specify for the time being as being one relating to a restrictive trade practice.

This list was interpreted by the Supreme Court of India as an inclusive list[32] in view of the general definition of RTP in Section 2(o) of the MRTP Act. Registration of agreements deemed to be RTP is compulsory. The MRTPC can, however, inquire into any RTP, irrespective of whether the agreement is registered, and pass a 'cease and desist' order if the practice is found to be prejudicial to public interest. An RTP is deemed to be prejudicial to public interest unless it falls in a negative list, which is broad enough to take the sting out of these provisions. Maintenance of re-sale price found special provision in the law and was strictly prohibited unless exemption was granted by the MRTPC on the grounds of maintaining quality and services required after sale.

32 AIR 1995 SC 1881 *Voltas Ltd.*

Provisions relating to UTPs were added to the mandate of the MRTPC by the 1984 amendments and broadly cover 'unfair method or unfair or deceptive practices'. As a result, misleading advertisements or advertisements disparaging products of rivals are considered unfair. Although, impact of most cases brought before the MRTPC are limited, resource requirement is high since the procedures for dealing with RTPs have been adopted for UTPs.

The director general[33] is to assist the MRTPC in investigation but has no power to compel attendance or evidence. The power of dawn raids vests with the central government, which can appoint an inspector for investigation.[34] The MRTPC or the DG do not have any role in this and it is difficult to understand how the government is expected to get the necessary information.

Penal provisions of civil imprisonment and fines are incorporated in the law, but the authority to penalize the offenders lies with sessions court, which has little experience of the complexities of this kind of economic law. This is, perhaps, the weakest link in the armoury. Reportedly, cases filed in the civil courts drag for years and make the law considerably less effective. The law has a confidentiality clause. Appeals against the orders of the MRTPC lie with the Supreme Court of India, the highest court in the country.

High Level Committee on Competition Policy and Law (Raghavan Committee)

The Raghavan Committee was set up in 1999.[35] The TOR inter alia included the following:

> a suitable legislative framework, in the light of international developments and the need to promote competition, relating to competition law, including law relating to mergers and demergers. Such a legislative framework could entail a new law or appropriate amendments to the MRTP Act, 1969.

The Raghavan Committee noticed that the word 'competition' has been used sparsely in the MRTP Act[36] and effectively finds place only at two places; while defining restrictive trade practice in Section 2(o) and in

[33] Original enactment had a registrar, which was re-designated director general in 1984.

[34] The inspector has powers to search under Sections 240 and 240A of the Companies Act, 1956.

[35] Order No. 1/9/99-CL-V of 25 October 1999.

[36] p. 68 of the report.

Section 38(1)(h). While a generic definition of competition is provided in Section 2(o) of the MRTP Act, precise definitions of anticompetitive practices like abuse of dominance, cartel, collusion, boycott, refusal to deal, bid rigging, predatory pricing, and so on, are necessary to effectively detect such behaviour and impose sanctions against them. Lack of precise definitions had led to different judicial interpretations, sometimes contradictory. These judicial pronouncements are binding precedents for future amendment to the MRTP Act. The MRTPC itself is constrained to fit anticompetitive behaviour into one or more of the provisions of the law in the absence of precise definitions. The Raghavan Committee noted that '[c]artels, to give another illustration, are not mentioned or defined in any of the clauses of Section 33(1) of the MRTP Act, though the MRTP Commission has attempted to fit such offences under one or more clauses of Section 33(1) by way of interpretation of the language used therein'.[37] The existing law was found to be inadequate to deal with implementation of the WTO agreements. The MRTP Act does not have merger control provisions since 1991.[38] The Committee recognized the necessity of having specific merger control provisions at par with other modern competition laws.[39] Provisions dealing with unfair trade practices overlap with similar provisions in the Consumers Protection Act, 1986, and in the MRTP Act. The Raghavan Committee found the MRTP Act to be falling short of squarely addressing competition and anticompetitive practices. It emphatically stated that '... the MRTP Act, in comparison with Competition Laws of many countries, is inadequate for fostering competition in the market and trade and for reducing, if not eliminating, anticompetitive practices in the country's domestic and international trade'.[40] Based on this analysis, the Raghavan Committee found it expedient to have a new competition law.[41] It will be useful to understand the underlying principles that led to the new enactment.

The Committee desired the focus of the new law to be on preventing anticompetitive practices that reduce welfare. While free markets produce desired outcomes, they do so only when protected from abuses. Therefore, '... the only legitimate goal of Competition Law is the maximization of economic

[37] p. 70 of the report.

[38] The merger control powers were with the central government until 1991.

[39] Merger control under the general provisions of monopolization in the Sherman Act had not succeeded in the US, leading to introduction of specific provisions in the Clayton Act.

[40] p. 68 of the report.

[41] The details of the enactment are in another chapter in this book.

welfare'.[42] The Committee further desired that the competition authority should be governed by established competition principles. The Committee was aware of the pitfalls and recommended a cautious approach to achieve a balance between over-intervention and exemption from sanction in the name of 'public interest'. The role of industrial organization theory in competition analysis was recognized and it recommended incorporation of a host of factors to be considered by the competition authority in competition assessment.

The Raghavan Committee was determined to have merger control provisions in the new legislation. It sought to make a distinction between horizontal mergers, vertical mergers, and conglomerate mergers on the basis of their differing degrees of impact on competition. But it chose to opt for a soft regime which has voluntary notification for mergers above rather high threshold limits and time-bound decisions to reduce transaction cost. The Committee perhaps felt that provision for action in law up to one year after merger would provide sufficient deterrence.

The Committee was convinced that government enterprises as well as departments should be brought under the purview of competition law. The only exception should be sovereign functions of the government like defence. The policy of purchase or price preference to government owned enterprises was recommended to be discontinued. These recommendations were in spite of the fact that many countries exempt government enterprises from purview of competition law.

The Committee also recommended that there should be no distinction between ultimate consumer and intermediate consumer.

While the Committee presumed some anticompetitive behaviour to be injurious to competition, it recognized the primacy of *rule of reason* test for the rest. This was expected to provide a real chance to an enterprise to put forth defence in terms of the many factors that the competition authority is to take into account in its competition assessment. The primacy of *rule of reason* test over *per se* rule is universal among modern competition laws; the latter is invoked only against hard-core anticompetitive behaviour like cartelization.

While competition cases are tried by courts in many countries, the Raghavan Committee did not find it suitable for India, given the inexperience of the judiciary in dealing with free market problems. According to the Committee, a specialized agency is preferable in developing countries.[43]

The Committee made detailed recommendations regarding the administrative set up of a competition authority. Its main objectives should be to

42 p. 29 of the report.

43 p. 57 of the report.

administer the competition law and engage 'proactively in Governmental policy formulation'.[44] In order to achieve these objectives, it should be manned by experts in various fields who can be removed only with the concurrence of the Supreme Court of India. The body should be independent and autonomous. Its investigative, prosecutorial, and adjudicative functions need to be separate and its proceedings should be transparent and rule-bound. The competition authority's reach should be extra-territorial and it should have powers to punish the guilty and levy fines.

The Raghavan Committee laid great emphasis on a competition advocacy role for the competition authority, and rightly so. The low awareness of competition issues among stakeholders and the governments (central as well as states) in India clearly requires intensive advocacy initiative.

Competition Law and Competition Commission of India

The new competition law, that is, Competition Act, 2002, was enacted in January 2003 after taking into consideration the recommendations of the Raghavan Committee and deliberations of the Standing Committee on Finance.

The preamble of the Competition Act provides for establishment of the Competition Commission of India (CCI). The CCI was established on 14 October 2003. The chairman and a member were appointed by the government and the member entered office in the same month.

Writ petitions were filed in the Supreme Court and Chennai High Court challenging certain provisions of the new Act. The government undertook to carry out certain amendments to the Act in its affidavits filed before the Supreme Court. The Petition was disposed of by the Supreme Court on 20 January 2005. The government has introduced an amendment bill in Parliament in March 2006 for carrying out certain amendments to the Competition Act, 2002. The Bill is under consideration in Parliament as of writing this chapter.

During this period, all the sections of the Competition Act have not been notified, including the sections relating to undertaking inquiries and regulatory work. However, the provision dealing with competition advocacy has been notified; CCI has undertaken this work seriously in spite of constraints of manpower and financial independence. A brief summary of the work done is given below and will throw light on its achievements.

[44] p. 57 of the report.

The current mandate of CCI is competition advocacy, public awareness, and training. It has taken many steps for the capacity building of the stakeholders, including its staff. Seminars and workshops with business associations like Confederation of Indian Industry and Federation of Chambers of Commerce and Industry, professional institutions like Indian Chartered Accountants Institute, state governments, central government ministries/departments like Planning Commission, National Manufacturing Competitiveness Council, and the like have been conducted. A Competition Forum has been set up as a platform for inviting experts in competition and trade-related matters to talk to the staff as part of the capacity building initiative. Draft course curriculum has been sent to over 140 universities/institutions to be incorporated in degree courses to build future competition experts.

General regulations for conduct of business have been drafted. There are many innovative features in the regulations. Provisions for consent order, time limit for pronouncement of order, restrictions on number of adjournments, electronic filing of complaints, and confidentiality of information collected are a few illustrations. A draft regulation on predatory pricing is under preparation. These are primarily aimed at being in a state of readiness and to be able to take on enforcement work as soon as the relevant sections are notified.

Competition authorities are interested in understanding market structure. Experts from various universities and institutions are taking up market studies. These studies would cover sectors like transport, cement, steel, automotive tyre, paints, energy, and so on. The outcomes are expected to be useful in the competition advocacy programme of the Competition Commission of India.

23

India*

The Competition Act and Its Enforcement

Vinod Dhall

India's competition law, the Competition Act, 2002 (hereinafter referred to as 'the Act'), was passed by the Parliament in December 2002 and received the assent of the president of India on 13 January 2003,[1] thereby becoming the law of the land from that date.

The finance minister of India in his budget speech delivered in February 1999 had stated that the Monopolies and Restrictive Trade Practices Act, 1969 (MRTP Act), had become obsolete in certain areas in the light of international economic developments, and the government had decided to appoint a committee to propose a modern competition law.[2] Subsequently, a High Level Committee on Competition Law and Policy was constituted which submitted its report to the government in May 2000. After consultations

* The author wishes to record his appreciation for the assistance given by Ms Mansi Tewari.

[1] See Gazette of India, Extraordinary, dated Tuesday, 14 January 2003.

[2] See Budget Speech (Union Budget 1999–2000), 27 February 1999, para 23. Available at http://finmin.nic.in/topics/union_budget/oldbudgets/budget1999-2000/b5/b5.htm.

with all concerned, including the trade and industry associations and the general public, the government decided to enact a new law on competition, that is, the Competition Act, 2002. The Act is a central law in India, that is, a law of the Union Government, and there is no corresponding law enacted at the level of the constituent states.

The Act was part of India's economic reform and globalization process started in the early nineties which necessitated aligning the economic laws of the country with the new economic scenario. The Statement of Objects and Reasons[3] annexed to the Competition Bill, 2001, stated the reasons for enacting the new law in the following words:

> In the pursuit of globalization, India has responded by opening up its economy, removing controls and resorting to liberalization. The natural corollary to this is that the Indian market should be geared to face competition from within the country and outside. The Monopolies and Restrictive Trade Practices Act, 1969 has become obsolete in certain respects in the light of international economic developments, relating more particularly to competition laws, and there is a need to shift our focus from curbing monopolies to promoting competition.

The objective of the Act may be gathered from its preamble[4] which states as follows:

> An Act to provide, keeping in view the economic development of the country, for the establishment of a Commission to prevent practices having adverse effect on competition, to promote and sustain competition in markets, to protect the interests of consumers and to ensure freedom of trade carried on by other participants in markets, in India, and for matters connected therewith or incidental thereto.

Section 18 of the Act further states that 'it shall be the duty of the Commission to eliminate practices having adverse effect on competition, to promote and sustain competition, protect the interests of consumers and ensure freedom of trade carried on by other participants, in markets in India'. In light of this, the Hon'ble Supreme Court of India in the case of *Commission* v. *Steel Authority of India Limited*[5] interpreted the principal objects of the Act as being to eliminate practices having adverse effects on competition, to promote and sustain

[3] See Statement of Objects & Reasons annexed to Competition Bill, 2001.

[4] See the Indian Competition Act, 2002. Available at http://www.competition-commission.gov.in/Act/competition_act2002.pdf.

[5] Civil Appeal No. 7779 of 2010 decided on 9 September 2010.

competition in the market, to protect the interests of the consumers and ensure freedom of trade carried on by the participants in the market, in view of the economic development of the country. The apex court also stated that 'the Act requires not only protection of trade but also protection of consumer interest'. The preamble and Section 18 read together would suggest that the Act seeks to achieve its objectives through the establishment of the Competition Commission of India (hereafter referred to as 'the Commission'), the enforcing authority, which in turn is given the mandate spelt out as above in Section 18.

The previously mentioned objectives are not unique and these appear in the competition laws of other jurisdictions as well. The principal objective of a competition law is to maintain and protect the competitive process; this figures as a core objective of the Act and also as a principal duty of the Commission. Economic theory asserts that competition itself maximizes consumer interest; nevertheless the protection of the interests of the consumers has been emphasized as a distinct objective of the Act. Ensuring the freedom of trade also figures as a separate objective of the Act. This may be seen in the light of the fundamental right to carry on any trade or business that is guaranteed in the Indian Constitution.[6] This view corresponds to the school of thought that regards competition law as being important to the preservation of economic freedom, much as political democracy is important to the protection of fundamental personal freedom. In Germany, the Act against Restraints of Competition is regarded by some as the 'constitution of the free market economy'.[7] The US Supreme Court noted in *Topco*, 'Antitrust laws in general, and the Sherman Act in particular, are the Magna Carta of free enterprise. They are as important to the preservation of economic freedom and our free-enterprise system as the Bill of Rights is to the protection of our fundamental personal freedoms. And the freedom guaranteed each and every business, no matter how small, is the freedom to compete—to assert with vigor, imagination, devotion, and ingenuity whatever economic muscle it can muster.'[8]

The Act regulates:

1. anticompetitive agreements, prohibited by Section 3 of the Act;
2. abuse of dominant position, prohibited by Section 4 of the Act; and
3. combinations, regulated by Sections 5 and 6 of the Act.

[6] Article 19(1)(g) of the Constitution of India guarantees the fundamental right of citizens 'to practice any profession, or to carry on any occupation, trade or business'.

[7] See chapter 'Competition Law in Germany' by Ulf Böge.

[8] *United States* v. *Topco Associates Inc. 405 US 593(1972).*

Sections 3 and 4 of the Act came into force on 20 May 2009[9] while Sections 5 and 6 came into force on 1 June 2011.[10] The Commission has reviewed anti-competitive practices in diverse sectors such as stock exchanges, infrastructure, travel, automobile, real estate, pharmaceuticals, financial sector, publishing, manufacturing, mining, telecom, and entertainment since the provisions were notified and has gone on to impose significant financial penalties.

References have been made in this chapter to the development of jurisprudence in India and to competition laws in other countries, which might help in better understanding the provisions of this Act. However, references to foreign laws should not be construed to mean that the provisions of the Act carry identical meanings as in those laws. An uncritical importation of concepts or ideas from foreign laws without regard to the context in which these concepts or ideas were developed in India would be a mistake. As far as possible, the Commission has tried to contextualize these laws for the Indian market and apply the language of the Act. Also, this chapter is concerned primarily with the substantive provisions of the Act; other provisions, though important, are not the subject of discussion here.

Anticompetitive Agreements

Section 3(1) prohibits any agreement with respect to production, supply, distribution, storage, acquisition or control of goods or provision of services which causes or is likely to cause an appreciable adverse effect on competition within India.[11] Further, Section 3(2) provides that any agreement in contravention of this provision shall be void.[12] Section 3(3) prohibits agreements, including cartels, between competitors. Section 3(4) deals with vertical agreements that have an appreciable adverse effect on competition.

The Commission has interpreted Section 3(1) not just as a declaratory provision but as a provision that can be invoked independently.[13]

[9] Government of India Notification, dated 15 May 2009, S.O 1241 E in the Extraordinary Gazette of India. Available at http://cci.gov.in/images/media/notifications/cf3.pdf.

[10] Government of India Notification, dated 4 March 2011, S.O. 479 E in the Extraordinary Gazette of India. Available at http://cci.gov.in/images/media/notifications/SO479(E),480(E),481(E),482(E)240611.pdf.

[11] Section 3(1), Indian Competition Act, 2002.

[12] Section 3(2), Indian Competition Act, 2002.

[13] Case No. 39 of 2012, *Ramakant Kini* v. *Dr. L.H. Hiranandani Hospital, Powai, Mumbai*, order dated 5 February 2014. Available at http://www.cci.gov.in/May2011/OrderOfCommission/27/392012.pdf.

Significantly, the Commission has noted that 'Section 3(3) and section 3(4) are expansion of section 3(1) but are not exhaustive of the scope of section 3(1). There can be various kinds of agreements among enterprises which may fall under Section 3(1) including agreements which are against the interests of consumers, affect freedom of trade and cause or are likely to cause appreciable adverse effect on competition in India. Section 3(3) carves out only an area of Section 3(1). The scope of Section 3(1) is thus vast and has to be considered keeping in view the aims and objects of the Act i.e. freedom of trade, consumer welfare etc. by ensuring that the markets are not distorted and made anti-competitive by such agreements of the enterprises which appreciably adversely affect the market or are likely to adversely affect the market.'[14] In this way, the Commission has read a very wide scope into Section 3(1) and has used this wide interpretation of the section to hold agreements in certain cases which are neither horizontal (Section 3[3]) nor vertical (Section 3[4]) as being in violation of the Act.

The term 'agreement' itself is defined in Section 2(b) of the Act; it includes any arrangement or understanding or action in concert whether or not it is formal or in writing or it is intended to be enforceable by legal proceedings. Clearly, the definition which is inclusive and not exhaustive, is a wide one. The agreement does not necessarily have to be in the form of a formal document executed by the parties. It may include even what is commonly called a 'gentlemen's agreement'.

As in the Indian law, in competition laws generally, the term 'agreement' is given a wide definition or meaning.[15] This is because the parties often choose not to formalize the agreement; in fact sometimes they go to great lengths to hide the agreement or any trace of it. In particular, cartels are usually shrouded in secrecy. The World Bank/OECD Glossary states that agreements 'may be implicit, and their boundaries are nevertheless understood and observed by convention among the different members' and 'most agreements which give rise to anticompetitive prices tend to be covert arrangements that are not easily detected by competition

[14] Case No. 39 of 2012, *Ramakant Kini* v. *Dr. L.H. Hiranandani Hospital, Powai, Mumbai*, order dated 5 February 2014. Available at http://www.cci.gov.in/May2011/OrderOfCommission/27/392012.pdf.

[15] For instance, according to Section 1(ii) of South Africa's Competition Act, 1998, 'agreement when used in relation to a prohibited practice, includes a contract, arrangement or understanding, whether or not legally enforceable'. Available at http://www.compcom.co.za/thelaw/ConsolidatedAct.doc.

authorities'.[16] In *Technip S.A.* v. *S.M.S. Holding Pvt. Ltd.*,[17] the court took note of *Guinness Plc* v. *Distillers Co. Plc* where the Takeover Panel was to determine whether Guinness had acted in concert with Piptec when Piptec purchased shares in Distillers Co. Plc. The Panel observed, 'The nature of acting in concert requires the definition to be drawn in deliberately wide terms. It covers an understanding as well as an agreement, and an informal as well as a formal arrangement which leads to the purchase of shares to acquire control of a company. This is necessary as arrangements are often informal, and the understanding may arise from a hint. The understanding may be tacit, and the definition covers situations where the parties act on the basis of a nod or a wink...unless persons formally declare this agreement or understanding, there is rarely direct evidence of action in concert and the panel must draw upon its experience and common sense to determine whether those involved in any dealings have some form of understanding and are acting in cooperation with each other.' In *Registrar of Restrictive Trade Agreements* v. *W.H.Smith and Sons*,[18] the court observed, 'people who combine together to keep up prices do not shout it from the house tops. They keep it quiet. They make their own arrangements in the cellar, where no one can see. They will not put anything into writing nor even into words. A nod or wink will do. Parliament as well is aware of this. So it included not only an "agreement" properly so called but any "arrangement", however informal.' However, in the EU in some recent cases, for example, *Bayer*[19] *&* *Volkswagen*,[20] the court disagreed with the EC's expansive interpretation of 'agreement' and has effectively toughened the standards for proof of agreement in cases of restrictive distribution.

Following a similar approach, the Commission too has given a wide interpretation to 'agreement' and concurs that 'existence of a written agreement is not necessary to establish common understanding, common design, common motive, common intent or commonality of approach among the parties to an anti-competitive agreement'.[21] In *Re Director*

[16] World Bank/OECD. 'Glossary of Industrial Organisation Economics and Competition Law'.

[17] (2005) 5 SCC 465, 485.

[18] (1968) 3 All ER 721.

[19] *Bundesverband der Arzneimittel – Importeure and Commission of the European Communities* v. *Bayer AG C-2/01P and C-3/01P.*

[20] *European Commission* v. *Volkswagen Case No. C-74/04P*

[21] *All India Tyre Dealers Federation* v. *Tyre Manufacturers. MRTP Case RTPE No. 20/2008.* Available at http://www.cci.gov.in/May2011/OrderOfCommission/202008.pdf

General (Supplies & Disposals), Ministry of Commerce v. *M/s Puja Enterprises and Others*,[22] it further clarified that 'the definition, being inclusive and not exhaustive, is a wide one. The understanding may be tacit, and the definition covers situations where the parties act on the basis of a nod or a wink. There is rarely a direct evidence of action in concert and the Commission has to determine whether those involved in such dealings had some form of understanding and were acting in co-operation with each other. In the light of the definition of the term "agreement", the Commission has to find sufficiency of evidence on the basis of benchmark of "preponderance of probabilities"'.[23]

Although rare, the Commission has discovered direct evidence in some cases. In *Re: Bengal Chemist and Druggist Association and in Re Director, Directorate of Drugs*, the Commission found clear evidence from the minutes of meeting of the Bengal Chemists and Druggists Association (BCDA) that it had taken concerted action against retailers who were providing discounts on the maximum retail price to customers.[24] In *FICCI—Multiplex Association of India* v. *United Producers/Distributors Forum and others*[25] the Commission found evidence that the film distributors' forum had 'brought together direct competitors who exchanged analysis of the market conditions, and shared information in dealing with multiplex owners in "one to one" negotiations'.[26] Further evidence of collusive action was established when one of the defendants pleaded that it was not aware that such discussions were unlawful and that it would never have participated if it was so aware.[27] The Commission, however, rightly refused to accept ignorance of law as a plea and imposed penalties.

[22] Ref. Case No. 01/2012 of *Director General (Supplies & Disposals), Ministry of Commerce, Government of India* v. *M/s Puja Enterprises and Others*. Available at http://www.cci.gov.in/May2011/OrderOfCommission/012012.pdf

[23] Ibid.

[24] In *Re: Bengal Chemists and Druggists Association and Reference Case No. 01 of 2013 Re: Reference Case No. 01 of 2013* filed under Section 19(1)(b) of the Competition Act, 2002 by Dr. Chintamoni Ghosh, Director, Directorate of Drugs, para 45-46. Available at http://www.cci.gov.in/May2011/OrderOfCommission/27/022012.pdf, last accessed on 25 September 2014.

[25] Case No. 1 of 2009. Available at http://www.cci.gov.in/May2011/OrderOfCommission/FICCIOrder260511.pdf, last accessed on 25 September 2014.

[26] Case No. 1 of 2009. Available at http://www.cci.gov.in/May2011/OrderOfCommission/FICCIOrder260511.pdf.

[27] Case No. 1 of 2009. Available at http://www.cci.gov.in/May2011/OrderOfCommission/FICCIOrder260511.pdf

In the *Ref. Case of Director General (Supplies & Disposals), Ministry of Commerce, Government of India* v. *M/s Puja Enterprises and Others*, the Commission also noted that even when there is documentary evidence in the form of minutes of a meeting, it is sparse and fragmentary and generally not sufficient to establish proof of an agreement directly; thus in most cases the existence of such agreement has to be inferred from a number of coincidences and other indicators which have no other plausible explanation.[28]

Once an agreement has been determined as causing or likely to cause an appreciable adverse effect on competition, such agreement, being void, cannot be enforced by the parties in a court of law. This could lead to serious difficulties for a party in trying to enforce any claim under such agreement in a court of law; therefore the consequences of an agreement being held to be anticompetitive, could be far reaching for the parties.

The term 'appreciable adverse effect on competition', used in Section 3(1), has not been defined in the Act. However, Section 19(3) states that while determining whether an agreement has an appreciable adverse effect on competition under Section 3, the Commission shall have due regard to all or any of the following factors: (a) creation of barriers to new entrants in the market; (b) driving existing competitors out of the market; (c) foreclosure of competition by hindering entry into the market; (d) accrual of benefits to consumers; (e) improvements in production or distribution of goods or provision of services; (f) promotion of technical, scientific, and economic development by means of production or distribution of goods or provision of services.[29] The first three factors relate to negative effects on competition while the remaining three relate to beneficial effects. Thus, in assessing whether an agreement has an appreciable adverse effect on competition, both the harmful and beneficial effects, as reflected in the previously mentioned factors, are to be considered and weighed against each other. 'Barriers to new entrants' can be created, for example, through an agreement to set unduly high standards. 'Driving existing competitors out of the market' could happen if an enterprise enters into an exclusive supply agreement with distributors that obliges them to discontinue their trade with other suppliers, or if certain suppliers enter into agreement to sharply reduce the prices with a view to drive out competitors who are not party to the agreement.

[28] Ref. Case No. 01/2012 of *Director General (Supplies & Disposals), Ministry of Commerce, Government of India* v. *M/s Puja Enterprises and Others*.

[29] It may be noted that there is a separate set of factors given in Section 20(4) for determining appreciable adverse effect on competition in respect of combinations.

Competition may be 'foreclosed' if an enterprise enters into a long-term agreement with a raw material or components supplier, thereby adversely affecting supplies to the competitors. 'Accrual of benefits to consumers' can arise from lower prices or improved quality or more efficient delivery of services. 'Improvements in production or distribution' can be reflected in rapid after-sale service or in a broader range of products being stocked by distributors. 'Promotion of technical, scientific and economic development' may result from agreements relating to research and development or specialization in production. This approach to determining the 'appreciable adverse effect on competition' is similar to the rule of reason that is common in the competition laws of most countries.

The World Bank/OECD Glossary states that the rule of reason is '[a] legal approach—where an attempt is made to evaluate the pro-competition features of the restrictive business practice against its anticompetitive effects in order to decide whether or not the practice should be prohibited'.[30] *Black's Law Dictionary* defines the rule of reason in antitrust law as a 'judicial doctrine holding that a trade practice violates the Sherman Act only if the practice is an unreasonable restraint of trade, based on economic factors'.[31] In the US, the rule of reason is applied in a more specific way. The principal question is whether the agreement will increase market power; if there is no significant indication to this effect, there is no case. On the other hand, if the indication is very strong, and there are no obvious efficiencies from the agreement and no good explanation that the agreement is a response to the market or is helping to produce or deliver something better or at lower prices, there is a presumption of anticompetitive effects and the defendant must come forward to show that there is no market harm. If there is no presumption, the plaintiff must produce more evidence of market power or its increase. In India, in *Tata Engineering & Locomotive Co. Ltd.*,[32] the Supreme Court of India observed that to determine whether the restraint promoted or suppressed competition, it was necessary to consider three matters: 'First, what facts are peculiar to the business to which the restraint is applied. Second, what was the condition

[30] World Bank/OECD. 'Glossary of Industrial Organisation Economics and Competition Law'.

[31] *Black's Law Dictionary*, 7th ed., p. 1033.

[32] *Tata Engineering and Locomotive Company Ltd.* v. *Registrar of Restrictive Trade Agreements* (1977) 47 Com. Cas 520 (SC*): (1977) 2 SCR 685:* (1977) 2 SCC 55. See also *Board of Trade of City of Chicago* v. *United States 246 US 231(1918)*. Available at http://caselaw.lp.findlaw.com/scripts/getcase.pl?navby=case&court=us&vol=246&page=231.

before and after the restraint was imposed. Third, what is the nature of the restraint and what is its actual and probable effect.'

Competition law usually places anticompetitive agreements in two categories—horizontal agreements and vertical agreements, with horizontal agreements being viewed more seriously than vertical agreements. The Act does not specifically use the terms horizontal agreement and vertical agreement. However, the agreements referred to in Section 3(3) are horizontal agreements and those referred to in Section 3(4) are vertical agreements.

Horizontal agreements of the types described in Section 3(3) are presumed to have an appreciable adverse effect on competition. These are agreements, including cartels, which (a) directly or indirectly determine purchase or sale prices; (b) limit or control production, supply, markets, technical development, investment, or provision of services; (c) share the market or source of production or provision of services by way of allocation of geographical market, or type of goods or services, or number of customers in the market; (d) directly or indirectly result in bid rigging or collusive bidding. Thus, cartels and similar horizontal agreements are placed in a special category and are subject to the adverse presumption of being anticompetitive. This approach is similar, but is not necessarily identical, to the per se rule in the US law.

The per se rule and its rationale were explained by the US courts in a number of cases, for example, *Northern Pacific Railway Co* v. *United States*,[33] *Arizona* v. *Maricopa County Medical Society*,[34] and *Continental T.V.* v. *GTE Sylvania Inc.*[35] In *Northern Pacific Railway*, the court observed that 'there are certain agreements or practices which because of their pernicious effects on competition and lack of any redeeming virtue are conclusively presumed to be unreasonable and, therefore illegal without any elaborate inquiry as to the precise harm they have caused or the business excuse for their use. This principle of per se unreasonableness not only makes the type of restraints that are proscribed by the Sherman Act more certain to the benefit of everyone concerned, but it also avoids the necessity for an incredibly complicated and prolonged economic investigation into the entire history of the industry involved, as well as related industries, in an effort to determine at large whether a particular restraint has been unreasonable—an inquiry so often wholly fruitless when undertaken.'[36] In *Jefferson Parish Hospital*, the court observed that the rationale for per se rule, in part, is to avoid a burdensome

[33] 356 US 1 (1958).

[34] 457 US 332 (1982).

[35] 433 US 36 (1977).

[36] 356 US 1 (1958).

inquiry into the actual market conditions in situations where the likelihood of anticompetitive conduct is so great as to render unjustified the costs of determining whether the particular case at bar involves anticompetitive conduct.[37] The per se rule, as opposed to the rule of reason, has been applied by the courts in respect of particularly harmful agreements such as agreements relating to price fixing, allocation of territories, bid rigging, group boycotts, and concerted refusal to deal, similar to the situations covered by Section 3(3). It should be noted, however, that in recent years the approach of the US courts has undergone a transition from a dichotomous approach based on two distinct rules, the per se rule and the rule of reason, to a more nuanced and case-specific inquiry tailored to the suspect conduct in each particular case.[38]

The principle of 'shall presume', used in Section 3(3), has been explained by the courts in India in numerous cases, such as in *Sodhi Transport Co* v. *State of Uttar Pradesh*[39] and *R. S. Nayak* v. *A. R. Antulay.*[40] In *Sodhi Transport Co*, the court observed that 'the words "shall presume" have been used in the Indian judicial lore for over a century to convey that they lay down a rebuttable presumption in respect of matters with reference to which they are used … and not laying down a rule of conclusive proof'. The court also observed that 'a presumption is not in itself evidence but only makes a prima facie case for the party in whose favour it exists. It indicates the person on whom the burden of proof lies. When the presumption is conclusive, it obviates the production of any other evidence. But when it is rebuttable, it only points out the party on which lies the duty of going forward on the evidence on the fact presumed, and when that party has produced evidence fairly and reasonably tending to show that the real fact is not as presumed, the purpose of presumption is over.'[41] This suggests that in the case of horizontal agreements listed in Section 3(3), once it is established that such an agreement exists, it will be presumed that the agreement has an appreciable adverse effect on competition; the burden of proof would then shift to the defendant.

The Commission has taken into account that in India there are only civil penalties for cartel arrangements and hence the standard of proof

[37] *Jefferson Parish Hospital Distt. No. 2* v. *Hyde* 466 US 2(1984).

[38] See *Polygram Holding Inc.* v. *FTC 416F.3d 29(D.C.Cir.2005)* referred to in Fox, Eleanor M., Lawrence A. Sullivan, and Rudolph J.R. Peritz. 2004. 'Cases and Materials for U.S. Antitrust in Global Context', 2nd ed. Thomson/West.

[39] AIR 1980 SC 1099.

[40] AIR 1986 SC 2045.

[41] AIR 1986 SC 1099, 1105.

need not be as high as in criminal matters. It noted that the test of proof will be the 'balance of probability' and 'liaison of intentions' which can be established with the support of indirect or circumstantial evidence.[42] In the case of *Builders Association of India* v. *Cement Manufacturers' Association and Others*,[43] the Commission found that cement prices had increased by similar margins in all regions of the country without any regard for demand and supply in different territories, local taxes, etc. This was one of the corroborative links in the case which brought the Commission to a finding of infringement. The cement companies were not able to provide explanation for the 'price parallelism' that was observed. Since the cost of production, freight charges, local taxes, etc. were not the same, the conclusion that the Commission arrived at pointed towards prior consultation before fixing prices. Another observation in this case was that prices seemed to increase almost immediately after a meeting of the Cement Manufacturers' Association.[44] All of these coincidences and circumstantial proofs of liaison, once taken together, were indicative that there was indeed collusion between the cement manufacturers. The test of 'preponderance of probabilities' was held to be satisfied.

Section 3(3) also covers cartels. A cartel is defined in Section 2(c), which states that a cartel 'includes an association of producers, sellers, distributors, traders, or service providers, who, by agreement amongst themselves, limit, control, or attempt to control the production, distribution, sale or price of, or, trade in goods or provision of services'. This definition is inclusive and wide. A cartel of producers or sellers usually seeks to do two things: raise prices and limit output. A cartel is regarded as the most pernicious offence since it has no redeeming feature, and there is no question about the harm that it causes to the consumers and to the economy.

Most competition laws treat practices such as those mentioned in Section 3(3) as particularly grave violations of the law and, as stated earlier, usually subject these to the per se rule. Price fixing may not refer necessarily to setting a uniform and inflexible price; it can also refer to setting an administered

[42] Suo-Moto Case No. 03 of 2011 (In Re: suo-motu case against LPG cylinder manufacturers). Order dated 6 August 2014. Available at http://www.cci.gov.in/May2011/OrderOfCommission/LPGMainfeb2.pdf.

[43] Case No. 29 of 2010, *Builders Association of India* v. *Cement Manufacturers' Association and Others*. Order dated 20 June 2012. Available at http://www.cci.gov.in/May2011/OrderOfCommission/292011.pdf.

[44] Case No. 29 of 2010, *Builders Association of India* v. *Cement Manufacturers' Association and Others*. Order dated 20 June 2012. Available at http://www.cci.gov.in/May2011/OrderOfCommission/292011.pdf.

price, which does not vary according to market conditions as competitive prices do. Thus, the prices might be controlled by formulae, agreements, or price leadership.[45] Geographic market sharing is considered by many as highly restrictive as it eliminates the need to police the pricing practices of the companies that are party to the agreement. Bid rigging has been defined in the Act itself in the Explanation to Section 3(3) as 'any agreement between enterprises or persons referred to in Subsection (3) engaged in identical or similar production or trading of goods or provision of services, which has the effect of eliminating or reducing competition for bids or adversely affecting or manipulating the process for bidding'. According to Meyerman et al., bid-rigging can take several forms such as bid suppression, complementary bidding, and bid rotation.[46]

The Commission has looked at a number of cases relating to bid-rigging in government tenders, an indication of the extent to which this practice appears to be prevalent in Indian markets, especially in relation to tenders floated by the government or governmental organizations or public sector companies. In the *suo-motu case against LPG cylinder manufacturers*[47] (hereinafter referred to as the LPG case) the Commission noted that certain factors could create a conducive environment for collusion in tenders. It went on to observe that the following factors will have to be taken into consideration, '1) Market conditions: A constant predictable flow of demand from the public sector tends to increase chances of collusion while significant changes in demand and supply tend to destabilise such arrangements; 2) Number of suppliers: Bid-rigging is more likely to occur in a concentrated market with a small number of suppliers because smaller numbers make it easier to collude and reach an agreement; 3) Few new entrants: In markets where few firms have recently entered, or are likely to enter, the chances of collusion increase; 4) Active trade association: Trade associations can step beyond the boundaries set by competition law because they involve meetings, discussions and cooperation between all (or most) of the competitors; 5) Repetitive bidding: Procurement of similar products on a recurring basis increases the chances of collusion; 6) Identical products: if the products or services being offered by companies are identical

[45] Mittal, D.P. 2003. *Taxmann's Competition Law*, p. 95, Taxmann Allied Services, New Delhi.

[46] Meyerman Gerald, Mary Jean Moltenbrey, and Judy Whalley, et al. 1999. 'Agreements', in World Bank/OECD. 1999. *A Framework for the Design & Implementation of Competition Law and Policy*, World Bank/OECD, p. 23.

[47] Suo-Moto Case No. 03/2011 (In Re: suo-motu case against LPG cylinder manufacturers), order dated 6 August 2014. Available at http://www.cci.gov.in/May2011/OrderOfCommission/LPGMainfeb2.pdf.

(or similar) in nature, the chances of collusion increase; 7) Few substitutes: If there are few or no substitutes for the product or service in question, bidders are more secure from competitive restraints and thus more likely to collude; and 8) Technological Changes: If there has been no change in product design over a long period of time it acts as an additive factor for firms to be able to reach an agreement which can be maintained for a significant duration.'

In *All India Tyre Dealers Federation* v. *Tyre Manufacturers*,[48] the Commission cautioned against trends of a particular industry that may show superficial signs of collusive activity, which though may not be enough to conclude the existence of a cartel. The Commission did not accept the Director General's conclusion that the price rise, despite a fall in the prices of natural rubber, that is, the raw material, was indicative of collusive conduct as the prices of other raw materials like NTC fabric and carbon black were not factored in. The companies were also able to justify price parallelism given that the products sold are homogenous which makes it difficult for businesses to charge different prices to customers.[49]

There may be horizontal agreements for activities other than those mentioned in Section 3(3), for example, for research and technology development, setting standards, or specialization. Such agreements may have efficiency enhancing effects. Horizontal agreements that do not fall in any of the categories listed in Section 3(3) would be covered by Section 3(1), and would therefore be subject to the rule of reason as against the 'shall presume' rule. In some jurisdictions, block exemptions are notified in favour of certain classes of agreements that may be efficiency enhancing; for example, in the EU, block exemptions have been notified in respect of agreements relating to specialization, and research and development.[50]

It is common for enterprises to enter into or form joint ventures for specific or agreed purposes. The proviso to Section 3(3) excludes any joint venture from the 'shall presume' rule if such 'joint venture' is efficiency enhancing. A 'joint venture' has nowhere been defined in the Act. In fact, there is no

[48] MRTP Case RTPE No. 20/2008, *All India Tyre Dealers Federation* v. *Tyre Manufacturers*, order dated 16 January 2013. Available at http://www.cci.gov.in/May2011/OrderOfCommission/202008.pdf.

[49] MRTP Case RTPE No. 20/2008, *All India Tyre Dealers' Federation* v. *Tyre Manufacturers'*, order dated 16 January 2013. Available at http://www.cci.gov.in/May2011/OrderOfCommission/202008.pdf.

[50] The European Commission has adopted block exemptions for agreements relating to specializations (Regulation 2658/2000), research and development (Regulation 2659/2000), technology transfer (Regulation 772/2004), motor vehicle distribution (Regulation 1400/2002), and some others.

standard universally accepted definition of joint venture. Rather, the term is used to describe a range of activities between firms that fall short of a complete merger. For example, Williamson defines a joint venture as 'two or more bodies cooperating for some common purpose. Beyond that it is really a matter of precise description rather than definition, for joint venture is really a convenient label for a variety of activities, which may be undertaken in a variety of ways, with a variety of legal consequences.'[51] Similarly, Harrison notes that the 'term "joint venture" covers a variety of forms of cooperation. The term is vague enough to include all situations in which two or more persons or companies join forces to achieve some common goal.'[52] The Australian law does define 'joint venture', but even that definition can encompass a huge class of arrangements.[53] In order to narrow the range of activities under consideration, some authors restrict attention to joint ventures that involve the explicit creation of a new entity.

Thus, an issue could arise in a case under Section 3 whether a particular agreement amounts to a joint venture or not. There is, therefore, the possibility that enterprises could use the proviso to Section 3(3) as a gateway to escape from the 'shall presume' rule of that subsection. There have not been many such cases decided by the Commission so far.

Section 3(4) deals with vertical agreements. It lists, in particular, five categories of vertical agreements which would be in contravention of Subsection (1) if these cause or are likely to cause an appreciable adverse effect on competition in India. Vertical agreements are therefore subject to the rule of reason, and not to the 'shall presume' rule of Subsection (3). This softer treatment acknowledges that vertical agreements can have beneficial aspects as well, and these need to be weighed against the harmful effects

[51] Williamson D. 1977. 'Trade Practices Law—Its Implications For Mining and Petroleum Joint Ventures', *Australian Mining and Petroleum Law Journal*, 1 (59–108): 85; King, Stephen P. 'Short of a Merger: The Competitive Effects of Horizontal Joint Ventures'. *Competition and Consumer Law Journal*, 6, 227. Available at http://www.economics.unimelb.edu.au/sking/Joint_Ventures.pdf.

[52] Harrison, F. 1975. 'Joint Ventures and the Trade Practices Act 1974: The American Approach and Its Applicability to Australia', *Australian Business Law Review*, 3 (117–31): 117. Quoted in King ibid.

[53] Section 4J(a) of the Trade Practices Act, 1974 defines joint venture as 'an activity in trade or commerce (i) carried out jointly by two or more persons, whether or not in partnership; or (ii) carried on by a body corporate formed by two or more persons for the purpose of enabling those persons to carry on that activity jointly by means of their joint control, or by means of their ownership of shares in the capital, of that body corporate'.

to see if the agreement is on balance anticompetitive. The harmful effects may include restrictions on inter-brand competition, foreclosure of competition, and compartmentalization of markets; and the pro-competitive effects can include efficiency gains, increase in inter-brand competition, and prevention of free-riding.[54] The five vertical agreements particularly listed in Subsection (4) are: (a) tie-in arrangement; (b) exclusive supply agreement; (c) exclusive distribution agreement; (d) refusal to deal; and (e) resale price maintenance. Each of these categories of agreements has been explained in the Explanations below Subsection (4).

Explanation (a) states that a 'tie-in arrangement' includes any agreement requiring a purchaser of goods (called the tying product), as a condition of such purchase, to purchase some other goods (called the tied product). This practice is often resorted to by enterprises to use the popularity of a product (tying product) to promote the sale of a less popular product. In the antitrust cases that Microsoft faced in the US and the EU, one of the allegations was that Microsoft used its dominance in personal computer operating systems (tying product) to push the sale of its other products, specifically its internet browser and media player systems (tied products).[55] According to Fox, tying-in arrangements (and exclusive dealing) can have net negative effects if they fence off so much of the market that not even a few efficient-sized competitors can survive or can bring their products to market efficiently. In such cases, consumer prices are likely to rise and the practice is likely to be found to be illegal under a market-based rule of reason.[56] In *Jefferson Parish Hospital*, the Supreme Court observed that the essential characteristic of an invalid tie-in arrangement lies in the seller's exploitation of its control over the tying product to force the buyer into the purchase of a tied product that the buyer either did not want at all, or might have preferred to purchase elsewhere on different terms.[57] In *Kodak*, the Supreme Court held that the questions to be asked in a tie-in case were: first, whether two separate products were involved; secondly, whether the defendant had required the tied product to be purchased with the tying product; thirdly, whether a substantial amount of inter-state commerce had been affected; and finally, whether the

[54] See Rodger, Barry J., and Angus MacCulloch. 2004. *Competition Law and Policy in the EC and UK*, 3rd ed., pp. 176–8, Routledge-Cavendish Publishing Ltd.

[55] *United States* v. *Microsoft Corporation 258 F. 3d. 34(DC Cir, 2001);* and Case No. COMP/C-3/37.792-Microsoft.

[56] See Fox, Eleanor M. 2002. 'Competition Law', in Lowenfeld, A., *International Economic Law*, Oxford University Press, UK.

[57] 466 US 2(1982).

defendant had market power in the tying product.[58] Tying, in the US, has been subject to the modified per se rule, under which it is per se unlawful whenever the seller has sufficient economic power with respect to the tying product to restrain appreciably free competition in the market for the tied-in product.[59] The recent trend, however, is towards dilution of this approach, and courts seem willing to hear and weigh the defendant's arguments that the tie was efficient and did not cause competitive harm.[60]

The Commission has taken a similar view while stipulating the following conditions as necessary for anticompetitive tying: (a) presence of two separate products or services capable of being tied, (b) the seller must have sufficient economic power with respect to the tying product to appreciably restrain free competition in the market for the tied product, and (c) the tying arrangement must affect a 'not insubstantial' amount of commerce.[61] The Commission has observed further that there are pro-competitive rationales for tying which include assembly benefits arising from both economies of scale and scope and therefore, tying arrangements would not be generally perceived as being anticompetitive unless a substantial portion of the market is affected.

Explanation (b) states that 'exclusive supply agreement' includes any agreement restricting in any manner the purchaser in the course of his trade from acquiring or otherwise dealing in any goods other than those of the seller or any other person. It is thus an agreement placing restrictions on the buyer in favour of the seller, prohibiting the buyer to deal in the goods of any competitor of the seller. For example, such a restriction may be placed by the producer of a product (like motor vehicles) on its distributors or retail showrooms. In certain circumstances, an exclusive supply agreement may contribute to efficiencies though, which must be weighed against the adverse effects.

Explanation (c) states that 'exclusive distribution agreement' includes any agreement to limit, restrict, or withhold the output or supply of any goods or allocate any area or market for the disposal or sale of goods. Such a restriction is, for example, resorted to by producers to demarcate the areas or customers for the operations of their distributors; often such a restriction may be required

[58] *Eastman Kodak Co.* v. *Image Technical Services Inc* 504 US 451, 461–2 (1992) referred to in Whish, Richard. 2005. *Competition Law*, 5th ed., p. 659. Oxford University Press, New York.

[59] *Northern Pacific Railway Co. et al.* v. *United States 356 US* 1(1958).

[60] See Fox, Eleanor M. 2002. 'Competition Law', in Lowenfeld, A. 2002. *International Economic Law*. Oxford University Press, New York.

[61] Case No. 24 of 2011, *Sonam Sharma* v. *Apple Inc.* decided on 19 March 2013. Available at http://www.cci.gov.in/May2011/OrderOfCommission/242011.pdf.

by a distributor itself in order to gain sufficiently from its business development efforts. Exclusive distribution agreements cause concern because these could dilute intra-brand competition and partition the market. This would be particularly so if inter-brand competition is weak between the supplier and its competitors; where this competition is robust, the dilution of intra-brand competition may be outweighed by the strengthened inter-brand competition.[62] In *Tata Engineering and Locomotive Co.* v. *Registrar of Restrictive Trade Practices*,[63] a case under the MRTP Act, the Supreme Court did not find the distribution of areas between the company's distributors as being restrictive.

The Commission analysed exclusive distribution agreements in the case of *Shamsher Kataria* v. *Honda Siel Cars India and Others*,[64] where car manufacturers were found to have imposed restrictive covenants on authorized dealers and original equipment suppliers leading to foreclosure of the aftermarket for supply of spare parts and diagnostic tools. The Commission noted, while ruling against the car manufacturers in this high profile and much debated case that the analysis has to be done in the context of the fact that the consumers do not have access to any competitive products because the exclusive dealers are the only dealers who are selling the manufacturer's products. In this case, the spare parts were found to be unique and not exchangeable with spare parts made by other car manufacturers.

Explanation (d) states that 'refusal to deal' includes any agreement that restricts, or is likely to restrict, by any method the persons or classes of persons to whom goods are sold or from whom goods are bought'. Refusal to deal by a dominant firm with say any of its distributors could have a damaging effect on the business of the distributor. In United Brands, the court held that the refusal to deal by United Brands with its distributor in Denmark was an abuse of its dominance.[65] Similarly, the court upheld EC's decision that Commercial Solvents had abused its dominant position by refusing to supply nitropropane to Zoja.[66]

[62] See Whish. 2005. *Competition Law*, 5th ed. p. 604.

[63] (1977) 47 Com. Cas 520 (SC); (1977) 2 SCR 685, (1977) 2 SCC 55.

[64] Case No. 03 of 2011, *Shamsher Kataria* v. *Honda Siel Cars India and Others,* decided on 25 August 2014. Available at http://www.cci.gov.in/May2011/OrderOfCommission/27/032011.pdf.

[65] *United Brands Co. and United Brands Continental BV* v. *Commission of the European Communities* (1978) 1 CMLR 429 See paras 163, 191, 202, 203, 294. Available at http://www.bailii.org/eu/cases/EUECJ/1978/C2776.html.

[66] Zoja/CSC-ICI JO[1972] L 299/51, [1973] CMLR referred to in Whish. 2005. *Competition Law*, 5th ed., p. 204.

Explanation (e) states that 'resale price maintenance' includes any agreement to sell goods on the condition that the prices to be charged on the resale by the purchaser shall be the prices stipulated by the seller unless it is clearly stated that prices lower than those may be charged. Resale price maintenance can reduce intra-brand competition and increase transparency of prices, which may facilitate collusion.[67] In the EU, price-fixing restrictions on the buyer/reseller are not permitted under the Block Exemption Regulation for vertical agreements. It perceives resale price maintenance as a hardcore restriction which is prohibited and hence excludes it from the purview of the said regulations.[68] On the other hand, the US Supreme Court has moved to a more effects-based analysis by adopting the rule of reason in the *Leegin* case. It is likely that the Commission may pursue a more strict approach to retail price maintenance.

Section 3(5) provides for exemption from the provisions of Section 3 for intellectual property rights (IPRs). It states that nothing in the section shall restrict the right of any person to restrain any infringement of, or to impose reasonable conditions, as may be necessary, for protecting any of his rights which have been or may be conferred upon him under the six laws mentioned in the section, such as the Patents Act, 1970, and the Copyright Act, 1957. Thus, like many competition laws, the Act recognizes the value of IPRs as an incentive to creativity and economic growth. However, to benefit from Section 3(5), the restrictions must be reasonable and necessary to protect the IPR. In some countries, restrictions held to be unreasonable include agreements restricting price, quantity of goods that may be manufactured, and competition between the licensee and the licensor, agreements providing for payment of royalty after the license period and certain types of exclusivity conditions.[69] The Commission in *FICCI—Multiplex Association of India* v. *United Producers/Distributors Forum and others*[70] has held that intellectual

[67] See Whish. 2005. *Competition Law*, 5th ed., p. 591.

[68] Commission Regulation (EU) No. 330/2010 of 20 April 2010 on the application of Article 101(3) of the Treaty on the Functioning of the European Union to categories of vertical agreements and concerted practices. Available at http://eur-lex.europa.eu/legal-content/EN/ALL/?uri=CELEX%3A32010R0330.

[69] See Anderson, Robert, Timothy Daniel, and Alberto Heimler, et al. 1999. 'Abuse of Dominance', in World Bank/OECD. 1999. *A Framework for the Design and Implementation of Competition Law and Policy*, pp. 80–1. World Bank/OECD; and Fox. 2002. *International Economic Law*, pp. 360–2.

[70] Case No. 01 of 2009, *FICCI—Multiplex Association of India* v. *United Producers/Distributors Forum and Others* decided on 25 May 2011. Available at *http://www.cci.gov.in/sites/default/files/FICCIOrder260511_0.pdf*.

property laws do not have any absolute overriding effect on the competition law. The extent of non-obstante clause in Section 3(5) of the Act is not absolute and it exempts the right holder from the rigours of competition law only to protect his rights from infringement and enables the right holder to impose reasonable conditions, as may be necessary, for protecting such rights.

Many countries exempt anticompetitive agreements relating to exports from the operation of the law; this is presumably on the ground that such anticompetitive agreements harm only overseas consumers and are therefore of no concern to the national authorities. A further argument for this could be to support the export efforts of domestic companies and thereby increase national export earnings. In a similar provision, Section 3(5) states that nothing in Section 3 shall restrict the right of any person to export goods from India to the extent to which the agreement relates exclusively to the production, supply, distribution, or control of goods or provision of services for such exports. Thus, the exemption applies only to the extent that the agreement relates to exports, and is not intended to cover the effect that the agreement might have in the domestic market. According to Meyerman et al., 'In the course of reaching agreement on export prices or terms of sale, for example, the participants may exchange information about domestic prices or output, that would permit them to reach an explicit or tacit agreement affecting the domestic market.' They note that while the export cartels may be lawful in exporting countries, they may be prosecuted by the importing countries, depending on the extraterritoriality provisions of their competition laws. However, they expect that increased cooperation between competition authorities and pressures to harmonize competition policy worldwide are likely to result in the elimination of export cartel exemptions or at least make them impractical.[71]

Abuse of Dominant Position

Section 4(1) prohibits any enterprise from abusing its dominant position. The term 'dominant position' has been defined in Explanation (a) below Section 4(e) which states that dominant position 'means a position of strength, enjoyed by an enterprise in the relevant market in India, which enables it to (i) operate independently of competitive forces prevailing in the relevant market; or (ii) affect its competitors or consumers or the relevant market in its favour'.

[71] See Meyerman Gerald, Mary Jean Moltenbrey, and Judy Whalley et al. 1999. 'Agreements', in World Bank/OECD. 1999. *'A Framework for Design and Implementation of Competition Law and Policy'*, p. 36. World Bank/OECD.

Dominant position has been defined in broadly similar terms in the competition laws of several other jurisdictions. The European Commission's Glossary states that 'a firm is in a dominant position if it has the ability to behave independently of its competitors, customers, suppliers and ultimately, the final consumer.'[72] In United Brands, the court stated: 'The dominant position thus referred to by Article 82 relates to a position of economic strength enjoyed by an undertaking which enables it to prevent effective competition being maintained on the relevant market by affording it the power to behave to an appreciable extent independently of its competitors, customers and ultimately of its consumers.'[73]

The Commission in the case of *Belaire Owners' Association* v. *DLF Limited* observed that if an enterprise has the ability to influence its competitors or the consumers in a relevant market, there could be little doubt in its ability to influence the market itself in its favour. In this case it was found that an announcement of several large projects by real estate company DLF could make its competitors react by holding back some of their own projects to avoid market saturation. Similarly, prospective consumers could also react by deferring their demand in expectation of availability of projects to be offered. Thus, the possibility to influence both the supply and demand in the relevant market by DLF indicated that DLF held a position of strength as envisaged in Explanation (a)(ii) to Section 4 of the Act.[74]

Dominant position defined in Explanation (a) relates to the relevant market and it is therefore necessary first to determine the relevant market in which the dominant position is alleged. The term 'relevant market' itself has been defined in Section 2(r) as 'the market which may be determined by the Commission with reference to the relevant product market or the relevant geographic market or with reference to both the markets'. The terms 'relevant geographic market' and 'relevant product market' have also been defined in the Act.

Section 2(s) states that the relevant geographic market 'means a market comprising the area in which the conditions of competition for supply of

[72] Glossary of Terms used in EU Competition Policy, Antitrust and Control of Concentrations, Director General for Competition, Brussels, July 2002.

[73] *United Brands Co. and United Brands Continental BV* v. *Commission of the European Communities (1978)1 CMLR 429*. Available at http://nnw.bailii.org./eu/cases/EUECJ/1978/C2776.html.

[74] Case No. 19 of 2010, *Belaire Owner's Association* v. *DLF Limited Haryana Urban Development Authority Department of Town and Country Planning, State of Haryana*, decided on 12 August 2011. Available at http://cci.gov.in/May2011/OrderOfCommission/DLFMainOrder110811.pdf.

goods or provision of services or demand of goods or services are distinctly homogeneous and can be distinguished from the conditions prevailing in the neighbouring areas'. The factors which are to be considered while determining the relevant geographic market have been listed in Section 19(6) of the Act, namely: '(a) regulatory trade barriers; (b) local specification requirements; (c) national procurement policies; (d) adequate distribution facilities; (e) transport costs; (f) language; (g) consumer preferences; and (h) need for secure or regular supplies or rapid after-sales services.' 'Regulatory trade barriers' could arise, for instance, from trade barriers such as import tariffs or quantitative restrictions or restrictions, if any, placed by state governments in India on inter-state movement of goods, thereby leading to segmentation of the market. Local specification requirements may be legal or cultural or arise from local business traditions; the language barrier in the case of newspapers is an example. National procurement policies sometimes stipulate giving preference to local manufacturers or suppliers. Inadequate distribution facilities or after-sales services in remote geographical areas or high transport costs could also lead to segmentation of the market; in the merger case of Lafarge-Holcim, the Commission defined the relevant geographic market as Eastern India comprising of five regional states of Chhattisgarh, Jharkhand, Orissa, Bihar, and West Bengal.[75] Sometimes, local consumers may have preference for a particular brand and therefore other brands of the same product may not be regarded as substitutable by those consumers. Interestingly, the Commission has understood the geographic market as limited to the territory of India in cases under Section 4 given that the Act defines dominant position to mean a position of strength enjoyed by an enterprise in the relevant market in India.[76] This sets a rather odd precedent that no relevant geographic market wider than India can be defined by the CCI.

Similarly, the relevant product market is defined in Section 2(t) as 'a market comprising all those products or services which are regarded as interchangeable or substitutable by the consumer, by reason of characteristics of

[75] Combination Registration No. C-2014/07/190 order dated 30 March 2015. Available at http://www.cci.gov.in/sites/default/files/C-2014-07-190_0.pdf.

[76] *Shri Bijoy Poddar* v. *Coal India Limited and Ors.* Case No. 59 of 2013 at para 42; 'From a plain reading of the Explanation to section 4 of the Act, "dominant position" means a position of strength, enjoyed by an enterprise, in the relevant market, in India, which enables it to operate independently of competitive forces prevailing in the relevant market or affect its competitors or consumers or the relevant market in its favour.' Available at http://www.cci.gov.in/May2011/OrderOfCommission/27/592013.pdf.

the products or services, their prices and intended use'. The factors that are to be considered while determining the relevant product market are listed in Section 19(7): namely '(a) physical characteristics or end-use of goods; (b) price of goods or service; (c) consumer preferences; (d) exclusion of in-house production; (e) existence of specialized producers; and (f) classification of industrial products.' A product may not be interchangeable with, or substitutable by, another product because of its certain peculiar physical characteristics or end-use, for example, in United Brands, the European Commission regarded a banana, because of its softness and its use for feeding infants, as not substitutable by an apple and it may, therefore, constitute a separate market from the apple market. The market for a highly priced luxury car may be different from that of a low end inexpensive car. One kind of industrial fuel may not be substitutable by another fuel if the furnace is designed only for a specific fuel and change over costs are prohibitive. Intermediate goods produced exclusively for in-house use for the manufacture of the end-product, and which the producer is unable to divert to other uses, may not be a substitute for other such goods in the market. Producers of a highly specialized product sometimes may not be considered in the market of non-specialized products due inter alia to their inability to switch to the production of non-specialized products.

In a case against Coal India, the Commission had noted that imported coking coal cannot be a substitute for the domestic variety due to reasons of price, 'size, quality, quantity and specifications'.[77] In another case,[78] the Commission found that 'imported coal is not a viable substitute or alternative for the Indian thermal power plants in view of the boilers used by them as well as on account of fact that the imported coal is very costly as raw material'.[79]

The determination of the relevant market is generally the starting point of the analysis of a particular case. According to World Bank/OECD Glossary, 'If markets are defined too narrowly in either product or geographic terms, meaningful competition may be excluded from the analysis. On the other hand, if the product and geographic markets are too broadly defined the degree of competition may be overstated. Too broad or too narrow market definitions lead to understating or overstating market share and concentration

[77] See Gazette of India, Extraordinary, dated Tuesday, 14 January 2003.

[78] See Budget Speech (Union Budget 1999–2000), para 23. 27 February 1999. Available at http://finmin.nic.in/topics/union_budget/oldbudgets/budget1999-2000/b5/b5.htm.

[79] See Statement of Objects & Reasons annexed to Competition Bill, 2002.

measures.'[80] Competition authorities frequently use certain economic tools to determine the relevant market. One of these is the small but significant non-transitory increase in price (SSNIP) test, also referred to as the hypothetical monopolist test; the investigator asks whether, if the hypothetical monopolist raises the price of the product by a 'small but significant amount' for a 'non-transitory' continuous period, a sufficient number of buyers would switch to other products so as to make the price increase unprofitable for the hypothetical monopolist. If such substitutes exist, they are included in a new provisional product market and the original question is repeated until no more close substitutes can be identified.[81]

It is necessary, however, to avoid the 'cellophane fallacy' in determining the relevant market in cases of abuse of dominance; this was an error committed by the US Supreme Court in *du Pont*. It refers to the situation where a dominant enterprise has already raised the price to a non-competitive level; a further rise of say 5–10 per cent may result in demand substitution by a product which might not have been a substitute at a lower competitive price. This could lead to an unjustifiably broad determination of the market, which would be favourable to the defence of the dominant firm.[82]

Once the relevant market has been determined, the next stage would be to inquire whether the enterprise enjoys a dominant position. The Act does not prohibit the mere possession of a dominant position, but only its abuse, thus recognizing that a dominant position may have been achieved through superior economic performance. Section 19(4) provides that while inquiring whether an enterprise enjoys a dominant position or not under Section 4, the Commission shall have due regard to all or any of the following factors, namely: (a) market share of the enterprise; (b) size and resources of the enterprise; (c) size and importance of the competitors; (d) economic power of the enterprise including commercial advantages over competitors; (e) vertical integration of the enterprises or sale or service network of such enterprises; (f) dependence of consumers on the enterprise; (g) monopoly or dominant position whether

[80] World Bank/OECD. 'Glossary of Industrial Organization Economics and Competition Law', World Bank/OECD.

[81] See also John Clark, et al. 1999. 'Market Definition and Assignment of Market Shares', in World Bank/OECD. 1999. *A Framework for the Design and Implementation of Competition Law and Policy*', pp. 10–18. World Bank/OECD; and *Black's Law Dictionary*, 7th ed.

[82] *United States* v. *E.I. du Pont de Neumours and Co. 351 US 377 (1956)*, referred to in Whish. 2005. *Competition Law*, 5th ed. pp. 30–2; also see 'Overview of Competition Law', in Vinod Dhall. 2007. *Competition Law Today: Concepts, Issues, and the Law in Practice*', 1st ed. Oxford University Press, New Delhi.

acquired as a result of any statute or by virtue of being a government company or a public sector undertaking or otherwise; (h) entry barriers including barriers such as regulatory barriers, financial risk, high capital cost of entry, marketing entry barriers, technical entry barriers, economies of scale, high cost of substitutable goods or service for consumers; (i) countervailing buying power; (j) market structure and size of market; (k) social obligations and social costs; (l) relative advantage, by way of the contribution to the economic development, by the enterprise enjoying a dominant position having or likely to have an appreciable adverse effect on competition; (m) any other factor which the Commission may consider relevant for the inquiry.

Factors similar to some of those enumerated in Section 19(4) are considered in many jurisdictions in determining dominance or market power. In *Hoffmann-La Roche*, the court listed the following as relevant factors in determining the existence of a dominant position: the relationship between the market shares of the undertaking concerned and of its competitors, especially those of the next largest, technological lead of an undertaking over its competitors, the existence of a highly developed sales network, and the absence of potential competition.[83] The court further explained why each of the aforementioned factors was relevant; and it observed that the first factor is relevant 'because it enables the competitive strength of the undertaking in question to be assessed, the second and third because they represent in themselves technical and commercial advantages and the fourth because it is the consequence of the existence of obstacles preventing new competitors from having access to the market'.[84] The court also noted that an 'undertaking which has a very large market share and holds it for some time, by means of the volume of production and the scale of supply which it stands for is by virtue of that share in a position of strength which makes it an unavoidable trading partner and which, already because of this secures for it, at the very least during relatively long periods, that freedom of action which is the special feature of a dominant position'.[85]

In *United Brands*, the court noted that in general a dominant position derives from a combination of several factors which, taken separately, are not necessarily determinative.[86] The court approvingly observed that,

[83] See *Hoffman La Roche AG* v. *Commission of European Communities [1979]* 3 CMLR 211, para 48.

[84] Ibid.

[85] Para 41, ibid.

[86] See *United Brands Company & United Brands Continental BV* v. *Commission of the European Communities (1978)* 1 CMLR 429, para 66. Available at http://www.bailii.org/eu/cases/EUECJ/1978/C2776.html.

'The Commission bases its view that UBC has a dominant position on the relevant market on a series of factors which, when taken together, give UBC unchallengeable ascendancy over all its competitors: its market share compared with that of its competitors, the diversity of its sources of supply, the homogeneous nature of its product, the organization of its production and transport, its marketing system and publicity campaigns, the diversified nature of its operations, and finally its vertical integration.'[87] The court also noted the high entry barriers arising from the exceptionally large capital investments required, the need to increase sources of supply, the introduction of essential system of logistics, economies of scale, and high general expenses in organizing an adequate commercial network and advertising campaign. Further, the court took note of the company's technical advantage in banana ripening methods, improving productivity, and combating plant disease.

In *Akzo Chemie*, the court observed, 'With regard to market shares the Court has held that very large shares are in themselves, and save in exceptional circumstances, evidence of the existence of a dominant position. That is the situation where there is a market share of 50% such as that found to exist in this case. Further, the court noted that Akzo regarded itself as the world leader in the peroxides market, and Akzo also admitted that it had the most highly developed marketing organization, both commercially and technically, and wider knowledge than that of its competitors with regard to safety and toxicology; thus the court concluded that Akzo was in a dominant position in the organic peroxides market and rejected Akzo's pleas to the contrary'.[88] EC's Guidance on the enforcement priorities in applying Article 102 to abusive exclusionary conduct by dominant undertakings states that market shares provide useful first indications of the market structure and of the competitive importance of various undertakings active in the market. If the undertaking concerned has a high market share compared to other players on the market, it is an indication of dominance provided that this market share has been held for some time.[89] Whish observes that assessing market power in practice requires a number of issues to be taken into account, like,

[87] Para 58, ibid.

[88] *Akzo Chemie B V* v. *Commission of European Communities (1991) EUECJ C-62/86*. Available at http://www.bailii.org/cgi-bin/markup.cgi?doc=/eu/cases/EUECJ/1991/C6286.html.

[89] EC, 'DG Competition Discussion Paper on the Application of Article 82 of the Treaty to Exclusionary Abuses' can be seen at http://ec.europa.eu/comm/competition/antitrust/others/discpaper2005.pdf.

market share, concentration of the market, barriers to entry and exit, and the degree of countervailing buyer power.[90]

Section 19(4), after listing a series of factors for determination of dominant position, also includes '(m) any other factor which the Commission may consider relevant for the inquiry'. Thus, discretion has been given to the Commission to take into account other relevant factors, for example, technical advancement of the enterprise, which has not been listed in Section 19(4), but which was an important factor for the courts in cases such as United Brands and Akzo. This could be of particular relevance in high technology industries.

The Commission in *MCX Stock Exchange Ltd.* v. *National Stock Exchange of India Ltd.* noted that what has to be seen is whether a particular player in a relevant market has clear comparative advantages in terms of financial resources, technical capabilities, brand value, historical legacy etc. to be able to do things which would affect its competitors who, in turn, would be unable to do or would find it extremely difficult to do so on a sustained basis. The Commission further noted that the question is not whether the enterprise is doing so but whether all the indicative facts point out that it has the ability to do so. A dominant enterprise can force its competitors into taking a certain position in the market which would make the market and consumers respond or react in a certain manner which is beneficial to the dominant enterprise but detrimental to the competitors.[91]

In the case of *Belaire Owner's Association* v. *DLF Limited and Haryana Urban Development Authority Department of Town and Country Planning*, the Commission observed that dominance is neither acquired nor asserted in a transient moment in time.[92] It went on to observe that it could take many years for an enterprise to acquire a position of strength and therefore its conduct has to be examined over a period of time. It also cautioned against use of snapshot data of market shares or market presence based on current active stock figures since it could present a false picture and if applied in the context of the Act, may cause avoidable harm to the market. Therefore, according to the Commission, the assessment of dominant position would be based on the

[90] Whish. 2005. *Competition Law*, 5th ed.

[91] Case No. 13 of 2009, *MCX Stock Exchange Ltd. v. National Stock Exchange of India Ltd.* decided on 23 June 2011. Available at http://www.cci.gov.in/May2011/OrderOfCommission/MCXMainOrder240611.pdf.

[92] Case No. 19 of 2010, *Belaire Owner's Association* v. *DLF Limited Haryana Urban Development Authority Department of Town and Country Planning, State of Haryana*, decided on 12 August 2011. Available at http://cci.gov.in/May2011/OrderOfCommission/DLFMainOrder110811.pdf.

profile, presence, and achievements of the enterprise over the years as well as its conduct in relation to consumers, over a period of time.

The next question that arises is whether there has been an abuse of dominant position. Section 4(2) states that 'there shall be an abuse of dominant position' if an enterprise indulges in any of the activities listed in the sub-section, these being: unfair or discriminatory condition or price including predatory pricing, limiting or restricting production or technical or scientific development, denying market access, imposing supplementary obligations having no connection with the subject of the contract, or using dominance in one market to enter into or protect another relevant market. The list of abuses is exhaustive, and not merely illustrative.

The abuses in Section 4(2) include exploitative abuses such as unfair or discriminatory conditions or prices as well as exclusionary abuses such as denial of market access and predatory pricing. According to Anderson et al., with exploitative abuses it is often difficult to say what amounts to an exploitative exercise of market power, and competition authorities should seek to minimize the extent to which they regulate prices of individual firms and focus more on seeking to prevent dominant firms from engaging in exclusionary acts that threaten competition.[93]

The Commission has examined exploitative abuses in the case of Coal India. The customers of Coal India had to enter into Fuel Supply Agreements (FSAs) for coal supply without any opportunity to negotiate the terms and conditions. The Commission held that any agreement which has a long lock-in period with express inability to negotiate by one of parties to it, is sufficient to attract prohibitory provisions of Section 4(2)(a) of the Act.[94] Similarly, in *Wardha Power* the Commission took note of the fact that the FSAs could be finalized without a bilateral process and held this to be an indication of dominance being abused.[95] Other unfair conditions that the Commission noted were with regard to the pricing mechanism which was unfair and non-transparent, arbitrary requirements of additional bank guarantees and unfair clauses related to the quality checks on the coal supplied.

[93] Anderson, Robert, Timothy Daniel, and Alberto Heimler, et al. 1999. 'Abuse of Dominance', in World Bank/OECD. 1999. *A Framework for the Design and Implementation of Competition Law and Policy*, World Bank/OECD.

[94] Case nos. 03, 11, and 59 of 2012, *M/s Maharashtra State Power* v. *M/s Coal India Ltd.*, M/s Western Coalfields Ltd., decided on 9 December 2013. Available at http://cci.gov.in/May2011/OrderOfCommission/27/592012.pdf.

[95] Case No. 88 of 2013, *M/s Sai Wardha Power Company Ltd.* v. *M/s Western Coalfields Ltd. and M/s Coal India Ltd.*, decided on 27 October 2014. Available at http://cci.gov.in/May2011/OrderOfCommission/27/C.%20No.%2088%20of%202013%20Final%20%20Order%20Dt.%2016%20Oct.pdf, paras 130 and 131.

The laws of many other jurisdictions are not very different from Section 4 in respect of the practices that are treated as abuse of dominant position. The term 'abuse of dominant position' has been incorporated in the competition laws such as those of EC, UK, Canada, and Germany. Article 102 of the Treaty of the EC specifically enumerates the following as being abuse of dominant position: unfair prices or conditions, limiting production, markets or technical development, applying dissimilar conditions to equivalent transactions, and making contracts subject to supplementary obligations having no connection with the subject of the contracts; the list is not exhaustive. Practices which have generally been treated as abusive include: charging unreasonable or excessive prices, price discrimination, predatory pricing, refusal to deal/sell, tied-selling or product bundling, and pre-emption of facilities.[96] It has been stated earlier that in *United Brands*, the court held that the company's refusal to sell to a long-standing customer who abides by regular commercial practice would limit markets to the prejudice of the consumers and would amount to discrimination.[97] The court also held that the company's policy of differing prices enabling it to apply dissimilar conditions to equivalent transactions with other trading parties, thereby placing them at a competitive disadvantage, was an abuse of dominant position. Further, the court laid down the principle that charging a price which is excessive because it has no reasonable relation to the economic value of the product supplied may be an abuse of dominant position.[98] In *Hoffmann—La Roche*, the court held that fidelity rebates by a dominant undertaking may result in application of dissimilar conditions to equivalent transactions, and therefore, amount to abuse of dominant position; it made a similar observation in respect of exclusive purchase contracts imposed by a dominant undertaking.[99]

In the US, the corresponding term for abuse of dominance is 'monopolization or attempt to monopolize', prohibited under Section 2 of the

[96] World Bank/OECD. 'Glossary of Industrial Organisation Economics and Competition Law', World Bank/OECD.

[97] The Court observed at para 182 that '...it is advisable to assert positively from the outset that an undertaking in a dominant position for the purpose of marketing a product—which cashes in on the reputation of a brand name known to and valued by the consumers—cannot stop supplying a long standing customer who abides by regular commercial practice, if the orders placed by that customer are in no way out of the ordinary'.

[98] Para 234, *United Brands Co. and United Brands Continental BV* v. *Commission of the European Communities (1978) 1 CMLR 429*. Available at http://www.bailii.org/eu/cases/EUECJ/1978/C2776.html.

[99] *Hoffman La Roche AG* v. *Commission of European Communities [1979] 3 CMLR 211*.

Sherman Act. Monopolization has two elements: one, the possession of monopoly power, and two, the wilful acquisition or maintenance of that power as distinguished from growth or development as a consequence of a superior product, business acumen, or historic accident.[100] A party can be said to have monopoly power if it has, over 'any part of the trade or commerce among the several States a power of controlling prices or unreasonably restricting competition'.[101] On the other hand, in order to demonstrate attempted monopolization, a plaintiff must prove (a) that the defendant has engaged in predatory or anticompetitive conduct with (b) a specific intent to monopolize and (c) a dangerous probability of achieving monopoly power.[102] The US does not have an excessive pricing violation, while predatory pricing and refusal to deal are hard to prove. Discriminatory pricing is barred under Section 2 of the Clayton Act, as amended by the Robinson–Patman Act, unless it is justified by cost savings or the need to meet the competition.[103] Similarly, the explanation below Section 4(2)(a) states that unfair or discriminatory conditions or price, shall not be regarded as an abuse if it has been adopted to meet the competition.

In *Microsoft* it was found by the EC that the company enjoyed a dominant position in the client PC operating system market and in the work group server operating system market, and that it indulged in abusive conduct by refusing to provide its competitors with 'inter-operability information' and refusing to allow its use for the purpose of developing and distributing products competing with Microsoft's own products on the work group server

[100] *United States* v. *Grinnel Corp. 384 US 563(1966)*. See also *Black's Law Dictionary*, p. 1023.

[101] *United States* v. *E.I. du Pont de Neumours and Co.* 351US 377(1956).

[102] *Spectrum Sports, Inc* v. *McQauillan,* 506 U.S.447 (1993). See also *Black's Law Dictionary*, p. 1023.

[103] See 'Competition Law in the United States of America' by Stephen Calkins. Also Section 2(b) of the Clayton Act reads as follows: 'Upon proof being made, at any hearing on a complaint under this section, that there has been discrimination in price or services or facilities furnished, the burden of rebutting the prima-facie case thus made by showing justification shall be upon the person charged with a violation of this section, and unless justification shall be affirmatively shown, the Commission is authorized to issue an order terminating the discrimination: Provided, however, that nothing herein contained shall prevent a seller rebutting the prima-facie case thus made by showing that his lower price or the furnishing of services or facilities to any purchaser or purchasers was made in good faith to meet an equally low price of a competitor, or the services or facilities furnished by a competitor.'

operating system market.[104] In *Tetra Pak*, the court observed that Tetra Pak used its dominant position in the aseptic market to gain advantages in the non-aseptic markets.[105] In *United States* v. *Griffith et al.*,[106] the US Supreme Court held it unlawful for the operator of a circuit of a motion picture theatre to use his monopoly in towns in which he has no competitors to obtain exclusive rights to films for towns in which he has competitors, thereby denying access to the competitors.

In the case of *Surinder Singh Barmi* v. *Board for Control of Cricket in India*, the Commission penalized BCCI, the governing body for cricket in India, for exclusionary conduct. Apart from its regulatory functions, BCCI also organizes the India Premier League (IPL). BCCI used its regulatory powers to obtain a commercial advantage by way of its agreements to deny market access to potential competitors of IPL by agreeing with the media rights holders that it will not allow any other private professional league in India during the period of the agreement. The Commission concluded that BCCI abused its regulatory position to obtain unfair commercial advantage by contractually agreeing to deny market access to any potential competitor, thereby violating the Act.[107] It may be noted that the COMPAT has set aside the order of the Commission on the grounds that principles of natural justice were not complied with and remanded the matter for fresh disposal.

The COMPAT has held that the abuse of denial of market access under Section 4(2) (c) is occasioned only to a competitor. In the case of *Fast Way Transmission and Others* v. *Kansan News*, it was found that the Fast Way group (engaged in the business of distribution of cable network channels of

[104] Commission Decision in COMP/C-3/37, 792 Microsoft.

[105] *Tetra Pak International* v. *Commission of European Communities [1996] EUECJ C-333/94P*. Available at http://www.bailii.org/eu/cases/EUECJ/1996/C33394.html. The Court noted at para 31 that 'the Court of First Instance was right to accept the application of Article 86 of the Treaty in this case, given that the quasi-monopoly enjoyed by Tetra Pak on the aseptic markets and its leading position on the distinct, though closely associated, non-aseptic markets placed it in a situation comparable to that of holding a dominant position on the markets in question as a whole'.

[106] 334 US 100 (1948). The Court observed that 'A man with a monopoly of theatres in any one town commands the entrance for all films into that area. If he uses that strategic position to acquire exclusive privileges in a city where he has competitors, he is employing his monopoly power as a trade weapon against his competitors'.

[107] Case No. 61 of 2010, decided on 8 February 2013. Available at http://cci.gov.in/May2011/OrderOfCommission/612010.pdf.

broadcasters) had denied market access to a broadcaster of a news channel by refusing to transmit the latter's news channel on its cable network. The COMPAT noted that the two were not competitors in the supply chain and held that there was no abuse of denial of market access.[108]

Abusing a dominant position to deny market access could be particularly harmful in the case of an 'essential facility', that is, a facility to which a competitor must have access, in order to compete effectively. The term 'essential facility' usually refers to infrastructure such as electricity transmission line, a gas or oil pipeline, a port, or an airport. But it has also sometimes been used to include an intellectual property or an essential raw material. The 'essential facility' doctrine is considered to have originated in the US where it was probably first used in *Terminal Railroad Association of St. Louis*,[109] though the term itself was not employed in the case. However, after *Trinko*, in the US, the doctrine would appear to have been watered down and hard to prove.[110] In the EC competition law, the doctrine has been invoked in a number of cases, like *Sealink/B&I-Holyhead* and *Commercial Solvents* and *Microsoft Corp.* v. *Commission*.[111] In *De Montis Catering Roma* v. *Aeroporti de Roma*, the state-owned airport controlling company that had an exclusive licence to provide maintenance and ground services denied access to the airport premises to a company wishing to compete for airline catering; this was found to be unjustified by the Italian competition authority.[112] In Australia, the doctrine has been regarded important enough to be incorporated into the law as a generic principle.[113]

[108] Appeal No. 116 of 2012, *M/s. Fast Way Transmission Pvt. Ltd. and Others* v. *Kansan News Pvt. Ltd. and Competition Commission of India*, decided on 2 May 2014. Available at http://compat.nic.in/upload/PDFs/mayordersApp2014/02_05_14.pdf.

[109] *224 US 383(1912)* referred to in Whish. 2005. *Competition Law*, 5th ed. p. 667.

[110] See 'Competition Law in the United States of America' by *Stephen Calkins, and Verzion Communications Inc.* v. *Law Offices of Curtis* v. *Trenko*, LLP 540 U.S. 682(2004).

[111] For an explanation of the 'essential facilities' doctrine, see Whish, Richard. 2005. *Competition Law*, 5th ed. pp. 667–77. Sealink/B&I-Holyhead and Commercial Solvents have been referred to therein.

[112] Anderson, Robert, Timothy Daniel and Alberto Heimler et al. 1999. 'Abuse of Dominance', in World Bank/OECD. 1999. *'A Framework for the Design and Implementation of Competition Law and Policy'*, World Bank/OECD, p. 77.

[113] The Competition Policy Reform Act 1995 inserts new Part IIIA into the Trade Practices Act, 1974 which establishes a legal regime providing for third party access to a range of facilities of national importance. A single facility might provide

One of the abuses listed in Section 4(2)(a)(ii) is predatory pricing, defined in Explanation (b) below Section 4(2)(e) as 'the sale of goods or provision of services at a price which is below cost, as may be determined by regulations, of production of the goods or provision of services, with a view to reduce competition or eliminate the competitors'. By using the term, 'with a view to reduce competition or eliminate the competitors', intention has been included as an ingredient of the violation. The COMPAT has taken a view that there is no requirement for any actual foreclosure to happen. For the application of Section 4(2)(a)(ii), it is sufficient if there is any possibility of the competition being affected.[114]

According to Anderson et al.,

> Predatory pricing is the practice of a dominant firm selling its product at prices so low as to drive competitors out of a market, prevent new entry, and successfully monopolize the market. The cost can be high, but a predator expects future discounted profits to outweigh present losses and foregone profits. Predation is condemned not because it results in lower prices now but because it is likely to lead to reduced output and higher prices in future.[115]

In the US, the ability of the predator to subsequently recoup the loss incurred in selling below cost is considered integral to the practice of predation. In *Brooke Group Limited* v. *Brown and Williamson Tobacco Corp.*,[116] the US Supreme Court observed that when a claim alleges predatory pricing under Section 2 of the Sherman Act, there are two prerequisites to recovery: 'First, a plaintiff seeking to establish competitive injury resulting

---

a number of services to which access may be essential for enhanced competition in some cases but not in others. For this reason, the legislation focuses on access to a *service* provided by means of a facility rather than access to a facility itself. See OECD. 1996. 'The Essential Facilities Concept'. Available at http://www.oecd.org/dataoecd/34/20/1920021.pdf; also Part IIIA of the Australian Trade Practices Act, 1974, and Steinwall, Ray. 2005. 'Annotated Trade Practices Act, 1974', Lexis Nexis, Butterworth.

[114] Appeal No. 15 of 2011, *The National Stock Exchange of India Ltd.* v. *Competition Commission of India MCX Stock Exchange Limited*, decided on 5 August 2014. Available at http://compat.nic.in/upload/PDFs/augustordersApp2014/05_08_14.pdf.

[115] Anderson, Robert, Timothy Daniel, and Alberto Heimler, et al. 1999. 'Abuse of Dominance', in World Bank/OECD. 1999. *A Framework for the Design and Implementation of Competition Law and Policy*, World Bank/OECD, p. 77.

[116] *Brooke Group Ltd.* v. *Brown Williamson Tobacco Corp., 509 US 209(1993)*. Available at http://caselaw.lp.findlaw.com/scripts/getcase.pl?navby=case&court=us&vol=509&page=209.

from a rival's low prices must prove that the prices complained of are below an appropriate measure of its rival's costs. The second prerequisite to holding a competitor liable under the antitrust laws for charging low prices is a demonstration that the competitor had under Section 2 of the Sherman Act, a dangerous probability, of recouping its investment in below-cost prices.' Under the EC law, the courts have held that prices below average variable cost are always abusive while prices below average total costs but above average variable costs are abusive if intention to eliminate competition can be shown. Further, the prospect of recoupment is not always necessary to be shown. In *Tetra Pak International*, the court held, 'First, prices below average variable costs must always be considered abusive. In such a case, there is no conceivable economic purpose other than the elimination of a competitor, since each item produced and sold entails loss for the undertaking. Secondly, prices below average total costs, but above average variable costs are only to be considered abusive if an intention to eliminate can be shown.'[117] The court further observed that, 'It would not be appropriate, in the circumstances of the present case, to require any additional proof that Tetra Pak had a realistic chance of recouping its losses. It must be possible to penalize predatory prices whenever there is a risk that competitors will be eliminated.'[118] In *Akzo Chemie BV*, the court held 'Prices below average variable cost (that is to say, those which vary depending on the quantities produced) by means of which a dominant undertaking seeks to eliminate a competitor must be regarded as abusive. A dominant undertaking has no interest in applying such prices except that of eliminating competitors so as to enable it subsequently to raise its prices by taking advantage of its monopolistic position, since each sale generates a loss, namely the total amount of the fixed costs (that is to say, those which remain constant regardless of the quantities produced) and, at least, part of the variable costs relating to the unit produced. Moreover, prices below average total cost, that is to say, fixed costs plus variable costs, but above average variable costs, must be regarded as abusive if they are determined as part of a plan for eliminating a competitor. Such prices can drive from the market undertakings which are perhaps as efficient as the dominant

[117] See *Tetra Pak International SA* v. *Commission of the European Communities[1996] EUECJ C 333/94P*, case C-333/94P, Judgment of the Court (5th Chamber) of 14 November 1996, para 41. Available at http://www.bailii.org/eu/cases/EUECJ/1996/C33394.html.

[118] See *Tetra Pak International SA* v. *Commission of the European Communities*, case C-333/94P, Judgment of the Court (5th Chamber) of 14 November 1996, para 44. Available at http://www.bailii.org/eu/cases/EUECJ/1996/C33394.html.

undertaking but which, because of their smaller financial resources, are incapable of withstanding the competition waged against them.'[119]

The Act does not say how 'cost' is to be determined; this has been left to be laid down in regulations. Accordingly, the Commission has enacted the Competition Commission of India (Determination of Cost of Production) Regulations in 2009.[120] It provides that 'cost' shall, generally, be taken as average variable cost, as a proxy for marginal cost. However the Commission can consider any other relevant cost concept such as avoidable cost, long run average incremental cost, and market value after it has recorded its reasons in writing for doing so.

In *National Stock Exchange of India Ltd. (NSE)* v. *Commission*, the NSE waived the brokerage fee for trading in currency futures in order to keep MCX out of the market and it was contended that the average variable cost was zero. The COMPAT noted that 'average variable cost' was derived from the 'total variable cost' which is the 'total cost' as defined in Regulation 2(1)(c)(i) minus the fixed cost and share of fixed overheads, if any. Any situation of zero average variable cost can come only by first arriving at the total variable cost being zero. The COMPAT held in appeal that in this case, there was good evidence available to suggest that the total variable cost could not be zero in order to justify the zero variable cost.

In competition laws, generally, for an act to be an abuse of dominant position, it is required that it should be shown to have an anticompetitive effect in the market. Anderson et al. have stated, 'a thorough economic analysis of the anticompetitive effect of alleged abusive behaviour is needed even when a firm clearly enjoys a dominant position'. They further advise that 'competition agencies should also be aware that potentially the abusive act can in some circumstances yield efficiencies, even for firms with large market shares. Thus, efficiency considerations should always be taken into account in analyzing the competitive effects of business practices.'[121] Article 102 of the EC Treaty provides that an abuse of a dominant position shall be prohibited 'in so far as it may affect trade between Member States'. Reynolds has pointed out that 'a dominant undertaking will infringe article 82 if it abuses its

[119] *Akzo Chemie BV* v. *Commission of European Communities* C-62/86, Judgment of the Court (5th Chamber) of 3 July 1991, paras 71 and 72. Available at http://www.bailii.org/eu/cases/EUECJ/1991/C6286.html.

[120] See http://www.cci.gov.in/images/media/Regulations/cost_pro.pdf.

[121] Anderson, Robert D., Timothy Daniel, and Alberto Heimler et al. 1999. 'Abuse of Dominance', in World Bank/OECD. 1999. *A Framework for the Design & Implementation of Competition Law & Policy*, World Bank/OECD, pp. 72–4.

dominant position and there is an effect on trade between EC Member States.'[122] Anderson and Heimler have explained that abuse of dominance provisions typically embody three common elements: first, the existence of dominant position which requires delineation of the 'relevant market'; second, identifying specific harmful practices; and third, 'their overall effects in the relevant market(s)' are assessed.[123]

The EC Guidance Paper on enforcement priorities in applying Article 102 to abusive exclusionary conduct by dominant undertakings also seems to reflect a movement away from an approach that prohibits certain categories of conduct by dominant enterprises towards an approach based on evaluating the likely or actual effects of the practice on competition and consumer welfare.

This shifts the attention more towards competition, away from competitors, and gives greater recognition, in principle, to the potential pro-competitive effects of the practice in question.[124] The US position, for long, has been to focus more on effects, and less on form.

Anderson et al. have pointed out that in some legal systems there is a presumption that certain practices by dominant firms are inherently unfair and that this approach has the merit of facilitating the design and enforcement of new competition laws.[125] Significantly, in Section 4 of the Act, there is no reference to 'appreciable adverse effect on competition', that is to say that in the abuses listed at items (a)–(e) of Section 4(2), the Act does not stipulate that any of these activities shall amount to an abuse of dominant position only if it causes or is likely to cause an 'appreciable adverse effect on competition'. This suggests that once it has been determined in accordance with Section 19(4) that an enterprise enjoys a dominant position (in the relevant market) and it is proved to be indulging in any of the activities listed in Section 4(2), the conclusion follows that it amounts to an abuse of dominant position.

[122] See chapter 'EC Competition Law Modernization: The First Experiences' by Michael Reynolds.

[123] See chapter 'Abuse of Dominant Position: Emerging Enforcement Issues and Approaches' by Robert D. Anderson and Alberto Heimler.

[124] EC, 'DG Competition Discussion Paper on the Application of Article 82 to Exclusionary Abuses' can be seen at http://ec.europa.eu/comm/competition/antitrust/others/discpaper2005.pdf.

[125] Anderson, Robert, Timothy Daniel and Alberto Heimler et al. 1999. 'Abuse of Dominance', p. 72. World Bank/OECD. 1999. '*A Framework for the Design & Implementation of Competition Law & Policy*, World Bank/OECD.

Remedies and Leniency

The remedies that can be ordered by the Commission in cases of contravention of Section 3 (relating to anticompetitive agreements) or Section 4 (relating to abuse of dominant position), as the case may be, have been provided in Section 27 of the Act. The Commission may pass a 'cease and desist' order (Section 27(a)) and impose a penalty not exceeding 10 per cent of the average turnover of the preceding 3 years (Section 27(b)). In the case of a cartel, the penalty could be 10 per cent of the turnover or three times of the amount of profits made out of the cartel agreement, whichever is higher (Proviso to Section 27[b]); thus, cartels could attract higher penalties than other contraventions. Previously there was an obligation on the Commission to impose this quantum of penalty. However, the word 'shall' in the proviso was replaced with 'may'[126]; thus giving the Commission flexibility in regard to the quantum of penalties. Section 28 further allows the Commission to direct the division of an enterprise enjoying dominant position; this power has not been invoked so far by the Commission; it is rarely used in other jurisdictions as well presumably because it is harsh in nature, is difficult to execute, and could have high economic costs. Section 27(c), read with Section 34, used to provide for award of compensation for any loss or damage suffered as a result of any contravention of the provisions of the Act relating to prohibition of anticompetitive agreements, abuse of dominant position, or regulation of combinations. Through an amendment this power was shifted to the Competition Appellate Tribunal under Section 53N of the Act; this provision has not been used so far in the enforcement of the Act.[127]

The Act also allows the Commission to direct the enterprise to abide by such other orders or directions as the Commission may give (Section 27[e]), including payment of costs, if any, and the Commission may also pass such other orders as it may deem fit (Section 27[g]). It is worth noting that the COMPAT in the case of *DLF Ltd.* v. *Commission and other*, has observed that the Act gives the Commission power to modify only those agreements which are in contravention of Section 3 of the Act. In the Tribunal's view, for contraventions of Section 4, the Commission can only direct the guilty party to discontinue the abuse and impose a penalty. While Section 27(d) specifically allows the Commission to modify any agreement under Section 3 of the Act, Sections 27 (e) and (g) give wider powers to the Commission to pass 'such other orders' as may be warranted. The intent of the Act clearly is

[126] Act 39 of 2007, Section 20(i) (w.e.f. 20 May 2009).

[127] Chapter VIIIA (containing Sections 52A to 53U) inserted by Act 39 of 2007, Section 43.

to allow the Commission flexibility in dealing with situations that do not fall squarely within the narrow wordings of the other provisions of the Act. The interpretation given by COMPAT is likely to significantly fetter the powers of the Commission in abuse of dominance cases, unless overruled by the Hon'ble Supreme Court of India.

Section 48 provides that not only the company that contravenes any provision of the law, or order or direction given thereunder, is liable to be proceeded against and punished, but also any person who, at the time of the contravention, was in charge of and was responsible to the company, unless such person can show that the contravention was committed without his knowledge or that he had exercised all due diligence to prevent such contravention. Similarly, every director, manager, secretary, or other officer of the company shall be deemed guilty and liable to action under the law if it is proved that the contravention took place with his consent or connivance, or is attributable to any neglect on his part. Thus the liability of the directors and the officers of the company can be very heavy and the punishment that they can receive can be severe. The Act makes no distinction between the penalty that can be imposed on a company and on an individual, which is unlike some other jurisdictions, for example, the US and Australia, where the penalty imposable on an individual is lower than on a company. The Commission has been examining the role of individuals involved in infringement and has imposed penalties on such individuals in certain cases; usually these penalties have been a percentage of the income of the individual concerned.

The Act includes a leniency programme in the case of a cartel. Section 46 states that if a party to a cartel makes a full and true disclosure in respect of the alleged violations and such disclosure is vital, and provided that the party continues to cooperate in the inquiry, such a party may be given a lesser penalty as the Commission deems fit. According to the original wording of the second proviso to Section 46 only the first producer, seller, distributor, trader, or service provider included in the cartel may benefit from the leniency provision. However after an amendment,[128] lesser penalty would be considered for subsequent applicants also provided these subsequent applicants provide significant added value to the evidence already in the possession of the Commission or the Director General, as the case may be. Under the Competition Commission of India (Lesser Penalty) Regulations, 2009[129] framed by the Commission to elaborate the process and conditions for lesser penalty, the first eligible applicant may be granted benefit

[128] Act 39 of 2007, s. 39 (b) (w.e.f. 20 May 2009).

[129] No. L-3(4)/Reg-L.P./2009-10/CCI published in the Extraordinary Gazette of India on 13 August 2009. Available at http://cci.gov.in/May2011/Home/regulation/regu_lesser.pdf; last accessed 10 September 2014.

of reduction in penalty up to or equal to 100 per cent, the second applicant a reduction of up to or equal to 50 per cent and the third applicant a reduction of up to or equal to 30 per cent of the penalty. It is worth noting that the leniency provision may save the cooperating party from a larger penalty, but it does not protect the party from a claim for compensation for loss or damage suffered by a person on account of the alleged violation by the party, or from any other direction or order of the Commission.

Leniency programmes exist in several competition laws such as in the US, EC and several of its Member States, Canada, Korea, Japan, and Mexico. Experience with the leniency programme is that it has proved an effective tool in unearthing, investigating, and punishing cartels. Since cartels operate usually in considerable secrecy, evidence is often hard to come by; the leniency tool has proved valuable in uncovering vital evidence against cartels and has greatly enhanced the success rate in the fight against cartels.[130] A very high proportion of cartel cases in jurisdictions such as the US and EU have been started on the basis of a leniency applicant or such applicants have come forward during the course of the proceedings; this has proved to be immensely helpful in proving and punishing the cartels.

The Commission had been concerned that applicants were not coming forward to take benefit of the leniency provision in reporting cartels. It had undertaken efforts to popularize this provision and to incentivize its use. There was some sign of relief in the Commission when the first such application was received and currently, several leniency cases are under processing in the Commission. Recently, the Commission also passed its first leniency decision. The application for leniency was made after the Commission's prima facie order had been passed and therefore, the applicant was granted a 75 per cent reduction in the penalty imposed. It is important to note that the benefit of the leniency provision was also extended to the individual who was responsible for the conduct of the enterprise.

Regulation of Combinations[131]

The Act contains provisions for regulation of combinations, that is, for 'merger control'. A combination has been defined in Section 5, and it includes an 'acquisition', 'acquiring of control', and any 'merger or amalgamation'

[130] For a more exhaustive treatment of the leniency programme refer to chapter 'Leniency Programmes in Competition Law' by Paul Crampton and Graham Reynolds.

[131] See 'Merger Control Regime under the Competition Law in India' by Vinod Dhall for a detailed analysis of the Indian merger control regime.

(Sections 5[a], [b] and [c], respectively). The word 'control' has been explained in Explanation (a) below Section 5 according to which it includes controlling the affairs or the management by one or more enterprises, either jointly or singly, over another enterprise or group, or by one or more groups, either jointly or singly, over another group or enterprise. The section also sets certain size-related thresholds and only an acquisition, acquiring of control, merger, or amalgamation above these thresholds, is covered by the definition of combination. Section 20(3) provides that these thresholds are subject to periodic revision by the central government so as to account inter alia for inflation and exchange rate fluctuations.

Merger control is an ingredient of the competition laws of most countries. In the US, the Sherman Act does not contain specific provisions relating to merger control and this led to numerous difficulties in dealing with mergers; consequently, the Clayton Act was enacted in 1914 which incorporated inter alia specific provisions for merger control. In the EC, merger control was introduced through a Council Regulation in 1989, which was later replaced by Council Regulation of 2004.

Section 5 does not make specific reference to joint ventures. However, if a joint venture arrangement satisfies all the conditions set out in Section 5, such a joint venture would be caught in the definition of combination and would accordingly be liable to scrutiny by the Commission. That could be the case in many countries. In Canada, it is by far the provisions of the competition law with respect to mergers which are the most relevant to a discussion of the anticompetitive effects of joint ventures. The broad definition of the term merger in the law fully encompasses the features inherent in joint venture contractual arrangements. This is also the case in the US.[132] Whish has explained that where the parties to an agreement establish a joint venture company to carry out their objectives this may amount to a 'merger' under the EC or UK competition law; it may even be the case that contractual integration without the establishment of a joint venture company will amount to a merger under the EC law. [133]

While the definition of combination is contained in Section 5, the regulation thereof is provided in Section 6. Section 6(1) states that no person or

[132] See Sotiriadis, Bob H: 'Reflections on Competition and Antitrust Laws: Joint Ventures and the Canadian and American Markets'. Available at www.robic.ca/publications/Pdf/129-BHS.pdf; also see King, Stephen P:, 'Short of a Merger: the Competitive Effects of Horizontal Joint Ventures'. Available at www.economics.unimelb.edu.au/sking/Joint_Ventures.pdf; and Ramappa T. 2006. *Competition Law in India—Policy, Issues and Developments*, Oxford University Press, India, pp. 224, 228.

[133] Whish, Richard. 2005. *Competition Law*, 5th ed., pp. 545–6.

enterprise shall enter into a combination which causes or is likely to cause an appreciable adverse effect on competition within the relevant market in India, and such a combination shall be void.

Section 6(2) provided for a notice to be given to the Commission disclosing the details of the proposed combination within seven days of approval by the board of directors of the enterprise concerned or execution of any agreement for acquisition or acquiring of control; in the original Act such a notice 'may' have been given by the person or enterprise concerned at his or its option. However, under the amended Act, the word 'may' was replaced with 'shall'.[134] Thus, the Act makes giving of notice to the Commission mandatory. (Only a few countries such as UK have a voluntary notification regime.) The time within which the notice has to be given was increased from 7 days (of approval of proposed merger by the board of directors or execution of any agreement or document for acquisition) to 30 days.[135]

The provisions regarding prohibition of anticompetitive combinations and giving notice to the Commission do not apply to share subscription or financing facility or acquisition pursuant to the covenants of a loan agreement or investment agreement by a public financial institution, foreign institutional investor, bank, or venture capital fund. However, such organizations are required, within seven days from the date of the acquisition, to notify the Commission in respect of such acquisition. Exemption to such financial organizations is provided in other competition regimes as well. For example, under the EC law, a concentration is not deemed to arise when a credit institution, financial institution, or insurance company, as part of its normal business, holds securities for a short time with a view to sell them and does not exercise any voting right in respect of those securities.[136]

Section 6(1) prohibits a combination having an 'appreciable adverse effect on competition within the relevant market in India'. Therefore, the first step in the analysis of a combination is the determination by the Commission of the relevant market in India. The exercise is similar to that for determining the relevant market in the case of abuse of dominant position, with however, one point of difference according to some authorities. Unlike in the analysis of abuse of dominance, the inquiry relating to the competitive effects of mergers is forward-looking and the main concern is whether the merger will

[134] Subs. By Act 39 of 2007, s. 5(a) (w.e.f. 1 June 2011).

[135] Subs. By Act 39 of 2007, s. 5(b) (w.e.f. 1 June 2011).

[136] See Ramappa, T. 2006. *Competition Law in India—Policy, Issues and Developments,* Oxford University Press, India, p. 193.

cause the prices to rise above the prevailing level, though that level may be above the competitive level. Thus, according to these authorities, the cellophane fallacy, which is pertinent in the case of abuse dominance, is not relevant in merger cases.[137]

Once the relevant market has been determined, the Commission has to determine whether the combination causes or is likely to cause an appreciable adverse effect in that relevant market. The factors which are to be considered by the Commission in making this inquiry are set out in Section 20(4), namely, actual and potential level of competition through imports in the market; extent of barriers to entry into the market; level of combination in the market; degree of countervailing power in the market; likelihood that the combination would result in the parties to the combination being able to significantly and sustainably increase prices or profit margins; extent of effective competition likely to sustain in a market; extent of which substitutes are available or likely to be available in the market; market share, in the relevant market, of the persons or enterprise in a combination, individually and as a combination; likelihood that the combination would result in the removal of a vigorous and effective competitor in the market; nature and extent of vertical integration in the market; possibility of a failing business; nature and extent of innovation; relative advantage, by way of the contribution to the economic development, by any combination having or likely to have appreciable adverse effect on competition; whether the benefits of the combination outweigh the adverse impact of the combination, if any.

The factors listed in Section 20(4) contain both negative and positive factors and the last factor, that is, (n) specifically states 'whether the benefits of the combination outweigh the adverse impact of the combination, if any.' This recognizes that a merger can have adverse effects, but it could also have positive gains for the economy such as economies of scale and increased efficiency. There is thus a rule of reason approach in inquiring into a combination. Factors similar to those listed in Section 20(4) are considered by competition authorities in many jurisdictions in appraising a merger. In UK, mergers are to be analysed according to the 'substantial lessening of competition' test. The merger guidelines issued by the OFT and the Competition Commission in UK (as these organisations existed at that time) require that the relevant market be defined, and the analysis of the merger's effect in the market take into consideration factors like degree of concentration, market

[137] See Bishop, Simon and Mike Walker. 2002. *The Economics of EC Competition Law: Concepts, Application and Measurement*, 2nd ed., pp. 98–100. Sweet & Maxwell; and Whish, Richard. 2005. *Competition Law*, 5th ed., pp. 30–2.

shares, removal of a maverick competitor, possibility of increase in prices as a result of loss of competition, barriers to entry and exit, degree of countervailing power, efficiencies and the failing firm defence.[138] The EC law requires determination of the relevant market, and the factors considered include the market structure, actual or potential competition, economic and financial power, barriers to entry, technical and economic progress, countervailing power, efficiency and failing firm defence.[139]

The 2010 US Department of Justice Horizontal Merger Guidelines describe the principal factors to analyse mergers which include market definition and description, identification of firms, their market shares and market concentration, potential adverse effects (unilateral or coordinated), buyer power, ease of market entry, and efficiencies that might arise.[140] Under the efficiency defence, the 'failing firm' factor is also considered which is similar to the factor (k) in Section 20(4), that is, 'the possibility of a failing business'. In *Staples Inc. and Office Depot Inc.*[141] the Court noted that the proposed merger between Staples and Office Depot will lead to undue concentration in the market and it will allow Staples to increase prices or otherwise maintain prices at an anticompetitive level. Further, the court noted the significant entry barriers on account of extremely high sunk costs and difficulty in achieving economies of scale, and it considered and rejected the efficiencies defence. It would be observed that in this case, several of the factors similar to those listed in Section 20(4) were considered by the court. However, in the US, the major question in merger analysis (as well as in analysis of anticompetitive agreements and abuse of dominance) is whether the merger is likely to artificially increase prices and lower output. The Commentary on the Horizontal Merger Guidelines of March 2006 (which still remains a valuable supplement to these Guidelines) issued by the US DoJ/FTC emphasizes the integrated nature of the merger analysis, the Guidelines being viewed not simply as a mechanical check-list, but as setting out a holistic approach focusing on the likely competitive effect of the transaction.[142]

[138] Whish, Richard. 2005. *Competition Law*, 5th ed. pp. 908–13.

[139] Pp. 833–47, Whish, Richard. 2005. *Competition Law*, 5th ed., pp. 833–47.

[140] Horizontal Merger Guidelines, 19 August 2010. Available at https://www.justice.gov/atr/horizontal-merger-guidelines-08192010.

[141] *Federal Trade Commission* v. *Staples Inc. and Office Depot Inc.*, Civ. No. 97–701(TFH).

[142] DoJ/ FTC 'Commentary on the Horizontal Merger Guidelines (March 2006)'. Available at http://www.ftc.gov/os/2006/03/CommentaryontheHorizontalMergerGuidelinesMarch2006.pdf.

The procedure for inquiry into a combination is laid down in Sections 29 and 31 of the Act. The investigation can commence either on the basis of a notification given by the parties to the Commission or it can be undertaken *suo motu* by the Commission up to one year after the combination has taken place (Section 20[3]). The Commission may approve the combination, deny approval, or approve it with modifications. Sections 29 and 31 set time caps for different stages of the investigation of the combination, and Section 31 provides that if the Commission fails to give its decision on the combination within 210 days from the date of notice given to the Commission, the combination shall be deemed to have been approved by the Commission.

In 2011 the Commission notified the Competition Commission of India (Procedure in regard to the transaction of business relating to combinations) Regulations, 2011[143] (Combinations Regulations). These regulations are amended from time to time and they essentially lay down the details of the procedure for regulating combinations. Among other things the regulations prescribe the forms that need to be submitted for filings, the scrutiny of such submissions, fee requirements, modifications to the notification, etc.

Extra Territoriality

The Act has extra-territorial jurisdiction. Section 32 provides that the Commission shall have the power to inquire into an agreement or abuse of dominant position or combination even if the act has taken place outside India or the party or enterprise is outside India provided that it has an appreciable adverse effect on competition in the relevant market in India. Thus, the governing factor is the effect in the domestic market; this is also referred to as the effects doctrine. Further, the Commission is allowed under the proviso to Section 18 to enter into memorandum or arrangement with any agency of any foreign country, with the prior approval of the central government. This provision is in support of the extra-territorial jurisdiction of the Commission. The Commission has entered into Memoranda of Understanding with a few countries such as Canada, the USA, and Australia. These provide for

[143] The Competition Commission of India (Procedure in regard to the transaction of business relating to combinations) Regulations, 2011 as amended up to 4 April 2013. Available at http://cci.gov.in/images/media/Regulations/CCICombination%20Regulations%20asat%20040413.pdf (last accessed 15 November 2013) *Vide* notification No. 1-1/ Combination Regulations/2011-12/CD/CCI, dated 11 May 2011.

cooperation and sharing of information between the two sides in competition matters and also for training.

The effects doctrine is now well accepted in competition law. It was first used in any significant manner in the US where the position now is that the US courts can intervene provided that there is a direct, substantial, and foreseeable effect on domestic or certain export commerce. Similarly, courts in the EU have asserted the effects doctrine in several cases involving overseas firms. The OECD Guidelines for Multinational Enterprises expressly caution these enterprises to take into account the competition laws of not only the countries in which they operate, but also of those countries where their acts are likely to have effect.[144]

Regulated Sectors

The jurisdiction of the Competition Act extends to all sectors of the economy and sectors regulated by sector-specific laws such as telecommunications or electricity or insurance are not excluded. Also Sections 21 and 21A contain provisions for consultation between the Commission and a sector regulator, where, in the course of proceedings before any statutory authority (that will include a sectoral regulator), an issue is raised by any party that any decision which the statutory authority has taken or proposes to take is, or would be, contrary to any of the provisions of the Act, then such statutory authority may make a reference in respect of such issue to the Commission. The statutory authority can also make a reference to the Commission *suo moto*. On receipt of such a reference, the Commission, after hearing the parties to the proceedings, shall give its opinion within 60 days to the statutory authority which shall thereafter pass such order as it deems fit. Section 21A contains similar provisions for the Commission to make a reference to a statutory authority. Implicit in these provisions is an encouragement for mutual consultations between sector regulators and the Commission. In practice, though there have been a number of cases before the Commission relating to regulated sectors, there have been very few instances of cross references between the Commission and sector regulators. There is also no instance of a broad policy level Memorandum of Understanding having been signed between the Commission and a sector regulator recognizing the spirit of Sections 21 and 21A.

[144] Fox, Eleanor M. 2002. *Competition Law* in Lowenfeld, A. 2002. *International Economic Law*, Oxford University Press; See also chapter 'Overview of Competition Law' by Vinod Dhall and chapter 'Conflicts, Convergence, Cooperation, and World Competition Law' by Eleanor M. Fox.

Exemptions

The Act covers enterprises irrespective of their ownership. Thus, private enterprises, as well as government enterprises, and also government departments are covered by the Act. However, the Act excludes activities of the government related to its sovereign functions and specifically excludes all activities carried on by the departments of the central government dealing with atomic energy, currency, defence, and space (Section 2[h]). What constitutes 'sovereign functions' has not been elaborated in the Act. However, there is a substantial body of case law in India on the subject. Broadly, sovereign functions are those that relate to matters such as maintenance of law and order, defence of the country, and administration of justice. In the US the 'state-action doctrine' refers to the principle that 'the antitrust laws do not prohibit a state's anticompetitive acts, or official acts directed by a state'.[145] Thus, prima facie, the Indian law extends less protection to the acts of the state than in the US. In India, any act of the state of a commercial nature described in the definition of the term 'enterprise' would, if anticompetitive in nature, be as much liable to action as a similar act by a private party. The Act is thus neutral in this respect. In fact, there have been a number of cases before the Commission relating to government-owned enterprises as well as some relating to government departments carrying on economic activities where the Commission had to determine whether at all the role of the government can be considered as an 'enterprise' under the Act. In one case, it was alleged that the Ministry of Civil Aviation (MOCA)[146] framed guidelines imposing unfair terms which limit and restrict the provisions of air transport services. Further, MOCA being the regulator as well as the provider of air transport services through its units/division, namely, Air India was in a position to provide unfair advantage to its units. The Commission held that the regulation of civil aviation sector by the MOCA per se cannot be considered a commercial activity under the term 'enterprise' defined in the Act.

In another case, the Commission held that Central Bureau of Narcotics (CBM) and Narcotics Control Bureau (NCB) are not 'enterprises' as defined under the Act[147]; both being regulatory agencies appointed by the

[145] See *Black's Law Dictionary*, 7th ed.

[146] Case No. 18 of 2013, *Shri Vineet Kumar* v. *Ministry of Civil Aviation*. Available at http://www.cci.gov.in/sites/default/files/182013_0.pdf.

[147] Case No. 41 of 2013, *Om Prakash* v. *Central Bureau of Narcotics, Ministry of Finance and Others*. Available at http://www.cci.gov.in/sites/default/files/412013_0.pdf.

government. The activities of CBM and NCB cannot be compared to a commercial organization and hence they are not 'enterprises'. In a case related to alleged abuse of dominance by the Department of Industrial Policy & Promotion (DIPP) in the 'formulation, promotion, approval and facilitation of Foreign Direct Investment (FDI) policy in civil air transport services in India', the Commission held, somewhat inexplicably that the DIPP is an 'enterprise' as the policy of pronouncement on FDI through Press Notes by DIPP amounts to 'control of provision of services'. However, while stating that the DIPP is constitutionally empowered to frame policy on FDI, the Commission held that it is not in violation of the Act since there was no appreciable adverse effect on competition in India.

The Act exempts two categories of agreements, namely, intellectual property rights in so far as they impose reasonable conditions (Section 3[5][i]), and export trade (Section 3 [5][ii]). Joint ventures, that enhance efficiency, are exempt only from the application of Section 3(3), that is, from the 'shall presume' rule, but not from the application of Section 3(1). Further, Section 54 allows the central government, not the Commission, to notify three other types of exemptions, these being: (a) 'any class of enterprises' in the interest of security of the State or public interest; (b) 'any practice or agreement' arising out of and in accordance with any obligation assumed by India under any treaty, agreement, or convention; and (c) 'any enterprise' which performs a sovereign function (the exemption being confined only to the activities relatable to the sovereign function). The period for which the exemption is given can also be specified in the notification.

Exemptions are provided under the competition laws of various jurisdictions. These exemptions relate to certain sectors or areas of the economy, for example, export trade, financial services, labour, agriculture, and telecommunications, or to certain categories of agreements, for example, agreements regarding research and development, setting of standards, or information exchange. In some jurisdictions, the exemptions are specified in the law itself while in others these may be notified on the basis of authority given by the law, like the authority given to the EC to notify block exemptions.

Under Section 54, exemption to individual enterprises can be given only in respect of a sovereign function, while in the case of a class of enterprises it can be exempted only on grounds of security of the State or of public interest. In respect of a practice or agreement, it can be exempted only if it arises out of any obligation assumed under any treaty, agreement, or convention. Thus, it appears that agreements such as those relating to research and development or standards setting that are exempted in the EU, cannot be exempted under Section 54, unless these arise out of some treaty obligation.

It may be noted that Section 54 allows public interest as a ground for exempting any class of enterprise. Public interest is a term with a broad meaning, leaving open the possibility of a wide range of exemptions being sought under this provision. Also Section 54 does not lay down any procedure to be followed by the central government before notifying an exemption, such as providing for public hearings or consultation with the Commission. While exemptions are at times warranted, and are being granted in practically all jurisdictions, it is important that such exemptions are granted only after a careful assessment of their necessity and their overall effect in the market. Khemani has suggested some useful procedures and principles in the granting of exemptions: a limited time period should be provided for the exemption along with periodic review; there should be analysis of the impact of the exemption on economic efficiency and consumer welfare; public hearings should be conducted with participation of the interested and affected parties; the exemption should be as least restrictive of competition as possible; and the exemption should be generic in nature.[148]

So far the power of exemption under Section 54 of the Act has been sparingly used by the government. The Ministry of Corporate Affairs issued a notification on 4 March 2011 providing for the target de minimis exemption for mergers; this exemption was extended for further five years in March 2016. On 8 January 2013, the Ministry issued a notification[149] exempting loss-making and failing banks from the purview of the Commission until the year 2018 with regard to mergers and takeovers. On 11 December 2013, the Ministry also exempted vessel-sharing agreements in the shipping industry from the purview of Section 3 of the Act for a period of one year from the date of issue.[150] This was last extended on 2 February 2016 for another year.

Who Can Approach the Commission?

According to Section 19 (1), the Commission can commence an inquiry into any contravention of Section 3(1) or Section 4(1) either on its own motion or on receipt of any information from any person, consumer, or their association,

[148] See chapter 'Exemptions, Exceptions, and Differential Application under Competition (Antitrust) Law' by R. Shyam Khemani.

[149] S.O.93(E) Notification dated 8 January 2013. Available at http://cci.gov.in/images/media/notifications/S.O.%2093%20(E)_08012013.pdf, (last accessed 15 November 2013).

[150] S.O. 3641 (F) dated 11 December 2013. Available at http://www.cci.gov.in/images/media/notifications/11Dec2013_SO_3641.pdf.

or trade association. The relevant terms in this section have been defined in the Act. The term 'person' has been defined in Section 2(l) and it is a broad category that includes an individual, a company, and a firm; it also includes an association, corporation, body corporate, cooperative society, or a local authority. Item (x) in Section 2(l) further includes every artificial juridical person not falling within any of the preceding sub-clauses. Thus, any person within or outside India or any association or body of persons incorporated in or outside India, or any company incorporated in or outside India, is eligible to approach the Commission against an anticompetitive act prohibited under Section 3 or Section 4.

The term consumer is defined in Section 2(f). It covers any person who buys any goods for a consideration or hires or avails of any service for a consideration. It includes an end-user of the product or service as well as any person or entity that purchases the goods or avails of the service for resale or for any commercial purpose. The condition is that the transaction must be for a consideration. Thus any commercial enterprise that procures goods or services for processing or its own use will be covered by the definition of consumer, unlike under the consumer protection law.

The Commission can be approached by an association of consumers or by a trade association. The term 'trade' has been defined in Section 2(x) and it includes trade in any goods or services, and also any profession or occupation relating to such trade. There have been cases brought before the Commission by trade associations. An inquiry into any alleged contravention of Section 3(1) or 4(1) can also be commenced on the basis of a reference made to the Commission by the central government or a state government or a statutory authority. A few cases have been referred by the government to the Commission for inquiry, and the Commission has acted on the same.

Further, the Commission can commence an inquiry on its own motion without a complaint or a reference. Thus, if the Commission comes to know of any alleged contravention under Section 3(1) or Section 4(1), the Commission can *suo motu* begin the inquiry. The Commission has taken note of certain media reports or information that has come to its notice to commence an inquiry. For instance, the Commission relied on multiple media reports alleging hoarding, price manipulation, and cartelization by onion traders to initiate an investigation to determine any anticompetitive behaviour.

The jurisdiction of the civil courts is excluded by Section 61 in respect of any matter which the Commission is empowered by or under the Act to determine and no injunction can be granted by any court or other authority in this respect. Thus, no private party can approach any civil court with a complaint under the Act. This situation is quite different, for example, from the position in the US where private action also is permissible in respect of antitrust matters, and in fact constitutes the majority of antitrust cases.[151]

Parties have, however, been taking recourse to the writ jurisdiction of the High Courts to challenge the proceedings in the Commission on procedural or jurisdictional issues and there have been several cases in which the High Courts have stayed the Commission's proceedings for extended periods of time.

Entities against Whom Action Lies?

The prohibition against abuse of dominant position extends only to an enterprise. Thus any enterprise which is in a dominant position is prohibited from indulging in any of the abuses listed in Section 4(2). On the other hand, the prohibition against anticompetitive agreements under Section 3(1) extends not only to an enterprise but also to an association of enterprises or person or association of persons. Similarly, the prohibition against anticompetitive combinations extends both to persons and to enterprises (Section 6[1]). The term enterprise has been given a broad definition in the Act and it includes a person (as defined in Section 2[l]) and a department of the government, other than a department having sovereign functions and the departments of the central government dealing with atomic energy, currency, defence, and space. Such departments excluded in the definition of the term enterprise will, therefore, not be liable to action under the Act.

Confidentiality of Information

The Act provides the protection of confidentiality to enterprises. Section 57 says that no information relating to any enterprise shall be disclosed without the prior written permission of the enterprise, except in compliance with or for the purposes of this Act or any other law for the time being in force. The Act thus recognizes that information obtained under the Act could be commercially sensitive and its disclosure could result in harm to the enterprise. The Commission, in its regulations, has elaborated on which information would be entitled to confidentiality and what criteria would be applied by the Commission before granting confidentiality. The Commission has progressively been tightening its processes for granting confidentiality.

[151] See chapter 'Competition Law in the United States of America' by Stephen Calkins.

Powers of the Commission and Judicial Challenges

The Commission has the power to regulate its own procedure and it is not bound by the procedure laid down in the Code of Civil Procedure 1908, which gives the general procedure for civil courts. However, the Commission must be guided by the principles of natural justice (Section 36), that is to say that a person against whom action is sought to be taken or whose right or interest is being affected has a right to be heard and should be given a reasonable opportunity to defend himself, and the authority deciding the matter should be free from bias. Further, the procedure shall also be subject to the rules made by the central government under the Act. The Commission has the power to summon witnesses, require production of documents, receive evidence on affidavits, and issue commissions for the examination of witnesses or documents.[152] The same powers are available to the Director General when carrying out investigations under the Act. The Director General may also undertake search of premises (dawn raids) with the permission of the magistrate having jurisdiction.[153]

The Commission, while exercising its powers has faced numerous challenges in the judiciary. The Commission's jurisdiction in examining abuses by standard essential patent holders was challenged before the High Court.[154] Similarly, the Commission also faced opposition in relation to the large volume of penalties being imposed by it on companies, with the courts granting some relief to the parties by staying the penalty order. The legality of the Commission's first dawn raid was also challenged before the High Court of Delhi.[155] The same High Court has also limited the scope of the Director General's investigation power to only those allegations made in the information or the reference received by the Commission.[156] The COMPAT has also been critical of the Commission for not adhering to the principles of natural justice and on this ground alone has remanded a number of matters to the Commission for fresh consideration.[157]

[152] See Section 36.

[153] See Section 42.

[154] *Ericsson* v. *Competition Commission of India,* W.P.(C) 464/2014.

[155] *JCB* v. *Competition Commission of India & Ors.*, W.P.(C) 2244/2014.

[156] *Grasim Industries Limited* v. *Competition Commission of India* 206 (2014) DLT 42.

[157] See Appeal No. 58 of 2015, *Himachal Pradesh Society of Chemist & Druggist Alliance* v. *Rohit Medical Store*; Appeal No. 21 of 2016 *Sunil Bansal and Others* v. *M/s Jaiprakash Associates Ltd. and Others*; Appeal No. 105 of 2012 & I.A. No. 36/2013 *Builder Association of India* v. *Cement Manufacturers*; Appeal No. 17 of 2013 with I.A. No. 26 of 2013, *The Board of Control for Cricket in India* v. *Competition Commission of India and Others.*

Competition Advocacy

The mandate given to the Commission under the Act includes a competition advocacy role. Section 49(3) states that the Commission shall take suitable measures, as may be prescribed, for the promotion of competition advocacy, creating awareness, and imparting training about competition issues, that is, activities that could strengthen the competition culture in the market.

Section 49 also states that in formulating a policy on competition (including review of laws related to competition), the central government and a state government may make a reference to the Commission for its opinion, and the Commission is required to furnish such an opinion to the government. The provisions of Section 21 of the Act, which have been referred to earlier, also provide a broad means to the Commission for providing a competition perspective to other statutory authorities, including sector regulators.

Advocacy has been defined in Black's Law Dictionary as the 'act of pleading for or actively supporting a cause or proposal'.[158] Khemani and Clark point out that a competition authority must 'participate more broadly in the formulation of its own country's economic policies, which may adversely affect competitive market structure, business conduct and economic performance. It must assume the role of competition advocate, acting proactively to bring about government policies that lower barriers to entry, promote deregulation and trade liberalization, and otherwise minimize unnecessary government intervention in the marketplace.'[159] They further state that 'the aim of competition advocacy is to foster conditions that will lead to a more competitive market structure and business behaviour without the direct intervention of the competition authority'. According to the ICN's Advocacy Working Group,[160] competition advocacy refers to those activities conducted by the competition authority related to the promotion of a competitive environment for economic activities by means of non-enforcement mechanisms. Enforcement and advocacy are regarded as complementary activities which are mutually reinforcing. According to some, competition advocacy is compliance without enforcement.

[158] *Black's Law Dictionary*, 7th ed.

[159] Khemani, R Shyam and Johan Clark et al. 1999. 'Competition Advocacy', in World Bank/OECD. 1999. *A Framework for the Design and Implementation of Competition, Law and Policy*, p. 93. World Bank/OECD. Also see chapter 'Competition Advocacy and Interface with Government' by Philip Lowe and Geraldine Emberger.

[160] See ICN report 'Advocacy and Competition Policy', 2002 by ICN's Advocacy Working Group. Available at http:/www.internationalcompetitionnetwork.org/advocacyfinal.pdf.

Competition advocacy has been an important area of activity of several competition authorities both in terms of creating general awareness about the law amongst the enterprises and thereby promoting self-compliance and also in terms of influencing government and regulatory policies in a pro-competition direction. In some of these countries, the advocacy role is supported by a statutory provision in the law, as in India, while in some other countries, it is undertaken as an administrative measure.

In the US, the FTC 'has a robust programme of non-litigation competition work, which includes doing studies, conducting hearings and workshops, widely advocating competition principles, giving advice as to the legality of various arrangements and distributing amicus briefs in state and federal courts'.[161] In the UK, the erstwhile OFT provided advice to government departments and regulators on avoidance of anticompetitive regulations and pro-competition design of laws. New legislative or regulatory proposals are required to be put through the 'competition filter'; the OFT was actively involved in the regulatory impact analysis of such proposals. In Canada, the competition law permits the competition authority to intervene in proceedings before regulatory bodies on issues relating to competition. In Turkey, the competition law allows the competition authority to give its opinion relating to amendments to the competition law.[162] In addition, in Turkey, a communique issued by the prime minister in 1998 urges other government agencies and ministries to consult the competition authority in advance about proposed regulations and decisions that may have implications for competition policy. In the EU, apart from the enforcement role, advocacy is the core tool available to the EC to promote competitive markets, and the European Court of Justice has encouraged competition authorities in the EU to take a critical approach towards legislation which frustrates the objectives of the European competition rules. [163]

The importance of advocacy tool has been underlined in the activities of international organizations like OECD, ICN, and UNCTAD. OECD's 'Guiding Principles on Regulatory Quality and Performance' suggest that competition authorities be provided with the authority and capacity to advocate

161 See chapter 'Competition Law in the United States of America' by Stephen Calkins. Also see chapter 'Competition Advocacy and Interface with Government' by Philip Lowe and Geraldine Emberger.

162 See Sections 125 and 126 of the Canadian Competition Act 1986, and Article 27 of the Turkish Competition Act.

163 See chapter 'Competition Advocacy and Interface with Government' by Philip Lowe and Geraldine Emberger. The chapter describes the advocacy role and activities of competition authorities in several countries and also of international bodies like the OECD, ICN, and UNCTAD.

reform and support public awareness of the role and benefits of competition. It is further advised to design sector regulations in all sectors as to stimulate competition ... .'[164] ICN's Advocacy Working Group in its report brought out certain suggestions on strengthening advocacy work, which include mandatory consultation with the competition authority in legislative and regulatory procedures, enhanced transparency of consultation procedures, greater autonomy to competition authorities, dissemination of the benefits of competition, and promotion of competition issues through websites and press offices.[165]

Since it was established, the Commission has been undertaking work relating to competition advocacy and institutional building. The Commission has undertaken awareness programmes with industry chambers and other bodies and has interacted or intervened with the central and state governments relating to competition issues in government policies and laws. The Commission has also brought out competition advocacy literature. It has been interacting with academic institutions for inclusion of study of competition policy and law in the curriculum for law, economics, and management courses. It has undertaken competition assessment studies through reputed institutions in various areas of the economy. The Commission has arranged training programmes for its staff and other stakeholders within and outside the country.

Recently, the Commission has issued guidelines for competition assessment of economic legislation and bills. The objective of these Guidelines is to facilitate objective and transparent assessment of select economic legislations enacted by the Parliament or State Legislatures. According to the Guidelines, the Commission would suggest, if necessary, appropriate modifications, along with the reasons for the same from the competition perspective, to the relevant stakeholders, including Parliament/State Legislatures, the Administrative Ministry or the Department of the Government which has piloted the legislation/bill, and the Standing/Select Committee of the Parliament/State Legislature that examines the bill.

***

The competition law enforcement in India is currently in its eighth year. During this relatively short period, the Commission armed with the mandate to eliminate anticompetitive practices and check anticompetitive mergers has

164 Ibid.

165 See ICN report 'Advocacy and Competition Policy', 2002 by ICN's Advocacy Working Group. Available at http:/www.internationalcompetitionnetwork.org/advocacyfinal.pdf.

been vigorously pursuing breaches of the law and has imposed, by Indian standards, very heavy penalties that created a significant impact on businesses and forced them to take note of the need for compliance with this new law. Its enforcement has covered various sectors like media, travel, pharmaceutical and healthcare, real estate, steel, cement, telecom, mining, and petroleum amongst many others. As of March 2016, the Commission had received over 700 cases against anticompetitive behaviour of which over 180 cases have been decided after investigation. A large majority of the cases that the Commission receives are disposed of at the prima facie stage where the Commission does not find grounds for ordering an investigation; this also allows the Commission to conserve its scarce resources from being diluted on inconsequential or weak cases. In addition, it would be worthwhile for the Commission to prioritize antitrust cases that cause the greatest harm such as cartels and exclusionary abuse of dominance.

Under merger control, the Commission had received a total of 363 cases as of March 2016 out of which 343 had been decided. A very small percentage of the total cases (about 2 per cent) had been initiated through *sou motu* action by the Commission. The Commission regularly scans business transactions reported in the media and where it finds that the merger application had not been filed in the Commission, it sends out notices to parties to explain why such filing had not been made. In cases of failure to file, the Commission has been imposing penalties on the delinquent parties.

It has also been the endeavour of the Commission to engage with Governments and regulators through advocacy initiatives to advise or incentivize them to avoid stifling competition in the market place. The Commission has been actively interacting with competition agencies in other jurisdictions to collaborate in enforcement of competition law and learn from their experiences. It also reaches out to various stakeholders such as the research community, legal practitioners, and industry and trade associations to develop a competition culture in the country.

The Commission is aware of the importance of creating a dynamic competition law regime that, while deterring anticompetitive practices, meets the emerging needs of the business community and does not create unnecessary hurdles in business activities. From time to time, it undertakes amendments to its regulations with a view to provide greater clarity and certainty based on its own experience of administration of the regulations, learnings from international experience, evolving best practices in tune with other jurisdictions, and consultation with the stakeholders.

Notwithstanding the progress made by the Commission, it faces daunting challenges. There have been concerns among the business community about the process in the Commission as being often bureaucratic and many of the staff not being sensitive to how a particular business model works. Further, there have also been challenges to its jurisdiction and powers before various courts. Several of its high-profile decisions have been overturned in appeal largely on issues of proper procedure. In several cases, the courts have put on hold the proceedings before the Commission for long periods on jurisdictional or procedural grounds. This could be the result of insufficient appreciation in judicial fora of the need for a market-facing regulator to come to speedy decisions and order relevant remedies. At the same time, the Commission needs to look inwards at its procedures both to satisfy judicial scrutiny and to establish its reputation as a state-of-the-art competition authority.

24

Re-viewing Competition Regime in Pakistan*

Rahat Kaunain Hassan

'It is not because things are difficult that we do not dare; it is because we do not dare that things are difficult.' This is the simple belief that the Competition Commission of Pakistan (CCP) seems to have followed while fiercely enforcing the law—across all sectors—since its establishment in 2007. The enforcement action paced up till mid-2013 enabling the CCP to become a worthy competitor for the Global Competition Review (GCR) Agency of the Year—Asia Pacific Middle East and Africa, twice in a row for the years 2011 and 2012. This, however, was followed by a lull spreading over a year and a half, when virtually no enforcement action was seen. Since December 2014, however, there has been a change of guard at the CCP, and we have seen some enforcement activity, albeit not at the pace of enforcement witnessed in the first six years. The GCR, in its review of the CCP for the year 2015,[1] cites the current chairperson to have 'touted the commission's success with merger reviews and advocacy' in her effort to 'make up for lost ground' as an immediate priority. While the CCP has been upgraded to a three-star rating, the 'Performance' assessment being downwards, points towards the

* The author is a former chairperson of the Competition Commission of Pakistan.

[1] Global Competition Review Rating Enforcement, 'Pakistan's Competition Commission', 28 July 2016.

need to focus on other underperformed areas. However, consensus regarding the CCP's remaining 'a relatively open and transparent body' in comparison to other governmental bodies is encouraging.

I may add with a sense of delight that the CCP remains 'an office that the government can justly be proud of. In fact the CCP can be advertised as a model … to adopt ….There's a definite touch of good feng shui about the place. Open, bright and clean.'[2]

Pakistan has remained, in some measure, familiar with competition law since the 1970s when the Monopolies and Restrictive Trade Practices (Control and Prevention) Ordinance, 1970 (MRTPO) was promulgated. However, the mandate under the MRTPO, through the Monopoly Control Authority (MCA), was only 'to provide for measures against undue concentration of economic power, growth of unreasonable monopoly power and unreasonably restrictive trade practices', which were reasoned to be 'injurious to the economic well-being, growth and development of Pakistan'. In contrast, the competition regime introduced in 2007 as an ordinance and attaining permanence as an Act in 2010 provides for 'free competition in all spheres of commercial and economic activity to enhance economic efficiency and to protect consumers from anti competitive behaviour'.

In tracing the origin and evolution of competition law, some of the striking provisions that have been introduced are the new tools of enforcement in particular, the power to conduct forcible entry to search any premises and the power to grant leniency. These considerably strengthened the investigative capacity of the CCP. Also, penalties under the new law are much higher, that is, 10 per cent of the turnover or PKR 75 million, as compared to the meagre penalty of PKR 100,000 under the MRTPO. The earlier lower penalty under the MRTPO was manifestly not a material deterrent; rather than dissuading formation of cartels, it could have facilitated the same.

Then, there is a sharp contrast in the scope of the two laws. The Competition Act is all encompassing and sector blind. It applies to all undertakings including governmental bodies, regulatory bodies, natural or legal persons, bodies corporate, partnerships, associations, trusts, or other entities engaged directly or indirectly in the production, supply, or distribution of goods and provision or control of services. Earlier, the MRTPO had a sector-specific application and envisaged exclusion of regulatory authorities in key sectors like energy, oil and gas, and telecom and also envisaged further exclusions to undertakings notified by the government.

[2] Anjum Niaz. 2013. 'Catching Business Barracudas', *Dawn*, 14 April 2013. Available at http://www.dawn.com/news/802506.

The exclusion of all federal and provincial governmental bodies as well as persons or undertakings acting in pursuance of their orders was, perhaps, critical in undermining MCA's regulatory remit. There is not much to ponder over why the MCA became passive, and is remembered as a toothless agency—a proverbial 'slumbering regulator'.

The statutory obligation to undertake advocacy coupled with the power to issue policy notes upon review of policy frameworks by other government agencies with a view to foster competition is another notable addition. The concept of holding open hearings on matters affecting the state of competition also supplements and facilitates the CCP in discharging its functions. The CCP has meaningfully utilized these powers not only to provide a platform for bringing diverse views but also enhancing its status as a key player in economic regulation.

Another key aspect of the Competition Act is the express recognition of its independence. The law recognizes it as an 'administratively and functionally independent' body, while also stating that the 'Federal Government shall use its best efforts to promote, enhance and maintain the independence of the Commission'. There is no denying that the power of independence is only felt and becomes visible when exercised. The latter indeed can do little without the former being in place but having a solid legal foundation for an independent structured agency goes a long way in making it robust. While legislating the Competition Act, Pakistan had a late mover's advantage, and happily Pakistan did benefit a great deal from global precedence. Examining the MRTPO and the Competition Act in juxtaposition, and then appreciating the work done at the CCP since its inception, it becomes quite clear that the perception rightly changed from a 'toothless' regulator to one with fangs.

'Independence' or 'autonomy' does not necessarily mean being opposed to the government. I have always maintained that with respect to organizations, it is essentially the ability to act independently and responsibly, and to remain accountable for those actions. In my view, there is a lot of hard work that earned Pakistan the reputation of a 'surprise success story'.[3] The International Clearing House (ICH)[4] case, in my assessment, serves the best example where the CCP visibly struggled to demonstrate its independence on both counts: advocacy and enforcement.

[3] Rosalind Donald. 2010. 'The Tortoise and the Hare', *Global Competition Review* 13(10), 18 November. Available at https://globalcompetitionreview.com/benchmarking/november-2010/1053128/the-tortoise-and-the-hare (access is limited to members or through purchase of the article).

[4] LDI Operators Order, 30 April 2013. Available at http://www.cc.gov.pk/images/Downloads/ich_order_30_april_2013.pdf.

The ICH is clearly a landmark case in terms of the autonomy exercised and the perseverance with which the CCP pursued the matter towards its logical conclusion. The peculiarities of the case reveal how the CCP countered not only the legal challenges but also both political as well as tactical. The CCP was not only confronted with the powerful telecom industry, which was backed by influential cadres, including at the Ministry of Information Technology (MOIT) and other powerful lobbies protecting vested interests with a trail of legal battles intended to halt the progress of proceedings before the CCP. The CCP was engaged in the matter for almost one and a half year—from October 2011 to April 2013. It started with the filing of an exemption application by long distance and international (LDI) operators with the CCP.

The ICH case presented a situation where there was agreement amongst all 14 LDI operators to terminate all incoming international traffic on the exclusive network of Pakistan Telecommunication Company Limited (PTCL). It required suspending all interconnection capacities of the remaining LDI operators. It involved price fixing stipulating a fixed settlement rate of 8.8 cents per minute and the revenue had to be shared amongst the LDI operators as per agreed quota allocated to each LDI operator (which was based on the average volume of traffic received by them in the past). Apart from price fixing and quota allocation, which are viewed as per se violations of competition law, there were other significant competition concerns. Competition was being restricted in the bandwidth market from 2 players to 1. In the LDI market from 14 players to 1; this not only amounted to rolling back to PTCL monopoly but also exposed increased risk of failure, as all local loop operators were being made completely dependent on one operator's circuit for international incoming calls. Thus, the ICH agreement foreclosed the market and killed the choice or even the option of a choice for local loop operators' vis-à-vis LDIs. Such arrangement was evidently a barrier to entry for any new entrants in the relevant market. The worst part was that there was no service being rendered by the 13 LDI's and the charges were enhanced with LDI share from 2.04 cents per minute to 5.9 cents.

Before the Courts, the LDI operators conveniently divided themselves, taking diametrically opposed views. First, they were caught in the Lahore High Court where one of the local loop operators had challenged the ICH arrangement. The Court granted stay against the ICH with the observation that the ICH agreement seemed to have been entered with undue haste and deliberately bypassed the CCP's concern expressed in its policy note and other communications. It was to avoid facing the piercing probe of the Honorable Justice Ijaz ul Ahsan, that a few of the LDIs filed an appeal with Supreme Court challenging the High Court's jurisdiction and there they touted the CCP's jurisdiction to handle the matter. Subsequently, the Honourable Supreme Court, with consent of parties, directed the CCP to treat the petition as a representation and to decide the matter after hearing all parties concerned within a given time period of 30 days. However, soon after issuance of a Show Cause Notice, the CCP was dragged to Sindh High Court where some of the LDIs asserted that not all LDIs had given their consent to the CCP's jurisdiction. The CCP's jurisdiction as well as issuance of Show Cause Notice without conducting an enquiry was challenged and a stay was obtained. It was then that the CCP took the bold step of taking these LDIs head on by initiating contempt proceedings before the Honourable Supreme Court. The matter finally was put to rest to the extent of the CCP being allowed to conclude the initiated proceedings. In fact, the then Honourable Chief Justice of Pakistan, Tassaduq Hussain Jillani, could see through the respondents conduct and the counsel for the LDIs tendered an unqualified apology, which was accepted by the Supreme Court. This in itself was no ordinary feat. This achievement by the CCP raised the bar for a legal contest the CCP was prepared to undertake with those who were inclined to undermine or avoid the impact of the competition paradigm.

Interestingly, initially all LDI operators filed an application to seek exemption from application of Section 4. Sections 5 and 9 envisage grant of exemption on account of: promoting technical or economic progress, improving production or distribution or where the benefits clearly outweigh the adverse effects of absence or lessening of competition in relation to practices/agreements otherwise prohibited under Section 4. However, when the LDIs were unable to justify the ICH arrangement and well into the fifth month of the application review, they decided to withdraw the application citing that the ICH parties 'do not consider this a live case'. The CCP, however, proceeded with the matter and concluded the hearings. While allowing withdrawal, it clearly warned and stipulated that any future ICH agreement shall be subject to prior clearance owing to prima facie serious competition concerns.

The MOIT, ignoring these concerns entirely and without taking the CCP on board, issued a policy directive endorsing the establishment of the ICH and announced it to be effective from 1 October 2012. The cornerstone of the policy directive issued by MOIT was purportedly to prevent evasion of access promotion charge payments and to recover its dues along with the pretext to curb grey traffic. In response, the CCP issued a policy note under Section 29 of the Competition Act, where the MOIT Directive and proposed the ICH Arrangement were stated to promote price fixation and quota allocation and thus per se illegal being the most pernicious of anticompetitive conducts.

It should not come as a surprise that the ICH matter persisted and all parties vigorously contested. The major arguments included: (a) that matter falls within the purview of the sector-specific regulator, that is, the telecom authority which regulates the special law relating to telecom operators; (b) incoming international telephony originates outside Pakistan and therefore beyond the CCP's territorial jurisdiction; (c) no inquiry was conducted before issuing show cause; (d) the division of revenue was a commercial issue and the ICH would divert balance of foreign exchange payments and positively impact the economy; (e) it would curb grey traffic; and (f) even if the ICH violated Competition Act they could not be held liable as they were following directions of MOIT.

The CCP addressed all these aspects giving its findings in a very detailed 89-page order in April 2013. It declared the ICH to be void in terms of sub-section (3) of Section 4 holding that it stood annulled. The LDI operators were directed to cease and desist from carrying on the prohibited practices of such nature and the telecom authority was advised to restore competition, as it existed prior to the implementation of the ICH. While the CCP did not accept the state conduct defence, it also did not impose the maximum penalty. A constrained penalty equivalent to 7.5 per cent of the annual turnover for the last preceding year was imposed on all LDIs. PTCL alone was penalized with a sum of PKR 8.3 billion. Full vindication of the CCP's stance was manifest in the Federal Government's decision to abolish the ICH arrangement in June 2014, citing ironically that such measure was 'in the wake of rampant increase in grey trafficking'.[5]

It would certainly be worthwhile to share that as per the data submitted by LDI operators to PTA, incoming call volumes went down by 70 per cent. Pre-ICH, during September 2012 the call volumes were at 1.9 billion whereas in February 2013 the volumes stood at 579 million. The LDI share of revenue under the ICH increased considerably to $34.14 million in February 2012 as opposed to the previous figure of $8.37 million, despite the sharp decrease in traffic for incoming. The key reason being the higher Approved Settlement Rate (ASR) (8.8 cents up from 6.25) and the absence of the permissible range, which was 80 per cent pre-ICH, allowing LDI's to compete and the actual rate was 1.68 cents per PTA in September 2012.

The ICH case is also an example of the international outreach of effective action by a competition agency. The CCP's policy note was relied upon by foreign undertakings in their jurisdiction, including in particular those in the

[5] 'Incoming calls to Pakistan to cost less', *The News*, 18 June 2014. Available at https://www.thenews.com.pk/archive/print/638571-incoming-calls-to-pakistan-to-cost-less.

US, to seek relief from the Federal Communications Commission (FCC). The FCC ordered that all facilities-based carriers shall not pay the increment above the negotiated settlement or termination rate by which such prior rate was increased effective on or around 1 October 2012, until such time such prohibition is removed.

That legal battles to enforce a change in behaviour of anticompetitive tendencies are long drawn is true for Pakistan experience as well. Currently, two matters in relation to the ICH arrangement remain pending before the Supreme Court and the Sindh High Court. Some LDI operators still persist in pursuit of the ICH challenging government's withdrawal while others have challenged the penalties imposed by the CCP. However, since then the Competition Appellate Tribunal (CAT) has become effectively operational. Complete closure of the ICH matter may still take a few if not several years. The important point is that despite formidable odds, the CCP did duly guard its 'precious independence'. As rightly observed by GCR in its Rating Enforcement, 2013, '[t]he CCP finds itself having to combat these contrary forces at almost every stage, which makes the progress it has made even more noteworthy in the eyes of Pakistan's competition bar'. In fact, one of the lawyers cited it as a 'testament to its commitment to maintaining its independence'.[6]

The peer review undertaken by UNCTAD in 2012[7] at the CCP's request states that '[i]n previous analyses of the progress of the CCP, experienced and respected commentators have called attention to what the agency has done, with outstanding competence in ascending a steep learning curve, concluding that it is to be considered one of the best-performing newly established agencies in the developing world'. But the observation that 'CCP struggles against difficulties that often challenge competition agencies in economies with a long tradition of strong government control, including a deficient public understanding of competition policy, slow judicial review and incomplete support from other parts of the Government, mainly translated into the lack of adequate financial autonomy' holds valid even for the current times.

Reverting to the legislative transition, the process of revamping the MRTPO into the Competition Ordinance, 2007 and its subsequent enactment as the Competition Act, 2010, remains one of the earliest and perhaps the biggest challenge faced. This challenge is not yet over or closed in the sense that the constitutionality of the law in terms of the legislation being

[6] Global Competition Review Rating Enforcement. 2013. Pakistan's Competition Commission.

[7] United Nations Conference on Trade and Development. 2013. 'Voluntary Peer Review of Competition Law and Policy-Pakistan'. Available at http://unctad.org/en/PublicationsLibrary/ditcclp2013d4_en.pdf

a Federal or a Provincial statute remains pending adjudication before the Courts. It is intriguing as to why there is procrastination in deciding such a basic question. This law is not unique to Pakistan; it exists in some form or the other in over 125 countries. There are indeed precedents highlighting the evolved jurisprudence on the subject. While the constitutional provisions may vary, the underlying thrust and spirit for application of competition law invariably remains the same. In any case, it calls for an urgent determination of the issue owing to the economic impact. One can't deny that the success of the enforcement of the competition law is dependent on timely decisions of such cases by the courts.

The CCP cases are pending and increasing in number for the last 8 years. The cases involving constitutional challenges have been heard at length several times but the final decision has been elusive due to elevation or substitution of the Honourable Judges or on account of adjournments that are endemic in the sluggish justice system typical to developing countries. In fact, when the matter was argued last,[8] in the Lahore High Court, Lahore, the Honourable Court instructed the office of the Attorney General of Pakistan to seek clarification as to whether the Government would be inclined to re-draft the Competition Act, 2010, and that certain sections (with particular emphasis laid on 'relevant market') were pointed out as very wide and thus 'could be beyond the competence of the Parliament'. Also, the Court wanted to know if the Federal Government would consider adopting the procedure available in Article 144 of the Constitution of Islamic Republic of Pakistan, 1973, that is, to seek ratification from the Provinces.

The Federal Government has held firm. It asserted that the Parliament enjoys the constitutional mandate to enact the Competition Act, 2010, by virtue of the powers vested in it under Article 151 of the Constitution, which, among others, empowers the Parliament to impose restrictions by law in relation to trade, commerce, or intercourse not merely between one Province and another but importantly, 'within any part of Pakistan as may be required in the public interest'. It also stated that the Competition Act provides for anticompetition regulation on the basis of 'business markets', 'undertakings', and 'economic and commercial activities' within any or all parts of the country. Accordingly, the Competition Act was stated to reflect national economic coordination and a consistent policy towards trade and commerce in the country. The clarity with which the Federal Government has responded is indeed admirable. Nonetheless, while the

[8] W.P. No 9518/2009 titled '*LPG Association of Pakistan vs. Federation of Pakistan*' along with other connected 13 writ petitions in the Lahore High Court, Lahore.

arguments were concluded and heard last in November 2015, a final determination on the constitutionality aspect is still awaited. It is learnt that the CCP is pursuing the matter but it is difficult to foretell how and in which direction the Lahore High Court may proceed. However, keeping in view that the Honourable Bench has in a way disclosed its mind; would the circumstances not call for constitution of a larger Bench to deliberate and conclude the matter?

It needs to be appreciated that prolonging of this determination is prejudicial to consumer interest. All enforcement actions taken in the past against the powerful players are having a fading effect in creating deterrence for cartels and those involved in anticompetitive practices. The fate of the penalties imposed, be it banks (PKR 205 million), cement (PKR 6.402 billion),[9] sugar (recommending a maximum penalty),[10] jute mills (PKR 23 million),[11] poultry (PKR 50 million),[12] cooking oil (PKR 50 million),[13] LPG & JJVL (PKR 318 million),[14] telecom sector (as detailed earlier), urea/fertilizer companies (PKR 8.64 billion)[15] is crucial from all perspectives. Also, actions initiated such as proceedings against electrical equipment manufacturers, that is., of switchgears, transformers[16] where the CCP to their credit received the first and so far the only leniency application, which was termed as a 'regulatory

[9] All Pakistan Cement Manufacturer Association (APCMA) and member undertakings, 27 August 2009. Available at http://www.cc.gov.pk/images/Downloads/Cement%20(final%20order)%2027-08-2009.pdf

[10] Owing to the injunctive relief granted by the Supreme Court that no final penal order could be passed, and only proceedings could be concluded, the CCP decided to pass a provisional order recommending the highest penalty in view of the conduct of the parties and restraint imposed by the Court.

[11] Pakistan Jute Mills Association and Member's Mills, 3 February 2011. Available at http://www.cc.gov.pk/images/Downloads/pjma_order_3%20feb_2011.pdf.

[12] M/s. Pakistan Poultry Association, 16 August 2010. Available at http://www.cc.gov.pk/images/Downloads/ppa_order_16_august_2010.pdf.

[13] Pakistan Vanaspati Manufacturers Association Order, 30 June 2011. Available at http://www.cc.gov.pk/images/Downloads/pvma_30_june.pdf.

[14] LPG Association of Pakistan Jamshoro Joint Venture Ltd, 14 December 2009. Available at http://www.cc.gov.pk/images/Downloads/lpg_final_order_proof_15_december_2009.pdf.

[15] Urea Manufacturers Order, 29 March 2013. Available at http://www.cc.gov.pk/images/Downloads/urea_manufacturers_orderr.pdf.

[16] Leniency Application filed by M/S. Siemens (Pakistan) Engineering Company Ltd Order, 3 April 2012. Available at http://www.cc.gov.pk/images/Downloads/leniency_application_filed_by_ms_siemens_engineering.pdf.

breakthrough',[17] remains in a limbo despite the admission of guilt by as big a corporate giant as Siemens who submitted 233 documents to corroborate the CCP's case. Such disclosure to date has not helped in vacation of stays granted by the Courts against the CCP proceedings against the remaining cartel participants. It is yet another feather in the CCP's cap that the decision that awarded leniency to Siemens itself was nominated for (though not awarded) GCR's 'Behavioural Matter of the Year' Award in Asia Pacific Middle East and African region.

The judicial review of the CCP decisions will have a true and real impact in determining the efficacy of the agency's work and lend a better understanding as to what role competition law will have in the state's economy. The enforcement actions taken currently are viewed without force to bring any corrective behaviour when the vested interests strongly hold to the belief that the fait accompli of such actions will not go beyond the status quo order in the years to come.

Notwithstanding the constitutional aspect, two major recent developments have been to the CCP's good fortune in receiving some share of the statutorily assured share of three per cent of the fees and charges levied by other regulatory agencies and equally important is the new appointment of the Members of the Competition Appellate Tribunal (CAT) by the present government who for the time being are viewed as effectively discharging their functions.

Under the law, five regulatory bodies[18] were notified to contribute three per cent of fees and charges charged by them to the CCP Fund to ensure its financial autonomy. The CCP in the past, and currently as well, has been struggling with low budget allocations. Recovering these contributions from designated regulatory bodies is a huge challenge. However, efforts have after several years borne fruit. The Securities and Exchange Commission of Pakistan (SECP) under the able leadership of the then chairman, Zafar Ul Haq Hijazi, had started making such contribution albeit in part. SECP was not only a major and powerful economic regulator but was at that time perceived as the best performing regulator. SECP's vision to strengthen other regulators is most worthy of mention. In the past two years, SECP alone has contributed around 40 per cent of the approved annual budget of the CCP. Apart from generating goodwill inter se key regulatory bodies, such

[17] BR Research, 'CCP's regulatory breakthrough', *Business Recorder*, 5 April 2012. Available at http://fp.brecorder.com/res/44-miscellaneous/2411-ccps-/.

[18] SECP; National Electric Power Regulatory Authority (NEPRA); Oil and Gas Regulatory Authority (OGRA); Pakistan Telecommunication Authority (PTA); and Pakistan Electronic Media Regulatory Authority (PEMRA).

coordination represents a cohesive and integrated approach of the government in creating the environment necessary for healthy business practices.

The law as originally framed did not envisage an appellate tribunal, and provided that all appeals from decisions of the CCP would lie before the Supreme Court. However, subsequent parliamentary debates resulted in providing for a special tribunal, where from appeals will be preferred to the Supreme Court. Initially, CAT did not take off, largely because of the delay in appointments and the provision of the administrative infrastructure for CAT. But now not only is the CAT membership complete, it has been provided the required infrastructure to attend to appeals, and it is no less than an icing on the cake that the current Members of CAT are expeditiously entertaining and disposing of appeals. CAT is widely well regarded and has earned a reputation of ensuring early disposal of cases with crisp orders.

It must be added that the establishment of the CAT is one of the four amendments that were introduced subsequent to the promulgation of the Competition Ordinance 2007 and incorporated in the enactment in 2010. At the time recommendation for establishing CAT was made, there were apprehensions relating to its efficacy but the majority regarded this a practical solution to save time taken for disposal of cases and pursuing them in different provinces of the High Court. With the appointment of the current Members of CAT, it is fair to comment that apprehensions and uncertainties have been laid to rest. Benefit of CAT has surfaced, in that while the Members are known to patiently hear cases at length, they are also known to take timely decisions on matters before them. Whether succeeding Members of CAT would continue this trend and the Honourable Supreme Court would also expeditiously decide appeals preferred from CAT's orders, is a question only time will answer.

In order to demonstrate the reach and impact of powerful lobbies, it is relevant to elaborate aspects preceding establishment of CAT. When the Competition Ordinance was promulgated in November 2007, the Supreme Court was designated as the Court of Appeal against the orders of the CCP Members. After the first re-promulgation of the Ordinance in 2008, through a corrigendum issued by the Law Ministry, the change was made in Section 42 and the Supreme Court was substituted with the High Court. This was patently not in order. A dozen of appeals were pending adjudication with the Supreme Court against the enforcement actions taken by the CCP and the Apex Court had not expressed any objection to preference of the appeals against the orders of the CCP. Being Member Legal, the CCP at that time, I recall deliberating and seeking advice from senior counsel who had opined that there was no constitutional issue with such direct right of appeal to the

Apex Court. However, within the legal fraternity this did raise a controversy. The settled law in Pakistan requires having at least one meaningful right of appeal be afforded. Therefore, even if the right of appeal before the Appellate Bench at the CCP (appeal from a single Member order to a bench of two or more Members) is not taken into account, the right of appeal before the Supreme Court, which is the court of unlimited jurisdiction, surely provided a 'meaningful right of appeal'. Had this change not been brought; and resultantly the CAT brought in as a substitute, the Supreme Court would have remained seized of the matter, and perhaps, by now the Apex Court would have pronounced its decision on the critical constitutional aspect, and things might have been altogether different.

Having seen the transition from temporary legislation to a formal enactment in 2010, I recall there were around 14 recommendations that were made by the Senate Standing Committee while considering passage of the Competition Act, 2010. These ranged inter alia from including a definition of 'Competition' in the legislation to advising the the CCP to keep advocacy, in particular media advocacy, at a minimum. It was also proposed that penalty be stipulated in a fixed amount rather than as a percentage of turnover. Some amendments, if incorporated, would have diluted the CCP's power or remit. The CCP with the support of the Ministry of Finance strongly resisted such proposals, including in particular to subject search and inspection power to prior approval of a magistrate by arguing that the law already provided due checks and balances and that if the CCP were required to seek such approval, the time lapse would provide an opportunity to the undertaking to conceal relevant records and, more importantly, take away the element of surprise which is critical to discovery of material evidence. Accordingly, power to order search and inspection was retained at the Commission level to ensure a considered and due exercise of authority. Section 34, which deals with the 'Power to enter and search premises', has been made subject to the requirement to have 'reasonable grounds to be recorded in writing' prior to authorizing entry and search of any premises.

Eventually, amendments were restricted to only four aspects, which if objectively looked at have resulted in bringing improvement to the law. The credit for passage of the law as an enactment is not only due to the then Prime Minister Yousaf Raza Gillani, who personally oversaw the presentation of the bill but also to Ishaq Dar, the chairman of the subject Senate Standing Committee, as he played a very positive role in resolving issues pertaining to the 14 proposed amendments and restricting it to only 4.

The power of the CCP to impose 'Penalties' (S. 38 of the Act) up to 15 per cent of the turnover was also subject to extended debate, and eventually, was brought down to 10 per cent, which threshold is closer in line with international practices. Against this, the CCP negotiated an increase in the fixed penalty from PKR 50 million to PKR 75 million. However, importantly, penalties collected by the CCP were to be deposited in the government treasury rather than with the CCP itself. This change dispelled any perception of conflict that may arise by linking imposition of high penalties to the CCP's financial interest. As a result, Section 20 titled 'Commission Fund' was amended to remove mention of 'penalties'. Instead, the Commission Fund now consists of inter alia grants by the Federal Government and charges and fees levied by the CCP and contributions recovered from designated regulatory bodies.

It has been 6 years to the enactment of the Competition Act, and there has not been a single amendment proposed since. Laws must evolve to ensure their efficacy. While the Competition Act sufficiently incorporates substantive aspects, benefitting from global best practices, there is perhaps a need to focus on further improvements aimed at ensuring quick disposal of pending cases before the CCP as well as the courts. There is need to make provision not only for the CCP's cases but also for other economic regulators. There already exist company benches in the High Courts, which aim at summary disposal of company matters. Likewise, dedicated Regulatory Benches may be considered for competition law issues, particularly where constitutional writs are filed.

The Tribunal being operational can be argued as offering an alternate adequate remedy, though not on determination of constitutional issues (which fall beyond its ambit), but these issues can be finally settled by the Supreme Court in the second appeal. For parties that would still pursue the writ remedy and keep their cases alive at the High Court or pursue the constitutional challenges, the procedures in this regard and even the ones before the Tribunal may specifically be streamlined for grant of stay. There should be a mandatory notice requirement by the Court before grant of interim relief, specific time period for lapse/vacation of stay, and deposit of adequate security for costs so that frivolous litigation is discouraged and there is efficient and effective disposal of cases. Invariably, in the CCP's cases stays have been obtained prior to hearing and giving notice to the CCP. The leniency case is one glaring example. Injunctive relief under the Code of Civil Procedure, 1908 is stipulated to be a maximum of 6 months. Nonetheless, these seem to continue forever.

No one seems to have gathered or is interested to determine the quantum of disputed claims pending before Courts in relation to the regulatory bodies, in particular the economic regulators. A very rough estimate would run into hundreds of billions of rupees. Matters of economic importance have to be prioritized. It is as important for the government as it is for the public at large and for ensuring that the arms of the government feel the pressure to perform. This would also generate a healthy debate on economic issues and provide impetus in development of economic jurisprudence.

Managing or reconciling the overlap of regulatory power by different regulatory bodies has been another predicament. The CCP has had to defend its jurisdiction vis-à-vis other sector-specific regulators, who may assert jurisdiction over competition issues in the garb of promoting competition and attempting to regulate that particular sector or service. In this respect, the CCP has stood by the ground[19] that a 'sector specific regulator owing to its limitations and restrictions in exercise of powers to "a sector alone" would not be able to regulate or enforce competition principles effectively'. Contrastingly, the competition agencies are sector blind regulators, and this principle is specifically endorsed by the preamble of the Competition Act itself, which does not exempt or restrict the scope of the Competition Act from or to any specific sector, but rather transcends all sectors.

In the ICH order, the CCP placed reliance on Article 18 of the Constitution to draw a distinction between the regulation of trade or profession 'by a licensing system' (Article 18 [a]) and the regulation of the same 'in the interest of free competition' (Article 18[b]). The CCP observed as far as 'free competition' is concerned, it remains only the domain of the CCP, whereas the 'licensing system', which altogether deals with a different aspect, is the domain of the respective sector-specific regulator, that is, the telecom authority.

In the CCP's experience, banks, securities market players, and the telecom sector (among others) have sought protection under the umbrella of sector-specific regulators. In early 2008, the State Bank of Pakistan had expressed its reservation to the Finance Ministry soon after the promulgation of law and sought exemption for the banking sector. The CCP, however, contested aggressively stating that it would not be in sync with the recognized global practice and can well be regarded as counterproductive. Such an exemption could neither be termed 'in the interest of the security of the state' nor could it be justified on grounds of 'public interest', which are necessary conditions for any class of undertaking invoking exemption from application of the competition law. The CCP argued that it would defeat the very objective of the law that is 'to provide for free competition in all spheres of commercial and economic activity'—the banking sector being the jugular vein of all commercial and economic activity.

[19] LDI Operators Order, 30 April 2013. Available at http://www.cc.gov.pk/images/Downloads/ich_order_30_april_2013.pdf.

Similarly, in the abuse of dominance case against the Karachi Stock Exchange Limited, the CCP resolved the issue of jurisdiction in its favour by observing that it 'can be best understood with reference to which law is relevant and applicable to an entity in a given context' (rather than getting into the debate of general versus special law, particularly, when two laws are special). It concluded the matter by stating that it is an established rule of construction/interpretation that even if both laws are considered special statutes, having non obstante clause, present in the Competition law and absent in the subject securities law, the subsequent enactment would have a prevailing effect. The issue of conflict of different laws was held not to arise in the absence of any provision on the competition aspect under review pursuant to the securities and companies' legislation.

The CCP's tenacity and perseverance earlier in establishing its writ has worked well. This would not be possible without the support provided by the government but to ensure that these issues do not resurface in one form or the other, and to conclusively settle the potential turf war inter se the regulators, an amendment in the Competition Act designating the CCP as 'the regulator' of free competition would consolidate CCP's position to settle such controversy with express obligation for other sector-specific regulators to provide support to the CCP in regulating free competition in their respective spheres.

As mentioned earlier, the outstanding recovery of the 3 per cent of fee and charges levied by the other regulatory agencies (OGRA, PTA, NEPRA, and PEMRA) has been pending since 2008. A firm measure at the government's end is required to ensure that the other regulatory bodies honour the long due statutory obligation. This will help CCP attain fully the financial autonomy envisaged under the statute and to reap the benefits by investing in and consolidating its human resource and the chartered scope of activities. Be it through an administrative direction or through an amendment in law a cut-off line for clearance of such dues is critical. The procedure for deposit and recovery of such contributions from the regulatory body needs to be incorporated in the Act itself. Unless there is some immediate threat or a penal consequence stipulated on the basis of which CCP may recover these dues, it will remain a stale claim. Clearly, effective advocacy is required on CCP's part; after having SECP on board they are far better placed to require compliance from other regulatory bodies and they must play this card well.

Lastly, what makes any organization strong is the human capital it employs. Over the years, CCP has developed a cadre of young and energetic professionals from a wide range of disciplines, ranging from law to economics, and from chartered accountants to technical experience in various sectors of economic enterprise. However, such cadre needs to be guided at the top by equally determined Members having diverse exposure and expertise. Currently, there are two vacant positions for Members. Due diversity, therefore, must be brought on board and timely appointment of such Members will provide due impetus. Perhaps an economist, a chartered accountant and a person from the industry or academia would result in value addition. Preferences apart, importantly these Members ought to be individuals of integrity having due competence and commitment to public service. It needs to be borne in mind that just as integrity without competence is lame, competence without integrity can be dangerous.

In my view, rather than having a competitive process for such appointments, the government may consider reverting back to exercising its prerogative of selection/appointment through invitation, albeit that selection process should be merit based adopting due procedures and taking into account all relevant aspects. Accordingly, both the government and the appointee should remain accountable. The competitive process appointment through open public invitation was recently introduced when the Supreme Court in one of the cases had asked the government to develop and provide guidelines in relation thereto. In such matters, the competitive process in countries like Pakistan is generally viewed by the public as farce—only a tool or a means to serve the desired end. Making individuals seek positions in public service could also place them in conflict to step down or part from that position (in case the need arises). If the government were to take conscious responsibility of duly selecting and appointing such Members, it would inevitably also duly provide support to them and thus the institution.

I would like to add that owing to the maximum ceiling placed on the Management Position (MP-1) Scale by the government as provided through the Rules, the salary of the Members has been on the real lower side when compared to the Members/Commissioners of the SECP. It is essential to remove this anomaly. Whether recognized or not, CCP is the regulator of regulators; accordingly, the remuneration and perks must also correspond to the envisioned status.

25

Merger Control Regime under the Competition Law in India*

Vinod Dhall

Until the merger control provisions contained in the Competition Act, 2002, (Competition Act) came into effect on 1 June 2011, there was no definitive merger control regime in India. Though the Monopolies and Restrictive Trade Practices Act, 1969 (MRTP Act), which was repealed once the Competition Act was brought into force, had limited powers for regulating mergers which had an anticompetitive effect on the market, these provisions were deleted in 1991 as part of the economic reforms introduced by the government.[1] In any case, the provisions of the MRTP Act were focused on controlling monopolies or large businesses than on promoting competition in the markets. Subsequently,

* The author wishes to record his appreciation for the assistance given by Ms Kabyashree Chaharia.

[1] On receiving an application for a merger, the government could refer the same to the Monopolies and Restrictive Trade Practices Commission (MRTPC) for conducting an inquiry under Section 23(6)(b) of the MRTP Act. The MRTPC was to furnish a report of its opinion to the government, after a hearing. As per Section 24, the government could consult with the MRTPC before imposing a penalty on undertakings in violation of Section 23.

mergers and acquisitions mainly fell within the ambit of the Companies Act, 1956 and SEBI Act, 1992; however, these legislations primarily protected the interests of shareholders, and creditors, and other stakeholders, and preventing adverse effects on competition was not the objective of these legislations.

As part of the government's initiative to replace the MRTP Act by a competition regime more in sync with a market-based economy, the Raghavan Committee on Competition Policy and Law in India, set up to recommend a new competition law, in its report also examined the necessity of assessing the effect of mergers and acquisitions on the market as a whole. The Committee concluded, '[M]ergers beyond a threshold limit in terms of assets will require pre-notification. If no reasoned order, prohibiting the merger is received within 90 days it should be deemed to have been approved. In adjudicating a merger, potential efficiency losses from the merger should be weighed against potential gains.'[2] Following this recommendation, the new Competition Act incorporated a merger control regime.

The present regime requires a mandatory notice to be filed to the Competition Commission of India (Commission) for those mergers, acquisitions, and amalgamations that exceed the thresholds under the Competition Act. The regime is also suspensory in nature, that is, there is a standstill obligation on parties to refrain from completing a transaction until clearance by the Commission.

As of 31 March 2016, the Commission had received about 363 applications and had approved 343 of them, with some still under review.[3] Of these, nine cases were cleared by the Commission post modification of certain terms and three cases were subjected to divestment; till date no transaction has been blocked by the Commission.

The manner in which the Commission regulates mergers, acquisitions, and amalgamations which cause or are likely to cause an appreciable adverse effect on competition (AAEC) in accordance with the powers given by the Competition Act and its own merger regulations (Combination Regulations) has been explained ahead.

Types of Transactions 'Caught' by the Merger Regulations

Any acquisition or merger or amalgamation that exceeds the financial thresholds prescribed in the Competition Act and the Government of India notification

[2] Report of High Level Committee on Competition Policy and Law, 2000. Chapter 4, Section D (para 4.8.8 of the Summary).

[3] Quarterly Newsletter of Competition Commission of India, January–March 2016, vol. 16, p. 8, available at http://www.cci.gov.in/sites/default/files/Newsletter_document/nl16.pdf.

dated 4 March 2016 amounts to a 'combination' which is reportable to the Commission, unless expressly exempted under the Combination Regulations.

Types of Transactions

Acquisition

Section 2(a) of the Competition Act defines an 'acquisition' as directly or indirectly acquiring or agreeing to acquire:

(i) shares, voting rights or assets of an enterprise;[4] or
(ii) control over management or control over assets of any enterprise.

Acquisition of Shares, Voting Rights, or Assets of an Enterprise

In this case, there is no requirement under the Competition Act to prove acquisition of control. Thus, technically an acquisition of even a single share or asset could be notifiable under the Competition Act, unless the transaction falls within the exemptions provided in the Combination Regulations.

Under Section 2(v) of the Competition Act, 'Shares' includes any security which entitles the holder to receive shares with voting rights; thus on a plain reading, convertible instruments and options would also constitute 'shares' and accordingly their acquisition would be notifiable. However, interestingly, the Commission's decisions in past cases indicate that holding of a mere option to receive shares in the future does not lead to the presumption of acquisition of 'shares' which can only be conclusively ascertained on examining the nature of the convertible instruments.

In *IMT/Network 18*,[5] the acquisition of Zero Optionally Convertible Debentures was found to be notifiable as they gave the holder an absolute

[4] Under Section 2(h) of the Competition Act, 'enterprise' means a person or a department of the Government who or which is, or has been, engaged in any activity, relating to the production, storage, supply, distribution, acquisition or control of articles or goods, or the provision of services, of any kind, or in investment, or in the business of acquiring, holding, underwriting or dealing with shares, debentures or other securities of any other body corporate, either directly or through one or more of its units or divisions or subsidiaries, whether such unit or division or subsidiary is located at the same place where the enterprise is located or at a different place or at different places, but does not include any activity of the Government relatable to the sovereign functions of the Government including all activities carried on by the departments of the Government dealing with atomic energy, currency, defence and space.

[5] Combination Registration No. C-2012/03/47, available at http://cci.gov.in/sites/default/files/C-2012-03-47.pdf.

entitlement to receive shares of the target companies with voting rights by converting them into equity at any time before the expiry of 10 years. In contrast, in *Reliance/Bharti AXA*,[6] the Commission held that the option to acquire was dependant on the FDI regulations and would therefore be examined at a later date when such option was exercised.

Therefore, it appears that if a convertible instrument gives the holder an unrestricted option to receive shares in the future, it will amount to an acquisition of 'shares' under the Competition Act.

Acquisition of Control over Management or Control over Assets of any Enterprise

The term 'control' has been defined in Explanation (a) to Section 5 and includes controlling the affairs or the management by one or more enterprises, either jointly or singly, over another enterprise or group, or by one or more groups, either jointly or singly, over another group or enterprise. The Commission has adopted a very expansive approach in interpreting the term 'control' to cover all rights giving the acquirer the ability to exercise influence over the management or affairs of an enterprise. Some of these include:

1. acquisition of shares with veto rights over strategic commercial decisions[7];
2. existence of common promoter group, directors, and management[8];

[6] Combination Registration No. C-2011/07/01, available at http://www.cci.gov.in/sites/default/files/RILOrder270711_0.pdf.

[7] *Alpha TC Holdings Pte Limited/Tata Capital Growth Fund I*, Combination Registration No. C-2014/07/192, available at http://www.cci.gov.in/sites/default/files/C-2014-07-192_0.pdf; In this case, the following veto rights over the 'Reserved Matters' were considered to have resulted in a joint control scenario: (a) appointment and removal of the managing director and the chief financial officer of the enterprise, (b) increasing or decreasing the number of directors on the board or any committees, (c) approving, adopting, amending, or modifying the annual budget and business plan (including any capital expenditure budget, operating budget, and financing plan), (d) pay emoluments/bonuses to promoters or directors; and any amendment to the memorandum or articles of association of the enterprise. In addition, the acquirers were to acquire the following rights which further strengthened the Commission's conclusion on joint control: (a) appointment of one director on the board of directors (acquirer directors), (b) appoint one acquirer director as the chairman of the Audit, Remuneration and Recruitment Committees of the board of directors, and (c) in the event any Reserved Matters are to be discussed at any board meeting, then the quorum for a board meeting shall require the presence of at least one of the acquirer directors.

[8] Alok Industries/Grabal Alok Impex, Combination Registration No. C-2012/01/28, available at http://www.cci.gov.in/sites/default/files/NP-C-2012-01-28.pdf.

3. right to block special resolutions[9];
4. approval of business plans, annual operating plan, budget, commencing of a new line of activity, discontinuing an existing line of activity, and appointment of key managerial personnel.[10]

Though the past decisions of the Commission throw some light on the manner in which control is defined, there is no clarity on the degree of influence that would be necessary to trigger the requirement to notify a transaction. In practice, transactions giving control rights that do not confer any competitively significant influence may also require a notification. For instance, in *SAAB/Pipavav*,[11] the Commission found that the acquisition of a 3.3 per cent shareholding in Pipavav by SAAB amounted to control even though it was in the nature of a strategic technology partnership whereby SAAB was also granted certain affirmative rights including the right to nominate one director on the Board of Pipavav, to enable it to preserve the value of its investment in the company and prevent misuse of intellectual property rights. Given this very broad interpretation, even an acquisition of rights only for the purpose of protecting the investments of a party that would otherwise have benefitted from the exemption under the Combination Regulations, becomes reportable.

It is relevant also to note that there are multiple regulators in India such as the Securities Exchange Board of India (SEBI), Insurance Regulatory and Development Authority of India, Civil Aviation Regulator, etc. that may be required to adjudicate on the issue of control under their respective rules or regulations. It is therefore likely that different regulators interpret the term 'control' differently. For instance, in the acquisition of 24 per cent stake by *Etihad*[12] in Jet, the Commission and SEBI[13] had different views on the issue

[9] MSM India/SPE Holdings/SPE Mauritius, Combination Registration No. C-2012/06/63, available at http://www.cci.gov.in/sites/default/files/C-2012-06-63.pdf.

[10] Century Tokyo Leasing Corporation/Tata Capital Financial Services Limited, Combination Registration No. C-2012/09/78, available at http://www.cci.gov.in/sites/default/files/C-2012-09-78.pdf.

[11] Combination Registration No. C-2012/11/95, available at http://cci.gov.in/sites/default/files/C-2012-11-95.pdf.

[12] Combination Registration No. C-2013/05/122, available at http://www.cci.gov.in/sites/default/files/C-2013-05-122%20Order%20121113.pdf

[13] The expression 'control' has been defined under Regulation 2(1)(e) of the SEBI (Substantial Acquisition of Shares and Takeovers) Regulations, 2011 (*Code*). It includes 'the right to appoint majority of directors or to control the management or

of control. In this case, Etihad had the right to nominate only 2 out of 12 directors without any affirmative or veto rights. For SEBI, one of the tests for control includes the right to appoint 'majority directors', which was absent in the present case; accordingly, Etihad was not found to control Jet. In contrast, the Commission in its decision indicated that Etihad exercised joint control over Jet and went on to assess the deal under the competition rules.

Mergers and Amalgamations

The other types of transactions falling within the jurisdiction of the Competition Act are mergers and amalgamations. As the Competition Act provides no definition of a merger or an amalgamation, these terms are interpreted in accordance with their general commercial usage. A merger is generally understood to refer to a transaction where one entity merges into another and itself ceases to exist. An amalgamation is generally understood to refer to a transaction where two entities merge to form an entirely new entity and each of them ceases to exist separately.

Practically speaking, there is no distinction to be made between mergers and amalgamations as the financial thresholds for reporting both are the same.

Financial Thresholds

Section 5 of the Competition Act sets certain size-related thresholds and only an acquisition, merger, or amalgamation above these thresholds amounts to a combination and requires a mandatory notification to the Commission. Section 20(3) provides that these thresholds are subject to periodic revision by the government, so as to account inter alia, for inflation and exchange rate fluctuations. On 4 March 2011, the Government on the basis of the wholesale price index had increased the value of assets and turnover given in Section 5 of the Competition Act by 50 per cent[14] for the purposes of that section. On the same date it also exempted enterprises below a certain threshold from the provisions of Section 5.[15] Thus, the acquisition of any enterprise with assets

---

policy decisions exercisable by a person or persons acting individually or in concert, directly or indirectly, including by virtue of their shareholding or management rights or shareholders agreements or voting agreements or in any other manner'.

[14] S.O 480 (E) Notification dated 4 March 2011, available at http://www.cci.gov.in/images/media/notifications/SO479(E),480(E),481(E),482(E)240611.pdf.

[15] S.O 482(E) Notification dated 4 March 2011, available at http://www.cci.gov.in/images/media/notifications/SO479(E),480(E),481(E),482(E)240611.pdf.

of not more than INR 2.5 billion (approx. USD 37 million) or turnover of not more than INR 7.5 billion (approx. USD 112 million) was exempted for a period of five years from the date of notification. This is often referred to as the target de minimis exemption. It must be noted that this exemption was not available to mergers and amalgamations.

On 4 March 2016, the Section 5 thresholds were again increased to 100 per cent above the values given in the Competition Act,[16] making these among the highest thresholds in the world. Further, the de minimis exemption was renewed for a period of another five years and the exemption limits were increased to INR 3.5 billion (approx. USD 51 million) of assets and INR 10 billion (approx. USD 147 million) of turnover.[17] This revision was made with the view to further facilitate the ease of doing business in India.

The Section 5 thresholds, as they currently stand are[18]: INR 20 billion (approx. USD 300 million) in terms of assets or INR 60 billion (approx. USD 900 million) in terms of turnover in India, being the joint assets or turnover, as the case may be, of the parties to the combination. In the case of enterprises having assets or turnover within and outside India, the threshold is USD 1,000 million of assets (including at least INR 10 billion in India, that is, approx. USD 150 million) or USD 3,000 million of turnover (including at least INR 30 billion in India, that is, approx. USD 450 million). In case the combination involves a group[19] of enterprises, the corresponding threshold is INR 80 billion (approx. USD 1,199 million) of assets or INR 240 billion (approx. USD 3,596 million) of turnover in India, or in the case of enterprises having assets or turnover within and outside India, USD 4 billion of assets (including at least INR 10 billion in India, that is, approx. USD 150 million in India) or USD 12 billion of turnover (including at least INR 30 billion in India, that is, approx. USD 450 million). If any one of the above thresholds is exceeded, the transaction will require a notification in India.

[16] S.O 675(E) Notification dated 4 March 2016, available at http://www.cci.gov.in/sites/default/files/notification/SO%20673%28E%29-674%28E%29-675%28E%29.pdf.

[17] S.O 674(E) Notification dated 4 March 2016, available at http://www.cci.gov.in/sites/default/files/notification/SO%20673%28E%29-674%28E%29-675%28E%29.pdf.

[18] The exchange rate used for calculation of thresholds is USD 1 = INR 66.74.

[19] 'Group' is defined as two or more enterprises which, directly or indirectly, are in a position to exercise, in respect of another enterprise, either (i) at least 50% of the voting rights; (ii) appoint more than half of the directors; or (iii) control the management or affairs of the other enterprise' (Section 5, Indian Competition Act, 2002).

The thresholds are displayed in tabular form below.

		Assets		Turnover
Enterprise Level	India	> INR 2,000 crore	OR	> INR 6,000 crore
	Worldwide (with India component)	>USD 1 bn with at least INR 1,000 crore in India		> USD 3 bn with at least INR 3,000 crore in India
OR				
Group Level	India	> INR 8,000 crore	OR	> INR 24,000 crore
	Worldwide (with India component)	> USD 4 bn with at least INR 1,000 crore in India		> USD 12 bn with at least INR 3,000 crore in India

Section 5(c) of the Act explains the manner in which the value of assets is to be computed and this includes intangible assets like the value of goodwill, copyright, patent, and trademark. However, the basis on which the intangible assets will be valued is not laid down in the Act. Section 2(y) explains that turnover will include the value of sale of goods and services.

Entities to Be Taken into Account for Calculating Thresholds

The Commission has recently, in its release of FAQs,[20] stated that the following entities will be considered for calculating the financial thresholds under the Competition Act:

1. In case of an acquisition of assets, shares, voting rights, or control, the value of assets and turnover of the acquirer (or acquirer group, for calculating group-level thresholds) and the target enterprise, whose assets, shares, voting rights, or control are being acquired, are required to be taken into account for calculating jurisdictional thresholds.
2. In case of acquisition of control by a person over an enterprise when such person already has direct or indirect control over another enterprise engaged in production, distribution, or trading of a similar or identical or substitutable goods or provision of a similar or identical or substitutable service, the value of assets and turnover of the enterprise (or group to which the enterprise would belong, for calculating group-level thresholds)

20 See http://www.cci.gov.in/node/2847.

over which control has been acquired along with the enterprise over which the acquirer already has direct or indirect control, are required to be taken into account for calculating jurisdictional thresholds.

3. In case of mergers/amalgamations, the value of assets and turnover of the enterprise (or group, for calculating group-level thresholds) remaining after the merger or created as a result of the amalgamation should be taken into account for calculating jurisdictional thresholds.

Even prior to the above clarification, the Commission had in practice been assessing thresholds by considering the relevant entities in the manner as mentioned earlier.

Attribution and Substance Rules

During the implementation of the merger provisions, it was observed by the Commission that transactions could be structured in a manner so as to escape notification under the Competition Act. For instance, this could be achieved by splitting a transaction into multiple steps, each of which when analysed separately would not amount to a 'combination' reportable to the Commission.

In order to prevent transactions from escaping notification, the Commission in March 2013 introduced Regulation 5(9) of the Combination Regulations (also referred to as the 'attribution rule'), which catches transactions wherein a transfer of assets (tangible or intangible) by one enterprise to the second enterprise is undertaken to enable the second enterprise to implement an acquisition, merger, or amalgamation with a third enterprise.[21] In such transactions, the value of assets and turnover of the first enterprise will be added to the value of assets and turnover of the second enterprise for carrying out the jurisdictional analysis. As a result, even when an acquisition or merger/amalgamation is being effected through a special purpose vehicle or a shell company with no assets and turnover of its own, it may fall within the definition of a 'combination'.

[21] Regulation 5(9) of the Combination Regulations states:

> Where, in a series of steps or individual transactions that are related to each other, assets are being transferred to an enterprise for the purpose of such enterprise entering into an agreement relating to an acquisition or merger or amalgamation with another person or enterprise, for the purpose of Section 5 of the Act, the value of assets and turnover of the enterprise whose assets are being transferred shall also be attributed to the value of assets and turnover of the enterprise to which the assets are being transferred.

Another provision with a similar intent was introduced in the Combination Regulations on 28 March 2014, which requires that filing of a notice be determined having regard to the substance of the transaction (also referred to as the 'substance test'); any structure of the transaction that has the effect of avoiding notice in respect of the whole or a part of the Combination shall be disregarded.[22]

Treatment of Joint Ventures

There is no explicit guidance in the Competition Act or the Combination Regulations relating to joint ventures. A joint venture can be formed either by way of an acquisition or a merger or amalgamation, and will be treated as such under the Competition Act for the purposes of notification (for instance, the de minimis exemption will not be available to a joint venture formed by way of a merger). Both incorporated and contractual joint ventures are subject to merger control rules. In a recent decision of the Commission, a 'business partnership agreement' entitling the parties to exercise control over the strategic commercial decisions of a business unit of the other party, was considered to give rise to joint control over the business unit.[23]

Generally speaking and in absence of any transfer of assets to the joint venture by the parents, greenfield joint ventures are not notifiable; whereas brownfield joint ventures may require notification if the financial thresholds are met. In fact, the Commission has recently in its FAQs clarified that if one or more enterprises transfers its assets to a joint venture company, then the formation of a joint venture is treated as a notifiable combination, provided that jurisdictional thresholds are met after applying the rule of attribution.

Anomalies in the Application of Financial Thresholds

Though the financial thresholds are clearly specified in the Competition Act and the government notifications, there is a degree of uncertainty around

[22] Regulation 9(5) of the Combination Regulations states that, 'The requirement of filing notice under regulation 5 of these regulations shall be determined with respect to the substance of the transaction and any structure of the transaction(s), comprising a combination, that has the effect of avoiding notice in respect of the whole or a part of the combination shall be disregarded.'

[23] Century Tokyo Leasing Corporation/Tata Capital Financial Services Limited, Combination Registration No. C-2012/09/78, available at http://www.cci.gov.in/sites/default/files/C-2012-09-78.pdf.

the manner in which these are to be applied by the Commission, which have been explained later in the chapter.

Applicability of the De Minimis Exemption

The de minimis exemption requires an assessment of the assets and turnover of the 'target'; however, there is an anomaly in what is regarded as the 'target' by the Commission, that is, whether target would be the asset acquired from the seller or the seller itself. There is no problem in the case of acquisition of shares, voting rights, or control of an entity, which itself is regarded as the 'target'. However, difficulty arises in the case of an asset acquisition where irrespective of the value of the asset being acquired the Commission has been interpreting the seller as the 'target'. This is on account of the fact that the Competition Act states that the parties to the acquisition are 'the acquirer and the *enterprise* whose control, shares, voting rights or assets are being acquired' and the definition of 'enterprise' under the Competition Act requires it to be a 'person'. Notably the definition of 'person' under the Competition Act does not include business undertakings or assets which are not artificial juridical persons; thus the seller of the undertaking or assets is the enterprise in question. As a result of this interpretation, even small transactions sold by an enterprise above the thresholds require to be notified to the Commission, though this may be contrary to the objective/spirit of this exemption.

In addition, this exemption, though intended to exclude all small transactions from the purview of the Competition Act, has been made applicable only to acquisitions and not to mergers and amalgamations. Even after the recent amendment on 4 March 2016, the government did not address this anomaly. In the absence of any rationale for distinguishing between acquisitions and mergers and amalgamations, there is justification to include the latter within the scope of the de minimis exemption. Doing so will result in a reduction in the burden on companies to make merger notifications in India even for those transactions which do not have the requisite local nexus.

The wording of the de minimis exemption in some situations results in discrimination between Indian and foreign enterprises. A filing with the Commission becomes necessary only if the target has assets of more than INR 3.5 billion (approx. USD 52 million) and turnover of not more than INR 10 billion (approx. USD 150 million) in India. This may favour foreign enterprises as compared to Indian enterprises, since foreign enterprises may have large turnover in India but not substantial assets since their manufacturing facilities may be situated overseas, with the Indian demand being met mainly through imports. Consequently, in identical or similar transactions, while the Indian acquirer may have to obtain the Commission's approval, the foreign acquirer may not require such approval. This anomaly has not been rectified by the government in its notification dated 4 March 2016, regarding the de minimis exemption.

Meaning of Combined Entity under the Competition Act

A transaction is reportable to the Commission if the combined entity or the group to which the combined entity belongs post transaction exceeds the thresholds in Section 5 of the Competition Act. However, there is no clarity as to how the assets or turnover of the combined entity are to be computed, that is, whether the assets and turnover should include the value of the assets and turnover of the acquirer and the asset/business that is being acquired or that of the seller in entirety. For instance, if 'A' acquires asset 'B' from seller 'C', the assets and turnover 'jointly' held by the two parties should ideally be those of 'A' and 'B'. However, the practice being followed by the Commission is to treat the assets and turnover of the acquirer and the seller as the 'joint' entity (that is, 'A'+ 'C').

As mentioned earlier, this difficulty may be arising on account of the fact that the Competition Act states that the parties to the acquisition are 'the acquirer and the *enterprise* whose control, shares, voting rights or assets are being acquired' and the definition of 'enterprise' under the Competition Act requires it to be a 'person'. Notably, the definition of 'person' under the Competition Act does not include any business undertaking or assets which are not artificial juridical persons. Therefore, the Commission's interpretation might be based on the fact that the seller 'C' is the 'enterprise' whose asset 'B' is being acquired. This anomaly needs to be addressed by making suitable amendments to the Competition Act.

Exemptions

Under the merger control regulations, certain transactions that are 'ordinarily' not likely to cause an AAEC in the relevant market in India need not 'normally' be notified to the Commission. In practice, this is generally understood to mean that no notification is required for such transactions. These transactions include the following:

1. An acquisition of less than 25 per cent shares or voting rights of an enterprise solely as an investment or in the ordinary course of business, not leading to change in control. The most recent amendment to the Combination Regulations in 2016 has clarified that the term 'solely as an investment' means any acquisition resulting in less than 10 per cent of the total shares or voting rights of an enterprise, provided the acquirer after

acquisition has the ability to exercise only such rights that are exercisable by ordinary shareholders and does not have any board representation or any interpretation to have board representation or any intention to participate in the affairs or management of the target company. Even prior to this amendment, the Commission considered 'solely as an investment' to refer to 'passive investments' as opposed to 'strategic investments' with an 'intention of participating in the formulation, determination or direction of the basic business decisions of the target'.[24]

The application of this exemption has been diluted by the Commission to some extent. This is because it considers that even acquisitions of shares or voting rights below 25 per cent which give rise to horizontal overlaps or vertical relationships, can raise competition concerns and would not be treated 'solely as an investment' or 'an acquisition in the ordinary course of business'; consequently, parties may have to file a notification in such cases.[25]

2. Until the amendment of the Combination Regulations in 2016, the acquisition of shares or voting rights of not more than 5 per cent in a financial year (April–March) where the acquirer or its group already held 25 per cent (but less than 50 per cent) or more shares or voting rights, (except where the transaction resulted in change of control) was exempt from the requirement to file a notification; post amendment the limit of 5 per cent has been omitted, thereby widening the scope of the exemption as all share acquisitions beyond 25 per cent which do not result in the acquirer holding 50 per cent post acquisition are now exempt.
3. Acquisition of shares or voting rights, where the acquirer, prior to acquisition, has 50 per cent or more shares or voting rights in the enterprise whose shares or voting rights are being acquired, except in the cases where the transaction results in transfer from joint control to sole control.
4. Acquisition of assets not directly related to the business activity of the acquirer but solely as an investment or in ordinary course of business, not leading to control (except where the assets being acquired represent substantial business operations in a particular location or for a particular product/service of the enterprise, of which assets are being acquired, irrespective of whether such assets are organized as a separate legal entity or not).

[24] C-2014/06/181, Zuari Fertilisers and Chemicals/Mangalore Chemicals and Fertilisers, available at http://www.cci.gov.in/sites/default/files/C-2014-06-181-43A_0.pdf.

[25] C-2014/08/202, Abbot/Mylan, available at http://www.cci.gov.in/sites/default/files/C-2014-08-202_0.pdf.

5. Amended or renewed tender offer already filed with the Commission by the party making the offer.[26]
6. Acquisition of stock-in trade, raw materials, stores and spares, and other similar current assets in ordinary course of business.
7. Acquisition of shares or voting rights pursuant to a bonus issue or stock splits or consolidation of face value of shares or buy back of shares or subscription to rights issue of shares (except where the transaction results in acquisition of control).
8. Acquisition of shares or voting rights by a securities underwriter or registered broker of a stock exchange in the ordinary course of business.
9. Intra group acquisition of shares or voting rights or assets by one person or enterprise of another person or enterprise within the same group, except in cases where the acquired enterprise is jointly controlled by enterprises that are not part of the same group;
10. Intra group merger and amalgamation where, either (a) one of the enterprises has more than 50 per cent shares or voting rights of the other enterprise, and/or (b) more than 50 per cent shares or voting rights in each of such enterprises are held by enterprise(s) within the same group. However, *this exemption does not apply to those intra group mergers or amalgamations wherein there is a change from joint control to sole control.* Joint control is said to exist where two or more persons have the ability to affect the 'commercial decision' making power of an enterprise. As mentioned earlier, the Commission has considered (a) veto rights, (b) power to approve business/budget plans, (c) power to appoint key managerial personnel, etc. while assessing the 'commercial decision' making power of a person in an enterprise.
11. Acquisition of shares, control, voting rights, or assets by a purchaser approved by the Commission in accordance with an order for divestment.[27]

Interestingly, the wording of the Combination Regulations is such that the above are not absolute exemptions, that is, even where the transaction falls within the above categories, it may have to be notified if it causes or is likely to cause an AAEC in any market in India. Therefore, it becomes important to undertake a qualitative assessment on a case to case basis before ruling out the requirement of a filing.

[26] Provided that the intimation of change has been duly made to the Commission under Regulation 16 of the Combination Regulations.

[27] This exemption was added vide an amendment of the Combinations Regulations in March 2016.

Apart from the above, the government under Section 54 of the Competition Act also has the power to exclude certain combinations from the requirement of a notification. Pursuant to this provision, the government, by way of a notification dated 8 January 2013, has exempted, for a period of five years, that is, until 7 January 2018, mergers and takeovers of *loss-making and failing banks* (in respect of which the government has issued a notification under Section 45 of the Banking Regulation Act 1949) from the purview of the Commission.[28]

Test Applied by the Commission in Reviewing a Combination

The Competition Act prescribes that the Commission shall prohibit a combination which has, or is likely to have, an AAEC in the relevant market in India. It specifies certain factors that the Commission needs to consider when determining whether a combination has an AAEC. These include:

1. market shares of the parties and competitors;
2. sources of actual and potential competition (including imports);
3. whether a vigorous competitor would be removed by the combination;
4. whether the target is a failing firm;
5. vertical integration in the market;
6. extent of entry barriers into the market;
7. significance of innovation;
8. the combination's contribution to economic development;
9. whether the benefits of the combination outweigh the adverse impact.

The Commission has also relied on certain economic techniques to ascertain the likely impact of a combination on the market. For instance, in *Holcim Limited/Lafarge S.A*[29] *and Grasim Industries Limited/Aditya Birla Chemicals*[30] the Commission relied upon the Herfindahl Hirschman Index test for assessing the impact of the transaction.[31]

[28] S.O 674(E) Notification dated 8 January 2013, available at http://www.cci.gov.in/sites/default/files/notification/S.O.%2093%20%28E%29_08012013.pdf.

[29] Holcim Limited/Lafarge S.A., Combination Registration No. C-2014/07/190, available at http://www.cci.gov.in/sites/default/files/C-2014-07-190_0.pdf.

[30] *Grasim Industries Limited/Aditya Birla Chemicals*, Combination Registration No. C-2015/03/256, available at http://www.cci.gov.in/sites/default/files/Notice_order_document/C-2015-03-256.pdf.

[31] Holcim Limited/Lafarge S.A., Combination Registration No. C-2014/07/190, available at http://www.cci.gov.in/sites/default/files/C-2014-07-190_0.pdf.

While reviewing a combination (or any other matter), the Commission under regulation 34 of the Combination Regulations, is also empowered to seek the opinion of any other agency or statutory authority in relation to the combination under scrutiny. Similarly, Section 36 of the Competition Act allows the Commission to gather information and opinions from experts in relation to a combination. For instance, the Commission sought the opinion of the Rubber Board, Ministry of Commerce along with customers of chloroprene rubber in India while analysing the effect of the merger between Denki Kagaku Kogyo Kabushiki Kaisha and Mitsui & Co. Ltd.[32] Similarly, the Commission required Air India, a competitor of Jet, to furnish its view and comments on the Jet–Etihad deal.[33] The Commission also sought the opinion of medical experts while evaluating the deal between GSK and Novartis.

In fact, through a 2016 amendment of the Combination Regulations,[34] the Commission has increased the scope of receiving third-party comments in relation to a combination by making it necessary that a summary of every combination be published on its website. Prior to this amendment, stakeholders could only submit their comments during a Phase II investigation (explained later in the chapter).

Timeline for Reporting and Review Period

The Indian merger control regime is mandatory in nature, that is, a notice to the Commission is statutorily required to be given prior to proceeding with a combination as defined in the Act and not exempted under the Act or the merger regulations. The notice shall be given within 30 calendar days of:

1. the approval of the merger or amalgamation by the board of directors of the enterprise concerned; or
2. in the case of an acquisition, the execution of any binding agreement or other document. Under the Combination Regulations, the term 'other document' includes any document which would be binding and convey an agreement or decision to carry out a relevant transaction. Prior to the amendment in 2016, the Combination Regulations provided that this would also include any document communicating an intention to

[32] Combination Registration No. C-2015/01/239, available at http://www.cci.gov.in/sites/default/files/C-2015-01-239_0.pdf.

[33] Combination Registration No. C-2015/01/239, available at http://www.cci.gov.in/sites/default/files/C-2015-01-239_0.pdf.

[34] Regulation 13(1B) of the Combination Regulations 2016.

undertake the acquisition to a Statutory Authority (for example, the Foreign Investment Promotion Board or any other regulator). However, post amendment, the Commission has expressly narrowed the meaning of 'other document' in the context of public M&A (mergers and acquisitions) to a public announcement in terms of the Securities and Exchange Board of India (Substantial Acquisition of Shares and Takeovers) Regulations, 2011.

Earlier the Commission had 30 calendar days from the date of notification to form a prima facie opinion in Phase I on the existence of any AAEC in the relevant market. However, through an amendment of the Combination Regulations effective as of 1 July 2015, the Commission extended the duration of Phase I to 30 'working' days (instead of 30 'calendar' days) thereby excluding weekends and public holidays from the review period. Further, the Commission can stop the clock during Phase I for an additional 15 working days to seek comments from third parties. Thus, the Commission now has 45 working days to form its prima facie opinion in Phase I and this does not include the time taken by the parties to provide additional information and clarifications.

In the event that the Commission reaches a prima facie opinion that the proposed combination is likely to cause an AAEC in any of the markets in India, it issues a notice under Section 29 of the Competition Act, requiring the parties to explain how the combination would not adversely affect the market. In case the Commission is not satisfied by the response of the parties, it initiates a detailed Phase II investigation.

Under the Competition Act, if the Commission does not pass a final order within 210 calendar days from the date of notification, the combination is deemed to be approved. However, in practice, the Commission has cleared almost all the transactions in Phase I.

Delayed Filings or Failure to Notify

Failure to notify a transaction within the prescribed time period can result in a penalty which may extend to 1 per cent of the worldwide turnover or assets of the combination, whichever is higher. The penalty is imposed on the party responsible for the filing, that is, the acquirer, in case of an acquisition and all parties to the transaction in case of a merger or amalgamation.

During the first year of the implementation of the Combination Regulations, the Commission adopted a lenient approach in dealing with delayed filings and did not impose any penalties. Thereafter the Commission has been extremely vigilant in detecting delays and has frequently initiated investigations against defaulters, often even on a *suo motu* basis. For instance, on 1 August 2013, the Commission imposed a penalty of INR 5 million (approx. USD 73,513) on the Temasek group for a delay of around 399 days in notification of its acquisition of shares in DBS Group Holdings Limited. The highest penalty until date of INR 50 million (approx. USD 7,35,073) was imposed on General Electric for failure to notify its acquisition of Alstom's India assets within 30 days from the date of making a public announcement. The parties had argued that the public announcement did not constitute a 'binding agreement' and accordingly the 30 day time period ought to have started only once such a binding document was executed. The Commission while rejecting this argument held that under the Combination Regulations (as these existed at that time) a 'binding document' would include any public document conveying to a statutory authority the intention to acquire.[35]

In the case of an acquisition, there continues to be a degree of uncertainty around what is to be treated as the trigger event. Though this uncertainty had been reduced to some extent by the amendment of the Combination Regulations in 2016, the binding nature of a document is still interpreted on a case to case basis by the Commission. For instance, in *GE/SABIC*, the parties in 2007 had executed an agreement regarding the purchase and sale inter alia of certain assets; five years later, in 2012, the parties concluded an asset transfer agreement, which gave effect to the agreement of 2007.[36] The Commission found that the later agreement concluded in 2012 constituted the trigger event for the purposes of Section 6(2) of the Competition Act. In the *Aditya Birla* case,[37] the notice was invalidated as the parties were yet to finalize the precise scope of the assets to be acquired, the share entitlement ratios, and the valuation report. The Commission also found that the parties were still negotiating the terms of the Implementation Agreement and details of the transaction, and that the signing of the document between the

[35] For instance, the Commission imposed a penalty of approx. €397,428 on British retailer Tesco for delay in filing the notice in relation to its acquisition of 50 per cent stake in a Tata Group company, Trent Hypermarket. The notice was filed following the signing of a binding agreement between the parties. However, the Commission observed that the notice should have been filed within 30 calendar days of the application to the Foreign Investment Promotion Board for undertaking the FDI (which had been made earlier), as this would be regarded as the trigger event even when no binding agreement has been signed.

[36] Combination Registration No. C-2013/01/106, available at http://www.cci.gov.in/sites/default/files/C-2013-01-106.pdf.

[37] Combination Registration No. C-2012/07/69.

parties (a memorandum of understanding) was only the first step towards future negotiations for finalization of the scheme, the valuation, and the exact scope of assets to be acquired. Therefore, there is no bright line test for what would constitute a 'trigger event' in the case of an acquisition.

Gun Jumping

Apart from the mandatory nature of the merger control regime, there also exists a 'suspensory' or 'standstill' obligation; no combination, requiring a notice to the Commission, shall be given effect to until the Commission has approved the combination or the Commission has failed to pass an order within 210 days from the date of the notice to the Commission. Any violation in this respect could amount to 'gun jumping'. Though there is no specific provision relating to gun jumping under the Competition Act or the Combination Regulations, in practice, the Commission treats it as a failure to notify and is punishable under Section 43(A).

In December 2013, the Commission imposed its first gun-jumping penalty of INR 10 million (approx. USD 147,015) on Etihad in relation to its acquisition of a 24 per cent equity stake in Jet Airways. The Commission observed that certain provisions of the commercial cooperation agreement had already been implemented and the transfer of certain landing/take-off slots of Jet at the London Heathrow Airport was not notified before consummation.

Similarly the Commission imposed a penalty of INR 10 million (approx. USD 147,015) on Thomas Cook and Sterling Holidays for gun jumping in relation to a composite scheme for arrangement and amalgamation, whereby the business of Sterling Holidays would be amalgamated with Thomas Cook. Prior to the scheme, Thomas Cook also acquired a 9.93 per cent stake in Sterling Holidays through open market purchases. The Commission noted that the scheme of arrangement and the market purchases were authorized in the same meeting of the Board of Directors and were thus interdependant and inter-connected to each other; accordingly, the parties ought to have obtained the Commission's approval prior to making the open market purchases. This view of the Commission flowed from the Combination Regulations wherein the parties are required to notify inter-connected transactions through a single notice.[38] On appeal, the COMPAT[39] set aside the

[38] The term 'interdependant' was omitted from Regulation 9(4) of the Combination Regulations in 2016.

[39] Thomas Cook/Sterling Holidays, 26 August 2015, available from http://compat.nic.in/upload/PDFs/judgement-orders-2015/26.08.2015.pdf.

penalty on the grounds that the mere fact that the two transactions were authorized in the same board meeting could not be made a basis for holding that the actions were interdependent or interconnected. The COMPAT held that the open market purchases were not connected to the further acquisition of shares from the seller and on a standalone basis benefitted from the de minimis exemption.

Interestingly, in a recent order, the Commission has held that even part pre-payment of consideration, irrespective of whether it is refundable or not, amounts to part consummation of the transaction.[40] Thus, the Commission is adopting a very strict, somewhat excessive, approach for ascertaining what amounts to consummation of the combination. In fact, the Commission has taken a clear stance that global completion would not be permissible pending local clearance.

Modifications and Divestments

The Commission has powers to block a combination outright in cases where it is likely to cause an AAEC in the relevant market. However, under Section 31(3) of the Competition Act, the Commission may also approve a combination subject to the parties implementing certain structural modifications to the notified deal or undertaking behavioural commitments.

While there has been no instance of a transaction being blocked by the Commission to date, there have been several cases where the Commission has granted clearance subject to conditions (both structural and behavioural) including three cases where the Commission ordered divestment of certain assets, namely: (a) Sun/Ranbaxy, where the Commission ordered divestment of seven drug brands of the parties[41]; (b) Holcim/Lafarge, where the Commission initially ordered divestment of two cement plants; when this could not be implemented by the parties due to certain new provisions in the mining laws restricting the transfer of the limestone mines attached to these cement plants, this divestment order was modified to encompass the entire business of Lafarge India[42]; and (c) PVR/DT Cinema, where the Commission ordered that seven screens of DT Cinemas would not form a

[40] Hindustan Colas Private Limited, Combination Regulation No. C-2015/08/299, available at http://www.cci.gov.in/sites/default/files/Notice_order_document/Order%20under%20Section%2043A-299.pdf.

[41] Combination Registration No. C-2014/05/170, available at http://www.cci.gov.in/sites/default/files/C-2014-05-170_0.pdf.

[42] Combination Registration No. C-2014/07/190, available at http://www.cci.gov.in/sites/default/files/C-2014-07-190_0.pdf.

part of the combination and would continue to compete with PVR post the completion of the acquisition of DT Cinemas by PVR.[43]

The Commission has also resorted to behavioural remedies to address competition concerns. A majority of these behavioural remedies have related to the revision of the duration and scope of non-compete clauses between the parties. For instance, in September 2012, while clearing the sale of Orchid Chemicals' active pharmaceutical ingredients to Hospira Healthcare, the Commission required the parties to modify the non-compete under which Orchid and its promoter were not to undertake certain business activities pertaining to the transferred business for a period of eight years and five years, respectively. The non-compete clause also restricted research, development, and testing of certain pharmaceutical ingredients. The Commission, while reducing the scope and duration of the non-compete, held that such obligations should be reasonable, particularly in respect of (a) the duration over which such restraint is enforceable; and (b) the business activities, geographical areas, and person(s) subject to such restraint, so as to ensure that they do not result in any AAEC. Accordingly, the parties were required to limit the duration of the non-compete obligation to four years in the domestic market in India and allow Orchid to conduct research, development, and testing on such new molecules, which would result in the development of new drugs.[44]

Behavioural commitments were also accepted by the Commission in the *Gujarat Gas* case,[45] where the parties submitted an undertaking that the target would review the contracts with its customers to ensure that such contracts are in compliance with the provisions of the Competition Act and sectoral regulations, and submit a compliance report to the Commission within six months after consummation of the proposed combination. In the *MIAL* case,[46] it was the prima facie opinion of the Commission that the proposed joint venture of three oil Public Sector Undertakings may monopolize the market for supply of Aviation Turbine Fuel in the Mumbai Airport and foreclose the market for other players. The Commission approved the combination on the basis of voluntary commitments offered by the parties for non-discriminatory access to other players apart from other commitments of installing adequate capacity, taking transparency measures such as publishing details on the website and diluting the restriction on transfer of ownership over the joint venture, and other similar commitments.

[43] Combination Registration No. C-2015/07/288, available at http://www.cci.gov.in/sites/default/files/Notice_order_document/C-2015-07-288.pdf; the Commission resorted to both structural and behavioural remedies in the present case.

[44] Combination Registration No. C-2012/11/92.

[45] Combination Registration No. C-2012/11/88.

[46] Combination Registration No. C-2014/04/164.

Road Ahead

The merger control regime in India is still evolving. In recent months, the Commission has striven to bring clarity in certain ambivalent provisions, or reduce the burden of filing on parties or ease the procedural requirements on the filing parties. But several other anomalies remain as described earlier. Some of these could be rectified through the Combination Regulations (as has indeed been done by the Commission) while others will require amendments to the Act itself which can only be undertaken at the level of the government. It is understood that the Commission is in fact considering relaxations or changes to the regulations and even proposing amendments to the Act.

One of the biggest criticisms being faced by the merger control regime in India is that it continues to be one of the few jurisdictions in the world which have prescribed a timeline for filing. Given that the regime is mandatory and suspensory in nature, this requirement does not serve any purpose and is unnecessarily onerous on the parties. This is particularly irksome in the case of global mergers because parties are unable to plan their multi-jurisdictional filings in accordance with commercial priorities, but must file in India well before they are ready with filings in the commercially more important jurisdictions.

At present, the Act allows the Commission up to 210 days to decide on a combination; this period is too long by international standards. For any additional information that the Commission requires from the parties, it has the power to seek such additional information, and meanwhile the clock stops; thus the time taken for seeking additional information does not count towards the time limit of 210 days. A shorter period of 150 days should suffice for the Commission to complete its internal processes and form an opinion about approving or not approving the combination. It needs to be kept in mind that mergers are normal transactions taking place in the market, and it is desirable that the Commission's process for analysing the merger is as expeditious as possible.

Further, the Act states that no combination 'shall come into effect' until 210 days have passed from the day on which the notification has been made to the Commission or the Commission has passed an approval order, whichever is earlier. There is, however, no express guidance on the meaning and scope of the words to 'come into effect'. From competition law perspective, it is important that there is no change in control of the acquired enterprise or that the parties do not coordinate their decisions during the pendency of review by Commission. However, other steps that do not lead to change in control may be permitted. For instance, fulfilling of conditions precedent for closing of a transaction such as application for transfer of leasehold property by a party or issuing employment offer letters should not amount to a combination coming into effect. Issue of guidelines on what steps can be legitimately taken by the parties to a combination before receiving the Commission's approval would be helpful.

The Commission should also re-assess its stand towards minority investments. As explained earlier, often investor protection rights accorded to minority investors have been found to amount to control by the Commission. This wide interpretation makes it onerous on parties to even report a transaction which would otherwise have benefitted from the exemption under the Combination Regulations.

Finally, there is also need for greater clarity in the substantive competitive analysis, especially in cases which may require divestment. The Commission faced heavy criticism in the approach adopted for divestment in the Lafarge/Holcim deal as the remedies imposed by the Commission were regarded as excessive and the process leading to the remedies was insufficiently consultative with the parties. To avoid such situations, the Commission may consider a mandatory consultation with parties before issuing proposal for modification. In a Phase II investigation, the onus to propose modification under the Competition Act is on the Commission. This is in contrast to the position in mature jurisdictions, such as the EU and the USA, where the parties have the ability to propose modifications and these follow a process of mutual interaction between the Commission and the parties. Suitable amendments to the Act and the merger regulations need to be considered to enable this.

Select Bibliography

Books

Albors-Llorens, Albertina (2002): *EC Competition Law and Policy*, Willan Publishing, Cullompton, Devon.

Anderson, Robert D. and Frédèric Jenny (2005): 'Competition Policy, Economic Development and the Possible Role of a Multilateral Framework on Competition Policy: Insights from the WTO Working Group on Trade and Competition Policy', in Erlinda Medalla, (ed.), *Competition Policy in East Asia*, Routledge/Curzon.

Anderman, Steven D. (2000): *EC Competition Law and Intellectual Property Rights: The Regulation of Innovation*, Oxford University Press, Oxford.

Areeda, Phillip E. and Herbert Hovencamp (2004): *Fundamentals of Antitrust Law: 2003 Edition*, Aspen Publishers, New York.

Beato, Paulina and Jean-Jacques Laffont (2003): *Competition Policy in Regulated Industries: Approaches for Emerging Economies*, Inter-American Development Bank, Washington, DC.

Bhala, Raj (1996): *International Trade Law, Cases and Materials*, Michie Law Publishers, Charlottesville.

Bishop, Simon and Mike Walker (2002): *The Economics of EC Competition Law* (2nd ed.), Sweet and Maxwell, London.

Bork, Robert H. (1993): *The Antitrust Paradox: A Policy at War with Itself*, Free Press, New York.

Broder, Douglas F. (2005): *A Guide to U.S. Antitrust Law*, Sweet and Maxwell, London.

Brooks, Douglas H. and Simon J. Evenett (eds) (2005): *Competition Law and Development in Asia*, Palgrave, Basingstoke.

Brunt, Maureen (2003): *Economic Essays on Australian and New Zealand Competition Law* (International Competition Law, 8), Kluwer Law International, The Hague.

Cahill, Dermot (ed.) (2004): *The Modernisation of EU Competition Law Enforcement in the European Union: FIDE 2004 National Reports*, Cambridge University Press, Cambridge.

Clarke, Phillip and Stephen Corones (2005): *Competition Law and Policy: Cases and Materials*, (2nd ed.), Oxford University Press (Australian law), South Melbourne, VIC.

Cook Paul, Colin Kirkpatrick, Minogue, Martin and David Parker (2004): *Leading Issues in Competition Regulation and Development*, Edward Elgar Publishing Ltd, Cheltenham.

Corones, S.G. (1990): *Competition Law and Policy in Australia*, Law Book Co., Sydney.

Dabbah, Mahar M. (2004): *EC and UK Competition Law: Commentary, Cases and Materials*, Cambridge University Press, Cambridge.

———. (2003): *The Internationalization of Antitrust Policy*, Cambridge University Press, Cambridge.

Doern, G. Bruce and Stephen Wilks (eds.) (2001): *Comparative Competition Policy: National Institutions in a Global Market*, Oxford University Press, Oxford.

Epstein, Richard A. and Michael S. Greve (eds.) (2004): *Competition Laws in Conflict: Antitrust Jurisdiction in the Global Economy*, AEI Press, Washington, DC.

Esty, Daniel C. and Damien Geradin (2001): *Regulatory Competition and Economic Integration: Comparative Perspectives*, Oxford University Press, Oxford.

Evenett, Simon J., Alexander Lehmann, and Benn Steil (eds.) (2000): *Antitrust Goes Global: What Future for Transatlantic Cooperation?* Royal Institute of International Affairs, London.

Fox, Eleanor M., Lawrence A. Sullivan, and Rudolph J.R. Peritz (2004): *Cases and Materials for US Antitrust in Global Context: Update for Fall 2006*, Thomson-West, St. Paul, Minnesota.

Gavil, Andrew I, William E. Kovacic, and Jonathan B. Baker (2002): *Antitrust Law in Perspective: Cases, Concepts and Problems in Competition Policy*, 2003 (American Casebook Series), Thomson-West, St. Paul, Minnesota.

Gellhorn, Ernest, William Kovacic, and Stephen Calkins (2004): *Antitrust Law and Economics in a Nutshell* (5th ed.) ('NUTSHELL').

Gerber, David J. (1998): *Law and Competition in Twentieth Century Europe: Protecting Prometheus*, Oxford University Press, Oxford.

Ghidna, Gustavo (2006): *Intellectual Property and Competition Law: The Innovation Nexus*, Edward Elgar Publishing Ltd, Cheltenham.

Greaves, Rosa (ed.) (2003): *Competition Law*, The International Library of Essays in Law and Legal Theory (2nd Series), Dartmouth Publishing Co, Aldershot, UK.

Grossman, Peter Z. (ed.) (2004): *How Cartels Endure and How They Fail: Studies of Industrial Collusion*. Edward Elgar, Cheltenham.

Hawk, Barry (ed.) (2003): *EC Competition Law Reform*, Fordham University School of Law, Juris Publishing Inc., Huntington, NY.

Hoa, Tran Van (ed.) (2003): *Competition Policy and Global Competitiveness in Major Asian Economies*, Edward Elgar Publishing Ltd, Cheltenham.

Hoekman, Bernard, Aaditya Mattoo, and Philip English (eds.) (2002): *Development, Trade and the WTO: A Handbook,* World Bank, Washington, DC.

Hylton, Keith N. (2003): *Antitrust Law: Economic Theory and Common Law Evolution*, Cambridge University Press, Cambridge.

Jones, Alison and Brenda Sufrin (2004): *EC Competition Law: Text, Cases and Materials*, Oxford University Press, Oxford.

Jones, Clifford A. (1999): *Private Enforcement of Antitrust Law in the EU, UK and USA*, Oxford University Press, Oxford.

Keeling, David E. (2004): *Intellectual Property Rights in EU Law*: vol. 1: *Free Movement and Competition*, Oxford University Press, Oxford.

Kirkwood, John B. (ed.) (2004): *Antitrust Law and Economics*, 21, (1st ed.) (Research in Law and Economics), Elsevier Science.

Kwoka, John D. and Lawrence J. White (eds.) (2003): *The Antitrust Revolution: Economics, Competition and Policy* (4th ed.), Oxford University Press, New York.

Laffont, Jean-Jacques (2005): *Regulation and Development*, Cambridge University Press, Cambridge.

Leveque, François and Howard Shelanksi (eds.) (2004): *Merger Remedies in American and European Union Competition Law*, Edward Elgar Publishing Ltd, Cheltenham.

Livingstone, Dorothy (2001): *Competition Act, 1998: A Practical Guide*, Sweet and Maxwell, London.

Lowenfeld, Andreas F. (2002): *International Economic Law*, Oxford University Press, Oxford.

MacCulloch, Angus, Richard J. Bragg and John De Lacy (2004): *Enterprise Act, 2002 and Related SIs*, Sweet and Maxwell, London.

Matsushita, Mitsuo (1993): *International Trade and Competition Law in Japan*, Oxford University Press, Oxford.

Mittal, D.P. (2003): *Competition Law*, Taxmann, Delhi.

Motta, Massimo (2004): *Competition Policy: Theory and Practice*, Cambridge University Press, Cambridge.

Navarro, Edurne, Andrés Font, Jaime Folguera and Juan Briones (2005): *Merger Control in the EU: Law, Economics and Practice*, Oxford University Press, Oxford.

Nolan, Peter (2001): *China and the Global Business Revolution*, Palgrave, Basingstoke.

Ortiz-Blanco, Luis and Ben Van Houtte (1997): *EC Competition Law in the Transport Sector*, Oxford University Press, Oxford.

Pattishall, Beverly, W., David C. Hillard and Joseph Nye Welch (2005): *Trademarks and Unfair Competition* (6th ed.), Lexis Nexis, Butterworths.

Peritz, Rudolph J.R. (2001): *Competition Policy in America: 1888–1992: History Rhetoric, Law* (Revised ed.), Oxford University Press, New York.

Porter, Michael E. (1998): *The Competitive Advantage of Nations*, Palgrave, Basingstoke.

Posner, Richard A. (2001): *Antitrust Law* (2nd ed.) University of Chicago Press, Chicago.

———. (1978): *Antitrust Law: An Economic Perspective*, University of Chicago Press, Chicago.

Prosser, Tony (2005): *The Limits of Competition Law: Markets and Public Services* (Oxford Studies in European Law) Oxford University Press, Oxford.

Ramappa, T. (2006): *Competition Law in India: Policy, Issues and Developments*, Oxford University Press, New Delhi.

Ritter, Lennart and W. David Braun (2004): *European Competition Law: A Practitioner's Guide*, Kluwer Law International, The Hague.

Robinson, Colin (2003): *Competition and Regulation in Utility Markets*, Edward Elgar Publishing Ltd, Cheltenham.

Rodger Barry and Angus MacCulloh (2004): *Competition Law in the EC and UK*, Cavendish Publishing, London.

Rowley, J. William and Donald I. Baker (2000): *The Antitrust Process*, Sweet and Maxwell, London.

Schumpeter, J.A. (1943): *Capitalism, Socialism and Democracy*, George, Allen and Unwin Ltd, London.

Scott, Andrew, Morten Hviid, Bruce Lyons and Christopher Bright (2006): *Merger Control in the United Kingdom*, Oxford University Press, Oxford.

Taylor, Paul (1999): *EC and UK Competition Law and Compliance*, Sweet & Maxwell, London (practical guide for non specialists).

Ullrich, Hanns (ed.) (2006): *The Evolution of European Competition Law—Whose Regulation, Which Competition*? Edward Elgar Publishing Ltd, Cheltenham.

Viscusi, W. Kip, Joseph E. Harrington and John M. Vernon (2005): *Economics of Regulation and Antitrust* (4th ed.), MIT Press, Cambridge, MA.

Von Kalinowski, Juliano (1984): *Antitrust Counseling and Litigation Techniques*, Lexis Nexis, Butterworth, Malaysia.

Ward, Tim and Kassie Smith (2005): *Competition Litigation in the UK*, Sweet & Maxwell, London.

Whish, Richard (2005): *Competition Law*, Oxford University Press, Oxford.

Williams, Mark (2005): *Competition Policy and Law in China, Hong Kong and Taiwan*, Cambridge University Press, Cambridge.

World Bank/OECD (1999): *A Framework for the Design and Implementation of Competition Law and Policy*, World Bank, OECD, Washington, DC.

Wu, Lawrence (2004): *Economics of Antitrust: New Issues, Questions, and Insights*, NERA Economic Consulting, New York.

Articles, Papers, and Reports

ABA (2003): 'Report on Antitrust Policy Objectives', Antitrust Law Section, 12 February.

Ahn, Yong Seok and Youngjin Jung (2004): 'Merger Control in Korea', *Asia Pac. Antitrust Rev.* 62, 64. Available at http://www.lawleeko.com/pdf/ Article_YSA_ 1, pdf.

Anderson, Robert D. and Brian Rivard (1999): 'Antitrust Policy towards EFT Networks: the Canadian Experience in the *Interac* Case', *Antitrust Law Journal*, 16 (2).

Anderson, Robert D. and Peter Holmes (2002): 'Competition Policy and the Future of the Multilateral Trading System', 5 *J. Int'l Econ. L.*, 531.

Anderson, S., Dev Khosla, and Joseph Monteiro (1996): 'Market Definition in Abuse of Dominant Position Cases under the Canadian Competition Act'. Reprinted in *Canada*, OECD Committee on Competition Law and Policy, Proceedings of a Roundtable on Abuse of Dominant Position (Paris: OECD), pp. 89–112.

Areeda, Phillip (1989): 'Essential Facilities: An Epithet in Need of Limiting Principles', *Antitrust Law Journal*, 58, 841.

Arhel, Pierre: 'Pratique communautaire et nationale de l'Accord *ADPIC*', LGDJ/EFE, Paris, forthcoming.

Bain, Joe S. (1941): 'The Profit Rate as a Measure of Monopoly Power,' *Quarterly Journal of Economics*, 55, 291.

Baker, Jonathan (1999): 'Promoting Innovation and Competition through the *Aspen/Kodak* Rule,' *George Mason Law Review*, 7, 500–3.

Basant, Rakesh and Sebastian Morris (2000): 'Competition Policy in India, Issues for a Globalising Economy', *Economic and Political Weekly*, 29 July.

Baumol, William J. and Sydak Gregory, J. (1994): 'The Pricing of Inputs Sold to Competitors', *The Yale Journal of Regulation*, 11 (1).

Baumol, William J. and Willig, Robert (1995): 'Notes on the Efficient Component Pricing Rule', Paper presented at the Montreal Conference on Regulated Industries.

Beato, Paulina and Jean-Jacques Laffont (2003): 'Competition Policy in Regulated Industries: Approaches for Emerging Economies' (Inter-American Development Bank).

Böge/Ost (2006): 'Up and Running, or Is It? Private Enforcement—The Situation in Germany and Policy Perspectives', ECLR 2006, 197.

Bork, Robert H. (1998): 'The Most Misunderstood Antitrust Case', *The Wall Street Journal*, 22 May, A16.

Brennan, Timothy (1987): 'Why Regulated Firms Should Be Kept Out of Unregulated Markets: Understanding the Divestiture in *US* v. *AT&T*.' *Antitrust Bulletin*, 32 (3): 741–93.

Calkins, Stephen (1986): 'Summary Judgment, Motions to Dismiss, and Other Examples of Equilibrating Tendencies in the Antitrust System', *Geo L.J.*, 74, 1065.

———. (1997): 'Corporate compliance and the Antitrust Agencies' Bi-Modal Penalties', *Law and Contemporary Problems*, 60, 127, 131–2.

———. (2003): 'Perspectives on State and Federal Antitrust Enforcement', *Duke Law Journal*, 53, 673.

———. (2006): 'Civil Monetary Remedies Available to the Federal Government', *University of San Francisco Law Review*, 40 (3).

Carlton, Dennis W. (2001): 'A General Analysis of Exclusionary Conduct and Refusal to Deal—Why *Aspen* and *Kodak* Are Misguided', *Antitrust Law Journal*, 68 (3), 659.

Chandler, Harry and Robert Jackson (2000): 'Beyond Merriment and Diversion: the Treatment of Conspiracies under Canada's Competition Act', Presented at the Roundtable on Competition Act Amendments, Insight Conferences, Toronto, 25 May 2000, at Appendix 1, available at http://www.competitionbureau.gc.ca/internet/index.cfm?itemID=1197&lg=e.

Crampton, Paul (2003): 'Competition and Efficiency as Organizing Principles for all Economic and Regulatory Policy Making', OECD-IADB, April 2003.

Dervis, Kamal and John M. Page (1996): 'Industrial Policy in Developing Countries', *Journal of Comparative Economics*, 8, 436–51.

Dobson, Paul W. and Michael Waterson (1996): 'Vertical Restraints and Competition Policy', United Kingdom, Office of Fair Trading, Research Paper 12, December.

Dutz, Mark (2002): 'Competition Policy Issues in Developing and Transition Markets', Presentation to the OECD's February 2002 Global Forum on Competition, available at http://www.oecd.org/dataoecd/48/3/2073927.pdf.

Dutz, Mark and Aydin Hayri (2000): 'Does More Intense Competition Lead to Higher Growth?', World Bank, Development Research Group, April 2000, Working Paper #2320, available at http://www.worldbank.org/research/growth.

Easterbrook, Frank H. (1981): 'Predatory Strategies and Counter-Strategies', *University of Chicago Law Review*, 48.

Elhauge, Einer (2002): 'Tunney Act Comment on the Proposed Settlements between the United States and Microsoft', http://www.justice.gov/atr/cases/ms_tuncom/major/mtc-00027209.htm.

European Commission (2005): 'DG Competition Discussion Paper on the Application of Article 82 of the Treaty to Exclusionary Abuses', Public consultation version.

Evenett, Simon J. (2002): 'Private International Cartels and Developing Economies', Presentation to the OECD's February 2002 Global Forum on Competition, available at http://www.oecd.org/dataoecd/48/2/2073938.pdf.

———. (2003): 'Study on Issues Related to a Possible Multilateral Framework on Competition'. Document Number WT/WGTCP/W228.WorldTrade Organization, Geneva.

First, Harry (2001): 'The Vitamins Case: Cartel Prosecutions and the Coming of International Competition Law', *Antitrust L.J.*, 68, 711.

Fisher, Franklin M. and John McGowan (1983): 'On the Misuse of Accounting Rates of Return to Infer Monopoly Profits,' *American Economic Review*, 73 (I), 81–97.

Fox, Eleanor M. (1986): 'Monopolization and Dominance in the United States and the European Community: Efficiency, Opportunity, and Fairness', *Notre Dame L. Rev.*, 61, 981, 1014–15.

———. (1987): 'Extraterritoriality, Antitrust, and the New Restatement: Is Reasonableness the Answer?', 19 *Nyu J. Int'l & POl.*, 565.

———. (1998): 'The United States of Boeing Versus the European Union of Airbus', *Brookings Rev.*, 16, 30.

———. (1998a): 'International Antitrust: Against Minimum Rules; For Cosmopolitan Principles', *Antitrust Bull.*, 43 (5), 9.

———. (2002): 'What is Harm to Competition?—Exclusionary Practices and Anticompetitive Effect', *Antitrust L.J.*, 70, 371.

———. (2002a): 'Mergers in Global Markets: GE/Honeywell and the Future of Merger Control', *U. Pa. J. Int'l Econ. L.*, 23, 457.

Fox, Eleanor M. (2006): 'The European Court's Judgment in *GE/Honeywell*—Not a Poster Child for Comity or Convergence', *Antitrust*, 77.

Geroski, Paul A. (2005): 'Competition Policy and National Champions', available at http://www.competition-commission.org.ur.

Gilbert, Richard and Carl Shapiro (1996): 'An Economic Analysis of Unilateral Refusals to License Intellectual Property', *Proceedings of the National Academy of Sciences*, 93, 12749–55, November.

Godek, Paul (1992): 'Protecting Eastern Europe from Antitrust', *Regulation*, Fall.

Goldman, C., C. Hersh, and C. Witterick (2005): 'Comity after *Empagran* and *Intel*', *Antitrust* 19, 6, Summer.

Guzman, Andrew T. (2001): 'Antitrust and International Regulatory Federalism', *Nyu L. Rev.,* 76, 1142.

Hammond, Scott (2000): 'Fighting Cartels—Why and How? Lessons Common to Detecting and Deterring Cartel Activity', Presented at Modern Museum, Stockholm, 12 September 2000, 3–4, available at http://www.usdoj.gov/atr/public/speeches/6487.htm.

Hawk, Barry (ed.) (1993): *International Antitrust Law and Policy*, Annual Proceedings of the Fordham Corporate Law Institute, New York.

Heimler, Alberto (2005): 'Below-cost Pricing and Loyalty Discounts: Are They Restrictive and, If So, When?' *Competition Policy International*, 1(2), Autumn.

International Competition Network (2002): 'Advocacy and Competition Policy', available at http://www.internationalcompetitionnetwork.org/.

International Competition Network Merger Working Group (2004): Analytical Framework Subgroup, Project on Merger Guidelines, April 2004, available at: http://www.internationalcompetitionnetwork.org/seoul/analysisofmerger.html.

Ireland, Government of New York (2003): 'Competition Policy in Small Economies,' Submission to the OECD Global Forum on Competition, Document reference number CCNM/GF/COMP/WD (2003)18.

Jordan, W.A. (1972): 'Producer Protection, Prior Market Structure and the Effects of Government Regulation', *Journal of Law and Economics*, XV (1), 151–76.

Joskow, Paul L. and Alvin K. Klevorick (1979): 'A Framework for Analyzing Predatory Pricing Strategy', *Yale Law Journal*, 89, 1–26. November.

Jung, Youngjin and Seung Wha Chang (2006): 'Korean Competition Law and Polices in Perspective', *Nw. J. Int'l L. Bus.,* 26, 687.

Jung, Youngjin (2005): 'Korean Competition Law: First Step towards Globalization', *Journal of Korean Law*, 4 (2), 177–99.

Kahn, Alfred E. (2004): *Lessons from Deregulation,* AEI-Brookings Joint Center for Regulatory Studies, Washington, DC.

Korah, Valentine. (2005): 'The Interface between Intellectual Property Rights and Competition in Developed Countries', 2:4 SCRIPT-ed 462 available at http://www.law.ed.ac.uk/ahrb/script-ed/vol2–4/korah.asp

Kovacic, William E. (1999): 'Designing Antitrust Remedies for Dominant Firm Misconduct', *Connecticut Law Review*, 31, 1285–319.

———. (2003): 'The Modern Evolution of U.S. Competition Policy Enforcement Norms', *Antitrust L.J.* 71, 377.

Krueger, Anne O. (1974): 'The Political Economy of the Rent-seeking Society', *American Economic Review* 64 (3), 291–303.

Landes, William M. and Richard A. Posner (1981, March): 'Market Power in Antitrust Cases', *Harvard Law Review*, 5, 937–96.

Lao, Marina L. (forthcoming): '*Aspen Skiing* and *Trinko*: Antitrust Intent and Sacrifice', *Antitrust Law Journal.*

Lee, K.U. (2002): 'Economic Development and Competition Policy in Korea', 1 *Wash. U. Global Stud. L. Rev.*, 1 (67), 69–70.

Levenstein, Margaret and Valerie Suslow (2001): 'Private International Cartels and their Effect on Developing Countries', Background Paper for World Bank's World Development Report 2001, available at http://www.worldbank.org/wdr/2001/bkgroundpapers/levenstein.pdf

McDonald, J. Bruce (2004): 'Antitrust Division Update: Trinko and Microsoft', Before the Houston Bar Association Antitrust and Trade Regulation Section, April.

———. (2005): 'Section 2 and Article 82: Cowboys and Gentlemen', College of Europe Global Competition Law Centre, Second Annual Conference, The Modernization of Article 82, Brussels, 16–17 June.

Miller (1907): 'The Case of the Monopolies—Some of its Results and Suggestions', *Mich. L. Rev.*, 6 (1), 2.

OECD (2001): *Recommendation of the Council Concerning Structural Separation in Regulated Industries*, Paris.

———. (2001a): 'Global Forum on Competition: Summary of Cartel Cases Described by Invitees', available at http://www.oecd.org/dataoecd/41/30/2491386.pdf.

———. (2003): 'OECD Peer Review: Competition Law and Policy in South Africa', available at http://www.oecd.org/dataoecd/43/58/34823812.pdf.

———. (2004): 'Structural Reform in the Rail Industry: Should Train Operations be Separated from the Provision of Track Infrastructure?', DAF/COMP/WP2 (2004)6; CFC files DE-57–2001 and RA-50–2003, IO-05–2002, DC-01–2002 and RA-11–2004.

———. (2005): Global Forum on Competition: Key Issues for Discussion in Technical Sessions, DAF/COMP/GF/ (2005) 3/ANN1.

———. (2005): 'The Relationship between Competition Authorities and Sectoral Regulators', Document No. AF/COMP/GF (2005)2 for Global Forum on Competition, OECD February, p. 3, available at http://www.oecd.org/dataoecd/8/61/237607.pdf.

OFCOM (2004): 'Strategic Review, Phase 2 Consultation Document', 18 November 2004.

OFT (2005): 'How Your Business Can Achieve Compliance', available at http://www.oft.gov.uk/nr/rdonlyres/78ad1280–4eb8–46d4-a52b-207f9afeaae1/0/oft424.pdf

Pack, Howard and Kamal Saggi (2006): 'Is There a Case for Industrial Policy?', *The World Bank Research Observer.*

Pitofsky, Robert (1999): 'The Effect of Global Trade on United States Competition Law and Enforcement Policies', Speech given at the Fordham Corporate Law Institute, 15 October.

Pittman, Russell (1995): 'Some Practical Considerations in Geographic Market Definition', Remarks prepared for the Seminar on Antitrust Enforcement in Central and Eastern Europe, Vienna, Austria, 31 October.

Pugel, T. (1984): 'Japan's Industrial Policy: Instruments, Trends, and Effects', *Journal of Comparative Economics*, 8 (4), 420–35.

Ridyard, D. (2002): 'Exclusionary Pricing and Price Discrimination Abuses under Article 82—an Economic Analysis', *European Competition Law Review*, 286.

Schmidt, K.S. (1997): 'Managerial Incentives and Product Market Competition', *Review of Economic Studies*, 64, 277–84.

Singh, Ajit (2002): 'Competition and Competition Policy in Emerging Markets: International and Development Dimensions', G-24 Discussion Paper Series. No. 18, United Nations, 18 September.

Spratling, Gary (1999): 'Making Companies an Offer They Shouldn't Refuse, The Antitrust Division's Corporate Leniency Policy—An Update', Presented at The Bar Association of the District of Columbia's 35th Annual Symposium on Associations and Antitrust, 16 February 1999, available at http://www.usdoj.gov/atr/public/speeches/2247.htm.

Stigler, G.J. (1971): 'The Theory of Economic Regulation', *Bell Journal of Economics and Management Science* 2 (1): 3–21, Spring.

Tarullo, Daniel K. (2000): 'Norms and Institutions in Global Competition Policy', *Am. J. Int'l L.* 94 (478).

Vickers, J. (2005): 'Abuse of Market Power', *Economic Journal*, 115, 244–61.

Werden, Gregory (1987): 'The Law and Economics of the Essential Facilities Doctrine,' *Saint Louis University Law Journal*, 32, 432–80.

Whinston, Michael D. (1990): 'Tying, Foreclosure and Exclusion', *American Economic Review*, 80.

Winerman, Marc (2003): 'The Origins of the FTC: Concentration, Cooperation, Control, and Competition', 71 *Antitrust L.J.*, 71, 1.

Winston, (1998): 'U.S. Industry Adjustment to Economic Deregulation', *J. Econ. Persp.*, 12 (89), 100.

Wood, Diane P. (2003): 'Soft Harmonization and Competition Laws: Track Record and Prospects', *Antitrust Bull.*, 48, 305.

Editor and Contributors

Editor

Vinod Dhall is a leading expert and advisor in competition policy and law in India, recognized for the depth and scope of his experience in this field. He is identified with the origin and growth of the new Competition Act, having been instrumental in the introduction and enactment of the law and its subsequent development. He was the founding member and acting chairman of the Competition Commission of India and laid the foundation for the Commission's eventual functioning. He has held several senior positions with Government of India including (Permanent) Secretary; during his tenure in the government, he initiated several reforms such as the Competition Act, setting up Serious Frauds Investigation Office, setting up one of the first interactive portals for a government ministry, and reforms in corporate governance. He was also ex-officio member of the stock market regulator, Securities and Exchange Board of India. He has been advisor/consultant to the United Nations Industrial Development Organisation. He holds a law degree from the University of Delhi, India, and an MA in mathematics from the University of Allahabad, India, where he also received several student achievement awards.

Contributors

Robert D. Anderson is counsellor and team leader for Government Procurement and Competition Policy in the Intellectual Property, Government Procurement and Competition Division of the World Trade Organization (WTO) in Geneva, Switzerland, where he has worked for more than 20 years. He is also honorary professor in the School of Law at the University of Nottingham, UK, and is on the part-time external faculties of the World Trade Institute in Bern, Switzerland, and the International Law and Economic Policy (IELPO) Programme of the University of Barcelona, Spain. Prior to joining the WTO in 1997, Anderson held various senior positions in the national competition agency of Canada (the 'Competition Bureau'). He holds a juris doctor (JD) from Osgoode Hall Law School, York University, Toronto, Canada, and a BA (Hons) in economics from the University of British Columbia, Vancouver, Canada. He is the editor of three books and author/co-author of more than 50 articles/book chapters on topics in competition policy, international government procurement policy, intellectual property, and/or international trade policy.

Christopher Bellamy is the chairman of the Global Competition Practice of Linklaters LLP, London, UK. Previously, he was president of the Competition Appeal Tribunal, UK, from 1999 to 2007. After qualifying as a barrister, he practised mainly in the fields of competition law, EU, and public law. He was appointed Queen's Counsel in 1986. From 1992 to 1999, he was a judge of the Court of First Instance of the European Communities, now known as the General Court of the European Union. He also sat as a High Court judge, a judge of the Employment Appeal Tribunal, and a recorder of the Crown Court. He edited the first three editions of *Bellamy & Child European Union Law of Competition*, published by Oxford University Press, which is now in its 7th edition.

Sitesh Bhojani is a barrister and consultant. His areas of practice include competition and consumer law. He was engaged to advise and prepare the Australian Council for Private Education and Training's submission to the April 2005 Productivity Commission—Review of Australia's National Competition Policy. Previously, he completed two full terms as an inaugural commissioner of the Australian Competition and Consumer Commission from the commission's inception in November 1995. He holds BSc and LLB degrees from Monash University, Melbourne.

Ulf Böge is the president of the Federal Cartel Office (Bundeskartellamt), Germany, since 2000. Previously, he has worked in the Federal Ministry of Economics in the field of competition policy, and in the Office of the Federal President. He was also director of the Office of the Supervisory Board of Deutsche Investitions und Beteiligungsgesellschaft in Entwicklungsländern (DEG); head of section on Nuclear Energy, Federal Ministry of Economics; deputy assistant secretary for General Energy Policy Issues; director general for Energy Policy, Mineral Resources, and Economic Issues relating to the Environment; and director general for Economic Policy. He read economics at the Universities of Mainz and Bonn, Germany and got his doctorate in 1971.

Amit Bubna teaches economics and finance at the Indian School of Business (ISB), Hyderabad, India. Earlier, he was a senior managing economist at LECG, LLC, where he worked on projects relating to telecom spectrum auctions, antitrust matters, copyright infringement, and damages in litigation. He co-authored a report on the impact of a cap on non-economic damages in medical malpractice lawsuits on physicians' incentives, cost, and quality of healthcare. He completed his PhD in economics from Stanford University, California, USA, BA and MPhil in economics from University of Cambridge, UK; and BSc in economics from Presidency University, Kolkata, India. His research interests lie in institutional analysis, capital markets, and financial intermediation, including venture capital, informal finance, and microfinance. His article on venture capital syndication was published in *Research in Finance*.

Stephen Calkins is professor of law at the Wayne State University Law School, Michigan, USA, where he teaches courses and seminars in antitrust and trade regulation, consumer law, and torts. He has taught at the Universities of Michigan, Pennsylvania (USA), and Utrecht (The Netherlands), and served as Wayne State University's associate provost and as the Law School's interim dean. He has also served as the commissioner of the Irish Competition and Consumer Protection Commission and (before that) as a member of the Irish Competition Authority and director of the Authority's Mergers Division. While in Ireland he served as adjunct professor at the University College Dublin Sutherland College of Law, Republic of Ireland. During 1995–7, Calkins served as general counsel of the Federal Trade Commission. Calkins lectures widely throughout the US and abroad, is a journal editor, and has authored many publications on competition and consumer law and policy and related subjects, including the co-authored 4th edition of *Antitrust Law: Policy and Practice*, the co-authored 5th edition of *Antitrust Law and Economics in a Nutshell*, and the co-edited *Consumer Protection Law Developments* (2009). He is a life member of the American Law Institute, a fellow of the European Law Institute, a life fellow of the American Bar Foundation, and a member of the advisory board of the American Antitrust Institute. He served three three-year terms on the Council of the American Bar Association Section of Antitrust Law and is a former member of the Council of the ABA Section of Administrative Law and Regulatory Practice. He is also a former chair of the Association of American Law School's Antitrust and Economic Regulation Committee. He holds a BA from Yale University and a JD from Harvard University, Massachusetts, USA.

Dando B. Cellini is a senior trial attorney at the Antitrust Division of the US Department of Justice and has extensive experience in international competition law. He was the Justice Department's first long-term advisor to Romania's Competition Council, served as a long-term advisor to South Africa's Competition Commission, and has consulted with competition law authorities in South America, the Far East, and Europe. He is the recipient of the Antitrust Division's Award of Distinction and the Assistant Attorney General's Outstanding Contribution Award. Prior to entering government service, he was a senior partner in the law firm of McGlinchey, Stafford, Cellini, and Lang PC, where he maintained an international antitrust counselling and litigation practice.

Paul Crampton is a partner in the Competition/Antitrust Law Group in the Toronto Office of Osler, Hoskin, and Harcourt LLP. His practice focuses on international mergers and cartels. During 2002–4, he took a sabbatical from his private practice at the Organization of Economic Cooperation and Development (OECD), where he was head of Outreach in the Competition Division and was responsible for overseeing the OECD's work with non-OECD countries in the competition field. He has held various positions with the Canadian Competition Bureau including as special advisor to the Commissioner of Competition. He has authored *Mergers and Competition Act* (1990), a leading text on the merger provisions of the Competition Act (Canada), and has published a number of articles on competition issues in numerous journals worldwide.

Geraldine Emberger is member of the International Relations Unit of the Directorate General (DG) Competition of the European Commission, where she is in charge of its contributions to the work of the International Competition Network (ICN), the OECD, as well as European Commission (EC) cooperation with South Korea, Latin and Central America, the Mercosur, and India. She joined the DG Competition in 1998, where she served in the Mergers Task Force and the Antitrust Policy and Strategic Support Unit. She was sent as an exchange officer to the Canadian Competition Bureau and has worked on mergers and cartel cases. She graduated as Magister Juris at the Vienna University, Austria, and subsequently specialized in European and public international law.

Simon J. Evenett is professor of international trade and economic development at the University of St Gallen, Switzerland. In addition to his research into the determinants of international commercial flows, he is particularly interested in the relationships between international trade policy, national competition law and policy, and economic development. He obtained his PhD from Yale University, Connecticut, USA, and a BA (Hons) from the University of Cambridge, UK. He has been a (non-resident) senior fellow of the Economic Studies Programme in the Brookings Institution, Washington, DC, USA. Previously, he has taught at University of Oxford, UK, and Rutgers University, New Jersey, USA, and has served twice as a World Bank official.

Allan Fels is adjunct professor at University of Melbourne and Monash University, Australia, and University of Oxford, UK. He is former dean of the Australia and New Zealand School of Government, Carlton, Australia, and former chairman of the Australian Competition and Consumer Commission from 1995 to 2003. Before that he was chairman of its predecessor bodies, the Trade Practices Commission, from 1991 to 1995, and of the Prices Surveillance Authority, from 1989 to 1992. Fels has degrees in law and economics from the University of Western Australia, Perth, Australia, and a PhD in economics from Duke University, North Carolina, USA. While a research fellow in the Department of Applied Economics, University of Cambridge, UK, he wrote *The British Prices and Incomes Board* (1972). Following that, he held various academic positions including professor of administration and director, Graduate School of Management, Monash University, Australia.

Eleanor M. Fox is Walter J. Derenberg Professor of trade regulation at New York University School of Law, USA, where she specializes in antitrust law and international and comparative competition policy with a focus on Europe and developing countries. She was a partner in the New York law firm Simpson Thacher & Bartlett. She served as a member of international competition policy advisory commissions and committees under Presidents Carter and Clinton. Fox received her law degree from New York University School of Law in 1961 and an honorary doctorate degree from the University of Paris Dauphine, France in 2009. She was awarded an inaugural Lifetime Achievement award in 2011 by the Global Competition Review for 'substantial, lasting and transformational impact on competition policy and practice'. She received the inaugural award for outstanding contributions to the competition law community in 2015 by ASCOLA, the world network of professors of antitrust law and economics. She was awarded the Lifetime Achievement Award of the Antitrust & Economic Regulation Section of the Association of American Law Schools in 2017. Her books include *Global Issues in Antitrust and Competition Law* with Daniel Crane (2d ed. 2017), *EU Competition*

Law casebook with Damien Gerard (2017), *The Design of Competition Law Institutions* edited with Michael Trebilcock, (Oxford University Press, 2013), and *US Antitrust in Global Context* casebook (3d ed. 2012).

Shubhashis Gangopadhyay is founder-director of India Development Foundation (IDF) since 2002. He joined the Indian Statistical Institute as a lecturer in 1983 and became a full professor in 1991. He is currently chief editor of *Journal of Emerging Market Finance*, associate editor of *Journal of Financial Stability*, and a member on the Board of the Centre for Analytical Finance, ISB, Hyderabad, India. He has international experience in teaching and advising doctoral students in USA, Europe, and India and has a number of ongoing research collaborations with international faculty. He has published widely in journals on development economics, international trade, industrial organization, regulatory economics, and finance. He has also co-authored and co-edited a number of books on economics and finance. He holds a BA in economics from Presidency University, Kolkata, India, and a PhD in economics from Cornell University, Ithaca, New York, USA.

Alan H. Goldberg is president of the Australian Competition Tribunal. He was called to the Victorian Bar in 1965 and was appointed Queen's Counsel in 1978. He has practised extensively in commercial, corporate, administrative, and competition law, and has been an active advocate of human rights and civil liberties. He was appointed a judge of the Federal Court of Australia in 1997, and deputy president of the Australian Competition Tribunal in 1998. In 2005, he was appointed an officer in the General Division of the Order of Australia for service to the judiciary and to the community.

Lennart Göranson, after graduating from the Stockholm School of Economics as civilekonom (Business Administration), has spent most of his professional career in national and international competition institutions in managerial positions. He has been director for Competition of the EFTA Surveillance Authority, Brussels, Belgium, and deputy head of the Swedish Competition Authority. He joined the OECD's Competition Division in 2000, and in 2004 became head of OECD's Competition Outreach overseeing OECD's capacity building and policy dialogue in competition policy areas with non-OECD countries. After retirement from the OECD in 2005, he continued competition policy capacity building as international consultant. In 2007, he became member of the Swedish Market Court. When this Court of Justice was discontinued in 2016, he became member (economic expert) of the Swedish Patents and Market Court as well as the Patents and Market Court of Appeal. He is also member of the

Competition Commission, a private foundation vetting abusive practices in public procurement.

Rahat Kaunain Hassan is the founder and senior partner of Hassan Kaunain Nafees, Legal Practitioners & Advisers (HKN). As Britannia Chevening Scholar, she studied law at King's College London, UK, and was awarded the LLM degree. Hassan obtained her LLB degree from the University of Punjab and BA from Kinnaird College, Lahore, Pakistan. In recognition of her professional standing, Hassan was appointed as one of the founding members of the Competition Commission of Pakistan (CCP), and played a significant role in regulation of anticompetitive practices during her tenure from 2007 to 2013. For the later part of her term at CCP (2010–13), she served as chairperson. At the CCP, she was instrumental in the establishment of the Office of Fair Trading and helped CCP acquire international acclaim for distinctive competition law enforcement. Earlier, she also served at the Securities and Exchange Commission of Pakistan as general counsel/executive director. She was also a partner in Amhurst Brown—Solicitors and Barristers, Islamabad, Pakistan, before she founded HKN. She is also the chairperson of 'Women on Board Pakistan', a recent initiative of South Asian Federation of Exchanges (SAFE), promoting an inclusive approach towards empowering women. Hassan has also been recently appointed as member of the Honorary Advisory Council of the Pakistan Women Entrepreneur Network for Trade (WE-NET). She is a recipient of the Women of Achievement Award (2010), Wonder Women Award (2013), and was recognized as one of the 100 successful women in antitrust globally by Global Competition Review in 2013. She has the honour of being nominated/recommended for Sitara-e-Imtiaz for her work at CCP, both by her predecessor and the current chairperson. Hassan was also the first female founder director of the Pakistan Stock Exchange, and is currently director of two other listed compaines. She has recently been appointed as member of the Academic Council of GC University Lahore, Pakistan.

Alberto Heimler is professor of economics at the Italian School of Government, Rome, Italy. He is the chairman of the Working Party on Competition and Regulation of the Competition Committee of the OECD. He was director for research at the Italian Antirust Authority, a member of the Steering Group of the ICN, and co-chair of a number of ICN working groups. His academic articles on antitrust enforcement, economic regulation, and public procurement have appeared in the leading journals of the field. Heimler is the co-coordinator of the procurement programmes at the Italian School of Government and lectures frequently on antitrust, economic regulation, and public procurement both in Italy and abroad.

Youngjin Jung is a partner with Woo Yun Kang Jeong and Han. He was deputy director of the International Trade Ministry and worked at Steptoe and Johnson. He is adjunct professor of KDI International Policy School and taught at Georgetown University Law Center, Washington, DC, USA, and Korea University Business School, Seoul, South Korea. He has extensive experience in antitrust law and international trade. He is a member of the Cartel Advisory Board of the Fair Trade Commission and was a member of the Korean delegations to the OECD Competition Committee and the WTO Working Party on Interaction between Trade and Competition Policy. He is a graduate of Seoul National University, South Korea (LLB and LLM) and Yale Law School, Connecticut, USA (LLM and JSD). He has numerous publications including *Korean Competition Law and Policies in Perspective* (2006) and *Northwestern Journal of International Law and Business* (2006).

R. Shyam Khemani has extensive experience in the private–public sectors and academia in the fields of industrial organization-competition policy, economic regulation, and international trade. Currently he is special advisor, Competition Policy with the SKP Group, a business consulting advisory firm with offices and associates in major centres in India; Dubai; Chicago, US; and Toronto, Canada. Previously he was advisor and group manager, Competition Policy in the Finance and Private Sector Development-Vice Presidency, The World Bank Group, Washington, DC, USA. He is former chief economist and director, Economics and International Affairs, Canadian Competition Bureau, and director (Europe), LECG Paris, France. He has served full and part-time on the faculties of commerce, economics, and business at the universities of British Columbia, Carleton, Concordia, and Ottawa, and has provided expert advice to several governments and competition offices, and private sector firms around the world. He also served as an advisor to the chairman of the Raghavan Committee established by the Government of India to study and put forward recommendations relating to competition law and policy.

Valentine Korah, Professor Emeritus of Competition Law at University College London, UK, and honorary professor at the College of Europe, Belgium. She, was one of the first lawyers to co-teach competition law and policy with economists. Since the 1960s, she has encouraged lawyers to consider economic arguments and work with economists. She has taught full courses on competition at the College of Europe for nearly 20 years and at Fordham University School of Law, New York, USA, for 14 consecutive spring semesters. Her *An Introductory Guide to EC Competition Law and Practice* (1994) is in its 8th edition and she has written many other critical and influential books and comments.

Amitabh Kumar is director general of the Competition Commission of India. He has served as commissioner of income tax in the Ministry of Finance; director in the Department of Heavy Industries; director/deputy secretary in the Ministry of Finance; and deputy/assistant commissioner of income tax in the Ministry of Finance of the Government of India. He has had consultancy experience as a financial analyst, economist, and financial expert and has degrees in law, economics, financial management, and fiscal studies.

David Lewis is chairperson of the Competition Tribunal of South Africa since 1999. Previously, he was member of the Competition Board and was a member of the Task Team advising the Minister of Trade and Industry on the development of competition policy, and participated in the drafting of the Competition Act. He is the vice-chairman of the Steering Group of the International Competition Network. He has been the director of the Development Policy Research Unit of the School of Economics at the University of Cape Town, South Africa, specializing in trade and industrial policy, and has served as special advisor to the Minister of Labour. He is deputy chairman of the Industrial Development Corporation and has served on the Board of the National Research Foundation. He received his training in economics from the universities of the Witwatersrand and Cape Town, South Africa. He has published widely in the fields of industrial policy, labour market policy, and trade union history.

Philip Lowe read politics, philosophy, and economics at St John's College, Oxford, UK, and has an MSc from London Business School, UK. Following a stint in the manufacturing industry, he joined the European Commission in 1973, and held a range of senior posts such as chef de cabinet and director in the fields of regional development, agriculture, transport, and administration, before becoming director general of the Development DG in 1997. He took up his current appointment as director general of the Competition DG in September 2002.

Eduardo Pérez Motta is chairman of Mexico's Federal Competition Commission. He has been ambassador and permanent representative of Mexico to the World Trade Organization (WTO) where he chaired the

Council on Trade Related Aspects of Intellectual Property Rights and the Negotiating Group on Rules. He has also been the Ministry for Economy's representative to the European Union, responsible for the negotiation of the Mexico–EU Free Trade Agreement. He has a PhD in economics from the University of California, Los Angeles (UCLA), specializing in international trade, labour, and monetary policy. He has a number of publications on international trade and industrial policy and has delivered lectures on these issues at El Colegio de Mexico and the Instituto Technologico Autonomo de Mexico (IATM), Mexico.

Graham Reynolds is a partner in Osler, Hoskin, and Harcourt LLP's Competition and Antitrust Law Group in Toronto, Canada. He was formerly senior general counsel in the Competition Law Division and Ontario Regional Office of Canada's Federal Department of Justice. As such, he acted as counsel for the Attorney General of Canada and Competition Bureau in major international and domestic cartel prosecutions, and several multinational investigations. His practice involves representation of immunity applicants and targets of domestic and international cartel investigations. He is a frequent writer and speaker on a variety of antitrust and regulatory law issues.

Michael J. Reynolds is a partner of Allen and Overy LLP in Brussels since 1981 and has worked with the EC Commission's legal service. He specializes in all types of EC law, especially competition law cases, mergers, and joint ventures; telecommunications; and financial services. He has represented or defended major UK, US, Japanese, and other international clients in a number of important cases before the European Commission and European Court of Justice. He is past chair of the IBA—Antitrust Committee. Currently he is chair of the IBA's Legal Practice Division and the IBA's EU coordinate. He is visiting professor in European Competition Law at the University of Durham, UK. He obtained a BA from Keele University, UK, and qualified as a solicitor in 1977.

Richard Whish is Emeritus Professor of Law at King's College London, UK. He was appointed as the QC Honoris Causa in 2014. He was a non-executive director of the Office of Fair Trading in the UK from 2003 to 2009, and a non-executive director of the Singaporean Energy Markets Authority from 2005 to 2011. He is the co-author, with David Bailey, of *Competition Law*, 8th edition (Oxford University Press, 2015), and the author of many other books, articles, case-notes, and book reviews on various aspects of international competition law and policy.

Index